THE

FOUR-PART CHORALS OF J. S. BACH

*With the German Text of the Hymns
and English Translations*

Edited, with an historical Introduction, Notes
and critical Appendices, by

CHARLES SANFORD TERRY

Travis & Emery

Charles Sanford Terry:

The Four-Part Chorals of J.S. Bach.

Facsimile of 1929 edition.

First published Oxford University Press 1929.

Republished in as two volumes in one book
Travis & Emery 2009.

Published by
Travis & Emery Music Bookshop
17 Cecil Court, London, WC2N 4EZ, United Kingdom.
(+44) 20 7240 2129
neworders@travis-and-emery.com

ISBN Hardback: 978-1-906857-23-3   Paperback: 978-1-906857-24-0

Charles Sanford Terry (1864-1936), Historian and Bach Scholar.

He studied at St. Pauls Cathedral Choir School as a solo boy, King's College and Lancing. He studied history at Cambridge, He lectured in history at Durham College of Science and at Aberdeen. He spent much of his life devoted to Music and to Bach in particular. He started choral societies in both Newcastle and Durham. He wrote extensively on Bach. Walter Emery said that his biography of Bach was "the only one that is both detailed and readable".

More details available from
- Stanley Sadie: The New Grove Dictionary of Music and Musicians.(Walter Emery).
- Dictionary of National Biography

Works:
Bach's B Minor Mass (1915)
Bach's Chorals (1915-1921, reprint Travis & Emery 2009)
Forkell (Translated C.S.T.): Johann Sebastian Bach: His Life, Art and Work. (1920)
J.S. Bach's Original Hymn-Tunes for Congregational Use (edited by Terry. 1922)
Bach: The Mass in B Minor (1924)
Bach: Coffee and Cupid (edited by C.S. Terry 1924)
Bach: The Cantatas and Oratorios (1925)
Bach: The Passions (1926).
Joh. Seb. Bach: Cantata Texts, sacred and Secular (1926, reprint Travis & Emery 2009)
Bach: a Biography (1928)
Bach: the Magnificat, Lutheran Masses and Motets (1929)
The Four Part Chorals of J.S. Bach (edited C.S.T. 1924, reprint Travis & Emery 2009)
The Origin of the Family of Bach Musicians (1929, reprint Travis & Emery 2009)
John Christian Bach (1929, reprint Travis & Emery 2009)
Bach: the Historical Approach (1930)
Bach's Orchestra (1932)
The Music of Bach (1933)

THE FOUR-PART CHORALS
OF J. S. BACH

JOHANN SEBASTIAN BACH
(From the drawing by W. E. Hoffmann, copyright of Grauert & Zink, Berlin-Charlottenburg)

THE

FOUR-PART CHORALS OF J. S. BACH

*With the German Text of the Hymns
and English Translations*

Edited, with an historical Introduction, Notes
and critical Appendices, by

CHARLES SANFORD TERRY

(VOLUME I)

OXFORD UNIVERSITY PRESS

London: Amen House Warwick Square E.C.4
and 95 Wimpole Street W.1.
Amsterdam : Broekmans & Van Poppel
Paris : Editions Max Eschig
New York : 114 Fifth Avenue

1929

ENGRAVED AND PRINTED BY
HENDERSON AND SPALDING LTD.
SYLVAN GROVE
LONDON
S.E. 15

CONTENTS

ILLUSTRATIONS

PREFACE

My Introduction sufficiently elucidates the scope of this volume and its relation to earlier collections of Bach's Chorals. Here I need only state its purpose and explain its method. First and foremost it equips the Chorals for the use Bach intended them to serve—as hymns for mixed voices. This obvious view of his intention was not recognized for a century after Bach's death. It was Ludwig Erk who in 1850 and 1865 first put words to their musical texts, though rarely more than a single stanza. The Bachgesellschaft edition of 1892 and Breitkopf's of 1898 are no less economical of words, while the most recent, an English, edition excludes them altogether. In the present volume so many English and German stanzas are associated with each setting as permits it to be sung as a hymn, introit, or short anthem. The number provided necessarily is limited by their length: but I have been careful always to associate the particular verse selected by Bach with the musical setting he gave it.

For the German words I have preferably used *Unverfälschter Liedersegen: Gesangbuch für Kirchen, Schulen und Häuser* (Berlin, 1851), a comprehensive anthology referred to in these pages as U.L.S., from which comparatively few of Bach's hymns are absent. Otherwise I have quoted Tucher's *Schatz des evangelischen Kirchengesangs* (Pt. I, Leipzig, 1848); for the earlier period, Wackernagel's *Das deutsche Kirchenlied von der ältesten Zeit bis zu Anfang des XVII Jahrhunderts* (5 vols., Leipzig, 1864–77); for the seventeenth century, Fischer-Tümpel's *Das deutsche evangelische Kirchenlied des siebzehnten Jahrhunderts* (6 vols. Gütersloh, 1904–16); and occasionally, of necessity, the German Hymn-book in which a hymn of restricted vogue appeared. In every case the source of the text is acknowledged.

For the English words I have generally used my own translations of the German texts. Indeed, in most cases I had no alternative, for comparatively few hymns set by Bach have passed into English. I have, however, included several of Catherine Winkworth's translations and made use of George Macdonald's rhythmic and virile versions of Luther's stanzas. Where the number of settings of a melody permits variation, I have provided alternative English texts. Their author and source are always indicated.

The musical text of the Chorals is the product of a close collation of the early authoritative editions and manuscripts. Not infrequently the result has been to displace a reading which has passed into general use; for in all cases of doubt Bach's autographs at Berlin and elsewhere have been examined. His pause signs have been retained and should be treated as double-bars in modern Hymn-books. Not infrequently Bach (or his earliest editor) places a ⌢ at points which do not close a line of the stanza, and so confuses the metrical structure of the hymn. In such cases the ⌢ has been removed, an asterisk denoting its position.

The Chorals are printed in their original key, and, where more than one setting of a melody occurs, in ascending order of pitch. By that means, since settings of similar key are contiguous, the organist can vary the accompaniment, or with equal facility the choir can alternate the harmonic treatment. The stanzas have been distributed to aid this interchange.

The number of Chorals decorated by Bach with instrumental *obbligati* is small. It has not seemed necessary to print the latter, excepting No. 135, a text only found in Erk. But in every instance the existence of instrumental *obbligati* is stated, and they can be easily found in the Cantata vocal scores in which they occur. Their introduction into one or more of the verses of the hymn is advised. It is also suggested that when a Choral melody is treated in one of Bach's Organ Preludes, the movement be introduced as a voluntary.

The explanatory notes upon the pages containing each Choral are restricted to a bare record of its source, date, and authorship, withdrawing to the Appendices the critical apparatus which it is my further purpose to provide. Appendix I exhibits the results of an exhaustive collation of the early texts of each Choral, variant readings, and historical notes which expose the date and purpose of such as are not associated with extant Cantatas. It attempts a task which till now has not been undertaken. Largely owing to the unsatisfactory manner in which Bach's 'Vierstimmige Choralgesänge, Lieder und Arien' were edited for the Bachgesellschaft in 1892 (Jahrgang XXXIX), it has been assumed that the four-part settings in that volume alone merit consideration, and that others excluded from it as 'duplicates' are either repetitions or inferior versions of the preferred text. In fact, the excluded settings not only preserve authoritative variant readings, but in some cases are sufficiently distinct to demand their separate inclusion. In these pages they are restored or their variant readings recorded. For the first time also an attempt is made (Appendix I) to relate the unattached Chorals to a practical purpose. It is shown that almost all their hymns were popular during the years 1730–1750 and were admitted into the Leipzig Hymn-book in that period. It is to be concluded therefore that they were written for the Leipzig churches, in some cases for the projected expansion of Schemelli's Hymn-book, and that frequently they are the survivors of otherwise lost Cantatas: for it was not Bach's habit to introduce into his concerted music hymns and melodies unfamiliar to his congregation.

Appendix II provides a metrical index of melodies which will facilitate the task of those who desire to fit Bach's settings to original English hymns. It will be observed that the preference of Bach's period was for six, seven, and eight-line stanzas. Stanzas of ten, twelve, and even fourteen lines are not infrequent and are of complicated metrical structure. The student will find it instructive to follow the development of

PREFACE

Choral melody from its pre-Reformation form to the curve it assumed under Bach's modelling. Appendix III will be useful in that connexion. It is interesting to notice how largely the sixteenth century bulked in Bach's preference, and how sparingly he harmonized tunes of his own century. The attribution of melodies to Bach himself is a speculative task: he put his name to only one (No. 481 *infra*). Still, his idiom is so personal and distinguishing that the attempt may be essayed with some confidence. The melodies that can be attributed to him with considerable certainty are numbered under his name at the end of the Appendix. An index of composers (Appendix IV) will facilitate the historical enquiry along another avenue. Appendices V and VII permit a similar investigation of German hymnody. The melodies are printed in alphabetical order, but since they are frequently associated with hymns otherwise entitled, a separate index is provided in Appendix VI. In Appendix VIII the hymns are grouped according to their seasonal use.

I desire to record my particular obligation to Prof. Dr Wilhelm Altmann, Director of the Department of Music in the Preussische Staatsbibliothek, Berlin, for his unfailing readiness to assist my investigations. It has been necessary constantly to refer disputed readings to the MSS in his custody. I owe to him also a lengthy use of MS P.831, on whose significance and value I dwell in the Introduction. To Dr W. Meyer, Director of the Staats- und Universitäts-Bibliothek, Königsberg, I am indebted for the loan of the 1784–87 edition of the 'Vierstimmige Choralgesänge', of which the only English copy known to me is in the Fitzwilliam Museum at Cambridge. I cannot refrain from remarking upon the singular generosity which has enabled an English student to receive into his distant hands the rare contents of German libraries. I must also thank Dr. W. Herse, Librarian of the Fürstl. Stolbergsche Bibliothek, Wernigerode, for assistance in tracing the author and source of unfamiliar hymns; Messrs. Breitkopf & Härtel, Leipzig, for giving access to their archives in my search for letters elucidating their publication of the 'Choralgesänge' in 1784–87; to Prof. Dr Walther Schubring, Hamburg, and Dr Reinhard Fink, Leipzig University, who also have helped me in that quest. Finally, I am beholden to Dr W. G. Whittaker, Mr E. Stanley Roper, and Mr Hubert J. Foss for reading my proof-sheets, and for counsel and correction.

I gratefully acknowledge the courtesy of Messrs Grauert and Zink, of Charlottenburg, who have permitted me to use for my frontispiece W. E. Hoffmann's etched portrait of Bach.

C. SANFORD TERRY

King's College
   Old Aberdeen
     February, 1928

INTRODUCTION

Marpurg's MS (1763)

Bach's altitude as a composer was instantly admitted in two aspects of his genius: his Organ works circulated in copies originally made by his pupils, while his harmonized hymn tunes obtained so wide a vogue that two editions of them passed into print within thirty years of his death, a full generation before his other vocal works were similarly respected. Whether he had been at pains himself to assemble his Chorals cannot be decided. Certainly such a source was accessible to his second son, Carl Philipp Emanuel (1714–88), who owned a MS containing more than four hundred of them, chiefly, according to Kirnberger[1], in his own handwriting. That Carl Philipp's collection was not formed by diligent individual search in his father's autographs is evidenced by the omission of many that exist in scores he inherited on his father's death.[2] It can be shown that others made copies of his manuscript. Thus, in his New Year's catalogue for 1764, the Leipzig publisher, Bernhard Christoph Breitkopf, a friend of the younger Bach, announced for sale:[3]

Bachs, J. S. Vollständiges Choralbuch mit in Noten aufgesetzten Generalbasse an 240 in Leipzig gewöhnlichen Melodien. 10 thl.
Bach, J. S. Capellmeisters und Musikdirectors in Leipzig, 150 Choräle, mit 4 Stimmen. a 6 Thlr.

These texts[4], however, did not furnish the first printed edition of the Chorals. Its history is detailed by Joh. Philipp Kirnberger (1721–83), Kapellmeister to Princess Amalia of Prussia, in a letter to Johann Gottlob Immanuel Breitkopf, who controlled the Leipzig firm after his father Bernhard Christoph's death on March 26, 1777. Kirnberger's correspondence with Breitkopf opened in May 1777; it reveals that he desired to interest the new head of the firm forthwith in the production of a new edition of Bach's Chorals. Meanwhile, in a long letter, dated June 19, 1777[5], he detailed the circumstances that led to the earlier one he now desired to supersede. He reveals the unsuspected fact that the immediate agent in its publication was Friedrich Wilhelm Marpurg (1718–95), composer, theorist, critic, who, in 1762 or early in 1763, induced the Berlin publisher, Fr. Wilhelm Birnstiel, to print two hundred of Bach's four-part Chorals from a manuscript in his possession. Marpurg's fortunes, according to Kirnberger, were at a low ebb, and Birnstiel's offer to pay him twelve hundred groschen for seeing the work through the press was accepted. He gave up the task when Kirnberger's influence, probably exerted through Princess Amalia, obtained him in 1763 the Directorship of the Prussian State Lottery. Thereupon, the first hundred Chorals being now in type, Birnstiel invited Carl Philipp Emanuel Bach, at that time in Berlin in Frederick the Great's service, to complete Marpurg's task. Demanding and receiving thrice Marpurg's fee, Carl Philipp consented; in 1765, with a brief Preface by the new editor and a formidable Table of 'Druckfehler,' the volume appeared.

The second Part of Marpurg's MS still remained unprinted, for Birnstiel, who thought Carl Philipp's demands extortionate, and had published Part I only 'mit Angst und Noth', writes Kirnberger, was not willing again to incur a similar charge. However, after an interval, and perhaps taking advantage of Carl Philipp's migration to Hamburg in 1767, Birnstiel invited Kirnberger to prepare the second hundred of Marpurg's Chorals for the press. Kirnberger declined, partly to avoid a quarrel with Carl Philipp, partly because he lacked time and inclination to correct a text alleged to be faulty. Birnstiel therefore turned to Johann Fr. Agricola (1720–74), Frederick the Great's Kapellmeister, a pupil of Johann Sebastian's, who fulfilled the commission with care, but not without blemish. In April or May 1769, four years after the first, the second Part of Marpurg's MS was published. It lacked a Preface, Carl Philipp's name was removed from the title-page, and Agricola's association with it was not made public.

Carl Philipp, who received a copy of the new volume at Hamburg, perused it with indignation. He ' seized the occasion,' says Kirnberger[6], 'to revenge himself on Birnstiel, and all because of the fee he had failed to draw into his own pocket. So he inserted a paragraph in a Hamburg paper, declaring Birnstiel's second volume to be full of mistakes, and even of containing Chorals of which his father was not the composer. So damaging was his action that the whole edition became so much waste paper.' Kirnberger's memory failed him in only one particular: C. P. E. Bach did not accuse the volume of containing spurious settings, but on the ground of its general faultiness flagellated it in a ' Nachricht für das Publikum ' published in the ' Staats- und Gelehrte Zeitung des Hamburgischen unpartheyeschen Correspondenten ', No. 85, on May 30, 1769:

NOTICE TO THE PUBLIC

With audacity that excels even his ignorance of music Herr Birnstiel has just published Part II of Johann Sebastian Bach's four-part Chorals, which I myself originally brought together, without giving me any hint of his intention.[7]

---

[1] *Bach-Jahrbuch* 1918, p. 142.
[2] e.g., Cantatas 59, 66, 79, 92, 97, 130, 175, 185, 195.
[3] Spitta iii, 108, 115.
[4] The possibility cannot be excluded that one of these collections came from Bach's eldest son, Wilhelm Friedemann. See *infra*, p. vii. The title of the larger manuscript suggests that it contained the settings prepared by Bach for Schemelli. Probably they were included in C. P. E. Bach's MS. See *infra*, p. viii.
[5] *Bach-Jahrbuch* 1918, p. 143
[6] *Bach-Jahrbuch* 1918, p. 144.
[7] This is not true. Kirnberger says that Birnstiel's invitation to him to edit the volume was made in Carl Philipp's presence.

I have examined the text sufficiently to see that it contains a mass of mistakes of all kinds. Disgust and indignation withhold me from giving closer attention to it; for I find in it errors that not even a beginner in composition would make. I shall be glad to show my original MS to anyone who cares to see it, and to point out the blunders of which I complain. Seeing that my distinguished father's reputation is hereby belittled, not to speak of my own as the original collector, I give public notice that I am not responsible, and earnestly beg that no one will circulate this libel by purchasing the book. I would ask every friend of my late father to prevent it from getting into public use. For the work inflicts a posthumous slur upon his credit, all the greater because this collection was planned to be a manual affording unimpeachable examples of the utmost value to students. As if we had not enough text-books already that teach false principles and print incorrect examples.

Hamburg, May 29, 1769.   C. P. E. BACH[1].

Before examining Birnstiel's edition of the Chorals, a preliminary problem needs to be investigated. Kirnberger's letter already quoted states that it was printed from a MS purchased by Birnstiel for thirty thalers[2]. The sum clearly included the right to print, for, as we have seen, 240 Chorals were offered by Breitkopf for ten thalers in 1764, whereas Marpurg's MS contained only 200. Whence had Marpurg acquired the right to dispose of a collection certainly not made by himself? Facts and inference alike declare it a transcript of Parts I and II of Carl Philipp Emanuel's larger collection. The outer sheet of his MS states its contents to have been ' collected by Carl Philipp Emanuel Bach '; the title-page of Birnstiel's first volume repeats the acknowledgement; its Preface promises still more Parts to follow, i.e., Marpurg's Part II, and, evidently, Parts III and IV of Carl Philipp's manuscript. Moreover, a collation of Marpurg's MS with Carl Philipp's collection as published by Breitkopf in 1784–1785 establishes the correspondence; for not only are their contents identical, but their order is identical, too[3]. Further, though in 1769 Carl Philipp condemned the errors in Birnstiel's second volume, he did not impugn his right to print; while his offer to prove its inaccuracies by a reference to his own MS, and his insistence that his personal reputation was involved, put the conclusion beyond doubt. Corroborative evidence, however, can be adduced. Marpurg's relations with Carl Philipp dated back at least to 1756, when he included three of the latter's songs in a volume of ' Oden und Melodien ' published by Bernhard Christoph Breitkopf. A year later Carl Philipp apparently obtained through him an introduction to the Leipzig firm, for Marpurg writes to Breitkopf in March 1757: ' In regard to Herr Bach, you need not doubt his friendly feelings towards you. All the same, it is money that he thinks most about, and unless you are ready to part with a hundred ducats or so, you will find it hard to do business with him '. In fact, it was not until 1766 that Breitkopf published a complete original work by Carl Philipp, the first of many and the foundation of a friendship which lasted till Breitkopf's death and was continued by his son[4]. These facts not only establish an earlier relationship between Carl Philipp and Marpurg, but indicate a situation in 1757 closely repeated in 1762 or 1763. It must, therefore, be regarded as established that Marpurg's MS was derived from Carl Philipp. His indirect approach to a publisher would be less easy to understand had he not taken that course again in connexion with his father's Chorals twenty years later. If Carl Philipp was under an obligation to Marpurg, then in poor circumstances, we may discover in the transaction an example of his not disinterested generosity.

Is Marpurg's MS extant? The Musik-Abteilung of the Preussische Staatsbibliothek owns an MS (P.831), unnoticed hitherto, whose outer sheet is thus inscribed:

Johann Sebastian Bachs vierstimmige Choralgesaenge gesamlet von Carl Philipp Emanuel Bach. Erster und Zweyter Theil.

The MS consists of 107 numbered pages, $8\frac{3}{4}$ by $14\frac{1}{2}$ inches in size and stout in texture, on which in very clear and careful script are written the two hundred Chorals printed by Birnstiel in 1765 and 1769. No. 100 is followed by the intimation: ' Ende des ersten Theiles ', while No. 101, on a new page, is prefaced by the heading: ' Zweyter Theil '. A pencilled note on the outer sheet poses the query: ' Von Hering geschrieben ? ' Since J. Hering was a pupil of Carl Philipp Emanuel's at Hamburg the question is relevant. In fact, he was not the writer. The two Parts of the MS correspond with the contents of Birnstiel's two volumes. But Nos. 11 and 12 of Part I are transposed, No. 11 of the MS being No. 12 of the printed Part I, while Nos. 137 and 138 are similarly transposed in Part II. The Preface contributed by Carl Philipp Emanuel to Birnstiel's Part I in 1765 is not in the MS as originally copied, but is inserted upon two smaller sheets between pages 1 and 2.

The question arises: Is P.831 a transcript of Birnstiel's volumes, or is it the original from which they were set up? An answer to two preliminary queries will help to a conclusion:

1 Why did the copyist omit Carl Philipp Emanuel's Preface?

2 Why is the order of the Chorals varied in the instances noted above?

Since it has been shown that Carl Philipp Emanuel's editorial association with the 1765 print was an accident, his Preface cannot have formed part of the MS submitted by Marpurg to Birnstiel. Indeed, its language

[1] C. H. Bitter, *Carl Philipp Emanuel und Wilhelm Friedemann Bach und deren Brüder* (Berlin, 1868), i, 167, regards the letter as a genuine expression of filial concern. His whole chapter on the topic is misinformed. I am obliged to Prof. Dr Schubring, who aided my search for the letter in the Hamburg newspaper files. Bitter's transcript is not textually correct.

[2] *Bach-Jahrbuch* 1918, p. 144.

[3] As will appear, this statement requires slight correction.

[4] See Dr H. von Hase's article on the relations of C. P. E. Bach and J. G. I. Breitkopf in the *Bach-Jahrbuch* 1911, pp. 86 ff.

Title-page of F. W. Marpurg's MS

makes this clear. Hence its omission from P.831 is explicable if P.831 is older than the printed volume and as clearly the reverse if it is not. In regard to the transposed Chorals, Nos. 11 and 12, 137 and 138, each pair fills a whole page of the printed edition, Nos. 11 and 12 on page 6 of 1765, Nos. 137 and 138 on page 73 of 1769. There is no apparent reason why the copyist should vary the order of the print, but there is a clear reason why the compositor should have done so with his manuscript ' copy ', for the transposition placed the lengthier Choral more conveniently at the top of his page.

On both these grounds, therefore, probability inclines to the conclusion that in 1765 and again in 1769 the compositor set up his type from P.831[1]—in other words, P.831 is the actual document put into Birnstiel's hands by Marpurg. Inference, however, can be pushed to certainty: Birnstiel's earlier (1765) volume contains a formidable Table of Errors, the result of Carl Philipp Emanuel's belated revision, which enumerates and corrects fifty-nine typographical misprints in the text of the first hundred Chorals.[2] Forty-one of them are printers' errors not found in P.831, the remainder (eighteen) are common to it and the printed text. Supposing the print and its list of exposed errors to have been before the writer of the MS, his omission to correct nearly one-third of them is difficult to understand. On the other hand, if the print was set up from P.831 the circumstances are clear: Carl Philipp Bach, coming late into touch with the print, detected, exposed in a Table, and corrected forty-one errors to conform with the MS. He recorded also eighteen more common to it and the print. No Table of Errors was published with Birnstiel's Part II (1769). But a collation of it with P.831 again indicates that the MS is the older document; for, as we should expect, in view of the more careful editorial work on it, the print (1769) is the more accurate. In ten Chorals P.831 exhibits errors which are not repeated in the print[3], while in only one case[4] the error is not shared by it. Every line of approach therefore, leads to the conclusion that P.831 is the original MS in Marpurg's possession from which the prints of 1765 and 1769 were set up in type. The supposition that it is a duplicate of Marpurg's MS is countered by the fact that Birnstiel paid thirty thalers for it, a price far in excess of its market value, as has been shown, unless the copyright of publication passed with the transaction. Birnstiel would not have paid such a sum for a manuscript of which a duplicate was vendible; for in that case he exposed himself to the risk of competition. It may be objected that Birnstiel's copyright did not prevent Breitkopf from publishing a competing edition in 1784–1787. But it will be shown that Breitkopf's was a fuller collection, and that its publication actually was delayed until Birnstiel withdrew from the field.

Birnstiel's Edition (1765–1769)

The circumstances attending the publication of Birnstiel's first volume have been detailed. Containing Part I of Marpurg's MS (Chorals 1–100) it was published in 1765 with the following title-page[5]:

Johann Sebastian Bachs vierstimmige Choralgesänge gesammlet von Carl Philipp Emanuel Bach. Erster Theil. Berlin und Leipzig, gedruckt und zu finden bey Friedrich Wilhelm Birnstiel, Königl. privil. Buchdrucker, 1765.

The volume is an oblong folio of fifty numbered pages, each of which normally contains two Chorals. They are preceded by Carl Philipp Emanuel's brief Preface, which throws little light on the history of the volume but speaks of its contents with filial respect:

The care of this collection was entrusted to me by the publisher after several sheets had been printed off. Hence it contains four Chorals which were not harmonized by my father, namely, Nos. 6, 15, 18, 31.[6] All the rest, in this volume and others to follow, were written by my father on four staves for four voices.[7] Here they are printed on two staves for the convenience of Organ and Clavier players. If they are sung, they will sometimes be found beyond the compass of particular voices and can be transposed. When the Bass part descends so low that it is played on the pedals, the voice may sing the octave above. Similarly, if the Bass rises above the Tenor, the lower octave may be played. Indeed, the composer was wont to accompany the Chorals with a sixteen-foot instrument in order to meet these conditions.[8] To help singers who otherwise might not readily follow the composer's intentions, the crossing of the parts is shown by single or double lines.

I am so sure that this collection of Chorals will give pleasure and be found useful that I do not attempt to enlarge upon its harmonic beauties. Indeed, the composer needs no testimonial from me to a public which has learnt to expect only masterpieces from his pen. There is no doubt whatever that every instructed user of these Chorals will place them in that category, whether he observes the easy and natural progression of their inner parts, or their Basses. For instructional purposes they will prove no less valuable. As an introduction to composition they are obviously to be preferred to stiff and pedantic counterpoint.

In conclusion, I take particular pleasure in announcing that this volume is the first instalment of a complete Choral Book. Two more Parts are to follow, and the whole will contain more than three hundred settings. C. P. E. BACH

Carl Philipp's Preface touches two matters which call for comment. He remarks that, contrary to his father's habit, the Chorals are set up on two staves for the convenience of players. But his short score differs from that in modern usage, which restricts the Soprano and Alto parts to the upper, and the Tenor and Bass

[1] An examination of the prints establishes the fact that they are examples of musical type printing. In Bach's own lifetime, less than twenty years earlier, such of his works as were printed were engraved on copper.

[2] The inference to be drawn is that either Birnstiel would not sanction the expense involved in correcting the type on the plates, or, more probably, that the sheets were printed off before the errors were discovered. Carl Philipp's Preface expressly says so in regard to the earlier portions of the book which contained the Chorals he denounced as spurious

[3] Cf. Appendix I, Nos. 39, 44, 129, 231, 235, 248, 294, 317, 319, 345.

[4] Appendix I, No. 341. In the cases of Nos. 96 and 348, P. 831 gives a preferable reading.

[5] A copy is in the British Museum.

[6] They are omitted from this volume

[7] See the illustration at p. xii.

[8] See Terry, *Bach's Cantatas and Oratorios* (O.U.P.), Bk. II, 33.

to the lower stave. In the 1765–1769 prints, while the Soprano and Bass parts are so confined, the middle parts are printed on the upper or lower stave according as they fall above or below the middle C, the bottom line of the upper stave, which serves as a bridge over which each part passes into the other system:

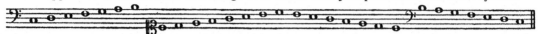

Simple, in that it abolishes duplicating ledger lines, the method tends on occasion to overload the stave, and was discarded by Breitkopf in 1784. In the second place, Carl Philipp's reference to the Bass part draws attention to the fact that for Chorals drawn from a Cantata, Motet, or Oratorio, the instrumental (continuo) and not the vocal Bass is generally provided. Comment upon the essentially instrumental purpose of the edition will be offered later.

An interval of four years intervened between the publication of Part I and Part II of Birnstiel's edition, in the duration of which Carl Philipp Emanuel migrated (1767) from Berlin to Hamburg. In April or May 1769, Part II (Nos. 101–200) made its appearance, uniform with its predecessor, paged consecutively (pp. 51–104), and with the following title-page:

Johann Sebastian Bachs vierstimmige Choralgesänge, Zweyter Theil. Berlin und Leipzig. gedruckt und zu finden. bey Friderich (sic) Wilhelm Birnstiel. Königl. privil. Buchdrucker. 1679.

Breitkopf's Edition (1784–1787)

Carl Philipp's strictures upon it and the admittedly defective text of its predecessor suggested the need for a more authoritative edition of the Chorals. Hence, soon after the appearance of Carl Philipp's advertisement, Kirnberger wrote to him on the matter. Carl Philipp replied on July 21, 1769[1]:

Like you, I am anxious to see a correct edition of my father's Chorals, and am ready to do all I can in the matter, but I leave you to take the necessary steps. I stipulate that Part II must be cleared of its errors and I will attend to Parts III and IV, you yourself undertaking the general revision of the whole. But my name must appear on Part I and the three following parts[2]; thereby I become responsible for the text. And this is essential—I must be paid in advance.

According to his own statement, Carl Philipp handed his manuscript to Kirnberger in 1771. As six years elapsed thereafter before the latter approached Breitkopf, it is possible that he first made overtures to Birnstiel, who, perhaps discouraged by the sales of his own edition, was disinclined to run further risks. At length, on May 10, 1777, Kirnberger wrote to Joh. Gottlob Immanuel Breitkopf:[3]

I have here the Chorals of Johann Seb. Bach which Herr Birnstiel published in two faulty Parts, along with two hundred more, over four hundred in all, which Her Highness [Princess Amalia] bought [1771] from Capellmeister Bach, of Hamburg. He has sold his right to publish them, which I alone now possess. On all sides I am urged to print them, but I am not in a position to bear the cost. If you are inclined to publish them I will gladly discuss terms with you; for the world will be the poorer if these Chorals are not preserved for posterity.

Apparently Breitkopf did not reply. Kirnberger therefore wrote again a month later (June 7, 1777):[4]

Regarding Bach's Chorals, of which I own more than four hundred, collected and for the most part copied by Herr Bach, of Hamburg: their publication for the benefit of future generations of musicians lies very close to my heart. I am not looking for profits from publisher or bookseller, nor do I want to sell them. You may have them for nothing if only you will make them accessible in worthy type in the cause of knowledge and for the use of young students. If any profit is forthcoming, it is yours, not mine. All I ask are a few copies for myself and Herr Bach, who begged for some when the Chorals are published, though he has already been paid twelve gold 'Fredericks', given me by my generous Princess for the purpose.

Breitkopf thought it prudent to seek information regarding Birnstiel's edition. For, a fortnight later (June 19, 1777), Kirnberger writes to him again, detailing the circumstances already narrated and bringing the story down to Carl Philipp's public denunciation of the 1769 print. He proceeds[5]:

To return to myself. I always longed to own every single Choral that can be attributed to Bach. So I begged my gracious Princess to buy the unpublished settings from Herr Bach, which she did. He asked for and was paid twelve louis d'or, handing over to me [1771] his complete MS. At the same time he sent me a letter, which I pass on to you, containing these words: 'Subject to your revision and correction, I consent to your publishing these, along with the others printed by Birnstiel, to form a complete Choral Book.' So, you see, I have his unqualified consent. It is so important that these splendid compositions should be available for all, and especially for students, and I am so disinclined to reap any reward for myself, that they are yours for nothing if you will print them to the eternal honour of Joh. Sebastian Bach. It is understood that the Chorals already published by Birnstiel must be included: they bring the total to more than four hundred. Of course, if you wish to make me some acknowledgement, I shall accept it gratefully. But whatever you do, you are free to print the Chorals as if you had bought them. If you do so, I undertake to read the proofs; there is no one in Leipzig I would trust with that task, not even Herr [Johann Adam] Hiller,[6] judging from the music he writes.

At this point the negotiations were complicated by Breitkopf's acquisition of a smaller collection of Chorals 'from Bach's heirs' ('von den Bachischen Erben'), containing precisely the number advertised for sale at six thalers in 1764; it was probably a duplicate of that manuscript. The reference to Bach's heirs clearly points to Wilhelm Friedemann Bach, who in 1764 gave up his Halle appointment, and entered upon

---

[1] Bach-Jahrbuch 1918, p. 143.
[2] Clearly Kirnberger had suggested, as eventually happened, that the Chorals should be published in four separate issues.
[3] Bach-Jahrbuch 1918, p. 142.
[4] Ibid.
[5] Ibid., p. 144.
[6] Hiller, who later became Cantor of the Thomasschule, depreciated Bach as a composer.

The Choral 'In dich hab ich gehoffet, Herr' in Marpurg's MS

INTRODUCTION

a chequered career which drove him to procure money by the sale of his father's manuscripts. Breitkopf informed Kirnberger of his acquisition and was answered on July 1 1777:[1]

> Regarding the Bach Chorals I sent you, I beg you to tell me without further delay whether you mean to publish them. You say that you have purchased another hundred and fifty from Bach's heirs, which may be duplicates of those in my collection. If they are not, it will be well to add them to it; but I should like to examine them first in order to determine whether they really are by Bach and to see that their text is accurate.

Reiterating his disinterestedness in the matter, Kirnberger informed Breitkopf that he had recently praised the technique of the Chorals ' at the close of my theoretical work ', his ' Kunst des reinen Satzes ', in which, discussing the treatment of the parts in four-part vocal harmony, he remarks:' In this characteristic the late Capellmeister Bach of Leipzig excels all other composers. And so, besides his larger works, I strongly recommend his Chorals to students, for they are the best models available '. And in a footnote: ' In view of the value of this great man's music to young composers, I propose shortly to publish one hundred of his Chorals'. Breitkopf held out some prospect of the promise being fulfilled. For, on July 26, 1777 Kirnberger writes again:[2]

> As the Chorals are to be published in their completeness, you had better arrange them in the order you think best. As to subscriptions in advance, I leave you to settle the rate, for I dissociate myself entirely from the finance aspect of the transaction, being content to know that I shall have performed a service to music, benefited Church and organist, enriched family devotions, and instructed young musicians by the publication of these incomparable examples of four-part harmony. If you can see your way to mention my name in the Preface, so that the world may recognize its debt to me, I am amply repaid.

Breitkopf's caution was sharpened by a visit from Birnstiel, who, coming to Leipzig in 1778 for the Easter Fair, announced his tardy decision to complete his edition of the Chorals in the ensuing summer. Whence he had obtained the materials is not known. But the news made Breitkopf pause. Hence, on October 31, 1778, his patience being exhausted, Kirnberger demanded the return of his manuscript, alleging the commands of his Princess[3]. Breitkopf complied. But the months passed without any movement on Birnstiel's part, and on March 17, 1779, Kirnberger wrote bitterly to Breitkopf: ' It seems that Johann Seb. Bach's sublime Chorals are fated never to be seen in print '[4]. A long interval of silence ensued, broken on March 27, 1781, by a letter from Kirnberger to Breitkopf:[5]

> That splendid collection of Joh. Seb. Bach's four-part Chorals which you looked at long ago is still lying here in manuscript. What a thousand pities it is not in print for the benefit of posterity. If you will only publish it and give me a single copy on good paper it is yours for nothing, for art's sake, and for the eternal glory of Bach.

Impressed by Kirnberger's insistence, or encouraged by Birnstiel's inactivity, Breitkopf at length accepted the gift, but refused to publish at his sole charge. ' The market for Choral Books is limited,' he explained. ' If within six months subscribers or guarantors do not come forward in sufficient numbers to meet the cost, the idea of printing must be dropped altogether.' Kirnberger was satisfied, and in the latter part of April 1781 again sent up his MS to Leipzig, in the charge of merchants attending the Easter Fair. He followed it in May with letters insisting upon its return in case the publication was abandoned, or alternatively, the receipt of the sum Princess Amalia had paid for it. The time-limit for intimation of subscriptions was fixed for Easter 1782, and an advertisement was drafted and published[5]. It received a moderate response. Kirnberger, however, now an invalid, protested against abandonment of publication on that ground. He wrote on November 5, 1782:[6]

> I cannot allow a work which posterity will receive with open arms to be lost merely because subscriptions do not provide the amount you require

And again on December 3, 1782[7]:

> I beg you to tell me how soon Part 1 of the Chorals will be published. We must name a definite date to those who are expecting it; for interest evaporates if a time limit is exceeded.

Six months passed. Part I still remained in manuscript, and on June 14, 1783, hopeless and disappointed, Kirnberger penned his last letter:[8]

> You have fooled me over and over again with the prospect, which I now know to have been groundless, of seeing the collection I gave you in print. I now demand the return of my MS. If you do not restore it within a fortnight, or failing a reply from yourself, I shall regard it as an intimation to me to send for it.

Six weeks later (July 27, 1783) Kirnberger died, his heart's desire unfulfilled. It would be unfair to lay the blame entirely upon Breitkopf's timidity. The publication of hymn-books of the conventional type received remarkable stimulus from the thirties of the century. But Carl Philipp Emanuel's collection was not in their category. A large number of its hymns were not in congregational use, yet no words were provided. The score was inconveniently arranged for singers, the parts were not phrased, their motions frequently obscure, and the Bass parts often non-vocal. Hence we must attribute the failure of Kirnberger's enthusiastic crusade partly to the unconventional character of Bach's ' Choralbuch '. Whether Breitkopf was restrained by Carl Philipp Emanuel at Hamburg cannot be decided.[9] It is at least curious that the tedious delays so disheartening to Kirnberger were replaced by an alacrity which published the first part of Carl Philipp's MS within

---

[1] *Bach-Jahrbuch* 1918, p. 145.   [2] *Ibid.*
[3] The possibility must not be excluded that Kirnberger had been drawn to approach Birnstiel by Breitkopf's dilatoriness.
[4] *Bach-Jahrbuch* 1918, p. 146.   [5] *Ibid.*   [6] *Ibid.* p. 147.
[7] *Ibid.*   [8] *Ibid.*
[9] Over two hundred letters from C. P. E. Bach to J. G. I. Breitkopf exist in the archives of the firm. Alike in those dealt with in Dr von Hase's article in *Bach-Jahrbuch* 1911, and in those still unpublished, the subject of his father's Chorals is not referred to.

a few months of the former's death. It made its appearance in 1784, contained 96 Chorals, and bore the following title-page:

Johann Sebastian Bachs vierstimmige Choralgesänge. Erster Theil. Leipzig, bey Johann Gottlob Immanuel Breitkopf. 1784.

As in 1765, Carl Philipp was invited to provide a Preface, but, with niggardly economy of effort, troubled himself no further than to re-write the first four sentences of his earlier ' Vorrede ', now twenty years old, repeating the rest of it verbatim:[1]

I have very carefully collated this text of the Chorals with the earlier edition, and have corrected the latter's errors. Herr Kirnberger, to whom I handed my collection in 1771, put it into the hands of its present publisher shortly before his death. From this new edition are excluded the unauthentic Chorals in the earlier one. Consequently, all that are printed here and in the other parts to follow may be accepted as my father's, and were written out by him, *etc., etc.*

Carl Philipp's reference to Kirnberger imperfectly conveys the facts as they are now known to us, and does scant justice to his patient loyalty and enthusiasm. A list of subscribers follows the Preface, whose meagre total (42) confirms Breitkopf's caution. Not a single Leipzig musician is named in it, though Weimar and Cöthen subscribed for the work of a composer formerly associated with both of them. Of the forty-two, the name of Johann Nikolaus Forkel alone has distinction. Parts II, III, IV of the work appeared at regular intervals in 1785, 1786, and 1787, the last with an index which brings the complete work to a total of 218 quarto pages. With the necessary typographical alterations and the provision of distinctive woodcuts, their title-pages are uniform with that of Part I. Breitkopf's catalogue for Michaelmas 1785 shows that each volume was sold for one thaler eight groschen.

Parts I (1784) and II (1785) reprint the contents of Birnstiel's volumes, minus the four (Nos. 6, 15, 18, 31) repudiated by Carl Philipp, No. 190 of Birnstiel's edition (a duplicate of his No. 68), and his No. 168, whose omission is against its authenticity, though Carl Philipp's earlier Preface sponsored its genuineness[2]. Thus Parts I and II of Breitkopf's edition contain 194 Chorals, revised by Carl Philipp, and purged of the errors in the earlier print[3]. The Chorals of the four Parts are numbered 1 to 370; Part I, Nos. 1–96; Part II, Nos. 97–194; Part III, Nos. 195–283; Part IV, Nos. 283–370. The actual total is 371 Chorals, since both the last Choral of Part III and the first of Part IV are numbered 283. It is observable that the total falls short of that frequently stated by Kirnberger as ' over 400 '. On the other hand, Carl Philipp himself, in 1765 and again in 1784, totalled his collection at ' more than 300 '. The discrepancy can be explained on the assumption that Kirnberger numbered the Schemelli arrangements, which, though included in Carl Philipp's MS, were not deemed by him appropriate to the ' Choral Buch '.

Though their texts are infrequently identical, twenty-three of the 371 Chorals have been disregarded hitherto as duplicates of others, a fact upon which comment will be offered later. They are as follows:

	Melody					Breitkopf's Edition	The Present Edition
1	Ach Gott, wie manches Herzeleid	...	...	...	...	156, 307	9
2	Allein Gott in der Höh sei Ehr	...	...	...	...	125, 325	17
3	Allein Gott in der Höh sei Ehr	...	...	...	...	312, 352	16
4	An Wasserflüssen Babylon	...	...	...	...	5, 308	24
5	Christus, der uns selig macht	...	...	...	...	198, 306	50
6	Das neugeborne Kindelein	...	...	...	...	52, 178	60
7	Durch Adams Fall ist ganz verderbt	...	...	...	100, 126	76
8	Ermuntre dich, mein schwacher Geist	...	...	...	9, 360	84
9	Freu dich sehr, o meine Seele	...	...	...	...	63, 256	106
10	Freu dich sehr, o meine Seele	...	...	...	...	254, 282	109
11	Heilig, heilig, heilig	...	...	...	...	235, 318	127
12	Helft mir Gotts Güte preisen	...	...	...	...	23, 88	128
13	Herr [O] Jesu Christ, meins Lebens Licht	...	...	236, 294	295
14	Herr, wie du willt, so schicks mit mir	...	...	...	144, 317	152
15	Hilf Gott, dass mirs gelinge	...	...	...	...	199, 301	176
16	Ich hab in Gottes Herz und Sinn	...	...	...	...	120, 348	361
17	Liebster Jesu, wir sind hier	...	...	...	...	131, 327	235
18	Nun lasst uns Gott dem Herren	...	...	...	...	93, 257	275
19	O Mensch, bewein dein Sünde gross	...	...	...	201, 305	297
20	Sei Lob und Ehr dem höchsten Gut	...	...	...	248, 353	93
21	Verleih uns Frieden gnädiglich	...	...	...	...	91, 259	332
22, 23	Wie schön leuchtet der Morgenstern	...	...	...	85, 195, 304	391

In three cases (Nos. 6, 7, 12 *supra*) the duplication occurs in Parts I. and II. In eleven (Nos. 1, 2, 4, 8, 9, 14, 16, 17, 18, 21, 22) the Choral is repeated from Parts I or II into a later Part. The remainder are within

[1] In fact, the word ' Kehle ' is substituted for ' Hälfe ' in the sentence: ' Wenn man sie vierstimmig absingen will, und einige davon den Umfang gewisser Hälfe überschreiten sollten: so kann mann sie übersetzen '. In the concluding sentence " drey," and not as earlier " zween," further Parts are promised.

[2] It is restored in the present edition (No. 55 *infra*).

[3] See Appendix I.

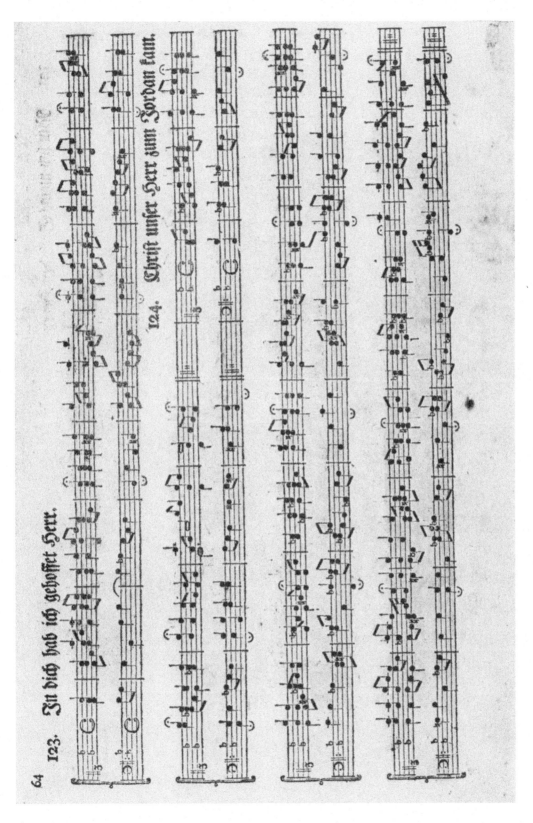

Parts III and IV. These duplications must not be regarded as due to carelessness. In most cases the duplicate pairs are associated with different hymns (Nos. 3, 4, 7, 8, 9, 10, 11, 12, 13, 14, 16, 18), while the third setting of ' Wie schön leuchtet der Morgenstern ' is distinguished from the others by association with a particular stanza. In four cases (Nos. 2, 4, 7, 9) the keys of the duplicates differ. There is, therefore, a strong presumption that each duplicate had a separate use and was extracted from a Cantata no longer extant. Almost exactly half (185) of the 371 are potentially in this category.

Breitkopf's edition is distinguished from Birnstiel's by its adoption of the modern short score. Otherwise it repeats its predecessor's bad qualities: the vocal parts are not phrased to the metre of the hymn, no words are provided, and the Bass is usually the instrumental Continuo.

Breitkopf's Third Edition (1832)

For nearly half a century the 1784–1787 edition satisfied the requirements of the public. It had passed out of print in the twenties of the nineteenth century, when interest in Bach revived, and was unprocurable except at second hand[1]. Hence, in 1832, Breitkopf and Härtel published a ' third edition ' of the Chorals in a single volume of 211 pages, with the following title-page:

371 vierstimmige Choralgesänge von Johann Sebastian Bach. Dritte Auflage. Eigenthum der Verleger. Leipzig, bei Breitkopf & Härtel. Pr. 3 Thlr.

The short Preface signed (' Leipzig, den 9 December 1831 ') by Carl Ferdinand Becker (1804–77), at that time organist of St Peter's, Leipzig, deprecates the tendency of the earlier editions to exhibit Bach's Chorals as technical models or instrumental pieces. Insisting that they were written for the use of the Thomanerchor and as movements within Cantatas, Motets, and similar works, he urges their use in public worship, whether as solos, quartets, or congregational hymns. It is the more regrettable, therefore, that the vocal parts are not phrased, a defect which seriously depreciated the volume for the use to which Becker desired to put it. Becker himself was not responsible; for, as in 1765, a practical musician was called in only at the last moment, when the book was in type and revision impracticable[2]. The volume exactly reproduces the contents, but not invariably the order, of the 1784–87 edition. No. 283b of that collection becomes 284, and the total numeration is thus expanded from 370 to 371. Throughout, the modern G clef replaces the C clef on the upper stave.

Friese's Edition (1843)

The third edition served for a decade. In 1841 Robert Friese, head of a general publishing firm which still exists, published the first ' Lieferung ' of an octavo edition of Bach's Chorals. It was followed by five others, the six forming a volume of x + 279 pages, issued in 1843 with the following title-page:

Joh. Seb. Bachs vierstimmige Kirchengesänge. Geordnet und mit einem Vorwort begleitet von C. F. Becker, Organisten an der Nicolaikirche und Lehrer an der Musikschule zu Leipzig. Eingetragen in das Archiv des Vereins. Mit Johann Sebastian Bach's Portrait. Leipzig, 1843. Verlag von Robert Friese.

As its title declares, the volume is definitely a hymn-book. The vocal parts are written out in full score, the customary vocal C clef is restored to the three upper parts, and the notes are phrased to fit the (unprinted) words. To the same practical purpose, but with excessive licence, many of the Chorals are transposed from their original key, while their Basses are treated in the manner recommended in C. P. E. Bach's original Preface. Otherwise, too, Becker used a freedom with his text which is regrettable, though here and there (see Appendix I) he corrected errors undetected in earlier editions. Nor is the volume a faithful reprint of Breitkopf's previous texts. Several Chorals common to them all are omitted—they are noted in Appendix I. Several are admitted from other sources: in the present edition they are Nos. 188, 205, 211, 235, 276, 416, 422, 438, 444, 459; notes upon them are in Appendix I. Becker also includes the Organ Prelude ' Wenn wir in höchsten Nöthen sein ' from Bach's ' Kunst der Fuge '.

Peters' Edition (1850–65)

Riemann characterizes Becker as unscholarly, a judgement probably sound. Yet in the period of his activity materials were inadequately available for a scholarly revision of the Choral texts. Ludwig Christian Erk (1807–83) was more fortunate. A teacher in the Berlin Seminar für Stadtschulen, conductor of male and mixed-voice choirs, and in 1857 Kgl. Musikdirektor, his name is not among the original members of the Bachgesellschaft, nor was he at any period upon its ' Directorium '. But his work is instinct with its scholarly spirit and, like its own, was aided by the concentration in Berlin of Bach's autographs hitherto dispersed. In 1850 he published with Peters the first volume of a new edition of Bach's Chorals, entitled:

Johann Sebastian Bachs mehrstimmige Choralgesänge und geistliche Arien. Zum ersten Mal unverändert nach authentischen Quellen mit ihren ursprünglichen Texten und mit den nöthigen Kunsthistorischen Nachweisungen herausgegeben von Ludwig Erk. In dieser Bearbeitung Eigenthum des Verlegers. Eingetragen in das Vereins-Archiv. Leipzig, C. F. Peters.

Erk's Preface (December 8, 1850) emphasizes the fact advertised on his title-page—his text is not a reprint of earlier editions, but is based on Bach's autographs and other authoritative manuscripts. Twenty-two of

---

[1] C. F. Becker writes (p. viii) in the Preface of the 1843 edition: ' Gedultig nahm das Publikum jedoch auch dieses Werk auf und im Lauf der Jahre war es so selten geworden, dass es längst nicht mehr auf dem Wege des Buchhandels zu erhalten war '.

[2] Becker makes this statement in his 1843 Preface.

its 150 numbers Erk claimed to publish for the first time. Three of them (Erk, Nos. 48, 149, 150) are extended Chorals (i.e., with orchestral interludes) excluded from the present edition. Three others—Erk, Nos. 43, 44, 111 (Nos. 429, 430, 471 *infra*)—are from Anna Magdalena Bach's 'Notenbuch'. One—Erk, No. 73 (No. 211 *infra*)—had, in fact, already been printed by Becker in 1843 (p. 147). The remaining fifteen —Erk, Nos. 11 (29 *infra*), 22 (72), 29 (86), 54 (161), 80 (226), 85 (126), 87 (243), 88 (254), 91 (259), 98 (273), 125 (351), 128 (357), 130 (360), 136 (372), 148 (402)—are extracted from Cantatas whose scores were not published by the Bachgesellschaft until many years after Erk's volume appeared.

Fifteen years later (Preface dated October 8, 1865) Erk published a second Part, containing numbers 151 to 319. Two of the Chorals are numbered 171. Hence the total in Part II is 170, and in the two volumes, 320. Part II includes thirty-one Chorals not found in previous editions. Of that number. Nos. 201, 233, 271, 298 and 319 are elaborate movements. Of the remaining twenty-six, six already had been published by the Bachgesellschaft—Nos. 174 (Cantata 7, No. 43 *infra*), 207 (Christmas Oratorio, No. 115 *infra*), 253 (Cantata 52, No. 193 *infra*), 260 (Cantata 195, No. 230 *infra*), 297 (Christmas Oratorio, No. 334 *infra*), 312 (Cantata 1, No. 393 *infra*). Nineteen are from Cantatas whose scores were as yet unpublished by the Bachgesellschaft—Nos. 159 (14 *infra*), 164 (29), 171a (36), 186 (72), 205 (102), 218 (134), 221 (138), 229 (155), 240 (189), 256 (225), 264 (252), 274 (138a), 275 (274), 279 (288), 303 (358), 304 (369), 308 (383), 310 (382), 314 (404). No. 220 (135 *infra*) is not found elsewhere than in Erk.

Erk's Prefaces severely criticize the editorial work of his predecessors, especially their neglect to present the Chorals as vocal pieces and to provide words for them. He rebukes Becker for his liberties with Bach's music. But he exaggerates the general inaccuracy of Carl Philipp Emanuel's texts revealed by his collation of them with the original autographs. He alleges alterations in the descant, tampering with the inner parts, substitution of the instrumental Continuo for the vocal Bass, or of a compound of both, in preference to Bach's own text. Appendix I *infra* reveals the extent to which these charges are justified. In regard to the Chorals for which Carl Philipp's MS is the only authority Erk's judgement was hasty and injudicious. Upon the ground that their texts are not ' as free as possible from arbitrary alterations and additions ' he excluded ninety-two of the 185. In the present volume they are Nos. 20, 22, 33, 37, 38, 42, 50, 56, 59, 63, 64, 65, 68, 69, 81, 88, 98, 111, 114, 117, 120, 133, 137, 139, 140, 141, 142, 151, 152, 154, 164, 173, 174, 176, 177, 181, 183, 187, 191, 196, 201, 203, 204, 208, 231, 232, 235, 236, 237, 240, 241, 246, 248, 253, 256, 260, 267, 277, 278, 280, 281, 289, 290, 294, 295, 297, 299, 303, 305, 309, 312, 320, 321, 322, 324, 337, 338, 339, 345, 347, 349, 364, 366, 367, 368, 371, 374, 375, 377, 388, 392, 398. In regard to some of these excluded settings it might be supposed that Erk reserved them for a concluding volume, did not his second Preface state expressly that a third Part was not in view owing to the failure of owners of Bach MSS to provide him with materials. While in general his criticism is hypercritical, the merits of his edition are, its care to refer the Choral texts to the original Cantatas whence they are derived, and its addition of words to the several settings.

The Bachgesellschaft Edition (1892)

The date of Erk's first Preface preceded by exactly one week the formal institution (December 15, 1850) of the Bachgesellschaft. By the end of 1891 all (190) of Bach's Cantatas then known to be extant had been published by that Society, except six whose Scores are incomplete, and four of doubtful authenticity. The Passions and Oratorios had also been published. Hence, excepting the Motets, every simple four-part Choral in Bach's concerted music had been published in its proper context. Deeming it unnecessary to reprint them in a complete collection, the committee of the Society decided to publish the 185 in C. P. E. Bach's collection which could not be referred to extant Cantatas and for whose text it was the sole source. The work was entrusted to Franz Wüllner (1832-1902), who fulfilled it in 1892 in Jahrgang XXXIX, a volume which also contained the Motets. Unfortunately Wüllner merely reprinted the texts in Breitkopf's 1784-87 edition, between some of which and others already printed by the Society an affinity exists which he was careless to explore. He was equally neglectful to collate those of the 185 which he associated as duplicates[1], of which he printed but one of each pair, though in two cases only (Nos. 50 and 152 *infra*) the duplicates are identical. He did not examine Birnstiel's edition, and Marpurg's MS was unknown to him. His texts are therefore uncritical reprints of Breitkopf's edition, into which he introduced several errors of his own[2]. His reversion to a four-line stave is neither convenient nor was demanded by his original text.

Breitkopf and Härtel's Edition (1898)

In 1894 the Bachgesellschaft issued (Jahrgang XLI: ed. Alfred Dörffel) a supplementary volume of Bach's Church music, containing the supplementary Cantatas already mentioned. The tale of Bach's Chorals being complete[3], Breitkopf and Härtel published them in 1898 as a separate volume of their octavo edition of his works, entrusting its editing to Professor Bernhard Fr. Richter (1850-), of Leipzig. It contains 389 Chorals, 204 of which are from the Cantatas, Passions, Oratorios, and Motets, while the remaining 185 reproduce Wüllner's text. Admirably convenient in its format, it is too meagrely supplied with words to be of practical use to choirs.

---

[1] See *supra* p. viii.

[2] Woldemar Bargiel, however, adopted it in an edition (Bote and Bock, 1891-93) for school use, which contains 438 Chorals, including those in Schemelli (*infra*). A 'Fortsezung' of it, by Siegfried Ochs, is in progress.'

[3] One Church Cantata has since been found.

No 118 of the 1785 Edition

INTRODUCTION
The Figured Chorals

So far only those Chorals fully harmonized by Bach have been dealt with. There survive also a number of hymn tunes to which he added a Bass, figured or unfigured, and a few melodies which can be attributed to him. By far the larger number of the former occur in Schemelli's Hymn-book. A few are found in Bach's Organ music, others in his wife's 'Notenbuch', and six in the MS of his pupil, Joh. Ludwig Krebs. Every Choral from these sources is included in the present collection.

Georg Christian Schemelli was Cantor at Zeitz, some thirty miles from Leipzig, formerly the seat of the Dukes of Sachsen-Zeitz, and since 1718 in the possession of the Saxon Elector. Following the habit of his period, Schemelli compiled a Hymn-book for the 'evangelical congregations' of Zeitz and Naumburg, a town fifteen miles distant, which before the Reformation was the capital of the See of Naumburg-Zeitz. The book was published in 1736 and bears the following title-page:

Musicalisches Gesang-Buch, Darinnen 954 geistreiche, sowohl alte als neue Lieder und Arien, mit wohlgesetzten Melodien, in Discant und Bass, befindlich sind; Vornemlich denen Evangelischen Gemeinen im Stifte Naumburg-Zeitz gewidmet . . . herausgegeben von Georg Christian Schemelli, Schloss-Cantore daselbst. Mit Allergnädigster Freyheit, weder mit, noch ohne Noten nachzudrucken. Leipzig, 1736. Verlegts Bernhard Christoph Breitkopf, Buchdr.

The book, a squat octavo, contains 954 hymns and sixty-nine melodies fitted by Bach with a figured Bass. Forty-seven of the tunes are of earlier origin. To one Bach attached his name as composer (No. 481 *infra*). Sixteen of the remaining twenty-one can also be attributed to him, though they are not similarly distinguished as his. Schemelli's Preface announced that Bach had prepared two hundred more settings in anticipation of an enlarged edition of the Hymn-book. In fact, they were not called for, but, it is possible, survived in Carl Philipp's MS and also in the collection advertised by Breitkopf in 1764. Forkel does not mention the Schemelli tunes, which passed out of recollection until C. F. Becker published them in April, 1832, in a small book of thirty-three pages uniform with his contemporary volume and bearing the following title-page:

69 Choräle mit beziffertem Bass von Johann Sebastian Bach, herausgegeben von C. F. Becker. Zweite nach dem Originaldrucke vom Jahre 1736 durchsehne Ausgabe. Leipzig, Breitkopf & Härtel.

More than thirty years later (Preface dated April 24, 1868) J. G. Lehmann, of Schloss Elsterwerda, printed the Schemelli tunes as an Appendix to his

Choralbuch, enthaltend eine Auswahl von 272 der schönsten und gebräuchlichsten Kirchengesänge in vierstimmiger Bearbeitung und mit vielen Zwischenspielen. Nebst einem Anhange, bestehend aus 69 von Joh. Seb. Bach 'theils ganz neu componirten, theils im Generalbass verbesserten Melodien'.[1]

Lehmann's Appendix was published separately by Breitkopf and Härtel and a third edition of it was called for in February, 1874. Becker's passed into its twelfth edition in June, 1921. Wüllner included the Schemelli settings in Jahrgang XXXIX of the Bachgesellschaft, and the earliest task of its successor, the Neue Bachgesellschaft, was to print them in practical form. In 1901 Karl Ernst Naumann (1832–1910) arranged them as solos with pianoforte accompaniment (Jahrgang I, Heft 1), and Franz Wüllner edited them for a four-part mixed choir (Jahrgang I, Heft 2). More recently, an edition of Naumann's arrangement, transposed for a lower voice, has been published (Preface dated Christmas, 1923) by Breitkopf and Härtel, and Dr Max Seiffert (1868–) has made a new arrangement of them as vocal solos (Leo Liepmannssohn, 1925).

Soon after his second marriage, Bach prepared for his wife, Anna Magdalena, a 'Notenbuch' containing vocal and instrumental movements. Its green cover bears in gold the inscription: 'A.M.B. 1725', and within are eight Chorals (*infra* Nos. 70, 429, 430, 466, 471, 482, 485). Only one of them (No. 70) is fully harmonized. The rest are melodies with continuo and, excepting No. 466, their tunes are by Bach. Nos. 429, 430, and 471 were printed by Erk in 1850. The rest (except No. 70) were first published by Wüllner in Jahrgang XXXIX (1892).

As an Appendix to his *Life of Bach* Spitta printed 'Sechs geistliche Lieder, wahrscheinlich von Seb. Bachs Composition'. They were discovered at Altenburg in a MS written by Joh. Ludwig Krebs, whom Bach regarded as one of his best pupils at the Thomasschule in the period when Schemelli's Hymn-book was in preparation. Of one of the six (No. 414 *infra*) only the figured Bass can be attributed to Bach. The others (Nos. 437, 482, 488, 489, 490) are wholly his.

Lastly, among the sources explored, the Organ Works have yielded a few figured Chorals (Nos. 188, 413, 484) which cannot be excluded.

The Oxford Edition (1928)

The present volume offers a complete and critical edition of Bach's four-part Chorals, along with an adequate equipment of English and German words. It contains every genuine example and admits a few which, though their authenticity is questionable, occur in scores printed by the Bachgesellschaft. Similarly complete is the tale of Chorals whose harmonization is outlined in a figured or unfigured Bass, while three of Bach's unharmonized melodies are also included. The result is a collection of nearly five hundred examples of Bach's genius in this form, a total which far exceeds the largest number hitherto assembled.

The perverse inclination of their earliest editors regarded these vocal gems either as instrumental pieces or as composition exercises. So little did they value them as hymns, that they neither provided words nor regarded Bach's phrasing of the vocal parts. Becker (1843) phrased the parts but withheld the words. Erk

---
[1] The quotation is from Schemelli's Preface.

attached a single stanza to each setting, rarely more. In the present volume the Chorals furnish a comprehensive Hymn-book. Each setting is associated with such a number of its proper stanzas as permits it to be sung as a hymn, introit, or short anthem. When more than one setting of a melody is included, care has been taken to enlarge the number available. In every case the stanza that inspired Bach's setting is associated with it, and is indicated by an asterisk in the German text.

Previous editors, to whom Marpurg's MS was unknown, have failed to observe that Birnstiel's edition not infrequently exhibits variations of the 1784–87 edition deserving consideration in the attempt to construct an authoritative text. The 1784–87 edition is generally to be preferred; its authority would be even firmer if Carl Philipp Emanuel's revision could be postulated. Occasionally, therefore, the earlier text affords an alternative and even a better reading. Moreover, later editors have followed Wüllner in superficially concluding that Chorals with identical or closely similar Basses are duplicates, one of which consequently can be neglected. Indeed, even looser correspondence has sufficed to excuse the obliteration of a setting. For instance, Erk, printing the concluding Choral of Cantata 178 (No. 403 *infra*) labels it as the counterpart of No. 335 in Breitkopf's 1787 volume. In fact, the two represent different settings of their common melody. So, too, Franz Wüllner excluded a number of Chorals which he bracketed as duplicates of others already published in the Cantata volumes. Consequently authentic Chorals have till now been buried out of sight which exhibit interesting variants of published and familiar texts. The decision of the Bachgesellschaft to print the Chorals invited a critical edition which Wüllner failed to provide, an omission the more regrettable in view of the meticulously careful work generally expended upon the Society's earlier publications. In the present volume it is sought to provide the critical apparatus withheld in 1892.

Wherever the instrumental Bass (Continuo) differs from the vocal Bass the former is printed in small notes. Not infrequently the vocal Bass is inconveniently low or crosses the Tenor; while occasionally chords are incomplete owing to the absence of the obbligato instruments. In both cases alternative small notes are printed within a bracket.

Because the music is here set to several stanzas, whereas Bach's original setting served only one, a simple adjustment of the note values of their final chord has been necessary in the case of a few Chorals.

For example, crotchets replace minims in Nos. 39, 68, 82, while becomes in Nos. 140 and 220.

The Chorals in question are Nos. 19, 39, 46, 47, 68, 82, 112, 140, 155, 180, 188B, 196, 220, 232, 257, 299, 303, 313, 321, 331, 350, 364.

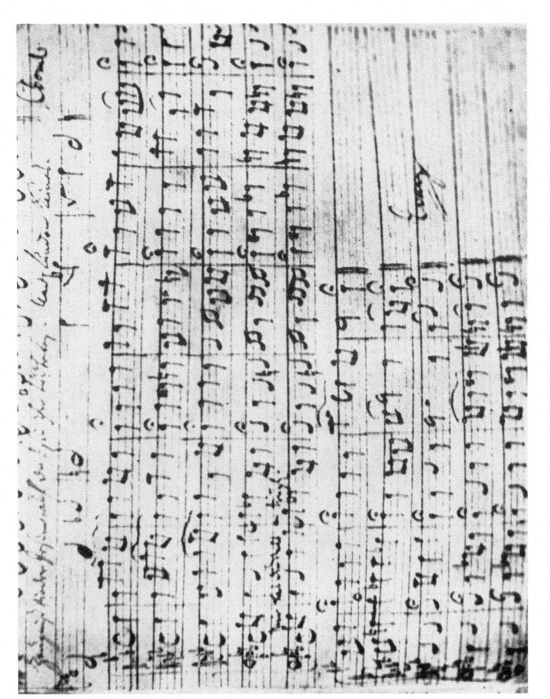

The Choral 'In dich hab ich gehoffet, Herr' (from the Autograph Score of the *Matthäus Passion*)

ACH, BLEIB BEI UNS, HERR JESU CHRIST

Hymn anonymous, in three 6-line stanzas (1601). Melody, anonymous (1589), to 'Danket dem Herrn heut und allzeit'.

i Uns ist ein Kindlein heut geborn
  Von einer Jungfrau auserkorn,
  Ein wahrer Mensch und wahrer Gott,
  Dass er uns helf aus aller Noth:
  Sein Nam ist wunderbar und Rath,
  Durch ihn wir haben funden Gnad.

ii Was hätt uns Gott mehr können thun,
  Denn dass er uns schenkt seinen Sohn,
  Der von uns weggenommen hat
  All unser Sünd und Missethat,
  Erlöst uns von der Sünd und Pein,
  Darein wir sollten ewig sein.

iii Freu dich du werthe Christenheit
  Und dank es Gott in Ewigkeit,
  Hass aber alle Sünd und List,
  Davon du theur erlöset bist,
  Sei fortan gottfürchtig und rein,
  Zu Ehrn dem neug'born Kindelein!
             Tucher.[1]

i This day to us a Child is born,
  A gentle Babe, a Virgin's Son;
  Both God and Man in flesh comes He
  That He may learn our misery.
  His name is Wonderful and Wise,
  And favour wins us in God's eyes.

ii What more for us could God have done
  Than make us brothers of His Son,
  Who now is born to set us free
  From all our sore infirmity,
  Relieving us from sin and pain,
  Wherein we else should e'er remain?

iii So then, rejoice, good Christians all,
  And loud to God your praises tell;
  Hence from you cast the weight of sin
  And eager your salvation win;
  Fear God and serve Him all your days,
  And to His Son confess your praise!
             Tr. C. S. T.

[1] Bd. i. No. 50.

ACH, BLEIB BEI UNS, HERR JESU CHRIST

Hymn, by Nikolaus Selnecker, in nine 4-line stanzas (1611).   Melody, anonymous (1589), to ' Danket dem Herrn heut und allzeit'

2

i Ach, bleib bei uns, Herr Jesu Christ,
 Weil es nun Abend worden ist :
 Dein Wort, o Herr, das ewig Licht,
 Lass ja bei uns auslöschen nicht.

ii In dieser letzt'n betrübten Zeit
 Verleih uns all'n Beständigkeit,
 Dass wir dein Wort und Sacrament
 Rein b'halten bis an unser End.

iii Herr Jesu, hilf, dein Kirch erhalt :
 Wir sind sicher, arg, faul und kalt ;
 Gib Glück und Heil zu deinem Wort,
 Damit es schall an allem Ort.

iv Erhalt uns nur bei deinem Wort
 Und wehr des Teufels Trug und Mord.
 Gib deiner Kirche Gnad und Huld,
 Fried, Einigkeit, Muth und Geduld.

ix Gib, dass wir lebn in deinem Wort
 Und darauf ferner fahren fort
 Von hinnen aus dem Jammerthal
 Zu dir in deinen Himmelssaal.

U.L.S. 207.

i Lord Jesu Christ, with us abide,
 For now, behold, 'tis eventide :
 And bring, to cheer us through the night,
 Thy Word, our true and only light.

ii In times of trial and distress
 Preserve our truth and steadfastness,
 And pure unto the end, O Lord,
 Vouchsafe Thy Sacraments and Word.

iii O Jesu Christ, Thy Church sustain ;
 Our hearts are wav'ring, cold, and vain :
 Then let Thy Word be strong and clear
 To silence doubt and banish fear.

iv O guard us all from Satan's wiles,
 From worldly threats and worldly smiles,
 And let Thy saints in unity
 Know Thee in God and God in Thee.

ix From these and all of God abhorred,
 O Christ, protect us by Thy Word ;
 Increase our faith and hope and love,
 And to Thy fold bring us above.

Tr. Benjamin Hall Kennedy.[1]

[1] *Hymnologia Christiana* (Lond. 1863), No. 41.

ACH GOTT, ERHÖR MEIN SEUFZEN UND WEHKLAGEN

Hymn, by Jakob Peter Schechs, in eight 5-line stanzas (1648). Melody, anonymous (1662); probably in earlier use.

i Ach Gott, erhör mein Seufzen und Wehklagen,
  Lass mich in meiner Noth nicht gar verzagen.
  Du weisst mein Schmerz,
  Erkennst mein Herz :
  Hast du mirs aufgelegt, so hilf mirs tragen.

ii Ohn deinen Willen kann mir nichts begegnen ;
  Du kannst verfluchen und auch wieder segnen.
  Bin ich dein Kind
  Und hab's verdient :
  Gieb wieder Sonnenschein nach trübem Regen.

iv Ich weiss, du hast meiner noch nicht vergessen,
  Dass ich vor Leid mir sollt mein Herz abfressen :
  Mitt in der Noth
  Denk ich an Gott,
  Wenn er mich schon mit Kreuz und Angst thut
    pressen.

viii Dass wir in Ewigkeit bleiben beisammen,
  Und ich allzeit dein auserwählten Namen
  Preis herziglich :
  Das bitt ich dich
  Durch Jesum Christum unsern Herren.   Amen.

U.L.S. 692.

i Give ear, O Lord, and mark my sore complaining,
  Nor leave me in my strait, my need disdaining !
  Thou know'st my smart,
  Thou read'st my heart :
  Then, help me bear my load : 'tis Thine ordaining.

ii For everything we do is of Thy willing ;
  'Tis Thou dost chide, 'tis Thou dost grant a blessing.
  Am I Thy son
  And grace have won ?
  Then send Thy light from out the cloud's dark lining.

iv I know that in Thy heart Thou ever lov'st me,
  That anxious thoughts torment my spirit vainly :
  Come aught that may,
  God is my Stay,
  E'en though a heavy cross of woe He sends me.

viii So may we one day joyous rise before Thee
  And with the blessèd ones above adore Thee !
  O rapture rare !
  Lord, hear my prayer,
  Through Jesus Christ our Saviour now in glory !

Tr. C. S. T.

ACH GOTT UND HERR

Hymn, attributed to Johann Major and Martin Rutilius, in six 6-line stanzas (1613). Melody, anonymous (1625).

i Ach Gott und Herr :
  Wie gross und schwer
  Sind mein begangne Sünden !
  Da ist Niemand,
  Der helfen kann,
  In dieser Welt zu finden.

* iv Solls ja so sein,
  Dass Straf und Pein
  Auf Sünde folgen müssen :
  So fahr hie fort
  Und schone dort ;
  Und lass mich ja jetzt büssen.

v Gieb auch Geduld,
  Vergiss der Schuld,
  Verleih ein g'horsam Herze ;
  Lass mich ja nicht,
  Wies wohl geschicht,
  Mein Heil murrend verscherzen.

vi Handel mit mir,
  Wies wohlg'fällt dir ;
  Durch dein Gnad will ichs leiden !
  Lass mich nur nicht
  Dort ewiglich
  Von dir sein abgescheiden !

i Alas ! my God !
  My sins are great,
  My conscience doth upbraid me ;
  And now I find
  That at my strait
  No man hath power to aid me.

iv If pain and woe
  Must follow sin,
  Then be my path still rougher.
  Here spare me not ;
  If heaven I win,
  On earth I gladly suffer.

v But curb my heart,
  Forgive my guilt,
  Make Thou my patience firmer ;
  For they must miss
  The good Thou will'st,
  Who at Thy teachings murmur.

vi Then deal with me
  As seems Thee best,
  Thy grace will help me bear it,
  If but at last
  I see Thy rest
  And with my Saviour share it.

U.L.S. 350.

Tr. Catherine Winkworth.[1]

[1] *Chorale Book for England* (Lond. 1865), No. 107.

ACH GOTT UND HERR

Hymn, attributed to Johann Major and Martin Rutilius, in six 6-line stanzas (1613). Melody, anonymous (1625).

i Ach Gott und Herr :
  Wie gross und schwer
  Sind mein begangne Sünden !
  Da ist Niemand,
  Der helfen kann,
  In dieser Welt zu finden.

ii Lief ich gleich weit
  Zu solcher Zeit
  Bis an der Welt ihr Ende
  Und wollt los sein
  Des Elends mein,
  Würd ich doch solchs nicht wenden.

iii Zu dir flieh ich :
  Verstoss mich nicht,
  Wie ichs wohl hab verdienet !
  Ach Gott, zürn nicht,
  Geh nicht ins Gricht :
  Dein Sohn hat mich versühnet.

U.L.S. 350.

i Alas ! my God !
  My sins are great,
  My conscience doth upbraid me ;
  And now I find
  That at my strait
  No man hath power to aid me.

ii If fled I hence,
  In my despair,
  In some lone spot to hide me,
  My griefs would still
  Be with me there,
  Thy hand still hold and guide me.

iii Nay, Thee I seek ;
  I merit nought,
  Yet pity and restore me ;
  Be not Thy wrath,
  Just God, my lot ;
  Thy Son hath suffered for me.

Tr. Catherine Winkworth.

ACH GOTT VOM HIMMEL, SIEH DAREIN

Hymn, by Martin Luther, in six 7-line stanzas (1524). Melody, anonymous (1524).

Psalm xii.

i Ach Gott vom Himmel, sieh darein
   Und lass dich dess erbarmen :
   Wie wenig sind der Heilgen dein,
   Verlassen sind wir Armen.
   Dein Wort man lässt nicht haben wahr,
   Der Glaub ist auch verloschen gar
   Bei allen Menschenkindern.

iii Gott woll ausrotten alle Lahr,
     Die falschen Schein uns lehren ;
     Dazu ihr Zung stolz offenbar
     Spricht : trotz ! wer wills uns wehren ?
     Wir haben Recht und Macht allein,
     Was wir setzen, das gilt gemein :
     Wer ist, der uns soll meistern ?

* vi Das wollst du, Gott, bewahren rein
      Vor diesem argen G'schlechte ;
      Und lass uns dir befohlen sein,
      Dass sichs in uns nicht flechte.
      Der gottlos Hauf sich umher findt,
      Wo diese lose Leute sind
      In deinem Volk erhaben.

U.L.S. 209.

i Ah God, from heaven, look down and view;
   Let it Thy pity waken ;
   Behold Thy saints how very few !
   We wretches are forsaken.
   Thy Word they will not grant it right,
   And faith is thus extinguished quite
   Amongst the sons of Adam.

iii God will outroot the teachers all
     Who false appearance teach us ;
     Besides, their proud tongues loudly call—
     ' What care we ?—Who can reach us ?
     We have the right and might in full ;
     And what we say, that is the rule ;
     Who dares to give us lessons ?'

vi God will its purity defend
    Against this generation.
    Let us ourselves to Thee commend,
    Lest we fall from our station ;
    The godless rout is all around
    Where these rude wanton ones are found
    Against Thy folk exalted.

Tr. George Macdonald.[1]

[1] *Exotics* (Lond. 1876), p. 62.

ACH GOTT VOM HIMMEL, SIEH DAREIN

Hymn, by Martin Luther, in six 7-line stanzas (1524). Melody, anonymous (1524).

i Ach Gott vom Himmel, sieh darein
  Und lass dich dess erbarmen :
  Wie wenig sind der Heilgen dein,
  Verlassen sind wir Armen.
  Dein Wort man lässt nicht haben wahr,
  Der Glaub ist auch verloschen gar
  Bei allen Menschenkindern.

ii Sie lehren eitel falsche List,
  Was eigen Witz erfindet ;
  Ihr Herz nicht Eines Sinnes ist,
  In Gottes Wort gegründet.
  Der wählet dies, der ander das ;
  Sie trennen uns ohn alle Mass ;
  Und gleissen schön von aussen.

v Das Silber, durchs Feur siebenmal
  Bewährt, wird lauter funden :
  An Gottes Wort man warten soll
  Desgleichen alle Stunden.
  Es will durchs Kreuz bewähret sein ;
  Da wird sein Kraft erkannt und Schein
  Und leucht stark in die Lande.

U.L.S. 209.

i Ah God, from heaven, look down and view;
  Let it Thy pity waken ;
  Behold Thy saints how very few !
  We wretches are forsaken.
  Thy Word they will not grant it right,
  And faith is thus extinguished quite
  Amongst the sons of Adam.

ii They teach a cunning false and fine,
  In their own wits they found it ;
  Their heart in one doth not combine,
  Upon God's Word well grounded.
  One chooses this, another that ;
  Division endless they are at,
  And yet they keep smooth faces.

v Silver that sevèn times is tried
  With fire is found the purer ;
  God's Word the same test will abide,
  It still comes out the surer.
  It shall by crosses provèd be ;
  Men shall its strength and glory see
  Shine strong upon the nations.

Tr. George Macdonald.[1]

[1] *Exotics* (Lond. 1876), p. 62.   In Cantata 77 the Choral is sung to an unauthorized text—St. viii. of
David Denicke's *Wenn einer alle Ding verstünd* (1657).

ACH GOTT VOM HIMMEL, SIEH DAREIN

Hymn, attributed to David Denicke, in eight 7-line stanzas (1646). Melody, anonymous (1524).

8

*i Schau, lieber Gott, wie meine Feind,
Damit ich stets muss kämpfen,
So listig und so mächtig seind,
Dass sie mich leichtlich dämpfen.
Herr, wo mich deine Gnad nicht hält,
So kann der Teufel und die Welt
Das Fleisch geschwind verführen.

v Nun muss ich Armer immerfort
Mit diesen Feinden streiten.
Sie ängsten mich an allem Ort
Und sein mir stets zur Seiten.
Der Satan setzt mir heftig zu,
Die Welt lässt mir gar keine Ruh,
Mein Fleisch zur Sünd mich reitzet.

vii Lass diesen deinen guten Geist
Mich innerlich regieren,
Dass ich allzeit thu, was du heisst,
Und mich nichts lass verführen,
Dass ich dem Argen widersteh
Und nicht von deinem Weg abgeh
Zur Rechten oder Linken.

Fischer-Tümpel.[1]

i How many they, how mighty rail,
The foes who press upon me !
Sore grievously do they assail,
My spirit faints within me.
Lord, with Thy grace my soul refresh !
So shall the Devil, World, and Flesh
No more prevail against me.

v Here must I, poor and helpless wight,
'Gainst foemen countless set me ;
On every hand they challenge fight
And on my paths molest me.
While Satan would mine armour test,
The hard World giveth me no rest,
And Flesh to sin doth tempt me.

vii O grant Thy Holy Spirit's grace
To govern and direct me !
Toward heavèn guide and set my face,
Let nought from Thee distract me !
Bring swift to ruin all my foes,
And set me on the path that goes
To where Thou reign'st in glory !

Tr. C. S. T.

[1] Bd. ii. No. 383.

ACH GOTT, WIE MANCHES HERZELEID

Hymn, attributed to Martin Moller and Conrad Hojer, in twelve 6-line stanzas (1587), also in eighteen 4-line stanzas
Melody, anonymous (1625).

9

*The Alto and Tenor parts may be interchanged here.

Jesu dulcis memoria.

i Ach Gott, wie manches Herzeleid
  Begegnet mir zu dieser Zeit.
  Der schmale Weg ist Trübsal voll,
  Den ich zum Himmel wandeln soll.

ii Wie schwer doch lässt sich Fleisch und Blut
  Bezwingen zu dem ewgen Gut !
  Wo sollt ich mich denn wenden hin ?
  Zu dir, Herr Jesu, steht mein Sinn.

xvi Drum will ich, weil ich lebe noch,
  Das Kreuz dir fröhlich tragen nach :
  Mein Gott, mach mich dazu bereit ;
  Es dient zum besten allezeit.

xvii Hilf mir mein Sach recht greifen an,
  Dass ich mein Lauf vollenden kann.
  Hilf mir auch zwingen Fleisch und Blut,
  Vor Sünd und Schanden mich behüt ;

*xviii Erhalt mein Herz im Glauben rein :
  So leb und sterb ich dir allein.
  Jesu, mein Trost, hör mein Begier :
  O mein Heiland, wär ich bei dir !

           U.L.S. 734.

i O Lord ! how many miseries
  Assault and discompose my peace ;
  The path that leads to Sion's gate
  Is full of thorns and very strait.

ii How hard it is for flesh and blood
  To seek the everlasting Good ;
  I know not where to turn my face,
  But, Christ, to Thy redeeming grace.

xvi So then, as long as life shall be,
  I'll bear the Cross and follow Thee :
  O Lord, prepare this heart of mine,
  Let it to nothing else incline.

xvii Assist me with Thy mighty grace,
  With joy to run my Christian race ;
  Help me to conquer flesh and blood,
  And make my Christian warfare good.

xviii Preserve my faith from error free,
  That I may live and die in Thee.
  Lord Jesus Christ, hear my desire,
  To hymn Thee in the heavenly choir.

           Tr. John Christian Jacobi.[1]

[1] *Psalmodia Germanica* (Lond. 1722), p. 76.

ACH GOTT, WIE MANCHES HERZELEID

Hymn, by Martin Behm, in fourteen 4-line stanzas (1611). Melody, anonymous (1625).

i O Jesu Christ, meins Lebens Licht,
  Mein Hort, mein Trost, mein Zuversicht :
  Auf Erden bin ich nur ein Gast,
  Und drückt mich sehr der Sünden Last.

ii Ich hab vor mir ein schwere Reis
   Zu dir ins Himmels Paradeis ;
   Da ist mein rechtes Vaterland,
   Darauf du hast dein Blut gewandt.

iii Zur Reis ist mir mein Herz sehr matt,
    Der Leib gar wenig Kräfte hat ;
    Allein mein Seele schreit in mir :
    Herr, hol mich heim, nimm mich zu dir !

xii Am jüngsten Tag erweck mein Leib ;
    Hilf, dass ich dir zur Rechten bleib,
    Dass mich nicht treffe dein Gericht,
    Welchs das erschrecklich Urtheil spricht.

xiv Wie werd ich dann so fröhlich sein,
    Werd singen mit den Engelein
    Und mit der Auserwählten Schaar
    Ewig schauen dein Antlitz klar !

i Lord Jesus Christ, my Life, my Light,
  My strength by day, my trust by night,
  I'm but on earth a passing guest,
  And sorely with my sins oppressed.

ii Far off I see my fatherland,
   Where through Thy grace I hope to stand,
   But ere I reach that Paradise
   A weary way before me lies.

iii My heart sinks at the journey's length,
    My wasted flesh has little strength,
    Only my soul still cries in me,
    'Lord, fetch me home, take me to Thee !'

xii And when the last great Day is come,
    And Thou our Judge shalt speak the doom,
    Let me with joy behold the light
    And set me then upon Thy right !

xiv Ah then I'll have my heart's desire,
    When, singing with the angels' choir
    Among the ransomed of Thy grace,
    For ever I behold Thy face !

U.L.S. 835.

Catherine Winkworth.[1]

[1] *Lyra Germanica* (2nd Series : Lond. 1863), p. 213.   In Cantata 153 the melody is set to
stanzas xvi, xvii, xviii of No. 9.

ACH, WAS SOLL ICH SÜNDER MACHEN

Hymn, by Johann Flittner, in seven 6-line stanzas (1661). Melody, an adaptation (1661) of the secular ' Silvius ging durch die Matten ' (1653).

i Ach ! was soll ich Sünder machen ?
  Ach, was soll ich fangen an ?
  Mein Gewissen klagt mich an :
  Es beginnet aufzuwachen.
  Dies ist meine Zuversicht :
  Meinen Jesum lass ich nicht !

iii Ob gleich schweres Kreuz und Leiden,
  So bei Christen oft entsteht,
  Mir sehr hart entgegen geht,
  Soll michs doch von ihm nicht scheiden :
  Er ist mir ins Herz gericht ;
  Meinen Jesum lass ich nicht !

v Sterb ich bald, so komm ich aber
  Von der Welt Beschwerlichkeit,
  Ruhe bis zur vollsten Freud
  Und weiss, dass im finstern Grabe
  Jesus ist mein helles Licht :
  Meinen Jesum lass ich nicht !

vii Drum, Herr Jesu, sollst mein bleiben,
  Bis ich komme an den Ort,
  Welcher ist des Himmels Pfort ;
  Wo du dann wirst einverleiben
  Meine Seele deinem Licht :
  Meinen Jesum lass ich nicht !

i What shall I, a sinner, do, Lord ?
  Whither shall I turn for aid ?
  Sins that make me sore afraid
  Conscience waking brings to view, Lord.
  This my confidence shall be,
  Jesus, I will cleave to Thee.

iii Here the Christian oft must bear, Lord,
  Many a cross and bitter smart ;
  Shall I waver or depart
  If their lot in this I share, Lord ?
  Loyal still my heart shall be,
  Jesus, still I cleave to Thee.

v If I die, I do but cease, Lord,
  Sooner from this toil and care ;
  In the grave, since Thou wert there.
  Shall I rest in perfect peace, Lord.
  There Thy light shall comfort me,
  There, too, I will cleave to Thee.

vii Then, Lord Jesu, Thou art mine, Lord,
  Till Thou bring me to that place
  Where I'll ever see Thy face,
  In Thy light for ever shine, Lord.
  Blessèd will that haven be !
  Jesus, I will cleave to Thee.

U.L.S. 357.

Tr. Catherine Winkworth (adapted).[1]

[1] *Chorale Book for England* (Lond. 1865), No. 110.

ACH WIE FLÜCHTIG, ACH WIE NICHTIG

Hymn, by Michael Franck, in thirteen 5-line stanzas (1652). Melody, by Michael Franck (1652).

12

* **Bach has a 𝄐 here.**

i Ach wie flüchtig, ach wie nichtig
Ist des Menschen Leben !
Wie ein Nebel bald entstehet,
Und bald wiederum vergehet :
So ist unser Leben, sehet !

ii Ach wie nichtig, ach wie flüchtig
Sind der Menschen Tage !
Wie ein Strom beginnt zu rinnen,
Und mit Laufen nicht hält innen :
So fährt unsre Zeit von hinnen.

iv Ach wie nichtig, ach wie flüchtig
Ist der Menschen Schöne !
Wie ein Blümlein bald vergehet,
Wenn ein rauhes Lüftlein wehet :
So ist unsre Schöne, sehet !

* xiii Ach wie flüchtig, ach wie nichtig
Sind der Menschen Sachen !
Alles, alles was wir sehen,
Das muss fallen und vergehen :
Wer Gott fürcht, bleibt ewig stehen.

U.L.S. 803.

i O how cheating, O how fleeting,
Is our earthly being !
'Tis a mist in wintry weather,
Gathered in an hour together,
And as soon dispersed in ether.

ii O how cheating, O how fleeting,
Are our days departing !
Like a deep and headlong river
Flowing onward, flowing ever.
Tarrying not and stopping never.

iv O how cheating, O how fleeting,
Is all earthly beauty !
Like a summer flow'ret flowing,
Scattered by the breezes, blowing
O'er the bed on which 'twas growing.

xiii O how cheating, O how fleeting,
All—yes, all that's earthly !
Every thing is fading, flying,
Man is mortal, earth is dying,
Christian ! live on heaven relying.

Tr. Sir John Bowring.[1]

[1] *Hymns* (Lond. 1825), No. 35.

ALLE MENSCHEN MÜSSEN STERBEN

Hymn, by Joh. Georg Albinus, in eight 8-line stanzas (1652).   Melody, by Jakob Hintze (1678).

i Alle Menschen müssen sterben,
  Alles Fleisch vergeht wie Heu ;
  Was da lebet muss verderben,
  Soll es anders werden neu.
  Dieser Leib, der muss verwesen,
  Wenn er ewig soll genesen
  Der so grossen Herrlichkeit,
  Die den Frommen ist bereit.

iv Da wird sein das Freudenleben,
   Da viel tausend Seelen schon
   Sind mit Himmelsglanz umgeben,
   Dienen Gott vor seinem Thron ;
   Da die Seraphinen prangen
   Und das hohe Lied anfangen :
   Heilig, heilig, heilig, heisst
   Gott der Vater, Sohn und Geist !

vi O Jerusalem, du Schöne !
   Ach wie helle glänzest du !
   Ach wie lieblich Lobgetöne
   Hört man da in sanfter Ruh !
   Ach der grossen Freud und Wonne :
   Jetzund gehet auf die Sonne,
   Jetzund gehet an der Tag,
   Der kein Ende nehmen mag.

U.L.S. 804.

i Hark ! a voice saith, 'All are mortal,
  Yea, all flesh must fade as grass ;
  Only through Death's gloomy portal
  To a better life ye pass ;
  For this body's doomed to anguish,
  Here must linger and must languish
  Ere it rise in glorious might,
  Fit to dwell with saints in light.'

iv There is joy beyond our telling
   Where so many saints are gone ;
   Thousand thousands there are dwelling,
   Worshipping before the throne :
   There the seraphim adoring
   Brightly shine, are ever calling :
   ' Holy, Holy, Holy, Lord !
   Three in One for aye adored ! '

vi O Jerusalem, how clearly
   Dost thou shine, thou city fair !
   Lo ! I hear the tones more nearly
   Ever sweetly sounding there !
   Oh what peace and joy surpassing !
   Lo, the sun is brightly rising,
   And the breaking day I see
   That shall never end for me !

Tr. Catherine Winkworth (adapted).[1]

[1] *Chorale Book for England* (Lond. 1865), No. 196.

ALLE MENSCHEN MÜSSEN STERBEN

Hymn, by Joh. Georg Albinus, in eight 8-line stanzas (1652). Melody, anonymous (1715).

i Alle Menschen müssen sterben,
  Alles Fleisch vergeht wie Heu ;
  Was da lebet muss verderben,
  Soll es anders werden neu.
  Dieser Leib, der muss verwesen,
  Wenn er ewig soll genesen
  Der so grossen Herrlichkeit,
  Die den Frommen ist bereit.

ii Drum so will ich dieses Leben,
   Wenn es meinem Gott beliebt,
   Auch ganz willig von mir geben ;
   Bin darüber nicht betrübt.
   Denn in meines Jesu Wunden
   Hab ich schon Erlösung funden,
   Und mein Trost in Todesnoth
   Ist des Herren Jesu Tod.

* vii Ach ich habe schon erblicket
   Alle diese Herrlichkeit :
   Jetzo werd ich schön geschmücket
   Mit dem weissen Himmelskleid,
   Mit der güldnen Ehrenkrone ;
   Stehe da vor Gottes Throne,
   Schaue solche Freude an,
   Die kein Ende nehmen kann.

i Hark ! a voice saith, 'All are mortal.
  Yea, all flesh must fade as grass ;
  Only through Death's gloomy portal
  To a better life ye pass ;
  For this body's doomed to anguish,
  Here must linger and must languish
  Ere it rise in glorious might,
  Fit to dwell with saints in light.'

ii Therefore, since my God doth choose it,
   Willingly I yield my life,
   Nor I grieve that I should lose it,
   For with sorrows it was rife ;
   And my Saviour suffered for me
   That I might not faint nor weary ;
   Since for me He bore my load
   And hath trod the same dark road.

vii Yea, I see what here was told me,
    See that wondrous glory shine,
    Feel the spotless robes enfold me,
    Know a golden crown is mine ;
    So before the throne I place me,
    One amid that glorious army,
    Gazing on that joy for aye
    That shall never pass away !

U.L.S. 804.

Tr. Catherine Winkworth (adapted).[1]

[1] *Chorale Book for England* (Lond. 1865), No. 196.

ALLEIN GOTT IN DER HÖH SEI EHR

Hymn, by Nikolaus Decius, in four 7-line stanzas (1525). Melody, an adaptation (1539) of the Easter plainsong 'Gloria in excelsis.'

15

Gloria in excelsis Deo.

i Allein Gott in der Höh sei Ehr !
  Und Dank für seine Gnade :
  Darum dass nun und nimmermehr
  Uns rühren kann ein Schade.
  Ein Wohlgefalln Gott an uns hat ;
  Nun ist gross Fried ohn Unterlass,
  All Fehd hat nun ein Ende.

ii Wir loben, preisn, anbeten dich,
   Für deine Ehr wir danken,
   Dass du, Gott Vater, ewiglich
   Regierst ohn Alles Wanken.
   Ganz ungemessen ist dein Macht,
   Fort g'schieht, was dein Will hat bedacht :
   Wohl uns des seinen Herren !

iii O Jesu Christ, Sohn eingeborn
    Deines himmlischen Vaters,
    Versöhner der, die warn verlorn,
    Du Stiller unsers Haders :
    Lamm Gottes, heilger Herr und Gott,
    Nimm an die Bitt von unsrer Noth,
    Erbarm dich unser Armen.

iv O Heilger Geist, du grösstes Gut,
   Du allerheilsamst Tröster :
   Vors Teufels G'walt fortan behüt
   Die Jesus Christ erlöset
   Durch grosse Mart'r und bittern Tod !
   Abwend all unser Jamm'r und Noth !
   Dazu wir uns verlassen.

U.L.S. 185.

i All glory be to God on high,
  Who hath our race befriended !
  To us no harm shall now come nigh,
  The feud at last is ended ;
  God showeth His goodwill t'ward men,
  And peace shall dwell on earth again ;
  Oh thank Him for His goodness.

ii We praise, we worship Thee, we trust
   And give Thee thanks for ever,
   O Father, that Thy rule is just
   And wise, and changes never :
   Thy boundless power o'er all things reigns,
   Done is whate'er Thy will ordains ;
   Well for us that Thou rulest !

iii O Jesu Christ, our God and Lord,
    Son of Thy heavenly Father,
    O Thou Who hast our peace restored
    And doth the lost sheep gather,
    Thou Lamb of God, to Thee on high
    From out our depths we sinners cry,
    Have mercy on us, Jesus !

iv O Holy Ghost, Thou precious gift,
   Thou Comforter unfailing,
   O'er Satan's snares our souls uplift,
   And let Thy power availing
   Avert our woes and calm our dread ;
   For us the Saviour's blood was shed :
   We trust in Thee to save us.

Tr. Catherine Winkworth.[1]

[1] *Chorale Book for England* (Lond. 1865), *No.* 1.

ALLEIN GOTT IN DER HÖH SEI EHR

Hymn, by Wolfgang Meusel, in five 7-line stanzas (1531). Melody, an adaptation (1539) of the Easter plainsong 'Gloria in excelsis'.

[Obbligato for 2 Horns]   *Psalm xxiii.*

i Der Herr ist mein getreuer Hirt,
  Hält mich in seiner Hute,
  Darin mir gar nichts mangeln wird
  Irgend an einem Gute.
  Er weidet mich ohn Unterlass,
  Darauf wächst das wohlschmeckend Gras
  Seines heilsamen Wortes.

ii Zum reinen Wasser er mich weist,
   Das mich erquicken thue.
   Das ist sein frohnheiliger Geist,
   Der macht mich wohlgemüthe.
   Er führet mich auf rechter Strass
   Seiner Geboten ohn Ablass,
   Von wegen seines Namens.

* v Gutes und die Barmherzigkeit
    Folgen mir nach im Leben,
    Und ich werd bleiben allezeit
    Im Haus des Herren eben :
    Auf Erd'n in christlicher Gemein,
    Und nach dem Tod da werd ich sein
    Bei Christo, meinem Herren.

              Bach's Text.

i The Lord my Shepherd deigns to be,
  My footsteps safe He guideth ;
  His goodness never faileth me,
  His bounty e'er provideth.
  He leadeth me by mead and rill,
  And in my heart He doth instil
  His Word and His Commandment.

ii Where streams of living water flow
   To meadows green He leadeth,
   And where the verdant pastures grow
   With food celestial feedeth.
   My feet in surety doth He guide
   Nor lets me wander from His side,
   But holds me for His Name's sake.

v And so, throughout my length of days
  His goodness faileth never,
  And fain am I to sing His praise
  Within His courts for ever.
  His Church doth us on earth sustain,
  And after death in heaven we'll reign,
  From Jesus parted never.

              Tr. C. S. T.

ALLEIN GOTT IN DER HÖH SEI EHR

Hymn, by Cornelius Becker, in three 7-line stanzas (1598). Melody, an adaptation (1539) of the Easter plainsong 'Gloria in excelsis'.

17

Psalm xxiii.

* i Der Herr ist mein getreuer Hirt,
  Dem ich mich ganz vertraue ·
  Zur Weid er mich, sein Schäflein, führt,
  Auf schöner grüner Aue,
  Zum frischen Wasser leit't er mich,
  Mein Seel zu laben kräftiglich
  Durchs selig Wort der Gnaden.

ii Er führet mich auf rechter Bahn
  Von seines Namens wegen :
  Obgleich viel Trübsal geht heran
  Auf Todes finstern Stegen ;
  So grauet mir doch nicht dafür,
  Mein treuer Hirt ist stets bei mir,
  Sein Steckn und Stab mich tröstet.

iii Ein köstlich'n Tisch er mir bereit't,
  Sollts auch die Feind verdriessen,
  Schenkt mir voll ein, das Öl der Freud
  Über mein Haupt thut fliessen :
  Sein Güte und Barmherzigkeit
  Werden mir folgen alle Zeit,
  In seinem Haus ich bleibe.

Tucher.[1]

i The Lord my Shepherd is and true,
  To Him my trust I render.
  He leadeth me to pastures new,
  To meadows green and tender.
· By waters clear He guides me still,
  He doth my soul with gladness fill,
  Through His great love and favour.

· ii My feet in surety doth He guide
  And for His Name's sake lead me :
  Though troubles sore do here abide
  And Death stalks on beside me.
  No matter what may happen here,
  My Shepherd hath me in His care,
  His rod and staff shall guide me.

iii He hath a table for me spread,
  My foes are vexed to madness ;
  He doth with oil anoint my head
  And fill my soul with gladness.
  His goodness never faileth me,
  And one day soon at home I'll be
  Within His house for ever !

Tr. C. S. T.

[1]Bd. i. No. 191.

ALLEIN ZU DIR, HERR JESU CHRIST

Hymn, by Johannes Schneesing, in four 9-line stanzas (c. 1540). Melody, anonymous (? 1541).

i Allein zu dir, Herr Jesu Christ,
Mein Hoffnung steht auf Erden !
Ich weiss, dass du mein Tröster bist ;
Kein Trost mag mir sonst werden.
Von Anbeginn ist nichts erkorn,
Auf Erden war kein Mensch geborn,
Der mir aus Nöthen helfen kann :
Ich rufe dich an,
Zu dem ich mein Vertrauen han.

ii Mein Sünd sind schwer und übergross
Und reuen mich von Herzen ;
Derselben mach mich frei und los
Durch deinen Tod und Schmerzen ;
Und zeig mich deinem Vater an,
Dass du hast gnug für mich gethan,
So werd ich quitt, der Sünden los.
O Herr, halt mir fest,
Wess du dich mir versprochen hast.

* iv Ehr sei Gott in dem höchsten Thron,
Dem Vater aller Güte,
Und Jesu Christ, seim liebsten Sohn,
Der uns allzeit behüte,
Und Gott dem Heiligen Geiste,
Der uns sein Hilf allzeit leiste,
Damit wir ihm gefällig sein,
Hier in dieser Zeit
Und folgend in der Ewigkeit.

i Alone in Thee, Lord Jesu Christ,
My hope on earth resideth.
That Thou my Saviour art I wist ;
Help nowhere else abideth.
Not ever since the world began
Hath on this earth been born the man
Who can from Satan rescue me.
I call, Lord, to Thee,
Alone Who can from bondage free.

ii My sin is sore and very great,
With all my heart I mourn it ;
Release me from its grievous weight !
In Jesu's Name I ask it.
O plead for me at God's high throne,
Thou Who for me salvation won !
So shall I see His face at last.
O Lord, hold me fast
Till all sin's storms are overpast !

iv Praise God upon His heavenly throne,
The Father, God Almighty ;
And Jesus Christ, His only Son,
Who for us careth dearly ;
And God the Holy Ghost also,
Who doth on us His grace bestow.
Both now and through eternity
Sing ever Their praise,
To Them in heaven your voices raise.

U.L.S. 361.

Tr. C. S. T.

ALLEIN ZU DIR, HERR JESU CHRIST

Hymn, by Johannes Schneesing, in four 9-line stanzas (c. 1540. Melody, anonymous (? 1541).

i Allein zu dir, Herr Jesu Christ,
  Mein Hoffnung steht auf Erden !
  Ich weiss, dass du mein Tröster bist ;
  Kein Trost mag mir sonst werden.
  Von Anbeginn ist nichts erkorn,
  Auf Erden war kein Mensch geborn,
  Der mir aus Nöthen helfen kann :
  Ich rufe dich an,
  Zu dem ich mein Vertrauen han.

iv Ehr sei Gott in dem höchsten Thron,
   Dem Vater aller Güte,
   Und Jesu Christ, seim liebsten Sohn,
   Der uns allzeit behüte,
   Und Gott dem Heiligen Geiste,
   Der uns sein Hilf allzeit leiste,
   Damit wir ihm gefällig sein,
   Hier in dieser Zeit
   Und folgend in der Ewigkeit.

U.L.S. 361.

i Alone in Thee, Lord Jesus Christ,
  My hope on earth resideth.
  That Thou my Saviour art I wist ,
  Help nowhere else abideth.
  Not ever since the world began
  Hath on this earth been born the man
  Who can from Satan rescue me.
  To Thee, Lord, I call,
  Who can sustain my trusting soul.

iv Praise God upon His heavenly throne,
   The Father, God Almighty ;
   And Jesus Christ His only Son,
   Who for us careth dearly;
   And God the Holy Ghost also,
   Who doth on us His grace bestow.
   Both now and through Eternity
   Sing ever Their praise,
   To Them in heaven your voices raise.

Tr. C. S. T.

ALLES IST AN GOTTES SEGEN

Hymn, anonymous, in six 6-line stanzas (1676). Melody, by J. Löhner (1691), reconstructed by (?) Bach.

20

i Alles ist an Gottes Segen
  Und an seiner Gnad gelegen,
  Über alles Geld und Gut.
  Wer auf Gott sein Hoffnung setzet,
  Der behält ganz unverletzet
  Einen freien Heldenmuth.

ii Der mich hat bisher ernähret
   Und so manches Glück bescheret,
   Ist und bleibet ewig mein.
   Der mich wunderlich geführet
   Und noch leitet und regieret,
   Wird forthin mein Helfer sein.

v Er weiss schon nach seinem Willen
  Mein Verlangen zu erfüllen ;
  Es hat alles seine Zeit.
  Ich hab ihm nichts vorzuschreiben :
  Wie Gott will, so muss es bleiben :
  Wann Gott will, bin ich bereit.

vi Soll ich hier noch länger leben,
   Will ich ihm nicht widerstreben ;
   Ich verlasse mich auf ihn :
   Ist doch nichts, das lang bestehet ;
   Alles Irdische vergehet
   Und fährt wie ein Strom dahin.

i All things move as God hath made them,
  As His bounteous grace hath laid them.
  Nought man's puny arts avail.
  He whose trust on God is founded
  Shall on earth be ne'er confounded,
  But his course in freedom sail.

ii He Whose care so long hath blessed me,
   And with happy gifts hath pressed me,
   Is and always shall be mine.
   He Whose eye from youth hath watched me,
   And from danger's path hath snatched me,
   Will not now His charge resign.

v Well He knows what best is for me,
  Giveth kindly, wisely, surely,
  At His own good time in need.
  Claim His favour never dare I,
  As He wills so shall it e'er be ;
  When He calls I come with speed.

vi So, if longer years are given,
   Ne'er I'll doubt my Lord in heavèn,
   But surrender all to Him.
   Nought there is that fast remaineth,
   All that's mortal onward straineth,
   Like a stream, the port to win.

U.L.S. 488.

Tr. C. S. T.

ALS DER GÜTIGE GOTT

Hymn, a translation, in twelve 5-line stanzas, of the Sequence ' Mittit ad virginem', by Michael Weisse (1531). Melody, that of the Sequence (12th cent), adapted by Bach

Mittit ad virginem.

i Als der gütige Gott
  Vollenden wollt sein Wort,
  Sandt er ein Engel schnell,
  Des Namen Gabriel,
  Ins galiläisch Land,

ii In die Stadt Nazareth,
  Da er ein Jungfrau hatt,
  Die, Maria genannt,
  Joseph nie hatt erkannt,
  Dem sie vertrauet war.

iii Als der Bot vor sie kam,
  Fing er mit Freuden an,
  Machet ihr offenbar,
  Was ihm befohlen war,
  Sprechend freundlich zu ihr :

iv Sei gegrüsst, holdselig !
  Gott, der Herr allmächtig,
  Ist mit dir aliezeit,
  O du gebenedeit
  Unter allen Frauen !

ix Maria glaubet ihm
  Und sprach : Wohlan, ich bin
  Willig des Herren Magd ;
  Er thu, wie du gesagt,
  Mit mir, was ihm behagt.

x Bald wirket Gottes Kraft
  In ihrer Jungfrauschaft
  Und sie empfing zuhand
  Christum, der Welt Heiland,
  Und der Engel verschwand.

xi Preis, Lob und Herrlichkeit,
  Danksagung und Klarheit
  Sei dir in Ewigkeit,
  O Herre Jesu Christ,
  Der du Mensch worden bist.

i The story famed is told,
  How God sometime of old
  An angel bright sent down
  To Nazareth's fair town
  In Galilee's broad land,

ii Where dwelt a maid so fair ;
  She was beyond compare,
  And Mary was her name.
  With her, too, Joseph came :
  For spouses twain were they.

iii And Gabriel, when he came,
  With speed did there proclaim
  The tidings he did bring
  To Mary there and then,
  And joyously did sing :

iv ' Hail, hail, O maid so fair !
  Favoured right well ye are !
  For God doth call you blest,
  Yea more than all the rest
  Of women that appear.'

ix And Mary mild did say :
  ' Do with me as you may ;
  For as God wills I'll do,
  Nor ever shal't me rue
  His bidding to obey.'

x So did it then befall
  In Bethlehem's poor stall
  That Christ was born on earth,
  A wondrous mortal birth,
  As Gabriel did say.

xi Praise, glory now be sung
  While endless ages run
  To Thee, Lord Jesu Christ,
  Who in a manger liest,
  Sweet Mary's gentle Son !

Zahn, 1645.[1]

Tr. C. S. T.

[1] *Die Melodien der deutschen evangelischen Kirchenlieder* (Gütersloh. 1889).

ALS JESUS CHRISTUS IN DER NACHT

Hymn, by Johann Heermann, in nine 4-line stanzas (1636). Melody, by Johann Crüger (1649).

i Als Jesus Christus in der Nacht,
   Darin er ward verrathen,
   Auf unser Heil ganz war bedacht
   Dasselb uns zu erstatten,

ii Da nahm er in die Hand das Brot
   Und brachs mit seinen Fingern,
   Sah auf gen Himmel, danket Gott,
   Und sprach zu seinen Jüngern :

iii Nehmt hin und esst : Das ist mein Leib,
   Der für euch wird gegeben,
   Und dankt, dass ich der euer bleib
   Im Tod und auch im Leben.

iv Desgleichen nahm er auch den Wein
   Im Kelch und sprach zu allen :
   Nehmt hin und trinket in gemein,
   Wollt ihr Gott recht gefallen.

ix O Jesu, dir sei ewig Dank
   Für deine Treu und Gaben.
   Ach lass durch diese Speis und Trank
   Auch mich das Leben haben.

Fischer-Tümpel.[1]

i Upon that night of mirk and gloom,
   Before He was betrayèd
   And passed to Calv'ry's awful doom,
   Sat Jesus undismayèd.

ii Within His hands He took the bread
   And in His fingers brake it,
   Then up to heavèn raised His head,
   And to the Twelve He gave it :

iii ' This is My Body, take and eat,
   For your good it is given ;
   So, thankful be, as is most meet,
   And share Me with high heavèn.'

iv Thereafter did He take the cup
   And thus did speak unto them :
   ' Now drink ye this full goblet up ;
   Think on My words and do them.'

ix Lord Jesus, thanks to Thee be said
   For Thy dear love and merit ;
   And may we through this wine and bread
   Thy heavenly home inherit.

Tr. C. S. T.[2]

[1] Bd. i. No. 369.
[2] *Johann Crüger's Hymn-Tunes* (Lond. 1923).

ALS VIERZIG TAG NACH OSTERN WARN

Hymn, by Nikolaus Herman, in fourteen 5-line stanzas (1560). Melody, by Nikolaus Herman (1560).

23

i Als vierzig Tag nach Ostern warn
Und Christus wollt gen Himmel fahrn,
B'schied er sein Jünger auf ein Berg,
        Alleluja!
Vollend hat er sein Amt und Werk.
        Alleluja!

ii Er sprach : All Ding erfüllet sind
Die man von mir geschrieben find
In Propheten und Moses Lahr;
        Alleluja!
Die Schrift er euch ausleget klar,
        Alleluja!

iii Also sprach er : Hats müssen sein,
Dass Christus leidet Todes Pein,
Und musst wider vom Tod aufstehn
        Alleluja!
Durchs Kreuz und Tod in sein Reich gehn.
        Alleluja!

v Geht hin, predigt in meinem Nam
Vergebung der Sünd jedermann,
Tauft und lehrt alle Völker gleich
        Alleluja!
Und sammlet mir ein ewigs Reich.
        Alleluja!

vi Wer glaubet und sich taufen lässt,
Derselb die Seligkeit empfängt,
Wer aber nicht glaubt wird verdammt
        Alleluja!
Macht solchs in aller Welt bekannt.
        Alleluja!

Wackernagel.[1]

i Four days had passed since Christ arose,
Triumphant over all His foes;
The Twelve He callèd to Him there:
        Alleluja!
His days on earth all finished were.
        Alleluja!

ii And thus did He unto them say :
' All things are finished that you may
In Moses and the prophets read,
        Alleluja!
Or of Me ever were decreed.'
        Alleluja!

iii Also spake He : ' On Me was laid
The price of sin that must be paid.
But from the grave I rose again,
        Alleluja!
And through the Cross have conquered pain.'
        Alleluja!

v ' Now go ye forth and through the world
Preach all the tidings ye have heard.
Baptize and teach ye in My name
        Alleluja!
Till to My kingdom all have come.'
        Alleluja!

vi ' Whoso believes and is baptized
For life eternal is designed :
Whoso no faith has he is damned :
        Alleluja!
This let all people understand.'
        Alleluja!

Tr. C. S. T.

[1] Bd. iii. No. 1357.

AN WASSERFLÜSSEN BABYLON

Hymn, by Wolfgang Dachstein, in five 10-line stanzas (1525). Melody, attributed to Dachstein (1525).
Psalm cxxxvii.

i An Was-ser-flüs-sen Ba-by-lon Da sas-sen wir mit Schmer-zen:
Als wir ge-dach-ten an Zi-on, Da wein-ten wir von Her-zen;
iv Ja, wenn ich nicht mit ganz-em Fleiss, Je-ru-sa-lem, dich eh-re,
Im An-fang mei-ner Freu-den Preis, Von itzt und im-mer-meh-re!

i By wa-ter-side in Ba-by-lon We sat down bit-ter cry--ing;
E'er when we thought up-on Zi-on, Our hearts to her were fly--ing.
iv O shall I not with all my soul, Je-ru-sa-lem, la-ment thee?
And shall I not pre-fer thee whole To ev'-ry oth-er ci-ty?

i Wir häng-ten auf mit schwerem Muth Die Har-fen und die Or-geln gut An
iv Ge-denk der Kin-der E-dom sehr Am Tag Je-ru-sa-lem, o Herr, Die

i We hang-ed up our harps on high Up-on the trees that were near by The
iv Think, Lord, on they of E-dom, who Did mock Je-ru-s'lem's bit-ter rue, And

i ih-re Bäum der Wei-den, Die drin-nen sind in ih-rem Land; Da
iv in ihr Bos-heit sprech-en: Reiss ab, reiss ab zu al-ler Stund, Ver-

i ri-ver's mar-ges sha--ded. We mourn-ed deep full many a day, And
iv all un-kind-ly jeer--ed: 'Down with it, down, de-stroy it all, To

AN WASSERFLÜSSEN BABYLON

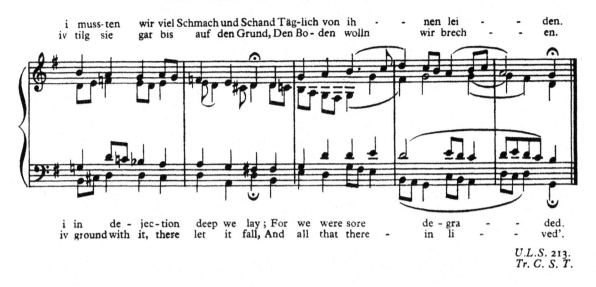

i muss-ten wir viel Schmach und Schand Täg-lich von ih - - nen lei - - den.
iv tilg sie gar bis auf den Grund, Den Bo - den wolln wir brech - - en.

i in de - jec - tion deep we lay; For we were sore de - gra - - ded.
iv ground with it, there let it fall, And all that there - in li - - ved'.

U.L.S. 213.
Tr. C. S. T.

Hymn, by Paul Gerhardt, in ten 10-line stanzas (1647). Melody, attributed to Wolfgang Dachstein (1525).

i Ein Lämmlein geht und trägt die Schuld
Der Welt und ihrer Kinder ;
Es geht und büsset in Geduld
Die Sünden aller Sünder.
Es geht dahin, wird matt und krank,
Ergiebt sich auf die Würgebank,
Verzeiht sich aller Freuden,
Es nimmet an Schmach, Hohn und Spott,
Angst, Wunden, Striemen, Kreuz und Tod,
Und spricht : Ich wills gern leiden.

i The Lamb of God for mortals' sakes,
Ourselves and all our children,
Our load of sin upon Him takes
That so we may be shriven.
For us He suffered shame and loss,
He knew the burden of the Cross,
And death itself endurèd.
By wicked men was He decried,
By torment cruel was He tried,
Yet for us gladly suffered.

vi Ich will von deiner Lieblichkeit
Bei Nacht und Tage singen,
Mich selbst auch dir zu aller Zeit
Zum Freudenopfer bringen.
Mein Bach des Lebens soll sich dir
Und deinem Namen für und für
In Dankbarkeit ergiessen :
Und was du mir zu gut gethan,
Das will ich stets, so tief ich kann,
In mein Gedächtniss schliessen.

vi O blessèd Lamb, to Thee always
A hymn of thanks I'm singing,
A joyful anthem in Thy praise
That heavenward's ever winging.
To Thee and to Thy blessèd Name,
Exalting high Thy glorious fame,
Thankoff'ring shall be flowing.
Yea, all for me that Thou hast done,
And all for man that Thou hast won,
Will I be ever showing.

U.L.S. 95.

Tr. C. S. T.

AUF, AUF, MEIN HERZ

Hymn, by Martin Opitz, in ten 4-line stanzas (1625); also in five 8-line stanzas. Melody, reconstructed by (?) Bach, attributed (1663) to Johann Staden.

25

* **Bach has a ⌒ here.**

i Auf, auf, mein Herz, und du mein ganzer Sinn :
  Wirf alles das, was Welt ist, von dir hin !
  Wo das du willt, was göttlich ist, erlangen,
  So lass den Leib, in dem du bist gefangen.

vi Wer aber ganz dem Leib ist abgethan,
   Und nimmt sich nur der Himmelssorgen an,
   Setzt allen Trost auf seines Gottes Gnaden :
   Dem kann nicht Welt, noch Tod, noch Teufel
     schaden.

x Vollbringst du das, mein Herz, und du, mein Sinn,
  Und legst die Last der Erden von dir hin,
  Sagst ab dem Leib, in dem du bist gefangen :
  So wird Gott dich, und du wirst Gott erlangen.

U.L.S. 295.

i Now, wake my heart, and all my soul within,
  Put from thee earth's poor dross, and heavèn win!
  And if thou'lt choose thee rather what is godly,
  Then break the fleshly chains that bind and hold thee!

vi For know that he whom passion ne'er controls,
   Whose gaze is fixed where God's high heavèn rolls,
   Who puts his trust in Jesu's love availing,
   Shall see nor Death, nor World, nor Hell prevailing.

x Be this thy care, my heart and soul, within :
  Put off earth's mire, heaven's greater glories win ;
  Cast off this flesh that like a vice hath bound thee ;
  So shall for evermore God's love surround thee !

Tr. C. S. T.

26

AUF MEINEN LIEBEN GOTT

Hymn, by Johann Heermann, in eleven 6-line stanzas (1630). Melody, anonymous (1609), of secular origin (1574).

26

i Wo soll ich fliehen hin,
  Weil ich beschweret bin
  Mit viel und grossen Sünden ?
  Wo kann ich Rettung finden ?
  Wenn alle Welt her käme :
  Mein Angst sie nicht wegnähme.

ix Dein Blut, der edle Saft,
   Hat solche Stärk und Kraft :
   Dass auch ein Tröpflein kleine
   Die ganze Welt kann reine,
   Ja gar aus Teufels Rachen
   Frei, los und selig machen.

* xi Führ auch mein Herz und Sinn
     Durch deinen Geist dahin,
     Dass ich mög alles meiden,
     Was mich und dich kann scheiden,
     Und ich an deinem Leibe
     Ein Gliedmass ewig bleibe

i O whither shall I flee,
  Depressed with misery ?
  Who is it that can ease me,
  And from my sins release me ?
  Man's help I vain have provèd,
  Sin's load remains unmovèd.

ix Christ, Thine atoning blood,
   The sinner's highest good,
   Is pow'rful to deliver
   And free the soul for ever
   From all claim of the devil,
   And cleanse it from all evil.

xi Lord, strengthen Thou my heart ;
   Such grace to me impart,
   That nought which may await me
   From Thee may separate me ;
   Let me with Thee, my Saviour,
   United be for ever.

U.L.S. 397.

Tr. Anon.[1]

[1] *Moravian Hymn-book,* 1754 (Ed. 1877), No. 286.

AUF MEINEN LIEBEN GOTT

Hymn, by Johann Heermann, in eleven 6-line stanzas (1630). Melody, anonymous (1609), of secular origin (1574).

27

i Wo soll ich fliehen hin,
  Weil ich beschweret bin
  Mit viel und grossen Sünden ?
  Wo kann ich Rettung finden ?
  Wenn alle Welt her käme :
  Mein Angst sie nicht wegnähme.

iii Ich, dein betrübtes Kind,
  Werf alle meine Sünd,
  So viel ihr in mir stecken
  Und mich so heftig schrecken,
  In deine tiefen Wunden,
  Da ich stets Heil gefunden.

* vii Mir mangelt zwar sehr viel :
  Doch was ich haben will,
  Ist alles mir zu Gute
  Erlangt mit deinem Blute ;
  Damit ich überwinde
  Tod, Teufel, Höll und Sünde.

U.L.S. 397.

i O whither shall I fly ?
  To Thee, O Lord, I cry.
  My heavy sins dismay me,
  Whence cometh help to stay me ?
  Though all the wide world aideth,
  'Tis Christ my need provideth.

iii A heavy load of sin,
  Saviour, to Thee I bring ;
  Whate'er the tasks that daunt me,
  The fear and doubts that haunt me,
  From out Thy wounds love floweth
  And saving grace bestoweth.

vii How poor's my life indeed !
  How grievous is my need !
  And yet, how rich in blessing
  Am I, Jesu possessing !
  Death vanquished, sin enchainèd,
  Hell, Sin, and Satan shamèd !

Tr. C. S. T.

AUF MEINEN LIEBEN GOTT

Hymn, by Johann Heermann, in eleven 6-line stanzas (1630). Melody, anonymous (1609), of secular origin (1574).

28

i Wo soll ich fliehen hin,
   Weil ich beschweret bin
   Mit viel und grossen Sünden ?
   Wo kann ich Rettung finden ?
   Wenn alle Welt her käme :
   Mein Angst sie nicht wegnähme.

ix Dein Blut, der edle Saft,
   Hat solche Stärk und Kraft :
   Dass auch ein Tröpflein kleine
   Die ganze Welt kann reine,
   Ja gar aus Teufels Rachen
   Frei, los und selig machen.

* xi Führ auch mein Herz und Sinn
   Durch deinen Geist dahin,
   Dass ich mög alles meiden,
   Was mich und dich kann scheiden,
   Und ich an deinem Leibe
   Ein Gliedmass ewig bleibe.

              U.L.S. 397.

i O whither shall I fly?
   To Thee, O Lord, I cry.
   My heavy sins dismay me,
   Whence cometh help to stay me ?
   Though all the wide world aideth,
   'Tis Christ my need provideth.

ix Of Jesu's blood the flow
   With might availeth so :
   One drop from out His torn Side
   Can throughly cleanse the world wide,
   From Satan's jaws can snatch us
   And to Himself can match us.

xi Lord, guide my heart and will,
   Thy strength in me instil !
   From all my sins deliver
   Which Thee from me dissever ;
   Until, from evil parted,
   In Thee I am engrafted !

              Tr. C. S. T.

AUF MEINEN LIEBEN GOTT

Hymn, attributed to Sigismund Weingärtner, in five 6-line stanzas (1607, Melody, anonymous (1609), of secular origin (1574).

i Auf meinen lieben Gott
  Trau ich in Angst und Noth.
  Der kann mich allzeit retten
  Aus Trübsal, Angst und Nöthen ;
  Mein Unglück kann er wenden :
  Steht all's in seinen Händen.

iii Ob mich der Tod nimmt hin,
  Ist sterben mein Gewinn,
  Und Christus ist mein Leben ;
  Dem thu ich mich ergeben.
  Ich sterb heut oder morgen :
  Mein Seel wird er versorgen.

vi Amen zu aller Stund
  Sprech ich aus Herzensgrund.
  Du wollest selbst uns leiten,
  Herr Christ, zu allen Zeiten.
  Auf dass wir deinen Namen
  Ewiglich preisen. Amen.

U.L.S. 694.

i In God, my faithful God,
  I trust when dark my road ;
  Though many woes o'ertake me,
  Yet He will not forsake me ;
  His love it is doth send them,
  And when 'tis best will end them.

iii If death my portion be,
  Then death is gain to me,
  And Christ my life for ever,
  From Whom death cannot sever ;
  Come when it may, He'll shield me ;
  To Him I wholly yield me.

vi ' So be it,' then I say,
  With all my heart each day ;
  ' Guide us while here we wander,
  Till, safely landed yonder,
  We too, dear Lord, adore Thee,
  And sing for joy before Thee.'

Tr. Catherine Winkworth.[1]

[1] *Chorale Book for England* (Lond. 1865), No. 147.

AUF MEINEN LIEBEN GOTT

Hymn, by Johann Heermann, in eleven 6-line stanzas (1630). Melody, anonymous (1609), of secular origin (1574).

30

[Obbligato for Violin]

i Wo soll ich fliehen hin,
  Weil ich beschweret bin
  Mit viel und grossen Sünden ?
  Wo kann ich Rettung finden ?
  Wenn alle Welt her käme :
  Mein Angst sie nicht wegnähme.

* ix Dein Blut, der edle Saft,
  Hat solche Stärk und Kraft :
  Dass auch ein Tröpflein kleine
  Die ganze Welt kann reine,
  Ja gar aus Teufels Rachen
  Frei, los und selig machen.

xi Führ auch mein Herz und Sinn
  Durch deinen Geist dahin,
  Dass ich mög alles meiden,
  Was mich und dich kann scheiden,
  Und ich an deinem Leibe
  Ein Gliedmass ewig bleibe.

  U.L.S. 397.

i O whither shall I fly ?
  To Thee, O Lord, I cry.
  My heavy sins dismay me,
  Whence cometh help to stay me ?
  Though all the wide world aideth,
  'Tis Christ my need provideth.

ix Of Jesu's blood the flow
  With might availeth so :
  One drop from out His torn Side
  Can throughly cleanse the world wide,
  From Satan's jaws can snatch us,
  And to Himself can match us.

xi Lord, guide my heart and will,
  Thy strength in me instil !
  From all my sins deliver
  Which Thee from me dissever ;
  Until, from evil parted,
  In Thee I am engrafted !

  Tr. C. S. T.

AUS MEINES HERZENS GRUNDE

Hymn, by (?) Johannes Mathesius, in seven 8-line stanzas (1592). Melody, anonymous (1598); probably of greater antiquity.

31

i Aus meines Herzens Grunde
  Sag ich dir Lob und Dank
  In dieser Morgenstunde,
  Dazu mein Leben lang,
  O Gott ! in deinem Thron,
  Dir zu Lob, Preis und Ehren
  Durch Christum, unsern Herren,
  Dein eingebornen Sohn.

ii Dass du mich hast aus Gnaden
  In der vergangnen Nacht
  Vor G'fahr und allem Schaden
  Behütet und bewacht.
  Ich bitt demüthiglich :
  Wollst mir mein Sünd vergeben,
  Womit in diesem Leben
  Ich hab erzürnet dich.

vii Darauf so sprech ich Amen
  Und zweifle nicht daran :
  Gott wird es all's zusammen
  Ihm wohlgefallen lan.
  Und streck nun aus mein Hand,
  Greif an das Werk mit Freuden,
  Dazu mich Gott bescheiden
  In meim Beruf und Stand.

i My inmost heart now raises,
  In this fair morning hour,
  A song of thankful praises
  To Thine Almighty power ;
  And as I have begun
  This day, my God, my life be
  Begun and closed to praise Thee,
  Through Christ Thy only Son.

ii For Thou from me hast warded
  All perils of the night ;
  From every harm hast guarded
  My soul till morning's light ;
  Humbly to Thee I cry,
  Do Thou the sins forgive me
  That as I live offend Thee ;
  Have mercy, Lord most High !

vii Amen ! I say, not fearing
  That God rejects my prayer;
  I doubt not He is hearing
  And granting me His care ;
  And so I go my way,
  And put my hands forth joyful
  To do His bidding cheerful,
  And serve Him through this day.

U.L.S. 440.

Tr. Catherine Winkworth (adapted).[1]

[1] *Chorale Book for England* (Lond. 1865), No. 164.

AUS TIEFER NOTH SCHREI ICH ZU DIR

Hymn, by Martin Luther, in five 7-line stanzas (1524). Melody, by (?) Luther (1524).

Psalm cxxx.

i Aus tiefer Noth schrei ich zu dir,
 Herr Gott, erhör mein Rufen !
 Dein gnädig Ohren kehr zu mir
 Und meiner Bitt sie öffen.
 Denn so du willt das sehen an,
 Was Sünd und Unrecht ist gethan :
 Wer kann, Herr, vor dir bleiben ?

ii Bei dir gilt nichts denn Gnad und Gunst,
 Die Sünde zu vergeben.
 Es ist doch unser Thun umsonst
 Auch in dem besten Leben.
 Vor dir niemand sich rühmen kann ;
 Dess muss dich fürchten jedermann
 Und deiner Gnaden leben.

*v Ob bei uns ist der Sünden viel :
 Bei Gott ist viel mehr Gnaden ;
 Sein Hand zu helfen hat kein Ziel,
 Wie gross auch sei der Schaden.
 Er ist allein der gute Hirt,
 Der Israel erlösen wird
 Aus seinen Sünden allen.

i From trouble deep I cry to Thee ;
 Lord God, hear Thou my crying ;
 Thy gracious ear O turn to me,
 Open it to my sighing.
 For if Thou mean'st to look upon
 The wrong and evil that is done,
 Who, Lord, can stand before Thee ?

ii With Thee availeth nought but grace
 To cover mortal weakness ;
 Our good deeds cannot show their face,
 Not one is there who's stainless.
 Before Thee no one glory can,
 And so must tremble every man,
 And live by Thy grace only.

v Although our sin be great, God's grace
 Is greater to relieve us ;
 His hand in helping nothing stays,
 The hurt however grievous.
 The shepherd good alone is He,
 Who will at last set Israel free
 From all and every trespass.

U.L.S. 362.

Tr. George Macdonald.[1]

[1] *Exotics* (Lond. 1876), p. 101.

BEFIEHL DU DEINE WEGE

Hymn, by Paul Gerhardt in twelve 8-line stanzas (1653); an acrostic on Luther's Ps. xxxvii. 5. Melody, by (?) Bartholomäus Gesius (1603), originally set to 'Lobet Gott, unsern Herren'.

i Befiehl du deine Wege
  Und was dein Herze kränkt,
  Der allertreusten Pflege
  Dess, der den Himmel lenkt;
  Der Wolken, Luft und Winden
  Giebt Wege, Lauf und Bahn,
  Der wird auch Wege finden,
  Da dein Fuss gehen kann.

v Und ob gleich alle Teufel
  Hie wollten widerstehn,
  So wird doch ohne Zweifel
  Gott nicht zurücke gehn.
  Was er ihm vorgenommen
  Und was er haben will,
  Das muss doch endlich kommen
  Zu seinem Zweck und Ziel.

vii Auf! auf! gieb deinem Schmerze
  Und Sorgen gute Nacht;
  Lass fahren, was das Herze
  Betrübt und traurig macht!
  Bist du doch nicht Regente,
  Der alles führen soll:
  Gott sitzt im Regimente
  Und führet alles wohl.

xii Mach End, o Herr, mach Ende
  An aller unser Noth;
  Stärk unsre Füss und Hände
  Und lass bis in den Tod
  Uns allzeit deiner Pflege
  Und Treu empfohlen sein:
  So gehen unsre Wege
  Gewiss zum Himmel ein.

U.L.S. 620.

i Commit thou all thy going,
  And all that grieves thy soul,
  To God's most gracious doing
  Who doth the heavens control!
  The winds and tides obey Him,
  All own His sovereign will;
  Then trust thy ways unto Him;
  He will with blessing fill.

v What though the power of Satan
  To raise its head should dare?
  It shall be broke and shaken
  And driven to its lair.
  For God's word ever standeth
  And alway must prevail,
  Fulfil what He commandeth,
  No matter who may rail.

vii Up, then! lay all thy sorrow,
  E'er trustful, in His care!
  Swift dawns a fair to-morrow
  When grief shall disappear.
  Man's wit is unavailing
  And little power may claim.
  But God's might is prevailing
  And will thy courses frame.

xii In Thy good time, O Father,
  Make mortal cares to cease,
  And guide our feet to enter
  The perfect paths of peace!
  So, when Death's voice shall call us
  To end this life of woe,
  Thy light may shine before us
  As unto heaven we go.

Tr. C. S. T.

CHRIST, DER DU BIST DER HELLE TAG

Hymn, by Erasmus Alber, in seven 4-line stanzas (c. 1556). Melody, anonymous (1568).

* **The fourth line of each stanza is repeated.**

Christe qui lux es et dies.

i { Christe,
{ Christ, der } du bist der helle Tag,
Vor dir die Nacht nicht bleiben mag.;
Du leuchtest uns vom Vater her
Und bist des Lichtes Prediger.

ii Ach lieber Herr, behüt uns heut
In dieser Nacht vorm bösen Feind;
Und lass uns in dir ruhen fein
Und vor dem Satan sicher sein.

vi Befiehl dem Engel, dass er komm
Und uns bewach, dein Eigenthum;
Gieb uns die lieben Wächter zu,
Dass wir vorm Satan haben Ruh.

vii So schlafen wir im Namen dein,
Dieweil die Engel bei uns sein.
Du heilige Dreieinigkeit,
Wir loben dich in Ewigkeit.

U.L.S. 507.

i O Christ, Thou art our Lamp and Light,
Who dost disperse the shades of night;
Thy rays from heaven upon us shine,
And speak to us of love divine!

ii O Saviour dear, so guard our sleep,
And watch upon us wakeful keep,
That no ill foes disturb our rest,
Nor hell its power manifest!

vi O let Thine angels vigil keep
While we Thy children are asleep;
And guard our slumbers through the night,
That Satan do us no despite!

vii So shall our bodies sleep in Thee
While that bright band guards sleeplessly.
O holy, blessèd Three in One,
Thy praises evermore be sung!

Tr. C. S. T.

CHRIST IST ERSTANDEN

Hymn, ancient, in three 4-line stanzas (1529). Melody, ancient.

i Christ ist er - stan - - - den Von der Mar - ter al - - -
i Christ is a - ris - - - en From the grave's dark pri - - -

le Des solln wir al - le froh sein, Chri - -
son! So let us all be joy - ful; He

stus will un - ser Trost sein. Ky - rie - e - leis!
is our Sa - viour faith - ful. Al - le - lu - ja!

ii Wär er nicht er - stan - den, So wär die Welt ver - gan - gen: Seit
ii Had He not a - ris - en We had been still in pri - son. But

dass er nun er - stan - den ist, So lo - ben wir den Her - ren Christ.
now He's van - quished Hell and Death, We laud Him with our loud - est breath!

Ky - rie e - leis!   iii Al - le - lu - ja, Al - le - lu - ja, Al -
Al - le - lu - ja!   iii Al - le - lu - ja, Al - le - lu - ja, Al -

le - lu - ja! Des solln wir al - le froh - sein, Chri -
le - lu - ja! Come, let us all be joy - ful; Christ -

stus will un - ser Trost sein. Ky - rie e - leis!
is our Sa - viour faith - ful. Al - le - lu - ja!

* iii Al - le - lu - ja, Al - le - lu - ja, Al - le - lu - ja! Des solln wir al - le
iii A - le - lu - ja, Al - le - lu - ja, Al - le - lu - ja! Come, let us all be

froh sein, Chri-stus will unser Trost sein. Ky - rie e - leis.
joy - ful; Christ is our Sa-viour faith - ful. Al - le - lu - ja!

U.L.S. 126.   Tr. C. S. T.

37

CHRIST LAG IN TODESBANDEN

Hymn, by Martin Luther, in seven 8-line stanzas (1524); a free revision of 'Christ ist erstanden'. Melody, an adaptation (1524) of 'Christ ist erstanden'.

i Christ lag in Todesbanden
  Für unser Sünd gegeben,
  Der ist wieder erstanden
  Und hat uns bracht das Leben :
  Des wir sollen fröhlich sein,
  Gott loben und ihm dankbar sein
  Und singen ihm Hallelujah,
        Hallelujah !

ii Den Tod niemand bezwingn konnt
  Bei allen Menschenkindern :
  Das machte alles unsr' Sünd,
  Kein Unschuld war zu finden.
  Davon kam der Tod so bald
  Und nahm auch über uns Gewalt,
  Hielt uns in seim Reich gefangen.
        Hallelujah !

iii Jesus Christus, wahr Gott'ssohn,
  An unser Statt ist kommen,
  Und hat die Sünde abg'than,
  Damit dem Tod genommen
  All sein Recht und sein Gewalt ;
  Da bleibet nichts denn Tods Gestalt,
  Den Stachel hat er verloren.
        Hallelujah !

U.L.S. 127.

i Christ lay in Death's grim prison ;
  He for our sins was given.
  But now to-day He's risen
  And brings us life from heavèn !
  Wherefore let us joyful be,
  Praising our God with hearty glee,
  And endless Allelujas sing !
        Alleluja !

ii O'er Death no man could conquer,
  No mortal dared to meet him ;
  Through sin our strength's the weaker,
  We could not e'er defeat him.
  Therefore Death did lead us thrall,
  His slaves did make us, one and all,
  And had us in his awful power.
        Alleluja !

iii Now Jesus Christ, God's true Son,
  From earth hath high arisen.
  His death for man did atone,
  So Death is bound in prison.
  All his might must Death forego.
  His powèr boasted's vain, a show,
  His sting is to derision brought !
        Alleluja !

Tr. C. S. T.

CHRIST LAG IN TODESBANDEN

Hymn, by Martin Luther, in seven 8-line stanzas (1524); a free revision of 'Christ ist erstanden'. Melody, an adaptation (1524) of 'Christ ist erstanden

38

i Christ lag in Todesbanden
  Für unser Sünd gegeben,
  Der ist wieder erstanden
  Und hat uns bracht das Leben :
  Des wir sollen fröhlich sein,
  Gott loben und ihm dankbar sein
  Und singen ihm Hallelujah.
        Hallelujah !

ii Den Tod niemand bezwing'n konnt
  Bei allen Menschenkindern :
  Das machte alles unsr' Sünd,
  Kein Unschuld war zu finden.
  Davon kam der Tod so bald
  Und nahm auch über uns Gewalt,
  Hielt uns in seim Reich gefangen.
        Hallelujah !

iii Jesus Christus, wahr Gott'ssohn,
  An unser Statt ist kommen,
  Und hat die Sünde abg'than,
  Damit dem Tod genommen,
  All sein Recht und sein Gewalt ;
  Da bleibet nichts denn Tods Gestalt,
  Den Stachel hat er verloren.
        Hallelujah !

i Christ lay in Death's grim prison ;
  He for our sins was given.
  But now to-day He's risen
  And brings us life from heavèn !
  Wherefore let us joyful be,
  Praising our God with hearty glee,
  And endless Allelujas sing !
        Alleluja !

ii O'er Death no man could conquer,
  No mortal dared to meet him ;
  Through sin our strength's the weaker,
  We could not e'er defeat him.
  Therefore Death did lead us thrall,
  His slaves did make us one and all,
  And had us in his awful power.
        Alleluja !

iii Now Jesus Christ, God's true Son,
  From earth hath high arisen.
  His death for man did atone,
  So Death is bound in prison.
  All his might must Death forego.
  His powèr boasted's vain, a show,
  His sting is to derision brought !
        Alleluja !

U.L.S. 127.

Tr. C. S. T.

CHRIST LAG IN TODESBANDEN

Hymn, by Martin Luther, in seven 8-line stanzas (1524); a free revision of ' Christ ist erstanden '. Melody, an adaptation (1524) of ' Christ ist erstanden '

39

i Christ lag in Todesbanden
  Für unser Sünd gegeben,
  Der ist wieder erstanden
  Und hat uns bracht das Leben :
  Des wir sollen fröhlich sein,
  Gott lobn und ihm dankbar sein
  Und singen ihm Hallelujah,
      Hallelujah !

iv Es war ein wunderlich Krieg,
  Da Tod und Leben rungen :
  Das Leben, das b'hielt den Sieg,
  Es hat den Tod verschlungen.
  Die Schrift hat verkündet das,
  Wie ein Tod den andern frass :
  Ein Spott aus dem Tod ist worden.
      Hallelujah !

* vii Wir essen und wir lebn wohl
  In rechten Osterfladen ;
  Der alte Saurteig nicht soll
  Sein bei dem Wort der Gnaden.
  Christus will die Koste sein
  Und speisen die Seel allein,
  Der Glaub will keins andern leben.
      Hallelujah !

U.L.S. 127.

i Christ lay in Death's grim prison;
  He for our sins was given.
  But now to-day He's risen
  And brings us life from heavèn !
  Wherefore let us joyful be,
  God praising with hearty glee,
  And endlèss Allelujas sing !
      Alleluja !

iv It was a wondrous fight, so
  That Death's dominion rended;
  Now Life hath bound His grim foe
  And Death's long reign is ended.
  As to us the Scripture saith :
  In death Christ hath conquered Death,
  And hell itself is brought to scorn.
      Alleluja !

vii With loving hearts receive now
  The feast that God hath given.
  Before His Word see hence go
  The old and evil leaven.
  Christ Himself the feast hath spread,
  By Him hungry souls are fed
  With living Bread come down from heaven.
      Alleluja!

Tr. C. S. T.

CHRIST LAG IN TODESBANDEN

Hymn by Martin Luther, in seven 8-line stanzas (1524); a free revision of ' Christ ist erstanden '. Melody, an adaptation (1524) of ' Christ ist erstanden '.

i Christ lag in Todesbanden
  Für unser Sünd gegeben,
  Der ist wieder erstanden
  Und hat uns bracht das Leben :
  Des wir sollen fröhlich sein,
  Gott loben und ihm dankbar sein
  Und singen ihm Hallelujah,
      Hallelujah !

* v Hie ist das rechte Ost'rlamm,
  Davon Gott hat geboten,
  Das ist einst an des Kreuz's Stamm
  In heisser Lieb gebraten :
  Dess Blut zeichnet unser Thür,
  Das hält der Glaub dem Tode für,
  Der Würger kann uns nicht rühren.
      Hallelujah !

vi So feiern wir das hoh Fest
  Mit Herzen Freud und Wonne,
  Das uns der Herre schein'n lässt.
  Er ist selber die Sonne,
  Der durch seiner Gnaden Glanz
  Erleuchtet unser Herzen ganz :
  Der Sünden Nacht ist vergangen.
      Hallelujah !

i Christ lay in Death's grim prison ;
  He for our sins was given.
  But now to-day He's risen
  And brings us life from heaven !
  Wherefore let us joyful be,
  Praising our God with hearty glee,
  And endless Allelujas sing !
      Alleluja !

v And now the Paschal Lamb see,
  As God of old ordainèd,
  Who hung for us on Calv'ry ;
  Our sin 'twas Him constrainèd !
  His blood's sprinkled on our door,
  And Satan, foilèd, passes o'er,
  The tyrant ne'er can harm us more.
      Alleluja !

vi So let us keep our Easter
  With joy and jubilation !
  The rising Sun in splendour
  Now bringeth us salvation.
  In His ever glorious grace
  Behold we all His radiant face :
  Sin-laden night before Him flies.
      Alleluja !

U.L.S. 127.

Tr. C. S. T.

CHRIST LAG IN TODESBANDEN

Hymn, by Martin Luther, in seven 8-line stanzas (1524); a free revision of 'Christ ist erstanden'. Melody, an adaptation (1524) of 'Christ ist erstanden'.

41

i Christ lag in Todesbanden
　Für unser Sünd gegeben,
　Der ist wieder erstanden
　Und hat uns bracht das Leben :
　Des wir sollen fröhlich sein,
　Gott loben und ihm dankbar sein
　Und singen ihm Hallelujah,
　　　　Hallelujah !

ii Den Tod niemand bezwing'n konnt
　Bei allen Menschenkindern :
　Das machte alles unsr' Sünd,
　Kein Unschuld war zu finden.
　Davon kam der Tod so bald
　Und nahm auch über uns Gewalt,
　Hielt uns in seim Reich gefangen.
　　　　Hallelujah !

iii Jesus Christus, wahr Gott'ssohn,
　An unser Statt ist kommen,
　Und hat die Sünde abg'than,
　Damit dem Tod genommen
　All sein Recht und sein Gewalt ;
　Da bleibet nichts denn Tods Gestalt,
　Den Stachel hat er verloren.
　　　　Hallelujah !

i Christ lay in Death's grim prison ;
　He for our sins was given.
　But now to-day He's risen
　And brings us life from heavèn !
　Wherefore let us joyful be,
　Praising our God with hearty glee,
　And endless Allelujas sing !
　　　　Alleluja !

ii O'er Death no man could conquer,
　No mortal dared to meet him ;
　Through sin our strength's the weaker,
　We could not e'er defeat him.
　Therefore Death did lead us thrall,
　His slaves did make us, one and all,
　And had us in his awful power.
　　　　Alleluja !

iii Now Jesus Christ, God's true Son,
　From earth hath high arisen.
　His death for man did atone,
　So Death is bound in prison.
　All his might must Death forego.
　His powèr boasted's vain, a show,
　His sting is to derision brought !
　　　　Alleluja !

U.L.S. 127.

Tr. C. S. T.

CHRIST UNSER HERR ZUM JORDAN KAM

Hymn, by Martin Luther, in seven 9-line stanzas (1541). Melody, by Johann Walther (?), originally (1524) to Luther's ' Es wollt uns Gott genädig sein ', set to ' Christ unser Herr' in 1543.

i Christ unser Herr zum Jordan kam
  Nach seines Vaters Willen,
Von sanct Johanns die Taufe nahm,
  Sein Werk und Amt zu 'rfüllen.
Da wollt er stiften uns ein Bad,
  Zu waschen uns von Sünden,
Ersäufen auch den bittern Tod
  Durch sein selbs Blut und Wunden ;
  Es galt ein neues Leben.

ii So hört und merket alle wohl,
  Was Gott heisst selbs die Taufe ;
Und was ein Christen glauben soll,
  Zu meiden Ketzerhaufen :
Gott spricht und will, dass Wasser sei,
  Doch nicht allein schlecht Wasser ;
Sein heiligs Wort ist auch dabei
  Mit reichem Geist ohn Massen :
  Der ist allhie der Täufer.

vii Das Aug allein das Wasser sieht,
  Wie Menschen Wasser giessen ;
Der Glaub im Geist die Kraft versteht
  Des Blutes Jesu Christi ;
Und ist vor ihm ein rothe Fluth
  Von Christi Blut gefärbet,
Die allen Schaden heilen thut,
  Von Adam her geerbet,
  Auch von uns selbs begangen.

i To Jordan when our Lord had gone,
  His Father's pleasure willing,
He took His baptism of St. john,
  His work and task fulfilling ;
Therein He would appoint a bath
  To wash us from defilement,
And also drown that cruel Death
  In His blood of assoilment :
  'Twas no less than a new life.

ii Let all then hear and right receive
  The baptism of the Father,
And what a Christian shall believe,
  To shun where heathen gather.
Water indeed, not water mere,
  In it can do His pleasure,
His Holy Word is also there
  With Spirit rich, unmeasured :
  He is the one Baptizer.

vii The eye but water doth behold,
  As from man's hand it floweth ;
But inward faith the power untold
  Of Jesus Christ's blood knoweth.
Faith sees therein a red flood roll,
  With Christ's blood dyed and blended,
Which hurts of all kinds maketh whole,
  From Adam here descended,
  Or by ourselves brought on us.

U.L.S. 258.

George Macdonald.[1]

[1] *Exotics* (Lond. 1876), p. 98.

43

CHRIST UNSER HERR ZUM JORDAN KAM

Hymn, by Martin Luther, in seven 9-line stanzas (1541). Melody, by Johann Walther (?), originally (1524) to Luther's 'Es wollt uns Gott genädig sein', set to 'Christ unser Herr' in 1543.

43

i Christ unser Herr zum Jordan kam
　Nach seines Vaters Willen,
　Von sanct Johanns die Taufe nahm,
　Sein Werk und Amt zu 'rfüllen.
　Da wollt er stiften uns ein Bad,
　Zu waschen uns von Sünden,
　Ersäufen auch den bittern Tod
　Durch sein selbs Blut und Wunden;
　Es galt ein neues Leben.

iii Solchs hat er uns beweiset klar
　Mit Bilden und mit Worten;
　Des Vaters Stimm man offenbar
　Daselbst am Jordan hörte.
　Er sprach: Das ist mein lieber Sohn,
　An dem ich hab Gefallen;
　Den will ich euch befohlen han,
　Dass ihr ihn höret alle
　Und folget seinem Lehren.

* vii Das Aug allein das Wasser sieht,
　Wie Menschen Wasser giessen:
　Der Glaub im Geist die Kraft versteht
　Des Blutes Jesu Christi;
　Und ist vor ihm ein rothe Fluth
　Von Christi Blut gefärbet,
　Die allen Schaden heilen thut,
　Von Adam her geerbet,
　Auch von uns selbs begangen.

i Christ baptized was in Jordan's flood;
　To John the Baptist came He,
　To wash away our sinfulness
　And cleanse us pure and throughly.
　For Death is drowned and Hell oppressed
　When holy water floweth;
　Therein we find th' eternal rest
　That God to mankind giveth,
　Receiving life immortal.

iii So hath He taught us well and clear
　By word and by example.
　Then to the words incline your ear:
　He spake of our Example:
　Said He, ' This is My dear loved Son
　In Whom am I well pleasèd,
　In all His ways He hath well done;
　So, follow what He teacheth,
　And hearken well unto Him.'

vii By faith and powèr from on high
　'Tis Christ's own blood that floweth,
　Celestial elements there lie,
　As water it appeareth.
　By it the penitent is purged
　Of Adam's sin and 'scapes Hell,
　And our low nature's upward urged
　To meet Almighty God's Self
　In raiment pure and spotless.

U.L.S. 258.

Tr. C. S. T.

CHRIST UNSER HERR ZUM JORDAN KAM

Hymn, by Paul Gerhardt, in eight 9-line stanzas (1653). Melody, by Johann Walther (?), originally (1524) to Luther's ' Es wollt uns Gott genädig sein ', set to ' Christ unser Herr ' in 1543, to ' Was alle Weisheit ' in 1653.

44

i Was alle Weisheit in der Welt
　Bei uns hier kaum kann lallen,
　Das lässt Gott aus dem Himmelszelt
　In alle Welt erschallen,
　Dass er alleine König sei
　Hoch über alle Götter,
　Gross, mächtig, freundlich, fromm und treu,
　Der Frommen Schutz und Retter :
　Ein Wesen, drei Personen.

★ viii Auf dass wir also allzugleich
　Zur Himmelspforte dringen
　Und dermaleins in deinem Reich
　Ohn alles Ende singen,
　Dass du alleine König seist
　Hoch über alle Götter,
　Gott Vater, Sohn und Heilger Geist,
　Der Frommen Schutz und Retter :
　Ein Wesen, drei Personen.

Fischer-Tümpel.[1]

i Our lips are mute, our wisdom dumb,
　God's wonders here beholding.
　No tongue can speak, nor mortal ken
　The glories He's unfolding.
　Yet in them God stands manifest,
　Of other gods Creator ;
　He's true and loving, mightiest,
　Our Friend and sure Protector,
　One Godhead in Three Persons !

viii So let our voices with accord,
　To heaven's high portals winging,
　Acclaim His might, our God and Lord,
　His endless praises singing !
　Alone He's King of heavèn's host,
　Of other gods Creator !
　God Father, Son, and Holy Ghost,
　Our Mediator, Saviour,
　One Godhead in Three Persons !

Tr. C. S. T.

[1] Bd. iii. No. 415.

CHRISTE, DER DU BIST TAG UND LICHT

Hymn, attributed to Wolfgang Meusel, in seven 4-line stanzas (1526). Melody, an adaptation (1535) of 'Christe qui lux es et dies'.

Christe qui lux es et dies.

i Christe, der du bist Tag und Licht,
  Vor dir ist, Herr, verborgen nichts :
  Du väterliches Lichtes Glanz,
  Lehr uns den Weg der Wahrheit ganz.

ii Wir bitten dein göttliche Kraft :
   Behüt uns, Herr, in dieser Nacht ;
   Bewahr uns, Herr, vor allem Leid,
   Gott Vater der Barmherzigkeit.

iii Vertreib des schweren Schlafens Frist,
    Dass uns nicht schad des Feindes List :
    Das Fleisch in Züchten reine sei,
    So sind wir mancher Sorgen frei.

vii Gott Vater sei Lob, Ehr und Preis,
    Auch seinem Sohne gleicherweis,
    Des Heilgen Geistes Gütigkeit :
    Von nun an bis in Ewigkeit.

U.L.S. 507.

i O Christ, that art the light and day,
  The Light of Lights Thou art alway ;
  Thou dost illume the shades of night,
  Show us the path of truth aright.

ii Thou holy Lord, to Thee we pray :
   Let us have rest in Thee alway ;
   Defend us in our darksome sight,
   And grant us all a quiet night.

iii Let heavy sleep not on us fall,
    Nor let our flesh consent withal
    To make us guilty, night or day,
    Nor let our foe take us away.

vii Now God the Father evermore,
    And Holy Ghost the Comforter,
    And Jesus Christ the Only Son,
    Be praisèd loud by everyone.

Myles Coverdale (adapted).[1]

[1] *Remains of Myles Coverdale* (Parker Society, 1846), p. 584.

CHRISTE, DU BEISTAND DEINER KREUZGEMEINDE

Hymn, by Matthäus Apelles von Löwenstern, in four 4-line stanzas (1644). Melody, by Löwenstern (1644).

*A pause here in 1786.
**The last line of each stanza is repeated.

i Christe, du Beistand deiner Kreuzgemeinde,
  Eile ! mit Hilf und Rettung uns erscheine !
  Steure den Feinden : ihre Blutgedichte
  Mache zu nichte !

ii Streite doch selber für dein arme Kinder,
   Wehre dem Teufel, seine Macht verhinder :
   Alles, was kämpfst wider deine Glieder,
   Stürze darnieder !

iii Friede bei Kirch und Schulen uns beschere ;
    Friede zugleich der Polizei verehre ;
    Friede dem Herzen, Friede dem Gewissen
    Gieb zu geniessen.

iv Also wird zeitlich deine Güt erhoben,
   Also wird ewig und ohn Ende loben
   Dich, o du Wächter deiner armen Heerde,
   Himmel und Erde.

                                        U.L.S. 215.

i O Christ, strong Champion of all souls that own Thee,
  Speed to our aid and comfort, we implore Thee !
  Our foes, disperse them, all their shouts of vict'ry
  Do Thou quench swiftly !

ii For Thine afflicted, Lord, gird on Thine armour,
   Curb Satan's malice, all his plotting hinder !
   He who dare come forth threat'ning Thine elected,
   Let him not prosper !

iii Peace to true doctrine and Thy Church assure us,
    Peace to Thy servants who direct and rule us,
    Peace in our borders, peace in all our doing,
    Be t'ward us flowing !

iv Great God in heavèn, ever then we'll hymn Thee,
   In songs of praise will evermore exalt Thee,
   Mighty Protector, Who this world created,
   In heaven now seated !

                                        Tr. C. S. T.

CHRISTUM WIR SOLLEN LOBEN SCHON

Hymn, by Martin Luther, trans. of Coelius Sedulius' ' A solis ortus cardine ', in eight 4-line stanzas (1524). Melody of the Latin hymn.

A solis ortus cardine.

i Christum wir sollen loben schon,
Der reinen Magd Marien Sohn,
So weit die liebe Sonne leucht
Und an aller Welt Ende reicht.

v Die edle Mutter hat geborn,
Den Gabriel verhiess zuvorn,
Den Sanct Johanns mit Springen zeigt,
Da er noch lag im Mutterleib.

vii Des Himmels Chör sich freuen drob
Und die Engel singen Gott Lob,
Den armen Hirten wird vermeldt
Der Hirt und Schöpfer aller Welt.

* viii Lob, Ehr und Dank sei dir gesagt,
Christ, geborn von der reinen Magd,
Mit Vater und dem Heilgen Geist,
Von nun an bis in Ewigkeit.

U.L.S. 25.

i Now must we Jesus laud and sing,
The maiden Mary's Son and King,
Far as the blessèd sun doth shine,
And reaches earth's most distant line.

v The noble mother hath brought forth
Whom Gabriel promised to the earth ;
Him John did greet in joyous way,
While in His mother's womb He lay.

vii Therefore the heavenly choir is loud ;
The angels sing their praise to God,
And tell poor men their flocks who keep
He's come Who makes and keeps the sheep.

viii Praise, honour, thanks, to Thee be said,
Christ Jesus, born of holy maid !
With Father and with Holy Ghost,
Now and for ever, ending not.

Tr. George Macdonald.[1]

[1] *Exotics* (Lond. 1876), p. 42.

CHRISTUS, DER IST MEIN LEBEN

Hymn, anonymous, in seven 4-line stanzas (1609), st. viii (1612). Melody, by Melchior Vulpius (1609).

i Christus, der ist mein Leben,
  Sterben ist mein Gewinn ;
  Dem thu ich mich ergeben,
  Mit Fried fahr ich dahin.

ii Mit Freud fahr ich von dannen
  Zu Christ, dem Bruder mein,
  Auf dass ich zu ihm komme
  Und ewig bei ihm sei.

iii Ich hab nun überwunden
  Kreuz, Leiden, Angst und Noth :
  Durch sein heilig fünf Wunden
  Bin ich versöhnt mit Gott.

vi Alsdann fein sanft und stille,
  Herr, lass mich schlafen ein
  Nach deinem Rath und Willen,
  Wenn kommt mein Stündelein ;

vii Und lass mich an dir kleben,
  Wie eine Klett am Kleid,
  Und ewig bei dir leben
  In himmlisch Wonn und Freud !

U.L.S. 808.

i My life is hid in Jesus,
  And death is gain to me ;
  Then, whensoe'er He pleases,
  I meet it willingly.

ii For Christ, my Lord and Brother,
  I leave this world so dim,
  And gladly seek that other
  Where I shall be with Him.

iii My woes are nearly over,
  Though long and dark the road ;
  My sins His merits cover,
  And I have peace with God.

vi In my last hour, O grant me
  To slumber soft and still,
  No doubts to vex or haunt me,
  Safe anchored on Thy will ;

vii And so, to Thee still cleaving
  Through all death's agony,
  To fall asleep believing,
  And wake in heaven with Thee.

Tr. Catherine Winkworth.[1]

[1] *Chorale Book for England* (Lond. 1865), No. 186.

CHRISTUS, DER IST MEIN LEBEN

Hymn, anonymous, in seven 4-line stanzas (1609), st. viii (1612). Melody, by Melchior Vulpius (1609).

49

* **Bach has a 𝄐 here.**

i Christus, der ist mein Leben,
   Sterben ist mein Gewinn ;
   Dem thu ich mich ergeben,
   Mit Fried fahr ich dahin.

iii Ich hab nun überwunden
   Leiden, Kreuz, Angst und Noth :
   Durch sein heilig fünf Wunden
   Bin ich versöhnt mit Gott.

v Wenn mein Herz und Gedanken
   Zergehn als wie ein Licht,
   Das hin und her thut wanken,
   Wenn ihm die Flamm gebricht :

vi Alsdann fein sanft und stille,
   Lass mich, Herr, schlafen ein
   Nach deinem Rath und Willen,
   Wenn kommt mein Stündelein.

U.L.S. 808.

i My life is hid in Jesus,
   Dying is gain to me ;
   Then, whensoe'er He pleases,
   I meet death willingly.

iii My woes are nearly over,
   Dreary and dark the road ;
   My sins His merits cover,
   And I have peace with God.

v When mind and thought, O Saviour,
   Flicker, as doth a light,
   That to and fro doth waver
   Ere 'tis extinguished quite,

vi In that last hour, O grant me
   Slumber so soft and still,
   No doubts to vex or haunt me,
   Safe anchored on Thy will.

Tr. Catherine Winkworth.[1]

[1] *Chorale Book for England* (Lond. 1865), No. 186.

CHRISTUS, DER UNS SELIG MACHT

Hymn, a free trans., by Michael Weisse, in eight 8-line stanzas (1531), of ' Patris sapientia, veritas divina '. Melody of the ancient hymn, adapted (1531).

Patris sapientia, veritas divina.

i Christus, der uns selig macht,
  Kein Bös hat begangen,
  Der ward für uns in der Nacht
  Als ein Dieb gefangen,
  Geführt vor gottlose Leut,
  Und fälschlich verklaget,
  Verlacht, verhöhnt und verspeit,
  Wie denn die Schrift saget.

ii In der ersten Tagesstund
  Ward er unbescheiden
  Als ein Mörder dargestellt
  Pilato dem Heiden,
  Der ihn unschuldig befand,
  Ohne Sach des Todes,
  Ihn derhalben von sich sandt
  Zum König Herodes.

iii Um drei ward der Gottessohn
  Mit Geisseln geschmissen
  Und sein Haupt mit einer Kron
  Von Dornen zerrissen ;
  Gekleidet zu Hohn und Spott
  Ward er sehr geschlagen,
  Und das Kreuz zu seinem Tod
  Musst er selber tragen.

viii O hilf, Christe, Gottes Sohn,
  Durch dein bitter Leiden,
  Dass wir stets dir unterthan
  All Untugend meiden,
  Deinen Tod und sein Ursach
  Fruchtbarlich bedenken,
  Dafür, wiewohl arm und schwach,
  Dir Dankopfer schenken.

i Christ, Who died mankind to right,
  Suffered for us guiltless,
  Taken as a thief at night
  That we might go blameless.
  Judged was He by wicked men
  Shamefully who used Him,
  Buffeted and spat on Him,
  Mocked Him sore and bruised Him.

ii In the early morning hour
  Was He led before them,
  And in haste to Pilate brought,
  Who found no fault in Him.
  Then was He, though innocent
  Of all accusation,
  Forthwith thence to Herod sent
  For his condemnation.

iii Then the holy Son of God
  Beaten was with lashes,
  Felt the cruel cutting rod,
  Wore a crown of ashes,
  In a purple robe was dressed,
  He all pure and stainless,
  And the Cross, upon Him pressed,
  Bore to Calv'ry blameless.

viii Grant us, Jesu, God's dear Son,
  By Thy bitter Passion,
  True to Thee our course to run
  And our lives to fashion,
  E'er reflecting that Thy death
  Opens heavèn to us !
  So shall our too feeble breath
  Laud Thy purpose glorious.

U.L.S. 89.

Tr. C. S. T.

CHRISTUS, DER UNS SELIG MACHT

Hymn, a free trans., by Michael Weisse, in eight 8-line stanzas (1531), of 'Patris sapientia, veritas divina'. Melody of the ancient hymn, adapted (1531).

Patris sapientia, veritas divina.

* i Christus, der uns selig macht,
   Kein Bös hat begangen,
   Der ward für uns in der Nacht
   Als ein Dieb gefangen,
   Geführt vor gottlose Leut,
   Und fälschlich verklaget,
   Verlacht, verhöhnt und verspeit,
   Wie denn die Schrift saget.

iv Um sechs ward er nackt und bloss
   An das Kreuz geschlagen,
   An dem er sein Blut vergoss,
   Betet mit Wehklagen :
   Die Zuseher spotten sein,
   Auch die bei ihm hingen,
   Bis die Sonn auch ihren Schein
   Entzog solchen Dingen.

v Jesus schrie zur neunten Stund,
   Klaget sich verlassen ;
   Bald war Gall in seinen Mund
   Mit Essig gelassen ;
   Da gab er auf seinen Geist,
   Und die Erd erbebet,
   Des Tempels Vorhang zerreisst,
   Und manch Fels zerklöbet.

viii O hilf, Christe, Gottes Sohn,
   Durch dein bitter Leiden,
   Dass wir stets dir unterthan
   All Untugend meiden,
   Deinen Tod und sein Ursach
   Fruchtbarlich bedenken,
   Dafür, wiewohl arm und schwach,
   Dir Dankopfer schenken.

i Christ, Who died mankind to right,
   Suffered for us guiltless,
   Taken as a thief at night
   That we might go blameless.
   Judged was He by wicked men
   Shamefully who used Him,
   Buffeted and spat on Him,
   Mocked Him sore and bruised Him.

iv 'Twas at noon the Son of God
   To the Cross was nailèd,
   Prayed for them who shed His blood
   And o'er Him prevailèd.
   They that stood by wagged their heads,
   Laughing in derision,
   Till the sun lamenting fled
   From the saddening vision.

v At the ninth hour Jesus cried :
   ' Lord, I am forsaken,'
   Swift a sponge upon a reed
   Offered consolation.
   So to God His spirit went
   While the earth was rended,
   And the Temple veil was rent
   As His life was ended.

viii Grant us, Jesu, God's dear Son,
   By Thy bitter Passion,
   True to Thee our course to run
   And our lives to fashion,
   E'er reflecting that Thy death
   Opens heavèn to us !
   So shall our too feeble breath
   Laud Thy purpose glorious.

U.L.S. 89.

Tr. C. S. T.

CHRISTUS, DER UNS SELIG MACHT

Hymn, a free trans., by Michael Weisse, in eight 8-line stanzas (1531), of 'Patris sapientia, veritas divina'. Melody of the ancient hymn, adapted (1531).

52

Patris sapientia, veritas divina.

i Christus, der uns selig macht,
  Kein Bös hat begangen,
  Der ward für uns in der Nacht
  Als ein Dieb gefangen,
  Geführt vor gottlose Leut,
  Und fälschlich verklaget,
  Verlacht, verhöhnt und verspeit,
  Wie denn die Schrift saget.

vi Da hat man zur Vesperzeit
  Die Schächer zerbrochen,
  Ward Jesus in seiner Seit
  Mit eim Speer gestochen,
  Daraus Blut und Wasser rann,
  Die Schrift zu erfüllen,
  Wie Johannes zeiget an,
  Nur um unsertwillen.

vii Da der Tag sein Ende nahm,
  Der Abend war kommen,
  Ward Jesus vons Kreuzes Stamm
  Durch Joseph genommen,
  Herrlich, nach Jüdischer Art,
  In ein Grab geleget,
  Allda mit Hütern verwahrt,
  Wie Matthäus zeiget.

* viii O hilf, Christe, Gottes Sohn,
  Durch dein bitter Leiden,
  Dass wir stets dir unterthan
  All Untugend meiden,
  Deinen Tod und sein Ursach
  Fruchtbarlich bedenken,
  Dafür, wiewohl arm und schwach,
  Dir Dankopfer schenken.

i Christ, Who died mankind to right,
  Suffered for us guiltless,
  Taken as a thief at night
  That we might go blameless.
  Judged was He by wicked men
  Shamefully who used Him,
  Buffeted and spat on Him,
  Mocked Him sore and bruised Him.

vi On the Cross, when evening came,
  Soldiers drew around Him,
  Piercèd deep His broken frame
  Ere the ghost had left Him.
  Thereout blood and water ran,
  As the Book doth tell us;
  Yea, St. John, who by did stand,
  Testifieth to us.

vii So, as shades of nightfall fell,
  There the Lord hung lifeless;
  Joseph came, who loved Him well,
  Begged the body precious,
  Laid Him softly in the tomb,
  Sweetest spices round Him,
  Watched Him in Death's narrow room :
  Matthew so has written.

viii Grant us, Jesu, God's dear Son,
  By Thy bitter Passion,
  True to Thee our course to run
  And our lives to fashion,
  E'er reflecting that Thy death
  Opens heavèn to us !
  So shall our too feeble breath
  Laud Thy purpose glorious.

U.L.S. 89.

Tr. C .S. T

CHRISTUS IST ERSTANDEN

Hymn, by Michael Weisse, in thirteen 8-line stanzas (1531), after ' Surgit in hac die '. Melody of the Latin hymn, adapted (1531).

Surgit in hac die.

i Christus ist erstanden,
  Hat überwunden !
  Gnad ist nun vorhanden,
  Wahrheit wird funden !
  Darum, lieben Leute,
  Freut euch heute !
  Lobet euren Herren,
  Jesum, den König der Ehren !

xii Seht an, lieben Leute,
  Den König und Held,
  Und höret ihn heute,
  Thut, was ihm gefällt !
  Denn es wird vernommen,
  Dass er kommen
  Jedermann belohnen,
  Keines Bösen will verschonen.

xiii Singet alle Zungen,
  Sprecht : Halleluja !
  Lob sei dir gesungen
  Und Halleluja !
  Der du erstanden bist,
  O Jesu Christ !
  Preis sei deinem Namen
  Nun und in Ewigkeit.   Amen.

i Christ to-day is risen,
  Hath broke Death's prison,
  Grace to man hath given
  And sent truth from heaven !
  Be ye therefore joyous,
  Praise Him glorious,
  Loud His praises singing,
  Jesu Who on high is reigning !

xii People all, behold Him,
  Who is your Lord King,
  Give your ear unto Him,
  Serve in everything !
  For He came to save us,
  Not enslave us,
  Every one rewarding,
  All that's evil from us warding.

xiii Sing then with loud voices
  Your Alleluja !
  Tell your heart rejoices
  With Alleluja !
  To Him, with the Highest,
  Jesus Lord Christ,
  Praise be sung by all men
  Henceforth now and ever !   Amen.

U.L.S. 128 (st. i., xiii).
Tucher, Bd. i.   No. 114 (st. xii).

Tr. C. S. T.

DA DER HERR CHRIST ZU TISCHE SASS

Hymn, by Nikolaus Herman, in twenty-eight 6-line stanzas (1560). Melody, anonymous (1611).

i Da der Herr Christ zu Tische sass,
Zuletzt das Osterlämmlein ass,
Und wollt von hinnen scheiden,
Sein Jüngern treulich er befahl,
Dass man allzeit verkünd'gen soll
Sein Tod und bitter Leiden.

xxvii Wir danken dir für deinen Tod,
Herr Jesu, und für solche Noth
Die du um unser Willen
Erleidten hast, denn sonst fürwahr,
Kein Opfer wo zu finden war
Das Gottes Zorn konnt stillen.

xxviii Erhalt dein liebe Kirch und Wort,
Dass zeitlich hie und ewig dort
Geheiligt wird dein Name.
Dein Leiden, Kreuz und bittrer Tod
Sei unser Trost in aller Noth,
Herr Christ, das hilf uns.   Amen.

Crüger.[1]

i Now when at supper they were met
Their Easter Passover to eat,
Did Jesus, sitting with them,
His twelve disciples all command
They forth should tell in every land
His bitter death and suffering.

xxvii Our praise to Thee, O Christ, we sound,
Who for us hath salvation found,
Thy precious death prevailing.
For we had suffered pain and loss
Hadst Thou not borne the cruel Cross,
Thy Father's anger staying.

xxviii Uphold Thy Church and Holy Word,
May everywhere Thy praise be heard,
And holy let Thy Name be !
For Thou from Satan hast us freed,
Our ever present Hope in need ;
O help us, Saviour, alway !

Tr. C. S. T.

[1] *Praxis Pietatis Melica* (Berlin : 1690), No. 452.

DA JESUS AN DEM KREUZE STUND

Hymn, by Johann Böschenstein, in nine 5-line stanzas (c.1515). Melody, anonymous (1545), to ' In dich hab ich gehoffet, Herr ',
but probably of earlier origin.

55

i Da Jesus an dem Kreuze stund
  Und ihm sein Leichnam war verwundt
  So gar mit bittern Schmerzen :
  Die sieben Wort, die Jesus sprach,
  Betracht in deinem Herzen.

ii Zum ersten sprach er inniglich
  Zu seinem Vat'r im Himmelreich,
  Da sie ans Kreuz ihn hiengen :
  Vergib ihn, Vat'r, sie wissen nicht,
  Was sie an mir verbringen !

viii Zum siebten rief der Gottes Sohn :
  Mein Vater, meinen Geist nimm an
  In dein göttliche Hände !
  Damit neigt er sein heiligs Haupt,
  Beschloss damit sein Ende.

ix Wer Gottes Mart'r in Ehren hat
  Und sich der tröst't in Todes Noth,
  Des will Gott eben pflegen
  Wohl hier auf Erd mit seiner Gnad
  Und dort im ewgen Leben.

Tucher.[1]

i When Jesus on the Cross was bound,
  His body pierced with many a wound,
  With torture very bitter ;
  The dying words, which then He spake,
  With a still heart consider.

ii First does He to His Father speak
  In heavèn's kingdom, sweetly meek :
  ' What they to Me are doing,
  Father, forgive ! they know it not.'
  Here He's love's pattern showing.

viii ' Father,' when all was at an end,
  Immanuel says, ' I recommend
  My spirit separated
  Into Thy hands.' His body dies,
  His soul's in life instated.

ix He who God's pains in honour has,
  To whom our Saviour gives the grace
  To be in heart possessing
  And weigh these seven Gospel words,
  Enjoys a noble blessing.

Tr. Moravian Hymn-book.[2]

[1] Bd. i. No. 103.   [2] Ed. 1746, Pt. ii, p. 714.

DANK SEI GOTT IN DER HÖHE

Hymn, by Johannes Mühlmann, in seven 8-line stanzas (1618). Melody, by (?) Bartholomäus Gesius (1605), originally to 'Jesus Christ unser Herre'.

56

i Dank sei Gott in der Höhe
In dieser Morgenstund,
Durch den ich wied'r aufstehe
Vom Schlaf frisch und gesund.
Mich hatte fest gebunden
Mit Finsterniss die Nacht :
Ich hab sie überwunden
Mit Gott, der mich bewacht.

v Gieb mildiglich dein Segen,
Dass wir nach deim Geheiss
Wandeln auf guten Wegen,
Thun unser Amt mit Fleiss,
Dass jeder seine Netze
Auswerf und auf dein Wort
Sein Trost mit Petro setze :
So geht hie Arbeit fort.

vii Wir sind die zarten Reben,
Der Weinstock selbst bist du,
Daran wir wachs'n und kleben
Und bringen Frucht darzu.
Hilf, dass wir an dir bleiben
Und wachsen immer mehr ;
Dein guter Geist uns treibe
Zu Werken deiner Ehr.

i While yet the morn is breaking
I thank my God once more,
Beneath Whose care awaking
I find the night is o'er ;
I thank Him that He calls me
To life and health anew,
I know, whate'er befalls me,
His care will still be true.

v O gently grant Thy blessing,
That we may do Thy will,
No more Thy ways transgressing,
Our proper task fulfil ;
With Peter's full affiance
Let down our nets again;
If Thou art our reliance
Our toil will not be vain.

vii Thou art the Vine,—O nourish
The branches graft in Thee,
And let them grow and flourish,
A fair and fruitful tree ;
Thy Spirit put within us,
And let His gifts of grace
To all good actions win us,
That best may show His praise.

U.L.S. 443.

Tr. Catherine Winkworth.[1]

[1] *Chorale Book for England* (Lond. 1865), No. 163.

DANKET DEM HERREN, DENN ER IST SEHR FREUNDLICH

Hymn, by Johann Horn (Roh), in six 2-line stanzas (1544). Melody, anonymous (1534), originally to ' Vitam quae faciunt'.

i Danket dem Herren, denn er ist sehr freundlich :
  Denn seine Güt und Wahrheit bleibet ewiglich.

ii Der als ein barmherziger gütiger Gott
  Uns dürftige Creaturen gespeiset hat.

iii Singet ihm aus Herzengrund mit Innigkeit :
  Nun Lob und Dank sei dir, Vater in Ewigkeit.

iv Der du uns als ein reicher, milder Vater
  Speisest und kleidest deine elenden Kinder.

v Verleih, dass wir dich recht lernen erkennen,
  Und nach dir, o ewigem Schöpfer, uns sehnen :

vi Durch Jesum Christum, dein allerliebsten Sohn,
  Welcher unser Mittler ist nun vor deinem Thron.

U.L.S. 493.

i Praise God, ye people, for His love is boundless,
  His truth is constant, steadfast, and is limitless.

ii He our Creator, bountiful to all men,
  Rich blessings show'reth e'er upon us every one.

iii Sing then, ye people, sing with heart and fervour,
  And praise the Father, Son, and Spirit evermore !

iv He as a Father all His children feedeth,
  He clotheth and man's every need He satisfieth.

v Grant then, O Father, that we rightly know Thee,
  And Thee our Saviour, throned in heavèn gloriously ;

vi Through Jesus Christ, Thy Son and most belovèd,
  Our Mediator now in heavèn worshippèd.

Tr. C. S. T.

DAS ALTE JAHR VERGANGEN IST

Hymn, attributed to Johann Steurlein and Jakob Tapp, in six 4-line stanzas (1588). Melody, by Steurlein (1588).

✻ The first and last lines of each stanza are repeated.

i Das alte Jahr vergangen ist :
   Wir danken dir, Herr Jesu Christ,
   Dass du uns in so gross Gefahr
   Bewahrt hast lange Zeit und Jahr.

ii Und bitten dich, ewigen Sohn
   Des Vaters in dem höchsten Thron,
   Du wollst dein arme Christenheit
   Bewahren ferner allezeit.

iii Entzeuch uns nicht dein heilsam Wort,
   Welchs ist der Seelen höchster Hort :
   Vors Papsts Lehr und Abgötterei
   Behüt uns, Herr, und steh uns bei.

vi Wir danken und wir loben dich
   Mit allen Engeln ewiglich.
   O Jesu ! unsern Glauben mehr,
   Zu deines Namens Lob und Ehr.

   U.L.S. 63.

i With this New Year we raise new songs
   To praise the Lord with hearts and tongues,
   For His support in troubles past,
   Wherewith our life was overcast.

ii To Thee, Lord Christ, we humbly press,
   To send us from the throne of grace
   Thy constant aid this instant year,
   To serve Thee with a filial fear.

iii Thy truth let never hence depart,
   Which is the comfort of our heart ;
   False doctrine, and idolatry,
   Remove from Christianity.

vi Then shall Thy praise anew begin,
   Without alloy of self and sin ;
   Increase, O Lord, our faith and love,
   Till Thou reveal'st Thy face above.

   Tr. John Christian Jacobi.[1]

[1] *Psalmodia Germanica* (Lond. 1722), p. 10.

DAS ALTE JAHR VERGANGEN IST

Hymn, attributed to Johann Steurlein and Jakob Tapp, in six 4-line stanzas (1588). Melody, by Steurlein (1588).

59

* The first and last lines of each stanza are repeated.

i Das alte Jahr vergangen ist:
   Wir danken dir, Herr Jesu Christ,
   Dass du uns in so gross Gefahr
   Bewahrt hast lange Zeit und Jahr.

iv Hilf, dass wir von der Sünd ablan
   Und fromm zu werden fahen an,
   Kein'r Sünd des alten Jahrs gedenk,
   Ein ghadenreich Neujahr uns schenk.

v Christlich zu leben, seliglich
   Zu sterben, und hernach fröhlich
   Am jüngsten Tag wied'r aufzustehn,
   Mit dir in Himmel einzugehn.

vi Zu danken und zu loben dich
   Mit allen Engeln ewiglich.
   O Jesu! unsern Glauben mehr,
   Zu deines Namens Lob und Ehr.

i With this New Year we raise new songs
   To praise the Lord with hearts and tongues,
   For His support in troubles past,
   Wherewith our life was overcast.

iv Thy Spirit keep us free from sin;
   Create us quite anew within:
   Remember no transgressions past,
   Thy mercy all our years outlast.

v Grant us to lead a Christian life;
   And when we leave this world of strife,
   Then raise us to that joyful day
   Where Thou wilt wipe all tears away.

vi Then shall Thy praise anew begin,
   Without alloy of self and sin.
   Increase, O Lord, our faith and love,
   Till Thou reveal'st Thy face above.

U.L.S. 63.

Tr. John Christian Jacobi.[1]

[1] *Psalmodia Germanica*, p. 10.

DAS NEUGEBORNE KINDELEIN

Hymn, by Cyriakus Schneegass, in four 4-line stanzas (1595). Melody, by Melchior Vulpius (1609).

i Das neugeborne Kindelein,
  Da herzeliebe Jeṣulein,
  Bringt abermal ein neues Jahr
  Der auserwählten Christenschaar.

ii Des freuen sich die Engelein,
  Die gerne um und bei uns sein :
  Sie singen in den Lüften frei,
  Dass Gott mit uns versöhnet sei.

iii Ist Gott versöhnt und unser Freund :
  Was kann uns thun der arge Feind ?
  Trotz Teufel und der Höllen Pfort !
  Das Jesulein ist unser Hort.

* iv Es bringt das rechte Jubeljahr ;
  Was trauern wir denn immerdar ?
  Frisch auf, itzt ist es Singens Zeit,
  Das Jesulein wendt alles Leid.

        U.L.S. 65.

i Sing we the birth of God's dear Son,
  From highest heaven to earth come down,
  Bringing to us a glad New Year,
  And to all people Christian cheer.

ii List to the angels what they tell,
  That Christ is born, Emanuel.
  All joyful do their voices sing,
  As in the heaven above they wing.

iii God is our friend and helper true ;
  What can fell Satan 'gainst us do ?
  Hell and its gates of brass must yield ;
  For this sweet Babe is Sword and Shield.

iv Come, let us hail this happy year,
  Put far away all doubt and fear,
  Raise our glad hearts to God's high throne,
  Saved by the grace of Christ, His Son !

        Tr. C. S. T.[1]

[1] *Bach's Cantata Texts, Sacred and Secular* (Lond. 1926).

DAS WALT GOTT VATER UND GOTT SOHN

Hymn, by Martin Behm (Böhm), in eleven 4-line stanzas (1608). Melody, anonymous (1713).

61

i Das walt Gott Vater und Gott Sohn,
Gott Heilger Geist ins Himmels Thron !
Man dankt dir, eh die Sonn aufgeht ;
Wenns Licht anbricht, man vor dir steht.

v Mein Gott, ich bitt durch Christi Blut,
Nimm mich auch diesen Tag in Hut :
Lass deine lieben Engelein
Mein Wächter und Gefährten sein.

vii Gieb, dass ich meine Werk und Pflicht
Mit Freuden diesen Tag verricht
Zu deinem Lob und meinem Nutz,
Und meinem Nächsten thue Guts.

x Behüt mich heut und allezeit,
Vor Schaden, Schand und Herzeleid ;
Tritt zwischen mich und meine Feind,
Die sichtbar und unsichtbar seind.

xi Mein Aus- und Eingang heut bewahr,
Dass mir kein Uebels widerfahr ;
Behüte mich vor schnellem Tod
Und hilf mir, wo mir Hilf thut noth.

U.L.S. 445.

i Thy will for evermore be done,
O God the Father, Spirit, Son !
We thank Thee at this morning hour
When light upon us Thou dost shower.

v We pray Thee, through Thy Son so dear,
This day to hold us in Thy care ;
And send Thine angels from Thy throne
To have us in their charge alone.

vii Whate'er our hands may find to do,
Let us with cheerful heart pursue,
E'er to Thy praise, and not for pelf,
And love our neighbour as ourself.

x O spread Thy shelt'ring wings around,
That with us sorrow ne'er be found :
Protect us by Thy wondrous power
From foes unseen and seen that are !

xi Our comings and our goings guide,
Nor let ill-fortune us betide ;
Prevent us from death's sudden call,
Afford Thine help when need befall !

Tr. C. S. T.

DAS WALT MEIN GOTT

Hymn, anonymous (? Basilius Förtsch), in eight 6-line stanzas (1613). Melody, anonymous (1648).

i Das walt mein Gott,
  Vater, Sohn und Heilger Geist,
  Der mich erschaffen hat,
  Mir Leib und Seel gegeben,
  Im Mutterleib das Leben,
  Gesund, ohn allen Schad.

ii Ach treuer Gott,
  Du dein Sohn aus Himmels Thron
  Für uns gegebn in Tod,
  Der für uns ist gestorben,
  Das Himmelreich erworben
  Mit seinem theuren Blut;

iii Dafür ich dir
  Aus Herzen, mit Zung und Mund,
  Lobsinge mit Begier,
  Und danke dir mit Schalle
  Für dein Wohlthaten alle
  Früh und spät, für und für.

Fischer-Tümpel.[1]

i Thy will be done,
  Father, Son, and Holy Ghost,
  Creation's Lord and Sun!
  Thou life to all men givest,
  Into man's nostrils breathest,
  And car'st for everyone.

ii O faithful God,
  Thy dear Son from heaven's high throne
  Came down to bear the rod,
  And death for us endurèd
  That we might be assoilèd
  Through His most precious blood.

iii Therefore to Thee
  From our hearts, with lips and voice,
  We sing out joyfully;
  We praise Thee now and ever,
  Whose goodness faileth never,
  On us poured endlessly!

Tr. C. S. T.

[1] Bd. i. No. 48.

DEN VATER DORT OBEN

Hymn, by Michael Weisse, in five 7-line stanzas (1531). Melody, anonymous (1531).

i Den Vater dort oben
 Wollen wir nun loben,
 Der uns, als ein milder Gott,
 Gnädiglich gespeiset hat,
 Und Christum seinen Sohn,
 Durch welchen der Segen kommt
 Vom allerhöchsten Thron.

iii Nimm an dies Dankopfer,
 O Vater und Schöpfer,
 Welchs wir deinem Namen thun
 In Christo deim lieben Sohn ;
 O lass dirs gefallen
 Und ihn mit seinem Verdienst
 Zahlen für uns alle.

v Herr, nimm an unsern Dank,
 Sammt diesem Lobgesang,
 Und vergieb, was noch gebricht,
 Zu thun bei unserer Pflicht !
 O, mach uns dir eben,
 Dass wir hier in deiner Gnad
 Und dort ewig leben.

i God in heaven Almighty,
 Hear the praise we sing Thee,
 Thou who hast Thy people led,
 Clothèd them and bounteous fed,
 Sent to them Thy dear Son,
 With salvation from above,
 From Thine ever bright throne !

iii Take the praise we proffer,
 Father, Lord, Creator,
 Which we offer in the name
 Of Thy Son who once was slain !
 May we, through His merit
 And the sacrifice He paid,
 Life with Thee inherit !

v Take, then, God Almighty,
 All the praise we give Thee,
 And forgive us our default
 If to Thee our song is nought.
 Grant us Thy grace alway
 Here to live and do Thy will,
 And see heavèn's glory.

U.L.S. 494.

Tr. C. S. T.

DER DU BIST DREI IN EINIGKEIT

Hymn, by Martin Luther, a translation, in three 4-line stanzas (1544), of ' O lux beata Trinitas '. Melody, an adaptation (1545) of the ancient tune.

O lux beata Trinitas.

i Der du bist drei in Einigkeit,
  Ein wahrer Gott von Ewigkeit :
  Die Sonn mit dem Tag von uns weicht :
  Lass uns leuchten dein göttlich Licht.

ii Des Morgens, Gott, dich loben wir,
  Des Abends auch beten vor dir :
  Unser armes Lied rühmet dich
  Jetzund immer und ewiglich.

iii Gott Vater, dem sei ewig Ehr,
  Gott Sohn, der ist der einig Herr,
  Und dem Tröster Heiligen Geist,
  Von nun an bis in Ewigkeit.

i Thou Who art Three in Unity,
  A true God from eternity,
  The sun with day withdraws his shine,
  Lighten us with Thy light divine.

ii At morn we praise Thee with the day,
  At evening, also, to Thee pray ;
  Our poor song glorifieth Thee
  Now, ever, and eternally.

iii To God the Father praise be poured,
  To God the Son, the only Lord,
  To the consoling Holy Ghost,
  Now and for ever, ending not.

U.L.S. 186.

Tr. George Macdonald.[1]

[1] *Exotics* (Lond. 1876), p. 61.

DER TAG DER IST SO FREUDENREICH

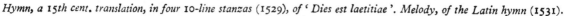

Hymn, a 15th cent. translation, in four 10-line stanzas (1529), of 'Dies est laetitiae'. Melody, of the Latin hymn (1531).

65

Dies est laetitiae.

i Der Tag der ist so freudenreich
 Aller Creature :
Denn Gottes Sohn vom Himmelreich
 Über die Natur
Von einer Jungfrau ist geborn :
Maria, du bist auserkorn,
 Dass du Mutter wärest :
Was geschah so wunderlich ?
Gottes Sohn vom Himmelreich,
 Der heut ist Mensch geboren.

ii Ein Kindelein so löbelich
 Ist uns geborn heute
Von einer Jungfrau säuberlich,
 Zu Trost uns arm'n Leuten.
Wär uns das Kindlein nicht geborn,
So wärn wir allzumal verlorn ;
 Das Heil ist uns'r aller.
Ei, du süsser Jesu Christ !
Der du Mensch geboren bist,
 Behüt uns vor der Hölle.

iv Die Hirten auf dem Felde warn,
 Erfuhren neu Mähre
Von diesen engelischen Schaarn,
 Wie Christ geborn wäre,
König üb'r alle Könge gross :
Herod die Red gar sehr verdross,
 Aussandt er sein Boten :
Ei ! wie gar ein falsche List
Erdacht er wid'r Jesum Christ !
 Die Kindlein liess er tödten.

i O hail this brightest day of days,
 All good Christian people !
For Christ is come upon our ways,
 Ring it from the steeple !
Of maiden pure is He the Son ;
For ever shall Thy praise be sung,
 Christ's fair mother Mary !
Ever was there news so great ?
God's own Son from heaven's high state
 Is born the Son of Mary !

ii This day the wondrous Child is born,
 Lent to earth from heavèn.
He comes to cheer a world forlorn,
 All its sin to leaven.
So, sing ye all the glorious birth
Which shall redeem our fallen earth
 And work our salvation !
Laud to Thee, Child Jesu Christ !
With mankind Thou'st kept the tryst,
 To save us from damnation.

iv The shepherds in amaze did stand,
 As from heaven came streaming
Bright angels in a flaming band,
 Christ the Babe proclaiming.
O Christ, the King of kings, where's He ?
False Herod, raging mightily,
 Everywhere doth seek Him,
Whom His mother Jesus dight,
Yea would slay, O wicked wight,
 The children for to catch Him.

U.L.S. 29.

Tr. C. S. T.

DES HEILGEN GEISTES REICHE GNAD

Hymn, a translation, attributed to Johannes Leon, in six 4-line stanzas (c. 1570), of 'Spiritus sancti gratia'. Melody, an adaptation (1627) of the ancient melody.

66

Spiritus sancti gratia.

i Des Heilgen Geistes reiche Gnad
　Die Herzen der Apostel hat
　Erfüllt mit seiner Gütigkeit,
　Geschenkt der Sprachen Unterscheid.

ii Er sandt sie aus in der Welt Kreis,
　Zu predigen mit allem Fleiss,
　Mit manchen Zungen, Gottes Wort
　Den Creatur'n an allem Ort.

iii Er sprach zu ihnen : Nehmet hin
　Den Heilgen Geist mit hohem Sinn,
　Der wird euch lehren ganz gewiss,
　Was vergangn und zukünftig ist.

vi Nun lobet all den Tröster werth,
　Der uns all Wahrheit hat gelehrt,
　Hat abgewandt all Ungenad,
　Viel Gaben uns geschenket hat.

U.L.S. 166.

i Filled with the Spirit's grace and love
　On them sent down from heaven above,
　Th' Apostles there were gathered all,
　On whom the gift of tongues did fall.

ii ' Go ye now forth,' the Spirit said,
　' Go preach the Word in every land,
　In every tongue, in every clime,
　Tell ye the Name of God sublime ! '

iii ' Receive ye, then, the Holy Ghost,
　And go ye forth, an earnest host !
　He shall direct you what to do,
　And in His wisdom shall ye go.'

vi Praise to the Comforter divine,
　He of all truth the Way, the Sign,
　Who fills our hearts with holy grace,
　And doth enrich earth's mortal race !

Tr. C. S. T.

DIE NACHT IST KOMMEN

Hymn, by Petrus Herbert, in five 7-line stanzas (1566). Melody, a reconstruction (1566) of ' Ipse cum solus '.

67

i Die Nacht ist kommen,
  Drin wir ruhen sollen :
  Gott walts zu Frommen
  Nach seim Wohlgefallen,
  Dass wir uns legen,
  In seim Gleit und Segen
  Der Ruh zu pflegen.

ii Treib, Herr, von uns fern
  Die unreinen Geister ;
  Halt die Nachtwach gern,
  Sei selbst unser Schutzherr.
  Schirm beid, Leib und Seel,
  Unter deine Flügel ;
  Send uns dein Engel.

iii Lass uns einschlafen
  Mit guten Gedanken,
  Fröhlich aufwachen
  Und von dir nicht wanken.
  Lass uns mit Züchten
  Unser Thun und Dichten
  Zu deim Preis richten.

v Vater, dein Name
  Werd von uns gepreiset ;
  Dein Reich zukomme,
  Dein Will werd beweiset.
  Frist unser Leben,
  Wollst die Schuld vergeben ;
  Erlös uns.   Amen !

i Night's darkness falleth,
  All creation sleepeth.
  God's wisdom ord'reth
  As to Him best seemeth.
  Beneath His blessing,
  His will e'er fulfilling,
  There's nought for fearing.

ii Drive from us far, Lord,
  Thoughts and sprites of evil.
  Watch o'er our sleep, Lord,
  Keep from us every ill.
  Both soul and body
  Hold in Thy safe keeping
  While we are sleeping !

iii Pure thoughts and holy
  In our sleep attend us ;
  And of Thee worthy
  May'st Thou at dawn find us,
  Thy will performing,
  As is to Thee seeming,
  Thy praises singing.

v Thy will, O Father,
  Be for e'er performèd ;
  Thy kingdom gather,
  Thy Name be worshippèd.
  Our bread provide us,
  From hell deliver us,
  Our sins forgive us !

U.L.S. 515.

Tr. C. S. T.

DIE SONN HAT SICH MIT IHREM GLANZ GEWENDET

Hymn, wrongly attributed to Josua Stegmann, in seven 4-line stanzas (1648). Melody, originally (1542) to ' O höchster Gott, O unser lieber Herre'.

68

✱ Bach has a 𝄐 here.

i Die Sonn hat sich mit ihrem Glanz gewendet
   Und, was sie soll, auf diesen Tag vollendet ;
   Die dunkle Nacht dringt allenthalben zu,
   Bringt Menschen, Vieh und alle Welt zur Ruh.

ii Ich preise dich, du Herr der Nächt und Tage,
   Dass du mich heut vor aller Noth und Plage
   Durch deine Hand und hochberühmte Macht
   Hast unverletzt und frei hindurch gebracht.

iii Vergieb, wo ich bei Tage so gelebet,
    Dass ich nach dem, was finster ist, gestrebet ;
    Lass alle Schuld durch deinen Gnadenschein
    In Ewigkeit bei dir verloschen sein.

vii Und lass hernach zugleich mit allen Frommen
    Mich zu dem Glanz des andern Lebens kommen,
    Da du uns hast den grossen Tag bestimmt,
    Dem keine Nacht sein Licht und Klarheit nimmt.

U.L.S. 518.

i The sun is set, in purple clouds descended,
   The sky is dark, another day is ended,
   Night closes round, in sable mantle dressed,
   The world is still, creation is at rest.

ii We praise Thee, Lord, sole God of day and darkness,
   Who'st led us safe, prevented by Thy goodness ;
   Nor pain nor woe our pathway has beset,
   Nor, by Thy might, ought hindered hath or let.

iii Forgive, O Lord, the sins we have committed,
    In Thy good time grant they be all remitted ;
    How foul the deed, still purge us clean and white,
    To stand in heaven soon meetly in Thy sight !

vii To where Thou reign'st bring us to live in glory,
    And in Thy sight to stand elect before Thee,
    When Death's loud trump its summons soundeth
       bright,
    In heaven above, where is nor day nor night !

Tr. C. S. T.

DIES SIND DIE HEILGEN ZEHN GEBOT

Hymn, by Martin Luther, in twelve 5-line stanzas (1524). Melody, the pilgrim song, ' In Gottes Namen fahren wir ' (1524).

69

*Bach has a pause here.

i Dies sind die heilgen zehn Gebot,
   Die uns gab unser Herre Gott
   Durch Mosen, seinen Diener treu,
   Hoch auf dem Berg Sinai.
          Kyrieleis.

ii Ich bin allein dein Gott der Herr,
   Kein Götter sollt du haben mehr ;
   Du sollt mir ganz vertrauen dich,
   Von Herzensgrund lieben mich.
          Kyrieleis.

ix Du sollt kein falscher Zeuge sein,
   Nicht lügen auf den Nächsten dein ;
   Sein Unschuld sollt auch retten du
   Und seine Schand decken zu.
          Kyrieleis.

xi Die G'bot all uns gegeben sind,
   Dass du dein Sünd, o Menschenkind,
   Erkennen sollt, und lernen wohl,
   Wie man vor Gott leben soll.
          Kyrieleis.

xii Das helf uns der Herr Jesus Christ,
   Der unser Mittler worden ist;
   Es ist mit unserm Thun verlorn,
   Verdienen doch eitel Zorn.
          Kyrieleis.

         U.L.S. 364.

i These are the holy ten commands,
   Which came to us from God's own hands
   By Moses, who obeyed His will,
   Standing upon Sin'i's hill.
          Have mercy, Lord !

ii I am the Lord thy God alone ;
   Of gods besides thou shalt have none ;
   Thou shalt thyself trust all to Me,
   Right heartily shalt love Me.
          Have mercy, Lord !

ix Thou shalt not lying stories bear,
   Nor 'gainst thy neighbour falsely swear ;
   His innocence thou shalt rescue,
   And hide his shame from man's view.
          Have mercy, Lord !

xi To us come these commands, that so
   Thou, son of man, thy sins may'st know,
   And with this lesson thy heart fill,
   That man must live for God's will.
          Have mercy, Lord !

xii May Christ our Lord help us in this,
   For He our Mediator is ;
   Our own work is a hopeless thing,
   Judgement alone it can bring.
          Have mercy, Lord !

        Tr. George Macdonald.[1]

[1] *Exotics* (Lond. 1876), p. 84.

DIR, DIR, JEHOVAH, WILL ICH SINGEN

Hymn, by Bartholomäus Crasselius, in eight 6-line stanzas (1697). Melody, by Bach (1725).

70

i Dir, dir, Jehovah, will ich singen ;
   Denn wo ist doch ein solcher Gott, wie du ?
   Dir will ich meine Lieder bringen :
   Ach gib mir deines Geistes Kraft dazu,
   Dass ich es thu im Namen Jesu Christ,
   So wie es dir durch ihn gefällig ist.

ii Zeuch mich, o Vater, zu dem Sohne,
   Damit dein Sohn mich wieder zieh zu dir ;
   Dein Geist in meinem Herzen wohne
   Und meine Sinne und Verstand regier ;
   Dass ich den Frieden Gottes schmeck und fühl
   Und dir darob im Herzen sing und spiel.

vii Wohl mir, dass ich dies Zeugnis habe !
   Drum bin ich voller Trost und Freudigkeit,
   Und weiss : dass alle gute Gabe,
   Die ich verlanget von dir jederzeit,
   Die gibst du und thust überschwenglich mehr,
   Als ich verstehe, bitte und begehr.

viii Wohl mir ! ich bitt in Jesu Namen,
   Der mich zu deiner Rechten selbst vertritt :
   In ihm ist alles Ja und Amen,
   Was ich von dir im Geist und Glauben bitt.
   Wohl mir ! Lob dir itzt und in Ewigkeit,
   Dass du mir schenkest solche Seligkeit !

U.L.S. 556.

i For Thee, Jehovah, are our praises ;
   There is not found on earth one like to Thee !
   Sweet hymns and songs our glad heart raises ;
   O may we show ourselves worthy of Thee !
   We praise Thee, pleading Thy Son, Jesus Christ,
   For Whose dear sake to our poor songs now list.

ii O call us, Father, up to heavèn,
   Up to Thy Son who draws all men to Thee !
   O let Thy Spirit our hearts leaven,
   Make all our thoughts of Thee worthy to be !
   Let heavenly peace, one and all, in us dwell
   That we may all Thy praises loud forth tell !

vii My trust is firmly on Thee grounded,
   For Thy word faithful stands, constant and sure !
   Thy mercies gracious are unbounded,
   Giving with love all our hearts dare implore ;
   Yea, scatt'ring gifts with so lavish a hand,
   Beyond our merit or can understand.

viii O God, in Jesu's dear name pray we,
   Who at Thy right hand for sinners doth plead ;
   O find our merits through Him worthy
   As up to Thee in faith our prayers do speed.
   How blest are we ! Lord, loud praises be Thine,
   Who dost for man such blessings rich design.

Tr. C. S. T.

DU FRIEDEFÜRST, HERR JESU CHRIST

Hymn, by Jakob Ebert, in seven 7-line stanzas (1601). Melody, by (?) Bartholomäus Gesius (1601).

71

<table>
<tr><td>

*i Du Friedefürst, Herr Jesu Christ,
  Wahr Mensch und wahrer Gott,
  Ein starker Nothhelfer du bist
  Im Leben und im Tod.
· Drum wir allein
  Im Namen dein
  Zu deinem Vater schreien.

ii Recht grosse Noth uns stösset an
  Von Krieg und Ungemach,
  Daraus uns niemand helfen kann,
  Denn du. Drum führ die Sach ;
  Dein Vater bitt,
  Dass er ja nitt
  Im Zorn mit uns woll fahren.

iv Verdient haben wir alles wohl,
  Und leidens mit Geduld:
  Doch deine Gnad grösser sein soll
  Denn unsre Sünd und Schuld;
  Darum vergib nach deiner Lieb,
  Die du fest zu uns trägest.

vii Erleucht auch unser Sinn und Herz
  Durch den Geist deiner Gnad,
  Dass wir nicht treibn daraus ein Scherz,
  Der unsrer Seelen schad.
  O Jesu Christ,
  Allein du bist,
  Der solchs wohl kann ausrichten.

</td><td>

i Lord Jesu, blessèd Prince of Peace,
  True God, and very Man !
  Thou mak'st our troubles rise and cease,
  Whose life is but a span.
  Thy Saviour's name
  Is what we claim
  Before Thy heavenly Father.

ii We are beset with great distress
  Of war and pestilence ;
  Who can restore our happiness
  But, Lord, Thy providence ?
  Be pleased to plead
  For us in need,
  Avert th' impending judgement.

iv We own our guilt deserves yet more
  From Thy provokèd hands ;
  But grace is greater, we implore,
  Than sins of all the lands.
  O Lord, forgive,
  Let sinners live,
  That we may praise Thy goodness.

vii Enlighten with forgiving grace
  The darkness of our heart,
  That we may hate the scoffer's ways
  Nor take the atheist's part.
  Christ, Thee we own,
  Thou art alone
  Our strength and our Redeemer.

</td></tr>
</table>

U.L.S. 585.

Tr. John Christian Jacobi.[1]

[1] *Psalmodia Germanica* (Lond. 1722), p. 121.

DU FRIEDEFÜRST, HERR JESU CHRIST

Hymn, by Jakob Ebert, in seven 7-line stanzas (1601). Melody, by (?) Bartholomäus Gesius (1601).

72

i Du Friedefürst, Herr Jesu Christ,
  Wahr Mensch und wahrer Gott,
  Ein starker Nothhelfer du bist
  Im Leben und im Tod.
  Drum wir allein
  Im Namen dein
  Zu deinem Vater schreien.

iii Gedenk, Herr, jetzund an dein Amt,
  Dass du ein Friedfürst bist,
  Und hilf uns gnädig allensammt
  Jetzund zu dieser Frist.
  Lass uns hinfort
  Dein göttlich Wort
  Im Fried noch länger schallen.

*vii Erleucht auch unser Sinn und Herz
  Durch den Geist deiner Gnad,
  Dass wir nicht treibn daraus ein Scherz,
  Der unsrer Seelen schad.
  O Jesu Christ,
  Allein du bist,
  Der solchs wohl kann ausrichten.

U.L.S. 585.

i Lord Christ, Thou art the Prince of Peace,
  True God and Man in One,
  Thou'rt strong to help when foes increase,
  Through life and when life's done !
  In Thy dear name
  Our prayers we frame,
  Thy Father's love invoking.

iii Bethink Thee, Jesu, that indeed
  The Prince of Peace Thou art ;
  O help us in our every need,
  And ne'er from us depart !
  Still year by year
  Grant us to hear
  Thy Word in peace and keep it.

vii So, let Thy Spirit us inflame,
  Our hearts and minds O stay
  That we may ne'er be put to shame,
  Nor fall on evil's day.
  Lord Jesu Christ,
  In Thee we trust,
  'Tis Thou wilt judge and save us.

Tr. C. S. T.

DU GROSSER SCHMERZENSMANN

Hymn, by Adam Thebesius, in seven 8-line stanzas (1663). Melody, by (?) Martin Janus (1663).

i Du grosser Schmerzensmann,
  Vom Vater so geschlagen,
  Herr Jesu, dir sei Dank
  Für alle deine Plagen :
  Für deine Seelenangst,
  Für deine Banden-Noth,
  Für deine Geisselung,
  Für deinen bittern Tod.

iv Dein Kampf ist unser Sieg,
  Dein Tod ist unser Leben ;
  In deinen Gnaden ist
  Die Freiheit uns gegeben.
  Dein Kreuz ist unser Trost,
  Die Wunden unser Heil,
  Dein Blut das Lösegeld,
  Der armen Sünder Theil.

vii Lass deine Wunden sein
  Ein Arznei unsern Sünden,
  Lass uns auf deinen Tod
  Den Trost im Tode gründen.
  O Jesu, lass an uns
  Durch dein Kreuz, Angst und Pein,
  Dein Leiden, Kreuz und Angst
  Ja nicht verloren sein.

Fischer-Tümpel.[1]

i O Christ, Who on the Tree
  The sins of mankind beared'st,
  Lord Jesu, thanks to Thee
  For anguish, keenest, rarest,
  For all the agony
  That stilled Thy panting breath,
  The buffeting and scorn,
  Thy Crucifixion, death !

iv Thy Passion was our gain,
  Thy Cross salvation gave us,
  Thine agony and pain
  From death and torment saved us,
  Hath reconcilèd God
  The Father with mankind,
  And brought salvation down
  To earth and freedom gained.

vii So let Thy Passion cleanse
  Our tempers weak and sinning,
  And by Thy death may we
  Through death to heaven be winning !
  O Jesu, grant us all,
  That through Thine Agony
  And bitter Cross of woe
  We ne'er Thine anger see !

Tr. C. S. T.

[1] Bd. i. No. 399.

DU, O SCHÖNES WELTGEBÄUDE

Hymn, by Johann Franck, in eight 8-line stanzas (1653). Melody, by Johann Crüger (1649).

74

i Du, o schönes Weltgebäude
  Magst gefallen, wem du willt :
  Deine scheinbarliche Freude
  Ist mit lauter Angst umhüllt.
  Denen, die den Himmel hassen,
  Will ich ihre Weltlust lassen :
  Mich verlangt nach dir allein,
  Allerschönstes Jesulein !

* vi Komm, o Tod, du Schlafes Bruder,
  Komm, und führe mich nur fort ;
  Löse meines Schiffleins Ruder,
  Bringe mich in sichern Port.
  Es mag, wer da will, dich scheuen :
  Du kannst mich vielmehr erfreuen :
  Denn durch dich komm ich hinein
  Zu dem schönsten Jesulein !

viii Doch, weil ich die Seelenauen
  Und den güldnen Himmelssaal
  Jetzt nicht kann nach Wünschen schauen,
  Sondern muss im Thränenthal
  Noch am Kummerfaden spinnen :
  Ei so sollen meine Sinnen
  Unterdess doch bei dir sein,
  Allerschönstes Jesulein !

i Things of nought are earth's vain treasures,
  Let who will find gain therein !
  Mingled with its glittering pleasures
  Are delusion, sorrow, sin.
  Some there be who love not heavèn ;
  Earth their hopes doth throughly leaven.
  But my heart is fixed on Thee,
  Jesus, Who art all to me !

vi Come, O Death, soft Sleep's kind brother,
  Haste, I pray thee, quickly come !
  Guide my vessel's drifting rudder,
  Bring me to my haven home !
  Many souls of thee are fearful,
  Joy thou bring'st me ; no more tearful,
  Through thy gates alone I'll see
  Jesus, only prize for me !

viii But, alas, heaven's golden portals
  Not yet may I enter in ;
  Still must I among the mortals
  Life's dark thread persist to spin.
  Yet while here below I'm moiling,
  All my thoughts are heavenward toiling,
  Where at rest I'd be with Thee,
  Jesus, Who art all to me !

U.L.S. 810.

Tr. C. S. T.

DU, O SCHÖNES WELTGEBÄUDE

Hymn, by Johann Franck, in eight 8-line stanzas (1653). Melody, by Johann Crüger (1649).

75

i Du, o schönes Weltgebäude !
  Magst gefallen, wem du willt :
  Deine scheinbarliche Freude
  Ist mit lauter Angst umhüllt.
  Denen, die den Himmel hassen,
  Will ich ihre Weltlust lassen :
  Mich verlangt nach dir allein,
  Allerschönstes Jesulein !

vii Ach dass ich den Leibeskerker
  Heute noch verlassen müsst,
  Und käm an den Sternenerker,
  Wo das Haus der Freuden ist :
  Da wollt ich mit Wortgepränge
  Bei der Engel grosser Menge
  Rühmen deiner Gottheit Schein,
  Allerschönstes Jesulein !

viii Doch, weil ich die Seelenauen
  Und den güldnen Himmelssaal
  Jetzt nicht kann nach Wünschen schauen,
  Sondern muss im Thränenthal
  Noch am Kummerfaden spinnen :
  Ei so sollen meine Sinnen
  Unterdess doch bei dir sein,
  Allerschönstes Jesulein !

Vainly, world, dost boast thy treasures :
Let who will find gain therein !
Lurketh ever in thy pleasures
Grief of heart and taint of sin.
Gladly them do I surrender
For my hope of heavèn yonder :
All my soul's athirst for Thee,
Jesus, only prize for me !

vii O, if death this day would call me
From my house of bondage here,
High among the stars instal me,
Where the songs of joy I'd hear !
There would I, mid angels hymning,
Homage, praise, and worship bringing,
Thee adore with ecstasy,
Jesus, Who art all to me !

viii Distant still is heavèn's glory,
Distant still its golden halls ;
Still life's journey lies before me,
Still the voice of duty calls.
Let not, Lord, my sore misdoing
In Thy sight ordain my ruin,
Take me hence to be with Thee,
Jesus, only prize for me !

U.L.S. 810.

Tr. C. S. T.

DURCH ADAMS FALL IST GANZ VERDERBT

Hymn, by Lazarus Spengler, in nine 10-line stanzas (1524). Melody (1535), sung at the Battle of Pavia (1529) to the song, 'Was wöll wir aber heben an'.

76

i Durch Adams Fall ist ganz verderbt
Menschlich Natur und Wesen :
Dasselb Gift ist auf uns geerbt,
Dass wir nicht mochtn genesen
Ohn Gottes Trost,
Der uns erlöst
Hat von dem grossen Schaden,
Darein die Schlang
Evam bezwang,
Gotts Zorn auf sich zu laden.

vii Wer hofft in Gott und dem vertraut,
Wird nimmermehr zu Schanden ;
Denn wer auf diesen Felsen baut,
Ob ihm gleich geht zuhanden
Viel Unfalls hie :
Hab ich doch nie
Den Menschen sehen fallen,
Der sich verlässt
Auf Gottes Trost ;
Er hilft sein Gläubgen allen.

* viii Ich bitt, o Herr, aus Herzengrund,
Du wollst nicht von mir nehmen
Dein heilges Wort aus meinem Mund,
So wird mich nicht beschämen
Mein Sünd und Schuld ;
Denn in dein Huld
Setz ich all mein Vertrauen :
Wer sich nur fest
Darauf verlässt,
Der wird den Tod nicht schauen.

i When Adam fell, the human race
Was doomed to condemnation ;
Bereft were we of innocence,
Sin's poison wrought destruction.
But thanks to God,
Who spares the rod,
From death have we been taken.
The Serpent Eve
Did once deceive
Beholds his power shaken.

vii Who hopes in God and trusts Him fast
Shall never be confounded,
If on that Rock his cares be cast
When stormy seas surround him.
Yet ne'er I saw
Or rich or poor,
If righteous, perish ever.
Who puts his trust
In God's Word must
From Him be parted never.

viii O Lord, I pray Thee from my heart,
Ne'er let Thy Word pass from me,
Nor let my sin hold me apart
From Thine abounding mercy !
My sins are great,
And sore my guilt ;
Yet e'er Thy love excelleth.
Who holdeth fast
To Thee, at last
One day in heavèn dwelleth.

U.L.S. 409

Tr. C. S. T.

EIN FESTE BURG IST UNSER GOTT

Hymn, by Martin Luther, in four 9-line stanzas (1529). Melody, by Luther (1529).

77

Psalm xlvi.

i Ein feste Burg ist unser Gott,
  Ein gute Wehr und Waffen
  Er hilft uns frei aus aller Noth,
  Die uns jetzt hat betroffen.
  Der alt böse Feind
  Mit Ernst ers jetzt meint;
  Gross Macht und viel List
  Sein gräusam Rüstung ist;
  Auf Erd ist nicht seins Gleichen.

ii Mit unsrer Macht ist nichts gethan
   Wir sind gar bald verloren:
   Es streit für uns der rechte Mann,
   Den Gott hat selbs erkoren.
   Fragst du, wer der ist?
   Er heisst Jesus Christ,
   Der Herr Zebaoth,
   Und ist kein andrer Gott;
   Das Feld muss er behalten.

iii Und wenn die Welt voll Teufel wär
    Und wollt uns gar verschlingen:
    So fürchten wir uns nicht so sehr,
    Es soll uns doch gelingen.
    Der Fürst dieser Welt,
    Wie saur er sich stellt,
    Thut er uns doch nicht;
    Das macht, er ist gericht:
    Ein Wörtlein kann ihn fällen.

i A stronghold sure our God is He,
  A coat of mail and weapon;
  He sets us free, our help will be
  From aught of ill can happen.
  Our old crafty foe
  Plots in wrath our woe.
  His might and craft sly
  Have driv'n him from the sky;
  Not earth can boast his fellow.

ii Our might alone do nothing can,
   Soon were we lost for ever.
   But fights for us the Perfect Man,
   Whom God sent to deliver.
   Ye ask who He is?
   Know then, Jesus Christ,
   Lord of Sabaoth,
   Of other gods sole God,
   'Tis He doth fight our battle!

iii If all the world with devils swarmed,
    All eager to devour us,
    Ne'er need it fear us to be harmed,
    No foe can overpower us.
    This world's Prince of Hell,
    Strive how much he will,
    Can do us no scathe;
    Doomed now is he by fate,
    The Word of God confounds him.

U.L.S. 218.

Tr. C. S. T.

EIN FESTE BURG IST UNSER GOTT

Hymn, by Martin Luther, in four 9-line stanzas (1529). Melody, by Luther (1529).

78

i Ein feste Burg ist unser Gott,
  Ein gute Wehr und Waffen ;
  Er hilft uns frei aus aller Noth,
  Die uns jetzt hat betroffen.
  Der alte böse Feind
  Mit Ernst ers jetzt meint ;
  Gross Macht und viel List
  Sein grausam Rüstung ist ;
  Auf Erd ist nicht seins Gleichen.

ii Mit unsrer Macht ist nichts gethan,
  Wir sind gar bald verloren :
  Es streit für uns der rechte Mann,
  Den Gott hat selbs erkoren.
  Fragst du, wer der ist ?
  Er heisst Jesus Christ,
  Der Herr Zebaoth,
  Und ist kein andrer Gott ;
  Das Feld muss er behalten.

iv Das Wort sie sollen lassen stan,
  Und kein Dank dazu haben.
  Er ist bei uns wohl auf dem Plan
  Mit seinem Geist und Gaben.
  Nehmen sie den Leib,
  Gut, Ehr, Kind und Weib ;
  Lass fahren dahin,
  Sie habens kein Gewinn ;
  Das Reich muss uns doch bleiben.

Psalm xlvi

i A stronghold sure our God is He,
  A coat of mail and weapon ;
  He sets us free, our help will be
  From aught of ill can happen.
  Our old crafty foe
  Plots in wrath our woe.
  His might and craft sly
  Have driv'n him from the sky ;
  Not earth can boast his fellow.

ii Our might alone do nothing can,
  Soon were we lost for ever.
  But fights for us the Perfect Man,
  Whom God sent to deliver.
  Ye ask who He is ?
  Know then, Jesus Christ,
  Lord of Sabaoth,
  Of other gods sole God,
  'Tis He doth fight our battle !

iv God's Word unshaken e'er shall stand,
  Though men no thanks give for it.
  He fights for us at our right hand,
  And lends His strength and Spirit.
  Though foes take our life,
  Honour, child, and wife,
  Let them be all gone !
  'Tis little hath been won ;
  For us the crown remaineth !

U.L.S. 218.

Tr. C. S. T.

EIN FESTE BURG IST UNSER GOTT

Hymn, by Martin Luther, in four 9-line stanzas (1529). Melody, by Luther (1529).

Psalm xlvi.

i Ein feste Burg ist unser Gott,
　Ein gute Wehr und Waffen ;
　Er hilft uns frei aus aller Noth,
　Die uns jetzt hat betroffen.
　Der alte böse Feind
　Mit Ernst ers jetzt meint ;
　Gross Macht und viel List
　Sein grausam Rüstung ist ;
　Auf Erd ist nicht seins Gleichen.

iii Und wenn die Welt voll Teufel wär
　Und wollt uns gar verschlingen :
　So fürchten wir uns nicht so sehr,
　Es soll uns doch gelingen
　Der Fürst von dieser Welt,
　Wie saur er sich stellt,
　Thut er uns doch nicht ;
　Das macht, er ist gericht :
　Ein Wörtlein kann ihn fällen.

* iv Das Wort sie sollen lassen stan,
　Und kein Dank dazu haben.
　Er ist bei uns wohl auf dem Plan
　Mit seinem Geist und Gaben.
　Nehmen sie uns den Leib,
　Gut, Ehr, Kind und Weib :
　Lass fahren dahin,
　Sie habens kein Gewinn ;
　Das Reich muss uns doch bleiben.

U.L.S. 218

i A stronghold sure our God is He,
　A coat of mail and weapon ;
　He sets us free, our help will be
　From aught of ill can happen.
　Our old and crafty foe
　Plots in wrath our woe.
　His might and craft sly
　Have driv'n him from the sky ;
　Not earth can boast his fellow.

iii And though the world with devils raged,
　Their horrid spite declaring,
　Their hate right soon shall be assuaged ;
　No cause is there for fearing.
　Hell's prince for nevermore
　May display his power,
　Nought can he harm us.
　He's fall'n inglorious ;
　The Word of God confounds him.

iv God's Word unshaken e'er shall stand,
　Though men no thanks give for it.
　He fights for us at our right hand,
　And lends His strength and Spirit.
　Our foes may take our life,
　Honour, child, and wife !
　Let them be all gone !
　'Tis little hath been won ;
　For us the crown remaineth !

Tr. C. S. T.

EINS IST NOTH, ACH HERR, DIES EINE

Hymn, by Johann Heinrich Schröder, in ten 8-line stanzas (1697). Melody, reconstruction (1704) of Joachim Neander's (?) ' Grosser Prophete, mein Herze begehret ' (1680).

i Eins ist noth! Ach Herr, dies Ei - ne Leh - re mich er - ken - nen doch!
i One thing, Lord, a - lone I cov - et More than aught the world can boast :

Al - les an - dre, wie's auch schei - ne, Ist ja nur ein schwe - res Joch,
Teach my soul to seek and love it, Prize it more than things of cost,

Dar - un - ter das Her - ze sich na - get und pla - get, Und
Than earth's glit - t'ring toy that the heart vain - ly seek - eth, That

den - noch kein wah - res Ver - gnü - gen er - ja - get. Er - lang ich dies
nought to the soul of true hap - pi - ness speak - eth; To long for that

Ei - ne, dass al - les er - setzt, So werd ich mit Ei - nem in al - lem er - götzt.
one thing all oth - ers out - shines, My soul for it pant - eth, nor elsewhere in - clines.

x Drum auch, Jesu, du alleine
Sollst mein End und Alles sein ;
Prüf, erfahre, wie ichs meine,
Tilge allen Heuchelschein.
Sieh, ob ich auf bösem betrüglichem Stege,
Und leite mich, Höchster, auf ewigem Wege ;
Gieb, dass ich hier alles nur achte für Koth
Und Jesum gewinne : dies Eine ist noth.

x Yea, Thee only, none but Thee, Lord,
Would my eager soul possess ;
Try me throughly, probe my heart, Lord,
Purge it clean of naughtiness !
Then, guide Thou my footsteps from pathways of error,
And show me the one road that leads to my Saviour,
Despising earth's splendour, so tarnished with stain,
And seeking for Jesus, my Saviour, my Gain !

U.L.S. 302.

Tr. C. S. T.

G

ERBARM DICH MEIN, O HERRE GOTT

Hymn, by Erhart Hegenwalt, in five 8-line stanzas (1524). Melody, by (?) Johann Walther (1524).

i Erbarm dich mein, o Herre Gott,
Nach deiner grossn Barmherzigkeit.
Wasch ab, mach rein mein Missethat,
Ich kenn mein Sünd und ist mir leid.
Allein ich dir gesündigt han,
Das ist wider mich stetiglich ;
Das Bös vor dir mag nicht bestan,
Du bleibst gerecht, ob urtheilst mich.

ii Sieh, Herr, in Sünd bin ich geborn,
In Sünd empfing mich mein Mutter ;
Die Wahrheit liebst, thust offenbarn
Deiner Weisheit heimlich Güter.
Bespreng mich, Herr, mit Isopo,
Rein werd ich, wo du wäschest mich,
Weisser denn Schnee, mein G'hör wird froh,
All mein Gebein wird freuen sich.

v Kein leiblich Opfer von mir heischst,
Ich hätte dir das auch geben :
So nimm nun den zerknirschten Geist,
Betrübts, traurigs Herz darneben.
Verschmäh nicht, Gott, das Opfer dein,
Thu wohl in deiner Gütigkeit
Dem Berg Zion, da Christen sein,
Die opfern dir Gerechtigkeit.

Psalm li.

i Have mercy, Lord, my sin forgive ;
For Thy long-suffering is great !
O cleanse and make me fit to live,
My sore offence do Thou abate !
With shame do I my fault confess,
'Gainst Thee alone, Lord, have I sinned.
Thou art the Source of righteousness,
And I the sinner just condemned.

ii Behold, in sin, Lord, was I born,
Within my mother's womb conceived.
Thou, righteous Master, wilt not scorn
One who hath wisdom not received.
With hyssop, Lord, O sprinkle me,
And wash me clean and thoroughly ;
So shall I white as snowflakes be,
And all my members sing to Thee.

v No sacrifice dost Thou require,
Else would I give it unto Thee ;
A broken heart Thou dost desire,
Nor shall it e'er despisèd be.
Rebuild, O Lord, Jerusalem,
Let Zion's walls rise up again,
And on her altars to Thy name
The sacrificial beast be slain !

U.L.S. 366.

Tr. C. S. T

ERHALT UNS, HERR, BEI DEINEM WORT

Hymn, by Martin Luther, in three 4-line stanzas (1542). Melody, anonymous (1543).

i Erhalt uns, Herr, bei deinem Wort,
Und steur des Papsts und Türken Mord,*
Die Jesum Christum deinen Sohn
Stürzen wollen von seinem Thron.

* ii Beweis dein Macht, Herr Jesu Christ,
Der du Herr aller Herren bist :
Beschirm dein arme Christenheit,
Dass sie dich lob in Ewigkeit.

iii Gott Heilger Geist, du Tröster werth,
Gib deim Volk ein'rlei Sinn auf Erd :
Steh bei uns in der letzten Noth,
G'leit uns ins Leben aus dem Tod.

U.L.S. 220.

i Uphold us, Lord, by Thy dread Word,
Make all to know that Thou art God,
To worship Jesus Christ Thy Son,
Confounding them who'd raze His throne !

ii Lord Jesus Christ, Thy might display,
Thou God of gods, Whom all obey !
Thy faithful flock on earth defend,
That we may praise Thee to the end !

iii O Holy Ghost, Who comfort art,
Make all on earth of Thee a part,
Stand by us in our last dread hour,
Through life and death to own Thy power !

Tr. C. S. T.

* Oder : Und steure deiner Feinde Mord,

ERMUNTRE DICH, MEIN SCHWACHER GEIST

Hymn, by Johann Rist, in fourteen 8-line stanzas (1641). Melody, by Johann Schop (1641).

i Du Lebensfürst, Herr Jesu Christ,
Der du bist aufgenommen
Gen Himmel, da dein Vater ist
Und die Gemein der Frommen :
Wie soll ich deinen grossen Sieg,
Den du uns durch den schweren Krieg
Erworben hast, recht preisen
Und dir gnug Ehr erweisen?

* iv Nun lieget alles unter dir,
Dich selbst nur ausgenommen.
Die Engel müssen für und für
Dir aufzuwarten kommen.
Die Fürsten stehn auch auf der Bahn,
Und sind dir willig unterthan.
Luft, Wasser, Feur und Erden
Muss dir zu Dienste werden.

xiii Zieh uns dir nach, so laufen wir ;
Gib uns des Glaubens Flügel.
Hilf, dass wir fliehen weit von hier
Auf Israelis Hügel.
Mein Gott, wann fahr ich doch dahin,
Wo ich ohn Ende fröhlich bin ?
Wann werd ich vor dir stehen,
Dein Angesicht zu sehen.

Fischer-Tümpel.[1]

i Lord Jesus Christ, Thou Prince of Life,
In heaven Thou reign'st in glory.
Finished is here Thine earthly strife,
There all Thy saints adore Thee.
How shall my mouth Thy victory sing ?
Heaven's arches with Thy praises ring,
Thy gracious might e'er telling,
Thy risen Self extolling.

iv Prone at Thy feet creation lies,
Thy sovereign will obeying.
Angelic hosts haste through the skies,
Thy dread commands obeying.
Princes and kings before Thee bow,
All Thy dread power and might allow ;
Earth, heavèn, fire, and ocean
Lie prostrate in devotion.

xiii Draw us to Thee without delay,
On wings of faith hence flying ;
Help us from earth to turn away,
Its nets and snares defying.
My God, when shall I see Thy face,
When rest content upon Thy grace,
And ever stand before Thee,
Mid angels who adore Thee ?

Tr. C. S. T.

[1] Bd. ii. No. 188.

ERMUNTRE DICH, MEIN SCHWACHER GEIST

Hymn, by Johann Rist, in twelve 8-line stanzas (1641). Melody, by Johann Schop (1641).

84

i Ermuntre dich, mein schwacher Geist,
  Und trage gross Verlangen,
  Ein kleines Kind, das Vater heisst,
  Mit Freuden zu empfangen.
  Dies ist die Nacht, darin es kam
  Und menschlich Wesen an sich nahm,
  Dadurch die Welt mit Treuen,
  Als seine Braut zu freien.

iii O grosser Gott ! wie konnt es sein,
  Dein Himmelreich zu lassen,
  Zu springen in die Welt hinein,
  Da nichts denn Neid und Hassen ?
  Wie konntest du die grosse Macht,
  Dein Königreich, die Freudenpracht,
  Ja dein erwünschtes Leben,
  Für solche Feind hingeben ?

* ix Brich an, du schönes Morgenlicht,
  Und lass den Himmel tagen ;
  Du Hirtenvolk, erschrecke nicht,
  Weil dir die Engel sagen,
  Dass dieses schwache Knäbelein
  Soll unser Trost und Freude sein,
  Dazu den Satan zwingen
  Und letztlich Friede bringen.

xii Lob, Preis und Dank, Herr Jesu Christ,
  Sei dir von mir gesungen,
  Dass du mein Bruder worden bist
  Und hast die Welt bezwungen :
  Hilf, dass ich deine Gütigkeit
  Stets preis in dieser Gnadenzeit,
  Und mög hernach dort oben,
  In Ewigkeit dich loben.

i Look up, faint heart, exult with joy !
  From heavèn tidings speedeth :
  To-day is born the Saviour Boy
  That man's salvation needeth ;
  To-day of old to earth He came
  And took on Him a mortal frame,
  Drawn down by love surpassing,
  A Bridegroom earth entrancing.

iii O Mighty One, how cometh it
  Thou leav'st the halls of heavèn ?
  Descend'st to earth and blessest it
  Whose ways with strife are riven ?
  Thou leavest an immortal throne
  To shine upon a world of gloom,
  Fair Paradise exchanging
  For glories that are waning.

ix Shine forth, O beauteous Morning Light,
  Of heaven thou bring'st the dawning !
  Ye shepherds, never show affright,
  But heed the angels' warning !
  They tell this infant Child shall be
  Our Hope and Joy eternally,
  The power of Satan breaking,
  And peace for mankind making.

xii Then, praise to Thee, Lord Jesu Christ,
  From every heart be sounded,
  Who now to be our Brother deign'st,
  And earth with honour's crownèd !
  O help us in this day of grace
  Thy gift surpassing to embrace,
  And one day, prone before Thee,
  To sing Thy praise in glory !

U.L.S. 32.

Tr. C. S. T.

ERMUNTRE DICH, MEIN SCHWACHER GEIST

Hymn, by Johann Rist, in fourteen 8-line stanzas (1641). Melody, by Johann Schop (1641).

85

* i Du Lebensfürst, Herr Jesu Christ,
    Der du bist aufgenommen
    Gen Himmel, da dein Vater ist
    Und die Gemein der Frommen :
    Wie soll ich deinen grossen Sieg,
    Den du uns durch den schweren Krieg
    Erworben hast, recht preisen
    Und dir gnug Ehr erweisen ?

iv Nun lieget alles unter dir,
    Dich selbst nur ausgenommen.
    Die Engel müssen für und für
    Dir aufzuwarten kommen.
    Die Fürsten stehn auch auf der Bahn,
    Und sind dir willig unterthan.
    Luft, Wasser, Feur und Erden
    Muss dir zu Dienste werden.

* xiii Zieh uns dir nach, so laufen wir ;
    Gib uns des Glaubens Flügel.
    Hilf, dass wir fliehen weit von hier
    Auf Israelis Hügel.
    Mein Gott, wann fahr ich doch dahin,
    Wo ich ohn Ende fröhlich bin ?
    Wann werd ich vor dir stehen,
    Dein Angesicht zu sehen.

i Lord Jesus Christ, Thou Prince of Life,
    In heaven Thou reign'st in glory.
    Finished is here Thine earthly strife,
    There all Thy saints adore Thee.
    How shall my mouth Thy victory sing ?
    Heaven's arches with Thy praises ring,
    Thy gracious might e'er telling,
    Thy risen Self extolling.

iv Prone at Thy feet creation lies,
    Thy sovereign will obeying.
    Angelic hosts haste through the skies,
    Thy dread commands obeying.
    Princes and kings before Thee bow,
    All Thy dread power and might allow ;
    Earth, heavèn, fire, and ocean
    Lie prostrate in devotion.

xiii Draw us to Thee without delay,
    On wings of faith hence flying ;
    Help us from earth to turn away,
    Its nets and snares defying.
    My God, when shall I see Thy face,
    When rest content upon Thy grace,
    And ever stand before Thee,
    Mid angels who adore Thee ?

Fischer-Tümpel.[1]

Tr. C. S. T.

[1] Bd. ii. No. 188.

ERSCHIENEN IST DER HERRLICH TAG

Hymn, by Nikolaus Herman, in fourteen 5-line stanzas (1560). Melody, by Herman (1560).

86

* i Erschienen ist der herrlich Tag,
Dran sich niemand gnug freuen mag !
Christ unser Herr heut triumphirt,
All sein Feind er gefangen führt.
                Alleluja !

ii Die alte Schlang, die Sünd und Tod,
Die Höll, all Jammer, Angst und Noth,
Hat überwunden Jesus Christ,
Der heut vom Tod erstanden ist.
                Alleluja !

iii Am Sabbath früh mit Specerei
Kamen zum Grab der Weiber drei,
Dass sie salbten Marien Sohn,
Der vom Tod war erstanden schon.
                Alleluja !

iv Wen sucht ihr da ? der Engel sprach ;
Christ ist erstanden, der hie lag ;
Hie seht ihr die Schweisstücherlein :
Geht hin, sagts bald den Jüngern sein.
                Alleluja !

xiv Drum wir auch billig fröhlich sein,
Singen das Hallelujah fein
Und loben dich, Herr Jesu Christ :
Zu Trost du uns erstanden bist.
                Alleluja !

U.L.S. 134.

i On earth has dawned this day of days,
Whereon let all men give God praise !
For Christ is risen from the tomb,
And on His foes declared just doom.
                Alleluja !

ii The Serpent old, and Sin, and Death,
And Hell, and all man threateneth,
Have been laid low by Christ the Lord,
Who from the tomb to heaven hath soared.
                Alleluja !

iii At early morn, with spices rare,
The women three assembled there,
All to anoint fair Mary's Son,
Who over Death had victory won.
                Alleluja !

iv ' Whom seek ye here ? ' the angel said ;
' He risen is, He is not dead ;
Here lies the cloth that covered Him ;
The tomb is empty : enter in ! '
                Alleluja !

xiv So let our songs to heavèn wing,
The vault with Allelujas ring,
In praise of Him, our risen Lord,
Who doth salvation man afford.
                Alleluja !

Tr. C. S. T.

ERSCHIENEN IST DER HERRLICH TAG

Hymn, by Nikolaus Herman, in fourteen 5-line stanzas (1560). Melody, by Herman (1560)

i Erschienen ist der herrlich Tag,
Dran sich niemand gnug freuen mag !
Christ unser Herr heut triumphirt,
All sein Feind er gefangen führt.
　　　Allelujah !

x Heut gehn wir aus Egyptenland,
Aus Pharaonis Dienst und Band,
Und das recht Osterlämmelein
Wir essen heut im Brod und Wein.
　　　Allelujah !

xii Der schlagend Eng'l vorüber geht,
Kein Erstgeburt er bei uns schlägt ;
Unser Thürschwell hat Christi Blut
Bestrichen, das hält uns in Hut.
　　　Allelujah !

xiii Die Sonn, die Erd, all Creatur,
Alls, was betrübet war zuvor,
Das freut sich heut an diesem Tag,
Da der Welt Fürst darnieder lag.
　　　Allelujah !

* xiv Drum wir auch billig fröhlich sein,
Singen das Hallelujah fein
Und loben dich, Herr Jesu Christ :
Zu Trost du uns erstanden bist.
　　　Allelujah !

i On earth has dawned this day of days,
Whereon let all men give God praise !
For Christ is risen from the tomb,
And on His foes declared just doom.
　　　Alleluja !

x From Egypt's bondage are we free,
And Pharaoh's cruel slavery ;
The Lord's Passover now we eat,
With staff in hand and shoon on feet.
　　　Alleluja !

xii Th' avenging angel flieth o'er ;
Not on the first-born will he draw ;
For on the lintel-posts he sees
The blood of Christ that Israel frees.
　　　Alleluja !

xiii The sun, and earth, and all that lives,
A mighty shout of victory gives
To-day, when Christ His stubborn foe,
The Prince of this world, hath laid low.
　　　Alleluja !

xiv So let our songs to heavèn wing,
The vault with Allelujas ring,
In praise of Him, our risen Lord,
Who doth salvation man afford.
　　　Alleluja !

U.L.S. 134.

Tr. C. S. T.

ERSTANDEN IST DER HEILIG CHRIST

Hymn, anon. translation of ' Surrexit Christus hodie ', in nineteen 4-line stanzas (1544). Melody, that of the Latin hymn (1555).

88

Surrexit Christus hodie.

i Erstanden ist der heilig Christ,
    Alleluja ! Alleluja !
Der aller Welt ein Tröster ist.
    Alleluja ! Alleluja !

ii Und wäre er nicht erstanden,
  So wäre die Welt vergangen.

iii Und seit dass er erstanden ist,
  Lobn wir den Herren Jesum Christ.

iv Es gingn drei heilige Frauen
  Des Morgens frühe im Thauen.

vi Sie funden da zween Engel schon,
  Die tröstn die Frauen lobesan.

vii Erschrecket nicht, und seid all froh,
  Denn, den ihr sucht, der ist nicht da.

ix Er ist erstanden aus dem Grab,
  Heut an dem fröhlich'n Ostertag.

xviii Nun singet all zu dieser Frist :
  Erstanden ist der heilig Christ.

xix Dess solln wir alle fröhlich sein,
  Und Christ soll unser Tröster sein.

U.L.S. 135.

i Lord Christ from death is ris'n to-day,
    Alleluja ! Alleluja !
And hath to heavèn led the way.
    Alleluja ! Alleluja !

ii Now, had He not to heaven aris'n,
  We still had lain in Death's dark pris'n.

iii But He is risen to the skies :
  Wherefore to Him we raise glad cries.

iv Him holy women weeping sought,
  And with them costly spices brought.

vi Two angels in the tomb they found,
  Who did their tim'rous fears confound:

vii ' Be not afraid, but joyous be ;
  He is not here, as you may see.'

ix ' He hath arisen from the grave :
  A joyous Easter ye may have.'

xviii So sing we all on this high feast,
  When ris'n on high is Jesus Christ,

xix And let us all right joyous be,
  And praise our Saviour heartily.

Tr. C. S. T.

ES IST DAS HEIL UNS KOMMEN HER

Hymn, by Paul Speratus, in fourteen 7-line stanzas (1524). Melody, that of the 15th century Easter hymn, 'Freu dich, du werthe Christenheit'.

89

i Es ist das Heil uns kommen her
  Von Gnad und lauter Güten ;
  Die Werke helfen nimmermehr,
  Sie mögen nicht behüten ;
  Der Glaub sieht Jesum Christum an ;
  Der hat gnug für uns all gethan,
  Er ist der Mittler worden.

* xi Die Hoffnung ward der rechten Zeit,
  Was Gottes Wort zusaget ;
  Wenn das geschehen soll zu Freud,
  Setzt Gott kein g'wisse Tage.
  Er weiss wohl, wenns am besten ist,
  Und braucht an uns kein arge List :
  Dess solln wir ihm vertrauen.

xii Ob sichs anliess, als wollt er nicht :
  Lass dich es nicht erschrecken ;
  Denn wo er ist am besten mit,
  Da will ers nicht entdecken.
  Sein Wort lass dir gewisser sein ;
  Und ob dein Fleisch spräch lauter Nein :
  So lass doch dir nicht grauen.

i Salvation now is come to earth,
  Bounty and grace bestowing.
  No man by works can prove his worth,
  Or win by his own doing.
  'Tis faith sees Jesus Christ alone,
  Who for our sins did once atone ;
  To God His Manhood joined us.

xi Hope looketh for the dawning day
  Which God's own Word foretelleth.
  The hoped-for hour may e'en delay ;
  God hath ordained and willeth.
  He knoweth what for us is best,
  Nor will our patience hardly test ;
  So therefore let us trust Him.

xii Should e'er His face seem turned from thee,
  Still be thou not affrighted !
  For when He seems most far from thee
  Then art thou least benighted.
  So, let His Word thy heart restore,
  And, e'en when doubting, still the more
  Be sure thou art not slighted !

U.L.S. 411.

Tr. C. S. T.

ES IST DAS HEIL UNS KOMMEN HER

Hymn, by Paul Speratus, in fourteen 7-line stanzas (1524). Melody, that of the 15th century Easter hymn, 'Freu dich, du werthe Christenheit'.

90

i Es ist das Heil uns kommen her
Von Gnad und lauter Güten ;
Die Werke helfen nimmermehr,
Sie mögen nicht behüten ;
Der Glaub sieht Jesum Christum an ;
Der hat gnug für uns all gethan,
Er ist der Mittler worden.

xi Die Hoffnung ward der rechten Zeit,
Was Gottes Wort zusaget ;
Wenn das geschehen soll zu Freud,
Setzt Gott kein g'wisse Tage.
Er weiss wohl, wenns am besten ist,
Und braucht an uns kein arge List :
Dess solln wir ihm vertrauen.

*xii Ob sichs anliess, als wollt er nicht :
Lass dich es nicht erschrecken ;
Denn wo er ist am besten mit,
Da will ers nicht entdecken.
Sein Wort lass dir gewisser sein ;
Und ob dein Fleisch spräch lauter Nein :
So lass doch dir nicht grauen.

i Salvation now is come to earth,
Bounty and grace bestowing.
No man by works can prove his worth,
Or win by his own doing.
'Tis faith sees Jesus Christ alone,
Who for our sins did once atone ;
To God His Manhood joined us.

xi Hope looketh for the dawning day
Which God's own Word foretelleth.
The hoped-for hour may e'en delay ;
God hath ordained and willeth.
He knoweth what for us is best,
Nor will our patience hardly test ;
So therefore let us trust Him.

xii Should e'er His face seem turned from thee,
Still be thou not affrighted !
For when He seems most far from thee
Then art thou least benighted.
So, let His Word thy heart restore,
And, e'en when doubting, still the more
Be sure thou art not slighted !

U.L.S. 411.

Tr. C.S.T.

ES IST DAS HEIL UNS KOMMEN HER

Hymn, by Paul Speratus, in fourteen 7-line stanzas (1524). Melody, that of the 15th century Easter hymn, ' Freu dich, du werthe Christenheit '.

91

j Es ist das Heil uns kommen her
Von Gnad und lauter Güten ;
Die Werke helfen nimmermehr,
Sie mögen nicht behüten ;
Der Glaub sieht Jesum Christum an ;
Der hat gnug für uns all gethan,
Er ist der Mittler worden.

xi Die Hoffnung ward der rechten Zeit,
Was Gottes Wort zusaget ;
Wenn das geschehen soll zu Freud,
Setzt Gott kein g'wisse Tage.
Er weiss wohl, wenns am besten ist,
Und braucht an uns kein arge List :
Dess solln wir ihm vertrauen.

* xii Ob sichs anliess, als wollt er nicht :
Lass dich es nicht erschrecken ;
Denn wo er ist am besten mit,
Da will ers nicht entdecken.
Sein Wort lass dir gewisser sein ;
Und ob dein Fleisch spräch lauter Nein :
So lass doch dir nicht grauen.

i Salvation now is come to earth,
Bounty and grace bestowing.
No man by works can prove his worth,
Or win by his own doing.
'Tis faith sees Jesus Christ alone,
Who for our sins did once atone ;
To God His Manhood joined us.

xi Hope looketh for the dawning day
Which God's own Word foretelleth.
The hoped-for hour may e'en delay ;
God hath ordained and willeth.
He knoweth what for us is best,
Nor will our patience hardly test ;
So therefore let us trust Him.

xii Should e'er His face seem turned from thee,
Still be thou not affrighted !
For when He seems most far from thee
Then art thou least benighted.
So, let His Word thy heart restore,
And, e'en when doubting, still the more
Be sure thou art not slighted !

U.L.S. 411.   *Tr. C. S. T.*

ES IST DAS HEIL UNS KOMMEN HER

Hymn, by Johann Jakob Schütz, in nine 7-line stanzas (1675). Melody, that of the 15th century Easter hymn, 'Freu dich, du werthe Christenheit'.

92

[Obbligato for 2 Horns]

*i Sei Lob und Ehr dem höchsten Gut,
Dem Vater aller Güte,
Dem Gott, der alle Wunder thut,
Dem Gott, der mein Gemüthe
Mit seinem reichen Trost erfüllt,
Dem Gott, der allen Jammer stillt :
Gebt unserm Gott die Ehre !

iii Was unser Gott geschaffen hat,
Das will er auch erhalten ;
Darüber will er früh und spat
Mit seiner Gnade walten.
In seinem ganzen Königreich
Ist alles recht, ist alles gleich :
Gebt unserm Gott die Ehre !

iv Ich rief dem Herrn in meiner Noth :
Ach Gott, vernimm mein Schreien !
Da half mein Helfer mir vom Tod
Und liess mir Trost gedeihen.
Drum dank, ach Gott, drum dank ich dir ;
Ach, danket, danket Gott mit mir :
Gebt unserm Gott die Ehre !

i Sing praise to God Who dwells on high,
The Father of Creation,
The God Who worketh wondrously,
Who giveth consolation,
The God our soul with solace fills,
The God Who every sorrow stills ;
To Him be praise and glory !

iii What God's almighty power hath done
For ever He upholdeth.
His founts of mercy ever run,
His favour us enfoldeth.
Yea, all within His kingdom's right,
No evil standeth in His sight ;
To Him be praise and glory !

iv I seek the Lord in my sore need ;
O God, now hear my crying !
'Tis for Thy comfort rare I plead,
For Thy support when dying.
A grateful heart I lift to Thee ;
Thank God, ye people all, with me ;
To Him be praise and glory !

U.L.S. 721.

Tr. C. S. T.

ES IST DAS HEIL UNS KOMMEN HER

Hymn, by Johann Jakob Schütz, in nine 7-line stanzas (1675). Melody, that of the 15th century Easter hymn,
'Freu dich, du werthe Christenheit'

i Sei Lob und Ehr dem höchsten Gut,
  Dem Vater aller Güte,
  Dem Gott, der alle Wunder thut,
  Dem Gott, der mein Gemüthe
  Mit seinem reichen Trost erfüllt,
  Dem Gott, der allen Jammer stillt :
  Gebt unserm Gott die Ehre !

vii Ich will dich all mein Leben lang,
  O Gott, von nun an ehren ;
  Man soll, o Gott, dein Lobgesang
  An allen Orten hören.
  Mein ganzes Herz ermuntre sich ;
  Mein Seel und Leib erfreue dich :
  Gebt unserm Gott die Ehre !

* ix So kommet vor sein Angesicht
  Mit jauchzenvollem Springen ;
  Bezahlet die gelobte Pflicht,
  Und lasst uns fröhlich singen :
  Gott hat es alles wohl bedacht
  Und alles, alles recht gemacht :
  Gebt unserm Gott die Ehre !

i Sing praise to God Who dwells on high,
  The Father of Creation,
  The God Who worketh wondrously,
  Who giveth consolation,
  The God our soul with solace fills,
  The God Who every sorrow stills ;
  To Him be praise and glory !

vii Yea, all my earthly life along
  I'll sing, O God, Thy praises.
  All men shall hear the happy song
  To Thee my glad heart raises.
  My heart, lift up a cheerful voice !
  O soul and body, both rejoice !
  To God be praise and glory !

ix Then, come ye all into His courts
  With glad and grateful singing ;
  Ne'er from His service loose your thoughts,
  To Godward set them winging !
  All things He hath most wisely planned,
  And fashioned them with His right hand ;
  To God be praise and glory !

U.L.S. 721.

Tr. C. S. T.

ES IST GENUG

Hymn by Franz Joachim Burmeister, in five 9-line stanzas (1662). Melody, by Joh. Rodolph Ahle (1662).

94

* **Bach has a 𝄐 here.**

i Es ist genug ;
　So nimm, Herr, meinen Geist
　Zu Zions Geistern hin.
　Lös auf das Band,
　Das allgemächlich reisst,
　Befreie diesen Sinn,
　Der sich nach seinem Gotte sehnet,
　Der täglich klagt, der nächtlich thränet.
　Es ist genug ! (*bis*)

iii Es ist genug
　Des Kreuzes, das mir fast
　Den Rücken Wund gemacht.
　Wie schwer, o Gott,
　Wie hart ist diese Last !
　Ich schwemme manche Nacht
　Mein hartes Lager durch mit Thränen ;
　Wie lang, wie lange muss ich sehnen ?
　Wann ist's genug ? (*bis*)

* v Es ist genug ;
　Herr, wann es dir gefällt,
　So spanne mich doch aus !
　Mein Jesus kömmt ;
　Nun gute Nacht, o Welt !
　Ich fahr ins Himmels Haus.
　Ich fahre sicher hin in Frieden,
　Mein feuchter Jammer bleibt darnieden.
　Es ist genug ! (*bis*)

　　　　　Fischer-Tümpel.[1]
　　　　　[1] Bd. iv. No. 533.

i It is enough !
　Lord, call my spirit home
　To Zion's halls above.
　Break down earth's ties,
　Receive the thoughts that roam
　T'ward Thee and Thy dear love,
　The heart's desire that calleth to Thee,
　The daily moan that riseth to Thee.
　It is enough ! (*bis*)

iii It is enough !
　My bitter Cross of pain
　Too grievous is.　I'm spent.
　My load is sore,
　To bear it is in vain ;
　With sobs my frame is rent.
　The whole night through I toss with weeping ;
　Now take me, Lord, into Thy keeping !
　It is enough ! (*bis*)

v It is enough !
　Lord, brace me to the test
　When Death knocks at the door.
　'Tis Jesus calls.
　Vain world, I go to rest
　Beyond earth's farthest shore,
　In peace and most exceeding happy,
　Leaving all sorrow far behind me.
　It is enough ! (*bis*)

　　　　　Tr. C. S. T.

ES SPRICHT DER UNWEISEN MUND WOHL

Hymn, by Martin Luther, translation of Psalm xiv, in six 7-line stanzas (1524). Melody, by (?) Luther (1524)·

95

Psalm xiv.

i Es spricht der Unweisen Mund wohl :
   Den rechten Gott wir meinen ;
   Doch ist ihr Herz Unglaubens voll,
   Mit That sie ihn verneinen.
   Ihr Wesen ist verderbet zwar,
   Vor Gott ist es ein Greuel gar :
   Es thut ihr keiner kein gut.

v Darum ist ihr Herz nimmer still
   Und steht allzeit in Fürchten.
   Gott bei den Frommen bleiben will,
   Dem sie mit Glaub'n gehorchen.
   Ihr aber schmäht des Armen Rath,
   Und höhnet alles, was er sagt,
   Dass Gott sein Trost ist worden.

vi Wer soll Israel dem armen
   Zu Zion Heil erlangen ?
   Gott wird sich seins Volks erbarmen
   Und lösen die Gefangnen ;
   Das wird er thun durch seinen Sohn,
   Davon wird Jakob Wonne han
   Und Israel sich freuen.

i Although the fools say with their mouth:
   ' Great God, we magnify Him,'
   Their heart cares nothing for the truth,
   In action they deny Him.
   Their being is corrupted quite ;
   To God it is a horrid sight ;
   Not one of them works goodness.

v Therefore their heart is never still,
   But always full of fearing.
   Dwell with the good the Father will,
   With them whose ears are hearing.
   But ye despise the poor man's ways,
   And scorn at everything he says
   Concerning God his comfort.

vi Who will to Israel's scattered flock,
   To Zion send salvation ?
   God will take pity on His folk,
   And free His captive nation ;
   That will He do through Christ His Son ;
   And then is Jacob's weeping done,
   And Israel filled with gladness.

U.L.S. 221.

Tr. George Macdonald.[1]

[1] *Exotics* (Lond. 1876), p. 64.

ES STEHN VOR GOTTES THRONE

Hymn, by Ludwig Helmbold, in seven 7-line stanzas (1585). Melody, by Joachim a Burck (1594).

96

i *Es stehn vor Gottes Throne,
   Die unser Diener sind,
   *Der in seim lieben Sohne
   Liebt aller Menschen Kind,
   Dass er auch nicht der eines
   Veracht will habn, so kleines
   *Als jemals ist geborn.

ii *Sie sehn sein Angesichte
   Und haben fleissig Acht,
   *Was er ihn auszurichten
   Befiehlet Tag und Nacht :
   Da sind die lieben Engel
   Geschwind, regen die Flügel,
   *Zu fahren hin und her.

iii *Wo Christenleute wohnen
   In Häusern gross und klein,
   *Da sie selber nicht können
   Vor Feinden sicher sein,
   Wo nicht ein englisch Lager
   Umher wird aufgeschlagen
   *In steter Hut und Wach.

vii *Auch Lazarus der Arme,
   Wenns gleich zum Sterben kömmt,
   *Gott, der sich sein erbarmet,
   Hat sein Engel bestimmt,
   Die ihn gen Himmel bringen :
   Dem lasst uns alle singen
   *Ewiges Lob und Preis.

i *God's mighty throne surrounding,
   The angels watchful stand,
   *By Him Whose purpose loving
   His Son to save us planned,
   Who suffers nought to perish,
   Who doth the meanest cherish
   *That e'er on earth was born.

ii *God's countenance to light them,
   They swift perform His will ;
   *His dread commands delight them
   To day and night fulfil.
   On speedy pinions plying,
   Like birds in ether flying,
   *They journey to and fro.

iii *Where Christian people gather
   In dwellings great or small,
   *It is their heavenly Father
   Whose angels heed their call.
   In legions close they ward us,
   They hold us safe and guard us
   *With constant watchful care.

vii *When Lazarus, the poor man,
   To death at last had come,
   *God sent an angel for him
   And brought him heavenward home.
   So let us lift our voices
   In song that God rejoices,
   *Enthroned in heaven above !

U.L.S. 203.

Tr. C. S. T.

* It is necessary to repeat the 1st, 3rd and 7th lines of each stanza.

ES WIRD SCHIER DER LETZTE TAG HERKOMMEN

Hymn, by Michael Weisse, in nineteen 4-line stanzas (1531). Melody, the Latin 'Felici peccatrici' adapted (1531).

97

i Es wird schier der letzte Tag herkommen,
   Denn die Bosheit hat sehr zugenommen :
   Was Christus hat vorgesagt,
   Das wird jetzt beklagt.

vi Lasst uns in den Bund des Herren treten,
   Und darinnen stets wachen und beten :
   Denn der letzte Tag geht her,
   Kömmt uns immer nähr.

xi Alsdann wird er zu sein'n Engeln sprechen :
   Nun will ich mich an mein'n Feinden rächen !
   Wer wider mich hat gethan,
   Wird nehmen sein'n Lohn !

xviii Aber sein Volk von diesen geschieden
   Wird er führen zu himmlischen Freuden,
   Wo es wie der Sonnenschein
   Ewiglich wird sein.

xix Ei nun, Herre, steh uns bei auf Erden,
   Und bereit uns, dass wir würdig werden
   Zu schauen in Ewigkeit
   Deine Herrlichkeit !

Tucher.[1]

i Day of doom, the Lord's great day approacheth,
   When to judge the world in wrath He cometh.
   Lo, the hour that Christ did tell
   Calls to heaven or hell !

vi Let us all as Christians then prepare us,
   Nor let careless sleep or sloth ensnare us :
   Soon our God from heaven will call
   And His vengeance fall.

xi Then shall He, His angel hosts assembling,
   On His foes proclaim His awful cursing :
   ' They who have against Me striven
   Shall their doom be given'.

xviii But His faithful, on His right before Him,
   God will call to heaven and joys entrancing,
   Where His light doth ever shine
   In the realms divine.

xix God, our Father, grant Thy help unto us,
   And prepare us for the vision glorious,
   That we, in eternity,
   May Thy glory see !

Tr. C. S. T.

[1] No. 562.

ES WOLLT UNS GOTT GENÄDIG SEIN

Hymn, by Martin Luther, in three 9-line stanzas (1524).   Melody, anonymous (1525).

98

Psalm lxvii.

i Es wollt uns Gott genädig sein
  Und seinen Segen geben :
  Sein Antlitz uns mit hellem Schein
  Erleucht zum ewgen Leben ;
  Dass wir erkennen seine Werk
  Und was ihm lieb auf Erden,
  Und Jesus Christus Heil und Stärk
  Bekannt den Heiden werden
  Und sie zu Gott bekehren.

ii So danken, Gott, und loben dich
  Die Heiden überalle ;
  Und alle Welt die freue sich
  Und sing mit grossem Schalle,
  Dass du auf Erden Richter bist
  Und lässest die Sünd nicht walten :
  Dein Wort die Hut und Weide ist,
  Die alles Volk erhalten,
  In rechter Bahn zu wallen.

iii Es danke, Gott, und lobe dich
  Das Volk in guten Thaten ;
  Das Land bringt Frucht und bessert sich :
  Dein Wort ist wohl gerathen.
  Uns segnen Vater und der Sohn,
  Uns segnen Gott der Heil'g Geist ;
  Dem alle Welt die Ehre thu,
  Vor ihm sich fürchte all'rmeist.
  Nun sprecht von Herzen : Amen.

i Would that the Lord would grant us grace,
  And in His volume write us,
  And with clear shining let His face
  To life eternal light us ;
  That we may know His work at length,
  And what men Him have faith in ;
  And Jesus Christ our health and strength
  Be known to all the heathen,
  And unto God convert them.

ii God then let thank, and Thee let praise
  The heathen with glad voices ;
  Let all the world for joy upraise
  A song with mighty noises,
  Because Thou art earth's Judge, O Lord,
  And sin no more prevaileth ;
  Thy Word it is both bed and board,
  And for all folk availeth
  In the right path to keep them.

iii Let them thank God, and Thee adore,
  The folk in deeds of grace full.
  The land grows fruitful more and more ;
  Thy Word it is successful.
  O bless us, God the Father, Son,
  O bless us, God the Spirit,
  To Whom by all be honour done.
  Let all men own Their merit.
  Now heartily say Amen.

U.L.S. 222.

Tr. George Macdonald [1]

[1] *Exotics* (Lond. 1876), p. 77.

ES WOLLT UNS GOTT GENÄDIG SEIN

Hymn, by Martin Luther, in three 9-line stanzas (1524).   Melody, anonymous (1525).

99

Psalm lxvii.

i Es wollt uns Gott genädig sein
Und seinen Segen geben :
Sein Antlitz uns mit hellem Schein
Erleucht zum ewgen Leben ;
Dass wir erkennen seine Werk
Und was ihm lieb auf Erden,
Und Jesus Christus Heil und Stärk
Bekannt den Heiden werden
Und sie zu Gott bekehren.

ii So danken, Gott, und loben dich
Die Heiden überalle ;
Und alle Welt die freue sich
Und sing mit grossem Schalle,
Dass du auf Erden Richter bist
Und lässest die Sünd nicht walten :
Dein Wort die Hut und Weide ist,
Die alles Volk erhalten,
In rechter Bahn zu wallen.

iii Es danke, Gott, und lobe dich
Das Volk in guten Thaten ;
Das Land bringt Frucht und bessert sich :
Dein Wort ist wohl gerathen.
Uns segnen Vater und der Sohn,
Uns segnen Gott der Heil'g Geist ;
Dem alle Welt die Ehre thu,
Vor ihm sich fürchte all'rmeist.
Nun sprecht von Herzen : Amen.   *U.L.S.* 222.

i Lord, in Thy love, look down on us
And shower on us Thy blessing ;
Send down Thy beams from heaven on us,
Be ever to us loving !
So shall we mortals own Thy sway,
Thy saving grace possessing,
And Jesus Christ by night and day
The heathen be confessing,
Their praise to God expressing.

ii Then let the heathen praise Thee, Lord,
In every climate dwelling !
Be Thou by mortals all adored,
Their grateful praises telling !
For Thou the Judge of all men art,
Who drivest sin before Thee ;
Thy Word prevails in every part,
It guides our path securely,
And leads to heavèn surely.

iii Come, praise ye God, our mighty Lord,
All folk on earth now dwelling !
He hath His favour on us poured,
And calls to joy excelling.
Now bless us, God the Father, Son,
Enlighten us, O Spirit !
Their praises sound, while ages run,
Let all men own Their merit.
So sing we, joyful, Amen.   *Tr. C. S. T.*

ES WOLLT UNS GOTT GENÄDIG SEIN

Hymn, by Martin Luther, in three 9-line stanzas (1524).   Melody, anonymous (1525).

100

[Trumpets I II III and Timpani obbligati.]   *Psalm lxvii.*

i Es wollt uns God genädig sein
  Und seinen Segen geben :
  Sein Antlitz uns mit hellem Schein
  Erleucht zum ewgen Leben ;
  Dass wir erkennen seine Werk
  Und was ihm belieb auf Erden,
  Und Jesus Christus Heil und Stärk
  Bekannt nun den Heiden werden
  Und sie zu Gott bekehren.

ii So danken, Gott, und loben dich
   Die Heiden überalle ;
   Und alle Welt die freue sich
   Und sing mit grossem Schalle,
   Dass du auf Erden Richter bist
   Und lässest die Sünd nicht walten :
   Dein Wort die Hut und Weide ist,
   Die alles dein Volk erhalten,
   In rechter Bahn zu wallen.

* iii Es danke, Gott, und lobe dich
    Das Volk in guten Thaten ;
    Das Land bringt Frucht und bessert sich :
    Dein Wort ist wohl gerathen.
    Uns segnen Vater und der Sohn,
    Uns segnen Gott der Heilig Geist ;
    Dem alle Welt die Ehre thu,
    Vor ihm sich fürchte allermeist.
    Nun sprecht von Herzen : Amen.

i Would that the Lord would grant us grace,
  And in His volume write us,
  And with clear shining let His face
  To life eternal light us ;
  That we may know His work at length,
  And who on Him their faith do place ;
  And Jesus Christ our health and strength
  Be known to all the heathen race,
  And unto God convert them.

ii God then let thank, and Thee let praise
   The heathen with glad voices ;
   Let all the world for joy upraise
   A song with mighty noises,
   Because Thou art earth's Judge, O Lord,
   And sin no more can e'er prevail ;
   Thy Word it is both bed and board,
   And for all folk it shall avail
   In the right path to keep them.

iii Let them thank God, and Thee adore,
    The folk in deeds of grace full.
    The land grows fruitful more and more ;
    Thy Word it is successful.
    O bless us, God the Father, Son,
    O bless us, God the Holy Ghost,
    To Whom by all be honour done.
    Before Him let men fear the most.
    Now heartily say Amen.

U.L.S. 222.

Tr. George Macdonald.[1]

[1] *Exotics* (Lond. 1876), p. 77.

ES WOLLT UNS GOTT GENÄDIG SEIN

Hymn, by Martin Luther, in three 9-line stanzas (1524). Melody, anonymous (1525).

i Es wollt uns Gott genädig sein
  Und seinen Segen geben :
  Sein Antlitz uns mit hellem Schein
  Erleucht zum ewgen Leben ;
  Dass wir erkennen seine Werk
  Und was ihm belieb auf Erden,
  Und Jesus Christus Heil und Stärk
  Bekannt nun den Heiden werden
  Und sie zu Gott bekehren.

ii So danken, Gott, und loben dich
   Die Heiden überalle ;
   Und alle Welt die freue sich
   Und sing mit grossem Schalle,
   Dass du auf Erden Richter bist
   Und lässest die Sünd nicht walten :
   Dein Wort die Hut und Weide ist,
   Die alles dein Volk erhalten,
   In rechter Bahn zu wallen.

iii Es danke, Gott, und lobe dich
    Das Volk in guten Thaten ;
    Das Land bringt Frucht und bessert sich :
    Dein Wort ist wohl gerathen.
    Uns segnen Vater und der Sohn,
    Uns segnen Gott der Heilig Geist ;
    Dem alle Welt die Ehre thu,
    Vor ihm sich fürchte allermeist.
    Nun sprecht von Herzen : Amen.

i Would that the Lord would grant us grace
  And in His volume write us,
  And with clear shining let His face
  To life eternal light us ;
  That we may know His work at length,
  And who in Him their faith do place ;
  And Jesus Christ our health and strength
  Be known to all the heathen race,
  And unto God convert them.

ii God then let thank, and Thee let praise
   The heathen with glad voices ;
   Let all the world for joy upraise
   A song with mighty noises,
   Because Thou art earth's Judge, O Lord,
   And sin no more can e'er prevail ;
   Thy Word it is both bed and board,
   And for all folk it shall avail
   In the right path to keep them.

iii Let them thank God, and Thee adore,
    The folk in deeds of grace full.
    The land grows fruitful more and more ;
    Thy Word it is successful.
    O bless us, God the Father, Son,
    O bless us, God the Holy Ghost,
    To Whom by all be honour done.
    Before Him let men fear the most.
    Now heartily say Amen.

U.L.S. 222.

Tr. George Macdonald.[1]

[1] *Exotics* (Lond. 1876), p. 77.

FREU DICH SEHR, O MEINE SEELE

Hymn, anonymous, in ten 8-line stanzas (1620). Melody, by Louis Bourgeois, originally (1551) to Psalm xlii, 'Ainsi qu'on oit le cerf bruire'.

102

i Freu dich sehr, o meine Seele,
  Und vergiss all Noth und Qual
  Weil dich nun Christus, dein Herre,
  Ruft aus diesem Jammerthal.
  Aus der Trübsal, Angst und Leid
  Sollt du fanren in die Freud
  Die kein Ohr jemals gehöret,
  Die in Ewigkeit auch währet.

ii Tag und Nacht hab ich gerufen
  Zu dem Herren meinem Gott,
  Weil mich stets viel Kreuz betroffen,
  Dass er mir hülf aus der Noth.
  Wie sich sehnt ein Wandersmann,
  Dass sein Weg ein End mög han :
  So hab ich gewünschet eben,
  Dass sich enden mög mein Leben.

* x Freu dich sehr, o meine Seele !
  Und vergiss all Noth und Qual ;
  Weil dich nun Christus, dein Herre,
  Rufet aus dem Jammerthal.
  Seine Freud und Herrlichkeit
  Sollt du sehn in Ewigkeit,
  Mit den Engeln jubilieren,
  In Ewigkeit triumphieren.

O my soul, be glad and joyful,
  Cast away thy care and woe !
  From this earth so sad and tearful
  Christ thy Lord doth call thee now.
  Pain no longer shalt thou know,
  But, where tears do never flow,
  Shalt thou peace enjoy surpassing,
  Joy and happiness entrancing.

ii Day and night my plaint has risen
  To God's throne in heaven above,
  Praying Him my woes to leaven
  With His mercy and His love.
  As the trav'ller, milestones passed,
  Sees his journey's end at last,
  So have I, sore spent and anguished,
  For life's instant ending languished.

x O my soul, be glad and joyful,
  Cast away thy care and woe !
  From this earth so sad and tearful
  Christ thy Lord doth call thee now.
  Through the ages shall thy sight
  Rest upon His power and might,
  With the angel choirs rejoicing,
  And their strains triumphant voicing.

U L.S. 814.

Tr. C. S. T.

FREU DICH SEHR, O MEINE SEELE

Hymn, by Paul Gerhardt, in twelve 8-line stanzas (1647).   Melody, by Louis Bourgeois, originally (1551) to Psalm xlii, ' Ainsi qu'on oit le cerf bruire'.

i Weg, mein Herz, mit dem Gedanken,
  Als ob du verstossen wärst !
  Bleib in Gottes Wort und Schranken,
  Da du anders reden hörst.
  Bist du bös und ungerecht :
  Ei, so ist Gott fromm und schlecht ;
  Hast du Zorn und Tod verdienet :
  Sinke nicht, Gott ist versühnet.

ix Kein See kann sich so ergiessen,
  Kein Grund kann so grundlos sein,
  Kein Strom so gewaltig fliessen :
  Gegen Gott ist alles klein.
  Gegen Gott und seine Huld,
  Die er über unsre Schuld
  Alle Tage lässet schweben
  Durch das ganze Sündenleben.

* xii Mein Gott, öffne mir die Pforten
  Solcher Wohlgewogenheit :
  Lass mich allzeit aller Orten
  Schmecken deine Süssigkeit !
  Liebe mich, und treib mich an,
  Dass ich dich, so gut ich kann.
  Wiederum umfang und liebe
  Und ja nun nicht mehr betrübe.

i Put all fear and doubt behind thee,
  Never think that prayer's unheard !
  Stake thy trust in God, confide thee
  In His ever faithful Word !
  Howsoe'er thy ways are ill,
  God is patient, loves thee still.
  Hast thou punishment deservèd ?
  Lift thy heart ! Thou art not spurnèd.

ix There is not an ocean rolleth,
  Not the widest tumbling stream,
  No abyss unfathomed yawneth
  God doth not as little deem.
  Measured by His patience, sin
  Is a small and petty thing ;
  For His mercy knows no limit
  To the sins that judgement merit.

xii Ope the gates of Zion before me,
  Let the founts of blessing flow !
  To Thy favour, Lord, restore me,
  Let me all Thy sweetness know !
  Shed on me Thy love divine,
  Take, O take this heart of mine !
  So it shall adore Thee ever,
  Sinful vex Thee henceforth never.

U.L.S. 436.

Tr. C. S. T.

FREU DICH SEHR, O MEINE SEELE

Hymn, by Johann Olearius, in four 8-line stanzas (1671).   Melody, by Louis Bourgeois, originally (1551) to Psalm xlii, ' Ainsi qu'on oit le cerf bruire'.

104

i Tröstet, tröstet meine Lieben,
  Tröstet mein Volk, spricht mein Gott,
  Tröstet, die sich jetzt betrüben
  Über Feindes Hohn und Spott.
  Weil Jerusalem wohl dran,
  Redet sie gar freundlich an,
  Denn ihr Leiden hat ein Ende ;
  Ihre Ritterschaft ich wende.

ii Ich vergeb all ihre Sünden,
   Ich tilg ihre Missethat,
   Ich will nicht mehr sehn noch finden,
   Was die Straf erwecket hat.
   Sie hat ja zweifältig Leid
   Schon empfangen ; ihre Freud
   Soll sich täglich neu vermehren
   Und ihr Leid in Freud verkehren.

* iii Eine Stimme lässt sich hören
   In der Wüsten weit und breit,
   Alle Menschen zu bekehren :
   Macht dem Herrn den Weg bereit,
   Machet Gott ein ebne Bahn ;
   Alle Welt soll heben an
   Alle Thäler zu erhöhen,
   Dass die Berge niedrig stehen.

Fischer-Tümpel.[1]

i Comfort, comfort ye My people,
  Speak ye peace, thus saith our God ;
  Comfort those who sit in darkness,
  Mourning 'neath their sorrows' load ;
  Speak ye to Jerusalem
  Of the peace that waits for them,
  Tell her that her sins I cover
  And her warfare now is over.

ii Yea, her sins our God will pardon,
   Blotting out each dark misdeed ;
   All that well deserved His anger
   He will no more see nor heed.
   She hath suffered many a day,
   Now her griefs have passed away,
   God will change her pining sadness
   Into ever-springing gladness.

iii For the Baptist's voice is crying
    In the desert far and near,
    Bidding all men to repentance,
    Since the kingdom now is here.
    O that warning cry obey,
    Now prepare for God a way ;
    Let the valleys rise to meet Him,
    And the hills bow down to greet Him.

Tr. Catherine Winkworth.[2]

[1] Bd. iv. No. 421.
[2] *Chorale Book for England* (Lond. 1865), No. 83.

FREU DICH SEHR, O MEINE SEELE

Hymn, by David Denicke, in eleven 8-line stanzas (1648).   Melody, by Louis Bourgeois, originally (1551) to Psalm xlii, ' Ainsi qu'on oit le cerf bruire'.

105

i Kommt, lasst euch den Herren lehren,
Kommt und lernet allzumahl,
Welche die sind, die gehören
In der rechten Christen Zahl :
Die bekennen mit dem Mund
Glaüben fest von Herzensgrund,
Und bemühen sich darneben,
Guts zu thun, so lang sie leben.

* vi Selig sind, die aus Erbarmen
Sich annehmen fremder Noth,
Sind mitleidig mit den Armen,
Bitten treulich für sie Gott ;
Die behülflich sind mit Rath,
Auch, wo möglich, mit der That,
Werden wieder Hülf empfangen
Und Barmherzigkeit erlangen.

viii Selig sind, die Friede machen
Und drauf sehn ohn Unterlass,
Dass man mög in allen Sachen
Fliehen Hader, Streit und Hass ;
Die da stiften Fried und Ruh,
Rathen allerzeits dazu,
Sich auch Friedens selbst befleissen,
Werden Gottes Kinder heissen.

Fischer-Tümpel.[1]

i Come, ye people, list and mark ye
What God's Word to us doth say !
Who are they in mansions heavenly
Dwell with Him eternally ?
They whose lips their Lord confess,
They whose faith doth Him profess,
They who kindness practise ever,
Do no evil to their neighbour.

vi Blest are they whose founts of mercy
Freely for another flow,
To the poor their alms disburse they,
Praying God to heal their woe.
Who the helpless aids with word,
Or to gen'rous acts is stirred,
Shall himself God's hand be given,
Stretched to lead him up to heavèn.

viii Blest are they e'er peace ensuing,
All who set them, early, late,
'Gainst the deeds that lead to ruin,
Anger, malice, strife, and hate ;
They whose counsel's gently given,
Ne'er to angry courses driven :
Such men sons of God are callèd,
For the ways of peace they've followed.

Tr. C. S. T.

[1] Bd. ii. No. 404.

FREU DICH SEHR, O MEINE SEELE

Hymn, by Johann Heermann, in twelve 8-line stanzas (1630).   Melody, by Louis Bourgeois, originally (1551) to Psalm xlii, 'Ainsi qu'on oit le cerf bruire'.

106

i Treuer Gott, ich muss dir klagen
  Meines Herzens Jammerstand,
  Ob dir wohl sind meine Plagen
  Besser, als mir selbst, bekannt :
  Grosse Schwachheit ich bei mir
  In Anfechtung selbst verspür,
  Wann der Satan allen Glauben
  Will aus meinem Herzen rauben.

* vi Heilger Geist im Himmelsthrone,
  Gleicher Gott von Ewigkeit
  Mit dem Vater und dem Sohne,
  Der Betrübten Trost und Freud !
  Der du in mir angezündt,
  So viel ich an Glauben findt :
  Über mir mit Gnaden walte,
  Ferner deine Gab erhalte.

* vii Deine Hilfe zu mir sende,
  O du edler Herzensgast !
  Und das gute Werk vollende,
  Das du angefangen hast.
  Blas das kleine Fünklein auf,
  Bis dass nach vollbrachtem Lauf
  Allen Auserwählten gleiche
  Ich des Glaubens Ziel erreiche.

i In Thy faithful help confiding,
  Lord, to Thee I bring my woe ;
  Knowing well from Thee's no hiding
  Of the griefs afflict me so.
  Lord, my spirit's faint and weak
  When would Satan crafty seek
  Of my faith in Thee to rob me,
  And from Thee, alas, to part me.

vi Holy Spirit, throned in heavèn,
  One with God eternally ;
  With the Son, for man's sin givèn,
  Source of joy and ecstasy.
  All my being is aflame
  With the love of Thy great name !
  Ever of Thy grace watch o'er me,
  And Thy precious gift restore me !

vii Send, O send Thy comfort to me,
  Sheltered deep within my heart ;
  Lord, fulfil Thy purpose in me,
  Make my will of Thine a part !
  In me kindle virtue's glow,
  Guide me whither I should go ;
  Till to join th' elect death calls me,
  And the victor's crown befalls me.

U.L.S. 430.

Tr. C. S. T.

FREU DICH SEHR, O MEINE SEELE

Hymn, anonymous, in ten 8-line stanzas (1620).   Melody, by Louis Bourgeois, originally (1551) to Psalm xlii, 'Ainsi qu'on oit le cerf bruire'.

107

[**Trumpets I, II, III, and Timpani obbligati**]

<table>
<tr><td>

i Freu dich sehr, o meine Seele,
  Und vergiss all Noth und Qual ;
  Weil dich nun Christus, dein Herre,
  Ruft aus diesem Jammerthal.
  Aus der Trübsal, Angst und Leid
  Sollt du fahren in die Freud
  Die kein Ohr jemals gehöret,
  Die in Ewigkeit auch währet.

</td><td>

i O my soul, be glad and joyful,
  Cast away thy care and woe !
  From this earth so sad and tearful
  Christ the Lord doth call thee now.
  Pain no longer shalt thou know,
  But, where tears do never flow,
  Shalt thou peace enjoy surpassing,
  Joy and happiness entrancing.

</td></tr>
<tr><td>

* ix Lass dein Engel mit mir fahren
  Auf Elias Wagen roth,
  Meine Seele wohl bewahren,
  Wie Lazarum nach seim Tod.
  Lass sie ruhn in deinem Schooss,
  Und erfülle sie mit Trost,
  Bis der Leib kommt aus der Erden,
  Und sie beid vereinigt werden.

</td><td>

ix Let Thine angel, Lord, attend me,
  As Elias, heavèn borne ;
  May my soul repose upon Thee,
  As once Laz'rus, poor, forlorn ;
  In Thy bosom me receive,
  Fill me full of trust and love,
  Till my risen soul and body
  Both unite above in glory !

</td></tr>
</table>

U.L.S. 814.   *Tr. C. S. T.*

FREU DICH SEHR, O MEINE SEELE

*Hymn, by Johann Heermann, in six 8-line stanzas (1644). Melody, by Louis Bourgeois, originally (1551) to Psalm xlii,
'Ainsi qu'on oit le cerf bruire'.*

108

i Jesu, deine tiefen Wunden,
  Deine Qual und bittrer Tod
  Geben mir zu allen Stunden
  Trost in Leibs- und Seelennoth.
  Fällt mir etwas Arges ein :
  Denk ich bald an deine Pein :
  Die erlaubet meinem Herzen
  Mit der Sünde nicht zu scherzen.

iv Ja, für alles, das mich kränket,
   Geben deine Wunden Kraft.
   Wenn mein Herz hinein sich senket,
   Krieg ich neuen Lebenshaft.
   Deines Trostes Süssigkeit
   Wendt in mir das bittre Leid,
   Der du mir das Heil erworben,
   Da du für mich bist gestorben.

v Auf dich setz ich mein Vertrauen :
  Du bist meine Zuversicht.
  Dein Tod hat den Tod zerhauen,
  Dass er mich kann tödten nicht.
  Dass ich an dir habe Theil,
  Bringet mir Trost, Schutz und Heil.
  Deine Gnade wird mir geben,
  Auferstehung, Licht und Leben.

i Christ, Thy wounds and bitter Passion,
  Bloody sweat, Cross, death, and tomb,
  Be my daily meditation,
  Till I to Thy presence come :
  When a sinful thought would start,
  Ready to seduce my heart,
  Thy sore pain my own doth rally,
  Me forbids with sin to dally.

iv Lord, in every sore oppression,
   Let Thy wounds be my relief ;
   When I seek Thy intercession,
   Add new strength to my belief :
   Ah, the feeling of Thy peace
   Sets my troubled heart at ease,
   And affords a demonstration
   Of Thy love and my salvation.

v All my hope and consolation,
  Christ, is on Thy bitter death ;
  At the hour of expiration,
  Lord, receive my dying breath ;
  Most of all, when I go hence,
  Let this be my confidence,—
  That Thy deep humiliation
  Has procurèd my salvation.

U.L.S. 103.

Tr. John Christian Jacobi.[1]

[1] *Moravian Hymn-Book* (Ed. 1877). No. 107.

FREU DICH SEHR, O MEINE SEELE

Hymn, by *Johann Heermann, in twelve 8-line stanzas* (1630). *Melody, by Louis Bourgeois, originally* (1551) *to Psalm xlii,*
'*Ainsi qu'on oit le cerf bruire*'

109

i Treuer Gott, ich muss dir klagen
　Meines Herzens Jammerstand,
　Ob dir wohl sind meine Plagen
　Besser, als mir selbst, bekannt :
　Grosse Schwachheit ich bei mir
　In Anfechtung selbst verspür,
　Wann der Satan allen Glauben
　Will aus meinem Herzen rauben.

vii Deine Hilfe zu mir sende,
　O du edler Herzensgast !
　Und das gute Werk vollende,
　Das du angefangen hast.
　Blas das kleine Fünklein auf,
　Bis dass nach vollbrachtem Lauf
　Allen Auserwählten gleiche
　Ich des Glaubens Ziel erreiche.

* xii Ich will alle meine Tage
　Rühmen deine starke Hand,
　Dass du meine Plag und Klage
　Hast so gnädig abgewandt.
　Nicht nur in der Sterblichkeit
　Soll dein Ruhm sein ausgebreit :
　Ich wills auch nachher erweisen
　Und dort ewiglich dich preisen.

i In Thy faithful help confiding,
　Lord, to Thee I bring my woe ;
　Knowing well from Thee's no hiding
　Of the griefs afflict me so.
　Lord, my spirit's faint and weak
　When would Satan crafty seek
　Of my faith in Thee to rob me
　And from Thee, alas, to part me.

vii Send, O send Thy comfort to me,
　Sheltered deep within my heart ;
　Lord, fulfil Thy purpose in me,
　Make my will of Thine a part !
　In me kindle virtue's glow,
　Guide me whither I should go ;
　Till to join th' elect death calls me,
　And the victor's crown befalls me !

xii All my days, O God, I'll praise Thee,
　And Thy mighty arm acclaim.
　Care and sorrow flee before Thee,
　Captives of Thy glorious Name.
　Lord, Thy praises will I sound
　While there's breath within me found,
　And hereafter shall my spirit
　Still proclaim Thy wondrous merit.

U.L.S. 430.

Tr. C. S. T.

FREUET EUCH, IHR CHRISTEN ALLE

Hymn, by Christian Keimann, in four 10-line stanzas (1646).   *Melody, by (?) Andreas Hammerschmidt (1646).*

110

i Freuet euch, ihr Christen alle !
  Freue sich, wer immer kan !
  Gott hat viel an uns gethan :
  Freuet euch mit grossem Schalle !
  Dass er uns so hoch geacht,
  Sich mit uns befreundt gemacht.
  Freude, Freude über Freude !
  Christus wehret allem Leide :
  Wonne, Wonne über Wonne !
  Er ist die Genadensonne.

iii Jesu, wie soll ich dir danken ?
  Ich bekenne, dass von dir
  Meine Seligkeit herrühr.
  Ach, lass mich von dir nicht wanken,
  Nimm mich dir zu eigen hin,
  So empfindet Herz und Sinn
  Freude, Freude über Freude !
  Christus wehret allem Leide :
  Wonne, Wonne über Wonne !
  Er ist die Genadensonne.

* iv Jesu, nimm dich deiner Glieder
  Ferner doch in Gnaden an ;
  Schenke, was man bitten kann,
  Zu erquicken deine Brüder ;
  Gieb der ganzen Christenschaar
  Frieden und ein seligs Jahr !
  Freude, Freude über Freude !
  Christus wehret allem Leide :
  Wonne, Wonne über Wonne !
  Er ist die Genadensonne.

i O rejoice, ye Christians, loudly,
  For your joy is now begun ;
  Wondrous things our God hath done.
  Tell abroad His goodness proudly,
  Who our race hath honoured thus
  That He deigns to dwell with us :
  Joy, O joy beyond all gladness !
  Christ hath done away with sadness !
  Hence, all sorrow and repining,
  For the Sun of grace is shining !

iii Lord, how shall I thank Thee rightly ?
  I acknowledge that from Thee
  Every blessing flows to me.
  Let me not forget it lightly,
  But to Thee through all things cleave ;
  So shall heart and mind receive
  Joy, yea, joy beyond all gladness.
  Christ hath done away with sadness !
  Hence, all sorrow, all repining,
  For the Sun of grace is shining !

iv Jesu, guard and guide Thy members,
  Fill Thy brethren with Thy grace,
  Hear their prayers in every place,
  Quicken now life's faintest embers ;
  Grant all Christians, far and near,
  Holy peace, a glad New Year !
  Joy, O joy beyond all gladness !
  Christ hath done away with sadness !
  Hence, all sorrow and repining,
  For the Sun of grace is shining !

U.L.S. 34.   *Tr. Catherine Winkworth.*[1]
[1] *Chorale Book for England* (Lond. 1865), No. 33.

FÜR FREUDEN LASST UNS SPRINGEN

Hymn .by Kasperl Peltsch, in six 6-line stanzas (1648).   Melody, anonymous (MS. 1648).

III

i Für Freuden lasst uns springen,
  Ihr Christen allzugleiche !
  Mit Mund und Herzen singen,
  Denn Christ vom Himmelreiche
  Von einer Jungfrau ist geborn ;
  Wer hat zuvor gehört von solchen Dingen ?

ii Der allem Fleisch bescheret
  Sein Speis, vom Himmelsthrone
  Dasselb erhält und nähret.
  Der ewig Gottes Sohne
  Von einer Jungfrau ist geborn.
  Ei ! wie gar freundlich er zu uns sich kehret.

iii Dem armen kleinen Kinde,
  Dem nichts ist zu vergleichen,
  Muss Meer und alle Winde
  Mit Furcht und Zittern weichen :
  Ihm dienen alle Engelein,
  Für ihm erschrickt der Teuf'l mit seim Gesinde.

v Thut euch zu ihm doch finden :
  Lasst ihn umsonst nicht rufen,
  Steht ab von euren Sünden,
  Weil noch die Thür ist offen.
  So werdt ihr zeitlich hie und dort
  Den Teufel und alls Unglück überwinden.

P. Wagner.[1]

i Good Christians all, rejoice ye,
  With hearts and voices singing ;
  For Christ, in heaven's full glory,
  Is now among us dwelling,
  The Offspring of a virgin's womb !
  Hath e'er been heard on earth such news excelling ?

ii He Who all flesh provideth
  With daily fare in plenty
  Himself as mortal liveth.
  The Son of God Almighty
  A virgin's babe now is He born.
  How great must be the love for us He beareth !

iii This Infant, poor and holy,
  Beyond all others precious,
  Doth rule the winds so mighty
  And tames the seas tempestuous.
  The angel hosts Him serve with awe,
  Proud Satan and his hosts in fear bend lowly.

v Good Christians, then, approach ye,
  Nor let Him call you vainly !
  Put every sin far from ye
  While still the time is ready !
  So shall you strength and grace receive,
  While Satan and misfortune ne'er shall daunt ye.

Tr. C. S. T.

[1] *Vollständiges Gesangbuch* (Leipzig 1701. Bd. i. p. 53).

GELOBET SEIST DU, JESU CHRIST

Hymn, by Martin Luther, a version of the Sequence 'Grates nunc omnes reddamus', in seven 5-line stanzas (1524). Melody, an adaptation (1524) of the Latin plainsong.

Grates nunc omnes reddamus.

i Gelobet seist du, Jesu Christ !
  Dass du Mensch geboren bist
  Von einer Jungfrau, das ist wahr,
  Dess freuet sich der Engel Schaar.
      Kyrieleis !

ii Des ewgen Vaters einig Kind
   Jetzt man in der Krippen findt,
   In unser armes Fleisch und Blut
   Verkleidet sich das ewig Gut.
      Kyrieleis !

vi Er ist auf Erden kommen arm,
   Dass er unser sich erbarm,
   Uns in dem Himmel machet reich
   Und seinen lieben Engeln gleich.
      Kyrieleis !

* vii Das hat er alles uns gethan,
    Sein gross Lieb zu zeigen an.
    Dess freu sich alle Christenheit
    Und dank ihm dess in Ewigkeit.
      Kyrieleis !

i Now praisèd be Thou, Jesu Christ,
  Who within a stable liest,
  Born of a virgin, wondrous true !
  The angel hosts their anthems blow.
      Alleluja ! [1]

ii The Father's Son, as was designed,
   In a manger you shall find.
   Concealed in man's poor flesh and blood
   He lieth there Who is our God.
      Alleluja !

vi Poor unto earth He cometh thus,
   For He pity takes on us,
   And in the heavèns makes us rich,
   Where angel hosts their voices pitch.
      Alleluja !

vii All this for us our God hath done,
    Whose great love gave us His Son.
    So, joyful let all Christians be,
    And give Him thanks eternally !
      Alleluja !

U.L.S. 36.

Tr. C. S. T.

[1] Pron. ' Al-le-lu-i-a '.

GELOBET SEIST DU, JESU CHRIST

Hymn, by Martin Luther, a version of the Sequence 'Grates nunc omnes reddamus', in seven 5-line stanzas (1524).   Melody, an adaptation (1524) of the Latin plainsong.

113

[Obbligati for Horns I, II, and Timpani]   *Grates nunc omnes reddamus.*

i Gelobet seist du, Jesu Christ !
Dass du Mensch geboren bist
Von einer Jungfrau, das ist wahr,
Dess freuet sich der Engel Schaar.
     Kyrieleis !

iii Den aller Welt Kreis nie beschloss,
Der liegt in Mariens Schoos ;
Er ist ein Kindlein worden klein,
Der alle Ding erhält allein.
     Kyrieleis !

iv Das ewig Licht geht da herein,
Giebt der Welt ein neuen Schein,
Es leucht wohl mitten in der Nacht
Und uns des Lichtes Kinder macht.
     Kyrieleis !

v Der Sohn des Vaters, Gott von Art,
Ein Gast in der Welt hier ward
Und führt uns aus dem Jammerthal,
Er macht uns Erben in seim Saal.
     Kyrieleis !

* vii Das hat er alles uns gethan,
Sein gross Lieb zu zeigen an.
Dess freu sich alle Christenheit
Und dank ihm dess in Ewigkeit.
     Kyrieleis !

i Now praisèd be Thou, Jesu Christ,
Who within a stable liest,
Born of a virgin, wondrous true !
The angel hosts their anthems blow.
     Alleluja ! [1]

iii He Who is Lord of earth and skies
On a mother's bosom lies.
A little babe, He cometh here
Who ruleth all things far and near.
     Alleluja !

iv Around Him see a light divine,
Which o'er all the earth doth shine !
Where it doth gleam there is no night,
And we become the sons of light.
     Alleluja !

v The Father's Son, whom none excel,
Deigns with man on earth to dwell.
He calleth us, in His great love,
To share with Him God's heaven above.
     Alleluja !

vii All this for us our God hath done,
Whose great love gave us His Son.
So, joyful let all Christians be,
And give Him thanks eternally !
     Alleluja !

U.L.S. 36.

Tr. C. S. T.

[1] Pron.' Al-le-lu-i-a'.

GELOBET SEIST DU, JESU CHRIST

Hymn, by Martin Luther, a version of the Sequence ' Grates nunc omnes reddamus ', in seven 5-line stanzas (1524). Melody, an adaptation (1524) of the Latin plainsong.

114

i Gelobet seist du, Jesu Christ !
  Dass du Mensch geboren bist
  Von einer Jungfrau, das ist wahr,
  Dess freuet sich der Engel Schaar.
        Kyrieleis !

ii Des ewgen Vaters einig Kind
   Jetzt man in der Krippen findt,
   In unser armes Fleisch und Blut
   Verkleidet sich das ewig Gut.
        Kyrieleis !

vi Er ist auf Erden kommen arm,
   Dass er unser sich erbarm,
   Uns in dem Himmel machet reich
   Und seinen lieben Engeln gleich.
        Kyrieleis !

vii Das hat er alles uns gethan,
    Sein gross Lieb zu zeigen an.
    Dess freu sich alle Christenheit
    Und dank ihm dess in Ewigkeit.
        Kyrieleis !

i Praisèd be Thou, O Jesus Christ,
  That a man on earth Thou liest !
  Born of a maiden—it is true—
  In this exult the heavens also.
        Alleluja !

ii The Father's only Son begot
   In the manger has His cot,
   In our poor dying flesh and blood
   Doth mask itself the endless Good.
        Alleluja !

vi Poor to the earth He cometh thus,
   Pity so to take on us,
   And make us rich in heaven above,
   And like the angels of His love.
        Alleluja !

vii All this for us did Jesus do,
    That His great love He might show.
    Let Christendom rejoice therefore,
    And give Him thanks for evermore.
        Alleluja !

U.L.S. 36.

Tr. George Macdonald.[1]

[1] *Exotics* (Lond. 1876), p. 43.

GELOBET SEIST DU, JESU CHRIST

Hymn, by Martin Luther, a version of the Sequence 'Grates nunc omnes reddamus', in seven 5-line stanzas (1524). Melody, an adaptation (1524) of the Latin plainsong.

115

i Gelobet seist du, Jesu Christ !
Dass du Mensch geboren bist
Von einer Jungfrau, das ist wahr,
Dess freuet sich der Engel Schaar.
                    Kyrieleis !

iv Das ewig Licht geht da herein,
Giebt der Welt ein neuen Schein,
Es leucht wohl mitten in der Nacht
Und uns des Lichtes Kinder macht.
                    Kyrieleis !

v Der Sohn des Vaters, Gott von Art,
Ein Gast in der Welt hier ward
Und führt uns aus dem Jammerthal,
Er macht uns Erben in seim Saal.
                    Kyrieleis !

* vii Das hat er alles uns gethan,
Sein gross Lieb zu zeigen an.
Dess freu sich alle Christenheit
Und dank ihm dess in Ewigkeit.
                    Kyrieleis !

i Due praises to th' incarnate love
Manifested from above !
All men and angels now adore
Nor we nor they have seen before.
                    Thanks, O Lord !

iv Th' eternal Splendour shows His sight,
Gives the world its saving light,
And drives the clouds of sin away,
To make us children of the day.
                    Thanks, O Lord !

v The Father's Son, by nature God,
Took amongst us His abode,
And opened through this world of strife
A way to everlasting life.
                    Thanks, O Lord !

vii Now this was done that He might prove
All the greatness of His love ;
Which makes all Christians join to sing
Praise to our new-born God and King.
                    Thanks, O Lord !

U.L.S. 36.

Tr. John Christian Jacobi.[1]

[1] *Psalmodia Germanica* (Lond. 1722), p. 6.

GIEB DICH ZUFRIEDEN UND SEI STILLE

Hymn, by Paul Gerhardt, in fifteen 7-line stanzas (1666). Melody, by Bach (1725).

116

i Gieb dich zufrieden und sei stille
In dem Gotte deines Lebens,
In ihm ruht aller Freuden Fülle,
Ohn ihn mühst du dich vergebens.
Er ist dein Quell und deine Sonne,
Scheint täglich hell zu deiner Wonne.
        Gib dich zufrieden (*bis*).

v Er hört die Seufzer deiner Seelen
Und des Herzens stilles Klagen,
Und was du keinem darfst erzählen,
Magst du Gott gar kühnlich sagen.
Er ist nicht fern, steht in der Mitten,
Hört bald und gern der Armen Bitten.
        Gib dich zufrieden (*bis*).

xiv Es ist ein Ruhe-Tag vorhanden,
Da uns unser Gott wird lösen:
Er wird uns reissen aus den Banden
Dieses Leibs und allem Bösen.
Es wird einmal der Tod herspringen
Und aus der Qual uns sämtlich bringen.
        Gib dich zufrieden (*bis*).

        Fischer-Tümpel.[1]

i Have faith in God, nor e'er distress thee,
Constant on His love relying;
In Him your joy is found in plenty,
His love stilleth all thy sighing.
He is our Sun, our Source, Light-giver,
Who lights us on our pathway ever.
        Faint heart, cease grieving (*bis*)!

v He hears thy sighs and knows thine anguish,
Every heart-beat loving heeding.
Though others scornful let thee languish,
Swiftly to thine aid God's speeding.
He is not far, by Thee is standing,
His gracious ear to thee inclining.
        Faint heart, cease grieving (*bis*)!

xiv The dawn's at hand when God shall call us
To His Father's home in glory,
And from the ills that here befall us
Will release our spirit surely.
No more may Death our spirit threaten:
God wipes away all tears in heaven.
        Faint heart, cease grieving (*bis*)!

        Tr. C. S. T.

[1] Bd. iii. No. 474.

GOTT, DER DU SELBER BIST DAS LICHT

Hymn, by Johann Rist, in fifteen 8-line stanzas (1641). Melody, by Johann Crüger (1648).

117

i Gott, der du selber bist das Licht,
Dess Güt und Treue stirbet nicht,
Dir sei itzt Lob gesungen,
Nach dem durch seine grosse Macht
Der helle Tag die finstre Nacht
So kräftig hat verdrungen,
Und deine Gnad und Wunderthat
Mich, da ich schlief, erhalten hat.

xiv Allein zu dir hab ich gesetzt
Mein Herz, o Vater, gib zuletzt
Auch mir ein seligs Ende,
Auf dass ich deinen jüngsten Tag
Mit grosser Freud erwarten mag,
Drauf streck ich aus die Hände :
Ach komm, Herr Jesu, komm, mein Ruhm,
Und nimm mich in dein Eigenthum.

xv Mein Gott und Vater segne mich ;
Der Sohn erhalte gnädiglich,
Was er mir hat gegeben ;
Der Geist erleuchte Tag und Nacht
Sein Antlitz über mich mit Macht
Und schütze mir mein Leben.
Nur dieses wünsch ich für und für :
Der Friede Gottes sei mit mir.

O God, Who art the Only Light,
Whose goodness ever shineth bright,
To Thee be praise unceasing !
For night's dark hours have passed away,
And brightly dawns another day,
Thy wonder-work displaying.
Thou'st held us safely while we slept,
And from our rest all evil kept.

xiv Thou only dost possess my heart :
O make me of Thyself a part
When life's last hour shall call me.
When sounds the last clear summons stern
May I heaven's joys still fuller learn
And find Thy hand to guide me.
O come, Lord Jesus, call me clear,
And make me Thy possession dear !

xv O God the Father, ever bless !
O Jesus Christ, e'er me confess
And to Thy grace elect me !
O God the Spirit, day and night,
Lift up Thy face on me with might
And with Thy love protect me !
And always, as I go my way,
May God His peace upon me lay !

Fischer-Tümpel.[1]

Tr. C. S. T.

[1] Bd. ii. No. 190.

GOTT DER VATER, WOHN UNS BEI

Hymn, by Martin Luther, in three 14-line stanzas (1524). Melody, anonymous (1524). Both Hymn and Melody are of pre-Reformation origin.

118

1 Gott der Vater, wohn uns bei
  Und lass uns nicht verderben,
  Mach uns aller Sünden frei
  Und helf uns selig sterben.
  Vor dem Teufel uns bewahr,
  Halt uns bei festem Glauben
  Und auf dich lass uns bauen,
  Aus Herzengrund vertrauen,
  Dir uns lassen ganz und gar,
  Mit allen rechten Christen
  Entfliehen Teufels Listen,
  Mit Waffen Gotts uns rüsten.
  Amen, Amen, das sei wahr,
  So singen wir Allelujah !

ii Jesus Christus, wohn uns bei
  Und lass uns nicht verderben, *etc.*

iii Der Heil'g Geiste, wohn uns bei
  Und lass uns nicht verderben, *etc.*

i God the Father, with us be,
  Let us not fall to badness ;
  Make us from all sinning free,
  And help us die in gladness.
  'Gainst the devil well us ware,
  And keep our faith from failing,
  Our hope in Thee from quailing.
  Our hearts upon Thee staying,
  Let us wholly trust Thy care,
  With all good Christians sharing,
  Escape the devil's snaring,
  Him with God's weapons daring.
  Amen, now ! so may we fare !
  Let us then sing Alleluja !

ii Jesus, Master, with us be,
  Let us not fall to badness ; *etc.*

iii Holy Spirit, with us be,
  Let us not fall to badness ; *etc.*

U.L.S. **187.**

Tr. George Macdonald.[1]

[1] *Exotics* (Lond. 1876), p. 60.

GOTT DES HIMMELS UND DER ERDEN

Hymn, by Johann Franck, in nine 6-line stanzas (1655). Melody, by Heinrich Albert (1642).

119

i Ihr Gestirn, ihr hohlen Lüfte
  Und du lichtes Firmament,
  Tiefes Rund, ihr dunklen Klüfte,
  Die der Widerhall zertrennt ;
  Jauchzet fröhlich, lasst das Singen
  Itzt bis durch die Wolken dringen.

iii Freude ! Freud in hohen Höhen !
  Freude, Freud im tiefen Thal !
  Freud und Wonne, wo wir gehen,
  Freud und Lachen ohne Zahl !
  Freude, Freud in unsern Thoren !
  Gott ist heut ein Mensch geboren !

v Bethlehem, uns wundert alle,
  Wie es immer zu mag gehn,
  Dass in deinem kleinen Stalle
  Kann der ganze Himmel stehn.
  Hat denn nun der Sterne Menge
  Raum in einer solchen Enge ?

* ix Zwar ist meine Herzenstube
  Wohl kein schöner Fürstensaal,
  Sondern eine finstre Grube ;
  Doch so bald dein Gnadenstrahl
  In denselben nur wird blinken,
  Wird es voller Sonnen dünken.

Fischer-Tümpel.[1]

i Starry aisles and heavenly spaces,
  Lofty, airy firmament,
  Ye, too, earth's remote recesses,
  All dark deeps with echoes rent,
  Come, rejoice ye, hearty singing,
  Till with sound the void is ringing !

iii Joy all happiness excelling,
  Joy in heavèn, joy on earth,
  Joy that's deep beyond all telling,
  Joy all eager, happy mirth,
  Sweetest joy has come to mortals :
  God descends from heaven's high portals !

v Bethlehem, thou favoured city,
  Wondrously hath it befell
  That within thy dwellings lowly
  God Himself is come to dwell !
  He Whom heaven nor earth containeth
  From an ox's manger reigneth.

ix Dark and cold the heart within me
  Till Thou deign'st to enter there.
  'Tis a dwelling black and gloomy,
  Not a palace bright and fair,
  Till Thy grace upon it beameth ;
  Then with radiance rare it gleameth.

Tr. C. S. T.

[1] Bd. iv. No. 109.

GOTT DES HIMMELS UND DER ERDEN

Hymn, by Heinrich Albert, in seven 6-line stanzas (1642). Melody, by Heinrich Albert (1642).

119a

i Gott des Himmels und der Erden,
  Vater, Sohn und Heilger Geist,
  Der es Tag und Nacht lässt werden,
  Sonn und Mond uns scheinen heisst;
  Dessen starke Hand die Welt,
  Und was drinnen ist, erhält.

iii Lass die Nacht auch meiner Sünden
   Jetzt mit dieser Nacht vergehn;
   O Herr Jesu, lass mich finden
   Deine Wunden offen stehn,
   Da alleine Hilf und Rath
   Ist für meine Missethat.

vi Meinen Leib und meine Seele
   Sammt den Sinnen und Verstand,
   Grosser Gott, ich dir befehle
   Unter deine starke Hand.
   Herr, mein Schild, mein Ehr und Ruhm,
   Nimm mich auf, dein Eigenthum.

vii Deinen Engel zu mir sende,
    Der des bösen Feindes Macht,
    List und Anschlag von mir wende
    Und mich halt in guter Acht;
    Der auch endlich mich zur Ruh
    Trage nach dem Himmel zu.

i God Who madest earth and heaven,
  Father, Son, and Holy Ghost,
  Who the day and night hast given,
  Sun and moon and starry host,
  All things wake at Thy command
  Held in being by Thy hand.

iii Let the night of sin that shrouded
   All my life, with this depart;
   Shine on me with beams unclouded!
   Jesu, in Thy loving heart
   Is my help and hope alone,
   For the evil I have done.

vi O my God, I now commend me
   Wholly to Thy mighty hand;
   All the powers that Thou dost lend me
   Let me use at Thy command;
   Thou my boast, my strength divine,
   Keep me with Thee, I am Thine.

vii Thus, afresh with each new morning,
    Save me from the power of sin,
    Hourly let me feel Thy warning
    Ruling, prompting me within,
    Till my final rest be come,
    And Thine angel bear me home.

U.L.S. 459.

Tr. Catherine Winkworth.[1]

[1] *Chorale Book for England* (Lond. 1865), No. 160.

GOTT HAT DAS EVANGELIUM

Hymn, by Erasmus Alber, in fourteen 5-line stanzas (1548). Melody, anonymous (1548).

120

i Gott hat das Evangelium
 Gegeben, dass wir werden fromm.
 Die Welt acht't solchen Schatz nicht hoch ;
 Der mehrer Theil fragt nicht darnach.
 Das ist ein Zeichen vor dem jüngsten Tag !

ii Man fragt nicht nach der guten Lehr ;
 Der Geiz und Wucher noch viel mehr
 Hat überhand genommen gar.
 Noch sprechen sie : Es hat kein G'fahr !
 Das ist ein Zeichen vor dem jüngsten Tag !

iv Man rühmt das Evangelium :
 Und will doch niemand werden fromm.
 Fürwahr, man spott den lieben Gott ;
 Noch sprechen sie : Es hat kein Noth !
 Das ist ein Zeichen vor dem jüngsten Tag !

xiv Darum, komm, lieber Herre Christ !
 Das Erdreich überdrüssig ist,
 Zu tragen solchen Höllebrand !
 Drum mach einmal mit ihm ein End ;
 Und lass uns sehn den lieben jüngsten Tag !

U.L.S. 655.

i God gave the Gospel unto men
 That they might worthy be of Him.
 Of little count the world it recks,
 Nor lets God's Word its conscience vex,
 So may we know the Day of Doom is near !

ii To words of truth man gives no heed,
 His mind is bent on gain and greed,
 And all that to the flesh is dear.
 He rashly deems there's nought to fear.
 So may we know the Day of Doom is near !

iv The Gospel's praise is on man's lips,
 But sin's sweet honey each one sips.
 Thus God they shame in very deed,
 For better doing find no need.
 So may we know the Day of Doom is near !

xiv So then, Lord Christ, do Thou appear,
 And from the earth right swiftly clear
 A race of sinners justly banned !
 The hour's at hand, their end is planned.
 Come then and speedy dawn, O God's Great
 Day !

Tr. C. S. T.

GOTT LEBET NOCH

Hymn, by Johann Friedrich Zihn, in eight 10-line stanzas (1692). Melody, anonymous (1714).

121

i Gott lebet noch :
　Seele, was verzagst du doch ?
　Gott ist gut, der aus Erbarmen
　Alle Hülf auf Erden thut,
　Der mit Macht und starken Armen
　Machet alles wohl und gut :
　Gott kann besser, als wir denken,
　Alle Noth zum Besten lenken :
　Seele, so bedenke doch,
　Lebt doch unser Herrgott noch.

ii Gott lebet noch :
　Seele, was verzagst du doch ?
　Soll der schlummern oder schlafen,
　Der das Aug hat zugericht ?
　Der die Ohren hat erschaffen,
　Sollte dieser hören nicht ?
　Gott ist Gott, der hört und siehet,
　Wo dem Frommen Weh geschiehet :
　Seele, so bedenke doch,
　Lebt doch unser Herrgott noch.

iii Gott lebet noch :
　Seele, was verzagst du doch ?
　Der den Erdenkreis verhüllet
　Mit den Wolken weit und breit,
　Der die ganze Welt erfüllet,
　Ist von uns nicht fern und weit ;
　Wer Gott liebt, dem will er senden
　Hülf und Trost an allen Enden :
　Seele, so bedenke doch,
　Lebt doch unser Herrgott noch.

i God lives ! He's near !
　See, my soul, and have no fear !
　God is good and full of mercy,
　Sendeth help in every need,
　With His arm will safe protect thee,
　And will all thy goings speed.
　Better than our fondest dreaming
　Is the good for us He's scheming.
　Soul, remember happily :
　God's in heaven and cares for thee !

ii God lives ! He's near !
　See, my soul, and have no fear !
　Can He slumber or lie sleeping
　Who the eye's far vision planned ?
　He Who gave to man his hearing
　Must too hear and understand.
　God is God ; He sees and shareth
　All the troubles mortal beareth.
　Soul, remember constantly :
　God's in heaven and cares for thee !

iii God lives ! He's near !
　See, my soul, and have no fear !
　He who heaven and earth controlleth,
　Whose behests each cloud conveys,
　He who all that lives disposeth
　Must be near to thee always.
　He who God sincerely loveth
　Help and hope he ever findeth.
　Soul, remember joyfully :
　God's in heaven and cares for thee !

C. C. J. Bunsen.[1]

Tr. C. S. T.

[1] *Gesang und Gebetbuch* (Hamburg 1833), No. 436.

GOTT SEI GELOBET UND GEBENEDEIET

Hymn, by Martin Luther, in three 10-line stanzas (1524). Melody, anonymous (1524). Hymn and melody are pre-Reformation in origin.

122

✱ **Bach has a ⌢ here.**

i Gott sei gelobet und gebenedeiet,
Der uns selber hat gespeiset
Mit seinem Fleische und mit seinem Blute;
Das gieb uns, Herr Gott, zu gute!
          Kyrieleison!
Herr! durch deinen heiligen Leichnam,
Der von dein Mutter Maria kam,
Und das heilige Blut:
Hilf uns, Herr, aus aller Noth.
          Kyrieleison!

ii Der heilig Leichnam ist für uns gegeben
Zum Tod, dass wir dadurch leben.
Nicht grösser Güte konnt er uns geschenken,
Dabei wir sein solln gedenken.
          Kyrieleison!
Herr, dein Lieb so gross dich g'zwungen hat,
Dass dein Blut an uns gross Wunder that
Und bezahlt unser Schuld,
Dass uns Gott ist worden hold.
          Kyrieleison!

iii Gott geb uns Allen seiner Gnaden Segen,
Dass wir gehn auf seinen Wegen
In rechter Lieb und brüderlicher Treue,
Dass die Speis uns nicht gereue.
          Kyrieleison!
Herr, dein heilig Geist uns nimmer lass,
Der uns geb zu halten rechte Mass,
Dass dein arm Christenheit
Leb in Fried und Einigkeit.
          Kyrieleison!
          U.L.S. 271.

i Let God be blest, be praisèd, and be thankèd,
Who to us Himself hath granted
This His own flesh and blood to feed and save us!
May we take well what He gave us.
          O hear us, Saviour!
By Thy body dear, once dead in shame,
Lord, which from Thy mother, Mary, came,
And by Thy holy blood
Ease us, Lord, from all our load.
          O hear us, Saviour!

ii Thy holy body is for us laid lowly
Down in death, that we live holy;
No greater goodness He to us could render,
To make think of His love tender.
          O hear us, Saviour!
Lord, Thy love so great in Thee hath wrought
That Thy blood to us hath marvels brought,
Paid our debt's so great sum,
That God gracious is become.
          O hear us, Saviour!

iii God on us all His blessing free bestow now,
That in His ways we may go now!
Right-hearted love and broth'rly truth ensuing,
Never so His Supper ruing.
          O hear us, Saviour!
Let Thy Spirit never us forsake,
Let Him teach us the just way to take,
That Thy poor Christendom
Into peace and union come.
          O hear us, Saviour!
          Tr. George Macdonald.[1]

[1] *Exotics* (Lond. 1876), p. 105.

GOTTES SOHN IST KOMMEN

Hymn, by Johann Roh (Horn), in nine 6-line stanzas (1544). Melody, ' Ave ierarchia celestis et pia ', adapted originally (1531) to M. Weisse's ' Menschenkind, merk eben '.

123

i Gottes Sohn ist kommen
Uns allen zu frommen
Hie auf diese Erden
In armen Gebärden,
Dass er uns von Sünde
Freiet und entbinde.

ii Er kommt auch noch heute
Und lehret die Leute,
Wie sie sich von Sünden
Zur Buss sollen wenden,
Von Irrthum und Thorheit
Treten zu der Wahrheit.

v Die also bekleiben
Und beständig bleiben,
Dem Herren in allem
Trachten zu gefallen,
Die werden mit Freuden
Auch von hinnen scheiden.

ix Ei nu Herre Jesu,
Schick unser Herzen zu,
Dass wir, alle Stunden
Rechtgläubig erfunden,
Darinnen verscheiden
Zur ewigen Freuden !

i Once He came in blessing,
All our ills redressing,
Came in likeness lowly,
Son of God most holy,
Bore the Cross to save us,
Hope and freedom gave us.

ii Still He comes within us,
Still His voice would win us
From the sins that hurt us ;
Would to truth convert us
From our foolish errors,
Ere He comes in terrors.

v But through many a trial,
Deepest self-denial,
Long and brave endurance,
Must thou win assurance
That His own He makes thee
And no more forsakes thee !

ix He who thus endureth
Bright reward secureth ;
Come then, O Lord Jesus,
From our sins release us.
Let us here confess Thee,
Till in heaven we bless Thee.

U.L.S. 6.

Tr. Catherine Winkworth.[1]

[1] *Chorale Book for England* (Lond. 1865). No. 26.

GOTTLOB, ES GEHT NUNMEHR ZUM ENDE

Hymn, by Christian Weise, in seven 6-line stanzas (1682). Melody, anonymous (1769), improbably by Bach.

124

i Gottlob, es geht nunmehr zum Ende,
   Das meiste Schrecken ist vollbracht :
   Mein Jesus reicht mir schon die Hände,
   Mein Jesus, der mich selig macht :
   Drum lasst mich gehn, ich reise fort,
   Mein Jesus ist mein letztes Wort.

v Mein Jesus hat den Tod bezwungen,
   Als er am Kreuze selbst verschied,
   Da ward mein Tod zugleich verschlungen,
   Er ist mein Haupt, ich bin sein Glied :
   Was Jesus hat, das hab ich dort :
   Drum sei er auch mein letztes Wort.

vi Gedenkt mir nicht an eitle Sachen,
   Der Höchste sorget für die Welt :
   Befehlt es ihm, er wirds wohl machen,
   Das Licht und Recht den Platz behält :
   Gott wende Jammer, List und Mord
   Durch Jesum als mein letztes Wort.

vii Nun freuet euch, es geht zum Ende,
   Mein Jesus heisst der letzte Ruhm :
   Wie fröhlich klopf ich in die Hände,
   Wo bleibst du doch, mein Eigenthum ?
   Ach, Jesu ! Jesu ! sei mein Wort :
   Nun schweig ich still und fahre fort.

C. C. J. Bunsen.[1]

i Life's radiant sun to rest is sinking,
   Earth and its troubles distant fade ;
   Jesus invites me to His keeping,
   He Who hath man's salvation made.
   My course is set, I go with glee :
   Jesus, my Lord, is all to me.

v Jesus o'er death triumphant conquered,
   On the cruel Cross for mortals bled.
   So death's among my foes not numbered,
   For I'm Christ's member, He's my Head.
   All that is His to me He gives ;
   Wherefore my soul in Him believes.

vi Turned are my thoughts from earth's vain treasure,
   God hath me ever in His care ;
   Leave all to Him, to me He'll measure
   Bounty and grace so rich and rare.
   If I to Jesus only cling,
   He will my soul to glory bring.

vii Then be of cheer, the journey's over,
   The last and great reward's in sight !
   How joyous heaven shall I discover
   Where Thou, Lord, reignest, glorious, bright.
   Ah, Jesu, Jesu, Thou art mine :
   To Thee my soul do I resign.

Tr. C. S. T.

[1] *Gesang und Gebetbuch* (Hamburg, 1833). No. 904.

HAST DU DENN, JESU, DEIN ANGESICHT GÄNZLICH VERBORGEN

Hymn, by Ahasuerus Fritsch, in twelve 5-line stanzas (1668). Melody, anonymous (1665), to ' Hast du denn, Liebster, dein Angesicht gänzlich verborgen ': perhaps of secular origin.

125

i Hast du denn, Jesu, dein Angesicht gänzlich verborgen,
Dass ich der Stunde der Hülfe muss warten bis morgen ?
Wie lässt du doch,
Süsser Herr Jesu, mich noch
Stecken in Aengsten und Sorgen !

* vi Richte dich, Liebste, nach meinem Gefallen und gläube,
Dass ich dein Seelenfreund immer und ewig verbleibe,
Der dich ergötzt,
Und in den Himmel versetzt
Aus dem gemarterten Leibe.

ix Drauf will ich fröhlich von zeitlichen Leiden abscheiden,
Drauf will ich fröhlich gesegnen die irdischen Freuden,
Weil mir bewusst
Süsser Herr Jesu, die Lust,
Die mich im Himmel wird weiden.

Fischer-Tümpel.[1]

i Hast Thou, Lord Jesus, Thy countenance far withdrawn
from me ?
Must I forsaken lie in my strait sore longing for Thee ?
Why, Saviour dear,
Is not Thy loving help near ?
Why do I call on Thee vainly ?

vi ' Walk in My ways and commandments, belovèd son.
Surely
Thou can'st on Me rely thy Friend in heaven to be alway.
Thou'rt My delight,
And evermore in My sight
Shalt thou in glory shine purely.'

ix So will I henceforth my earthly woes cheerfully bear
them,
And with the joys of hereafter resignèd compare them.
Wait me above
Jesus and His sweetest love,
Where with th' elect shall I share them.

Tr. C. S. T.

[1] Bd. v. No. 569.

HAST DU DENN, JESU, DEIN ANGESICHT GÄNZLICH VERBORGEN

Hymn, by Joachim Neander, in five 5-line stanzas (1680). Melody, anonymous (1665), to 'Hast du denn, Liebster, dein Angesicht gänzlich verborgen': perhaps of secular origin.

126

[Trumpets I, II, III, and Timpani obbligati]

i Lobe den Herren, den mächtigen König der Ehren,
Meine geliebete Seele ; das ist mein Begehren.
Kommet zu Hauf !
Psalter und Harfe wacht auf !
Lasset den Lobgesang hören !

ii Lobe den Herren, der alles so herrlich regieret,
Der dich auf Adelers Fittigen sicher geführet,
Der dich erhält,
Wie es dir selber gefällt :
Hast du nicht dieses verspüret ?

* iv Lobe den Herren, der deinen Stand sichtbar gesegnet,
Der aus dem Himmel mit Strömen der Liebe geregnet !
Denke daran,
Was der Allmächtige kann,
Der dir mit Liebe begegnet.

*v Lobe den Herren, was in mir ist, lobe den Namen !
Alles was Odem hat, lobe mit Abrahams Samen !
Er ist dein Licht.
Seele, vergiss es ja nicht !
Lobende schliesse mit Amen !

U.L.S. 687.

i Praise Him, the Highest, Omnipotent, King of creation !
Praise Him for ever, my spirit, thy Hope of salvation !
Come to His courts,
Songs and sweet music discourse,
Swelling in deep adoration !

ii Praise to the Highest, Who all things so wondrously
guideth,
Shelters thee under His wing and thy comfort provideth,
Holds thee upright,
Making thee glad in His sight !
Ever His goodness abideth.

iv Praise to the Highest, Who makes thee His own and thee
blesseth,
Looks down from heaven and showers of His love on thee
presseth !
Know ye all then,
Blessing He show'reth on him
Who His high favour possesseth !

v Praise ye the Highest, all people now living adore Him !
All that hath life and breath hasten with praises before
Him !
He is our Light,
Come then, make Him your delight,
Raising a jubilant Amen !

Tr. C. S. T.

HEILIG, HEILIG, HEILIG

Sanctus, Dominus Deus Sabaoth. Melody, anonymous (1726), reminiscent of the plainsong (1557).

127

Sanc - tus, sanc - tus, sanc - tus, Do - minus De - us Sa - ba -
Ho - ly, ho - ly, ho - ly, Lord God of Sa - ba -
Hei - lig, hei - lig, hei - lig bist du Herr Gott Ze - ba -

oth! Ple - ni sunt coe - li glo - ri - a tu - a.
oth! All the earth is full of Thy glo - ry.
oth! Al - le Lan - de sind sei - ner Eh - re voll.

O - san - na in ex - cel - sis. Bene - dic - tus qui ve - nit in
Ho - san - na in the high - est. Blessed is He that co - meth in
Ho - si - an - na in der Hö - he. Ge - lobt sei der da kommt im

no - mine Do - mi - ni. O - san - na in ex - cel - sis!
the name of the Lord. Ho - san - na in the high - est.
Na - men des Herrn. Ho - si - an - na in der Hö - he!

HELFT MIR GOTTS GÜTE PREISEN

Hymn, by Paul Eber, in six 8-line stanzas (c. 1580). Melody, the secular 'Ich ging einmal spazieren' (1569).

128

i Helft mir Gotts Güte preisen,
  Ihr lieben Kindelein,
  Mit G'sang und andre Weisen
  Ihm allzeit dankbar sein,
  Vornehmlich zu der Zeit,
  Da sich das Jahr thut enden,
  Die Sonn sich zu uns wenden,
  Das neu Jahr ist nicht weit.

iv Er hat unser verschonet
  Aus väterlicher Gnad;
  Wenn er sonst hätt belohnet
  All unser Missethat
  Mit gleicher Straf und Pein;
  Wir wären längst gestorben,
  In mancher Noth verdorben,
  Die wir voll Sünden sein.

*vi All solch dein Güt wir preisen,
  Vater ins Himmels Thron,
  Die du uns thust beweisen
  Durch Christum deinen Sohn,
  Und bitten ferner dich:
  Gib uns ein friedlichs Jahre,
  Vor allem Leid bewahre
  Und nähr uns mildiglich!

i Come, let us all with fervour,
  On whom heaven's mercies shine,
  To our supreme Preserver
  In tuneful praises join.
  Another year is gone,
  Of which the tender mercies
  Each pious heart rehearses
  Demand a grateful song.

iv 'Tis His eternal kindness
  That spares us from the rod.
  Though long our wilful blindness
  Has sore provoked our God
  To pour His vengeance down;
  Yet still His grace provides us,
  And still His mercy hides us
  From His own dreadful frown.

vi To Christ our peace is owing;
  Through Him Thou art appeased.
  Through Him Thy love's still flowing:
  O wilt Thou then be pleased,
  Through Christ, Thy grace to send,
  In all its strength and beauty,
  To keep us in our duty,
  Till these frail days shall end!

U.L.S. 68.
                                     Tr. John Christian Jacobi.[1]
[1] Psalmodia Germanica (Ed. 1765), p. 10.

HELFT MIR GOTTS GÜTE PREISEN

Hymn, by Paul Eber, in six 8-line stanzas (c. 1580). Melody, the secular ' Ich ging einmal spazieren' (1569).

129

i Helft mir Gotts Güte preisen,
  Ihr lieben Kindelein,
  Mit G'sang und andre Weisen
  Ihm allzeit dankbar sein,
  Vornehmlich zu der Zeit,
  Da sich das Jahr thut enden,
  Die Sonn sich zu uns wenden,
  Das neu Jahr ist nicht weit.

v Nach Vaters Art und Treuen
  Er uns so gnädig ist,
  Wenn wir die Sünd bereuen
  Glauben an Jesum Christ
  Herzlich ohn Heuchelei :
  Thut er all Sünd vergeben,
  Lindert die Straf daneben,
  Steht uns in Nöthen bei !

* vi All solch dein Güt wir preisen,
  Vater ins Himmels Thron,
  Die du uns thust beweisen
  Durch Christum deinen Sohn,
  Und bitten ferner dich :
  Gieb uns ein friedlichs Jahre,
  Vor allem Leid bewahre
  Und nähr uns mildiglich !

i Come, let us all with fervour,
  On whom heaven's mercies shine,
  To our supreme Preserver
  In tuneful praises join.
  Another year is gone,
  Of which the tender mercies
  Each pious heart rehearses
  Demand a grateful song.

v The Source of all compassion
  Pities our feeble frame,
  When, turning from transgression,
  We come in Jesu's name
  Before His holy face.
  Then every sinful motion
  Is cast into the ocean
  Of never failing grace.

vi These mercies we're adoring,
  O Lord Who dwell'st above,
  Which Thou hast been restoring
  Through Christ the Son of Love,
  In Whom Thou wilt be pleased
  To grant this year ensuing
  Grace, constant in well-doing,
  Till we're from sin released.

U.L.S. 68.

Tr. John Christian Jacobi.[1]

[1] *Psalmodia Germanica* (Ed. (1722), p. 11.

HELFT MIR GOTTS GÜTE PREISEN

Hymn, by Paul Gerhardt, in twelve 8-line stanzas (1653). Melody, the secular ' Ich ging einmal spazieren' (1569).

130

i Zeuch ein zu deinen Thoren,
  Sei meines Herzens Gast,
  Der du, da ich geboren,
  Mich neu geboren hast :
  O hochgeliebter Geist
  Des Vaters und des Sohnes,
  Mit beiden gleiches Thrones,
  Mit beiden gleich gepreist !

* v Du bist ein Geist, der lehret,
  Wie man recht beten soll :
  Dein Beten wird erhöret,
  Dein Singen klinget wohl ;
  Es steigt zum Himmel an,
  Es steigt und lässt nicht abe,
  Bis der geholfen habe,
  Der allen helfen kann.

vi Du bist ein Geist der Freuden,
  Vom Trauern hältst du nicht,
  Erleuchtest uns im Leiden
  Mit deines Trostes Licht.
  Ach ja, wie manches mal
  Hast du mit süssen Worten
  Mir aufgethan die Pforten
  Zum güldnen Freudensaal.

xii Richt unser ganzes Leben
  Allzeit nach deinem Sinn,
  Und wenn wirs sollen geben
  Ins Todes Hände hin,
  Wenns mit uns hie wird aus :
  So hilf uns fröhlich sterben
  Und nach dem Tod ererben
  Des ewgen Lebens Haus !

i Come, enter to Thy dwelling,
  And be my heart's sweet guest !
  For Thou with love excelling
  My soul new quickened hast.
  O God the Holy Ghost,
  To Thee and to the Father,
  And God the Son, we offer
  The praise Thou prizest most.

v Now teach our hearts, O Spirit,
  How rightly we should pray !
  So shall our prayers have merit,
  Our songs ascend alway,
  And mount to heavèn's throne,
  To where the Father reigneth,
  Who never prayer disdaineth,
  Who giveth help alone.

vi Of joy Thou art the giver,
  Before Thee sorrow flies.
  Sweet comfort send'st Thou ever
  In life's dark miseries.
  Ah yes, how much enthrals
  Thy Word in accents dearest,
  Wherewith to man Thou callest
  To enter heavèn's halls.

xii And so, while life is in us,
  E'er keep us in Thy love,
  And when death comes to call us,
  Still guard us from above !
  So shall we win with Thee
  Through death a glorious treasure,
  Full joy beyond all measure
  In God's eternity.

U.L.S. 184.

Tr. C. S. T.

HERR CHRIST, DER EINIG GOTTS SOHN

Hymn, by Elisabethe Cruciger, in five 7-line stanzas (1524). Melody, anonymous (1524).

131

i Herr Christ, der einig Gotts Sohn,
  Vaters in Ewigkeit,
  Aus seinem Herz'n entsprossen,
  Gleich wie geschrieben steht :
  Er ist der Morgensterne,
  Sein Glanze streckt er ferne
  Vor andern Sternen klar.

ii Für uns ein Mensch geboren
   Im letzten Theil der Zeit,
   Der Mutter unverloren
   Ihr jungfräulich Keuschheit,
   Den Tod für uns zerbrochen,
   Den Himmel aufgeschlossen,
   Das Leben wiederbracht.

* v Ertödt uns durch dein Güte,
    Erweck uns durch dein Gnad ;
    Den alten Menschen kränke,
    Dass der neu leben mag,
    Wohl hie auf dieser Erden
    Den Sinn und all Begehrden
    Und G'danken habn zu dir.

i Lord Christ, of God Supernal
  The one belovèd Son,
  Of very God eternal
  Before that time began,
  Thou art the Star of morning
  Whose beams declare the dawning
  When other stars must pale.

ii Thou deign'st to dwell among us !
   Now, at th' appointed time,
   Thou com'st, O mystery wondrous,
   Born of a Virgin's womb !
   To conquer death Thou comest,
   The gates of heaven wide op'nest,
   And life to man dost give.

v Awake us, Lord, and hasten,
  Thy Holy Spirit give,
  The old man in us chasten
  That our new man may live !
  So shall we, now and alway,
  With gladsome hearts bethank Thee
  Who hast us favour shown.

U.L.S. 37.

Tr. C. S. T.

HERR CHRIST, DER EINIG GOTTS SOHN

Hymn, by Elisabethe Cruciger, in five 7-line stanzas (1524). Melody anonymous (1524).

132

i Herr Christ, der einig Gotts Sohn,
　Vaters in Ewigkeit,
　Aus seinem Herz'n entsprossen,
　Gleich wie geschrieben steht :
　Er ist der Morgensterne,
　Sein Glanze streckt er ferne
　Vor andern Sternen klar.

iii Lass uns in deiner Liebe
　Und Kenntniss nehmen zu,
　Dass wir im Glauben bleiben,
　Und dienen im Geist so,
　Dass wir hie mögen schmecken
　Dein Süssigkeit im Herzen
　Und dürsten stets nach dir.

* v Ertödt uns durch dein Güte,
　Erweck uns durch dein Gnad ;
　Den alten Menschen kränke,
　Dass der neu leben mag,
　Wohl hie auf dieser Erden
　Den Sinn und all Begehrden
　Und G'danken habn zu dir.

i Lord Christ, of God Supernal
　The One belovèd Son,
　Of very God eternal
　Before that time began,
　Thou art the Star of morning
　Whose beams declare the dawning
　When other stars must pale.

iii Upon Thy love relying,
　And on Thy knowledge stayed,
　May we in faith keep striving,
　Our service to Thee paid !
　So shall we taste Thy sweetness,
　Thy love in its completeness,
　And in Thee live alone.

v Awake us, Lord, and hasten,
　Thy Holy Spirit give,
　The old man in us chasten
　That our new man may live !
　So shall we, now and alway,
　With gladsome hearts bethank Thee
　Who hast us favour shown.

U.L.S. 37.

Tr. C. S. T,

HERR GOTT, DICH LOBEN ALLE WIR

Hymn, by Paul Eber, trans. of Philipp Melanchthon's 'Dicimus grates tibi', in thirteen 4-line stanzas (c 1554).
Melody, Louis Bourgeois' 'Or sus, serviteurs du Seigneur' (1551): Old Hundredth.

133

Dicimus grates tibi.

i Herr Gott, dich loben alle wir,
  Und sollen billig danken dir
  Für dein Geschöpf der Engel schon,
  Die um dich schweben in deim Thron.

ii Sie glänzen hell und leuchten klar
   Und sehen dich ganz offenbar :
   Dein Stimm sie hören allezeit
   Und sind voll göttlicher Weisheit.

xi Darum wir billig loben dich
   Und danken dir, Gott, ewiglich,
   Wie auch der lieben Engel Schaar
   Dich preisen heut und immerdar.

xii Und bitten dich : wollst allezeit
    Dieselben heissen sein bereit,
    Zu schützen deine kleine Heerd,
    So hält dein göttlichs Wort in Werth.

U.L.S. 204.

Come praise ye all our mighty Lord,
Give thanks to Him and loud applaud,
For those bright hosts above the sky
Who round Him fly eternally !

ii How bright those glorious beings shine !
   They see and know His great design,
   They hear His voice and do His will,
   Who with His wisdom them doth fill.

xi We praise Thee, Lord, and Thee adore,
   We thank Thee now and evermore,
   Whose own dread angels swell the song
   That through the ages rolls along.

xii O may that bright angelic band
    Fulfil for ever Thy command,
    And help all people here on earth
    Thy Word to prize at highest worth !

Tr. C. S. T.

HERR GOTT, DICH LOBEN ALLE WIR

Hymn, by (?) William Kethe, in four 4-line stanzas (1560-1). Melody, Louis Bourgeois' ' Or sus, serviteurs du Seigneur ' (1551):
Old Hundredth.

[Trumpets I, II, III, and Timpani obbligati]   *Psalm c.*

i All people that on earth do dwell,
  Sing to the Lord with cheerful voice,
  Him serve with fear, His praise forth tell,
  Come ye before Him and rejoice.

ii The Lord ye know is God indeed,
  Without our aid He did us make,
  We are His folk, He doth us feed,
  And for His sheep He doth us take.

iii O enter then His gates with praise,
  Approach with joy His courts unto ;
  Praise, laud, and bless His name always,
  For it is seemly so to do.

iv For why ? the Lord our God is good,
  His mercy is for ever sure :
  His truth at all times firmly stood
  And shall from age to age endure.*

                             Catherine Winkworth.

* In Cantata 130 the melody is set to stanzas xi and xii of No. 133.

HERR GOTT, DICH LOBEN ALLE WIR

Hymn, by Paul Eber, trans. of Philipp Melanchthon's ' Dicimus grates tibi ', in thirteen 4-line stanzas (c. 1554). Melody, Louis Bourgeois' ' Or sus, serviteurs du Seigneur ' (1551): Old Hundredth.

Dicimus grates tibi.

i Herr Gott, dich loben alle wir,
   Und sollen billig danken dir
   Für dein Geschöpf der Engel schon,
   Die um dich schweben in deim Thron.

vii Indess wachet der Engel Schaar,
   Die Christo folgen immerdar,
   Und schützet deine Christenheit,
   Wehret des Teufels Listigkeit.

ix Der Massen auch des Feuers Glut
   Verschont und keinen Schaden thut
   Den Knaben in der heissen Flamm :
   Der Engel ihn zu Hilfe kam.

x Also schützt Gott noch heut bei Tag
   Vorm Uebel und vor mancher Plag
   Uns durch die lieben Engelein,
   Die uns zu Wächtern geben sein.

i To God let all the human race
   Bring humble worship mixed with grace,
   Who makes His love and wisdom known
   By angels that surround His throne.

vii These angels, whom Thy breath inspires,
   Thy ministers are, flaming fires ;
   And swift as thought their armies move
   To tear Thy vengeance or Thy love.

ix What did the three men in the flame,
   As soon their guardian angel came ?
   Did not the ov'n's devouring fire
   Resound the notes of heavenly choir ?

x Thus God defends us day by day
   From many mischiefs in our way,
   By angels which do always keep
   A watchful eye whene'er we sleep.

U.L.S. 204.

Tr. John Christian Jacobi.[1]

[1] *Psalmodia Germanica* (Lond. 1722), p. 28.

HERR GOTT, DICH LOBEN ALLE WIR

Hymn, by Bodo von Hodenberg, in fifteen 4-line stanzas (1646). Melody, Louis Bourgeois' ' Or sus, serviteurs du Seigneur'
(1551): Old Hundredth.

i Vor deinen Thron tret ich hiemit,
　O Gott, und dich demüthig bitt :
　Wend dein genädig Angesicht
　Von mir blutarmen Sünder nicht !

ii Du hast mich, o Gott Vater mild,
　Gemacht nach deinem Ebenbild ;
　In dir web, schweb, und lebe ich :
　Vergehen müsst ich ohne dich.

v Gott Sohn, du hast mich durch dein Blut
　Erlöset von der Höllenglut,
　Das schwer Gesetz für mich erfüllt,
　Damit des Vaters Zorn gestillt.

viii Gott Heilger Geist, du höchste Kraft,
　Dess Gnade in mir alles schafft :
　Ist etwas Guts am Leben mein,
　So ist es wahrlich lauter dein.

xi Drum danke ich mit Herz und Mund
　Dir, Gott, in dieser { Morgen- / Abend - } Stund
　Für alle Güte, Treu und Gnad,
　Die meine Seel empfangen hat.

i Before Thy throne, my God, I stand,
　Myself, my all, are in Thy hand ;
　O show me Thine approving face,
　Nor from me now withhold Thy grace.

ii O God, my Father, Thou hast laid
　Thy likeness on me, whom Thou'st made ;
　In Thee is all my being here,
　With Thee beside me nought I fear.

v Thou Son of God, through Thy dear blood
　Have I escaped from Hell's dark flood :
　'Tis Thou hast paid the price decreed,
　And of God's wrath my soul relieved.

viii O Holy Spirit, power divine,
　Fill full this erring heart of mine !
　Of good repute whate'er there be
　In me is found, it comes from Thee.

xi Wherefore I thank Thee, heavenly Three,
　Now { morning's sunlight / evening's shadows } fall(s) on me,
　For all the grace Thou dost bestow,
　For all the joy my soul doth know

U.L.S. 458.

Tr. C. S. T.

HERR GOTT, DICH LOBEN WIR

A free version of ' Te Deum laudamus ', by Martin Luther, in 52 lines for antiphonal singing (1529). Melody, a reconstruction (1529 ?) of the Latin plainsong.

HERR GOTT, DICH LOBEN WIR

[13]Thy god-like might and lord-ship go [14]wide o-ver heav'n and earth be-low.
[15]To Thee the ho-ly Twelve do call, [16]and Thy be-lov-ed pro-phets all.
[17]The pre-cious mar-tyrs with one voice [18]praise Thee, O Lord, with migh-ty noise.
[19]From all Thy wor-thy Chris-ten-dom [20]Thy prai-ses ev'-ry day do come.
[21]Thee, God, the Fa-ther, on heav'n's throne, [22]Thy true and on-ly got-ten Son,
[23]The Ho-ly Com-for-ter al-ways, [24]with ser-vice true they thank and praise.

[13]Dein gött-lich Macht und Herr-lich-keit [14]geht ü-ber Himm'l und Er-den weit.
[15]Der hei-li-gen zwölf Bo-ten Zahl [16]und die lie-ben Pro-phe-ten all,
[17]Die theu-ren Märt-rer all-zu-mal [18]lo-ben dich, Herr, mit gro-ssem Schall.
[19]Die gan-ze wer-the Christen-heit [20]rühmt dich auf Er-den al-le-zeit.
[21]Dich, Gott Va-ter im höchsten Thron, [22]dei-nen rech-ten und ein-gen Sohn,
[23]Den heil-gen Geist und Tröster werth [24]mit rech-tem Dienst sie lobt und ehrt.

[25]Thou, King of glo-ry, Christ, a-lone [26]the Fa-ther's One e-ter-nal Son,
[27]Did'st not the vir-gin's womb de-spise, [28]that so the hu-man race might rise;
[29]Thou on the might of death did'st tread, [30]and Chris-tians all to heaven hast led.
[31]Thou sit-test now at God's right hand, [32]with ho-nour in Thy Fa-ther's land.
[33]The hour shall come when Thou shalt yet [34]judge of the dead and li-ving sit.
[35]Now to Thy ser-vants help af-ford, [36]ran-somed with Thy dear blood, O Lord.

[25]Du Kön'g der Eh-ren, Je-su Christ, [26]Gott Va-ters ew-ger Sohn du bist;
[27]Der Jung-frau Leib nicht hast verschmäht, [28]zu'r lö-sen das mensch-lich Geschlecht;
[29]Du hast dem Tod zer-stört sein Macht [30]und all Chri-sten zum Him-mel bracht;
[31]Du sitzt zur Rech-ten Got-tes gleich [32]mit al-ler Ehr ins Va-ters Reich;
[33]Ein Rich-ter du zu-künf-tig bist [34]Al-les, das todt und le-bend ist.
[35]Nun hilf uns, Herr, den Die-nern dein, [36]die mit deim Blut er-lö-set sein.

[37]Let us in hea-ven have our dole, [38]and with the ho-ly e'er be whole. [39]Thy

[37]Lass uns im Him-mel ha-ben Theil [38]mit den Heil-gen am ew-gen Heil! [39]Hilf

folk, Lord Jes - us Christ, ad - vance, [40]and bless Thine own in - her - i - tance. [41]Them

dei - nem Volk, Herr Je - su Christ, [40]und seg - ne, was dein Erb - theil ist; [41]Wart'

watch and ward, Lord, ev' - ry day. [42]E - ter - nal - ly them raise, we pray. [43]Dai -

und pfleg ihr zu al - ler Zeit, [42]und heb sie hoch in E - wig - keit. [43]Täg -

- ly, Lord God, we ho - nour Thee, [44]and praise Thy name con - tin - ual - ly

- lich, Herr Gott, wir lo - ben dich, [44]und ehrn dein Na - men ste - tig - lich.

[45]O God of truth, keep us this day [46]from ev' - ry sin and e - vil way.
[47]Be gra - cious to us, Lord, we plead, [48]be gra - cious to us in all need.
[49]Show un - to us Thy pi - ty'ng grace, [50]for all our hope in Thee we place.

[45]Be - hüt uns heut, o treu - er Gott, [46]vor al - ler Sünd und Mis - se - that,
[47]Sei gnä - dig uns, o Her - re Gott, [48]sei gnä - dig uns in al - ler Noth!
[49]Zeig uns dei - ne Barm - her - zig - keit, [50]wie un - ser Hoffnung zu dir steht.

[51]Dear Lord, our hope is in Thy name; [52]let us be ne - ver

[51]Auf dich hof - fen wir, lie - ber Herr, [52]in Schan - den lass uns

put to shame. [2]

nim - mer - mehr. A - - - - - - - - - - - men. [1]

HERR GOTT, DICH LOBEN WIR

A free version of 'Te Deum laudamus', by Martin Luther, in 52 lines for antiphonal singing (1529). Melody, a reconstruction (1529?) of the Latin plainsong.

138

[39]Thy folk, Lord Jesus Christ, advance, [40]and bless Thine own inheritance. [41]Them watch and ward, Lord, ev'ry day. [42]Eternally them raise, we pray.[2]

★ [39]Hilf deinem Volk, Herr Jesu Christ, [40]und segne, was dein Erbtheil ist. [41]Wart und pfleg ihr zu aller Zeit, [42]und heb sie hoch in Ewigkeit. Amen.[1]

[1] *U.L.S.* 189.   [2] *Tr. George Macdonald, 'Exotics' (Lond. 1876), p. 112.*

HERR GOTT, DICH LOBEN WIR

A free version of ' Te Deum laudamus ', by Martin Luther, in 52 lines for antiphonal singing (1529). Melody, a reconstruction (1529?) of the Latin plainsong.

138ᵃ

35Now to Thy ser-vants help af-ford, 36ransomed with Thy dear blood, O Lord. 37Let

★ 35Nun hilf uns, Herr, den Die-nern dein, 36die mit deim Blut er - lö - set sein. 37Lass

us in heav - en have our dole, 38and with the ho - ly e'er be whole. 39Thy

uns im Him-mel ha - ben Theil 38mit den Heil - gen am ew - gen Heil. 39Hilf

folk, Lord Je - sus Christ, ad-vance, 40and bless Thine own in - he - ri - tance. 41Them

dei - nem Volk, Herr Je - su Christ, 40und seg - ne, was dein Erb-theil ist. 41Wart

watch and ward, Lord, ev' - ry day. 42E - ter - nal - ly them raise, we pray.(¹)

und pfleg ihr zu al - ler Zeit, 42und heb sie hoch in E - wig-keit.(²)

¹ *U.L.S.* 189.

²*Tr. George Macdonald, 'Exotics' (Lond. 1876), p. 112.*

HERR, ICH DENK AN JENE ZEIT

Hymn, by Georg Mylius, in seven 7-line stanzas (1640). *Melody, originally* (1566) *set to P. Herbert's ' Lob sei dir, gütiger Gott'*

i Herr, ich denk an jene Zeit,
Wenn ich diesem kurzen Leben
Wegen meiner Sterblichkeit
Gute Nacht soll geben,
Wenn ich werd auf dein Gebot
Durch den Tod
Alles überstreben.

v Dieser Leib und dies Gebein,
Ob ich noch so ängstlich zage,
Muss der Würmer Frass doch sein
Über wenig Tage.
Alles ist der Schlangen Raub,
Asch und Staub,
Was ich an mir trage.

vi Jesu, steh alsdann mir bei,
Lass mich Armen nicht verderben ;
Mach mich aller Aengsten frei
Durch dein Blut und Sterben.
Tröste mich durch deinen Geist,
Der mich heisst
Gottes Kind und Erben.

vii Hilf, dass ich dies Pilger-Land,
Dieses eitle Thun mög hassen,
Und mir recht den Himmels-Stand
Im Gemüte fassen.
Dann will ich in Fried und Wonn
Hie davon
Und die Welt verlassen.

i Lord, at all times doth my soul,
On this mortal life reflecting,
Mid the hours that graveward roll,
Think on death's swift coming ;
When the summons dread must call,
And a pall
Cover all man's doing.

v Comes the day when man's poor frame,
Silent to the tomb descending,
Food for worms is given, his fame
Perished past all mending.
Satan's prey must he become,
Meet his doom,
None from it escaping.

vi Jesu, save my soul from loss,
In my anguish never leave me !
Save me by the blessèd Cross
That did once redeem me !
In Thy pity look on me
Lovingly !
God His son hath called me.

vii Help me turn my thoughts away
From this life wherein I journey,
And toward heavèn's gates alway
Face me fair, serenely !
So shall I, above with Thee,
Joyfully
Know the joy awaits me.

Fischer-Tümpel.[1]

Tr. C. S. T.

[1] Bd. iii. No. 30.

HERR, ICH HABE MISSGEHANDELT

Hymn, by Johann Franck, in eight 6-line stanzas (1649). Melody, by Johann Crüger (1649).

140

i Herr, ich habe missgehandelt ;
  Ja, mich drückt der Sünden Last :
  Ich bin nicht den Weg gewandelt,
  Den du mir gezeiget hast ;
  Und jetzt wollt ich gern aus Schrecken
  Mich vor deinem Zorn verstecken.

ii Doch, wie könnt ich dir entfliehen ?
  Du wirst allenthalben sein.
  Wollt ich über See gleich ziehen,
  Stieg ich in die Gruft hinein,
  Hätt ich Flügel gleich den Winden :
  Gleichwohl würdest du mich finden.

iii Drum ich muss es nur bekennen :
  Herr, ich habe missgethan ;
  Darf mich nicht dein Kind mehr nennen :
  Ach, nimm mich zu Gnaden an !
  Lass die Menge meiner Sünden
  Deinen Zorn nicht gar entzünden.

viii Dir will ich die Last aufbinden :
  Wirf sie in die tiefste See ;
  Wasche mich von meinen Sünden,
  Mache mich so weiss wie Schnee.
  Lass dein guten Geist mich treiben,
  Einzig stets bei dir zu bleiben.

i Lord, to Thee I make confession,
  I have sinned and gone astray,
  I have multiplied transgression,
  Chosen for myself my way :
  Forced at last to see my errors,
  Lord, I tremble at Thy terrors.

ii But from Thee how can I hide me ;
  Thou, O God, art everywhere.
  Refuge from Thee is denied me,
  Or by land, or sea, or air.
  Nor death's darkness can enfold me
  So that Thou should'st not behold me.

iii Yet, though conscience' voice appal me,
  Father, I will seek Thy face ;
  Though Thy child I dare not call me,
  Yet admit me to Thy grace.
  Do not for my sins forsake me,
  Let not yet Thy wrath o'ertake me.

viii Then on Thee I cast my burden,
  Sink it in the depths below !
  Let me feel Thy inner pardon,
  Wash me, make me white as snow.
  Let Thy Spirit leave me never,
  Make me only Thine for ever !

U.L.S. 371.

Tr. Catherine Winkworth.[1]

[1] *Chorale Book for England* (Lond. 1865), No. 44.

HERR, ICH HABE MISSGEHANDELT

Hymn, by Johann Franck, in eight 6-line stanzas (1649). Melody, by Johann Crüger (1649).

141

i Herr, ich habe missgehandelt;
Ja, mich drückt der Sünden Last :
Ich bin nicht den Weg gewandelt,
Den du mir gezeiget hast ;
Und jetzt wollt ich gern aus Schrecken
Mich vor deinem Zorn verstecken.

ii Doch, wie könnt ich dir entfliehen ?
Du wirst allenthalben sein.
Wollt ich über See gleich ziehen,
Stieg ich in die Gruft hinein,
Hätt ich Flügel gleich den Winden :
Gleichwohl würdest du mich finden.

vii Jedoch, Christe, deine Beulen,
Ja ein einzig Tröpflein Blut :
Das kann meine Wunden heilen,
Löschen meiner Sünden Glut.
Drum will ich, mein Angst zu stillen,
Mich in deine Wunden hüllen.

viii Dir will ich die Last aufbinden :
Wirf sie in die tiefste See ;
Wasche mich von meinen Sünden,
Mache mich so weiss wie Schnee.
Lass dein guten Geist mich treiben,
Einzig stets bei dir zu bleiben.

U.L.S. 371

i Like a wayward sheep and wandering
From God's path I've gone astray ;
Little on His counsels pondering,
Still I follow evil's way.
Lord, to Thee I own my errors
And expect Thy judgment's terrors.

ii Lord, from Thee there is no hiding,
Thou can'st see me near and far,
Whether on this earth abiding,
Or remote as distant star.
Had I wings, in flight to hover,
Still would'st Thou my sin discover.

vii But Thy Son once died to save me,
On the Cross gave up His life,
In His precious blood did lave me,
Purged me clean of sin and strife.
He who in the tomb did languish
Hath redeemed me by His anguish.

viii Lord, on Thee I lay my burden ;
See, its weight no more I know !
Of Thy grace, accord me pardon,
Wash me, cleanse me, pure as snow !
Holy Spirit, guard me ever ;
From my side depart Thou never !

Tr. C. S. T.

HERR JESU CHRIST, DICH ZU UNS WEND

Hymn, by (?) Wilhelm II of Sachsen-Weimar, in four 4-line stanzas (1651). Melody, anonymous (1648).

142

i Herr Jesu Christ, dich zu uns wend,
  Dein Heilgen Geist du zu uns send ;
  Mit Lieb und Gnad er uns regier
  Und uns den Weg zur Wahrheit führ.

ii Thu auf den Mund zum Lobe dein,
   Bereit das Herz zur Andacht fein ;
   Den Glauben mehr, stärk den Verstand,
   Dass uns dein Nam werd wohl bekannt ;

iii Bis wir singen mit Gottes Heer :
    Heilig, heilig ist Gott der Herr !
    Und schauen dich von Angesicht
    In ewgem Heil und selgem Licht.

iv Ehr sei dem Vater und dem Sohn,
   Dem Heilgen Geist in einem Thron ;
   Der heiligen Dreifaltigkeit
   Sei Lob und Preis in Ewigkeit !

U.L.S. 225.

i Lord Jesus Christ, be present now !
  And let Thy Holy Spirit bow
  All hearts in love and fear to-day,
  To hear the truth and keep Thy way.

ii O make our lips to sing Thy praise,
   Our hearts in true devotion raise,
   Enlarge our faith, increase our light,
   That we may know Thy name aright :

iii Until we join the host that cry
    ' Holy, holy art Thou Most High,'
    And mid the light of that blest place
    Shall gaze upon Thee face to face.

iv Glory to God, the Father, Son,
   And Holy Spirit, Three in One !
   To Thee, O blessèd Trinity,
   Be praise throughout eternity !

Tr. Catherine Winkworth.[1]

[1] *Chorale Book for England* (Lond. 1865), No. 13.

HERR JESU CHRIST, DU HAST BEREIT

Hymn, by Samuel Kinner, in eight 7-line stanzas (1638). Melody, in MS. (1742).

143

i Herr Jesu Christ, du hast bereit
  Für unsre matten Seelen
  Dein Leib und Blut zur Liebsmahlzeit
  Zu Gästen uns zu wählen,
  Wir klagen unsre Sündenlast,
  Drum kommen wir zu dir zu Gast,
  Und suchen Rath und Hülfe.

ii Du sprichst : Nehmt hin, das ist mein Leib,
  Den sollet ihr hier essen,
  Trinckt mein Blut, der ich bei euch bleib,
  Ihr sollt mein nicht vergessen.
  Du hasts geredt, drum ist es wahr,
  Du bist allmächtig, auch so gar,
  Dass dir kein Ding unmöglich.

iv Ich glaub, o lieber Herr ! ich glaub,
  Hilf meinem schwachen Glauben !
  Ich bin doch nichts, als Asch und Staub,
  Dein Wort lass mir nicht rauben !
  Dein Wort, die Tauf, und Abendmahl
  Tröst mich in diesem Jammerthal.
  Da liegt mein Schatz begraben.

i Lord Jesus Christ, Thou hast in love
  Thy Flesh and Blood preparèd,
  And to Thy Table from above
  Thy guests on earth hast callèd.
  Our sins are great and manifold,
  But with Thy favour we are bold
  To seek Thy help and blessing.

ii Thou say'st : ' This is My Flesh ; take eat
  My Body for you given :
  And this My Blood, your drink and meat,
  Must prove Me not forgotten.'
  So hast Thou said : I know it true,
  It is Thy Word that sayeth so ;
  Thy might transcends our knowing.

iv I do believe Thy Word, O Lord,
  Help Thou mine unbelieving !
  Thy saving grace to me afford ;
  Without it I am nothing.
  Thy Holy Word and Sacrament
  Can every evil thing prevent :
  Of them no man can rob me.

P. Wagner.[1]

Tr. C. S. T.

[1] *Vollständiges Gesangbuch* (Leipzig, 1697). Bd. v. 950.

HERR JESU CHRIST, DU HÖCHSTES GUT

Hymn, by Bartholomäus Ringwaldt, in eight 7-line stansas (1588). Melody, anonymous (1593).

i Herr Jesu Christ, du höchstes Gut,
   Du Brunnquell aller Gnaden,
   Sieh, wie ich nach des Geistes Muth
   Mit Schmerzen bin beladen
   Und in mir hab die Pfeile viel,
   Die im Gewissen ohne Ziel
   Mich armen Sünder drücken.

ii Erbarm dich mein in solcher Last,
   Nimm sie aus meinem Herzen;
   Dieweil du sie gebüsset hast
   Am Holz mit Todesschmerzen:
   Auf dass ich nicht vor grossem Weh
   In meinen Sünden untergeh
   Und ewiglichen sterbe.

iv Aber dein heilsam Wort das macht
   Mit seinem süssen Singen,
   Dass mir das Herze wieder lacht
   Und schon beginnt zu springen;
   Dieweil es alle Gnad verheisst
   Denen, die mit zerknirschtem Geist
   Zu dir, o Jesu, kommen.

i Lord Jesus Christ, my sovereign good,
   Thou Fountain of salvation,
   Behold me bowed beneath the load
   Of sin and condemnation:
   My sins indeed are numberless;
   O Lord, regard my deep distress,
   Relieve my conscience guilty.

ii In pity look upon my need,
   Remove my sore oppression;
   Since Thou hast suffered in my stead,
   And paid for my transgression,
   Let me not yield to dark despair;
   A wounded spirit who can bear?
   O show me Thy salvation.

iv But Thy reviving Gospel-Word,
   Which leads me to salvation,
   Does joy unspeakable afford,
   And lasting consolation:
   It tells me Thou wilt not despise
   A broken heart, in sacrifice
   Upon Thine altar offered.

U.L.S. 372.

Tr. Anon.[1]

[1] *Moravian Hymn-Book* (Ed. 1877), No. 285.

HERR JESU CHRIST, DU HÖCHSTES GUT

Hymn, anonymous, in twelve 7-line stanzas (1620). Melody, anonymous (1593).

145

i Herr Jesu Christ, ich schrei zu dir
  Mit ganz betrübter Seele :
  Dein Allmacht lass erscheinen mir
  Und mich nicht also quäle.
  Viel grösser ist die Angst und Schmerz,
  So anficht und turbirt mein Herz,
  Als dass ich kann erzählen.

ii Herr Jesu Christ, erbarm dich mein
  Durch deine grosse Güte ;
  Mit Erquickung und Hülf erschein
  Meim traurigen Gemüthe,
  Welchs elendiglich wird geplagt
  Und, so du nicht hilfst, gar verzagt,
  Dieweil kein Trost kann finden.

* xii Herr Jesu Christ, einiger Trost,
  Zu dir will ich mich wenden ;
  Mein Herzleid ist dir wohl bewusst,
  Du kannst und wirst es enden.
  In deinem Willen seis gestellt,
  Machs, liebster Gott, wie dirs gefällt :
  Dein bin und will ich bleiben.

i Incline, O Lord, Thine ear to me,
  And heed my bitter crying !
  O let Thy favour shine on me,
  My grievous need supplying !
  The heavy woes that sore distress,
  And with their weight my soul oppress,
  Are more than I can number.

ii Lord Jesu Christ, O pity me,
  And show Thy loving kindness !
  Thy quick'ning help now send to me,
  My sufferings are endless !
  They press on me on every side
  And over me tormenting ride :
  Thy help alone can save me.

xii Lord Jesu Christ, man's surest Stay,
  Who comfort rare dispensest,
  My anguish sore is known to Thee,
  Alone 'tis Thou help sendest.
  But as Thou wilt, so let it be,
  In Thy sure wisdom deal with me ;
  Thine am I now and alway.

Fischer-Tümpel.[1]

Tr. C. S. T.

[1] Bd. i. No. 574.

HERR JESU CHRIST, DU HÖCHSTES GUT

Hymn, by Bartholomäus Ringwaldt, in eight 7-line stanzas (1588). Melody, anonymous (1593).

i Herr Jesu Christ, du höchstes Gut,
　Du Brunnquell aller Gnaden,
　Sieh, wie ich nach des Geistes Muth
　Mit Schmerzen bin beladen
　Und in mir hab die Pfeile viel,
　Die im Gewissen ohne Ziel
　Mich armen Sünder drücken.

v Und weil ich denn in meinem Sinn,
　Wie ich zuvor geklaget,
　Auch ein betrübter Sünder bin,
　Den sein Gewissen naget,
　Und wollte gern im Blute dein
　Von Sünden abgewaschen sein,
　Wie David und Manasse.

* viii Stärk mich mit deinem Freudengeist,
　Heil mich durch deine Wunden ;
　Wasch mich mit deinem Todesschweiss
　In meiner letzten Stunden :
　Und führ mich einst, wenn dirs gefällt,
　Im rechten Glauben aus der Welt
　Zu deinen Auserwählten.

U.L.S. 372.

i Lord Jesu Christ, pure Source of good,
　From Whom all grace proceedeth,
　Beneath sin's weight behold me bowed,
　My heart Thy pity needeth.
　With arrows sharp my soul is pierced,
　Accusing conscience, too, is vexed,
　And I, poor sinner, perish.

v Right sore my conscience doth reproach,
　My sins do hard beset me.
　How dare I to God's throne approach
　Or to my Judge submit me ?
　O, in Thy blood, Lord, wash me clean,
　However dark my sins have been,
　As David and Manasseh !

viii Fulfil me with Thy Spirit's glow,
　Have mercy, blessèd Saviour !
　O wash me, cleanse me, through and through,
　When death comes show me favour,
　And call me hence to Thy far home,
　To reign with Thee, blest Three in One,
　Among Thy saints for ever !

Tr. C. S. T.

HERR JESU CHRIST, DU HÖCHSTES GUT

Hymn, by Bartholomäus Ringwaldt, in eight 7-line stanzas (1588). Melody, anonymous (1593).

147

i Herr Jesu Christ, du höchstes Gut,
　Du Brunnquell aller Gnaden,
　Sieh, wie ich nach des Geistes Muth
　Mit Schmerzen bin beladen
　Und in mir hab die Pfeile viel,
　Die im Gewissen ohne Ziel
　Mich armen Sünder drücken.

vii O Herr, mein Gott ! vergieb mir doch
　Um deines Blutes willen,
　Und thu in mir das schwere Joch
　Der Uebertretung stillen ;
　Dass ich mein Seel zufrieden geb
　Und dir hinfort zu Ehren leb
　Mit kindlichem Gehorsam.

* viii Stärk mich mit deinem Freudengeist,
　Heil mich durch deine Wunden ;
　Wasch mich mit deinem Todesschweiss
　In meiner letzten Stunden :
　Und führ mich einst, wenn dirs gefällt,
　Im rechten Glauben aus der Welt
　Zu deinen Auserwählten.

i Lord Jesus Christ, my sovereign good,
　Thou Fountain of salvation,
　Behold me bowed beneath the load
　Of sin and condemnation :
　My sins indeed are numberless ;
　O Lord, regard my deep distress,
　Relieve my conscience guilty.

vii O pitying Lord, forgive me, pray,
　The sin Thy wrath's incurrèd,
　Now take its grievous load away
　Which hath me fast ensnarèd.
　So shall my heart find rest and peace,
　And in Thy praises never cease,
　Its gratitude forth telling.

viii Fulfil me with Thy Spirit's glow,
　Have mercy, blessèd Saviour !
　O wash me, cleanse me, through and through,
　When death comes show me favour,
　And call me hence to Thy far home,
　To reign with Thee, blest Three in One,
　Among Thy saints for ever !

U.L.S. 372.

Tr. C. S. T.

HERR JESU CHRIST, WAHR MENSCH UND GOTT

Hymn, by Paul Eber, in eight 6-line stanzas (1563). Melody, anonymous (1597).

148

i Herr Jesu Christ, wahr Mensch und Gott,
   Der du littst Marter, Angst und Spott,
*Für mich am Kreuz und endlich starbst
*Und mir deins Vaters Huld erwarbst :
   Ich bitt durchs bitter Leiden dein,
   Du wollst mir Sünder gnädig sein.

ii Wenn ich nun komm in Sterbensnoth
   Und ringen werde mit dem Tod ;
*Wenn mir vergeht all mein Gesicht,
*Und meine Ohren hören nicht ;
   Wenn meine Zunge nichts mehr spricht
   Und mir vor Angst mein Herz zerbricht ;

iii*Wenn mein Verstand sich nichts versinnt
   *Und mir all menschlich Hilf zerrinnt :
   So komm, o Herr Christ, mir behend
   Zu Hilf an meinem letzten End
   Und führ mich aus dem Jammerthal ;
   Verkürz mir auch des Todes Qual !

U.L.S. 820.

i Lord Jesu Christ, true Man and God,
   Who suffered torment, shame, the rod,
*Who bore the Cross, accursèd tree,
*To bring salvation down to me ;
   I pray Thee, by Thy bitter woe,
   Let not Thine anger overflow !

ii And when at length the moment comes,
   When sight is dim and vision glooms,
*To feel the icy hand of death ;
*When hands are weak and ears are deaf,
   When voice enfeebled no more speaks,
   And when the heart for anguish breaks ;

iii *When reason's light begins to pale,
   *When mortal aid's of no avail,
   O then, Lord Christ, Thy comfort send !
   Be with me as I near my end ;
   To take from death its dreaded sting,
   My soul to Thy safe harbour bring !

Tr. C. S. T.

* When the hymn is sung to the four-lined tune, omit the lines distinguished by an asterisk. Alternatively, repeat lines
3 and 4 of the melody.

HERR JESU CHRIST, WAHR MENSCH UND GOTT

Hymn, by Paul Eber, in eight 6-line stanzas (1563). Melody, by Louis Bourgeois, originally (1551) to Ps. cxxvii.

149

i Herr Jesu Christ, wahr Mensch und Gott,
   Der du littst Marter, Angst und Spott,
   *Für mich am Kreuz und endlich starbst
   *Und mir deins Vaters Huld erwarbst :
   Ich bitt durchs bitter Leiden dein,
   Du wollst mir Sünder gnädig sein.

iii *Wenn mein Verstand sich nichts versinnt
   *Und mir all menschlich Hilf zerrinnt :
   So komm, o Herr Christ, mir behend
   Zu Hilf an meinem letzten End
   Und führ mich aus dem Jammerthal ;
   Verkürz mir auch des Todes Qual !

* viii Ach Herr, vergib all unsre Schuld !
   Hilf, dass wir warten mit Geduld,
   *Bis unser Stündlein kommt herbei ;
   *Auch unser Glaub stets wacker sei,
   Deim Wort zu trauen festiglich,
   Bis wir einschlafen seliglich.

i Lord Jesu Christ, true Man and God,
   Who suffered torment, shame, the rod,
   *Who bore the Cross, accursèd tree,
   *To bring salvation down to me ;
   I pray Thee, by Thy bitter woe,
   Let not Thine anger overflow !

iii When reason's light begins to pale,
   When mortal aid's of no avail,
   O then, Lord Christ, Thy comfort send !
   Be with me as I near my end,
   *To take from death its dreaded sting,
   *My soul to Thy safe harbour bring !

viii Dear Lord, forgive us all our ill,
   Help us to wait upon Thy will.
   *Until death's solemn moment fall,
   *O make our souls on Thee to call,
   Upon Thy Word securely fast,
   And so to sleep in Thee at last !

U.L.S. 820.   *Tr. C. S. T.*

* When the hymn is sung to No. 148, omit the lines distinguished by an asterisk.

HERR, NUN LASS IN FRIEDE

Hymn by David Behme, in ten 6-line stanzas (c. 1663): based on the 'Nunc dimittis' Melody, anonymous (1694).

150

i Herr, nun lass in Friede,
  Lebenssatt und müde,
  Deinen Diener fahren
  Zu den Himmelsschaaren ;
  Selig und im Stillen ;
  Doch nach deinem Willen.

ii Gerne will ich sterben
  Und den Himmel erben ;
  Christus mich geleitet,
  Welchen Gott bereitet
  Zu dem Licht der Heiden,
  Das uns setzt in Freuden.

vii Mein Erlöser lebet,
  Und mich selber hebet
  Aus des Todes Kammer ;
  Da liegt aller Jammer.
  Fröhlich, ohne Schrecken,
  Will er mich aufwecken.

ix Ihm nun will ich singen,
  Lob und Ehre bringen,
  Rühmen seine Güte
  Mit Seel und Gemüthe,
  Preisen seinen Namen
  Ohn Aufhören. Amen.

i Lord, of life I'm weary,
  Fain would I be near Thee !
  Let me, all resigning,
  See Thy glory shining,
  With all joy fulfillèd,
  As Thyself hast willèd.

ii Death no terrors holdeth,
  Heaven rich treasures openeth.
  Christ my footsteps guideth,
  Christ Whom God provideth
  For the blinded heathen
  And of truth the Beacon.

vii My Redeemer liveth,
  And my spirit biddeth
  Leave death's gloomy chamber,
  Follow Him, my Saviour,
  And one day in heavèn
  Know that He is calling.

ix Therefore let us praise Him,
  Grateful anthems raising,
  For His favours many
  To man's soul and body.
  Praise Him loudly, all men,
  Praise Him ever ! Amen.

U.I.S. 821.

Tr. C. S. T.

HERR, STRAF MICH NICHT IN DEINEM ZORN

Hymn, anonymous, in six 7-line stanzas (1610): trans. Ps. xxxviii. Melody, by Johann Crüger (1640).

151

Psalm xxxviii.

i Herr, straf mich nicht in deinem Zorn,
 Das bitte ich von Herzen ;
 Sonst bin ich ganz und gar verlorn,
 Mit dir ist nicht zu Scherzen ;
 Auch züchtig mich nicht in deim Grimm,
 Der ich voller Betrübniss bin,
 Und leide grosse Schmerzen.

iii Ach wende dich, du lieber Herr,
 Errette meine Seele ;
 Hilf mir durch deine Güt und Ehr,
 Ich thu mich dir befehlen.
 Denn im Tod gedenkt man dein nicht,
 In der Hell dir kein Dank geschicht,
 Darin nichts ist denn quälen.

vi Ihr Übelthäter, weicht von mir,
 Der Herr erhört mein Flehen.
 Mein Feind zu Schanden werden schier ;
 Mein G'bet, zu Gott geschehen,
 Wird nicht vergeblich sein fürwahr :
 Dess ist gewiss und offenbar,
 Dess thu ich mich versehen.

i Lord, in Thy wrath O chide me not,
 Of Thy dear love I pray Thee !
 Could I survive Thine anger hot
 Or from Thy doom escape me ?
 Sore full of heaviness am I,
 By sin oppressed and like to die,
 But craving Thy sure mercy.

iii So bend to me, most gracious Lord,
 Lend comfort to my spirit,
 And, through Thy power, to grace restored,
 Thy Word let me inherit !
 In death no man rememb'reth Thee,
 Or from the pit can raisèd be
 Else rescued by Thy merit.

vi O men of mischief, give ye place !
 My God has heard my crying.
 My foes He'll bring to swift disgrace,
 On Him my soul's relying.
 Not ever from me will He turn,
 Or let my soul in terror burn,
 His love to me denying.

Fischer-Tümpel.[1]

Tr. C. S. T.

[1] Bd. i. No. 264.

HERR, WIE DU WILLT, SO SCHICKS MIT MIR

Hymn, by Sebald Heyd, in eight 7-line stanzas (1554): trans. of Ps. xci. Melody, anonymous, originally (1525) to ' Aus tiefer Noth schrei ich zu dir '.

Psalm xci,

i Wer in dem Schutz des Höchsten ist
  Und sich Gott thut ergeben,
  Der spricht : du, Herr, mein Zuflucht bist,
  Mein Gott, Hoffnung und Leben,
  Der du ja wirst erretten mich
  Vons Teufels Stricken gnädiglich
  Und von der Pestilenze.

ii Mit seinen Flügeln deckt er dich,
  Auf ihn sollt du vertrauen ;
  Sein Wahrheit schützt dich gwaltiglich,
  Dass dich bei Nacht kein Grauen
  Noch Betrübniss erschrecken mag,
  Auch kein Pfeil, der da fleugt bei Tag,
  Weil dir sein Wort thut leuchten.

vi Auf Löw'n und Ottern wirst du gehn
  Und treten auf die Drachen,
  Auf jungen Löwen wirst du stehn,
  Ihr Zähn und Gift verlachen ;
  Denn dir der'n keines schaden kann :
  Kein Seuch kommt den von andern an,
  Der auf Gott thut vertrauen.

viii 'Er ruft mich an als seinen Gott,
  Drum will ich ihn erhören,
  Ich steh ihm bei in aller Noth,
  Ich will ihm Hülf gewähren,
  Zu Ehren ich ihn bringen will,
  Langs Leben ihm auch geben viel,
  Mein Heil will ich ihm zeigen.'

Tucher.[1]

i Whoso doth rest in God's defence,
  Safe 'neath His care indwelling,
  May say : Lord, Thou'rt my refuge, whence
  Comes help and strength excelling.
  From Satan's jaws Thou savest me,
  From pestilence and misery :
  Thou art my Shield and Buckler !

ii Beneath Thy wings I sheltered lie,
  From every ill defended ;
  Thy faithfulness and truth alway
  My pathways have protected.
  Nor pestilence that walks by day
  Nor sickness that destroyeth may
  Prevail at all against me.

vi On lions and adders shalt thou go,
  And dragons dread shalt slay them ;
  The young lions swift shalt thou pursue,
  And 'neath thy feet shalt tread them.
  For He hath set His love on thee ;
  Thou canst not lie in jeopardy
  Who art by God protected.

viii Saith God : He calls and I will hear,
  Mine ear to him inclining.
  When troubles rise, then am I near,
  To honour will I bring him,
  With long life will I satisfy,
  With honour will I gratify,
  Salvation to him showing.

Tr. C. S. T.

[1] Bd. i. No. 246.

HERR, WIE DU WILLT, SO SCHICKS MIT MIR

Hymn, by Caspar Bienemann, in three 7-line stanzas (1582). Melody, anonymous, originally (1525) to 'Aus tiefer Noth schrei ich zu dir'.

153

*i Herr, wie du willt, so schicks mit mir
Im Leben und im Sterben.
Allein zu dir steht mein Begier ;
Lass mich, Herr, nicht verderben.
Erhalt mich nur in deiner Huld :
Sonst wie du willt, gieb mir Geduld :
Denn dein Will ist der beste.

ii Zucht, Ehr und Treu verleih mir, Herr,
Und Lieb zu deinem Worte :
Behüt mich, Herr, für falscher Lehr
Und gieb mir hier und dorte,
Was mir dienet zur Seligkeit :
Wend ab all Ungerechtigkeit
In meinem ganzen Leben.

iii Soll ich denn einmal nach deim Rath
Von dieser Welt abscheiden :
Verleih mir, Herr, nur deine Gnad,
Dass es gescheh mit Freuden.
Mein Leib und Seel befehl ich dir :
O Herr, ein selig End gieb mir
Durch Jesum Christum. Amen.

U.L.S. 578.

i Lord, as Thou wilt, so deal with me,
In living and in dying.
With Thee alone my soul would be,
On Thy dear love relying.
O hold me ever in Thy care,
And give me patience to declare
' Thy will be ever done, Lord '.

ii E'er keep me true in thought and deed,
Thy Holy Scripture loving,
O let it be my only creed,
The path of error showing.
O give me of Thy righteousness,
Take from me all ungodliness
In all my words and doing !

iii And when death's summons I must face
And from this world betake me,
O grant me, Lord, of Thy dear grace
My last end may be happy !
Into Thy hands do I resign
My soul and body : make them Thine,
Through Christ our Saviour ! Amen.

Tr. C. S. T.

HERZLICH LIEB HAB ICH DICH, O HERR

Hymn, by Martin Schalling, in three 12-line stanzas (1571). Melody, anonymous (1577).

154

*Bach has a 𝄐 here.

i Herzlich lieb hab ich dich, O Herr :
  Ich bitt, wollst sein von mir nicht fern
  Mit deiner Güt und Gnaden.
  Die ganze Welt nicht freuet mich,
  Nach Himmel und Erd nicht frag ich,
  Wenn ich dich nur kann haben.
  Und wenn mir gleich mein Herz zerbricht .
  So bist du doch mein Zuversicht,
  Mein Theil und meines Herzens Trost,
  Der mich durch sein Blut hat erlöst.
  Herr Jesu Christ (*bis*), mein Gott und Herr,
  In Schanden lass mich nimmermehr.

ii Es ist ja, Herr, dein G'schenk und Gab
  Mein Leib und Seel und was ich hab
  In diesem armen Leben :
  Damit ichs brauch zum Lobe dein,
  Zum Nutz und Dienst des Nächsten mein,
  Wollst mir dein Gnade geben.
  Behüt mich, Herr, vor falscher Lehr,
  Des Satans Mord und Lügen wehr ;
  In allem Kreuz erhalte mich,
  Auf dass ichs trag geduldiglich.
  Herr Jesu Christ (*bis*), mein Herr und Gott,
  Tröst mir mein Seel in Todesnoth.

i Thee, Lord, I love with sacred awe,
  Thy gracious presence ne'er withdraw
  From me, Thy feeble creature :
  The world is tasteless unto me,
  I find no comfort but in Thee,
  And in Thy loving nature :
  Yea, when the strings of life are broke
  Thou shalt remain my lasting Rock ;
  Thou art my Portion and my All,
  Whose blood redeemed me from the fall ;
  Lord Jesu Christ (*bis*), Thy saving name
  Preserve me from eternal shame !

ii All my desires are fixed on Thee,
  Lord Jesus ; Thou art more to me
  Than every earthly treasure :
  Were heaven itself without Thee, Lord,
  What could all heavenly bliss afford
  To yield me solid pleasure ?
  Did I not feel that Thou art near,
  Whene'er I mourn, my heart to cheer,
  Nought in this world could comfort me ;
  My wishes centre all in Thee :
  Lord Jesu Christ (*bis*), if Thou art gone,
  My every refuge is withdrawn.

U.L.S. 561.

Tr. John Christian Jacobi.[1]

[1] *Moravian Hymn-Book* (Ed. 1877), **No. 459.**

HERZLICH LIEB HAB ICH DICH, O HERR

Hymn, by Martin Schalling, in three 12-line stanzas (1571). Melody, anonymous (1577).

155

Bach has a 𝄐 here.

[Trumpets I II III and Timpani obbligati]

HERZLICH LIEB HAB ICH DICH, O HERR

i Herzlich lieb hab ich dich, O Herr :
  Ich bitt, wollst sein von mir nicht fern
  Mit deiner Güt und Gnaden.
  Die ganze Welt nicht freuet mich,
  Nach Himmel und Erd nicht frag ich,
  Wenn ich dich nur kann haben.
  Und wenn mir gleich mein Herz zerbricht :
  So bist du doch mein Zuversicht,
  Mein Theil und meines Herzens Trost,
  Der mich durch sein Blut hat erlöst.
  Herr Jesu Christ (bis), mein Gott und Herr,
  In Schanden lass mich nimmermehr.

ii Es ist ja, Herr, dein G'schenk und Gab
  Mein Leib und Seel und was ich hab
  In diesem armen Leben :
  Damit ichs brauch zum Lobe dein,
  Zum Nutz und Dienst des Nächsten mein,
  Wollst mir dein Gnade geben.
  Behüt mich, Herr, vor falscher Lehr,
  Des Satans Mord und Lügen wehr ;
  In allem Kreuz erhalte mich,
  Auf dass ichs trag geduldiglich.
  Herr Jesu Christ (bis), mein Herr und Gott,
  Tröst mir mein Seel in Todesnoth.

* iii Ach, Herr, lass dein lieb Engelein
  An meinem End die Seele mein
  In Abrahams Schooss tragen :
  Den Leib in seim Schlafkämmerlein
  Gar sanft ohn einig Qual und Pein
  Ruhn bis am jüngsten Tage.
  Alsdann vom Tod erwecke mich,
  Dass meine Augen sehen dich
  In aller Freud, o Gottessohn,
  Mein Heiland und mein Gnadenthron !
  Herr Jesu Christ (bis), erhöre mich :
  Ich will dich preisen ewiglich.

i Lord, all my heart is fixed on Thee,
  I pray Thee, be not far from me,
  With tender grace uphold me.
  The whole wide world delights me not,
  Of heaven or earth, Lord, ask I not,
  If but Thy love enfold me.
  Yea, though my heart be like to break,
  Thou art my trust that nought can shake,
  My portion and my hidden joy,
  Whose Cross could all my bonds destroy.
  Lord Jesu Christ (bis), my God and Lord,
  Forsake me not, who trust Thy Word !

ii Rich are Thy gifts ! 'Twas God that gave
  Body and soul and all I have
  In this poor life of labour.
  O grant that I may through Thy grace
  Use all my powers to show Thy praise,
  And serve and help my neighbour.
  From all false doctrine keep me, Lord ;
  All lies and malice from me ward,
  In every cross uphold Thou me,
  That I may bear it patiently.
  Lord Jesu Christ (bis), my God and Lord,
  In death Thy comfort still afford !

iii Ah, Lord, let Thy dear angels come
  At my last.end, to bear me home,
  That I may die unfearing.
  And in its narrow chamber keep
  My body safe in painless sleep
  Until my Lord's appearing.
  And then from death awaken me,
  That these mine eyes with joy may see,
  O Son of God, Thy glorious face,
  My Saviour and my Fount of Grace !
  Lord Jesu Christ (bis), receive my prayer :
  Thy love will I for aye declare.

U.L.S. 561.

Tr. Catherine Winkworth.[1]

[1] Chorale Book for England (Lond. 1865), No. 119.

HERZLICH LIEB HAB ICH DICH, O HERR

Hymn, by Martin Schalling, in three 12-line stanzas (1571). Melody, anonymous (1577).

156

* **Bach has a 𝆺 here.**

*i Herzlich lieb hab ich dich, O Herr :
  Ich bitt, wollst sein von mir nicht fern
  Mit deiner Güt und Gnaden.
  Die ganze Welt nicht freuet mich,
  Nach Himmel und Erd nicht frag ich,
  Wenn ich dich nur kann haben.
  Und wenn mir gleich mein Herz zerbricht :
  So bist du doch mein Zuversicht,
  Mein Theil und meines Herzens Trost,
  Der mich durch sein Blut hat erlöst.
  Herr Jesu Christ (*bis*), mein Gott und Herr,
  In Schanden lass mich nimmermehr.

ii Es ist ja, Herr, dein G'schenk und Gab
  Mein Leib und Seel und was ich hab
  In diesem armen Leben :
  Damit ichs brauch zum Lobe dein,
  Zum Nutz und Dienst des Nächsten mein,
  Wollst mir dein Gnade geben.
  Behüt mich, Herr, vor falscher Lehr,
  Des Satans Mord und Lügen wehr ;
  In allem Kreuz erhalte mich,
  Auf dass ichs trag geduldiglich.
  Herr Jesu Christ (*bis*), mein Herr und Gott,
  Tröst mir mein Seel in Todesnoth.

i Lord, take my heart, it beats for Thee,
  Stand at my side, nor distant be,
  Thy help and grace bestowing !
  In this world have I no delight,
  Nought else is pleasing in my sight,
  Thy love and favour knowing.
  And when my heart would break with grief,
  In Thee's my trust and sure belief.
  Thou art my Hope, my Trust, my Lord,
  Who hast redeemed me by Thy blood.
  Lord Jesu Christ (*bis*), O show Thy face,
  And let me never see disgrace !

ii Whate'er I have from Thee doth spring,
  My soul and body, everything
  That mortal man possesseth.
  That I may use it to Thy praise,
  And for my neighbour's good always,
  Nought but Thy help availeth.
  From all false doctrine keep me clean,
  From Satan's arts and tempting screen !
  Help me my daily ills to bear,
  And patiently my cross to wear !
  Lord Jesu Christ (*bis*), my God and Lord,
  In life's last hour Thy help afford !

U.L.S. 561.

Tr. C. S. T.

HERZLICH LIEB HAB ICH DICH, O HERR

Hymn, by Martin Schalling, in three 12-line stanzas (1571). Melody, anonymous (1577).

157

* **Bach has a 𝆒 here.**

i Herzlich lieb hab ich dich, O Herr :
  Ich bitt, wollst sein von mir nicht fern
  Mit deiner Güt und Gnaden.
  Die ganze Welt nicht freuet mich,
  Nach Himmel und Erd nicht frag ich,
  Wenn ich dich nur kann haben.
  Und wenn mir gleich mein Herz zerbricht :
  So bist du doch mein Zuversicht,
  Mein Theil und meines Herzens Trost,
  Der mich durch sein Blut hat erlöst.
  Herr Jesu Christ (*bis*), mein Gott und Herr,
  In Schanden lass mich nimmermehr.

* iii Ach, Herr, lass dein lieb Engelein
  An meinem End die Seele mein
  In Abrahams Schooss tragen :
  Den Leib in seim Schlafkämmerlein
  Gar sanft ohn einig Qual und Pein
  Ruhn bis am jüngsten Tage.
  Alsdann vom Tod erwecke mich,
  Dass meine Augen sehen dich
  In aller Freud, o Gottessohn,
  Mein Heiland und mein Gnadenthron !
  Herr Jesu Christ (*bis*), erhöre mich :
  Ich will dich preisen ewiglich.

U.L.S. 561.

i Lord, take my heart, it beats for Thee,
  Stand at my side, nor distant be,
  Thy help and grace bestowing !
  In this world have I no delight,
  Nought else is pleasing in my sight,
  Thy love and favour knowing.
  And when my heart would break with grief,
  In Thee's my trust and sure belief.
  Thou art my Hope, my Trust, my Lord,
  Who hast redeemed me by Thy blood.
  Lord Jesu Christ (*bis*), O show Thy face,
  And let me never see disgrace !

iii Lord, let Thy blessèd angels come,
  At my last end, when life is done,
  To bear my soul to heavèn !
  Asleep within the quiet tomb,
  There I'll await Thy Day of Doom,
  All fear and pain out-driven.
  One day from death awaken me
  To let my soul Thy beauty see
  In all Thy glory, God's dear Son,
  Who hath for me salvation won !
  Lord Jesu Christ (*bis*), receive my prayer,
  Who evermore Thy praise declare !

Tr. C. S. T.

HERZLICH THUT MICH VERLANGEN

Hymn, by Christoph Knoll, in eleven 8-line stanzas (1605). Melody, by Hans Leo Hassler, originally (1601) to the secular 'Mein Gmüt ist mir verwirret'.

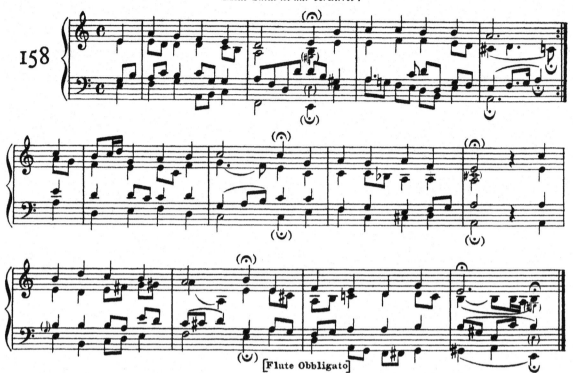

[Flute Obbligato]

i Herzlich thut mich verlangen
  Nach einem selgen End ;
  Weil ich hie bin umfangen
  Mit Trübsal und Elend.
  Ich hab Lust, abzuscheiden
  Von dieser argen Welt ;
  Sehn mich nach ewgen Freuden :
  O Jesu, komm nur bald.

* iv Der Leib zwar in der Erden
  Von Würmern wird verzehrt :
  Aber erwecket werden
  Durch Christum schön verklärt ;
  Wird leuchten als die Sonne
  Und lebn ohn alle Noth
  In himmlisch Freud und Wonne :
  Was schadet mir der Tod ?

xi Hilf, dass ich ja nicht wanke
  Von dir, Herr Jesu Christ ;
  Den schwachen Glauben stärke
  In mir zu aller Frist.
  Hilf mir ritterlich ringen,
  Dein Hand mich halte fest,
  Dass ich mag fröhlich singen
  Das Consummatum est.

i Lord, hear my deepest longing—
  To pass to Thee in peace,
  From earthly troubles thronging,
  From trials that never cease.
  For Thee my soul is thirsting,
  Above earth's dismal gloom
  To reach joy everlasting ;
  O Saviour, quickly come !

iv Though worms destroy my body
  Within its earth-bound grave,
  Yet Christ one day shall call me,
  And from the darkness save.
  Then, clothed in radiant glory,
  Before my God I'll sing
  Of His great love the story.
  O Death, where is thy sting !

xi O let not death's dark terror
  Disturb my faith in Thee ;
  But keep me from all error,
  In faith Thine loyally.
  With Thy dear hand to guide me
  Death firmly will I face,
  To wake, the tomb behind me,
  In heaven's appointed place.

U.L.S. 822.

Tr. C. S. T.

HERZLICH THUT MICH VERLANGEN

Hymn, by Paul Gerhardt, in twelve 8-line stanzas (1653). Melody, by Hans Leo Hassler, originally (1601) to the secular
' Mein Gmüt ist mir verwirret'.

159

i Befiehl du deine Wege
  Und was dein Herze kränkt,
  Der allertreusten Pflege
  Dess, der den Himmel lenkt ;
  Der Wolken, Luft und Winden
  Giebt Wege, Lauf und Bahn,
  Der wird auch Wege finden,
  Da dein Fuss gehen kann.

v Und ob gleich alle Teufel
  Hie wollten widerstehn,
  So wird doch ohne Zweifel
  Gott nicht zurücke gehn.
  Was er ihm vorgenommen
  Und was er haben will,
  Das muss doch endlich kommen
  Zu seinem Zweck und Ziel.

vi Hoff, o du arme Seele,
  Hoff, und sei unverzagt !
  Gott wird dich aus der Höhle,
  Da dich der Kummer plagt,
  Mit grossen Gnaden rücken :
  Erwarte nur der Zeit :
  So wirst du schon erblicken
  Die Sonn der schönsten Freud.

i Commit thy ways to Jesus,
  Lay on Him all thy woe,
  Thy cares and every grievance
  That doth disturb thee so !
  For He, the heavens Who ruleth,
  Whom winds and seas obey,
  Thy paths for thee controlleth,
  And will not say thee nay.

v When Satan's hosts provoke thee,
  And on thy pathway press,
  Not then will God forsake thee,
  But succours thy distress.
  Thyself, on Him relying,
  Pursue His purpose clear !
  So shalt thou, Satan flying,
  Fair course to heavèn steer.

vi Hope then, hope on eternal, -
  Nor ever be dismayed !
  From all the powers infernal
  Hath Christ deliverance made.
  Put sorrow then behind thee,
  Wait only on God's will :
  His sun, soon shining brightly,
  With joy thy heart shall fill !

U.L.S. 620.

Tr. C. S. T.

HERZLICH THUT MICH VERLANGEN

Hymn, by Paul Gerhardt, in ten 8-line stanzas (1656): a free version of 'Salve caput cruentatum'.   Melody, by Hans Leo Hassler, originally (1601) to the secular 'Mein Gmüt ist mir verwirret'.

160

Salve caput cruentatum.

i O Haupt voll Blut und Wunden,
  Voll Schmerz und voller Hohn !
  O Haupt, zum Spott gebunden
  Mit einer Dornenkron !
  O Haupt, sonst schön gezieret
  Mit höchster Ehr und Zier,
  Jetzt aber höchst schimpfiret :
  Gegrüsset seist du mir !

ii Du edles Angesichte,
  Davor sonst schrickt und scheut
  Das grosse Weltgewichte,
  Wie bist du so bespeit,
  Wie bist du so erbleichet,
  Wer hat dein Augenlicht,
  Dem sonst kein Licht nicht gleichet,
  So schändlich zugericht ?

* ix Wann ich einmal soll scheiden,
  So scheide nicht von mir ;
  Wann ich den Tod soll leiden,
  So tritt du dann herfür.
  Wann mir am allerbängsten
  Wird um das Herze sein,
  So reiss mich aus den Aengsten
  Kraft deiner Angst und Pein

i O sacred Head now wounded,
  With grief and shame weighed down,
  Now scornfully surrounded
  With thorns, Thy only crown !
  How pale art Thou with anguish,
  With sore abuse and scorn !
  How does that visage languish
  Which once was bright as morn !

ii O Lord of life and glory,
  What bliss till now was Thine !
  I read the wondrous story ;
  I joy to call Thee mine.
  Thy grief and bitter Passion
  Were all for sinners' gain :
  Mine, mine was the transgression,
  But Thine the deadly pain.
                    Tr. J. W. Alexander.

ix When life's last hour shall call me,
  Be present at my side ;
  Let no dread fears appal me ;
  Thy mercy, Lord, is wide.
  And when my heart must languish,
  Prepare the path I go,
  And let Thy Cross and anguish
  Assuage my deepest woe.
                    Tr. C. S. T.

HERZLICH THUT MICH VERLANGEN

Hymn, by Cyriakus Schneegass, in five 8-line stanzas (1597). Melody, by Hans Leo Hassler, originally (1601) to the secular 'Mein Gmüt ist mir verwirret'.

161

i Ach Herr, mich armen Sünder
  Straf nicht in deinem Zorn ;
  Dein ernsten Grimm doch linder,
  Sonst ists mit mir verlorn.
  Ach Herr, wollst mir vergeben
  Mein Sünd und gnädig sein,
  Dass ich mag ewig leben,
  Entfliehn der Höllenpein.

v Nun weicht ihr Uebelthäter :
  Mir ist geholfen schon.
  Der Herr ist mein Erretter ;
  Er nimmt mein Flehen an,
  Er hört meins Weinens Stimme ;
  Es müssen falln geschwind
  All sein und meine Feinde,
  Die schändlich kommen um.

U.L.S. 349.

* vi Ehr sei ins Himmels Throne
  Mit hohem Ruhm und Preis,
  Dem Vater und dem Sohne,
  Und auch zu gleicher Weis
  Dem heilgen Geist mit Ehren,
  In alle Ewigkeit !
  Der woll uns All'n bescheren
  Die ewge Seligkeit.

Addendum : 1625.

i A sinner, Lord, I pray Thee
  Recall Thy dread decree ;
  Thy fearful wrath O spare me.
  From judgement set me free !
  O dear Lord, grant compassion,
  And toward me turn Thy face,
  That I may dwell beside Thee
  In heaven's appointed place !

v Hence, all ye men of evil !
  My God my plaint hath heard,
  Hath rescued me from peril,
  Hath grace on me conferred.
  He's heard my bitter weeping,
  And put my foes to shame,
  Upon their heads wrath heaping
  Who doubt His sacred name.

vi All praise to Thy great merit,
  High God on heaven's throne,
  Father and Holy Spirit,
  And ever blessèd Son !
  Our eager voices praise Thee
  With joyful ecstasy,
  In hope to sing before Thee
  For all eternity.

Tr. C. S. T.

HERZLICH THUT MICH VERLANGEN

Hymn, by Paul Gerhardt, in ten 8-line stanzas (1653). Melody, by Hans Leo Hassler, originally (1601) to the secular 'Mein Gmüt ist mir verwirret'.

162

* i Wie soll ich dich empfangen ?
   Und wie begegn' ich dir ?
   O aller Welt Verlangen,
   O meiner Seelen Zier !
   O Jesu, Jesu, setze
   Mir selbst die Fackel bei,
   Damit, was dich ergötze,
   Mir kund und wissend sei.

ii Dein Zion streut dir Palmen
   Und grüne Zweige hin,
   Und ich will dir in Psalmen
   Ermuntern meinen Sinn.
   Mein Herze soll dir grünen
   In stetem Lob und Preis,
   Und deinem Namen dienen,
   So gut es kann und weiss.

x Er kommt zum Weltgerichte,
   Zum Fluch dem, der ihm flucht ;
   Mit Gnad und süssem Lichte
   Dem, der ihn liebt und sucht.
   Ach komm ! ach komm ! o Sonne,
   Und hol uns allzumal
   Zum ew'gen Licht und Wonne
   In deinen Freudensaal.

i Ah ! Lord, how shall I meet Thee,
   How welcome Thee aright ?
   All nations long to greet Thee,
   My hope, my sole delight !
   Brighten the lamp that burneth
   But dimly in my breast,
   And teach my soul, that yearneth
   To honour such high quest.

ii Thy Zion strews before Thee
   Her fairest buds and palms,
   And I too will adore Thee
   With sweetest songs and psalms ;
   My soul breaks forth in flowers
   Rejoicing in Thy fame,
   And summons all her powers
   To honour Jesu's name.

x He comes to judge the nations,
   A terror to His foes,
   A light of consolations
   And blessèd hope to those
   Who love the Lord's appearing :
   O glorious Sun, now come,
   Send forth Thy beams of cheering
   And guide us safely home !

U.L.S. 21.

Tr. Catherine Winkworth.[1]

[1] *Chorale Book for England* (Lond. 1865), No. 21.

HERZLICH THUT MICH VERLANGEN

Hymn, by Paul Gerhardt, in twelve 8-line stanzas (1653). Melody, by Hans Leo Hassler, originally (1601) to the secular 'Mein Gmüt ist mir verwirret'.

163

i Befiehl du deine Wege
　Und was dein Herze kränkt,
　Der allertreusten Pflege
　Dess, der den Himmel lenkt ;
　Der Wolken, Luft und Winden
　Giebt Wege, Lauf und Bahn,
　Der wird auch Wege finden,
　Da dein Fuss gehen kann.

* v Und ob gleich alle Teufel
　Hie wollten widerstehn,
　So wird doch ohne Zweifel
　Gott nicht zurücke gehn.
　Was er ihm vorgenommen
　Und was er haben will,
　Das muss doch endlich kommen
　Zu seinem Zweck und Ziel.

vi Hoff, o du arme Seele,
　Hoff, und sei unverzagt !
　Gott wird dich aus der Höhle,
　Da dich der Kummer plagt,
　Mit grossen Gnaden rücken :
　Erwarte nur die Zeit:
　So wirst du schon erblicken
　Die Sonn der schönsten Freud.

i Commit thy ways to Jesus,
　Lay on Him all thy woe,
　Thy cares and every grievance
　That doth disturb thee so!
　For He, the heavens Who ruleth,
　Whom winds and seas obey,
　Thy paths for thee controlleth,
　And will not say thee nay.

v When Satan's hosts provoke thee,
　And on thy pathway press,
　Not then will God forsake thee,
　But succour thy distress.
　Thyself, on Him relying,
　Pursue His purpose clear !
　So shalt thou, Satan flying,
　Fair course to heaven steer.

vi Hope then, hope on eternal,
　Nor ever be dismayed !
　From all the powers infernal
　Hath Christ deliverance made.
　Put sorrow then behind thee,
　Wait only on God's will :
　His sun, soon shining brightly,
　With joy thy heart shall fill !

U.L.S. 620.

Tr. C. S. T.

169

HERZLICH THUT MICH VERLANGEN

Hymn, by Paul Gerhardt, in twelve 8-line stanzas (1653). Melody by Hans Leo Hassler, originally (1601) to the secular 'Mein Gmüt ist mir verwirret'

164

i Befiehl du deine Wege
  Und was dein Herze kränkt,
  Der allertreusten Pflege
  Dess, der den Himmel lenkt ;
  Der Wolken, Luft und Winden
  Giebt Wege, Lauf und Bahn,
  Der Wird auch Wege finden,
  Da dein Fuss gehen kann.

vi Hoff, o du arme Seele,
  Hoff, und sei unverzagt !
  Gott wird dich aus der Höhle,
  Da dich der Kummer plagt,
  Mit grossen Gnaden rücken :
  Erwarte nur die Zeit :
  So wirst du schon erblicken
  Die Sonn der schönsten Freud.

xii Mach End, o Herr, mach Ende
  An aller unsrer Noth ;
  Stärk unsre Füss und Hände
  Und lass bis in den Tod
  Uns allzeit deiner Pflege
  Und Treu empfohlen sein :
  So gehen unsre Wege
  Gewiss zum Himmel ein.

i Commit thy ways to Jesus,
  Lay on Him all thy woe,
  Thy cares and every grievance
  That sore disturb thee so !
  For He, the heavens Who ruleth,
  Whom winds and seas obey,
  Thy paths for thee controlleth,
  And will not say thee nay.

vi Hope then, hope on eternal,
  Nor ever be dismayed !
  From all the powers infernal
  Hath Christ deliverance made.
  Put sorrow then behind thee,
  Wait only on God's will :
  His sun, soon shining brightly,
  With joy thy heart shall fill !

xii Make end, O Lord, in mercy,
  Of this our earthly strife;
  Uphold our hands to serve Thee
  While still there's in us life !
  So shall we neath Thy favour
  Our mortal course pursue,
  And one day do Thy pleasure
  In heaven's eternal blue.

U.L.S. 620.

Tr. C. S. T.

HERZLICH THUT MICH VERLANGEN

Hymn, by Paul Gerhardt, in twelve 8-line stanzas (1653). Melody, by Hans Leo Hassler, originally (1601) to the secular 'Mein Gmüt ist mir verwirret'.

165

* i Befiehl du deine Wege
Und was dein Herze kränkt,
Der allertreusten Pflege
Dess, der den Himmel lenkt ;
Der Wolken, Luft und Winden
Giebt Wege, Lauf und Bahn,
Der wird auch Wege finden,
Da dein Fuss gehen kann.

vii Auf ! auf ! gieb deinen Schmerzen
Und Sorgen gute Nacht ;
Lass fahren, was das Herze
Betrübt und traurig macht !
Bist du doch nicht Regente,
Der alles führen soll :
Gott sitzt im Regimente
Und führet alles wohl.

xi Wohl dir, du Kind der Treue ;
Du hast und trägst davon
Mit Ruhm und Dankgeschreie
Den Sieg und Ehrenkron !
Gott giebt dir selbst die Palmen
In deine rechte Hand ;
Und du singst Freudenpsalmen
Dem, der dein Leid gewandt.

i Commit thy ways to Jesus,
Lay on Him all thy woe,
Thy cares and every grievance
That sore disturb thee so !
For He, the heavens Who ruleth,
Whom winds and seas obey,
Thy paths for thee controlleth,
And will not say thee nay.

vii To all thy grief and sorrow
Now bid a long good-night !
The past is dead : to-morrow
Thou'lt see God's shining light.
'Tis not thy will provideth
What shall and shall not be,
But God above decideth
And ord'reth wondrously.

xi O happy, happy mortal !
Thy course on earth is run ;
Thou'lt pass through heavèn's portal,
The fight on earth is won.
Yea, God Himself will crown thee
With palms upon thy brow,
And hear thy song of victory
To Him Who bore thy woe.

U.L.S. 620.

Tr. C. S. T.

HERZLICH THUT MICH VERLANGEN

Hymn, by Paul Gerhardt, in twelve 8-line stanzas (1653). Melody, by Hans Leo Hassler, originally (1601) to the secular 'Mein Gmüt ist mir verwirret'.

166

i Befiehl du deine Wege
 Und was dein Herze kränkt,
 Der allertreusten Pflege
 Dess, der den Himmel lenkt;
 Der Wolken, Luft und Winden
 Giebt Wege, Lauf und Bahn,
 Der wird auch Wege finden,
 Da dein Fuss gehen kann.

xi Wohl dir, du Kind der Treue;
 Du hast und trägst davon
 Mit Ruhm und Dankgeschreie
 Den Sieg und Ehrenkron!
 Gott giebt dir selbst die Palmen
 In deine rechte Hand;
 Und du singst Freudenpsalmen
 Dem, der dein Leid gewandt.

xii Mach End, o Herr, mach Ende
 An aller unsrer Noth;
 Stärk unsre Füss und Hände
 Und lass bis in den Tod
 Uns allzeit deiner Pflege
 Und Treu empfohlen sein:
 So gehen unsre Wege
 Gewiss zum Himmel ein.

U.L.S. 620.

i Commit thy ways to Jesus,
 Lay on Him all thy woe,
 Thy cares and every grievance
 That sore disturb thee so!
 For He, the heavens Who ruleth,
 Whom winds and seas obey,
 Thy paths for thee controlleth,
 And will not say thee nay.

xi O happy, happy mortal!
 Thy course on earth is run;
 Thou'lt pass through heav'n's portal,
 The fight on earth is won.
 Yea, God Himself will crown thee
 With palms upon thy brow,
 And hear thy song of victory
 To Him Who bore thy woe.

xii Lord, in Thy mercy bring us
 From this world's trials free,
 And on our way attend us
 Until we sleep in Thee.
 That so, Thy will fulfilling,
 Our course toward heaven we take,
 And find there joy excelling
 When out of death we wake.

Tr. C. S. T.

HERZLICH THUT MICH VERLANGEN

Hymn, by Paul Gerhardt, in ten 8-line stanzas (1656): a free version of ' Salve caput cruentatum'. Melody, by Hans Leo Hassler, originally (1601) to the secular ' Mein Gmüt ist mir verwirret'.

Salve caput cruentatum.

i O Haupt voll Blut und Wunden,
   Voll Schmerz und voller Hohn !
   O Haupt, zum Spott gebunden
   Mit einer Dornenkron !
   O Haupt, sonst schön gezieret
   Mit höchster Ehr und Zier,
   Jetzt aber höchst schimpfiret :
   Gegrüsset seist du mir !

* v Erkenne mich, mein Hüter,
   Mein Hirte, nimm mich an !
   Von dir, Quell aller Güter,
   Ist mir viel Guts gethan,
   Dein Mund hat mich gelabet
   Mit Milch und süsser Kost,
   Dein Geist hat mich begabet
   Mit mancher Himmelslust.

* vi Ich will hier bei dir stehen,
   Verachte mich doch nicht !
   Von dir will ich nicht gehen,
   Wann dir dein Herze bricht ;
   Wann dein Haupt will erblassen
   Im letzten Todesstoss,
   Alsdann will ich dich fassen
   In meinen Arm und Schooss.

i O sacred head, encircled
   With crown of piercing thorn !
   O bleeding head empurpled,
   Reviled, insulted, torn !
   Thou once in highest glory
   With beauteous grace wast crowned ;
   Now wicked men revile Thee
   By shameful lashes bound.

v Regard me then, my Master,
   My Saviour, make me Thine !
   I dwell on heav'n's pasture
   If Thou but make me Thine.
   How oft Thyself hast fed me
   With love and heavenly food,
   How oft Thy spirit led me
   To seek th' eternal good.

vi I too will stand beside Thee,
   O bid me not depart !
   Nor ever I'll desert Thee
   Till Thou'st endured death's smart.
   So when Thou art o'ertaken
   By death's tremendous doom,
   Thou shalt not be forsaken,
   But to my fond arms come.

U.L.S. 109.

Tr. C. S. T.

HERZLICH THUT MICH VERLANGEN

Hymn, by Paul Gerhardt, in ten 8-line stanzas (1656): a free version of ' Salve caput cruentatum '. Melody, by Hans Leo Hassler, originally (1601) to the secular ' Mein Gmüt ist mir verwirret '.

168

⊙ **The Alto and Tenor parts may be interchanged to the** ⌢

Salve caput cruentatum.

*i O Haupt voll Blut und Wunden,
Voll Schmerz und voller Hohn !
O Haupt, zum Spott gebunden
Mit einer Dornenkron !
O Haupt, sonst schön gezieret
Mit höchster Ehr und Zier,
Jetzt aber höchst schimpfiret :
Gegrüsset seist du mir !

*ii Du edles Angesichte,
Davor sonst schrickt und scheut
Das grosse Weltgewichte,
Wie bist du so bespeit,
Wie bist du so erbleichet,
Wer hat dein Augenlicht,
Dem sonst kein Licht nicht gleichet,
So schändlich zugericht ?

ix Wann ich einmal soll scheiden,
So scheide nicht von mir ;
Wann ich den Tod søll leiden,
So tritt du dann herfür.
Wann mir am allerbängsten
Wird um das Herze sein,
So reiss mich aus den Aengsten
Kraft deiner Angst und Pein.

i O sacred Head now wounded,
With grief and shame weighed down,
Now scornfully surrounded
With thorns, Thy only crown !
How pale art Thou with anguish,
With sore abuse and scorn !
How does that visage languish
Which once was bright as morn !

ii O Lord of life and glory,
What bliss till now was Thine !
I read the wondrous story ;
I joy to call Thee mine.
Thy grief and bitter Passion
Were all for sinners' gain :
Mine, mine was the transgression,
But Thine the deadly pain.

ix Be near me, Lord, when dying ;
Show Thou Thyself to me ;
And, for my succour flying,
Come, Lord, to set me free.
These eyes, new faith receiving,
From Jesus shall not move ;
For he who dies believing
Dies safely through Thy love.

U.L.S. 109.

Tr. J. W. Alexander.

HERZLIEBSTER JESU, WAS HAST DU VERBROCHEN

Hymn, by Johann Heermann, in fifteen 4-line stanzas (1630).   Melody, by Johann Crüger (1640).

169

i Herzliebster Jesu, was hast du verbrochen,
   Dass man ein solch scharf Urtheil hat gesprochen?
   Was ist die Schuld? in was für Missethaten
   Bist du gerathen?

ii Du wirst gegeisselt, und mit Dorn gekrönet,
   Ins Angesicht geschlagen und verhöhnet:
   Du wirst mit Essig und mit Gall getränket:
   Ans Kreuz gehenket.

iii Was ist doch wohl die Ursach solcher Plagen?
   Ach, meine Sünden haben dich geschlagen!
   Ich, o Herr Jesu! hab dies wohl verschuldet,
   Was du erduldet!

*vii O grosse Lieb! o Lieb ohn alle Masse,
   Die dich gebracht auf diese Marterstrasse!
   Ich lebte mit der Welt in Lust und Freuden:
   Und du musst leiden!

U.L.S. 102.

i O dearest Jesu, wherefore hath man spoken
   'Gainst Thee Who never God's command hath broken?
   What is Thy crime? How hast Thou done transgression?
   When made confession?

ii Thy side is pierced, Thy head with thorns is crownèd,
   By cruel hands art struck, sore mocked and wounded.
   They give Thee gall to drink and foul deride Thee
   Who crucify Thee.

iii Dear Lord, who meekly bore such bitter anguish
   As none before, for which else must I languish,
   'Twas my dark sin to torture did enslave Thee,
   Who died to save me.

vii O feeling heart that torture's deeps hath sounded,
   Thou gav'st Thy life lest I should be confounded.
   While we stand heedless, with the world complying,
   Thou hangest dying.

Tr. C. S. T.

HERZLIEBSTER JESU, WAS HAST DU VERBROCHEN

Hymn, by Johann Heermann, in fifteen 4-line stanzas (1630).   Melody, by Johann Crüger (1640).

170

i Herzliebster Jesu, was hast du verbrochen,
  Dass man ein solch scharf Urtheil hat gesprochen?
  Was ist die Schuld? in was für Missethaten
  Bist du gerathen?

vii O grosse Lieb! o Lieb ohn alle Masse,
   Die dich gebracht auf diese Marterstrasse!
   Ich lebte mit der Welt in Lust und Freuden:
   Und du musst leiden!

*viii Ach grosser König, gross zu allen Zeiten,
    Wie kann ich gnugsam solche Lehr ausbreiten?
    Keins Menschen Herz vermag es auszudenken,
    Was dir zu schenken.

* ix Ich kanns mit meinen Sinnen nicht erreichen,
   Mit was doch dein Erbarmen zu vergleichen.
   Wie kann ich dir denn deine Liebesthaten
   Im Werk erstatten?

U.L.S. 102.

i O dearest Jesu, wherefore hath man spoken
  'Gainst Thee Who never God's command hath broken?
  What is Thy crime? How hast Thou done trans-
        gression?
  When made confession?

vii O feeling heart! O depths of love unsounded!
   Thou gav'st Thy life lest I should be confounded.
   While we stand heedless, with the world complying,
   Thou hangest dying.

viii Great King of heaven, Who ever reign'st in glory,
    Can mortal tongue rehearse Thy glorious story?
    What thankful gift of price is there to bring Thee?
    What song to hymn Thee?

ix The mind of man its debt can never measure,
   Nor plumb the deeps of God's eternal treasure.
   How can I ever by my feeble doing
   My love be showing?

Tr. C. S. T.

HERZLIEBSTER JESU, WAS HAST DU VERBROCHEN

Hymn, by Johann Heermann, in fifteen 4-line stanzas (1630). Melody, by Johann Crüger (1640).

171

*i Herzliebster Jesu, was hast du verbrochen,
　Dass man ein solch scharf Urtheil hat gesprochen?
　Was ist die Schuld? in was für Missethaten
　Bist du gerathen?

vii O grosse Lieb! o Lieb ohn alle Masse,
　Die dich gebracht auf diese Marterstrasse!
　Ich lebte mit der Welt in Lust und Freuden:
　Und du musst leiden!

viii Ach grosser König, gross zu allen Zeiten,
　Wie kann ich gnugsam solche Lehr ausbreiten?
　Keins Menschen Herz vermag es auszudenken,
　Wass dir zu schenken.

xii Alsdann so werd ich deine Huld betrachten,
　Aus Lieb an dich die Welt für nichtes achten,
　Bemühen werd ich mich, Herr, deinen Willen
　Stets zu erfüllen.

U.L.S. 102.

i Alas, dear Lord, what law then hast Thou broken,
　That such sharp sentence should on Thee be spoken?
　Of what great crime hast Thou to make confession —
　What dark transgression?

vii O wondrous love! whose depths no heart hath
　　　sounded,
　That brought Thee here by foes and thieves sur-
　　　rounded;
　All worldly pleasures, heedless, I was trying,
　While Thou wert dying!

viii O mighty King! no time can dim Thy glory!
　How shall I spread abroad Thy wondrous story?
　How shall I find some worthy gift to proffer?
　What dare I offer?

xii I'll think upon Thy mercy hour by hour,
　I'll love Thee so that earth must lose her power;
　To do Thy will shall be my sole endeavour
　Henceforth for ever.

Tr. Catherine Winkworth.[1]

[1] *Chorale Book for England* (Lond. 1865), No. 52.

HERZLIEBSTER JESU, WAS HAST DU VERBROCHEN

Hymn, by Johann Heermann, in fifteen 4-line stanzas (1630).   Melody, by Johann Crüger (1640).

172

i Herzliebster Jesu, was hast du verbrochen,
Dass man ein solch scharf Urtheil hat gesprochen?
Was ist die Schuld? in was für Missethaten
Bist du gerathen?

ii Du wirst gegeisselt, und mit Dorn gekrönet,
Ins Angesicht geschlagen und verhöhnet:
Du wirst mit Essig und mit Gall getränket:
Ans Kreuz gehenket.

* iv Wie wunderbarlich ist doch diese Strafe!
Der gute Hirte leidet für die Schafe;
Die Schuld bezahlt der Herre, der Gerechte,
Für seine Knechte!

xv Wann, Herre Jesu, dort vor deinem Throne
Wird stehn auf meinem Haupt die Ehrenkrone:
Da will ich dir, wenn alles wird wohl klingen,
Lob und Dank singen.

U.L.S. 102.

i Alas, dear Lord, what law then hast Thou broken,
That such sharp sentence should on Thee be spoken?
Of what great crime hast Thou to make confession—
What dark transgression?

ii They crown His head with thorns, they smite, they
scourge Him,
With cruel mockings to the Cross they urge Him,
They give Him gall to drink, they loud decry Him,
They crucify Him.

iv What strangest punishment is suffered yonder!
The Shepherd dies for sheep that wayward wander!
The Master pays the debts His servants owe Him,
Who would not know Him.

xv And when, dear Lord, before Thy throne in heavèn
The crown of joy to me at last is given,
Where sweetest hymns Thy saints for ever raise Thee,
I too shall praise Thee!

Tr. Catherine Winkworth.[1]

[1] *Chorale Book for England (Lond. 1865), No. 52.*

HEUT IST, O MENSCH, EIN GROSSER TRAUERTAG

Hymn, by Apelles von Löwenstern, in six 3-line stanzas, with a 'Vorgesang' and 'Nachgesang' (1644). Melody, by Löwenstern (1644).

173

*Bach has a 𝄐 here.

Vorgesang.

i Heut ist, o Mensch, ein grosser Trauertag,
  An welchem unser Heiland grosse Plag
  Erlitten hat, und tod darnieder lag.

ii Heut stirbet Gott ; wer ist, der solchs bedenkt ?
   Das Leben selbst heut an dem Kreuze hängt
   Und sich für uns zum Sündenopfer schenkt.

iii Komm, meine Seel, und tritt zum Kreuz herbei,
    Zu hören, was des Todes Ürsach sei,
    Und trage drob von Herzen Leid und Reu.

i O man, this day in darkest gloom doth lie,
  Wherein the Saviour suffered cruelly,
  The Cross endured, and gave Himself to die.

ii To-day He died ; God's Self 'twas suffered so,
   His life for man gave up.   O Cross of woe !
   He for our sins faced death, our deadly foe.

iii Come then, my soul, come, stand thou by His side,
    Mark well the tortured mien of Him Who died,
    And be thyself with Him in grief allied !

[Here follows No. 174.]
Nachgesang.

i Wir danken dir, o Jesu, Gottes Sohn,
  Dass du für uns gelitten Spott und Hohn
  Und uns dadurch geschenkt die Ehrenkron.

ii Hilf, dass dein Tod, o Herr, mein Leben sei ;
   Dein Blut mach uns von allen Sünden frei ;
   Nimm uns zu dir, durch dein Valet-Geschrei.

iii O Jesu mein, mein Geist befehl ich dir,
    Wie zu dem Schächer neige dich zu mir,
    Und mich am End ins Paradies einführ.

i We thank Thee, Lord, Christ Jesus, God's dear Son,
  The Cross for our salvation Thou hast borne ;
  For we thereby shall wear the victor's crown.

ii O through Thy death new life may all men see,
   Thy blood outpourèd make us sinless, free,
   And called to heaven by Thy departing cry !

iii O Jesu mine, my soul I give to Thee ;
    As once the robber, call me too on high,
    With Thee at last in Paradise to be !

Zahn.[1]

Tr. C. S. T.

[1] Bd. v.   No. 8569.

HEUT IST, O MENSCH, EIN GROSSER TRAUERTAG

Hymn, by Apelles von Löwenstern, in seven 8-line stanzas, with a 'Vorgesang' and 'Nachgesang' (1644). Melody, by Löwenstern (1644).

Christ speaks from the Cross.
(Christus redet am Kreuze.)

i Schaut, ihr Sünder,
   Ihr macht mir grosse Pein.
   Ihr sollt Kinder
   Des Todes ewig sein ;
   Durch mein Sterben
   Seid ihr hievon befreit
   Und nun Erben
   Der wahren Seligkeit.

iv Durch die Wunden,
   So mir geschlagen sein,
   Habt ihr funden
   Ein offnes Brünnelein ;
   Daraus fliessen
   Noch täglich Wass'r und Blut,
   Zu geniessen
   Euch, die ihr Busse thut.

vii Kommt, kommt alle,
   Umfasst im Glauben mich !
   Keiner falle,
   Wie Judas, hinter sich !
   Durch mein Leiden
   Soll weder Sünd noch Tod
   Euch nun scheiden
   Von mir und eurem Gott.

Zahn.[1]

i 'Sinners guilty,
   For you I suffered pain.
   Ruined were ye,
   And still in death had lain.
   Through My anguish
   Are ye now all made free,
   Nor shall languish
   In Satan's tyranny.'

iv See, blood floweth
   Where cruel men did smite !
   It bestoweth
   A fountain of delight.
   Blood and water
   Pour forth, a cleansing flood,
   To deliver
   Him who hath sin withstood.

vii 'Come ye to Me,
   And give Me your embrace ;
   Never falsely
   Receive My kiss of peace.
   Henceforth never
   Shall Satan, Death, or Sin
   You dissever
   From Me your soul did win.'

Tr. C. S. T.

(The *Nachgesang* (No. 173) follows.)

[1] Bd. v. No. 8569.

HEUT TRIUMPHIRET GOTTES SOHN

Hymn, attributed to Bartholomäus Gesius and Basilius Förtsch, in six 6-line stanzas (1601). Melody, by (?) Gesius (1601).

175

i Heut triumphiret Gottes Sohn,
　Der vom Tod ist erstanden schon,
　　　Alleluja ! Alleluja !
　Mit grosser Pracht und Herrlichkeit :
　Dess dankn wir ihm in Ewigkeit.
　　　Alleluja ! Alleluja !

ii Dem Teufel hat er sein Gewalt
　Zerstört, verheert ihm all Gestalt,
　　　Alleluja ! Alleluja !
　Wie pflegt zu thun ein starker Held,
　Der seinen Feind gewaltig fällt.
　　　Alleluja ! Alleluja !

v Dafür dankn wir ihm allzugleich
　Und sehnen uns ins Himmelreich.
　　　Alleluja ! Alleluja !
　Es ist am End : Gott helf uns All'n,
　So singen wir mit grossem Schall'n :
　　　Alleluja ! Alleluja !

vi Gott dem Vater im höchsten Thron,
　Sammt seinem eingebornen Sohn,
　　　Alleluja ! Alleluja !
　Dem Heiligen Geist gleicher Weis
　Sei Lob in Ewigkeit und Preis,
　　　Alleluja ! Alleluja !

i Jesus to-day rose triumphing ;
　He over death's proclaimèd King,
　　　Alleluja ! Alleluja !
　Glorious He reigns in majesty :
　We praise Him through eternity.
　　　Alleluja ! Alleluja !

ii Satan's fell power in dust lies low,
　Kingdom and might must he forgo.
　　　Alleluja ! Alleluja !
　For Israel's Lord has triumphèd,
　And laid His foes beneath Him dead.
　　　Alleluja ! Alleluja !

v So let us thank Him heartily
　Who calleth us with Him to be.
　　　Alleluja ! Alleluja !
　The fight is won : God help us all !
　With lusty shout on Him we call.
　　　Alleluja ! Alleluja !

vi To God the Father, Mighty One,
　To Christ, the One-begotten Son,
　　　Alleluja ! Alleluja !
　To Holy Ghost, the Spirit blest,
　Be praise by all the world confessed !
　　　Alleluja ! Alleluja !

U.L.S. 138.

Tr. C. S. T.

HILF, GOTT, DASS MIRS GELINGE

Hymn, by Heinrich Müller, in thirteen 7-line stanzas (1531 or earlier).   Melody, anonymous (1545), probably of secular origin.

i Hilf, Gott, dass mirs gelinge,
  Du edler Schöpfer mein,
  Die Silben reimen zwinge
  Zu Lob den Ehren dein !
  Dass ich mag fröhlich heben an
  Von deinem Wort zu singen,
  Herr, du wollst mir beistan !

x Und in denselben Tagen
  Jesus sein' Jünger lehrt,
  Allein sein Wort zu tragen,
  Pred'gen in aller Welt :
  Wer glauben thut und wird getauft,
  Der hat das ewig Leben,
  Ist ihm durch Christ erkauft.

xii Ein Tröster thät er senden,
  Das war der Heilig Geist,
  Von Gott thät er sie lenken
  In Wahrheit allermeist.
  Denselben wolln wir rufen an,
  Der wird uns nicht verlassen
  Und uns treulich beistan.

i O help me, Lord, to praise Thee,
  Great Shepherd of Thy sheep,
  In grateful phrases worthy
  Of Thee, Who watch dost keep !
  Help me in song my voice upraise
  For Thy blest Word so holy,
  And guide my feeble praise !

x When Jesus lived among us,
  The Twelve He all did teach
  The Word, of power glorious,
  And sent them forth to preach :
  He who's baptized and doth believe
  Shall be o'er death victorious
  And God's reward receive.

xii A Comforter He sent us,
  The Holy Ghost adored,
  In ways of truth to guide us
  And teach His holy Word.
  And whenso'er we call on Him,
  Be sure He'll show Him gracious
  And that our prayer is heard

Tucher.[1]

Tr. C. S. T.

[1] Bd. i. No. 88.

HILF, HERR JESU, LASS GELINGEN

Hymn, by Johann Rist, in sixteen 6-line stanzas (1642).   Melody, by Johann Schop (1642).

177

i Hilf, Herr Jesu, lass gelingen !
  Hilf, das neue Jahr geht an ;
  Lass es neue Kräfte bringen,
  Dass aufs neu ich wandeln kann.
  Neues Glück und neues Leben
  Wollest du aus Gnaden geben.

iii Meiner Hände Werk und Thaten,
  Meiner Zunge Red und Wort,
  Müssen nur durch dich gerathen
  Und ganz glücklich gehen fort.
  Neue Kraft lass mich erfüllen,
  Zu verrichten deinen Willen.

viii Lass dies sein ein Jahr der Gnaden,
  Lass mich büssen meine Sünd ;
  Hilf, dass sie mir nimmer schaden
  Und ich bald Verzeihung find,
  Herr, in dir ; nur du, mein Leben,
  Kannst die Sünd allein vergeben.

U.L.S. 70.

i On this New Year shed Thy blessing,
  Send us all prosperity !
  May it strength renewed be bringing,
  Speed us on our heavenly way !
  Help, O Lord, Thy help O give me,
  And into Thy grace receive me !

iii Every plan and undertaking,
  All I think and do and say,
  May it have Thy constant blessing,
  E'er Thy just commands obey !
  To my will give strength renewèd
  E'er to know Thy will and do it !

viii Send Thy bounteous grace from heavèn,
  Make me contrite for my sin !
  Never let me by't be driven
  Into shame, to know its sting !
  Thou alone my sin forgivest,
  Thou my life, my all, Who givest.

Tr C. S. T.

HILF, HERR JESU, LASS GELINGEN

Hymn, by Johann Rist, in sixteen 6-line stanzas (1642).   Melody, by Bach (1734).

178

i Hilf, Herr Jesu, lass gelingen !
  Hilf, das neue Jahr geht an ;
  Lass es neue Kräfte bringen,
  Dass aufs neu ich wandeln kann.
  Neues Glück und neues Leben
  Wollest du aus Gnaden geben.

iii Meiner Hände Werk und Thaten,
  Meiner Zunge Red und Wort,
  Müssen nur durch dich gerathen
  Und ganz glücklich gehen fort.
  Neue Kraft lass mich erfüllen,
  Zu verrichten deinen Willen.

* xv Jesus richte mein Beginnen,
  Jesus bleibe stets bei mir ;
  Jesus zähme mir die Sinnen,
  Jesus nur sei mein Begier ;
  Jesus sei mir in Gedanken ;
  Jesus lasse nie mich wanken.

i Shed, Lord, on this New Year blessing,
  Send us all prosperity !
  May it strength renewed be bringing,
  Speed us on our heavenly way !
  Help, O Lord, Thy help O give me,
  And into Thy grace receive me !

iii Every plan and undertaking,
  All I think and do and say,
  May it have Thy constant blessing,
  E'er Thy just commands obey !
  To my will give strength renewèd
  E'er to know Thy will and do it !

xv Jesus, lead my footsteps ever,
  Ever all my doings guide,
  From all ill my senses sever,
  Put all else than Thee aside !
  Jesu, let Thy grace attend me ;
  From all weakness e'er defend me !

U.L.S. 70.

Tr. C. S. T.

ICH BIN JA, HERR, IN DEINER MACHT

Hymn, by Simon Dach, in eight 8-line stanzas (1648). Melody, by Bach.

179

i Ich bin ja, Herr, in deiner Macht,
　Du hast mich an dies Licht gebracht,
　Du unterhältst mir auch das Leben,
　Du kennest meiner Monden Zahl,
　Weisst, wenn ich diesem Jammerthal
　Auch wieder gute Nacht muss geben.
　Wo, wie und wann ich sterben soll,
　Das weisst du, Vater, mehr als wohl.

vii Herr Jesu, ich, dein theures Gut,
　Bezeug es selbst mit deinem Blut,
　Dass ich der Sünden nicht gehöre ;
　Was schont denn Sathan meiner nicht
　Und schreckt mich durch das Zorn-Gericht ?
　Komm, rette deines Leidens Ehre.
　Was giebest du mich fremder Hand
　Und hast so viel an mich gewandt ?

viii Nein, nein, ich weiss gewiss, mein Heil,
　Du lässest mich, dein wahres Theil,
　Zu tief in deinen Wunden sitzen.
　Hie lach ich aller Macht und Not,
　Es mag Gesetz, Höll oder Tod
　Auf mich her donnern oder blitzen.
　Dieweil ich lebte, war ich dein,
　Jetzt kann ich keines Fremden sein.

Fischer-Tümpel.[1]

i Great God, I own Thy heavenly might.
　'Twas Thou that gav'st me life and light
　And every day my steps upholdest.
　Thou know'st the number of my days,
　Know'st when from earth my soul Thou'lt raise,
　When through the grave to me Thou callest.
　The hour is known alone to Thee
　When I must lay me down to die.

vii Lord Jesus, Thee do I beseech
　Thy loving hand to me outreach
　And by Thy Cross from sin to save me.
　Not then shall Satan's power affright,
　Nor need I fear Thine awful sight
　When Thou to Judgment hence shalt call me.
　So much I owe to all Thy care,
　That I need never know despair.

viii Nay, nay, I know, my Saviour dear,
　That I am Thine and Thou art near,
　That by Thy grievous wounds Thou'st won me.
　No matter then hell's power and might !
　Nor Satan nor can Death affright,
　Their thunders mighty ne'er can daunt me.
　For Thou on earth so lovèd me
　That joy in heaven awaiteth me.

Tr. C. S. T.

[1] Bd. iii. No. 105.

ICH DANK DIR, GOTT

Hymn, by Johann Freder, in three 10-line stanzas (1559). Melody, anonymous (1568).

180

i Ich dank dir, Gott,
  Für all Wohlthat,
  Dass du auch mich hast gnädiglich
  Die Nacht behüt't
  Durch deine Güt,
  Und bitt nun fort :
  O Gott, mein Hort,
  Für Sünd und G'fahr
  Mich heut bewahr,
  Dass mir kein Böses widerfahr !

ii Ich b'fehl dir, Herr,
  Mein Seel und Ehr,
  Herz, Sinn und Muth, mein Leib und Gut
  Und all das Mein :
  Der Engel dein
  Hab meiner acht,
  Dass nicht find Macht
  Der Feind an mir
  Nach seim Begier
  Noch mich in Sünd mit Lüsten führ.

iii Auch wollest, Herr,
  Vergeben mir
  Durch deine Huld mein Sünd und Schuld,
  Ich hab an dich,
  Vergriffen mich,
  Unrecht gethan !
  Herr, gnad und schon
  Zu aller Frist
  Durch Jesum Christ,
  Der unser einig Mittler ist !

Tucher.[1]

i Accept, O Lord,
  The praise outpoured,
  For all the joy Thou'st given to me !
  The night is o'er
  Beneath Thy care ;
  And now I pray
  That through the day
  From sin and sleep
  Thou safe wilt keep
  And let no evil on me creep.

ii To Thee I give
  My soul and breath ;
  Heart, thought, and song to Thee belong,
  My life, my all !
  Thine angel call
  To guide me right,
  That Satan's might
  May not prevail
  Nor me assail,
  Nor work me ill, poor sinner frail.

iii Forgive me, Lord,
  The sins abhorred
  That I have done against Thy Son !
  I own my ill
  Is grievous ; still,
  Lord, show Thy face
  Nor doom disgrace !
  Send mercy down,
  Through Christ Thy Son,
  Who hath for me salvation won !

Tr. C. S. T.

[1] Bd. i. No. 584.

ICH DANK DIR, LIEBER HERRE

Hymn, by Johann Kolross, in nine 8-line stanzas (c. 1535). Melody, anonymous (1544), of earlier secular origin.

181

i Ich dank dir, lieber Herre,
　Dass du mich hast bewahrt
　In dieser Nacht Gefährde,
　Darin ich lag so hart
　Mit Finsterniss umfangen,
　Dazu in grosser Noth ;
　Daraus ich bin entgangen,
　Halfst du mir, Herre Gott.

ii Mit Dank will ich dich loben,
　O du mein Gott und Herr,
　Im Himmel hoch dort oben.
　Den Tag mir auch gewähr,
　Warum ich dich thu bitten
　Und auch dein Will mag sein.
　Leit mich in deinen Sitten
　Und brich den Willen mein ;

iii Dass ich, Herr, nicht abweiche
　Von deiner rechten Bahn,
　Der Feind mich nicht erschleiche,
　Damit ich irr möcht gahn.
　Erhalt mich durch dein Güte,
　Das bitt ich fleissig dich,
　Vors Teufels List und Wüthen,
　Damit er setzt an mich.

i I thank Thee, Saviour dearest,
　Who watch hast o'er me kept,
　My Master, best and nearest,
　Who warded while I slept.
　While darkness closed around me
　Beside me hast Thou stood :
　No evil dared come near me.
　I thank Thee, Lord my God.

ii My heart with praise is fillèd
　To Thee, my God and Lord.
　In heavèn high exalted
　Thy help to me afford,
　That I may do Thy bidding
　This day before me lies,
　The pathway straight pursuing
　That leads to Paradise.

iii O keep me, Lord, so closely
　Within the narrow way,
　Nor let the foe entice me
　On other paths to stray !
　Strength give me that resisteth
　The devil's artful lure,
　That, through Thy grace that helpeth,
　My vict'ry may be sure !

U.L.S. 461.

Tr. C. S. T.

ICH DANK DIR, LIEBER HERRE

Hymn, by Johann Kolross, in nine 8-line stanzas (c. 1535).   Melody, anonymous (1544), of earlier secular origin.

182

i Ich dank dir, lieber Herre,
   Dass du mich hast bewahrt
   In dieser Nacht Gefährde,
   Darin ich lag so hart
   Mit Finsterniss umfangen,
   Dazu in grosser Noth ;
   Daraus ich bin entgangen,
   Halfst du mir, Herre Gott.

* iv Den Glauben mir verleihe
    An dein Sohn Jesum Christ ;
    Mein Sünd mir auch verzeihe
    Allhie zu dieser Frist.
    Du wirst mirs nicht versagen,
    Wie du verheissen hast,
    Dass er mein Sünd thut tragen
    Und löst mich von der Last.

vi Dein Wort lass mich bekennen
    Vor dieser argen Welt,
    Auch mich dein Diener nennen,
    Nicht fürchten G'walt noch Geld,
    Das mich bald möcht abwenden
    Von deiner Wahrheit klar ;
    Wollst mich auch nicht absenden
    Von der christlichen Schaar.

i I thank Thee, Saviour dearest,
   Who watch hast o'er me kept,
   My Master, best and nearest,
   Who warded while I slept.
   While darkness closed around me
   Beside me hast Thou stood :
   No evil dared come near me.
   I thank Thee, Lord my God.

iv Firm faith undoubting grant me
    In Jesus Christ my Lord ;
    May all my sins forgiven be
    And I to grace restored !
    For sure He'll not deny me,
    But His true word fulfil,
    Who died for me the guilty
    And freed me from sin's ill.

vi Let me, Thy Word confessing,
    Thee own before the world,
    Thy service e'er professing
    And Thee as my one Lord.
    And ne'er let earth's vain treasure
    Distract my soul from Thee,
    Nor barter for its pleasure
    The joy to live with Thee.

U.L.S. 461.

Tr. C. S. T.

ICH DANK DIR, LIEBER HERRE

Hymn, by Johann Kolross, in nine 8-line stanzas (c. 1535). Melody, anonymous (1544), of earlier secular origin.

183

i Ich dank dir, lieber Herre,
  Dass du mich hast bewahrt
  In dieser Nacht Gefährde,
  Darin ich lag so hart
  Mit Finsterniss umfangen,
  Dazu in grosser Noth ;
  Daraus ich bin entgangen,
  Halfst du mir, Herre Gott.

ii Mit Dank will ich dich loben,
   O du mein Gott und Herr,
   Im Himmel hoch dort oben.
   Den Tag mir auch gewähr,
   Warum ich dich thu bitten
   Und auch dein Will mag sein.
   Leit mich in deinen Sitten
   Und brich den Willen mein.

viii Herr Christ ! dir Lob ich sage
    Für deine Wohlthat all,
    Die du mir diese Tage
    Erzeigt hast überall.
    Dein Namen will ich preisen,
    Der du allein bist gut :
    Mit deinem Leib mich speise,
    Tränk mich mit deinem Blut.

i I thank Thee, Saviour dearest,
  Who watch hast o'er me kept,
  My Master, best and nearest,
  Who warded while I slept.
  While darkness closed around me
  Beside me hast Thou stood :
  No evil dared come near me.
  I thank Thee, Lord my God.

ii My heart with praise is fillèd
   To Thee, my God and Lord.
   In heavèn high exalted
   Thy help to me afford
   That I may do Thy bidding
   This day before me lies,
   The pathway straight pursuing
   That leads me to the skies.

viii Lord Christ, to Thee in heavèn
    Be endless praises sung
    For all the gifts Thou'st given,
    For all that Thou hast done !
    Thy name alone be praisèd ;
    For Thou alone art God.
    O feed me now, be pleasèd,
    With Thine own Flesh and Blood !

U.L.S. 461.

Tr. C. S. T.

ICH DANK DIR SCHON DURCH DEINEN SOHN

Hymn, anonymous, in seven 4-line stanzas (1586). Melody, anonymous (1595), to 'Ach, Herre Gott, mich treibt die Not'.

184

i Ich dank dir schon durch deinen Sohn,
  O Gott, für deine Güte,
  Dass du mich heut in dieser Nacht
  So gnädig hast behütet.

ii Darum bitt ich aus Herzens Grund,
  Du wollest mir vergeben
  All mein Sünd, die ich hab begunnt
  Mit meinem bösen Leben ;

iii Und wollest mich auch diesen Tag
  In deinem Schutz erhalten,
  Dass mir der Feind nicht schaden mag
  Mit Listen mannigfalten.

vii Allein Gott in der Höh sei Preis,
  Sammt seinem eingen Sohne
  In Einigkeit des Heilgen Geists,
  Der herrscht ins Himmels Throne.

  U.L.S. 462.[1]

i I thank Thee, Lord, through Thy dear Son,
  For all Thy loving-kindness,
  That yet another day has come
  To chase the hours of darkness.

ii I beg Thee, Lord, Thy pardon give
  For all I have committed
  That doth my heavenly Father grieve ;
  And be my sins remitted.

iii Shelter me, Lord, beneath Thy wing
  Throughout the day that dawneth,
  Nor let fell Satan plant his sting
  That soul and spirit woundeth.

vii In the height, Lord, to Thee be praise,
  And to Thy Son eternal,
  And to the Holy Ghost likewise,
  Of majesty supernal !

  Tr. C. S. T.

[1] St. ii, viii, x in *U.L.S.* are later additions.

ICH DANKE DIR, HERR GOTT, IN DEINEM THRONE

Hymn, anonymous, in two 6-line stanzas (1612). Melody, by Louis Bourgeois (1547), originally to Psalm xxiii.

185

i Now thanks to Thee, Lord God in heaven be sound - ed, Through

i Ich dan - ke dir, Herr Gott, in dei - nem Thro - ne Durch

Je - sus Christ Thy Son, our Lord be - lov - ed, That

Je - sum Chri - stum, dei - nen lie - ben Soh - ne, Dass

Thou through - out the night that's past hast guard - ed Our

du mich heut die - ser Nacht hast be - wah - ret Vor

rest and all that's e - vil from us ward - ed! And

al - lem Scha - den und vor al - ler G'fahr - ren, Und

ICH DANKE DIR, HERR GOTT, IN DEINEM THRONE

now we pray, through-out the hours of day - light Thou'lt

bit - te dich, wollst mich heut die - sem Ta - - ge Be -

keep us safe from sin and pure in Thy sight.

hü - ten auch vor Sün - den, Schand und Pla - - ge.

ii Dann ich dir, Herr, in deine Händ befehle
  Mein Leib und Gut und meine arme Seele.
  Dein heiliger Engel zu allen Zeiten
  Der sei und bleib bei mir auf allen Seiten,
  Auf dass der böse Feind, so arg und g'schwinde,
  Nimmermehr keine Macht an mir mög finden.

ii Now take, O Lord, my soul into Thy keeping,
  Thy grace from heaven and sure protection seeking ;
  Thy holy angel send for my protection,
  To guide me ever under his direction !
  So shall proud Satan ne'er prevail against me,
  Nor all his power avail from Thee to wrest me.

Also in this form as an Evening Hymn.

ABENDLIED.

i Ich danke dir, Herr Gott, in deinem Throne,
  Durch Jesum Christum, deinen lieben Sohne,
  Dass du mich heut diesen Tag hast bewahret
  Vor allem Schaden und vor aller G'fahren,
  Und bitte dich, wollst mir all Sünd vergeben,
  Behüt mich auch heut diese Nacht gar eben.

i Now thanks to Thee, O God, in heaven be sounded,
  Through Jesus Christ Thy Son, our Lord belovèd,
  That Thou throughout the day that's past hast guided
  Our course and all that's evil from us warded.
  Forgive me, Lord, the sins that have offended,
  And may I still this night by Thee be fended.

ii Dann ich dir, Herr, in deine Händ befehle
  Mein Leib und Gut und meine arme Seele.
  Dein heiliger Engel zu allen Zeiten
  Der sei und bleib bei mir auf allen Seiten,
  Auf dass der böse Feind, so arg und g'schwinde,
  Nimmermehr keine Macht an mir mög finden.

ii Now take, O Lord, my soul into Thy keeping,
  Thy grace from heaven and sure protection seeking ;
  Thy holy angel send for my protection,
  To guide me ever under his direction !
  So shall proud Satan ne'er prevail against me,
  Nor all his power avail from Thee to wrest me.

Fischer-Tümpel.[1]

Tr. C. S. T.

[1] Bd. i. No. 219A.

ICH FREUE MICH IN DIR

Hymn, by Caspar Ziegler, in four 8-line stanzas (1697). Melody, anonymous (1738), to ' O stilles Gotteslamm '.

186

i Ich freue mich in dir
　Und heisse dich willkommen,
　Mein liebstes Jesulein !
　Du hast dir vorgenommen
　Mein Brüderlein zu sein.
　Ach ! wie ein süsser Ton !
　Wie freundlich sieht er aus,
　Der grosse Gottes Sohn.

ii Gott senkt die Majestät,
　Sein unbegreiflich Wesen,
　In eines Menschen Leib ;
　Nun muss die Welt genesen.
　Der allerhöchste Gott
　Spricht freundlich bei uns ein,
　Wird gar ein kleines Kind,
　Und heisst mein Jesulein.

* iv Wohlan, so will ich mich
　An diesen Jesum halten,
　Und sollte gleich die Welt
　In tausend Stücken spalten.
　O Jesu ! dir, nur dir,
　Dir leb ich ganz allein.
　Auf dich, allein auf dich,
　O Jesu ! schlaf ich ein.

i In Thee do I rejoice
　And with a welcome greet Thee,
　O dearest Jesu mine !
　Thy promise giv'st Thou sweetly
　My brother e'er to stand.
　How dear the name doth sound !
　And O, th' unmeasured love
　In God's dear Son is found !

ii God veils His majesty
　And cometh down among us,
　Fruit of a virgin's womb,
　To bring salvation to us.
　The God of earth and sky,
　Whose is immortal fame,
　A mortal child is born,
　And Jesus is His name !

iv So, come whate'er betide,
　To Jesus I cling closely.
　Let earth to atoms break,
　Yet shall it not dismay me.
　Lord Jesus, 'tis on Thee
　Alone my heart is set.
　Firm founded on Thy love,
　Earth's ills can never fret.

U.L.S. 38.

Tr. C. S. T.

o

ICH HAB MEIN SACH GOTT HEIMGESTELLT

Hymn, by Johannes Leon, in eighteen 5-line stanzas (1589).   Melody, ' Ich weiss mir ein Röslein hübsch und fein ' (1589).

187

i Ich hab mein Sach Gott heimgestellt :
  Er machs mit mir, wies ihm gefällt.
  Soll ich allhier noch länger lebn :
  Nicht widerstrebn,
  Seim Willn thu ich mich ganz ergebn.

xi Und ob mich schon mein Sünd anficht,
   Dennoch will ich verzagen nicht,
   Ich weiss, dass mein getreuer Gott
   Für mich in Tod
   Sein lieben Sohn gegeben hat.

xiv Das ist mein Trost zu aller Zeit,
    In allem Kreuz und Traurigkeit :
    Ich weiss, dass ich am jüngsten Tag
    Ohn alle Klag
    Werd auferstehn aus meinem Grab.

xv Mein lieben Gott von Angesicht
   Werd ich anschaun, dran zweifl' ich nicht,
   In ewger Freud und Herrlichkeit,
   Die mir bereit :
   Ihm sei Lob, Preis in Ewigkeit.

U.L.S. 605.

i My cause is God's, and I am still,
  Let Him do with me as He will ;
  Whether for me the race is won,
  Or scarce begun,
  I ask no more—His will be done !

xi My sins are more than I can bear,
   Yet not for this will I despair ;
   I know to death and to the grave
   The Father gave
   His dearest Son, that He might save.

xiv This is my solace, day by day,
    When snares and death beset my way,
    I know that at the morn of doom
    From out the tomb
    With joy to meet Him I shall come.

xv Then I shall see God face to face,
   I doubt it not, through Jesu's grace,
   Amid the joys prepared for me !
   Thanks be to Thee
   Who givest us the victory !

Tr. Catherine Winkworth.[1]

[1] Chorale Book for England (Lond. 1865), No 127.

ICH HAB MEIN SACH GOTT HEIMGESTELLT

Hymn, by Johannes Leon, in eighteen 5-line stanzas (1589).   Melody, 'Ich weiss mir ein Röslein hübsch und fein' (1589).

ICH HAB MEIN SACH GOTT HEIMGESTELLT

i Ich hab mein Sach Gott heimgestellt :
  Er machs mit mir, wies ihm gefällt.
  Soll ich allhier noch länger lebn :
  Nicht widerstrebn,
  Seim Willn thu ich mich ganz ergebn.

xiv Das ist mein Trost zu aller Zeit,
  In allem Kreuz und Traurigkeit :
  Ich weiss, dass ich am jüngsten Tag
  Ohn alle Klag
  Werd auferstehn aus meinem Grab.

xv Mein lieben Gott von Angesicht
  Werd ich anschaun, dran zweifl' ich nicht,
  In ewger Freud und Herrlichkeit,
  Die mir bereit :
  Ihm sei Lob, Preis in Ewigkeit.

xviii Amen, mein lieber frommer Gott,
  Bescher uns all'n ein selgen Tod ;
  Hilf, dass wir mögen allzugleich
  Bald in dein Reich
  Kommen und bleiben ewiglich.

U.L.S. 605.

i My cause is God's, and I am still,
  Let Him do with me as He will ;
  Whether for me the race is won,
  Or scarce begun,
  I ask no more—His will be done !

xiv This is my solace, day by day,
  When snares and death beset my way,
  I know that at the morn of doom
  From out the tomb
  With joy to meet Him I shall come.

xv Then I shall see God face to face,
  I doubt it not, through Jesu's grace,
  Amid the joys prepared for me !
  Thanks be to Thee
  Who givest us the victory !

xviii Amen, dear God ! now send us faith,
  And at the last a happy death ;
  And grant us all ere long to be
  In heaven with Thee,
  To praise Thee there eternally.

Tr. Catherine Winkworth.[1]

[1] *Chorale Book for England* (Lond. 1865), No. 127.

ICH RUF ZU DIR, HERR JESU CHRIST

Hymn, by Johannes Agricola, in five 9-line stanzas (1529). Melody, anonymous (1529).

189

[Violin obbligato]

* i Ich ruf zu dir, Herr Jesu Christ,
Ich bitt : erhör mein Klagen ;
Verleih mir Gnad zu dieser Frist,
Lass mich doch nicht verzagen.
Den rechten Weg, o Herr, ich mein,
Denn wollest du mir geben,
Dir zu leben,
Meim Nächsten nütz zu sein,
Dein Wort zu halten eben.

iii Verleih, dass ich aus Herzengrund
Den Feinden mög vergeben ;
Verzeih mir auch zu dieser Stund,
Schaff mir ein neues Leben.
Dein Wort mein Speis lass allweg sein,
Damit mein Seel zu nähren,
Mich zu wehren,
Wenn Unglück gehet her,
Das mich bald möcht verkehren.

iv Lass mich kein Lust noch Furcht von dir
In dieser Welt abwenden ;
Beständig sein ins End gieb mir :
Du hasts allein in Händen ;
Und wem dus giebst, der hats umsonst ;
Es mag niemand erwerben
Noch ererben
Durch Werke deine Gnad,
Die uns errett vom Sterben.

i I call to Thee, Lord Jesus Christ,
O hear my sore complaining !
In Thy good time unto me list,
Thine ear to me inclining !
True faith in Thee, O Lord, I seek ;
O make me now and wholly
Love Thee solely,
My neighbour hold as self,
And keep Thy word e'er holy.

iii I pray Thee, from my deepest heart,
My foes be all forgiven ;
Lord, bid this hour my sins depart
And grant me rest in heavèn !
O feed me with Thy holy Word,
My soul restore and nourish,
Give it courage
When danger is abroad,
That so I may not perish ! ·

iv Whate'er befall or ill betide,
Ne'er let me from Thee wander.
O keep me ever by Thy side
Till I shall meet Thee yonder !
From Thee alone such grace doth come
As else none can inherit,
Nor can take it
By his own works alone,
Or have by his own merit.

U.L.S. 379.

Tr. C. S. T.

ICH RUF ZU DIR, HERR JESU CHRIST

Hymn, by Johannes Agricola, in five 9-line stanzas (1529). Melody, anonymous (1529).

190

i Ich ruf zu dir, Herr Jesu Christ,
  Ich bitt : erhör mein Klagen ;
  Verleih mir Gnad zu dieser Frist,
  Lass mich doch nicht verzagen.
  Den rechten Weg, o Herr, ich mein,
  Denn wollest du mir geben,
  Dir zu leben,
  Meim Nächsten nütz zu sein,
  Dein Wort zu halten eben.

ii Ich bitt noch mehr, o Herre Gott,
   Du kannst es mir wohl geben :
   Dass ich nicht wieder werd zu Spott,
   Die Hoffnung gieb daneben ;
   Voraus wenn ich muss hie davon :
   Dass ich dir mög vertrauen
   Und nicht bauen
   Auf all mein schwaches Thun ;
   Sonst wirds mich ewig reuen.

* v Ich lieg im Streit und widerstreb :
    Hilf, o Herr Christ, dem Schwachen !
    An deiner Gnad allein ich kleb ;
    Du kannst mich stärker machen.
    Kommt nun Anfechtung her, so wehr,
    Dass sie mich nicht umstosse.
    Du kannst machen,
    Dass mirs nicht bringt Gefähr ;
    Ich weiss : du wirsts nicht lassen.

i I call to Thee, Lord Jesus Christ,
  O hear my sore complaining !
  In Thy good time unto me list,
  Thine ear to me inclining !
  True faith in Thee, O Lord, I seek ;
  To make me now and wholly
  Love Thee solely,
  My neighbour hold as self,
  And keep Thy Word e'er holy.

ii Yet more from Thee, O God, I claim ;
   I know that Thou wilt grant it :
   O let me ne'er be put to shame !
   My hope on Thee's sure founded.
   And when from this world I must go,
   May I still find Thee near me,
   Ever hear Thee ;
   Whatever may ensue,
   May have Thy love to cheer me !

v In sore perplexity I lie ;
  My weakness, Lord, O strengthen !
  On Thee alone can I rely
  My halting steps to lengthen.
  If sore temptations should arise,
  'Tis Thou canst break their power
  When they glower,
  And rescue to me bring,
  My refuge and my tower.

IHR GESTIRN, IHR HOHLEN LÜFTE

Hymn, by Johann Franck, in nine 6-line stanzas (1655). Melody, by Christoph Peter (1655).

191

i Ihr Gestirn, ihr hohlen Lüfte
  Und du lichtes Firmament,
  Tiefes Rund, ihr dunklen Klüfte,
  Die der Wiederschall zertrennt :
  Jauchzet fröhlich, lasst das Singen
  Jetzt bis durch die Wolken dringen.

ii Aber du, o Mensch, für allen
  Hebe deine Stimm empor,
  Lass ein Freudenlied erschallen
  Dort mit jenem Engel-Chor,
  Das den Hirten auf der Weide
  Heut verkündet grosse Freude.

iv Bist willkommen! Heil der Erden,
  Bist willkommen, Jesulein!
  Dass wir möchten Herren werden,
  Stellst du als ein Knecht dich ein.
  Du verlässt die hohen Thronen
  Und willst nun hier unten wohnen.

ix Zwar ist meine Herzenstube
  Wohl kein schöner Fürstensaal,
  Sondern eine finstre Grube ;
  Doch so bald dein Gnadenstrahl
  In denselben nur wird blinken ;
  Wird es voller Sonnen dünken.

i Stars above in myriads shining,
  Spacious sky, God's firmament,
  Earth's round orb, and deeps dark lying,
  Caverns wild with echoes rent,
  Come, rejoice ye, loudly singing
  Till the arch of heaven is ringing !

ii But, above all others lusty,
  Man, upraise a thankful voice ;
  With the angel chorus shout ye,
  Show with them that we rejoice
  At the news to-day proclaimèd
  To the shepherd folk amazèd !

iv Welcome, welcome, earth's Salvation !
  Welcome, Lord, sweet Babe, to-day !
  To exalt us to high station
  Thou a poor child deign'st to be.
  Come from heav'n, where Thou reignest,
  Here on earth with man remainest.

ix Dark and cold the heart within me
  Till Thou deign'st to enter there ;
  'Tis a dwelling black and gloomy,
  Not a palace bright and fair.
  When Thy grace upon it beameth,
  Filled with radiance rare it gleameth.

Fischer-Tümpel.[1]

Tr. C. S. T.

[1] Bd. iv. No. 109.

IN ALLEN MEINEN THATEN

Hymn, by Paul Flemming, in fifteen 6-line stanzas (1642). Melody, anonymous (1679).

192

i In allen meinen Thaten
   Lass ich den Höchsten rathen,
   Der alles kann und hat :
   Er muss zu allen Dingen,
   Solls anders wohl gelingen,
   Selbst geben Rath und That.

ii Nichts ist es spat und frühe
   Um alle meine Mühe ;
   Mein Sorgen ist umsonst :
   Er mags mit meinen Sachen
   Nach seinem Willen machen ;
   Ich stells in seine Gunst.

iii Es kann mir nichts geschehen,
    Als was er hat versehen
    Und was mir selig ist :
    Ich nehm es, wie ers giebet ;
    Was ihm von mir geliebet,
    Das hab ich auch erkiest.

xv So sei nun, Seele, meine,
   Und traue dem alleine,
   Der dich geschaffen hat.
   Es gehe, wie es gehe :
   Dein Vater aus der Höhe
   Weiss allen Sachen Rath.

i Whate'er the task before me,
  To God's care I submit me,
  Who all things well did plan.
  Unless His will decree-eth,
  No thought or deed succeedeth,
  And fails the wit of man.

ii Vain's all my toil and striving,
   My trouble and contriving,
   My sorrow and distress.
   'Tis He alone controlleth,
   And all my ways disposeth :
   He shall my will possess.

iii There's nothing can befall me
    But what in love God sends me
    Who works my daily weal.
    I take what He conferreth,
    And do what He preferreth
    With thankful heart and leal.

xv Let nought, my soul, affright thee,
   Thy trust in God still plight thee !
   He hath thy being given.
   Whatever ills dismay thee,
   Thy Father's love will stay thee,
   And guide thee home to heaven.

Tr. C. S. T.

IN DICH HAB ICH GEHOFFET, HERR

Hymn, by Adam Reissner, a translation of Psalm xxxi, in seven 6-line stanzas (1533).   Melody, by (?) Sethus Calvisius (1581).

193

[Horns I.II. obbligati]

Psalm xxxi.

* i In dich hab ich gehoffet, Herr !
    Hilf, dass ich nicht zu Schanden werd,
    Noch ewiglich zu Spotte.
    Dess bitt ich dich :
    Erhalte mich
    In deiner Treu, Herr Gotte !

ii Dein gnädig Ohr neig her zu mir,
    Erhör mein Bitt, thu dich herfür,
    Eil bald, mich zu erretten.
    In Angst und Weh
    Ich lieg und steh :
    Hilf mir aus meinen Nöthen.

vii Glorie, Lob, Ehr und Herrlichkeit
    Sei Gott Vater und Sohn bereit,
    Dem Heilgen Geist mit Namen !
    Die göttlich Kraft
    Mach uns sieghaft
    Durch Jesum Christum.   Amen.

i In Thee, O Lord, I put my trust,
    O raise me, helpless, from the dust,
    Nor unregarded leave me.
    I pray Thee, Lord,
    Thy help afford,
    And in Thy truth sustain me.

ii Thy gracious ear incline to me ;
    O let my cry ascend to Thee,
    And swift Thine aid accord me !
    I languish here
    In pain and fear ;
    O speed ! Thy help afford me !

vii To Father, Son, and Trinity
    Be praise, be glory, majesty,
    To Persons Three, from all men !
    'Tis by their might
    We'll win the fight,
    Through Christ our Saviour.   Amen.

U.L.S. 629.

Tr. C. S. T.

IN DICH HAB ICH GEHOFFET, HERR

Hymn, by Georg Weissel, in six 6-line stanzas (1642).   Melody, by (?) Sethus Calvisius (1581).

194

i Nun liebe Seel, nun ist es Zeit,
  Wach auf, erwäg mit Lust und Freud,
  Was Gott an uns gewendet :
  Sein lieben Sohn
  Vom Himmelsthron
  Ins Jammerthal gesendet.

v O Jesu, unser Heil und Licht,
  Halt über uns dein Angesicht,
  Mit deinen Strahlen walte,
  Und mein Gemüth
  Durch deine Güt
  Bei deinem Licht erhalte.

* vi Dein Glanz all Finsterniss verzehr,
  Die trübe Nacht in Licht verkehr,
  Leit uns auf deinen Wegen :
  Dass dein Gesicht
  Und herrlich Licht
  Wir ewig schauen mögen.

i Arise, my soul, thy voice employ
  To sing God's praise with mirth and joy !
  Great things for us He planneth.
  His only Son
  From heaven's high throne
  To us poor folk He sendeth.

v O Jesu, Saviour, guiding Star,
  Preserve us ever in Thy care,
  Thy glorious beams e'er lead us !
  Beneath Thy light
  And in Thy sight,
  Upon Thy paths O speed us !

vi Black darkness flies before Thy face,
  Bright rays the clouds of night displace.
  O guide our footsteps ever !
  That in that bright
  And glorious light
  We journey, Saviour, ever !

U.L.S. 78.[1]

Tr. C. S. T.

[1] Here wrongly attributed to Joh. Christoph Arnschwanger.

IN DICH HAB ICH GEHOFFET, HERR

Hymn, by Adam Reissner, a translation of Psalm xxxi, in seven 6-line stanzas (1533).   Melody, by (?)Sethus Calvisius (1581).

195

Psalm xxxi.

i In dich hab ich gehoffet, Herr !
  Hilf, dass ich nicht zu Schanden werd,
  Noch ewiglich zu Spotte.
  Dess bitt ich dich :
  Erhalte mich
  In deiner Treu, Herr Gotte !

* v Mich hat die Welt trüglich gericht
  Mit Lügen und mit falschem G'dicht,
  Viel Netz und heimlich Stricken :
  Herr, nimm mein wahr
  In dieser G'fahr,
  B'hüt mich vor falschen Tücken.

vi Herr, meinen Geist befehl ich dir :
  Mein Gott, mein Gott, weich nicht von mir ;
  Nimm mich in deine Hände !
  O wahrer Gott,
  Aus aller Noth
  Hilf mir am letzten Ende.

                          U.L.S. 629.

i In Thee, O Lord, I put my trust,
  O raise me, helpless, from the dust,
  Nor unregarded leave me.
  I pray Thee, Lord,
  Thy help afford,
  And in Thy truth sustain me.

v How false a part the world doth play,
  What lies and evil thoughts doth say,
  So eager to condemn me !
  Lord, in my smart
  Take Thou my part,
  From lying tongues protect me !

vi O Lord, to Thee do I commend
  My soul, and know Thou wilt it tend,
  Nor stand aloof for ever.
  God of pity,
  In misery
  O haste Thee to deliver !

                          Tr. C. S. T.

IN DULCI JUBILO

Hymn, 14th or 15th cent., in three (and more) 7-line stanzas.   Melody (1535).

196

i *In dulci jubilo*
  Nun singet und seyd froh !
  Unsers Herzens Wonne
  Leit *in praesepio*
  Und leuchtet als die Sonne
  Matris in gremio.
  Alpha es et O ! (*bis*)

ii *O Jesu parvule,*
  Nach dir ist mir so weh !
  Tröst mir mein Gemüthe,
  O puer optime,
  Durch alle deine Güte,
  O princeps gloriae !
  Trahe me post te ! (*bis*)

iii *O patris caritas,*
  O nati lenitas !
  Wir wärn all verloren
  Per nostra crimina,
  So hat er uns erworben
  Coelorum gaudia.
  Eya, wärn wir da ! (*bis*)

iv *Ubi sunt gaudia ?*
  O nirgend mehr denn da,
  Da die Engel singen
  ♪♪ ♩
  Nova cantica,
  Und die Schellen all klingen
  In regis curia.
  Eya, wärn wir da ! (*bis*).

i *In dulci jubilo*
  Your praises hearty show,
  He our heart's sweet treasure
  Lies *in praesepio,*
  Is come to do God's pleasure
  Matris in gremio.
  Alpha es et O ! (*bis*)

ii *O Jesu parvule*
  How sore I long for Thee !
  Bring Thy love and blessing,
  O puer optime,
  To man all good expressing,
  O princeps gloriae !
  Trahe me post te ! (*bis*)

iii *O patris caritas,*
  O nati lenitas !
  We from heaven were driven
  Per nostra crimina ;
  To all men Christ hath given
  Coelorum gaudia.
  Would that we were there ! (*bis*)

iv *Ubi sunt gaudia ?*
  O surely are they there
  Where bright hosts are singing
  ♪♪ ♩
  Nova cantica,
  And sweet bells all are ringing
  In regis curia.
  Would that we were there ! (*bis*)

Tucher.[1]   *Tr. C. S. T.*

[1] Bd. i. No. 24.

204

IST GOTT MEIN SCHILD UND HELFERSMANN

Hymn, by Ernst Christoph Homburg, in seven 6-line stanzas (1659).   Melody, anonymous (1694).

197

i Ist Gott mein Schild und Helfersmann,
Was wird sein, das mir schaden kann ?
Weicht, alle meine Feinde,
Die ihr mir listiglich nachsteht ;
Ihr eurer Schmach entgegen geht,
Ich habe Gott zum Freunde. (*bis*)

ii Ist Gott mein Trost und Zuversicht,
Kein Leid kann sein, so mich anficht.
Weicht, alle meine Feinde,
Die ihr nur sinnet auf Gefahr ;
Ich achte solches keiner Haar,
Ich habe Gott zum Freunde. (*bis*)

* iv Ist Gott mein Schutz und treuer Hirt,
Kein Unglück mich berühren wird.
Weicht, alle meine Feinde,
Die ihr mir stiftet Angst und Pein ;
Es wird zu eurem Schaden sein,
Ich habe Gott zum Freunde. (*bis*)

vii Ist Gott mein Beistand in der Noth,
Was kann mir schaden Sünd und Tod ?
Weicht, alle meine Feinde !
Tod, Sünde, Teufel, Höll und Welt,
Ihr müsset räumen doch das Feld,
Ich habe Gott zum Freunde. (*bis*)

i While God is constant on my side,
Then all is well ; whate'er betide,
My foes shall fall before me.
Their crafty plots to nought must come,
In shame they'll stand before me dumb ;
For God above befriends me. (*bis*)

ii While God in heaven looks down on me,
I fear not pain nor misery ;
My foes shall fall before me.
Whatever mischief they may plan,
I dare defy them, every man ;
For God above befriends me. (*bis*)

iv While God's my Shield and Helper true,
There's nought can vex ; come all or few,
My foes shall fall before me.
On their own heads the pains shall fall
'Gainst me designed : I dare them all ;
For God above befriends me. (*bis*)

vii If God is present in my need,
Then sin and death are dead indeed ;
My foes shall fall before me.
The world, the devil, sin, and hell,
Upon their heads their darts recoil ;
For God above befriends me. (*bis*)

Fischer-Tümpel.[1]

Tr. C. S. T.

[1] Bd. iv. No. 342.

JESU, DER DU MEINE SEELE

Hymn, by Johann Rist, in twelve 8-line stanzas (1641).   Melody, anonymous, of secular origin (1642).

198

i Jesu, der du meine Seele
   Hast durch deinen bittern Tod
   Aus des Teufels finstern Höhle
   Und der grossen Sündennoth
   Kräftiglich herausgerissen,
   Und mich solches lassen wissen
   Durch dein angenehmes Wort :
   Sei doch jetzt, o Gott, mein Hort !

ii Treulich hast du ja gesuchet
   Die verlornen Schäfelein,
   Als sie liefen ganz verfluchet
   In den Höllenpfuhl hinein ;
   Ja, du Satans Ueberwinder,
   Hast die hochbetrübten Sünder
   So gerufen zu der Buss,
   Dass ich billig kommen muss.

vi Jesu, du hast weggenommen
   Meine Schulden durch dein Blut :
   Lass es, o Erlöser ! kommen
   Meiner Seligkeit zu gut ;
   Und dieweil du so zerschlagen
   Hast die Sünd am Kreuz getragen :
   Ei, so sprich mich endlich frei,
   Dass ich ganz dein eigen sei.

i Jesu, Who deliv'rance bought me
   By Thine own most bitter woe,
   In hell's chains had Satan bound me
   If Thou had'st not loved me so.
   From the tomb 'tis Thou wilt call me,
   And in heavèn wilt instal me.
   Through the strength Thy Word doth yield,
   Be Thou still, dear Lord, my Shield !

ii Thou hast searched for me and found me,
   Me Thine erring, wayward child,
   Tended me with love and turned me
   From the depths of hell defiled.
   Through the wiles of Satan's luring,
   As I hear Thine accents calling,
   Lord, my evil I perceive ;
   Me, Thy penitent, receive !

vi Jesu, Thou hast won salvation
   Through Thy cruel Passion's smart ;
   Enter not in condemnation,
   Hold me closely to Thy heart.
   On the Cross o'er sin Thou'rt victor,
   And through Thee man too may conquer :
   Speak then to me, Love divine,
   Tell me I am truly Thine !

U.L.S. 382.

Tr. C. S. T.

JESU, DER DU MEINE SEELE

Hymn, by Johann Rist, in twelve 8-line stanzas (1641).   Melody, anonymous, of secular origin (1642).

199

i Jesu, der du meine Seele
 Hast durch deinen bittern Tod
 Aus der Teufels finstern Höhle
 Und der grossen Sündennoth
 Kräftiglich herausgerissen,
 Und mich solches lassen wissen
 Durch dein angenehmes Wort :
 Sei doch jetzt, o Gott, mein Hort !

iii Ach, ich bin ein Kind der Sünden !
 Ach, ich irre weit und breit !
 Es ist nichts an mir zu finden,
 Als nur Ungerechtigkeit ;
 All mein Dichten, all mein Trachten
 Heisset : unsern Gott verachten ;
 Böslich leb ich ganz und gar
 Und sehr gottlos immerdar.

*xii Herr ! ich glaube ; hilf mir Schwachen,
 Lass mich ja verzagen nicht !
 Du, du kannst mich stärker machen,
 Wenn mich Sünd und Tod anficht.
 Deiner Güte will ich trauen,
 Bis ich fröhlich werde schauen
 Dich, Herr Jesu, nach dem Streit
 In der süssen Ewigkeit.

i Jesu, Who deliv'rance bought me
 By Thine own most bitter woe,
 In hell's chains had Satan bound me
 If Thou had'st not loved me so.
 From the tomb 'tis Thou wilt call me,
 And in heavèn wilt instal me.
 Through the strength Thy Word doth yield,
 Be Thou still, dear Lord, my Shield !

iii Yea, in paths of sin I've wandered,
 Practised all unrighteousness,
 What Thou gavest have I squandered
 On vile deeds and wrongfulness.
 All my thoughts and deeds are evil,
 Bring me justly into peril :
 Nothing good in me is found,
 All is rotten and unsound.

xii Lord, I trust Thee, help my weakness,
 Leave me not accursed to sigh !
 Thou with strength canst nerve my meekness,
 Give me courage e'en to die.
 Lord, Thy gracious love and blessing
 Will I set forth without ceasing
 Till, toil ended, I shall be
 Through eternity with Thee.

U.L.S. 382.

Tr. C. S. T.

JESU, DER DU MEINE SEELE

Hymn, by Johann Rist, in twelve 8-line stanzas (1641).   Melody, anonymous, of secular origin (1642).

200

i Jesu, der du meine Seele
   Hast durch deinen bittern Tod
   Aus des Teufels finstern Höhle
   Und der grossen Sündennoth
   Kräftiglich herausgerissen,
   Und mich solches lassen wissen
   Durch dein angenehmes Wort :
   Sei doch jetzt, o Gott, mein Hort !

iv Herr, ich muss es ja bekennen,
   Dass nichts Gutes wohnt in mir :
   Das zwar, was wir Wollen nennen,
   Halt ich meiner Seele für,
   Aber Fleisch und Blut zu zwingen
   Und das Gute zu vollbringen
   Folget gar nicht, wie es soll ;
   Was ich nicht will, thu ich wohl.

x Du ergründest meine Schmerzen,
   Du erkennest meine Pein.
   Es ist nichts in meinem Herzen,
   Als dein herber Tod allein,
   Dies mein Herz, mit Leid vermenget,
   Das dein theures Blut besprenget,
   So am Kreuz vergossen ist,
   Geb ich dir, Herr Jesu Christ !

i Jesu, Who deliv'rance bought me
   By Thine own most bitter woe,
   In hell's chains had Satan bound me
   If Thou had'st not loved me so.
   From the tomb 'tis Thou wilt call me,
   And in heavèn wilt instal me.
   Through the strength Thy Word doth yield,
   Be Thou still, dear Lord, my Shield !

iv Lord, I needs must make confession
   Of my deep unworthiness,
   I who am Thine own possession,
   Made by Thee for righteousness.
   But the flesh too strong hath provèd ;
   All too rare to virtue movèd,
   What I would not, that I do ;
   For my will doth fail me so.

x Lord, Thou hearest all my weeping,
   Understandest all my pain ;
   Constant in my soul is sleeping
   Grief that nothing can restrain.
   All my heart, with sorrow groaning,
   Cleansèd by Thy love atoning,
   Which upon the Cross was poured,
   Give I Thee, O Christ, my Lord !

U.L.S. 382.

Tr. C. S. T.

208

JESU, DER DU MEINE SEELE

Hymn, by Johann Rist, in twelve 8-line stanzas (1641). Melody, anonymous, of secular origin (1642).

201

i Jesu, der du meine Seele
　Hast durch deinen bittern Tod
　Aus des Teufels finstern Höhle
　Und der grossen Sündennoth
　Kräftiglich herausgerissen,
　Und mich solches lassen wissen
　Durch dein angenehmes Wort :
　Sei doch jetzt, o Gott, mein Hort !

ix Wenn ich vor Gericht soll treten,
　Da man nicht entfliehen kann,
　Ach, so wollest du mich retten
　Und dich meiner nehmen an.
　Du allein, Herr, kannst es stören,
　Dass ich nicht den Fluch darf hören :
　Ihr zu meiner linken Hand,
　Seid von mir noch nie erkannt !

xi Nun ich weiss : du wirst mir stillen
　Mein Gewissen, das mich plagt ;
　Es wird deine Treu erfüllen,
　Was du selber hast gesagt :
　Dass auf dieser weiten Erden
　Keiner soll verloren werden,
　‘Sondern ewig leben soll,
　Wenn er nur ist glaubensvoll.’

i Jesu, Who deliverance bought me
　By Thine own most bitter woe,
　In hell’s chains had Satan bound me
　If Thou had’st not loved me so.
　From the tomb ’tis Thou wilt call me,
　And in heav'n wilt instal me.
　Through the strength Thy Word doth yield,
　Be Thou still, dear Lord, my Shield !

ix When the Day of Judgment falleth,
　All we mortals must obey,
　Let it be Thy voice that calleth
　To me loving on that day.
　But for Thee, Lord, am I doomèd,
　Lost, in deepest hell confounded.
　Say not to me : ‘ Get you hence !
　Flee My sight, for your offence ! ’

xi Yea, I know that Thou wilt hear me,
　Ease my heavy load of sin,
　Thy sure promise, Lord, wilt grant me,
　Let it cure my heart within.
　Through our life’s long toilsome journey
　Ever shall Thy comfort cheer me :
　‘ Who on Me in faith believes
　My protection e’er receives.’

U.L.S. 382.

Tr. C. S. T.

JESU, DER DU SELBSTEN WOHL

Hymn, by Michael Babzien, in four 8-line stanzas (1663). Melody, anonymous (? 1668).

1 Jesu, der du selbsten wohl
  Hast den Tod geschmecket,
  Hilf mir, wann ich sterben soll,
  Wann der Tod mich schrecket.
  Wenn mich mein Gewissen plagt
  Und die Sünden nagen,
  Wenn der Satan mich verklagt,
  Lass mich nicht verzagen.

ii Jesu, zeige mir die Seit'
  Und die rothen Wunden
  In dem letzten scharfen Streit
  Meiner Todesstunden.
  Lass mir deinen bittern Tod,
  Blut und Angstschweiss nützen,
  Wenn ich in der letzten Noth
  Vor dem Tod soll schwitzen.

iv Jesu, meines Lebens-Licht,
  Dich nicht von mir wende ;
  Ach, Herr Jesu, lass mich nicht
  An dem letzten Ende.
  Jesu, reisse mich, mein Schutz,
  Aus der Höllen Rachen.
  Ach, ein Tröpflein deines Bluts
  Kann mich selig machen.

Fischer-Tümpel.[1]

i Jesu, Lord of life and death,
  Who the grave hast conquered,
  When I draw my latest breath
  Be Thy mercy offered !
  When my thoughts would go astray,
  Deeds of evil cherish,
  Or when Satan blocks my way,
  Let me, Lord, not perish !

ii Jesu, let me see Thy Side,
  Pierced and sorely wounded,
  When death standeth close beside
  And his call is sounded.
  Let Thy blood and anguish sore,
  Sacrifice atoning,
  Me to God and heaven restore,
  Thee my Saviour owning.

iv Jesu, Thou the only Light,
  Cast Thy beams upon me,
  Shine upon my glazing sight
  When death's pains are on me !
  Jesu, then be Thou my Shield
  'Gainst hell's power accursèd.
  Let the might Thy blood doth yield
  Draw me to Thee blessèd.

Tr. C. S. T.

[1] Bd. i. No. 452.

JESU, DU MEIN LIEBSTES LEBEN

Hymn, by Johann Rist, in thirteen 10-line stanzas (1641).   Melody, by Johann Schop (1642).

203

i Jesu, du mein liebstes Leben,
Meiner Seelen Bräutigam,
Der du dich vor mich gegeben
An des bittern Kreuzes Stamm;
Jesu, meine Freud und Wonne,
All mein Hoffnung, Schatz und Theil,
Mein Erlösung, Schmuck und Heil,
Hirt und König, Licht und Sonne :
Ach, wie soll ich würdiglich,
Mein Herr Jesu, preisen dich ?

ii O du allerschönstes Wesen,
O du Glanz der Herrlichkeit,
Von dem Vater ausserlesen
Zum Erlöser in der Zeit :
Ach ich weiss, dass ich auf Erden,
Der ich bin ein schnöder Knecht,
Heilig, selig und gerecht
Sonder dich kann nimmer werden.
Herr, ich bleib ein böser Christ,
Wo dein Hand nicht mit mir ist.

iii Ei so komm, du Trost der Heiden,
Komm, mein Liebster, stärke mich.
Komm, erquicke mich mit Freuden,
Komm und hilf mir gnädiglich.
Eile bald, mich zu erleuchten,
Gott, mein Herz ist schon bereit ;
Komm, mit deiner Süssigkeit
Leib und Seel mir zu befeuchten.
Komm, du klares Sonnen-Licht,
Dass ich ja verirre nicht.

Fischer-Tümpel.[1]

i Jesu, Thou my dearest treasure,
Bridegroom of my loving heart,
All Thou didst for me I measure
By Thy Passion's cruel smart.
Jesu, joy beyond all other,
All my heart and soul hast won.
Thou'rt my Master, Light, and Sun,
Saviour, Lord, and sweetest treasure.
Ah, how can I worthily
Jesu, sing my praise to Thee ?

ii O Thou great and glorious Presence,
Shining from Thy throne divine,
Of eternal good the Essence,
Once on earth to make men Thine !
Well I know that I am mortal,
Worthless, evil in Thy sight,
Dark my soul as blackest night.
Can I dare pass heavèn's portal?
Lord, no hope on earth I have
If Thou wilt not stoop to save.

iii Come, Thou Hope of nations, to me,
Strength unto my soul impart !
With Thy joy and spirit fill me,
Enter close into my heart !
See, it ready swept is for Thee,
Quickly come and make it Thine,
With Thy brightness on it shine,
Nurture both my soul and body !
Thou Whose light outshin'st the day,
Come, that I no more may stray !

Tr. C. S. T.

[1] Bd. ii. No. 206.

JESU, JESU, DU BIST MEIN

Hymn, anonymous, in eight 8-line stanzas (1687).   Melody, by Bach (1736).

204

i Jesu, Jesu, du bist mein,
   Weil ich muss auf Erden wallen,
   Lass mich ganz dein eigen sein,
   Lass mein Leben dir gefallen.
   Dir will ich mich ganz ergeben
   Und im Tode an dir kleben,
   Dir vertraue ich allein ;
   Jesu, Jesu, du bist mein.

iv Jesu, Jesu, du bist mein,
   Lass mich nimmer von dir wanken,
   Halt mir meinen Glauben rein,
   Gieb mir gute Bussgedanken,
   Lass mich Reu und Leid empfinden
   Über die begangnen Sünden.
   Dein Blut wäscht mich weiss und rein ;
   Jesu, Jesu, du bist mein.

viii Jesu, Jesu, du bist mein,
   Lass mich bei dir unterkommen,
   Nimm mich in den Himmel ein,
   Dass ich habe mit den Frommen
   Himmelsfreude, Lust und Wonne,
   Und ich seh die Gnadensonne
   Dort mit allen Engelein ;
   Jesu, Jesu, du bist mein.

i Jesu, Jesu, Thou art mine !
   While on earth I live and languish,
   Keep me ever only Thine,
   Thine alone in joy and anguish.
   Living do I make surrender,
   Nor shall death Thee from me sunder.
   All to Thee do I resign :
   Jesu, Jesu, Thou art mine !

iv Jesu, Jesu, Thou art mine !
   Never let me tire or falter,
   All my heart to Thee incline,
   Bring me contrite to Thine altar !
   Let the weight of sin oppress me
   And to penitence distress me.
   Lord, Thy blood hath washed me clean ;
   Jesu, Jesu, Thou art mine !

viii Jesu, Jesu, Thou art mine !
   Call me unto Thee in glory,
   Open heavèn, Love divine,
   That redeemed I may adore Thee !
   There, amid the seraphs winging,
   Holy, holy, holy, singing,
   I shall know that I am Thine :
   Jesu, Jesu, Thou art mine !

Schemelli.[1]

Tr. C. S. T.

[1] *Musicalisches Gesangbuch* (Leipzig, 1736), No 741.

JESU LEIDEN, PEIN UND TOD

Hymn, by Paul Stockmann, in thirty-four 8-line stanzas (1633). Melody, by Melchior Vulpius (1609), to ' Jesu Kreuz, Leiden und Pein '.

205

i Jesu Leiden, Pein und Tod,
Jesu tiefe Wunden
Haben Menschen, die nur Koth,
Heilsamlich verbunden :
Menschen, schafft die Sünde ab,
Wir sind Christen worden,
Sollen kommen aus dem Grab
In der Engel Orden.

* xxxiii Jesu, deine Passion
Ist mir lauter Freude,
Deine Wunden, Kron und Hohn
Meines Herzens Weide :
Meine Seel auf Rosen geht,
Wenn ich dran gedenke;
In dem Himmel eine Stätt
Mir deswegen schenke !

xxxiv Jesu, der du warest todt,
Lebest nun ohn Ende :
In der letzten Todesnoth
Nirgends mich hinwende,
Als zu dir, der mich versühnt,
O mein trauter Herre !
Gieb mir nur, was du verdient,
Mehr ich nicht begehre.

i Jesu, by His bitter Cross
And the wounds that flowèd,
Has redeemed mankind from loss,
Healing grace bestowèd.
Man, cast off the toils of sin,
As Christ's soldier show ye !
So to heavèn shall you win,
Share the angels' glory.

xxxiii Jesu, all Thy bitter pain
Was for my salvation ;
Thine the wounds, O Victim slain,
Mine sweet consolation.
Riseth up my soul with joy
Gratefully to thank Thee
For the bliss without alloy
That the Cross hath won me.

xxxiv Jesu, Thou Who knewest death
Livest now for ever.
When I draw my latest breath
Nought from Thee can sever.
'Twas for me Thou suffered'st pain,
Lord of life and glory.
What Thou willest is my gain ;
More I do not ask Thee.

U.L.S. 104.[1]

Tr. *C. S. T.*

[1] *U.L.S.* omits st. xxii and xxx.

JESU LEIDEN, PEIN UND TOD

Hymn, by Paul Stockmann, in thirty-four 8-line stanzas (1633). Melody, by Melchior Vulpius (1609), to 'Jesu Kreuz, Leiden und Pein'.

206

i Jesu Leiden, Pein und Tod,
Jesu tiefe Wunden
Haben Menschen, die nur Koth,
Heilsamlich verbunden :
Menschen, schafft die Sünde ab,
Wir sind Christen worden,
Sollen kommen aus dem Grab
In der Engel Orden.

* x Petrus, der nicht denkt zurück,
Seinen Gott verneinet,
Der doch auf ein ernsten Blick
Bitterlichen weinet :
Jesu, blicke mich auch an,
Wenn ich nicht will büssen,
Wenn ich Böses hab gethan,
Rühre mein Gewissen.

xxxiv Jesu, der du warest todt,
Lebest nun ohn Ende :
In der letzten Todesnoth
Nirgends mich hinwende,
Als zu dir, der mich versühnt,
O mein trauter Herre !
Gieb mir nur, was du verdient,
Mehr ich nicht begehre.

i Jesu, by His bitter Cross
And the wounds that flowèd,
Has redeemed mankind from loss,
Healing grace bestowèd.
Man, cast off the toils of sin,
As Christ's soldier show ye !
So to heavèn shall you win,
Share the angels' glory.

x Peter thoughtless, Christ denies,
E'en his God forswearing.
Jesus on Him turns His eyes ;
Peter's tears are flowing.
Jesu, turn Thy gaze on me,
When by sin I'm taken ;
Stir my conscience right to see
How I've Thee forsaken.

xxxiv Jesu, Thou Who knewest death
Livest now for ever.
When I draw my latest breath
Nought from Thee can sever.
'Twas for me Thou suffered'st pain,
Lord of life and glory.
What Thou willest is my gain ;
More I do not ask Thee.

U.L.S. 104.[1]   *Tr. C. S. T.*

[1] *U.L.S.* omits st. xxii and xxx.

JESU LEIDEN, PEIN UND TOD

Hymn, by Paul Stockmann, in thirty-four 8-line stanzas (1633). Melody, by Melchior Vulpius (1609), to 'Jesu Kreuz, Leiden und Pein'.

207

i Jesu Leiden, Pein und Tod,
  Jesu tiefe Wunden
  Haben Menschen, die nur Koth,
  Heilsamlich verbunden :
  Menschen, schafft die Sünde ab,
  Wir sind Christen worden,
  Sollen kommen aus dem Grab
  In der Engel Orden.

xxxiii Jesu, deine Passion
  Ist mir lauter Freude,
  Deine Wunden, Kron und Hohn
  Meines Herzens Weide :
  Meine Seel auf Rosen geht,
  Wenn ich dran gedenke,
  In dem Himmel eine Stätt
  Mir deswegen schenke !

* xx Er nahm alles wohl in Acht
  In der letzten Stunden,
  Seine Mutter noch bedacht,
  Setzt ihr ein Vormunden :
  O Mensch, mache Richtigkeit,
  Gott und Menschen liebe,
  Stirb darauf ohn alles Leid,
  Und dich nicht betrübe.

i Jesu, by His bitter Cross
  And the wounds that flowèd,
  Has redeemed mankind from loss,
  Healing grace bestowèd.
  Man, cast off the toils of sin,
  As Christ's soldier show ye !
  So to heavèn shall you win,
  Share the angels' glory.

xxxiii Jesus, all Thy bitter pain
  Was for my salvation ;
  Thine the wounds, O Victim slain,
  Mine sweet consolation.
  Riseth up my soul with joy
  Gratefully to thank Thee
  For the bliss without alloy
  That the Cross hath won me.

xx Still He planned for others' good
  As He hung there dying ;
  To His mother, where she stood,
  Comfort, love supplying.
  O my soul, the lesson learn :
  Love thy God and neighbour !
  So thy soul will He not spurn,
  But give life for ever.

U.L.S. 104.[1]

Tr. C. S. T.

[1] *U.L.S.* omits st. xxii and xxx.

JESU, MEINE FREUDE

Hymn, by Johann Franck, in six 10-line stanzas (1653). Melody, by Johann Crüger (1653).

208

i Jesu, meine Freude,
Meines Herzens Weide,
Jesu, meine Zier :
Ach wie lang, ach lange
Ist dem Herzen bange
Und verlangt nach dir !
Gottes Lamm,
Mein Bräutigam,
Ausser dir soll mir auf Erden
Nichts sonst Liebers werden.

ii Unter deinem Schirmen
Bin ich vor den Stürmen
Aller Feinde frei.
Lass den Satan wittern,
Lass die Welt erschüttern,
Mir steht Jesus bei.
Ob es itzt
Gleich kracht und blitzt,
Obgleich Sünd und Hölle schrecken :
Jesus will mich decken.

iii Trotz dem alten Drachen,
Trotz dem Todesrachen,
Trotz der Furcht dazu !
Tobe, Welt, und springe :
Ich steh hier und singe
In gar sichrer Ruh.
Gottes Macht
Hält mich in Acht.
Erd und Abgrund muss verstummen,
Ob sie noch so brummen.

i Jesu, Joy and Treasure,
Solace passing measure,
Precious gift to me !
Long, so long, I languish,
Torn with grief and anguish,
Yearning, Lord, for Thee.
Thine I am,
O spotless Lamb,
In Thine arms I'd ever hide me ;
Earth holds nought beside Thee.

ii While Thine arms are round me,
Let the foe surround me,
Him I do defy !
Satan's hosts may press me,
Powers of ill distress me,
Still is Jesus nigh !
Hell fires flash,
Their thunders crash,
Sin and Satan's might assail me ;
Jesus ne'er will fail me.

iii Hence, thou noisome serpent !
Hence ! I mock Death's torment.
Bow in fear thy crest !
Rage ye, world, wild leaping,
I stand here, and singing,
Calm, in peace, at rest.
'Tis God's arm
Protects from harm,
Earth and Satan rouse no terror,
Though in wrath they mutter.

U.L.S. 762.

Tr. C. S. T.

JESU, MEINE FREUDE

Hymn by Heinrich Müller, in nine 10-line stanzas (1659).   Melody, by Johann Crüger (1653).

209

i Selig ist die Seele,
　Die in ihrer Höhle
　Dich, o Jesu, liebt ;
　Du wirst sie umärmen
　Und mit Trost erwärmen,
　Wann sie ist betrübt.
　Du bist ihr
　Licht, Heil und Zier,
　Ihres Herzens süsse Weide,
　Leben, Schatz und Freude.

ii Ein Herz, das dich liebet,
　Ist stets unbetrübet
　Und von Sorgen frei.
　Unter tausend Waffen
　Kann es sicher schlafen,
　Denn du stehst ihm bei.
　Wann der Feind,
　Ders böse meint,
　Noch so grausam tobt und wütet,
　Wird es doch behütet.

* ix Muss ich sein betrübet ?
　So mich Jesus liebet,
　Ist mir aller Schmerz
　Über Honig-süsse :
　Tausend Zucker-Küsse
　Drücket er ans Herz.
　Wann die Pein
　Sich stellet ein :
　Seine Liebe macht zur Freuden
　Auch das bittre Leiden.

i Blessèd truly is he
　In this vale of mis'ry,
　Jesu, loves Thee well.
　Him Thou'lt ever cherish,
　Never shall he perish
　When life's tempests swell.
　For 'tis Thou
　A light wilt show,
　Comfort sweet beyond all measure :
　Jesu, Joy and Treasure !

ii Lord, the heart that loves Thee
　Standeth ever firmly,
　Free from every care.
　Foemen wildly raging,
　Him in fight engaging,
　Let them all beware !
　Satan's might
　Is broken quite ;
　Howsoever fierce he rageth,
　God his power tameth.

ix When dark cares oppress me,
　If my Lord possess me,
　Vanishes my woe.
　Honey is not sweeter,
　Passing joys are fleeter,
　Jesu's love I know.
　Grief and pain
　I do disdain ;
　Jesu's love can turn to gladness
　E'en the deepest sadness.

Fischer-Tümpel.[1]   *Tr. C. S. T.*

[1] Bd. v. No. 539.

JESU, MEINE FREUDE

Hymn, by Johann Franck, in six 10-line stanzas (1653).   Melody, by Johann Crüger (1653).

210

i Jesu, meine Freude,
  Meines Herzens Weide,
  Jesu, meine Zier :
  Ach wie lang, ach lange
  Ist dem Herzen bange
  Und verlangt nach dir !
  Gottes Lamm,
  Mein Bräutigam,
  Ausser dir soll mir auf Erden
  Nichts sonst Liebers werden.

iv Weg mit allen Schätzen :
   Du bist mein Ergötzen,
   Jesu, meine Lust.
   Weg ihr eitlen Ehren :
   Ich mag euch nicht hören ;
   Bleibt mir unbewusst.
   Elend, Noth,
   Kreuz, Schmach und Tod
   Soll mich, ob ich viel muss leiden,
   Nicht von Jesu scheiden.

* vi Weicht, ihr Trauergeister,
   Denn mein Freudenmeister,
   Jesus, tritt herein.
   Denen, die Gott lieben,
   Muss auch ihr Betrüben
   Lauter Zucker sein.
   Duld ich schon
   Hie Spott und Hohn :
   Dennoch bleibst du auch im Leide,
   Jesu, meine Freude.

i Jesu, Joy and Treasure,
  Solace passing measure,
  Precious gift to me !
  Long, so long, I languish,
  Torn with grief and anguish,
  Yearning, Lord, for Thee.
  Thine I am,
  O spotless Lamb,
  In Thine arms I'd ever hide me ;
  Earth holds nought beside Thee.

iv Nought on earth is lasting,
   Thou art joy surpassing,
   Jesu, my Delight !
   Hence, vain wealth's deceiving,
   Nought for you I'm grieving,
   Get thee from my sight !
   Death or pain
   Or Cross or shame,
   Jesu is beside me ever,
   Nor can aught us sever.

vi Banish fear and sadness,
   Come, sweet Lord of Gladness,
   Jesu, Master mine !
   Who do truly serve Thee
   Must by faith deserve Thee,
   Joyous bear Thy sign.
   Scorn and hate
   May be man's fate ;
   E'en in them Thy love I measure,
   Jesu, Joy and Treasure.

U.L.S. 762.

Tr. C. S. T.

JESU, MEINE FREUDE

Hymn, by Johann Franck, in six 10-line stanzas (1653). Melody, by Johann Crüger (1653).

ii. While Thine arms are round me, Let the foe sur - round me, Him I do de - fy!
Sa - tan's hosts may press me, Pow'rs of ill dis - tress me, Still is Je - sus nigh!
* Un - ter dei - nem Schir - men Bin ich vor den Stür - men Al - ler Feinde frei;
Lass den Sa - tan wit - tern, Lass die Welt er - schüt - tern, Mir steht Je - sus bei!

Hell fires flash, Their thun - ders crash
Ob es itzt Gleich kracht und blitzt,

Hell fires flash, fires flash, Their thun-ders crash, Hell and Sa - tan's
Ob es itzt Gleich kracht, gleich kracht und blitzt, Ob - gleich Sünd und

Hell fires flash, Their thun-ders crash, Hell fires flash, Hell and Sa - tan's
Ob es itzt Gleich kracht und blitzt, kracht und blitzt, Ob - gleich Sünd und

Hell fires flash, Their thun - ders crash, Sin and Sa - tan's
Ob es itzt Gleich kracht und blitzt, Ob - gleich Sünd und

might as - sail me; Je - sus ne'er will fail me.
Höl - le schre - - cken: Je - sus will mich de - - cken!

Tr. C. S. T.
U.L.S. 762.

JESU, MEINE FREUDE

Hymn, by *Johann Franck, in six* 10-*line stanzas* (1653).   Melody, by *Johann Crüger* (1653).

212

i Jesu, meine Freude,
  Meines Herzens Weide.
  Jesu, meine Zier :
  Ach wie lang, ach lange
  Ist dem Herzen bange
  Und verlangt nach dir !
  Gottes Lamm,
  Mein Bräutigam,
  Ausser dir soll mir auf Erden
  Nichts sonst Liebers werden.

* ii Unter deinem Schirmen
  Bin ich vor den Stürmen
  Aller Feinde frei.
  Lass den Satan wittern,
  Lass die Welt erschüttern :
  Mir steht Jesus bei.
  Ob es itzt
  Gleich kracht und blitzt,
  Obgleich Sünd und Hölle schrecken :
  Jesus will mich decken

v Gute Nacht, o Wesen,
  Das die Welt erlesen :
  Mir gefällst du nicht.
  Gute Nacht, ihr Sünden :
  Bleibet weit dahinten,
  Kömmt nicht mehr ans Licht.
  Gute Nacht,
  Du Stolz und Pracht :
  Dir sei ganz, o Lasterleben,
  Gute Nacht gegeben.

i Jesu, Joy and Treasure,
  Solace passing measure,
  Precious gift to me !
  Long, so long, I languish,
  Torn with grief and anguish,
  Yearning, Lord, for Thee.
  Thine I am,
  O spotless Lamb,
  In Thine arms I'd ever hide me ;
  Earth holds nought beside Thee.

ii While Thine arms are round me,
  Let the foe surround me,
  Him, I do defy !
  Satan's hosts may press me,
  Powers of ill distress me,
  Still is Jesus nigh !
  Hell fires flash,
  Their thunders crash,
  Sin and Satan's might assail me;
  Jesus ne'er will fail me.

v Fare thee well that's mortal ;
  Gaze I on heaven's portal,
  Earth's poor arts are vain !
  Fare ye well, temptation
  Sin and condemnation,
  Thee do I disdain !
  Fare thee well,
  Earth's pomp and spell !
  World, thy life and bonds I sever ;
  Fare thee well for ever !

U.L.S. 762.

Tr. C. S. T.

JESU, MEINE FREUDE

Hymn, by Johann Franck, in six 10-line stanzas (1653). Melody, by Johann Crüger (1653).

213

iv Nought on earth is last - - - ing,
Hence, vain wealth's de - ceiv - - - ing,

* Weg mit al - len Schä - - tzen,
Weg, ihr eit - len Eh - - ren,

iv Nought, nought on earth is last - - ing, on earth is
Hence, hence vain wealth's de - ceiv - - ing, vain wealth's de -

Weg, weg mit al - len Schä - - tzen, mit al - len
Weg, weg, ihr eit - len Eh - - ren, ihr eit - len

iv Nought,nought,nought,nought on earth is last - - ing, on earth is
Hence,hence,hence,hence,vain wealth's de - ceiv - - ing, vain wealth's de -

Weg, weg, weg, weg mit al - len Schä - - tzen, mit al - len
Weg, weg,weg, weg, ihr eit - len Eh - - ren, ihr eit - len

iv Nought,nought,nought,nought on earth is last - ing,
Hence,hence,hence,hence, vain wealth's de - ceiv - ing,

Weg, weg, weg, weg mit al - len Schä - tzen,
Weg, weg, weg, weg, ihr eit - len Eh - ren.

Thou art Joy sur-pass - - ing, Je - su, my De - light !
Nought for you I'm griev - - ing, Get thee from my sight !

Du bist mein Er - göt - - zen, Je - su, mei - ne Lust !
Ich mag euch nicht hö - - ren, Bleibt mir un - be-wusst !

lasting.Thou, Thou art Joy sur-pass - ing, Je - su, my De - light, my Delight !
ceiving,Nought,nought for you I'm griev - ing, Get thee from my sight, from my sight !

Schätzen, Du, du bist mein Er-göt - zen, Je - su, mei - ne Lust, mei-ne Lust !
Eh-ren, Ich, ich mag euch nicht hö - ren, Bleibt mir un - be - wusst, un - bewusst !

lasting, Thou,Thou art Joy sur-pass - ing, Je - su, my De - light !
ceiving, Nought,nought for you I'm griev - ing, Get thee from my sight !

Schätzen, Du, du bist mein Er - göt - zen, Je - su, mei - ne Lust !
Eh-ren, Ich,ich mag euch nicht hö - ren, Bleibt mir un - be - wusst !

Thou,Thou art Joy sur-pass - - - ing, Je - su, Je - su, my De - light, my Delight !
Nought,nought for you I'm griev - - ing, Get thee, get thee from my sight, from my sight !

Du, du bist mein Ergöt - - - zen, Je - su, Je - su, mei - ne Lust, mei - ne Lust !
Ich,ich mag euch nicht hö - - ren. Bleibt mir, bleibt mir un - be - wusst, un - bewusst !

JESU, MEINE FREUDE

Death or pain or Cross or shame, Je-su is be-
E - lend, Noth, Kreuz, Schmach und Tod Soll mich, ob ich

Death or pain or Cross or shame, Cross or shame, Je-su is
E - lend, Noth, Kreuz, Schmach und Tod, Schmach und Tod Soll mich, ob

Death or pain or Cross or shame, Cross or shame, Je-su is be - side
E - lend, Noth, Kreuz, Schmach und Tod, Schmach und Tod Soll mich, ob ich viel

Death or pain or Cross or shame, Je-su is be - side me
E - lend, Noth, Kreuz, Schmach und Tod Soll mich, ob ich viel muss

side me e - ver, Nought from Him can se - ver.
viel muss lei - den, Nicht von Je-su schei - den.

beside me e - ver, Nought, nought from Him can se - ver.
ich viel muss lei - den, Nicht, nicht von Je - su schei - den.

me e - ver, Nought, nought from Him can se - ver, can se - ver, se - ver.
muss lei - den, nicht, nicht von Je - su schei - den, von Je - su schei - den.

e - ver, Nought, nought, nought from Him can se - ver.
lei - den, Nicht, nicht, nicht, nicht von Je - su schei - den.

Tr. C. S. T.
U.L.S. 762.

JESU, MEINE FREUDE

Hymn, by Johann Franck, in six 10-line stanzas (1653).   Melody, by Johann Crüger (1653).

i Jesu, meine Freude,
   Meines Herzens Weide,
   Jesu, meine Zier :
   Ach wie lang, ach lange
   Ist dem Herzen bange
   Und verlangt nach dir !
   Gottes Lamm,
   Mein Bräutigam,
   Ausser dir soll mir auf Erden
   Nichts sonst Liebers werden.

*v Gute Nacht, o Wesen,
   Das die Welt erlesen :
   Mir gefällst du nicht.
   Gute Nacht, ihr Sünden :
   Bleibet weit dahinten,
   Kommt nicht mehr ans Licht.
   Gute Nacht,
   Du Stolz und Pracht :
   Dir sei ganz, o Lasterleben,
   Gute Nacht gegeben.

vi Weicht, ihr Trauergeister,
   Denn mein Freudenmeister
   Jesus, tritt herein.
   Denen, die Gott lieben,
   Muss auch ihr Betrüben
   Lauter Zucker sein.
   Duld ich schon
   Hie Spott und Hohn :
   Dennoch bleibst du auch im Leide,
   Jesu, meine Freude.

i Jesu, Joy and Treasure,
   Solace passing measure,
   Precious gift to me !
   Long, so long, I languish,
   Torn with grief and anguish,
   Yearning, Lord, for Thee.
   Thine I am,
   O spotless Lamb,
   In Thine arms I'd ever hide me ;
   Earth holds nought beside Thee.

v Fare thee well that's mortal ;
   Gaze I on heaven's portal,
   Earth's poor arts are vain !
   Fare ye well, temptation,
   Sin and condemnation,
   Thee do I disdain !
   Fare thee well,
   Earth's pomp and spell !
   World, thy life and bonds I sever ;
   Fare thee well for ever !

vi Banish fear and sadness,
   Come, sweet Lord of Gladness,
   Jesu, Master mine !
   Who do truly serve Thee
   Must by faith deserve Thee,
   Joyous bear Thy sign.
   Scorn and hate
   May be man's fate ;
   E'en in them Thy love I measure,
   Jesu, Joy and Treasure.

U.L.S. 762.

Tr. C. S. T.

JESU, MEINES HERZENS FREUD

Hymn, by Johann Flittner, in five 7-line stanzas (1660), a translation of 'Salve cordis gaudium'. Melody, by J. R. Ahle (1660).

215

Salve cordis gaudium.

i Jesu, meines Herzens Freud,
  Süsser Jesu,
  Meiner Seelen Seligkeit,
  Süsser Jesu,
  Des Gemüthes Sicherheit,
  Süsser Jesu,
  Jesu, süsser Jesu!

ii Tausendmal gedenk ich dein,
  Mein Erlöser,
  Und begehre dich allein,
  Mein Erlöser,
  Sehne mich, bei dir zu sein,
  Mein Erlöser,
  Jesu, mein Erlöser.

iii Nichts ist lieblicher als du,
  Liebste Liebe,
  Nichts ist freundlicher als du,
  Süsse Liebe;
  Auch ist süsser nichts als du,
  Süsse Liebe,
  Jesu, süsse Liebe.

v Ich bin krank, komm, stärke mich,
  Meine Stärke,
  Ich bin matt, erquicke mich,
  Süsser Jesu.
  Wenn ich sterbe, tröste mich,
  Du mein Tröster,
  Jesu, du mein Tröster.

Fischer-Tümpel.[1]

i Jesu, sweetest, loved, and best;
  Jesu, hail Thee!
  By Thee all my heart's possessed;
  Jesu, hail Thee!
  In Thee all my soul's expressed;
  Jesu, hail Thee,
  Jesu, sweetest Jesu!

ii All my heart and soul are Thine,
  Saviour dearest!
  'Tis for Thee alone I pine,
  Saviour dearest!
  Me a place in heaven assign,
  Saviour dearest,
  Jesu, Saviour dearest!

iii None is more beloved than Thee,
  Love entrancing!
  None so kind and good to me,
  Love entrancing!
  None so sweet and true can be,
  Love entrancing,
  Jesu, Love entrancing!

v Weak am I, O strengthen me,
  Great Defender!
  Languid am I, quicken me,
  Jesu, Saviour!
  When I die, call me to Thee,
  Blessèd Saviour,
  Jesu, blessèd Saviour!

Tr. C. S. T.

[1] Bd. iv. No. 542.

JESU, NUN SEI GEPREISET

Hymn, by (?) Johann Hermann, in three 14-line stanzas (1591). Melody, anonymous (1591).

216

i Je - su, come let us praise Thee, This new and hap - py year. Right
With what fair skies of bless - ing Dost dawn, O hap - py day, God's

i Je - su, nun sei ge - prei - set Zu die - sem neu - en Jahr, Für
Dass wir ha - ben er - le - bet Die neu fröh - li - che Zeit, Die

hear - ty an - thems raise Thee, Who gi - vest us good cheer!
full - est love ex - press - ing, To all of us, we pray!

dein Güt uns be - wei - set In al - ler Noth und G'fahr:
vol - ler Gna - den schwe - bet Und ew - ger Se - lig - keit;

We dwell at peace and rest - ful, In hap - pi - ness, con - tent - ful. We
Dass wir in gu - ter Stil - le Das alt Jahr habn er - fül - let. Wir

JESU, NUN SEI GEPREISET

ii Lass uns das Jahr vollbringen
Zu Lob dem Namen dein,
Dass wir denselben singen
In der Christen Gemein :
Wollst uns das Leben fristen
Durch deine starke Hand ;
Erhalt dein liebe Christen
Und unser Vaterland.
Dein Segen zu uns wende,
Gieb Fried an allem Ende :
Gieb unverfälscht im Lande
Dein seligmachend Wort;
Die Feinde mach zu Schande } (bis)
Hie und an allem Ort.

ii May this New Year before us
Add praises to God's name !
Good Christians all, in chorus
Your loudest carols frame !
Lord, by Thy might and power,
Grant us long days on earth ;
Thy richest blessing shower
On our dear land of birth !
O shield us 'neath Thy strong wing !
May this New Year firm peace bring !
Stablish among believers
Thine own Almighty realm,
And all earth's vain deceivers } (bis)
Right utterly o'erwhelm !

U.L.S. 71.

Tr. C. S. T.

JESU, NUN SEI GEPREISET

Hymn, by (?) Johann Hermann, in three 14-line stanzas (1591). Melody, anonymous (1591).

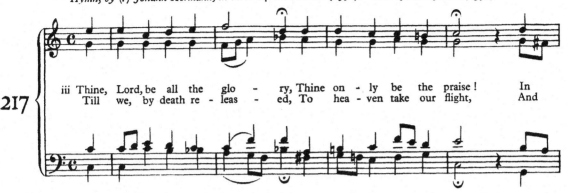

217

iii Thine, Lord, be all the glo - ry, Thine on - ly be the praise! In
Till we, by death re - leas - ed, To hea - ven take our flight, And

*iii Dein ist al - lein die Eh - re, Dein ist al - lein der Ruhm; Ge -
Bis wir fröh-lich ab - schei - den ins e - wig Him - mel - reich Zu

trou - ble ne'er we doubt Thee, Who gov - ern'st all our ways;
dwell, with joy in - creas - ed, For e - ver in God's sight.

duld im Kreuz uns leh - re Re - gier all un - ser Thun,
wah - rem Fried und Freu - den, Den Heil - gen Got - tes gleich.

Do with us, each and all, then, Ac - cord - ing to Thy wil - ling. Thy

In - dess machs mit uns al - len Nach dei - nem Wohlge - fal - len: Solchs

JESU, NUN SEI GEPREISET

faith-ful flock re - joi - ces, With Christ-ian glow and fear, And

sin - get heut ohn Scher - zen Die Christ-gläu - bi - ge Schaar, Und

lifts to Thee their voi - ces To beg a hap - py year,

wünscht mit Mund und Her - zen Ein se - lig neu - es Jahr,

And lifts to Thee their voi - ces To beg a hap - py year.

Und wünscht mit Mund und Her - zen Ein se - lig neu - es Jahr.

U.L.S. 71.   *Tr. C. S. T.*

JESU, NUN SEI GEPREISET

Hymn, by (?) Johann Hermann, in three 14-line stanzas (1591). Melody, anonymous (1591).

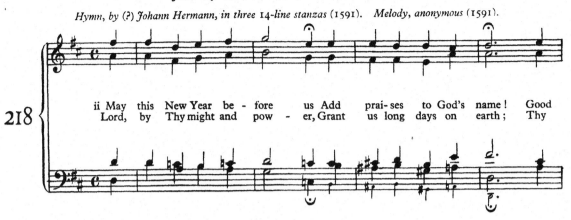

218

ii May this New Year be-fore us Add prai-ses to God's name! Good
Lord, by Thy might and pow-er, Grant us long days on earth; Thy

*ii Lass uns das Jahr voll-brin-gen, Zu Lob dem Na-men dein, Dass
Wollst uns das Le-ben fri-sten Durch dein all-mäch-tig Hand, Er

Christ-ians all, in chor-us Your loud-est car-ols frame!
rich-est bless-ing show-er On our dear land of birth!

wir den-sel-ben sin-gen In der Chri-sten Ge-mein;
halt dein lie-be Chri-sten Und un-ser Va-ter-land.

O shield us neath Thy strong wing! May this New Year firm peace bring!

Dein Se-gen zu uns wen-de, Gieb Fried an al-lem En-de;

JESU, NUN SEI GEPREISET

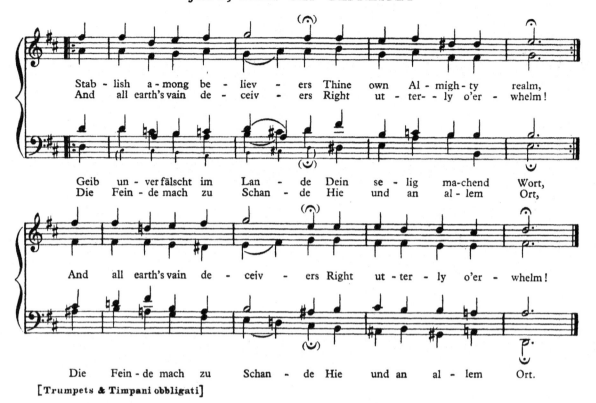

Stab - lish a - mong be - liev - ers Thine own Al - migh-ty realm,
And all earth's vain de - ceiv - ers Right ut - ter - ly o'er - whelm!

Geib un - ver fälscht im Lan - de Dein se - lig ma-chend Wort,
Die Fein - de mach zu Schan - de Hie und an al - lem Ort,

And all earth's vain de - ceiv - ers Right ut - ter - ly o'er - whelm!

Die Fein - de mach zu Schan - de Hie und an al - lem Ort.

[Trumpets & Timpani obbligati]

i Jesu, nun sei gepreiset
Zu diesem neuen Jahr,
Für dein Güt, uns beweiset
In aller Noth und G'fahr :
Dass wir in guter Stille
Das alt Jahr habn erfüllet.
Wir wolln uns dir ergeben
Jetzund und immerdar,
Behüt uns Leib und Leben
Hinfort das ganze Jahr !

i Jesu, come let us praise Thee,
This new and happy year ;
Right hearty anthems raise Thee,
Who givest us good cheer !
We dwell at peace and restful,
In happiness contentful.
We would to God be giving
As gifts ourselves, our fear,
Our heart, life, soul and being
Throughout the coming year.

JESUS CHRISTUS, UNSER HEILAND, DER DEN

Hymn, by Martin Luther, in three 5-line stanzas (1524). Melody, anonymous (1535).

219

i Jesus Christus, unser Heiland,
   Der den Tod überwand,
   Ist auferstanden ;
   Die Sünd hat er gefangen.
        Kyrie eleison !

ii Der ohn Sünden war geboren,
   Trug für uns Gottes Zorn ;
   Hat uns versöhnet,
   Dass uns Gott sein Huld gönnet.
        Kyrie eleison !

iii Tod, Sünd, Leben und Genade,
    Alls in Händen er hat :
    Er kann erretten
    Alle, die zu ihm treten.
        Kyrie eleison !

                U.L.S. 139.

i Jesus Christ, our Lord Redeemer
   O'er Death is now victor !
   To heaven He's risèn
   And Death hath put in prison.
        We thank Thee, Lord our God !

ii He Whom sinful mortals adore
   For us God's anger bore,
   And hath redeemed us :
   God hath His favour given us.
        We thank Thee, Lord our God !

iii Over Sin and Death He's Victor,
    Of mortals Controller.
    He will deliver
    All they who seek their Saviour.
        We thank Thee, Lord our God !

                Tr. C. S. T.

JESUS CHRISTUS, UNSER HEILAND, DER VON

Hymn, by Martin Luther, a version, in ten 4-line stanzas (1524), of John Hus's (?) 'Jesus Christus, nostra salus'. Melody, anonymous (1524).

Jesus Christus, nostra salus.

i Jesus Christus, unser Heiland,
  Der von uns den Gottes Zorn wandt,
  Durch das bitter Leiden sein
  Half er uns aus der Höllen Pein.

ii Dass wir nimmer dess vergessen,
  Gab er uns sein Leib zu essen,
  Verborgen im Brod so klein,
  Und zu trinken sein Blut im Wein.

iii Wer sich zu dem Tisch will machen,
  Der hab wohl Acht auf sein Sachen :
  Wer unwürdig hinzugeht,
  Für das Leben den Tod empfäht.

iv Du sollt Gott den Vater preisen,
  Dass er dich so wohl wollt speisen
  Und für deine Missethat
  In den Tod sein Sohn geben hat.

x Die Frucht soll auch nicht ausbleiben l
  Deinen Nächsten sollt du lieben,
  Dass er dein geniessen kann,
  Wie dein Gott an dir hat gethan.

U.L.S. 279.

i Christ our Saviour hath redeemed us,
  Turned His Father's anger from us,
  By the bitter Cross He bore,
  And saved us all from Satan's power.

ii That we never should forget it
  Giveth He His Flesh to eat it,
  Hid in bread, and, feast divine,
  His precious Blood to drink as wine.

iii He who to His table cometh
  Must be wary how he goeth :
  He who goes unworthily
  Not life but death will surely see.

iv God the Father therefore praise ye,
  Who this precious feast doth give thee,
  And that thou may'st go to heaven
  His Son a sacrifice hath given.

x Let thy faith be seen in doing :
  Good unto thy neighbour showing.
  Let Him in thy conduct see
  All that thy Lord hath done for thee.

Tr. C. S. T.

JESUS, MEINE ZUVERSICHT

Hymn, by Luise Henriette, Electress of Brandenburg, in ten 6-line stanzas (1653).   Melody, by (?) Johann Crüger (1653).

221

i Jesus, meine Zuversicht
  Und mein Heiland, ist im Leben !
  Dieses weiss ich : soll ich nicht
  Darum mich zufrieden geben ?
  Was die lange Todesnacht
  Mir auch für Gedanken macht ?

ii Jesus, er mein Heiland lebt ;
   Ich werd auch das Leben schauen,
   Sein, wo mein Erlöser schwebt :
   Warum sollte mir denn grauen ?
   Lässet auch ein Haupt sein Glied,
   Welches es nicht nach sich zieht ?

iii Ich bin durch der Hoffnung Band
    Zu genau mit ihm verbunden ;
    Meine starke Glaubenshand
    Wird in ihm gelegt gefunden,
    Dass mich auch kein Todesbann
    Ewig von ihm trennen kann.

x Nurr dass ihr den Geist erhebt
  Von den Lüsten dieser Erden
  Und euch dem schon jetzt ergebt,
  Dem ihr beigefügt wollt werden.
  Schickt das Herze da hinein,
  Wo ihr ewig wünscht zu sein.

i Jesus Christ, my sure defence
  And my Saviour, ever liveth ;
  Knowing this, my confidence
  Rests upon the hope it giveth,
  Though the night of death be fraught
  Still with many an anxious thought.

ii Jesus, my Redeemer, lives !
   I too unto life must waken ;
   He doth call me where He is ;
   Shall my courage then be shaken ?
   Shall I fear ?   Or could the Head
   Rise and leave its members dead ?

iii Nay, too closely am I bound
    Unto Him by hope for ever ;
    Faith's strong hand the Rock hath found,
    Grasped it, and will leave it never.
    Not the ban of death can part
    From its Lord this trusting heart.

x Only draw away your heart
  Swift from pleasures base and hollow ;
  Would ye there with Christ have part,
  Here His footsteps ye must follow ;
  Fix your hearts beyond the skies,
  Whither ye yourselves would rise !

U.L.S. 866.

Tr. Catherine Winkworth.[1]

[1] *Chorale Book for England* (Lond. 1865), No. 59.

JESUS, MEINE ZUVERSICHT

Hymn, by Caspar Neumann, in nine 6-line stanzas (c. 1700). Melody, by (?) Johann Crüger (1563).

222

*i Auf, mein Herz, des Herren Tag
   Hat die Nacht der Furcht vertrieben.
   Christus, der begraben lag,
   Ist im Tode nicht geblieben.
   Nunmehr bin ich recht getröst,
   Jesu hat die Welt erlöst.

ii Nunmehr ist er Gottes Sohn,
   Und hat dieses klar erwiesen.
   Allen Feinden auch zu Hohn,
   Sei er dafür hoch gepriesen,
   Denn es kommet in der That,
   Was sein Mund geredet hat.

viii Tod, wo ist nun deine Kraft ?
   Hölle, wo sind deine Ketten ?
   Hier ist Gott der Hülfe schafft ;
   Hier ist einer der kann retten,
   Wann gleich unser Fleisch und Bein
   Lange wird verweset sein.

ix Herr, dies glaub ich dir zu Ruhm,
   Und mein Trost ist nicht vergebens.
   Denn ich bin dein Eigenthum,
   Gleich wie du mein Fürst des Lebens.
   Dir auch sei viel Dank bereit,
   Jetzund und in Ewigkeit.

C. Neumann.[1]

i Up, my soul, 'tis God's great day,
   Death no longer can enthral us !
   He Who in the dark grave lay
   Ris'n and glorious goes before us.
   Ever will I trust in Him
   Who hath bought the world from sin.

ii Son of God, a mighty name,
   Reigns He now in highest heavèn,
   All His foes hath put to shame ;
   Thanks and praise to Him be given !
   What He did to man foretell
   Comes to pass, we know right well.

viii Death, where is thy vaunted might ?
   Hell, thy chains to dust are riven !
   God doth aid us in the fight,
   By Him help and strength are given ;
   Else must we poor mortals all
   Quick into destruction fall.

ix Lord, I lift my song of praise
   To my Saviour, loving, faithful.
   Thine I am for all my days,
   Thou the Prince of Life eternal.
   Thanks and glory be to Thee
   Now and through eternity !

Tr. C. S. T.

[1] *Vollkommenes Schlesisches G.B.* (Breslau and Liegnitz, 1727), p. 376.

KEINEN HAT GOTT VERLASSEN

Hymn, anonymous (?) Andreas Kesler, in eight 8-line stanzas (1611). Melody, anonymous (1609), to 'O Gott, ich thu dirs klagen'.

i Keinen hat Gott verlassen,
　Der ihm vertraut allzeit ;
　Und ob ihn gleich viel hassen,
　Geschicht ihm doch kein Leid.
　Gott will die Seinen schützen,
　Zuletzt erheben hoch ;
　Und geben, was ihn nützet
　Hie zeitlich und auch dort.

iv All's Glück und Ungelücke,
　Das kommt allein von Gott :
　Ich weiche nicht zurücke
　Und fleh in meiner Noth.
　Wie kann er mich denn hassen,
　Der treu Nothhelfer mein ?
　Ja, wenn die Noth am grössten,
　So will er bei mir sein.

vi Ihn hab ich eingeschlossen
　In meines Herzens Schrein.
　Sein Blut hat er vergossen
　Für mich arm's Würmelein,
　Mich damit zu erlösen
　Von ewger Angst und Pein :
　Wie könnt auf dieser Erden
　Doch grössre Liebe sein ?

viii Amen, nun will ich schliessen
　Dies schlichte Liedelein.
　Herr, durch dein Blutvergiessen
　Lass mich dein Erben sein :
　So hab ich all's auf Erden,
　Was mich erfreuet schon ;
　Im Himmel soll mir werden
　Die ewig Gnadenkron.

i His own God ne'er neglecteth,
　Who in Him put their trust,
　He who his sin repenteth
　He raiseth from the dust.
　God will protect His children
　And one day call them home,
　On earth let nothing harm them,
　But to their comfort come.

iv Both good and ill He sendeth ;
　He chooseth which alone.
　He foolish is that groaneth
　Or troubled makes his moan.
　How can God e'er reject me,
　My Helper, truest, best ?
　No, when care rubs most sorely,
　He'll give me quiet and rest.

vi Deep in my heart I shrine Him
　Who gave His blood for me.
　How deep His love inclined Him
　To stoop to rescue me !
　From hell and pain He saved me
　By His most precious death.
　For His so gracious bounty
　I raise my grateful breath.

viii Amen.　Now, Lord, is ended
　This duteous song of mine.
　Lord, by Thy love commended,
　Make me all wholly Thine !
　So shall I, here a mortal,
　Enjoy Thy bounteous grace,
　And one day pass heaven's portal
　To my appointed place.

U.L.S. 632.

Tr. C.S.T.

KOMM, GOTT SCHÖPFER, HEILIGER GEIST

Hymn, by Martin Luther, a translation of 'Veni Creator Spiritus', in seven 4-line stanzas (1524). Melody (1524), that of the Latin hymn.

Veni Creator Spiritus.

i Komm, Gott Schöpfer, Heiliger Geist,
  Besuch das Herz der Menschen dein,
  Mit Gnaden sie füll, wie du weisst,
  Dass dein Geschöpf soll vor dir sein.

iii Zünd uns ein Licht an im Verstand,
  Gieb uns ins Herz der Liebe Brunst,
  Des Fleisches Schwachheit, dir bekannt,
  Erhalt fest durch dein Kraft und Gunst.

v Des Feindes List treib von uns fern,
  Den Fried schaff bei uns deine Gnad,
  Dass wir dein'm Leiten folgen gern
  Und meiden, was der Seele schadt.

vi Lehr uns den Vater kennen wohl
  Und Jesum Christum, seinen Sohn,
  Dass wir des Glaubens werden voll,
  Dich, beider Geist, zu verstehen.

vii Gott unser Vater, sei allezeit
  Aus Herzensgrund von uns gepreist,
  Lob sei, Herr Jesu, dir bereit
  Mit Gott dem werten Heilgen Geist.

U.L.S. 172.

i Come, Holy Ghost, our souls inspire,
  And lighten with celestial fire ;
  Thou the anointing Spirit art,
  Who dost Thy sevenfold gifts impart.

iii Thy blessèd unction from above
  Is comfort, life, and fire of love.
  Enable with perpetual light
  The dulness of our blinded sight.

v Anoint and cheer our soilèd face
  With the abundance of Thy grace ;
  Keep far our foes ; give peace at home :
  Where Thou art Guide no ill can come.

vi Teach us to know the Father, Son,
  And Thee of Both, to be but One,
  That through the ages all along
  This may be our unending song :
  ' Praise unto Thee eternally,
  Father and Son, and Holy Three.'[1]

Tr. John Cosin.

[1] Repeat the second half of the tune.

KOMM, GOTT SCHÖPFER, HEILIGER GEIST

Hymn, by Martin Luther, a translation of 'Veni Creator Spiritus', in seven 4-line stanzas (1524). Melody (1524), that of the Latin hymn.

225

[Horns I & II Obbligati]   *Veni Creator Spiritus.*

* i Komm, Gott Schöpfer, Heiliger Geist,
   Besuch das Herz der Menschen dein,
   Mit Gnaden sie füll, wie du weisst,
   Dass dein Geschöpf soll vor dir sein.

iii Zünd uns ein Licht an im Verstand,
   Gieb uns ins Herz der Liebe Brunst,
   Des Fleisches Schwachheit, dir bekannt,
   Erhalt fest durch dein Kraft und Gunst.

v Des Feindes List treib von uns fern,
   Den Fried schaff bei uns deine Gnad,
   Dass wir dein'm Leiten folgen gern
   Und meiden, was der Seele schadt.

vi Lehr uns den Vater kennen wohl,
   Und Jesum Christum, seinen Sohn,
   Dass wir des Glaubens werden voll,
   Dich, beider Geist, zu verstehen.

vii Gott unser Vater, sei allezeit
   Aus Herzensgrund von uns gepreist,
   Lob sei, Herr Jesu, dir bereit
   Mit Gott dem werten Heilgen Geist.

i Come, Holy Ghost, our souls inspire,
   And lighten with celestial fire ;
   Thou the anointing Spirit art,
   Who dost Thy sevenfold gifts impart.

iii Thy blessèd unction from above
   Is comfort, life, and fire of love.
   Enable with perpetual light
   The dulness of our blinded sight.

v Anoint and cheer our soilèd face
   With the abundance of Thy grace ;
   Keep far our foes ; give peace at home :
   Where Thou art Guide no ill can come.

vi Teach us to know the Father, Son,
   And Thee of Both, to be but One,
   That through the ages all along
   This may be our unending song :
   ' Praise unto Thee eternally,
   Father and Son, and Holy Three.'[1]

Tr. John Cosin.

U.L.S. 172.

[1] Repeat the second half of the tune.

KOMM, HEILIGER GEIST, HERRE GOTT

Hymn, by Martin Luther, an expansion of the antiphon 'Veni Sancte Spiritus', in three 9-line stanzas (1524). Melody, anonymous (1524).

* Bach has a 𝄐 here.

KOMM, HEILIGER GEIST, HERRE GOTT

Tr. Catherine Winkworth.[1]

[Strings and Flutes obbligati]

U.L.S. 174.

[1] *Chorale Book for England* (Lond. 1865). No. 72.

KOMM, HEILIGER GEIST, HERRE GOTT

In Cantata 175 the melody is set to Johann Rist's ' O Gottes Geist, mein Trost und Rath ', a hymn of twelve 8-line stanzas (1651).

i O Gottes Geist, Trost und Rath,
 Mein treuer Hort und Advokat,
 Ich zweifle nicht, dass auf mein Beten
 Du wirst mich also vertreten,
 Dass ich für Gottes Angesicht
 Und Richterstuhl erschrecke nicht ;
 Ach lehre mich den Mittler kenn'n
 Den alle Welt muss Heiland nennen.
           Alleluja ! Alleluja !

* ix Nun werther Geist, ich folg dir ;
 Hilf, dass ich suche für und für
 Nach deinem Wort ein ander Leben,
 Das du mir willst aus Gnaden geb'n.
 Dein Wort ist ja der Morgenstern,
 Der herrlich leuchtet nah und fern.
 Drum will ich, die mich anders lehr'n,
 In Ewigkeit, mein Gott, nicht hören.
           Alleluja ! Alleluja !

xii Herr, tröste mich in mein Noth,
 Ja stärke mich, wenn nun der Tod
 Die Seele will vom Leibe scheiden :
 Alsdan versüsse mir mein Leid'n.
 Sei du mein Lehrer, Schutz und Rath,
 Dämpf alle meine Missethat,
 Hilf Noth und Tod mir überstreb'n
 Und lass mich ewig bei dir leben.
           Alleluja ! Alleluja !

             Fischer Tümpel.[1]

i O Holy Spirit, Counsel sweet,
 My only Hope and Advocate,
 Ne'er doubt I that Thou hear'st my crying,
 That Thou my soul wilt, when dying,
 Courage to meet her Lord supply,
 That without fear Thy face I see.
 O teach me ay the Christ to know
 Whom all the world as Saviour doth own.
           Alleluja ! Alleluja !

ix O Holy Spirit, Thee we pray
 Grant us Thy help that so we may
 A purer, better life be living,
 And win at last grace and blessing.
 God's word shines like the morning star
 Whose beams illumine near and far.
 No matter what the world murmur,
 We'll find in heaven love's fullest fervour.
           Alleluja ! Alleluja !

xii Lord, counsel give me in my need,
 Strengthen my soul when I am dead
 And from my body she hence wingeth,
 And cause her fearless heavenward speed.
 O be my Counsellor and Friend,
 And from me far misfortune send.
 Help me o'er death and ill conquer
 And one day live with Thee for ever.
           Alleluja ! Alleluja !

             Tr. C. S. T.

[1] Bd. ii. No. 247.

KOMM, HEILIGER GEIST, HERRE GOTT

Hymn, by Martin Luther, an expansion of the antiphon 'Veni Sancte Spiritus', in three 9-line stanzas (1524). Melody, anonymous (1524).

i Come, Ho - ly Spi - rit, God and Lord, Be all Thy gra - ces
ii Thou strong De - fend - er, Ho - ly Light, Teach us to know our
iii Thou Sa - cred Ar - dour, Com - fort sweet, Help us to wait with

i Komm, Hei - li - ger Geist, Her - re Gott, Er - füll mit dei - ner
ii Du Hei - li - ges Licht, ed - ler Hort, Lass uns leuch - ten des
* iii Du Hei - li - ge Brunst, sü - sser Trost, Nun hilf uns fröh - lich

now out-poured On the be - liev - er's mind and spi - rit, And touch our hearts with
God a - right, And call Him Fa - ther from out the heart. The Word of Life and
rea - dy feet And wil - ling heart at Thy dread com - mand, Nor tri - al fright us

Gna - den Gut Dein - er Glaü - bi - gen Herz, Muth und Sinn; Dein brün - stig Lieb ent -
Le - bens Wort, Und Lehr uns Gott - recht zu er kenn - en, Von Her - zen Va - ter
und getrost In deinem Dienst be - stän - dig blei - ben, Die Trübsal uns nicht

- liv - ing coal. Thy Light this day shone forth so clear, All tongues and na - tions
- Truth im - part, That we may love not doctrines strange, Nor e'er to oth - er
- from Thy band. Lord, make us rea - dy with Thy powers. Strengthen the flesh in

- zünd in ihn. O Herr, durch dei - nes Licht - es Glanz Zu dem glau - ben ver -
ihn nen - nen. O Herr, be - hüt vor frem - der Lehr Dass wir nicht Meister
ab - trei - ben! O Herr, durch dein Kraft uns bereit, Und stärk des Fleisches

*Bach has a 🐦 here.

KOMM, HEILIGER GEIST, HERRE GOTT

gathered near To learn the faith for which we bring Glad praise to Thee and
teachers range, But Je-sus for our Mas-ter own, And put our trust in
weaker hours, That as good war-riors we may force Through life and death, un -

sammelt hast Das Volk aus al - ler Welt Zung - en, Das sei dir, Herr, zu
su-chen mehr Denn Je - sum, mit recht - em Glau - ben, Und ihm aus ganz-er
Blö - digkeit, Dass wir hie rit - ter - lich rin - gen, Durch Tod und Le - ben

grateful - ly sing. Al - le - lu - ja, Al - le - lu - ja!
His grace a - - lone. Al - le - lu - ja, Al - le - lu - ja!
- to Thee our course. Al - le - lu - ja, Al - le - lu - ja!

Tr. Catherine Winkworth.[1]

Lob ge - sung - en. Al - le - lu - ja, Al - le - lu - ja!
Macht ver - trau - en. Al - le - lu - ja, Al - le - lu - ja!
zu dir dring - en! Al - le - lu - ja, Al - le - lu - ja!

U.L.S. 174.

[1] *Chorale Book for England* (Lond. 1865), No. 72.

KOMM, JESU, KOMM

Hymn, perhaps by Johann Christoph Schwedler, in eleven 7-line stanzas (1697). Melody, by Bach.

i Komm, Je - su, komm, mein Leib ist mü - de, Die Kraft ver -
* xi Drum schliess ich mich in dein - e Hän - de, Und sa - ge,

i Come, Je - su, come, my soul is wear - y, My heart is
xi Lord, take my heart in - to Thy keep - ing. The long day's

schwindt je mehr und mehr; Ich seh - ne mich nach dei - nem
Welt, zu gu - ter Nacht! Eilt gleich mein Le - bens - lauf zum

sick with troub - le sore. I fix my gaze on hea - ven's
o'er, now comes the night. The dark'-ning tomb my bod - y's

Frie - de, Der sau - re Weg Wird mir zu schwer. Komm, komm, ich
En - de, Ist doch der Geist Wohl an ge - bracht. Er soll bei

glo - ry, And long to see Thee more and more. Come, Lord, me
near - ing, My soul shall heaven - ward take its flight. There with my

243

KOMM, JESU, KOMM

will mich dir er-ge-ben, Du bist der rech - te
sei - nem Schö-pfer schwe-ben, Weil Je-sus ist und

Thine for e - ver mak - ing! Thou art the Way of
Sa - viour e - ver liv - ing. He is the Way of

Weg Die Wahrheit und das Le - ben, das Le - ben.
bleibt Der wah-re Weg zum Le - ben.

Truth And glor-ious life ex-cel - ling!
Truth And glor-ious life ex-cel - ling!

ii Wer an dich glaubt, wird nicht zu schanden,
Wer dich umfasst, hat wohlgethan,
Ja, mitten in des Todes Banden
Findt er die beste Lebensbahn.
Drum lass mich eifrig nach dir streben :
Du bist der rechte Weg,
Die Wahrheit und das Leben.*

P. Wagner.[1]

ii Whoso to Thee his faith hath given
Shall never into judgement fall ;
Yea, when the cords of life are riven,
Shall the more clearly hear Thy call.
So, Lord, to Thee my course I'm winging,
Thou art the way of Truth
And glorious life excelling ! *

Tr. C. S. T.

* Only the Soprano sings the first word of this line.

[1] *Vollständiges G.B. (Ed. 1697), viii. 326.*

KOMMT HER ZU MIR, SPRICHT GOTTES SOHN

Hymn, by Paul Gerhardt, in twelve 6-line stanzas (1653).   Melody, anonymous (1530).

229

i Gott Vater, sende deinen Geist,
   Den uns dein Sohn erbitten heisst,
   Aus deines Himmels Höhen !
   Wir bitten, wie er uns gelehrt ;
   Lass uns doch ja nicht unerhört
   Von deinem Throne gehen !

* ii Kein Menschenkind hier auf der Erd
   Ist dieser edlen Gabe werth,
   Bei uns ist kein Verdienen :
   Hier gilt gar nichts als Lieb und Gnad,
   Die Christus uns verdienet hat
   Mit Büssen und Versühnen.

x Der Geist, den Gott vom Himmel giebt,
   Der leitet alles, was ihn liebt,
   Auf wohlgebahnten Wegen ;
   Er setzt und richtet unsern Fuss,
   Dass er nicht anders treten muss,
   Als wo man findt den Segen.

U.L.S. 170

i O Father, hear our humble prayer,
   Send down to us the Comforter,
   Of Whom Thy Son foretold us !
   To ways of truth He all shall lead.
   Lord, bow Thine ear and give us heed,
   Nor from Thy grace expel us !

ii No child of man dwells here on earth
   Who of God's grace can boast his worth ;
   No one of it's deserving.
   We owe it to His love alone,
   And to the merits of His Son,
   Our grievous trespass bearing.

x His Spirit, Whom God sends at need,
   Us on His righteous paths will lead,
   Our footsteps e'er protecting.
   They shall not wander from His ways,
   Nor be ensnared in Satan's maze,
   Who follow His directing.

Tr. C. S. T.

KOMMT HER ZU MIR, SPRICHT GOTTES SOHN

Hymn, by Georg Grünewald, in sixteen 6-line stanzas (1530). Melody, anonymous (1530).

i Kommt her zu mir, spricht Gottes Sohn,
  All die ihr seid beschweret nun,
  Mit Sünden hart beladen :
  Ihr Jung und Alt, Frauen und Mann !
  Ich will euch geben, was ich han ;
  Will heilen euren Schaden.

xiv Ist euch das Kreuz bitter und schwer :
   Gedenkt, wie heiss die Hölle wär,
   Darein die Welt thut rennen,
   Mit Leib und Seel muss leidend sein
   Ohn Unterlass die ewig Pein
   Und mag doch nicht verbrennen !

xvi Und was der ewig gütig Gott
   In seinem Geist versprochen hat,
   Geschworen bei seim Namen :
   Das hält und giebt er g'wiss fürwahr ;
   Der helf uns an der Engel Schaar
   Durch Jesum Christum.   Amen !

U.L.S. 421.[1]

i O come to Me, saith God's dear Son,
  All ye who are with care weighed down,
  By load of sin sore laden !
  Both young and old, O come to Me,
  Come, tell Me all your misery,
  And in Me find your Haven !

xiv And should the Cross too heavy press,
   Then think on hell, and hell's distress
   That waits to rend the sinner.
   Therein must soul and body burn,
   Nor anywhere for comfort turn,
   But be consumed for ever.

xvi But what th' eternal God of peace
   Hath promised of His heavenly grace
   And for His name's sake sworn to,
   That will He well and true perform,
   And call us hence to His far throne,
   Through Christ our Saviour.   Amen.

Tr. C. S. T.

[1] Here attributed, wrongly, to Hans Witzstadt von Wertheim.   In Cantata 108 the melody is set to st. ii. of No. 229 *supra.*

KYRIE, GOTT VATER IN EWIGKEIT

Hymn, a version of ' Kyrie fons bonitatis ', in three unequal stanzas (1541). *Melody* (1525).

i Ky——— rie, Gott Va - ter in Ew - ig - keit! Gross ist
i O——— Lord our Fa - ther for ev - er - more! We Thy

dein Barm - herz - ig - keit, Al - ler Ding ein Schöp - fer
won - drous grace a - dore; We con - fess Thy pow'r, all

und Re - gie - - rer. E——— le - i - son!
worlds up - hold - - ing. Grant——— mer - cy, Lord.

ii Chri——— ste, Al——— ler Welt Trost,
ii O——— Christ, our——— Hope a - lone,

KYRIE, GOTT VATER IN EWIGKEIT

uns Sün - der al - lein du hast er - - löst. O——
Who with Thy blood didst for us a - -tone, O——

Je - su—— Got - tes Sohn! Un - ser
Je - su,—— Son of God! Our Re -

Mitt - ler bist in dem höch - sten Thron, Zu dir
-deem - - er! Our Ad - vo - cate on high! Lord, to

schrei - en wir aus Herz - ens be -
Thee a - lone in our need we

gier. E—— le - i - son.
cry, Grant—— mer - cy, Lord.

KYRIE, GOTT VATER IN EWIGKEIT

iii Ky — ri — — e! Gott —— Hei - li - ger Geist! Tröst, stärk
iii Ho — ly Lord, God —— the Ho - ly Ghost! Who of

uns im Glau - ben al — ler — meist, Dass
life im and light ben the foun - tain art, With

wir am letz - ten End Fröh - lich
faith sus - tain our heart. That at

ab - schei - den aus dies'm E - lend. ——
last we hence in peace de - part. ——

E —— le - i - - son! — *U.L.S.* 176.
Grant —— mer - cy, Lord! — *Tr. A. T. Russell.*[1]

[1] *Psalms and Hymns* (Camb. 1851), No. 14.

LASS, O HERR, DEIN OHR SICH NEIGEN

Hymn, by Martin Opitz, a translation of Psalm lxxxvi, in eight 8-line stanzas (1637).   Melody, by Louis Bourgeois (1547), to Psalm lxxxvi.

Psalm lxxxvi.

i Lass, o Herr, dein Ohr sich neigen,
  Dir mein Wort zu Herzen steigen ;
  Stoss mich ja nicht von dir hin,
  Weil ich arm und elend bin.
  Hüte meiner Seel und Leben,
  Die ich heilig dir ergeben ;
  Bringe deinen Knecht aus Noth,
  Der auf dich nur hofft, o Gott !

ii Gnade, Herr ; du siehst mein Beten
  Dich den ganzen Tag betreten.
  Spring mir, deinem Diener, bei,
  Dass mein Herz erfreuet sei.
  Dann zu dir geht mein Gemüte,
  Du bist gut und selbst die Güte
  Und verstösset keinen nicht,
  Welcher deinen Schutz bespricht.

iv Kein Gott, Herr, kann dir sich gleichen,
  Alle That muss deinen weichen ;
  Aller Heiden grosse Schaar,
  Die dein Werk sind ganz und gar,
  Werden, Herr, sich vor dir neigen,
  Deinem Namen Ehr erzeigen.
  Gross ist deiner Wunder Schein,
  Und du bist ein Gott allein.

Fischer-Tümpel.[1]

i Bow Thine ear, O Lord, unto me,
  From Thy presence do not spurn me ;
  For I needy am and poor,
  Weighed down with affliction sore.
  Keep my soul, for it is holy,
  Trusting in Thy goodness only.
  Lord, deliver in my need,
  Hasten to my help with speed !

ii Unto Thee, Lord, do I daily
  Tell my woes and beg Thy pity :
  Bid Thy servant to rejoice !
  Speak to me with loving voice !
  To forgive Thou'rt ever ready,
  Plentiful in love and mercy,
  And wilt in Thy grace instal
  All who on Thee truly call.

iv Of the gods there's no one like Thee,
  None that can in works vie with Thee.
  By the nations Thou hast made
  Homage shall to Thee be paid,
  Bending at Thy footstool lowly,
  Singing Holy, holy, holy
  To the God of gods and might,
  Sitting throned in splendour bright.

Tr. C. S. T.

[1] Bd. i. No. 304.

LIEBSTER GOTT, WANN WERD ICH STERBEN

Hymn, by Caspar Neumann, in five 8-line stanzas (c. 1700).   Melody, by Daniel Vetter (1713).

233

i Dear-est Lord, when wilt Thou sum - - mon? Days and
i Lieb-ster Gott, wann werd ich ster - - ben? Mein - e

i Dear-est Lord, when wilt Thou sum-mon?
i Lieb-ster Gott, wann werd ich ster-ben?

i Dear-est Lord, when wilt Thou sum - mon?
i Lieb-ster Gott, wann wird ich ster - ben?

i Dear-est Lord, when wilt Thou sum - mon?
i Lieb-ster Gott, wann werd ich ster - ben?

mo - ments quick - - - ly fly. 'Tis of A - dam's
Zeit läuft im - - - mer hin, Und des al - ten

Days and mo - ments quick - ly fly. 'Tis of
Mein - e Zeit läuft im - mer hin, Und des

Days and mo - ments quick - ly fly. 'Tis of
Mein - e Zeit läuft im - mer hin, Und des

Days and mo-ments quick - ly fly. 'Tis of
Mein - - e Zeit läuft im - mer hin, Und des

seed the bur - - den, Heirs of e - vil you and I.
A - dams Er - - ben, Un - ter de - nen ich auch bin,

A - dam's seed the bur - den, Heirs of e - vil, you and I.
al - ten A - dams Er - ben, Un - ter de - nen ich auch bin,

A - dam's seed the bur - den, Heirs of e - vil, you and I.
al - ten A - dams Er - ben, Un - ter de - nen ich auch bin,

A - dam's seed the bur - den, Heirs of e - vil, you and I.
al - ten A - dams Er - ben, Un - ter de-nen ich auch bin,

LIEBSTER GOTT, WANN WERD ICH STERBEN

Death's fell curse pur — sues the race, Dwell-ing here a lit — tle space, One day, af — ter toil and mourn — ing To the earth a — gain re — turn — ing.

Ha — ben dies zum Va — ter-theil, Dass sie ei — ne klein — e Weil Arm und e — lend sein auf Er — den. Und dann sel — ber Er — de wer — den.

* v Herrscher über Tod und Leben,
Mach einmal mein Ende gut,
Lehre mich den Geist aufgeben
Mit recht wohlgefasstem Muth.
Hilf, dass ich ein ehrlich Grab
Neben frommen Christen hab,
Und auch endlich in der Erde
Nimmermehr zu Schanden werde.

v Lord of all things dead and living,
Bring me spotless to the light !
Teach me how, my soul upgiving,
To show courage firm and right !
And one day an honoured grave
With the holy dead I crave,
Till death's bonds by God are riven
And I stand with Him in heavèn.

Bach's Text.

Tr. C. S. T.

LIEBSTER IMMANUEL, HERZOG DER FROMMEN

Hymn, by Ahasuerus Fritsch, in five 7-line stanzas (1679). Melody (1679), an adaptation of a Courante.

234

* Bach has a ⌢ here

i Liebster Immanuel, Herzog der Frommen,
  Du meiner Seelen Trost, komm, komm doch bald,
  Denn du hast mir, mein Schatz, das Herz genommen,
  So ganz vor Liebe brennt und nach dir wallt.
  Nichts kann auf Erden
  Mir liebers werden,
  Wenn ich, mein Jesu, dich nur stets behalt.

iv Will mich nun aller Welt Verfolgung hassen,
   Bin ich verachtet schon bei jedermann,
   Von meinen Freunden auch gänzlich verlassen,
   Nimmt sich mein Jesus dennoch meiner an
   Und stärkt mich Müden,
   Spricht : sei zufrieden,
   Ich bin der beste Freund, so helfen kann.

* v Drum fahret immerhin, ihr Eitelkeiten ;
    Du, Jesu ! du bist mein, und ich bin dein.
    Ich will mich von der Welt zu dir bereiten,
    Du sollt in meinem Mund und Herze sein.
    Mein ganzes Leben
    Sei dir ergeben,
    Bis man mich leget in das Grab hinein.

Fischer-Tümpel.[1]

i Hasten, Immanuel, Prince of the lowly !
  Thou'rt our salvation's hope ! Come, Lord, draw near !
  Thou know'st my heart is Thine, yea, Thine own only,
  Burns for Thee, trusts in Thee, waits without fear.
  Farewell, earth's treasure !
  Trivial thy pleasure !
  Cometh the day when Lord Christ shall appear.

iv What if the world in its envy doth hate me ?
   What if it thinks my poor lot to despise ?
   What if my neighbours and friends all berate me ?
   Jesus doth send me a look from His eyes :
   Be strong ! it sayeth,
   Courage it stayeth,
   Jesus, best friend of man, biddeth me rise.

v How ill content me now earth's hollow pleasures !
  Jesu, my life Thou art, and I am Thine.
  For Thee I gladly yield this world's vain treasures,
  Thou shalt direct my ways, be only mine.
  Thou hast my heart, Lord,
  Never we'll part, Lord,
  When from the grave to Thy far throne I climb.

Tr. C. S. T.

[1] Bd. v. No. 593.

LIEBSTER JESU, WIR SIND HIER

Hymn, by Tobias Clausnitzer, in three 6-line stanzas (1663).   Melody, by Johann Rodolph Ahle (1664), to 'Ja, er ists, das Heil der Welt'.

i Liebster Jesu, wir sind hier
  Dich und dein Wort anzuhören :
  Lenke Sinnen und Begier
  Auf die süssen Himmelslehren,
  Dass die Herzen von der Erden
  Ganz zu dir gezogen werden.

ii Unser Wissen und Verstand
  Ist mit Finsternis umhüllet,
  Wo nicht deines Geistes Hand
  Uns mit hellem Licht erfüllet.
  Gutes denken, thun und dichten,
  Musst du selbst in uns verrichten.

iii O du Glanz der Herrlichkeit,
  Licht vom Licht, aus Gott geboren :
  Mach uns allesammt bereit,
  Offne Herzen, Mund und Ohren :
  Unser Bitten, Fleh'n und Singen
  Lass, Herr Jesu, wohl gelingen.

i Blessèd Jesu, at Thy word
  We are gathered all to hear Thee ;
  Let our hearts and souls be stirred
  Now to seek and love and fear Thee,
  By Thy teachings sweet and holy
  Drawn from earth to love Thee solely.

ii All our knowledge, sense and sight
  Lie in deepest darkness shrouded,
  Till Thy Spirit breaks our night
  With the beams of truth unclouded ;
  Thou alone to God canst win us,
  Thou wilt work all good within us.

iii Glorious Lord, Thyself impart !
  Light of Light from God proceeding,
  Open Thou our ears and heart,
  Help us by Thy Spirit's pleading,
  Hear the cry Thy people raises,
  Hear, and bless our prayers and praises !

Tr. Catherine Winkworth.[1]

U.L.S. 232.

[1] *Chorale Book for England* (Lond. 1865), No. 12.

LOBET DEN HERREN, DENN ER IST SEHR FREUNDLICH

Hymn, anonymous, in seven 4-line stanzas (1568) : based on Psalm cxlvii. Melody, by Antonio Scandelli (1568).

236

*Bach has a ⌢ here

i Lobet den Herren (*bis*), denn er ist sehr freundlich.
Es ist sehr köstlich, | unsern Gott zu loben (*bis*) ;
Sein Lob ist schöne, lieblich anzuhören.
Lobet den Herren. (*bis*)

ii Singt gen einander (*bis*) dem Herren mit Danken.
Lobt ihn mit Harfen, | unsern Gott, den Werthen (*bis*);
Denn er ist mächtig und von grossen Kräften.
Lobet den Herren. (*bis*)

iii Er kann den Himmel (*bis*) mit Wolken bedecken,
Und giebet Regen, | wenn er will, auf Erden (*bis*).
Er lässt Gras wachsen hoch auf dürren Bergen.
Lobet den Herren. (*bis*)

iv Der allem Fleische (*bis*) giebet seine Speise,
Dem Vieh sein Futter | väterlicher Weise (*bis*),
Den jungen Raben, wenn sie ihn anrufen.
Lobet den Herren. (*bis*)

i Praise thy Creator (*bis*), for He owns and loves thee,
Sing praises to Him, | pleasant 'tis and comely (*bis*)
Within His courts to sing unto thy Maker :
Praise thy Creator ! (*bis*)

ii Sing ye together (*bis*) to the Lord with praises,
With harps and timbrels | and well tunèd voices. (*bis*)
For He is mighty and doth reign for ever :
Praise thy Creator ! (*bis*)

iii The heaven's broad spaces (*bis*) all with clouds He
spreadeth,
And for the earth's use | soft'ning rain prepareth. (*bis*)
The mountain tops with verdure He doth cover :
Praise thy Creator ! (*bis*)

iv To all that liveth (*bis*) meat and drink He giveth,
And as a Father | for all flesh provideth. (*bis*)
The fowls of air in vain call on Him never :
Praise thy Creator ! (*bis*)

U.L.S. 499.

Tr. C. S. T.

LOBT GOTT, IHR CHRISTEN ALLE GLEICH

Hymn, by Nikolaus Herman, in eight 4-line stanzas (1560). Melody, by Nikolaus Herman (1554), to his ' Kommt her, ihr lieben Schwesterlein '.

237

i Lobt Gott, ihr Christen alle gleich
In seinem höchsten Thron,
Der heut schleusst auf sein Himmelreich
Und schenkt uns seinen Sohn ! (*bis*)

ii Er kommt aus seines Vaters Schoos
Und wird ein Kindlein klein ;
Er liegt dort elend, nackt und bloss
In einem Krippelein. (*bis*)

iv Er liegt an seiner Mutter Brust,
Ihr Milch die ist sein Speis,
An dem die Engel sehn ihr Lust,
Denn er ist Davids Reis, (*bis*)

v Das aus sein'm Stamm entspriesen sollt
In dieser letzten Zeit,
Durch welchen Gott aufrichten wollt
Sein Reich, die Christenheit. (*bis*)

U.L.S. 47.

i Praise God, ye people one and all,
Raise anthems to His throne !
To-day His grace from heaven doth fall :
He sendeth us His Son. (*bis*)

ii A little Babe, from heaven above
He leaves His Father's hall,
And there He lies—O wondrous love !
Within an ox's stall. (*bis*)

iv There lies He at His mother's breast,
Soothed in her gentle arms.
He Whom the angels God confessed
A mortal maiden calms. (*bis*)

v Of David's lineage is He born,
A stem of Jesse's root;
From Him a mighty realm shall come,
And like a cedar shoot. (*bis*)

Tr. C. S. T.

LOBT GOTT, IHR CHRISTEN ALLE GLEICH

Hymn, by Nikolaus Herman, in eight 4-line stanzas (1560).   Melody, by Nikolaus Herman (1554), to his ' Kommt her, ihr lieben Schwesterlein '.

i Lobt Gott, ihr Christen alle gleich
  In seinem höchsten Thron,
  Der heut schleusst auf sein Himmelreich
  Und schenkt uns seinen Sohn ! (*bis*)

ii Er kommt aus seines Vaters Schoos
   Und wird ein Kindlein klein ;
   Er liegt dort elend, nackt und bloss
   In einem Krippelein. (*bis*)

vii Er wird ein Knecht und ich ein Herr,
    Das mag ein Wechsel sein !
    Wie könnt es doch sein freundlicher
    Das Herze-Jesulein. (*bis*)

*viii Heut schleusst er wieder auf die Thür
     Zum schönen Paradeis,
     Der Cherub steht nicht mehr dafür ;
     Gott sei Lob, Ehr und Preis ! (*bis*)

U.L.S. 47.

i Praise God, ye people one and all,
  Raise anthems to His throne !
  To-day His grace from heaven doth fall :
  He sendeth us His Son. (*bis*)

ii A little Babe, from heaven above
   He leaves His Father's hall,
   And there He lies—O wondrous love !
   Within an ox's stall. (*bis*)

vii O what a wondrous change is here !
    A servant there He lies,
    Yet me He makes a lord appear :
    What marv'llous love is this ! (*bis*)

viii Now open stands the once closed door
     Of Eden's garden ways ;
     The angel wardeth it no more :
     To God be thanks and praise ! (*bis*)

Tr. C. S. T.

LOBT GOTT, IHR CHRISTEN ALLE GLEICH

Hymn, by Paul Gerhardt, in nine 4-line stanzas (1647). Melody, by Nikolaus Herman (1554), to his ' Kommt her, ihr lieben Schwesterlein '.

239

[Horns I.II and Timpani obbligati]

* i Nun danket all und bringet Ehr,
    Ihr Menschen in der Welt,
    Dem, dessen Lob der Engel Heer
    Im Himmel stets vermeldt. (*bis*)

ii Ermuntert euch und singt mit Schall
    Gott, unserm höchsten Gut,
    Der seine Wunder überall
    Und grosse Dinge thut. (*bis*)

iii Der uns von Mutterleibe an
    Frisch und gesund erhält,
    Und wo kein Mensch nicht helfen kann,
    Sich selbst zum Helfer stellt. (*bis*)

vi Er lasse seinen Frieden ruhn
    In Israelis Land ;
    Er gebe Glück zu unserm Thun
    Und Heil in allem Stand. (*bis*)

viii So lange dieses Leben währt,
    Sei er stets unser Heil ;
    Und bleib auch, wenn wir von der Erd
    Abscheiden, unser Theil. (*bis*)

U.L.S. 716.

i Now, mortals all, your voices raise,
    Acclaim God lustily,
    Whom angel hosts throng with their praise
    Before His throne on high ! (*bis*)

ii Lift up your voice right heartily
    To Him Who reigns above,
    Who worketh for us wondrously
    And showers on us His love ! (*bis*)

iii He since our mother gave us birth
    In surety doth us hold,
    And when man's aid's of little worth
    Will in His care enfold. (*bis*)

vi He showers peace and plenteousness
    Upon our Motherland,
    With happiness He doth her bless
    And strengthens her right hand. (*bis*)

viii So long as we have life and breath
    His watch still may He keep !
    And when we hear the call of death
    In Jesus may we sleep ! (*bis*)

Tr. C. S. T.

LOBT GOTT, IHR CHRISTEN ALLE GLEICH

Hymn, by Nikolaus Herman, in eight 4-line stanzas (1560). Melody, by Nikolaus Herman (1554), to his 'Kommt her, ihr lieben Schwesterlein'

240

i Lobt Gott, ihr Christen alle gleich
   In seinem höchsten Thron,
   Der heut schleusst auf sein Himmelreich
   Und schenkt uns seinen Sohn! (*bis*)

iii Er äussert sich all seiner G'walt,
   Wird niedrig und gering,
   Und nimmt an sich eins Knechts Gestalt,
   Der Schöpfer aller Ding! (*bis*)

vi Er wechselt mit uns wunderlich:
   Fleisch und Blut nimmt er an,
   Und giebt uns in seins Vaters Reich
   Die klare Gottheit dran. (*bis*)

viii Heut schleusst er wieder auf die Thür
   Zum schönen Paradeis,
   Der Cherub steht nicht mehr dafür;
   Gott sei Lob, Ehr und Preis! (*bis*)

U.L.S. 47.

i Let all together praise our God
   Upon His lofty throne;
   He hath the heavens unclosed to-day,
   And given to us His Son. (*bis*)

iii He lays aside His majesty,
   And seems as nothing worth,
   He takes on Him a servant's form,
   Who made both heaven and earth. (*bis*)

vi Behold the wonderful exchange
   Our Lord with us doth make!
   Lo! He assumes our flesh and blood!
   We of His heaven partake! (*bis*)

viii The glorious gates of Paradise
   The cherub guards no more;
   This day again those gates unfold!
   With praise our God adore! (*bis*)

Tr. A. T. Russell.[1]

[1] *Psalms and Hymns* (Camb. 1851), No. 52.

MACHS MIT MIR, GOTT, NACH DEINER GÜT

Hymn, by Johann Hermann Schein, in five 6-line stanzas (1629).   Melody, by J. H. Schein (1629).

241

i Machs mit mir, Gott, nach deiner Güt,
  Hilf mir in meinem Leiden.
  Ruf ich dich an, versag mirs nit :
  Wenn sich mein Seel will scheiden,
  So, nimm sie, Herr, in deine Händ;
  Ist alles gut, wenn gut das End.

ii Gern will ich folgen, liebster Herr,
  Du wirst mich nicht verderben.
  Auch bist du doch von mir nicht fern,
  Wenn ich gleich hie muss sterben,
  Verlassen meine besten Freund,
  Die's mit mir herzlich gut gemeint.

v Was wollt ich denn lang traurig sein,
  Weil ich so wohl bestehe,
  Bekleidt mit Christi Unschuld fein,
  Wie eine Braut hergehe ?
  Gehab dich wohl, du schnöde Welt :
  Bei Gott zu leben mir gefällt.

U.L.S. 830.

i My soul is ever in Thy hand :
  Lord, hear my anxious crying !
  Incline Thine ear, Thy grace extend
  To comfort me when dying.
  O hold me close when death shall call;
  Then all is well, no fears appal.

ii Where'er Thou pointest will I go,
  I know Thou art beside me,
  And though my feet stray to and fro,
  Thy hand is near to guide me,
  E'en when at death's dread door I stand
  And friendless face an unknown land.

v No need is there for tears or woe,
  For joy entrancing waits me ;
  Yea, clothed in spotless robes I go
  In heavenly bridal glory.[1]
  So, earth, I bid thee long farewell;
  With God above my lot's to dwell.

Tr. C. S. T.

[1] The hymn was written for the funeral of a woman.

MACHS MIT MIR, GOTT, NACH DEINER GÜT

Hymn, by Johann Hermann Schein, in five 6-line stanzas (1629).   *Melody, by J. H. Schein (1629).*

242

i Machs mit mir, Gott, nach deiner Güt,
   Hilf mir in meinem Leiden.
   Ruf ich dich an, versag mirs nit :
   Wenn sich mein Seel will scheiden,
   So, nimm sie, Herr, in deine Händ ;
   Ist alles gut, wenn gut das End.

iii Ruht doch der Leib sanft in der Erd,
    Die Seel sich zu dir schwinget ;
    In deine Hand sie unversehrt
    Durch Tod ins Leben dringet.
    Hier ist doch nur ein Thränenthal :
    Angst, Noth, Müh, Arbeit überall.

iv Tod, Teufel, Höll, die Welt und Sünd
   Mir können nichts mehr schaden.
   An dir, o Herr, ich Rettung find ;
   Ich tröst mich deiner Gnaden.
   Dein eigner Sohn aus Lieb und Huld
   Für mich bezahlet alle Schuld.

U.L.S. 830.

i My soul is ever in Thy hand ;
   Lord, hear my anxious crying !
   Incline Thine ear, Thy grace extend
   To comfort me when dying.
   O hold me close when death shall call ;
   Then all is well ; no fears appal.

iii In earth's soft bed the spirit sleeps,
    The soul to heavèn soareth,
    Thou callest her from dungeon deeps,
    New life to her restoreth.
    She leaves behind a vale of tears,
    Her toil and care and anxious fears.

iv So, Hell and Satan, Death and Sin
   No more have power to fright me ;
   For Christ did my salvation win,
   I trust in Him completely.
   'Tis Jesus hath the ransom paid
   And on Himself my burden laid.

Tr. C. S. T.

Stanza, by Christian Heinrich Postel, from the ' Passion ' (1704).

* Durch dein Gefängnis, Gottes Sohn,
   Ist uns die Freiheit kommen,
   Dein Kerker ist der Gnadenthron,
   Die Freistatt aller Frommen ;
   Denn gingst du nicht die Knechtschaft ein,
   Müsst unsre Knechtschaft ewig sein.

Bach's Text.

Thy bonds, O God's Almighty Son,
To grace on high will lead us.
Thy prison is a royal throne
Whence Thou in love dost speed us ;
For hadst Thou not known bondage sore,
We had been slaves for evermore.

Tr. C. S. T.

MACHS MIT MIR, GOTT, NACH DEINER GÜT

Hymn, by Johann Christoph Rube, in five 6-line stanzas (1692). Melody, by Johann Hermann Schein (1629).

243

i Wohl dem, der sich auf seinen Gott
  Recht kindlich kann verlassen !
  Den mag gleich Sünde, Welt und Tod
  Und alle Teufel hassen,
  So bleibt er dennoch wohl vergnügt,
  Wenn er nur Gott zum Freunde kriegt.

ii Die böse Welt mag immerhin
  Mich hier und da befeinden;
  Kann sich nur mein Gemüth und Sinn
  Mit meinem Gott befreunden.
  So frag ich nicht nach ihrem Hass:
  Ist Gott mein Freund, wer thut mir was?

*v Dahero trotz der Höllenheer,
  Trotz auch des Todes Rachen,
  Trotz aller Welt, mich kann nicht mehr
  Ihr Pochen traurig machen.
  Gott ist mein Schutz, mein Hülf und Rath:
  Wohl dem der Gott zum Freunde hat.

             Vopelius.[1]

i 'Tis well with him who on his God
  Doth place his full reliance.
  He may to Satan, Death, the world
  With boldness bid defiance.
  He shall a blessing sure command
  Who on God's promise takes his stand.

ii The spiteful world doth vainly strive
  To do me ill and harm me.
  But only doth its spleen contrive
  To bring me near God closely.
  For little reck I of its hate:
  If God's my friend, then all is right.

v Of what avail the hosts of hell?
  They can no more affright me.
  The world no longer weaves its spell,
  I hold its glamour lightly.
  God speeds to help, He clasps my hand.
  On His sure Word I take my stand.

             Tr. C. S. T.

[1] *Leipziger G.B.* (ed. 1729), p. 342.

MEIN AUGEN SCHLIESS ICH JETZT IN GOTTES NAMEN ZU

Hymn, by Matthäus Apelles von Löwenstern, in six 4-line stanzas (1644).   Melody, by M. A. von Löwenstern (1644).

244

*Bach has a 𝄐 here

i Mein Augen schliess ich jetzt in Gottes Namen zu,
   Dieweil der müde Leib begehret seine Ruh,
   Weiss aber nicht, ob ich den Morgen möcht erleben ;
   Es könnte mich der Tod vielleicht noch heut umgeben.

ii Drum sag ich dir, o Gott, von Herzen Lob und Dank ;
   Ich will auch solches thun hinfort mein Leben lang,
   Weil du mich diesen Tag hast wollen so bewahren,
   Dass mir kein Ungelück hat können wiederfahren.

v Und wenn ja diese Nacht mein Ende käm herbei,
   So hilf, dass ich in dir, o Jesu, wacker sei,
   Auf dass ich seliglich und sanft von hinnen scheide ;
   Dann führe meine Seel hinauf zur Himmels-Freude.

   Fischer-Tümpel.[1]

i The hour is come, O Lord, to lay me down in sleep :
   The weary body droops, dark shadows round me creep.
   Perchance, another dawn Thou from mine eyes withholdest,
   And e'er the morning breaks to die my spirit callest.

ii So, lowly on my knees, I give Thee thanks and praise
   For all the loving care that's kept me all my days.
   And yet another's past, so hallowed by Thy blessing ;
   No ill has dared intrude, my peaceful life distressing.

v And so, if Thou dost will this night to call me home,
   In heaven to sing Thy praise, I ready am to come.
   But help me so to die, upon Thy grace relying,
   That swift my soul to Thee may heavènward be flying.

   Tr. C. S. T.

[1] Bd. i. No. 395.

MEINE SEELE ERHEBT DEN HERREN

St. Luke i. 46-55   Melody, Tonus peregrinus.

245

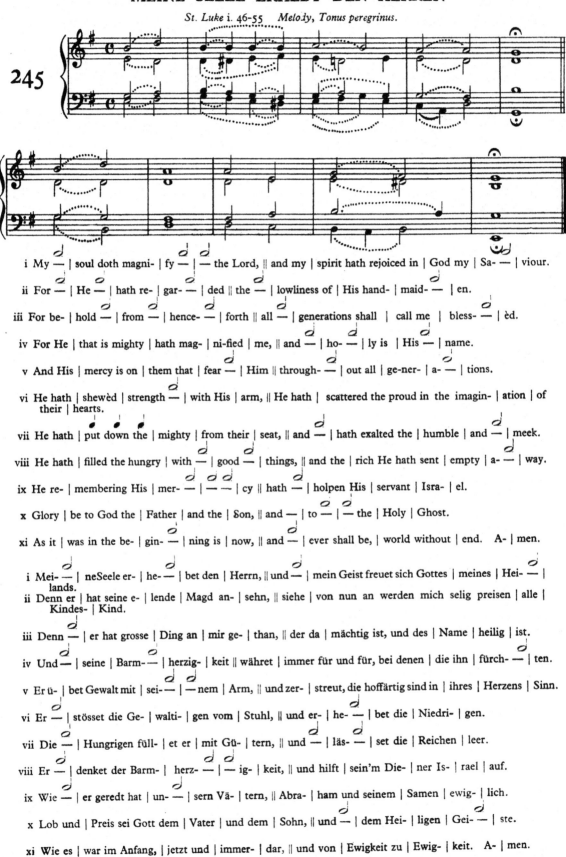

i My — | soul doth magni- | fy — | — the Lord, ‖ and my | spirit hath rejoiced in | God my | Sa- — | viour.

ii For — | He — | hath re- | gar- — | ded ‖ the — | lowliness of | His hand- | maid- — | en.

iii For be- | hold — | from — | hence- | forth ‖ all — | generations shall | call me | bless- — | èd.

iv For He | that is mighty | hath mag- | ni-fied | me, ‖ and — | ho- — | ly is | His — | name.

v And His | mercy is on | them that | fear — | Him ‖ through- — | out all | ge-ner- | a- — | tions.

vi He hath | shewèd | strength — | with His | arm, ‖ He hath | scattered the proud in the imagin- | ation | of
their | hearts.

vii He hath | put down the | mighty | from their | seat, ‖ and — | hath exalted the | humble | and — | meek.

viii He hath | filled the hungry | with — | good — | things, ‖ and the | rich He hath sent | empty | a- — | way.

ix He re- | membering His | mer- — | — — | cy ‖ hath — | holpen His | servant | Isra- | el.

x Glory | be to God the | Father | and the | Son, ‖ and — | to — | — the | Holy | Ghost.

xi As it | was in the be- | gin- — | ning is | now, ‖ and — | ever shall be, | world without | end.   A- | men.

i Mei- — | neSeele er- | he- — | bet den | Herrn, ‖ und — | mein Geist freuet sich Gottes | meines | Hei- — |
lands.

ii Denn er | hat seine e- | lende | Magd an- | sehn, ‖ siehe | von nun an werden mich selig preisen | alle |
Kindes- | Kind.

iii Denn — | er hat grosse | Ding an | mir ge- | than, ‖ der da | mächtig ist, und des | Name | heilig | ist.

iv Und — | seine | Barm- — | herzig- | keit ‖ währet | immer für und für, bei denen | die ihn | fürch- — | ten.

v Er ü- | bet Gewalt mit | sei- — | —nem | Arm, ‖ und zer- | streut, die hoffärtig sind in | ihres | Herzens | Sinn.

vi Er — | stösset die Ge- | walti- | gen vom | Stuhl, ‖ und er- | he- — | bet die | Niedri- | gen.

vii Die — | Hungrigen füll- | et er | mit Gü- | tern, ‖ und — | läs- — | set die | Reichen | leer.

viii Er — | denket der Barm- | herz- — | — ig- | keit, ‖ und hilft | sein'm Die- | ner Is- | rael | auf.

ix Wie — | er geredt hat | un- — | sern Vä- | tern, ‖ Abra- | ham und seinem | Samen | ewig- | lich.

x Lob und | Preis sei Gott dem | Vater | und dem | Sohn, ‖ und — | dem Hei- | ligen | Gei- — | ste.

xi Wie es | war im Anfang, | jetzt und | immer- | dar, ‖ und von | Ewigkeit zu | Ewig- | keit.   A- | men.

MEINE SEELE ERHEBT DEN HERREN

Numbers vi. 24-26.   Melody, Tonus peregrinus.

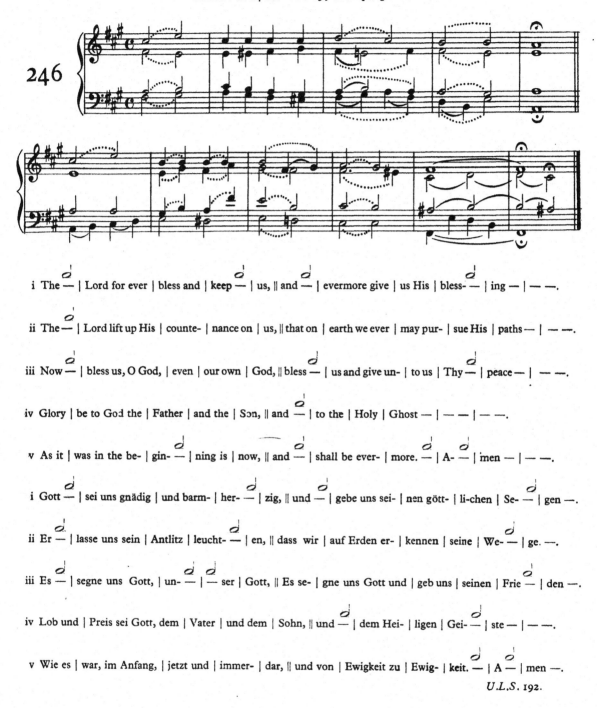

246

i The — | Lord for ever | bless and | keep — | us, ‖ and — | evermore give | us His | bless- — | ing — | — —.

ii The — | Lord lift up His | counte- | nance on | us, ‖ that on | earth we ever | may pur- | sue His | paths — | — —.

iii Now — | bless us, O God, | even | our own | God, ‖ bless — | us and give un- | to us Thy — | peace — | — —.

iv Glory | be to God the | Father | and the | Son, ‖ and — | to the | Holy | Ghost — | — — | — —.

v As it | was in the be- | gin- — | ning is | now, ‖ and — | shall be ever- | more. — | A- — | men — | — —.

i Gott — | sei uns gnädig | und barm- | her- — | zig, ‖ und — | gebe uns sei- | nen gött- | li-chen | Se- — | gen —.

ii Er — | lasse uns sein | Antlitz | leucht- — | en, ‖ dass wir | auf Erden er- | kennen | seine | We- — | ge. —.

iii Es — | segne uns Gott, | un- — | — ser | Gott, ‖ Es se- | gne uns Gott und | geb uns | seinen | Frie — | den —.

iv Lob und | Preis sei Gott, dem | Vater | und dem | Sohn, ‖ und — | dem Hei- | ligen | Gei- — | ste — | — —.

v Wie es | war, im Anfang, | jetzt und | immer- | dar, ‖ und von | Ewigkeit zu | Ewig- | keit. — | A- — | men —.

U.L.S. 192.

MEINE SEELE ERHEBT DEN HERREN

Doxology. Tonus peregrinus.

247

* Lob und Preis sei Gott dem Va - ter und dem Sohn und dem Heili - gen Gei - ste,
Glo - ry be to God the Fa - ther and the Son, and to the Ho - ly Ghost.

wie es war im An-fang jetzt und im - mer - dar und von
As it was in the be - gin - ning and is now, and shall

wie es war im An-fang jetzt und im-mer-dar
As it was in the be - gin - ning, is now
wie es war im An-fang jetzt und im - mer dar und von
As it was in the be - gin - ning, is now and shall

wie es war im An-fang jetzt und im - mer dar und von E - wig -
As it was in the be - gin-ning and is now, and shall be for

E-wigkeit zu E - wig-keit. A - men.
be for e - ver - more.

und von E - wig - keit zu E - wig - keit. A - men.
and shall be for e - ver - more.
E-wig-keit zu E - .wig-keit. A - men.
be for e - ver-more - .

keit zu E - wig-keit. A - men.
e - ver-more.

MEINEN JESUM LASS ICH NICHT, JESUS

Hymn, anonymous, in seven 6-line stanzas (1736). Melody, anonymous (1686), to 'Jesus ist mein Aufenthalt'.

248

i Meinen Jesum lass ich nicht,
  Jesus wird mich auch nicht lassen,
  Jesus hab ich mich verpflicht,
  Ich will ihn ins Herz fassen :
  Weiss gewiss und glaube fest,
  Dass mich Jesus auch nicht lässt.

vi Meinen Jesum lass ich nicht :
  Ich will nichts als Jesum wissen,
  Wenn mein Herz im Leibe bricht,
  Und ich muss die Augen schliessen;
  Wenn kein Mensch mir helfen kann,
  Nimmt sich Jesus meiner an.

vii Meinen Jesum lass ich nicht :
  Jesus wird mir helfen siegen,
  An dem letzten Weltgericht,
  Und in meinen Todeszügen :
  Ich weiss, nimmt der Tod mich hin,
  Dass ich doch bei Jesu bin.

G. C. Schemelli.[1]

i Ne'er from Jesus will I part,
  Nor will Jesus ever leave me.
  He shall own my very heart,
  To it now I press Him closely.
  And I know right well that He
  Never will depart from me.

vi Ne'er from Jesus will I part,
  He alone my soul desireth.
  When Death's hand is on my heart
  And my last faint breath expireth,
  When man's help's of no avail,
  Jesus, cannot, will not, fail.

vii Ne'er from Jesus will I part,
  He is by my side to help me
  When the Judgment Hall is set
  And a righteous God shall judge me.
  Death, come, call me hence away ;
  Jesus shall be mine alway !

Tr. C. S. T.

[1] *Musicalisches Gesangbuch* (1736), p. 99.

MEINEN JESUM LASS ICH NICHT, WEIL

Hymn, by Christian Keimann, in six 6-line stanzas (1658).   Melody, by (?) Andreas Hammerschmidt (1658).

249

[Strings Obbligati]

i Meinen Jesum lass ich nicht :
 Weil er sich für mich gegeben,
 So erfordert meine Pflicht,
 Klettenweis an ihm zu kleben.
 Er ist meines Lebens Licht :
 Meinen Jesum lass ich nicht.

ii Jesum lass ich nmmer nicht,
 Weil ich soll auf Erden leben ;
 Ihm hab ich voll Zuversicht,
 Was ich bin und hab, ergeben.
 Alles ist auf ihn gericht :
 Meinen Jesum lass ich nicht.

*v Nicht nach Welt, nach Himmel nicht,
 Meine Seele wünscht und stöhnet :
 Jesum wünscht sie und sein Licht ;
 Der mich hat mit Gott versöhnet,
 Der mich freit vom Gericht :
 Meinen Jesum lass ich nicht.

i Never Jesus will I leave !
 He Who bore the Cross to win me
 All my homage shall receive,
 Clinging close to Him so fondly.
 Jesus lights my soul and heart,
 From Him never will I part.

ii Never Jesus will I leave
 While on earth my course I follow.
 From Him doth my soul receive
 All its joy and e'en its sorrow.
 What He wills is good for me :
 Jesus, ne'er I'll part from Thee !

v Heaven nor earth are my delight,
 Other bourne my soul inviteth.
 Jesus is my Hope, my Light,
 God and man He reconcileth,
 He hath borne my load of sin,
 Never will I part from Him.

U.L.S. 323.

Tr. C. S. T.

MEINEN JESUM LASS ICH NICHT, WEIL

Hymn, by Christian Keimann, in six 6-line stanzas (1658).   Melody, by (?) Andreas Hammerschmidt (1658).

250

i Meinen Jesum lass ich nicht :
   Weil er sich für mich gegeben,
   So erfordert meine Pflicht,
   Klettenweis an ihm zu kleben.
   Er ist meines Lebens Licht :
   Meinen Jesum lass ich nicht.

iii Lass vergehen das Gesicht,
   Hören, Schmecken, Fühlen weichen,
   Lass das letzte Tageslicht
   Mich auf dieser Welt erreichen ;
   Wenn der Lebensfaden bricht,
   Meinen Jesum lass ich nicht.

vi Jesum lass ich nicht von mir,
   Geh ihm ewig an der Seiten ;
   Christus lässt mich für und für
   Zu dem Lebensbächlein leiten.
   Selig, wer mit mir so spricht :
   Meinen Jesum lass ich nicht.

i Never Jesus will I leave !
   He Who bore the Cross to win me
   All my homage shall receive,
   Clinging close to Him so fondly.
   Jesus lights my soul and heart,
   From Him never will I part.

iii Come what may ! let hearing, sight,
   Every sense and pleasure vanish !
   Let grim Death display his might,
   And from mortal ken me banish !
   When the summons tolls for me,
   Jesus, ne'er I'll part from Thee !

vi Jesus never will I leave.
   By His side my pathway treading,
   He will lead me to receive
   Waters fresh in meadows welling.
   Blessèd he who saith with me :
   ' Jesus, ne'er I'll part from Thee '.

U.L.S. 323.

Tr. C. S. T.

MEINEN JESUM LASS ICH NICHT, WEIL

Hymn, by Christian Keimann, in six 6-line stanzas (1658).   Melody, by (?) Andreas Hammerschmidt (1658).

251

i Meinen Jesum lass ich nicht :
   Weil er sich für mich gegeben,
   So erfordert meine Pflicht,
   Klettenweis an ihm zu kleben.
   Er ist meines Lebens Licht :
   Meinen Jesum lass ich nicht.

iv Ich werd ihn auch lassen nicht,
    Wenn ich nun dahin gelanget,
    Wo vor seinem Angesicht
    Meiner Väter Glaube pranget.
    Mich erfreut sein Angesicht :
    Meinen Jesum lass ich nicht.

*vi Jesum lass ich nicht von mir,
     Geh ihm ewig an der Seiten ;
     Christus lässt mich für und für
     Zu dem Lebensbächlein leiten.
     Selig, wer mit mir so spricht :
     Meinen Jesum lass ich nicht.

i Never Jesus will I leave !
   He Who bore the Cross to win me
   All my homage shall receive,
   Clinging close to Him so fondly.
   Jesus lights my soul and heart,
   From Him never will I part.

iv Never from Him will I stray.
    When the toil of earth is over,
    And there dawns the longed-for day,
    Then I shall Himself discover.
    In His presence all is joy :
    Jesus, ne'er I'll part from Thee !

vi Jesus never will I leave.
    By His side my pathway treading,
    He will lead me to receive
    Waters fresh in meadows welling.
    Blessèd he who saith with me :
    ' Jesus, ne'er I'll part from Thee '.

U.L.S. 323.

Tr. C. S. T.

MEINEN JESUM LASS ICH NICHT, WEIL

Hymn, by Christian Keimann, in six 6-line stanzas (1658). Melody, by (?) Andreas Hammerschmidt (1658).

252

i Meinen Jesum lass ich nicht :
  Weil er sich für mich gegeben,
  So erfordert meine Pflicht,
  Klettenweis an ihm zu kleben.
  Er ist meines Lebens Licht :
  Meinen Jesum lass ich nicht.

iv Ich werd ihn auch lassen nicht,
  Wenn ich nun dahin gelanget,
  Wo vor seinem Angesicht
  Meiner Väter Glaube pranget.
  Mich erfreut sein Angesicht :
  Meinen Jesum lass ich nicht.

*vi Jesum lass ich nicht von mir,
  Geh ihm ewig an der Seiten ;
  Christus lässt mich für und für
  Zu dem Lebensbächlein leiten.
  Selig, wer mit mir so spricht :
  Meinen Jesum lass ich nicht.

U.L.S. 323.

i Never Jesus will I leave !
  He Who bore the Cross to win me
  All my homage shall receive,
  Clinging close to Him so fondly.
  Jesus lights my soul and heart,
  From Him never will I part.

iv Never from Him will I stray.
  When the toil of earth is over,
  And there dawns the longed-for day,
  Then I shall Himself discover.
  In His presence all is joy :
  Jesus, ne'er I'll part from Thee !

vi Jesus never will I leave.
  By His side my pathway treading,
  He will lead me to receive
  Waters fresh in meadows welling.
  Blessèd he who saith with me :
  ' Jesus, ne'er I'll part from Thee '.

Tr. C. S. T.

MEINEN JESUM LASS ICH NICHT, WEIL

Hymn, by Christian Keimann, in six 6-line stanzas (1658).   Melody, by (?) Andreas Hammerschmidt (1658).

253

i Meinen Jesum lass ich nicht :
  Weil er sich für mich gegeben,
So erfordert meine Pflicht,
  Klettenweis an ihm zu kleben.
Er ist meines Lebens Licht,
Meinen Jesum lass ich nicht.

v Nicht nach Welt, nach Himmel nicht
  Meine Seele wünscht und stöhnet :
Jesum wünscht sie und sein Licht,
  Der mich hat mit Gott versöhnet,
Der mich freiet vom Gericht :
Meinen Jesum lass ich nicht.

vi Jesum lass ich nicht von mir,
  Geh ihm ewig an der Seiten ;
Christus lässt mich für und für
  Zu dem Lebensbächlein leiten.
Selig, wer mit mir so spricht :
Meinen Jesum lass ich nicht.

U.L.S. 323.

i Never Jesus will I leave !
  He Who bore the Cross to win me
All my homage shall receive,
  Clinging close to Him so fondly.
Jesus lights my soul and heart,
From Him never will I part.

v Heaven nor earth are my delight,
  Other bourne my soul inviteth.
Jesus is my Hope, my Light,
  God and man He reconcileth.
He hath borne my load of sin,
Never will I part from Him.

vi Jesus never will I leave.
  By His side my pathway treading,
He will lead me to receive
  Waters fresh in meadows welling.
Blessèd he who saith with me :
' Jesus, ne'er I'll part from Thee '.

Tr. C. S. T.

THE

FOUR-PART CHORALS OF J. S. BACH

*With the German Text of the Hymns
and English Translations*

Edited, with an historical Introduction, Notes
and critical Appendices, by

CHARLES SANFORD TERRY

(VOLUME II)

OXFORD UNIVERSITY PRESS

London: Amen House Warwick Square E.C.4
and 95 Wimpole Street W.1.
Amsterdam : Broekmans & Van Poppel
Paris : Editions Max Eschig
New York : 114 Fifth Avenue

1929

ENGRAVED AND PRINTED BY
HENDERSON AND SPALDING LTD.
SYLVAN GROVE
LONDON
S.E. 15

MEINEN JESUM LASS ICH NICHT, WEIL

Hymn, by Christian Keimann, in six 6-line stanzas (1658). Melody, by (?) Andreas Hammerschmidt (1658).

254

i Meinen Jesum lass ich nicht :
　　Weil er sich für mich gegeben,
　　So erfordert meine Pflicht,
　　Klettenweis an ihm zu kleben.
　　Er ist meines Lebens Licht :
　　Meinen Jesum lass ich nicht.

ii Jesum lass ich nimmer nicht,
　　Weil ich soll auf Erden leben ;
　　Ihm hab ich voll Zuversicht,
　　Was ich bin und hab, ergeben.
　　Alles ist auf ihn gericht :
　　Meinen Jesum lass ich nicht.

* vi Jesum lass ich nicht von mir,
　　Geh ihm ewig an der Seiten ;
　　Christus lässt mich für und für
　　Zu dem Lebensbächlein leiten.
　　Selig, wer mit mir so spricht :
　　Meinen Jesum lass ich nicht.

i Never Jesus will I leave !
　　He Who bore the Cross to win me
　　All my homage shall receive,
　　Clinging close to Him so fondly.
　　Jesus lights my soul and heart,
　　From Him never will I part.

ii Never Jesus will I leave
　　While on earth my course I follow.
　　From Him doth my soul receive
　　All its joy and e'en its sorrow.
　　What He wills is good for me :
　　Jesus, ne'er I'll part from Thee !

vi Jesus never will I leave.
　　By His side my pathway treading,
　　He will lead me to receive
　　Waters fresh in meadows welling.
　　Blessèd he who saith with me :
　　' Jesus, ne'er I'll part from Thee '.

U.L.S. 323.

Tr. C. S. T.

T

273

MEINEN JESUM LASS ICH NICHT, WEIL

Hymn, by Christian Keimann, in six 6-line stanzas (1658).   Melody, by (?) Andreas Hammerschmidt (1658).

255

i Meinen Jesum lass ich nicht :
  Weil er sich für mich gegeben,
So erfordert meine Pflicht,
  Klettenweis an ihm zu kleben.
Er ist meines Lebens Licht :
  Meinen Jesum lass ich nicht.

iii Lass vergehen das Gesicht,
  Hören, Schmecken, Fühlen weichen,
Lass das letzte Tageslicht
  Mich auf dieser Welt erreichen ;
Wenn der Lebensfaden bricht,
  Meinen Jesum lass ich nicht.

* vi Jesum lass ich nicht von mir,
  Geh ihm ewig an der Seiten ;
Christus lässt mich für und für
  Zu dem Lebensbächlein leiten.
Selig, wer mit mir so spricht :
  Meinen Jesum lass ich nicht.

i Never Jesus will I leave !
  He Who bore the Cross to win me
All my homage shall receive,
  Clinging close to Him so fondly.
Jesus lights my soul and heart,
  From Him never will I part.

iii Come what may ! let hearing, sight,
  Every sense and pleasure vanish !
Let grim Death display his might,
  And from mortal ken me banish !
When the summons tolls for me,
  Jesus, ne'er I'll part from Thee !

vi Jesus never will I leave.
  By His side my pathway treading,
He will lead me to receive
  Waters fresh in meadows welling.
Blessèd he who saith with me :
  ' Jesus, ne'er I'll part from Thee '.

U.L.S. 323.

Tr. C.S.T.

MEINES LEBENS LETZTE ZEIT

Hymn, anonymous, in seven 8-line stanzas (1726).   Melody, anonymous (1726).

256

i Meines Lebens letzte Zeit
   Ist nunmehro angekommen,
   Da der schnöden Eitelkeit
   Meine Seele wird genommen ;
   Wer kann widerstreben,
   Dass uns Menschen Gott das Leben
   Auf ein zeitlich Wiedernehmen
   Hat gegeben.

iii Ach ! wohin ? ach Weh ! wohin ?
    Ach wer kann mir Hülfe schicken ?
    Wo wird mein gequälter Sinn
    Sich mit rechtem Trost erquicken ?
    Alle Dinge lehren,
    Die sich itzo von mir kehren,
    Dass kein Menschenmittel kann dem
    Tode wehren.

iv Jesus ist allein der Mann,
    Der in Nöthen bei uns bleibet,
    Der im Tode helfen kann,
    Und uns alle Furcht vertreibet.
    Ach ! in Jesu Wunden
    Hat in seinen Jammerstunden
    Mancher Sünder seinen süssen
    Trost gefunden.

i Now at length the hour is near,
   On my soul is pressing closely,
   When Death sounds his call so clear,
   And from earth's mean joys invites me.
   Brief's our mortal journey ;
   God hath willed, and wisely, surely,
   That our life must, late or early,
   Know an ending.

iii Woe is me ! Ah, bitter woe !
    Who is there at hand to aid me ?
    Faint my spirit quaileth so,
    Is there none at hand to help me ?
    Everything that breatheth
    Graveward ever swiftly moveth :
    None can death resist ; so proveth
    All that liveth.

iv Jesus only, none but He,
    In our last great need availeth
    Over fear's proud mastery.
    He alone with might prevaileth.
    By His blood that flowèd
    Hath He to the soul restorèd
    Blessèd comfort, balm outpourèd,
    Joy assurèd.

G. C. Schemelli.[1]

Tr. C. S. T.

[1] *Musicalisches Gesangbuch* (1736), p. 601.

275

MIT FRIED UND FREUD ICH FAHR DAHIN

Hymn, by Martin Luther, a free version of 'Nunc dimittis', in four 6-line stanzas (1524).   Melody, by (?) Luther (1524).

257

Nunc dimittis.

i Mit Fried und Freud ich fahr dahin
   In Gottes Wille ;
   Getrost ist mir mein Herz und Sinn,
   Sanft und stille.
   Wie Gott mir verheissen hat :
   Der Tod ist mein Schlaf worden.

ii Das macht Christus, wahr Gottes Sohn,
   Der treue Heiland,
   Den du mich, Herr, hast sehen lan,
   Und macht bekannt,
   Dass er mir das Leben sei
   Und Heil in Nöth und Sterben.

iii Den hast du allen fürgestellt
    Mit grossen Gnaden,
    Zu seinem Reich die ganze Welt
    Heissen laden
    Durch dein theuer heilsam Wort,
    An allem Ort erschollen.

iv Er ist das Heil und selig Licht
   Für alle Heiden :
   Zu 'rleuchten, die dich kennen nicht,
   Und zu weiden.
   Er ist deins Volks Israel
   Der Preis, Ehr, Freud und Wonne.

i In peace and joy I now depart,
   As God would have me.
   At rest and still are mind and heart,
   He doth save me.
   As my God hath promised me,
   Death is become my slumber.

ii That is because Christ was God's Son,
   Our Redeemer true,
   Whom Thou, O Lord, to me hast shown,
   And made me know
   As the one eternal life,
   And health in pain and dying.

iii Thou hast Him in the forefront placed,
    In Him delighted ;
    The whole world to His kingdom blest
    Hast invited,
    Through Thy precious wholesome Word
    In every place resounding.

iv He is the health and happy light
   Of all the heathen,
   To feed them and their eyes make bright
   Thee to see then.
   Of Thy folk Israel is He
   The praise, joy, honour, pleasure.

U.L.S. 198.   *Tr. George Macdonald.*[1]

[1] *Exotics* (Lond. 1876), p. 109.

276

MIT FRIED UND FREUD ICH FAHR DAHIN

Hymn, by Martin Luther, a free version of ' Nunc dimittis ', in four 6-line stanzas (1524).   Melody, by (?) Luther (1524).

258

Nunc dimittis.

i Mit Fried und Freud ich fahr dahin
  In Gottes Wille;
  Getrost ist mir mein Herz und Sinn,
  Sanft und stille.
  Wie Gott mir verheissen hat:
  Der Tod ist mein Schlaf worden.

ii Das macht Christus, wahr Gottes Sohn,
   Der treue Heiland,
   Den du mich, Herr, hast sehen lan,
   Und macht bekannt,
   Dass er mir das Leben sei
   Und Heil in Nöth und Sterben.

iii Den hast du allen fürgestellt
    Mit grossen Gnaden,
    Zu seinem Reich die ganze Welt
    Heissen laden
    Durch dein theuer heilsam Wort,
    An allem Ort erschollen.

* iv Er ist das Heil und selig Licht
     Für alle Heiden:
     Zu 'rleuchten, die dich kennen nicht,
     Und zu weiden.
     Er ist deins Volks Israel
     Der Preis, Ehr, Freud und Wonne.

i In peace and joy I now depart,
  For God has callèd.
  I trust in Him with soul and heart,
  Calm, preparèd.
  God doth e'er His promise keep,
  And death's a few years' sleeping.

ii This Christ hath wrought, God's only Son,
   Our blessèd Saviour,
   Whom to mine eyes Thou makest known,
   My Redeemer.
   He's my Help in trouble's hour
   To comfort me when dying.

iii Him hast Thou in the face of all
    In love designèd
    The Gentiles to Thy light to call,
    Now benighted,
    By Thy ever sacred Word
    Throughout the world resounding.

iv To heathen folk He hath brought light
   From out of darkness.
   He leadeth them of blinded sight
   Into gladness.
   He's of His own Israel
   Her praise, her joy, her glory,

U.L.S. 198.

Tr. C. S. T.

MIT FRIED UND FREUD ICH FAHR DAHIN

Hymn, by Martin Luther, a free version of 'Nunc dimittis', in four 6-line stanzas (1524).   Melody, by (?) Luther (1524).

259

Nunc dimittis.

i Mit Fried und Freud ich fahr dahin
  In Gottes Wille ;
  Getrost ist mir mein Herz und Sinn,
  Sanft und stille.
  Wie Gott mir verheissen hat :
  Der Tod ist mein Schlaf worden.

ii Das macht Christus, wahr Gottes Sohn,
  Der treue Heiland,
  Den du mich, Herr, hast sehen lan,
  Und macht bekannt,
  Dass er mir das Leben sei
  Und Heil in Nöth und Sterben.

iii Den hast du allen fürgestellt
  Mit grossen Gnaden,
  Zu seinem Reich die ganze Welt
  Heissen laden
  Durch dein theuer heilsam Wort,
  An allem Ort erschollen.

* iv Er ist das Heil und selig Licht
  Für alle Heiden ;
  Zu 'rleuchten, die dich kennen nicht,
  Und zu weiden.
  Er ist deins Volks Israel
  Der Preis, Ehr, Freud und Wonne.

i In peace and joy I now depart,
  As God would have me.
  At rest and still are mind and heart,
  He doth save me.
  As my God hath promised me,
  Death is become my slumber.

ii That is because Christ was God's Son,
  Our Redeemer true,
  Whom Thou, O Lord, to me hast shown,
  And made me know
  As the one eternal life,
  And health in pain and dying.

iii Thou hast Him in the forefront placed,
  In Him delighted ;
  The whole world to His kingdom blest
  Hast invited,
  Through Thy precious wholesome Word
  In every place resounding.

iv He is the health and happy light
  Of all the heathen,
  To feed them and their eyes make bright
  Thee to see then.
  Of Thy folk Israel is He
  The praise, joy, honour, pleasure.

U.L.S. 198.

Tr. George Macdonald.[1]

[1] *Exotics* (Lond. 1876), p. 109.

MITTEN WIR IM LEBEN SIND

Hymn (st. ii. iii.), by Martin Luther, an expansion of the Antiphon ' Media vita in morte sumus ', in three 14-line stanzas (1524).
Melody, pre-Reformation, adapted (1524).

i Mit-ten wir im Le - ben sind   Mit dem Tod um-fan - - gen;
Wen suchn wir, der Hül - fe thu,   Dass wir Gnad er-lan - - gen?

ii Mit-ten in dem Tod an-ficht   Uns der Höl-le Ra - - chen:
Wer will uns aus sol-cher Noth   Frei und le-dig ma - - chen?

iii Mit-ten in der Höl-len Angst   Uns-er Sünd uns trei - - ben:
Wo solln wir denn flieh-en hin,   Da wir mö-gen blei - - ben?

i In the midst of life, we are   Aye in Death's em-bra - - ces.
Who is there who help us can,   And in fa-vour place us?

ii In the midst of death, be-hold   Hell's jaws ga-ping at us!
Who will from such dire dis-tress   Free and scatheless set us?

iii In the midst of pains of hell   Us our sins are bait - - ing;
Whither shall we flee a-way   Where a rest is wait - - ing?

i Das bist du, Herr, al - lei - - ne,   Uns reu-et uns-re
ii Das thust du, Herr, al - lei - - ne.   Es jam-mert dein Barm -
iii Zu dir, Herr Christ, al - lei - - ne.   Ver-gos-sen ist dein

i Thou art He, Lord, Thou on - - ly.   From ill deeds we sor -
ii That dost Thou, Lord, Thou on - - ly.   It fills Thy ten-der
iii To Thee, Lord Christ, Thee on - - ly.   Out-pour-èd is Thy

i Mis - se - that,   Die dich, Herr, er-zür-net hat.   Hei-
ii -herz-ig - keit   Un-ser Sünd und gros-ses Leid.   Hei-
iii theu-res Blut   Das gnug für die Sün-de thut.   Hei-

i -row-ing turn,   That have made Thy an-ger burn.   Ho-
ii heart with woe   We should sin and suf-fer so.   Ho-
iii pre-cious blood,   For our sins suf-fi-cing good.   Ho-

MITTEN WIR IM LEBEN SIND

i li - ger Her - re Gott! Hei - li - ger star - ker Gott! Hei - li - ger, barm - herz - i -
ii li - ger Her - re Gott! Hei - li - ger star - ker Gott! Hei - li - ger, barm - herz - i -
iii li - ger Her - re Gott! Hei - li - ger star - ker Gott! Hei - li - ger, barm - herz - i -

i -ly, ho - ly, Lord God, Ho - ly, migh - ty Lord God, Ho - ly Sa - viour with the
ii -ly, ho - ly, Lord God, Ho - ly, migh - ty Lord God, Ho - ly Sa - viour with the
iii -ly, ho - ly, Lord God, Ho - ly, migh - ty Lord God, Ho - ly Sa - viour with the

i ger Hei - land! Du e - - wi - ger Gott! Lass uns nicht ver - sin - -
ii ger Hei - land! Du e - - wi - ger Gott! Lass uns nicht ver - za -
iii ger Hei - land! Du e - - wi - ger Gott! Lass uns nicht ent - fal -

i ten - der heart, E - ver - last - ing God, Let us not be drown -
ii ten - der heart, E - ver - last - ing God, Let us not be ghas - -
iii ten - der heart, E - ver - last - ing God, Let us not fall from

i ken In des bit - tern To - des Noth. Ky - rie e - lei - - son!
ii gen Vor der tief - en Höll - en Glut. Ky - rie e - lei - - son!
iii len Von des recht - en Glau - bens Trost. Ky - rie e - lei - - son

U.L.S. 566.

i -èd in the pains of bit - ter death. O Lord, hear us - - now!
ii -ted By hell's hol - lows all a - glow. O Lord, hear us - - now!
iii Thee, From the com fort of Thy faith. O Lord, hear us - - now!

Tr. George Macdonald.[1]

[1] *Exotics* (Lond. 1876), p. 107.

NICHT SO TRAURIG, NICHT SO SEHR

Hymn, by Paul Gerhardt, in fifteen 6-line stanzas (1647).   Melody, by Bach (1736).

261

i Nicht so traurig, nicht so sehr,
Meine Seele, sei betrübt,
Dass dir Gott Glück, Gut und Ehr,
Nicht so viel wie andern giebt.
Nimm vorlieb mit deinem Gott :
Hast du Gott, so hats nicht Noth.

iii Bist du doch darum nicht hier,
Dass du Erden haben sollt ;
Schau den Himmel über dir :
Da, da ist dein edles Gold ;
Da ist Ehre, da ist Freud,
Freud ohn End, Ehr ohne Neid.

vii Ach, wie bist du doch so blind
Und im Denken unbedacht !
Augen hast du, Menschenkind,
Und hast doch noch nie betracht
Deiner Augen helles Glas :
Siehe, welch ein Schatz ist das !

xi Gott ist deiner Liebe voll
Und von ganzem Herzen treu ;
Wenn du wünschest, prüft er wohl,
Wie dein Wunsch beschaffen sei :
Ist dirs gut, so geht ers ein ;
Ists dein Schade, spricht er Nein !

xv Führe deinen Lebenslauf
Allzeit Gottes eingedenk :
Wie es kommt, nimmt alles auf
Als ein wohlbedacht Geschenk.
Geht dirs widrig : lass es gehn ;
Gott und Himmel bleibt dir stehn.

i Why so troubled, O my heart ?
Why with doubting care cast down ?
Think'st thou unregarded art,
Fearing God doth on Thee frown ?
Be content with what He sends :
Loving Him thy trouble ends.

iii Not on earth thy treasure lies,
In this life of pain and woe.
Seek it there beyond the skies
Where one day man's soul shall go.
There's your treasure, there your joy,
Happiness without alloy !

vii Why so blinded are thine eyes,
Thoughtless and ingrate thy mind ?
Learn what wealth above there lies,
All that God for thee's designed.
Use thy vision clear to see
All that He has done for thee.

xi God hath nought but love for thee,
Ever planning for thy good.
What is meet He gives to thee,
What is ill He will withhold.
All thy longings doth He test,
Granting only what is best.

xv Cheerfully then go thy way,
Showing God a grateful heart,
E'er reflecting, come what may,
That He alway takes thy part.
Should misfortune weave a spell,
God's in heaven and all is well !

U.L.S. 698.

Tr. C. S. T.

NUN BITTEN WIR DEN HEILIGEN GEIST

Hymn (st. ii, iii, iv), by Martin Luther, in four 5-line stanzas (1524).   Melody, pre-Reformation.

262

*Bach has a ⌒ here

i Nun bitten wir den Heiligen Geist
  Um den rechten Glauben allermeist,
  Dass er uns behüte an unserm Ende,
  Wenn wir heimfahren aus dieser Erde.
          Kyrie eleison !

ii Du werthes Licht, gieb uns deinen Schein,
   Lehr uns Jesum Christ kennen allein,
   Dass wir an ihm bleiben, dem treuen Heiland,
   Der uns bracht hat zum rechten Vaterland.
          Kyrie eleison !

*iii Du süsse Lieb, schenk uns deine Gunst,
    Lass uns empfinden der Liebe Brunst,
    Dass wir uns von Herzen einander lieben
    Und in Friede auf eim Sinne bleiben.
          Kyrie eleison !

iv Du höchster Tröster in aller Noth,
   Hilf, dass wir nicht fürchten Schand noch Tod :
   Dass in uns die Sinne nicht gar verzagen,
   Wenn der Feind wird das Leben verklagen.
          Kyrie eleison !

U.L.S. 177.

i Now let us pray to the Holy Ghost
  For the true faith, of all things the most,
  That He take care of us when we are dying,
  And are going from this vale of crying.
          Hear our prayer, O Lord !

ii Thou noble Light, shine as Thou hast shone,
   Teach us to know Jesus Christ alone,
   Saviour Lord most blessèd, to hold by His hand,
   Which has brought us to the right and true land.
          Hear our prayer, O Lord !

iii Thou sweet Love, favour us now, that so
    We of Thy love feel within the glow,
    That we from our hearts may be true to others,
    And in peace dwell with the minds of brothers.
          Hear our prayer, O Lord !

iv Thou Comforter, best in need or blame,
   Help us to fear neither death nor shame,
   Nor at last to tremble lest Thou refuse us,
   When the enemy comes to accuse us.
          Hear our prayer, O Lord !

Tr. George Macdonald.[1]

[1] *Exotics* (Lond. 1876), p. 59.

NUN BITTEN WIR DEN HEILIGEN GEIST

Hymn (st. ii, iii, iv), by Martin Luther, in four 5-line stanzas (1524).   Melody, pre-Reformation.

263

*Bach has a ⁀ here.

i Nun bitten wir den Heiligen Geist
  Um den rechten Glauben allermeist,
  Dass er uns behüte an unserm Ende,
  Wenn wir heimfahren aus dieser Erde.
            Kyrie eleison!

ii Du werthes Licht, gieb uns deinen Schein,
   Lehr uns Jesum Christ kennen allein,
   Dass wir an ihm bleiben, dem treuen Heiland,
   Der uns bracht hat zum rechten Vaterland.
            Kyrie eleison!

iii Du süsse Lieb, schenk uns deine Gunst,
    Lass uns empfinden der Liebe Brunst,
    Dass wir uns von Herzen einander lieben
    Und in Friede auf ein'm Sinne bleiben.
            Kyrie eleison!

iv Du höchster Tröster in aller Noth,
   Hilf, dass wir nicht fürchten Schand noch Tod:
   Dass in uns die Sinne nicht gar verzagen,
   Wenn der Feind wird das Leben verklagen.
            Kyrie eleison!

            U.L.S. 177.

i Now let us pray to God Holy Ghost
  For the true faith, of all things the most,
  That He take care of us when we are dying,
  And are going from this vale of crying.
            Hear our prayer, O Lord!

ii Thou noble Light, shine as Thou hast shone,
   Teach us know Lord Jesus Christ alone,
   The Saviour most blessèd, to hold by His hand,
   Which has brought us to the right and true land.
            Hear our prayer, O Lord!

iii Thou sweet Love, grant us favour, that so
    We of Thy love feel within the glow,
    That we from our true hearts may love the others,
    And in peace dwell with the minds of brothers.
            Hear our prayer, O Lord!

iv Thou Comfort, best in danger or blame,
   Help us all to fear nor death nor shame,
   Nor at last to tremble lest Thou refuse us,
   When the enemy comes to accuse us.
            Hear our prayer, O Lord!

            Tr. George Macdonald.[1]

¹ *Exotics* (Lond. 1877), p. 59.

NUN BITTEN WIR DEN HEILIGEN GEIST

Hymn, (st. ii, iii, iv), by Martin Luther, in four 5-line stanzas (1524). Melody, pre-Reformation.

264

*Bach has a 𝄐 here

i Nun bitten wir den Heiligen Geist
  Um den rechten Glauben allermeist,
  Dass er uns behüte an unserm Ende
  Wenn wir heimfahren aus dieser Erde.
          Kyrie eleison !

ii Du werthes Licht, gieb uns deinen Schein,
   Lehr uns Jesum Christ kennen allein,
   Dass wir an ihm bleiben, dem treuen Heiland,
   Der uns bracht hat zum rechten Vaterland.
          Kyrie eleison !

* iii Du süsse Lieb, schenk uns deine Gunst,
   Lass uns empfinden der Liebe Brunst,
   Dass wir uns von Herzen einander lieben,
   Und in Friede auf eim Sinne bleiben.
          Kyrie eleison !

iv Du höchster Troster in aller Noth,
   Hilf, dass wir nicht fürchten Schand noch Tod :
   Dass in uns die Sinne nicht gar verzagen,
   Wenn der Feind wird das Leben verklagen.
          Kyrie eleison !

                    U.L.S. 177.

i Now let us pray to the Holy Ghost
  For the true faith, of all things the most,
  That He take care of us when we are dying,
  And are going from this vale of crying.
          Hear our prayer, O Lord !

ii Thou noble Light, shine as Thou hast shone,
   Teach us to know Jesus Christ alone,
   Saviour Lord most blessèd, to hold by His hand,
   Which has brought us to the right and true land.
          Hear our prayer, O Lord !

iii Thou sweet Love, favour us now, that so
   We of Thy love feel within the glow,
   That we from our hearts may be true to others,
   And in peace dwell with the minds of brothers.
          Hear our prayer, O Lord !

iv Thou Comforter, best in need or blame,
   Help us to fear neither death nor shame,
   Nor at last to tremble lest Thou refuse us,
   When the enemy comes to accuse us.
          Hear our prayer, O Lord !

                    Tr. George Macdonald.[1]

[1] *Exotics* (Lond. 1876), p. 59.

NUN DANKET ALLE GOTT

Hymn, by Martin Rinkart, in three 8-line stanzas (1636).   Melody, by Johann Crüger, (1648).

[Horns I & II obbligati.]

* i Nun danket alle Gott	i Now thank we all our God,
Mit Herzen, Mund und Händen,	With heart, and hands, and voices,
Der grosse Dinge thut	Who wondrous things hath done.
An uns und allen Enden ;	In Whom His world rejoices ;
Der uns von Mutterleib	Who from our mother's arms
Und Kindesbeinen an	Hath blessed us on our way
Unzählig viel zu gut	With countless gifts of love,
Und noch jetzund gethan.	And still is ours to-day.
ii Der ewig reiche Gott	ii O may this bounteous God
Woll uns bei unserm Leben	Through all our life be near us,
Ein immer fröhlich Herz	With ever joyful hearts
Und edlen Frieden geben,	And blessèd peace to cheer us ;
Und uns in seiner Gnad	And keep us in His grace,
Erhalten fort und fort,	And guide us when perplexed,
Und uns aus aller Noth	And free us from all ills
Erlösen hier und dort.	In this world and the next.
iii Lob, Ehr und Preis sei Gott,	iii All praise and thanks to God
Dem Vater und dem Sohne	The Father now be givèn,
Und dem, der beiden gleich,	The Son, and Him Who reigns
Im höchsten Himmelsthrone :	With Them in highest heavèn,
Dem dreimaleinen Gott,	The One eternal God,
Als er ursprünglich war	Whom heaven and earth adore,
Und ist und bleiben wird	For thus it was, is now,
Jetzund und immerdar !	And shall be evermore !

U.L.S. 234.

Tr. Catherine Winkworth[1]

[1] *Chorale Book for England* (Lond. 1865), No. 11.

NUN DANKET ALLE GOTT

Hymn, by Martin Rinkart, in three 8-line stanzas (1636).   Melody, by Johann Crüger 1648).

266

i Nun danket alle Gott
Mit Herzen, Mund und Händen,
Der grosse Dinge thut
An uns und allen Enden ;
Der uns von Mutterleib
Und Kindesbeinen an
Unzählig viel zu gut
Und noch jetzund gethan.

ii Der ewig reiche Gott
Woll uns bei unserm Leben
Ein immer fröhlich Herz
Und edlen Frieden geben,
Und uns in seiner Gnad
Erhalten fort und fort,
Und uns aus aller Noth
Erlösen hier und dort.

iii Lob, Ehr und Preis sei Gott,
Dem Vater und dem Sohne,
Und dem, der beiden gleich,
Im höchsten Himmelsthrone :
Dem dreimaleinen Gott,
Als er ursprünglich war
Und ist und bleiben wird
Jetzund und immerdar !

i Now thank we all our God,
With heart, and hands, and voices,
Who wondrous things hath done,
In Whom His world rejoices ;
Who from our mother's arms
Hath blessed us on our way
With countless gifts of love,
And still is ours to-day.

ii O may this bounteous God
Through all our life be near us,
With ever joyful hearts
And blessèd peace to cheer us ;
And keep us in His grace,
And guide us when perplexed,
And free us from all ills
In this world and the next.

iii All praise and thanks to God
The Father now be givèn,
The Son, and Him Who reigns
With Them in highest heavèn,
The One eternal God,
Whom heaven and earth adore,
For thus it was, is now,
And shall be evermore !

U.L.S. 234.   *Tr. Catherine Winkworth.*[1]

[1] *Chorale Book for England* (Lond. 1865), No. 11.

NUN FREUT EUCH, GOTTES KINDER ALL

Hymn, by Erasmus Alber, in 29 (abridged to 16) 4-line stanzas (c. 1549). Melody, anonymous (1546), to 'Ihr lieben Christen, freut euch nun'.

267

i Nun freut euch, Gottes Kinder all,
   Der Herr führt euch mit grossem Schall;
   Lobsinget ihm, lobsinget ihm,
   Lobsinget ihm mit lauter Stimm!

ii Die Engel und all Himmelsheer
   Erzeigen Christo göttlich Ehr,
   Und jauchzen ihm mit frohem Schall,
   Das thun die lieben Engel all.

iv Der Herr hat uns die Stätt bereit,
   Da wir solln bleibn in Ewigkeit;
   Lobsinget ihm, lobsinget ihm,
   Lobsinget ihm mit lauter Stimm!

v Wir sind Erben im Himmelreich,
   Wir sind den lieben Engeln gleich,
   Das sehn die lieben Engel gern
   Und danken mit uns Gott dem Herrn.

vi Es hat mit uns nun nimmer Noth,
   Der Satan, Sünd und ewger Tod
   Allsammt zu Schanden worden sind,
   Durch Gottes und Marien Kind.

Tucher.[1]

i Rejoice now, Christians young and old,
   The highest heavens now Christ enfold!
   Come, praise ye Him, come, praise ye Him,
   And joyful in His honour sing!

ii The angel hosts their voices raise,
   And give the Lord ascended praise,
   Acclaiming loudly every one
   Him Who o'er death hath victory won.

iv He goes before us to prepare
   Our heavenly mansion, bright and fair.
   Come, praise ye Him, come, praise ye Him,
   And joyful in His honour sing!

v He makes us heirs of heaven above,
   And, like the angels, of His love.
   The angels mark His gracious plan
   And with delight their Master scan.

vi Now Death and Satan down are cast
   Our time of sorrow all is past.
   For Christ ascended hath prevailed
   O'er Sin and Death that man assailed.

Tr. C. S. T.

[1] Bd. i. No. 137.

NUN FREUT EUCH, LIEBEN CHRISTEN GMEIN

Hymn, by Martin Luther, in ten 7-line stanzas (1524). Melody, anonymous (1524), to 'Ach Gott vom Himmel, sieh darein'.

268

i Nun freut euch, lieben Christen gmein,
  Und lasst uns fröhlich springen,
  Dass wir getrost und all in ein
  Mit Lust und Liebe singen :
  Was Gott an uns gewendet hat,
  Und seine süsse Wunderthat ;
  Gar theur hat ers erworben.

ii Dem Teufel ich gefangen lag,
  Im Tod war ich verloren ;
  Mein Sünd mich qüalet Nacht und Tag,
  Darin ich war geboren ;
  Ich fiel auch immer tiefer drein,
  Es war kein Guts am Leben mein :
  Die Sünd hatt mich besessen.

iv Da jammert Gott in Ewigkeit
  Mein Elend übermassen ;
  Er dacht an sein Barmherzigkeit,
  Er wollt mir helfen lassen.
  Er wandt zu mir das Vaterherz ;
  Es war bei ihm fürwahr kein Scherz :
  Er liess sein Bestes kosten.

i Dear Christians, let us now rejoice,
  And dance in joyous measure !
  That, of good cheer, and with one voice,
  We sing in love and pleasure
  Of what to us our God hath shown,
  And wonder sweet that He hath done !
  Full dearly hath He wrought it.

ii Forlorn and lost in death I lay,
  A captive to the devil,
  My sin lay heavy, night and day,
  For I was born in evil.
  I fell but deeper for my strife,
  There was no good in all my life,
  For sin had all possessed me.

iv Then God was sorry on His throne
  To see such torment rend me ;
  His tender mercy He thought on
  His good help He would send me.
  He turned to me His father-heart ;
  Ah ! then was His no easy part,
  For of His best it cost Him.

U.L.S. 235.

Tr. George Macdonald.[1]

[1] *Exotics* (Lond. 1876), p. 80.

NUN FREUT EUCH, LIEBEN CHRISTEN GMEIN

Hymn, by Paul Gerhardt, in fifteen 7-line stanzas (1653). Melody (1535), of secular origin

269

*i Ich steh an deiner Krippen hier,
   O Jesulein, mein Leben,
   Ich stehe, bring und schenke dir,
   Was du mir hast gegeben.
   Nimm hin, es ist mein Geist und Sinn,
   Herz, Seel und Muth, nimm alles hin,
   Und lass dirs wohlgefallen,

ii Du hast mit deiner Lieb erfüllt
   Mein Adern und Geblüte ;
   Dein schöner Glanz, dein süsses Bild
   Liegt mir stets im Gemüthe.
   Und wie mag es auch anders sein,
   Wie könnt ich dich, mein Herzelein,
   Aus meinem Herzen lassen ?

iv Ich lag in tiefer Todesnacht,
   Du wurdest meine Sonne,
   Die Sonne, die mir zugebracht
   Licht, Leben, Freud und Wonne.
   O Sonne, die das werthe Licht
   Des Glaubens in mir zugericht,
   Wie schön sind deine Strahlen !

x O, dass doch ein so lieber Stern
   Soll in der Krippen liegen !
   Für edle Kinder grosser Herrn
   Gehören güldne Wiegen.
   Ach, Heu und Stroh sind viel zu schlecht ;
   Sammt, Seiden, Purpur wären recht,
   Dich, Kindlein, drauf zu legen.

i Beside Thy cradle, see, I stand,
  Child Jesus, Lord of heavèn.
  The gifts I offer in my hand
  Are by Thy bounty givèn.
  O take me then, my mind and heart,
  My soul, my strength, my every part,
  And be't in Thy sight pleasing !

ii Thou hast full filled me with Thy love,
   It floodeth all my being :
   Thy likeness, all things else above,
   My heart and soul is filling.
   And yet how else, Lord, should it be ?
   Could I endure the misery
   To lose Thee, O my Treasure ?

iv In deepest night of woe I lay
   Till Thou did'st shine upon me.
   My night's become the brightest day,
   And joy and light surround me !
   O Light of Heaven, come down to earth,
   Of Faith and Hope renewing birth,
   How lovely is Thy beauty !

x To think a Star so wondrous fair
  In yon poor manger lieth !
  To think the Lord of earth and air
  His Godhead now resigneth !
  How ill befits so poor a stall
  The Lord Who reigneth over all,
  In majesty enthronèd !

U.L.S. 39.

Tr. C. S. T.

NUN FREUT EUCH, LIEBEN CHRISTEN GMEIN

Hymn, by Bartholomäus Ringwaldt, in seven 7-line stanzas (c. 1556).   Melody (1535), of secular origin.

270

i Es ist gewisslich an der Zeit,
   Dass Gottes Sohn wird kommen
   In seiner grossen Herrlichkeit,
   Zu richten Bös und Frommen.
   Da wird das Lachen werden theur,
   Wenn alles wird vergehn im Feur,
   Wie Petrus davon schreibet.

ii Posaunen wird man hören gehn
   An aller Welte Ende,
   Darauf bald werden auferstehn
   All Todten gar behende ;
   Die aber noch das Leben han,
   Die wird der Herr von Stunden an
   Verwandeln und erneuen.

iv O weh demselben, welcher hat
   Des Herren Wort verachtet,
   Und nur auf Erden früh und spat
   Nach grossem Gut getrachtet !
   Der wird fürwahr ganz kahl bestehn,
   Und mit dem Satan müssen gehn
   Von Christo in die Hölle.

v O Jesu, hilf zur selben Zeit
   Von wegen deiner Wunden,
   Dass ich im Buch der Seligkeit
   Werd eingezeichnet funden.
   Daran ich denn auch zweifle nicht ;
   Denn du hast ja den Feind gericht
   Und meine Schuld bezahlet.

i Be sure that awful time will come,
   When Christ, the Lord of glory,
   Shall from His throne give men their doom
   And change things transitory.
   How dumb 'twill strike each impious jeer,
   When all things are consumed by fire,
   And heaven and earth dissolvèd.

ii The wakening trumpet all shall hear,
   The dead shall then be raisèd,
   And 'fore the judgement-seat appear,
   On right and left hand placèd.
   Those in the body at that time
   Shall, in a manner most sublime,
   Be altogether changèd.

iv Woe then to him that hath despised
   God's Word and revelation,
   And here done nothing but devised
   His lust's gratification ;
   Then, how confounded will he stand,
   When he must go, at Christ's command,
   To everlasting torment.

v When all with awe shall stand around
   To hear their doom allotted,
   O may my worthless name be found
   Within the Book unblotted !
   Grant me that firm, unshaken faith,
   That Thou, my Saviour, by Thy death
   Hast purchased my salvation.

U.L.S. 746.

Tr. John Christian Jacobi.[1]

[1] *Moravian Hymn-book* (Ed. 1877), No. 1215.

NUN KOMM, DER HEIDEN HEILAND

Hymn, by Martin Luther, a translation of St. Ambrose's ' Veni redemptor gentium ', in eight 4-line stanzas (1524). Melody, an adaptation (1524) of that of the Latin hymn.

271

Veni redemptor gentium.

i Nun komm, der Heiden Heiland,
Der Jungfrauen Kind erkannt,
Dass sich wunder alle Welt,
Gott solch Geburt ihm bestellt.

ii Nicht von Manns Blut noch von Fleisch,
Allein von dem Heilgen Geist
Ist Gotts Wort worden ein Mensch,
Und blüht ein Frucht Weibes Fleisch.

iii Der Jungfrau Leib schwanger ward,
Doch blieb Keuschheit rein bewahrt,
Leucht herfür manch Tugend schon,
Gott da war in seinem Thron.

iv Er ging aus der Kammer sein,
Dem Kön'glichen Saal so rein ;
Gott von Art und Mensch, ein Held,
Sein Weg er zu laufen eilt.

* viii Lob sei Gott dem Vater gthan,
Lob sei Gott seim eingen Sohn,
Lob sei Gott dem Heilgen Geist,
Immer und in Ewigkeit.

U.L.S. **17.**

i Come, Redeemer of our race,
Whom a virgin bore in grace !
Filled with wonder's all the earth
At its Saviour's mortal birth.

ii Not of mortal flesh or blood,
Through the Spirit come from God
Hath the Word a Man become,
Offspring of a virgin's womb.

iii Gentle mother of this Child
Spotless was and undefiled,
Forth from her all virtue shone,
There God reignèd on His throne.

iv See, He leaves His halls on high,
Royal state and majesty,
As the Hero of our race
Deigns to take a mortal's place.

viii Praise to God the Father be,
Glory, Holy Ghost, to Thee,
Praise and honour to the Son,
While eternal ages run !

Tr. C. S. T.

NUN KOMM, DER HEIDEN HEILAND

Hymn, by Martin Luther, a translation of St. Ambrose's ' Veni redemptor gentium', in eight 4-line stanzas (1524). Melody, an adaptation (1524) of that of the Latin hymn.

Veni redemptor gentium.

i Nun komm, der Heiden Heiland,
Der Jungfrauen Kind erkannt,
Dass sich wunder alle Welt,
Gott solch Geburt ihm bestellt.

v Sein Lauf kam vom Vater her,
Und kehrt wieder zum Vater,
Fuhr hinunter zu der Höll,
Und wieder zu Gottes Stuhl.

vi Der du bist dem Vater gleich,
Führ hinaus den Sieg im Fleisch,
Dass dein ewig Gotts Gewalt
In uns das krank Fleisch enthalt.

vii Dein Krippe glänzt hell und klar,
Die Nacht giebt ein neu Licht dar,
Dunkel muss nicht kommen drein,
Der Glaub bleibt immer im Schein.

* viii Lob sei Gott dem Vater gthan,
Lob sei Gott seim eingen Sohn,
I ob sei Gott dem Heilgen Geist,
Immer und in Ewigkeit.

U.L.S. 17.

i Come, Redeemer of our race,
Whom a virgin bore in grace !
Filled with wonder's all the earth
At its Saviour's mortal birth.

v From the Father cometh He,
And returneth speedily ;
Down to hell His road descends
Till again in heaven it ends.

vi To the Father equal, Thou
Canst our bodies frail endow
With Thy grace in plenteous store,
Flesh of our flesh evermore.

vii O how shines Thy cradle clear,
Brilliant as a new-born star !
Night and darkness flee away,
Faith is shining in the sky.

viii Praise to God the Father be,
Glory, Holy Ghost, to Thee,
Praise and honour to the Son,
While eternal ages run !

Tr. C. S. T.

NUN LASST UNS GOTT DEM HERREN

Hymn, by Ludwig Helmbold, in eight 4-line stanzas (1575).   Melody, by (?) Nikolaus Selnecker (1587).

273

i Nun lasst uns Gott dem Herren
 Dank sagen und ihn ehren
 Von wegen seiner Gaben,
 Die wir empfangen haben.

ii Den Leib, die Seel, das Leben
 Hat er allein uns geben ;
 Dieselbig zu bewahren,
 Thut er gar nichtes sparen.

iii Nahrung giebt er dem Leibe ;
 Die Seele muss auch bleiben,
 Wiewohl tödtliche Wunden
 Sind kommen von der Sünden.

iv Ein Arzt ist uns gegeben,
 Der selber ist das Leben :
 Christus, für uns gestorben,
 Hat uns das Heil erworben.

* v Sein Wort, sein Tauf, sein Nachtmahl
 Dient wider allen Unfall :
 Der Heilig Geist im Glauben
 Lehrt uns darauf vertrauen.

U.L.S. 500.

i Now praise we God Almighty
 With voices loud and lusty
 For all the grace and favour
 Which we His children savour !

ii Our body, soul and being,
 We owe them to His giving.
 His love He ne'er relaxes,
 But o'er our welfare watches.

iii To all flesh food He giveth,
 Our spirit too sustaineth,
 E'en though with sin 'tis scarrèd,
 With evil habits marrèd.

iv Christ, Lord of Life all glorious,
 Of every ill He cures us,
 Who by His Cross and Passion
 Hath won our full salvation.

v The font of grace, sin-cleansing
 The Word and love's outpouring,
 On these the Spirit guide us
 To rest, whate'er betide us.

Tr. C. S. T

NUN LASST UNS GOTT DEM HERREN

Hymn, by Ludwig Helmbold, in eight 4-line stanzas (1575).   Melody, by (?) Nikolaus Selnecker (1587).

274

[Horns I.II. & Timpani obbligati.]

i Nun lasst uns Gott dem Herren
Dank sagen und ihn ehren
Von wegen seiner Gaben,
Die wir empfangen haben.

vi Durch ihn ist uns vergeben
Die Sünd, geschenkt das Leben :
Den Himmel solln wir haben.
O Gott, wie grosse Gaben !

vii Wir bitten deine Güte :
Wollst uns hinfort behüten,
Uns Grosse mit den Kleinen ;
Du kannst's, nicht böse meinen.

★ viii Erhalt uns in der Wahrheit,
Gieb ewigliche Freiheit,
Zu preisen deinen Namen,
Durch Jesum Christum. Amen.

U.L.S. 500.

i Now praise we God Almighty
With voices loud and lusty
For all the grace and favour
Which we His children savour !

vi Our sins have been forgiven,
And we inherit heavèn
Through love's abounding plenty.
O God, how great Thy bounty !

vii We pray Thee, of Thy goodness,
To us henceforth be gracious !
Whatever Thou dost send us
We know is seemly for us.

viii Uphold us in the true faith,
In freedom and without scathe !
Thy name be praised by all men,
Through Christ Who saved us ! Amen.

Tr. C. S. T.

NUN LASST UNS GOTT DEM HERREN

Hymn, by Paul Gerhardt, in ten 4-line stanzas (1647).   Melody, by (?) Nikolaus Selnecker (1587).

275

i Wach auf, mein Herz, und singe
  Dem Schöpfer aller Dinge,
  Dem Geber aller Güter,
  Dem frommen Menschenhüter.

ii Heut als die dunkeln Schatten
   Mich ganz umfangen hatten,
   Hat Satan mein begehret ;
   Gott aber hats gewehret.

* ix Sprich Ja zu meinen Thaten ;
  Hilf selbst das Beste rathen ;
  Den Anfang, Mitt' und Ende,
  Ach Herr, zum besten wende.

* x Mit Segen mich beschütte :
  Mein Herz sei deine Hütte ;
  Dein Wort sei meine Speise,
  Bis ich gen Himmel reise.

  U.L.S. **475.**

i Awake, my soul, and sing ye
  The praise of God Who made thee,
  Of all good things the Giver,
  Of mortals their Protector !

ii The night is past and over :
   God's love my rest did cover,
   And Satan, prowling angry,
   In vain hath dared to harm me.

ix O Lord, confirm and guide me,
   And ever stand beside me !
   Throughout life's toilsome journey
   Thy sheltering care be with me !

x With Thy dear love console me,
  Come, Lord, and e'er control me,
  E'er let Thy Spirit feed me,
  In heaven at last receive me !

  Tr. C. S. T.

NUN LOB, MEIN SEEL, DEN HERREN

Hymn, by Johann Graumann, a translation of Psalm ciii, in four 12-line stanzas (1540). Melody, by (?) Johann Kugelmann (1540).

276

i Nun lob, mein Seel, den Herren ;
Was in mir ist, den Namen sein.
Sein Wohlthat thut er mehren :
Vergiss es nicht, o Herze mein !
Hat dir dein Sünd vergeben
Und heilt dein Schwachheit gross ;
Errett dein armes Leben,
Nimmt dich in seinen Schooss,
Mit rechtem Trost beschüttet,
Verjüngt dem Adler gleich.
Der Kön'g schafft recht, behütet
Die Leidenden im Reich.

* iii Wie sich ein Vat'r erbarmet
Über sein junge Kinderlein
So thut der Herr uns Armen,
So wir ihn kindlich fürchten rein.
Er kennt das arm Gemächte,
Und weiss, wir sind nur Staub,
Gleichwie das Gras, von Rechte,
Ein Blum und fallend Laub :
Der Wind nur drüber wehet,
So ist es nimmer da,
Also der Mensch vergehet,
Sein End das ist ihm nah.

Psalm ciii.

i My soul, now praise Thy Lord God,
Exalt on high His holy Sign !
His mercies have for e'er stood ;
Forget it not, O spirit mine !
He hath thy sins forgiven
That on thee grievous press,
Thy soul hath He clean shriven
And given thee His caress.
His care and love ne'er endeth,
Thy life He maketh fast,
He justice executeth
And rights the wronged at last.

iii Like as a father showereth
His tender care and pitying love,
So God His bounty poureth
On us His sons from heaven above.
Our frailty well He knoweth,
That out of dust we're made,
A flow'r decay that showeth,
A grass, a withered blade,
A wind that comes and goeth,
A dream, a passing breath,
A stream that quickly floweth,
Till all is quenched in death.

U.L.S. 238.

Tr. C. S. T

NUN LOB, MEIN SEEL, DEN HERREN

Hymn, by *Johann Graumann, a translation of Psalm ciii, in four 12-line stanzas* (1540). *Melody, by* (?)*Johann Kugelmann* (1540).

277

Psalm ciii.

i Nun lob, mein Seel, den Herren ;
  Was in mir ist, den Namen sein.
  Sein Wohlthat thut er mehren :
  Vergiss es nicht, o Herze mein !
  Hat dir dein Sünd vergeben
  Und heilt dein Schwachheit gross ;
  Errett dein armes Leben,
  Nimmt dich in seinen Schooss,
  Mit rechtem Trost beschüttet,
  Verjüngt dem Adler gleich.
  Der Kön'g schafft recht, behütet
  Die Leidenden im Reich.

ii Er hat uns wissen lassen
   Sein heilges Recht und sein Gericht,
   Dazu sein Gut ohn Massen ;
   Es mangelt an Erbarmung nicht.
   Sein Zorn lässt er wohl fahren,
   Straft nicht nach unser Schuld ;
   Die Gnad thut er nicht sparen,
   Den Blöden ist er hold.
   Sein Güt ist hoch erhaben
   Ob den, die fürchten ihn ;
   So fern der Ost vom Abend,
   Ist unser Sünd dahin.

i My soul, now praise Thy Lord God,
  Exalt on high His holy Sign !
  His mercies have for e'er stood ;
  Forget it not, O spirit mine !
  He hath thy sins forgiven
  That on thee grievous press,
  Thy soul hath He clean shriven
  And given thee His caress.
  His care and love ne'er endeth,
  Thy life He maketh fast,
  He justice executeth
  And rights the wronged at last.

ii He giveth us to treasure
   His righteousness, and judgement fair.
   He showers without measure
   Upon us all His loving care.
   His anger ne'er endureth,
   Forgives us all our ills,
   His love on us He poureth
   And e'en the wayward fills.
   Upon all them that serve Him
   His bounty is sent forth,
   And far as morn's from evening
   Removeth He His wrath.

U.L.S. 238.

Tr. C. S. T.

NUN LOB, MEIN SEEL, DEN HERREN

Hymn, by Johann Graumann, a translation of Psalm ciii, in four 12-line stanzas (1540).   *Melody, by* (?) *Johann Kugelmann* (1540).

Psalm ciii.

iv Die Gottes Gnad alleine
   Bleibt stät und fest in Ewigkeit
   Bei seiner liebn Gemeine,
   Die steht in seiner Furcht bereit,
   Die seinen Bund behalten.
   Er herrscht im Himmelreich :
   Ihr starken Engel waltet
   Sein's Lob's, und dient zugleich
   Dem grossen Herrn zu Ehren
   Und treibt sein heiligs Wort :
   Mein Seel soll auch vermehren
   Sein Lob an allem Ort !

iv God's grace alone endureth,
   Stands fast and true for evermore
   For him who truly loveth
   And always holdeth Him in awe.
   In heaven, 'mid seraphs soaring,
   He ruleth over all.
   The angel hosts adoring
   Before Him prostrate fall,
   His praises loudly singing,
   Fulfilling His dread Word.
   My soul, thy voice uplifting,
   Come, praise thy mighty Lord !

U.L.S. 238.

Tr. C. S. T.

NUN LOB, MEIN SEEL, DEN HERREN

Hymn, by Johann Graumann, a translation of Psalm ciii, in four 12-line stanzas (1540). St. v. circa 1555. Melody, by (?) Johann Kugelmann (1540).

279

[Trumpets I. II. III and Timpani obbligati]   *Psalm ciii.*

* v Sei Lob und Preis mit Ehren,
　　 Gott Vater, Sohn, Heiligem Geist !
　　 Der woll in uns vermehren,
　　 Was er uns aus Gnaden verheisst,
　　 Das wir ihm fest vertrauen,
　　 Gänzlich verlassn auf ihn,
　　 Von Herzen auf ihn bauen,
　　 Dass unsr' Herz, Muth, und Sinn
　　 Ihm tröstlich solln anhangen ;
　　 Drauf singen wir zur Stund :
　　 Amen wir werdens erlangen,
　　 Glaubn wir aus Herzensgrund.

v All glory, praise, and blessing
　 To Father, Son, and Holy Ghost,
　 Who ward us without ceasing,
　 And give us all that we need most.
　 Our faith in Them deep founded
　 Their favour sure hath won.
　 Their praise let e'er be sounded
　 While countless ages run.
　 On Them secure relying
　 We raise our joyous lay,
　 Amen, our voices glad crying
　 To praise this happy day.

NUN PREISET ALLE GOTTES BARMHERZIGKEIT

Hymn, by Matthäus Apelles von Löwenstern, in five 6-line stanzas (1644). Melody, by M. A. von Löwenstern (1644).

280

i Nun preiset alle
  Gottes Barmherzigkeit ;
  Lob ihn mit Schalle,
  Wertheste Christenheit !
  Er lässt dich freundlich zu sich laden :
  Freue dich, Israel, seiner Gnaden !

ii Der Herr regieret
   Über die ganze Welt ;
   Was sich nur rühret,
   Ihme zu Füssen fällt.
   Viel tausend Engel um ihn schweben ;
   Psalter und Harfen ihm Ehre geben.

iv Er giebet Speise
   Reichlich und überall,
   Nach Vaters Weise
   Sättigt er allzumal ;
   Er schaffet früh und späten Regen,
   Füllet uns alle mit seinem Segen.

v Drum preis und ehre
  Seine Barmherzigkeit,
  Sein Lob vermehre,
  Wertheste Christenheit !
  Uns soll hinfort kein Unfall schaden :
  Freue dich, Israel, seiner Gnaden !

i Come, all men, praise ye
  Our God so merciful !
  Sing anthems hearty,
  All who on earth do dwell !
  Sweet loving kindness He doth show ye :
  Sing now, O Israel, for His bounty !

ii For the Lord ruleth
   Over the whole world wide.
   What He commandeth
   Ever shall fast abide.
   Ten thousand angels round Him winging
   Loudly His praises ever are singing.

iv He food provideth
   Unto both man and beast,
   As He decideth
   Satisfies great and least.
   He sendeth down from heaven the showers
   Till with His blessing the green earth flowers.

v Wherefore, now praise Him,
  Merciful God and true !
  Anthems sing to Him,
  Who careth much for you !
  Henceforth misfortune harms us never :
  Sing now, O Israel, praise Him ever !

U.L.S. 717.

Tr. C. S. T.

NUN SICH DER TAG GEENDET HAT

Hymn, by Johann Friedrich Hertzog, in nine 4-line stanzas (1692). Melody, by Adam Krieger (1667), to a secular song similarly entitled.

281

i	Nun sich der Tag geendet hat Und keine Sonn mehr scheint, Schläft alles, was sich abgematt Und was zuvor geweint.	i	The day is over, night descends, The sun no more gives light, All nature sleeps, day's turmoil ends, And trouble's out of sight.
ii	Nur du, mein Gott, hast keine Rast, Du schläfst noch schlummerst nicht. Die Finsternis ist dir verhasst, Weil du bist selbst das Licht.	ii	But Thou, O God, no rest can know, Not ever dost Thou sleep. How can black night its shadows show Where lights eternal leap?
iii	Gedenke, Herr, doch auch an mich In dieser schwarzen Nacht, Und schenke mir genädiglich Den Schutz von deiner Wacht.	iii	Then turn Thy shelt'ing gaze on me Throughout the coming night, Look on me ever lovingly And keep me in Thy sight.
viii	Darauf thu ich mein Augen zu Und schlafe fröhlich ein. Mein Gott wacht jetzt in meiner Ruh : Wer wollt doch traurig sein ?	viii	So shall I close my eyes in peace To slumber quietly, Knowing Thy watch will never cease, And harm will pass me by.

Fischer-Tümpel.[1]

Tr. C. S. T.

[1] Bd. iv. No. 204.

O EWIGKEIT, DU DONNERWORT

Hymn, by Johann Rist, in sixteen 8-line stanzas (1642).   Melody, by Johann Schop (1642), to Rist's ' Wach auf, mein Herz, erhebe dich'.

282

i O Ewigkeit, du Donnerwort,
O Schwert, das durch die Seele bohrt,
O Anfang sonder Ende !
O Ewigkeit, Zeit ohne Zeit,
Ich weiss vor grosser Traurigkeit
Nicht, wo ich mich hinwende.
Mein ganz erschrocknes Herze bebt,
Dass mir die Zung am Gaumen klebt.

xiii Wach auf, o Mensch, vom Sündenschlaf ;
Ermuntre dich, verlornes Schaf,
Und bessre bald dein Leben.
Wach auf ! es ist doch hohe Zeit,
Es kommt heran die Ewigkeit,
Dir deinen Lohn zu geben.
Vielleicht ist heut der letzte Tag :
Wer weiss noch, wie man sterben mag ?

U.L.S. 770.

i Eternity, tremendous word,
A soul and body piercing sword,
Beginning without ending !
Eternity, thou timeless tide
On which nor grief nor sorrow ride,
Fain theeward I'd be wending !
My heart affrighted scarce can breathe,
My tongue doth to my palate cleave.

xiii Awake, O man, from sin's dull sleep,
Arouse thyself, poor wandering sheep,
Amend thy ways and living !
Awake, awake ! the hour is near
When God to judgement shall appear,
His sentence dread pronouncing.
To-day's perchance the day of doom
When into judgement thou shalt come.

Tr. C. S. T.

O EWIGKEIT, DU DONNERWORT

Hymn, by Johann Rist, in sixteen 8-line stanzas (1642). Melody, by Johann Schop (1642), to Rist's 'Wach auf, mein Geist, erhebe dich'

283

i O Ewigkeit, du Donnerwort,
  O Schwert, das durch die Seele bohrt,
  O Anfang sonder Ende !
  O Ewigkeit, Zeit ohne Zeit,
  Ich weiss vor grosser Traurigkeit
  Nicht, wo ich mich hinwende.
  Mein ganz erschrocknes Herze bebt,
  Dass mir die Zung am Gaumen klebt.

* xi So lang ein Gott im Himmel lebt
  Und über alle Wolken schwebt,
  Wird solche Marter währen ;
  Es wird sie plagen Kält und Hitz,
  Angst, Hunger, Schrecken, Feur und Blitz,
  Und sie doch nicht verzehren.
  Dann wird sich enden diese Pein,
  Wenn Gott nicht mehr wird ewig sein.

* xvi O Ewigkeit, du Donnerwort,
  O Schwert, das durch die Seele bohrt,
  O Anfang sonder Ende !
  O Ewigkeit, Zeit ohne Zeit,
  Ich weiss vor grosser Traurigkeit
  Nicht, wo ich mich hinwende.
  Nimm du mich, wenn es dir gefällt,
  Herr Jesu, in dein Freudenzelt.

U.L.S. 770.

i Eternity, tremendous word,
  A soul and body piercing sword,
  Beginning without ending !
  Eternity, thou timeless tide
  On which nor grief nor sorrow ride,
  Fain theeward I'd be wending !
  My heart affrighted scarce can breathe,
  My tongue doth to my palate cleave.

xi Though God our King from heaven, His place,
  Looks down upon the human race,
  Still Nature's ills affront us.
  The thunder's roll, the lightning's flash,
  Grim pain and want our bodies lash ;
  Yet shall they not confound us.
  For one day all our troubles cease
  When God's good time shall give release.

xvi Eternity, tremendous word,
  A soul and body piercing sword,
  Beginning without ending !
  Eternity, thou timeless tide
  On which nor grief nor sorrow ride,
  Fain theeward I'd be wending !
  Lord Jesu Christ, O grant it me
  That heaven's pure joys one day I see !

Tr. C. S. T.

O GOTT, DU FROMMER GOTT

Hymn, by Caspar Ziegler, in four 8-line stanzas (1697).   Melody, anonymous (1679), to ' Die Wollust dieser Welt.'

i Ich freue mich in dir
Und heisse dich willkommen,
Mein liebstes Jesulein !
Du hast dir vorgenommen
Mein Brüderlein zu sein :
Ach ! wie ein süsser Ton !
Wie freundlich sieht er aus,
Der grosse Gottes Sohn.

ii Gott senkt die Majestät,
Sein unbegreiflich Wesen,
In eines Menschen Leib ;
Nun muss die Welt genesen.
Der allerhöchste Gott
Spricht freundlich bei uns ein,
Wird gar ein kleines Kind
Und heisst mein Jesulein.

* iv Wohlan, so will ich mich
An diesen Jesum halten,
Und sollte gleich die Welt
In tausend Stücke spalten.
O Jesu ! dir, nur dir,
Dir leb ich ganz allein.
Auf dich, allein auf dich,
O Jesu, schlaf ich ein.

i In Thee do I rejoice
And with a welcome greet Thee,
O dearest Jesu mine !
Thy promise giv'st Thou truly
My Brother e'er to stand.
How dear the name doth sound !
And, O th' unmeasured love
In God's dear Son is found !

ii God sinks His majesty
And high mysterious being
Within a mortal frame,
A virgin pure conceiving.
God friendly deals with us :
How highly blest are we !
Jesus is born on earth
To win us liberty.

iv So, come whate'er betide,
On Jesus will I stay me.
Let earth to atoms break,
Yet shall it not dismay me.
Lord Jesus, 'tis on Thee
Alone my heart is set,
And, resting on Thy love,
Earth's ills can never fret.

U.L.S. 38.

Tr. C. S. T

O GOTT, DU FROMMER GOTT

Hymn, by Georg Michael Pfefferkorn, in eight 8-line stanzas (1671). Melody, anonymous (1679), to 'Die Wollust dieser Welt'.

285

*i Was frag ich nach der Welt,
Und allen ihren Schätzen,
Wenn ich mich nur an dir,
Herr Jesu, kann ergötzen ?
Dich hab ich einzig mir
Zur Wollust vorgestellt :
Du, du bist meine Ruh ;
Was frag ich nach der Welt !

iii Die Welt sucht Ehr und Ruhm
Bei hoch-erhabnen Leuten,
Und denkt nicht einmal drauf,
Wie bald doch diese gleiten.
Das aber was allein
Mein Herz für rühmlich hält,
Ist Jesus nur allein :
Was frag ich nach der Welt !

v Die Welt bekümmert sich,
Im Fall sie wird verachtet,
Als wann man ihr mit List
Nach ihren Ehren trachtet ;
Ich trage Christi Schmach,
So lang es ihm gefällt :
Wann mich mein Heiland ehrt,
Was frag ich nach der Welt !

Joh. Crüger.[1]

i The world I hold for nought,
Its vain and hollow pleasures ;
Jesu, my love for Thee
Contemns such empty treasures.
On Thee, and only Thee,
My every thought is stayed.
While on Thee I repose,
How can I be dismayed ?

iii To vain and empty show
The world doth give preferment.
How partial is its choice !
How doth it lack discernment !
No ! not on things of earth
Are my foundations laid ;
If Jesus calls me His,
How can I be dismayed ?

v How is the world provoked
If men flee its allurement,
Or haste not to pursue
The lure of its enchantment !
Lord Jesus by His Cross
All else pure dross hath made.
And, since He loved me so,
How can I be dismayed ?

Tr. C. S. T.

[1] *Praxis Pietatis Melica* (Ed. 1736), No. 830.

O GOTT, DU FROMMER GOTT

Hymn, by Georg Michael Pfefferkorn, in eight 8-line stanzas (1671).   Melody, anonymous (1679), to 'Die Wollust dieser Welt'.

286

i Was frag ich nach der Welt,
Und allen ihren Schätzen,
Wenn ich mich nur an dir,
Herr Jesu, kann ergötzen?
Dich hab ich einzig mir
Zur Wollust vorgestellt:
Du, du bist meine Ruh;
Was frag ich nach der Welt!

* vii Was frag ich nach der Welt
Im Hui muss sie vergehen,
Ihr Ansehn kann durchaus
Dem Tod nicht wiederstehen,
Die Güter müssen fort,
Und alle Lust verfällt!
Bleibt Jesus nur bei mir:
Was frag ich nach der Welt!

* viii Was frag ich nach der Welt,
Mein Jesus ist mein Leben,
Mein Schatz, mein Eigenthum,
Dem ich mich ganz ergeben,
Mein ganzes Himmelreich
Und was mir sonst gefällt.
Drum sag ich noch einmal:
Was frag ich nach der Welt!

i The world I hold for nought,
Its vain and hollow pleasures;
Jesu, my love for Thee
Contemns such empty treasures.
On Thee, and only Thee,
My every thought is stayed.
While on Thee I repose,
How can I be dismayed?

vii World, what art thou to me?
Thou fadest in a moment,
Nor 'gainst death's stern decree
Canst win an hour's postponement.
Thy glories soon decay,
Their lure in ashes laid.
But Jesu's at my side;
How can I be dismayed?

viii Vain earth's poor vanities!
'Tis Jesu doth enrich me.
My treasured All He is,
With love doth He bewitch me.
For me is heaven displayed;
The price hath Jesus paid.
Therefore I proudly cry:
'How can I be dismayed?'

Joh. Crüger.[1]   *Tr. C. S. T.*

[1] *Praxis Pietatis Melica* (Ed. 1736), No. 830.

O GOTT, DU FROMMER GOTT

Hymn, by Johann Heermann, in eight 8-line stanzas (1630). Melody, anonymous (1679), to 'Die Wollust dieser Welt'.

287

i O Gott, du frommer Gott,
   Du Brunnquell guter Gaben,
   Ohn den nichts ist, was ist,
   Von dem wir alles haben :
   Gesunden Leib gieb mir,
   Und dass in solchem Leib
   Ein unverletzte Seel
   Und rein Gewissen bleib.

* ii Gieb, dass ich thu mit Fleiss,
   Was mir zu thun gebühret,
   Wozu mich dein Befehl
   In meinem Stande führet.
   Gieb, dass ichs thue bald,
   Zu der Zeit, da ich soll ;
   Und wann ichs thu, so gieb,
   Dass es gerathe wohl.

vi Soll ich auf dieser Welt
   Mein Leben höher bringen,
   Durch manchen sauren Tritt
   Hindurch ins Alter dringen :
   So gieb Geduld ; vor Sünd
   Und Schanden mich bewahr,
   Dass ich mit Ehren trag
   All meine graue Haar.

i O ever faithful God,
   From Whom all blessing floweth,
   Without Whom nothing is,
   Who life on man bestoweth ;
   Give to my body health,
   And grant me too within,
   What richer is than wealth,
   A heart cleansed pure of sin.

ii Lord, grant me grace to do
   Whate'er Thou hast ordainèd,
   With ready heart and true,
   And by Thy grace sustainèd.
   Nor let me show delay,
   Or, fainting, fail to press
   Undaunted on, but stay
   My soul till victory bless.

vi And if long days on earth
   Thou should'st in wisdom grant me,
   And after troubles sore
   To old age wouldest bring me,
   Bear with me, Lord, I pray,
   Protect from shame and sin,
   That so my hoary head
   May life eternal win.

U.L.S. 568.

Tr. C. S. T.

O GOTT, DU FROMMER GOTT

Hymn, by Matthäus Avenarius, in six 8-line stanzas (1673). Melody, anonymous (1679), to 'Die Wollust dieser Welt'.

288

[Horns I & II obbligati]

i O Jesu, meine Lust,
   O Leben meiner Seelen,
   Wenn rafst du mich hervor
   Aus dieser Trauer-Höhlen ?
   Wenn werd ich einst befreit
   Dich, liebster Jesu, sehn,
   Und zu dir in dein Reich
   Mit Freuden-Springen gehn ?

ii O du mein Aufenthalt,
   Mein Leben, meine Wonne,
   Mein einziger Gewinn
   Und rechte Freuden-Sonne :
   Mein Herz und ganzer Geist
   Schreit stets, o Gott, zu dir :
   Wenn werd ich schauen dich,
   O Jesu, meine Zier ?

* iv Alsdann so wirst du mich
   Zu deiner Rechten stellen,
   Und mir, als deinem Kind,
   Ein gnädig Urtheil fällen,
   Mich bringen zu der Lust,
   Wo deine Herrlichkeit
   Ich werde schauen an
   In alle Ewigkeit.

Fischer-Tümpel.[1]

i O Jesu, Master mine,
   Thou essence of my being,
   When shall I hear Thy call
   That summons me to heavèn ?
   When shall my longing eyes
   Thy countenance behold,
   And in Thy house above
   These arms my Lord enfold ?

ii Thou art my soul's abode,
   My Hope and Joy surpassing.
   In heaven I'd be with Thee
   In glory everlasting.
   My heart and spirit call
   To Thee, O Lord, on high :
   When shall I see Thy face
   And join Thee in the sky ?

iv For Thou hast promised, Lord,
   On Thy right hand to place me ;
   With all a father's love
   One day Thou wilt embrace me
   In heavèn, where Thou art,
   Enthroned above the sky,
   And in Thy sight I'll stand
   For all eternity.

Tr. C. S. T.

[1] Bd. iv. No. 452.

O GOTT, DU FROMMER GOTT

Hymn, by Johann Heermann, in eight 8-line stanzas (1630).   Melody, anonymous (1693).

289

*i O Gott, du frommer Gott,
  Du Brunnquell guter Gaben,
  Ohn den nichts ist, was ist,
  Von dem wir alles haben :
  Gesunden Leib gieb mir,
  Und dass in solchem Leib
  Ein unverletzte Seel
  Und rein Gewissen bleib.

iii Hilf, dass ich rede stets,
  Womit ich kann bestehen :
  Lass kein unnützes Wort
  Aus meinem Munde gehen ;
  Und wenn in meinem Amt
  Ich reden soll und muss,
  So gieb den Worten Kraft
  Und Nachdruck, ohn Verdruss.

iv Findt sich Gefährlichkeit,
  So lass mich nicht verzagen :
  Gieb einen Heldenmuth :
  Das Kreuz hilf selber tragen.
  Gieb, dass ich meinen Feind
  Mit Sanftmuth überwind,
  Und wenn ich Rath bedarf,
  Auch guten Rath erfind.

i O God, Thou faithful God,
  Thou Fountain ever flowing,
  Without whom nothing is,
  All perfect gifts bestowing ;
  A pure and healthy frame
  O give me, and within
  A conscience free from blame,
  A soul unhurt by sin.

iii And let me promise nought
  But I can keep it truly,
  Abstain from idle words,
  And guard my lips still duly ;
  And grant, when in my place
  I must and ought to speak,
  My words due power and grace,
  Nor let me wound the weak.

iv If dangers gather round,
  Still keep me calm and fearless ;
  Help me to bear the Cross
  When life is dark and cheerless ;
  To overcome my foe
  With words and actions kind ;
  When counsel I would know,
  Good counsel let me find.

U.L.S. 568.

Tr. Catherine Winkworth.[1]

[1] *Chorale Book for England* (Lond. 1865), No. 115.

O GOTT, DU FROMMER GOTT

Hymn, by Johann Heermann, in eight 8-line stanzas (1630).   *Melody, anonymous* (1693).

290

i O Gott, du frommer Gott,
   Du Brunnquell guter Gaben,
   Ohn den nichts ist, was ist,
   Von dem wir alles haben :
   Gesunden Leib gieb mir,
   Und dass in solchem Leib
   Ein unverletzte Seel
   Und rein Gewissen bleib.

vii Lass mich an meinem End
   Auf Christi Tod abscheiden :
   Die Seele nimm zu dir
   Hinauf zu deinen Freuden ;
   Dem Leib ein Räumlein gönn
   Bei seiner Eltern Grab,
   Auf dass er seine Ruh
   An ihrer Seite hab.

viii Wenn du die Todten wirst
   An jenem Tag erwecken,
   So thu auch deine Hand
   Zu meinem Grab ausstrecken.
   Lass hören deine Stimm
   Und meinen Leib weck auf,
   Und führ ihn schön verklärt
   Zum auserwählten Hauf.

i O God, Thou faithful God,
   Thou Fountain ever flowing,
   Without whom nothing is,
   All perfect gifts bestowing ;
   A pure and healthy frame
   O give me, and within
   A conscience free from blame,
   A soul unhurt by sin.

vii Let nothing that may chance
   Me from my Saviour sever ;
   And, dying with Him, take
   My soul to Thee for ever ;
   And let my body have
   A little space to sleep
   Beside my fathers' grave,
   And friends that o'er it weep.

viii And when the Day is come,
   And all the dead are waking,
   O reach me down Thy hand,
   Thyself my slumbers breaking ;
   Then let me hear Thy voice,
   And change this earthly frame,
   And bid me aye rejoice
   With those who love Thy name.

U.L.S. 568.

Tr. Catherine Winkworth.[1]

[1] *Chorale Book for England* (Lond. 1865), No. 115.

O GROSSER GOTT VON MACHT

Hymn, by Balthasar Schnurr, in eight (ninth added 1633) 8-line stanzas (1632).   Melody, by (?) Melchior Franck (1632).

291

i O grosser Gott von Macht
  Und reich von Gütigkeit,
  Willt du das ganze Land
  Strafen mit Grimmigkeit ?
  Vielleicht möchten noch Fromme sein,
  Die thäten nach dem Willen dein ;
  Der wollest du verschonen,
  Nicht nach den Werken lohnen.

iii O grosser Gott von Rath,
  Lass die Barmherzigkeit
  Ergehen, und halt ein
  Mit der Gerechtigkeit.
  Der möchten fünf und vierzig sein,
  Die thäten nach dem Willen dein ;
  Der wollest du verschonen,
  N cht nach den Werken lohnen.

iv O grosser Gott von Stärk,
  Schau an das arme Land
  Und wende von der Straf
  Dein ausgestreckte Hand.
  Der möchten etwa vierzig sein,
  Die thäten nach dem Willen dein ;
  Der wollest du verschonen,
  Nicht nach den Werken lohnen.

*ix O grosser Gott von Treu,
  Weil vor dir Niemand gilt
  Als dein Sohn Jesus Christ,
  Der deinen Zorn gestillt.
  So sieh doch an die Wunden sein,
  Sein Marter, Angst, und schwere Pein :
  Um seinetwillen schone
  Uns nicht nach Sünden lohne.

i O God of power and might,
  And loving mercy too,
  Withdraw Thy vengeful hand,
  Nor with just wrath pursue.
  Perchance there are among us still
  A faithful few to do Thy will.
  For their sake, Lord, O hear us,
  And on Thy mercy bear us !

iii O God of wisdom rare,
  Thy pity condescend,
  Nor on us for our sins
  Swift judgment vengeful send !
  Perchance there are among us still
  A faithful few to do Thy will.
  For their sake, Lord, O hear us,
  And on Thy mercy bear us !

iv O God of strength and power,
  Look down upon our land,
  And let us shelter safe
  Beneath Thy loving hand !
  Perchance there are among us still
  A faithful few to do Thy will.
  For their sake, Lord, O hear us,
  And on Thy mercy bear us !

ix O Lord, Thou God of Truth,
  Before Whom none may stand
  If Jesus Christ Thy Son
  Stay not Thy wrathful hand.
  O, to His wounds have Thou regard,
  His anguish, pain, and body marred :
  For His dear sake, O spare us,
  And on Thy mercy bear us !

Fischer-Tümpel.[1]

Tr. C. S. T.

[1] Bd. iii.   No. 321.

O HERRE GOTT, DEIN GÖTTLICH WORT

Hymn, by (?) *Anark von Wildenfels, in eight 8-line stanzas* (1527). *Melody, anonymous* (1527).

*Bach has a ⌢ here

i O Herre Gott, dein göttlich Wort
  Ist lang verdunkelt blieben,
  Bis durch dein Gnad uns ist gesagt,
  Was Paulus hat geschrieben,
  Und andere Apostel mehr
  Aus dein'm göttlichen Munde ;
  Dess dankn wir dir mit Fleiss, dass wir
  Erlebet han die Stunde,

ii Dass es mit Macht an Tag ist bracht,
   Wie klärlich ist vor Augen.
   Ach Gott, mein Herr ! Erbarm dich der,
   Die dich noch itzt verleugnen
   Und achten sehr auf Menschenlehr,
   Darin sie doch verderben :
   Deins Worts Verstand mach ihn bekannt,
   Dass sie nicht ewig sterben.

viii Herr, ich hoff je, du werdest die
    In keiner Noth verlassen,
    Die dein Wort recht als treue Knecht
    Im Herz und Glauben fassen ;
    Giebst ihn bereit die Seligkeit
    Und lässt sie nicht verderben.
    O Herr, durch dich bitt ich : lass mich
    Fröhlich und willig sterben.

i O Lord our God, Thy holy Word
  By man is long forgotten,
  Till dawns Thy grace to us vouchsafed,
  As in Thy Book is written
  By them to whom Thy Word did come
  Forth from Thy mouth proceeding.
  Our praise we send to Thee w'thout end,
  Thy promise now fulfilling.

ii For, lo, with might doth it prevail,
   Of day proclaims the dawning.
   O God and Lord, may it avail
   To them Thy Word disowning !
   Make error clear, impose Thy fear
   On such as do not know Thee !
   Stablish Thy Word, let it be heard
   And flourish now and alway !

viii O Lord, in faith to Thee we pray,
    Ne'er of Thy help bereave us !
    For we are Thine, marked by Thy sign,
    And hold the faith bequeathed us.
    Grant here on earth we know its worth,
    Though angry foes assail us,
    In certainty Thy face to see
    When death's last trump shall hail us.

U.L.S. 241.

Tr. C. S. T.

O HERRE GOTT, DEIN GÖTTLICH WORT

Hymn, by (?) Anark von Wildenfels, in eight 8-line stanzas (1527).   Melody, anonymous (1527).

293

* Bach has a 𝄐 here

i O Herre Gott, dein göttlich Wort
   Ist lang verdunkelt blieben,
   Bis durch dein Gnad uns ist gesagt,
   Was Paulus hat geschrieben,
   Und andere Apostel mehr
   Aus dein'm göttlichen Munde ;
   Dess dankn wir dir mit Fleiss, dass wir
   Erlebet han die Stunde,

ii Dass es mit Macht an Tag ist bracht,
   Wie klärlich ist vor Augen.
   Ach Gott, mein Herr ! Erbarm dich der,
   Die dich noch itzt verleugnen
   Und achten sehr auf Menschenlehr,
   Darin sie doch verderben :
   Deins Worts Verstand mach ihn bekannt,
   Dass sie nicht ewig sterben.

* viii Herr, ich hoff je, du werdest die
   In keiner Noth verlassen,
   Die dein Wort recht als treue Knecht
   Im Herz und Glauben fassen ;
   Giebst ihn bereit die Seligkeit
   Und lässt sie nicht verderben.
   O Herr, durch dich bitt ich : lass mich
   Fröhlich und willig sterben.

i O Lord our God, Thy holy Word
   By man is long forgotten,
   Till dawns Thy grace to us vouchsafed,
   As in Thy Book is written
   By them to whom Thy word did come
   Forth from Thy mouth proceeding.
   Our praise we send to Thee w'thout end,
   Thy promise now fulfilling.

ii For, lo, with might doth it prevail,
   Of day proclaims the dawning.
   O God and Lord, may it avail
   To them Thy Word disowning !
   Make error clear, impose Thy fear
   On such as do not know Thee !
   Stablish Thy Word, let it be heard
   And flourish now and alway !

viii O Lord, in faith to Thee we pray,
   Ne'er of Thy help bereave us !
   For we are Thine, marked by Thy sign,
   And hold the faith bequeathed us.
   Grant here on earth we know its worth,
   Though angry foes assail us,
   In certainty Thy face to see
   When death's last trump shall hail us.

U.L.S. 241.

Tr. C. S. T.

O HERZENSANGST, O BANGIGKEIT UND ZAGEN

Hymn, by Fr. D. Gerh. Müller, in nine 4-line stanzas (1700).   Melody, by Bach.

294

*Bach has a 𝄐 here

i O Herzensangst, o Bangigkeit und Zagen !
  Was seh ich hier für eine Leiche tragen !
  Wess ist das Grab ? wie ist der Fels zu nennen ?
  Ich soll ihn kennen.

ii Ach, fliesst, ihr Thränen ! fliesst, ach fliesst, o wehe !
   Es ist der Herr, mein Liebster, ich vergehe !
   Mein traut'ster Schatz, der mir zu gut geboren,
   Und mich erkoren.

iii Halt still, ihr Träger ! wartet doch, halt stille,
    Bis ich zu letzen Treu an ihm erfülle,
    Und seinen Leichnam, liebreich mich zuletzen,
    Genug kann netzen.

viii Komm her, mein Herr ! Komm ruh in meinem Herzen,
     So fühl ich weiter keine Noth und Schmerzen,
     Schau, wie ich auch in brünstigem Verlangen
     Dich zu empfangen.

Paul Wagner.[1]

i Ah, woe is me ! What grief is mine past measure !
  Say, where's the grave that houseth my heart's Treasure ?
  Where doth He lie ? O whither have they borne Him ?
  I fain would find Him.

ii Weep, weep, sad eyes, hot tears in anguish falling !
   For 'tis my Lord, my dearest Lord, I'm calling,
   My dearest Joy, Who did for bliss create me
   And hath redeemed me.

iii Sad mourners, stay, nor venture now approach me,
    Till to my Lord my homage is paid meetly,
    And on His bier my heart's full love is pourèd,
    My Lord adorèd.

viii Come, Saviour mine, within my heart now rest Thee !
     So shall my woes not evermore distress me.
     See with what joy and eagerness I press me,
     Lord, to embrace Thee.

Tr. C. S. T.

[1] *Vollständiges Gesangbuch (Leipzig, 1697), ii, p. 813.*

O JESU CHRIST, MEINS LEBENS LICHT

Hymn, by Martin Behm, in fourteen 4-line stanzas (1610). Melody (1594), of 'Rex Christe factor omnium'.

295

i O Jesu Christ, meins Lebens Licht,
  Mein Hort, mein Trost, mein Zuversicht,
  Auf Erden bin ich nur ein Gast,
  Und drückt mich sehr der Sünden Last.

ii Ich hab vor mir ein schwere Reis
  Zu dir ins Himmels Paradeis;
  Da ist mein rechtes Vaterland,
  Darauf du hast dein Blut gewandt.

vii Wenn mein Mund nicht kann reden frei,
  Dein Geist in meinem Herzen schrei.
  Hilf, dass mein Seel den Himmel find,
  Wenn meine Augen werden blind.

xiv Wie werd ich dann so fröhlich sein,
  Werd singen mit den Engelein,
  Und mit der Auserwählten Schaar
  Ewig schauen dein Antlitz klar.

U.L.S. 835.

i Lord Jesus Christ, my life, my light,
  My guide, my hope, my dear delight,
  On earth here am I but a guest,
  With heavy load of sin oppressed.

ii The way is long and full of sighs
  That leads me to God's Paradise.
  Far off my Fatherland I see
  That Jesu's blood hath won for me.

vii Lord, when fast fails my halting breath,
  And sinks my spirit into death,
  O then Thine accents may I hear,
  And let my soul to heavèn soar.

xiv What happiness it then shall be
  Amid Thine angels' minstrelsy
  To take my place and evermore
  In Thy blest Presence to adore.

Tr. C. S. T.

C. P. E. Bach (1786) associates the melody with Johann Heermann's 'O Jesu, du mein Bräutigam', a hymn in twelve 4-line stanzas (1630).

i O Jesu, du mein Bräutigam,
  Der du aus Lieb am Kreuzesstamm
  Für mich den Tod gelitten hast,
  Genommen weg der Sünden Last;

ii Ich komm zu deinem Abendmahl
  Verderbt durch manchen Sündenfall.
  Ich bin krank, unrein, nackt und bloss,
  Blind und arm; ach, mich nicht verstoss!

iii Du bist der Arzt, du bist das Licht,
  Du bist der Herr, dem nichts gebricht;
  Du bist der Brunn der Heiligkeit:
  Du bist das rechte Hochzeitkleid.

iv Drum, o Herr Jesu, bitt ich dich:
  In meiner Schwachheit heile mich;
  Was unrein ist, das mache rein
  Durch deinen hellen Gnadenschein.

U.L.S. 283.

i O Jesu Christ, my heavenly Lord,
  Whose love for me Thy life-blood poured,
  Who gav'st Thy life upon the Cross
  To save my soul from sin and loss;

ii I come before Thine altar here
  Weighed down with sin, oppressed with fear,
  Unclean, unworthy of Thy grace;
  Yet drive me not, Lord, from Thy face.

iii Thou canst make whole the broken one,
  Shine on his darkness, heavenly Sun,
  Pure essence of all holiness,
  Canst clothe my soul in righteousness.

iv And so, O Lord, I pray Thee now,
  With strength my weakness to endow,
  Make cleanly what is still impure,
  And with Thy grace my good ensure.

Tr. C. S. T.

O LAMM GOTTES UNSCHULDIG

Hymn, by Nikolaus Decius, a translation of the 'Agnus Dei', in three 7-line stanzas (1531).   Melody, anonymous (1542).

296

Agnus Dei.

i O Lamm Gottes unschuldig
Am Stamm des Kreuzes g'schlachtet,
Allzeit gefunden duldig,
Wiewohl du wurdst verachtet :
All Sünd hast du getragen,
Sonst müssten wir verzagen !
Erbarm dich unser, o Jesu !

ii O Lamm Gottes unschuldig
Am Stamm des Kreuzes g'schlachtet,
Allzeit gefunden duldig,
Wiewohl du wurdst verachtet :
All Sünd hast du getragen,
Sonst müssten wir verzagen !
Erbarm dich unser, o Jesu !

iii O Lamm Gottes unschuldig
Am Stamm des Kreuzes g'schlachtet,
Allzeit gefunden duldig,
Wiewohl du wurdst verachtet :
All Sünd hast du getragen,
Sonst müssten wir verzagen !
Gieb uns dein Frieden, o Jesu.

i O Lamb of God, pure, spotless,
Who on the Cross didst languish,
Who suffered man's unkindness,
And knew the bitt'rest anguish ;
Our sin Thou bearest for us,
Else hell had triumphed o'er us :
Have mercy on us, O Jesu !

ii O Lamb of God, pure, spotless,
Who on the Cross didst languish,
Who suffered man's unkindness,
And knew the bitt'rest anguish ;
Our sin Thou bearest for us,
Else hell had triumphed o'er us :
Have mercy on us, O Jesu !

iii O Lamb of God, pure, spotless,
Who on the Cross didst languish,
Who suffered man's unkindness,
And knew the bitt'rest anguish ;
Our sin Thou bearest for us,
Else hell had triumphed o'er us :
Thy peace give to us, O Jesu.

U.L.S. 110.

Tr. C. S. T.

O MENSCH, BEWEIN DEIN SÜNDE GROSS

Hymn, by Sebald Heyd, in twenty-three 12-line stanzas (1525). Melody, by (?) Matthäus Greitter (1525), to ' Es sind doch selig alle ' (Ps. cxix).

297

i O Mensch, bewein dein Sünde gross,
  Darum Christus seins Vaters Schoos
  Aussert und kam auf Erden.
  Von einer Jungfrau zart und rein
  Für uns er hier geboren ward,
  Er wollt der Mittler werden.
  Den Todten er das Leben gab,
  Und legt dabei all Krankheit ab,
  Bis sich die Zeit herdrange,
  Dass er für uns geopfert würd,
  Trug unsrer Sünden schwere Bürd
  Wohl an dem Kreuze lange.

i O man, bewail thy grievous fall,
  For which Christ left His Father's hall
  And came to earth from heavèn.
  He of a virgin maiden pure
  Was born, of man the Saviour sure,
  And came earth's ills to leaven.
  The dead He raised again to life,
  The sick He loosed from pain and strife,
  Until the time appointed
  That He for us should shed His blood
  And take on Him our sins' dark load,
  Stretched on the Cross accursèd.

xxiii So lasst uns ihm nun dankbar sein
  Dass er für uns leid solche Pein,
  Nach seinem Willen leben.
  Auch lasst uns sein der Sünden Feind
  Weil uns Gotts Wort so helle scheint,
  Tag und Nacht darnach streben,
  Die Lieb erzeigen jedermann
  Wie Christus hat an uns gethan
  Mit seim Leiden und Sterben.
  O Menschenkind, betracht das recht,
  Wie Gottes Zorn die Sünde schlägt,
  Thu dich dafür bewahren.[1]

xxiii Then let us all, with one accord,
  Unite to praise our loving Lord
  Who took our blame upon Him,
  Cast off from us the bonds of sin,
  And strive His countenance to win,
  His Word and will fulfilling.
  And let our hearts toward Him burn
  With love, attempting due return
  For all He hath endurèd.
  O mortals all, the right ensue,
  Or surely shall God's wrath pursue
  All those who've Him rejected!

Tr. C. S. T.

[1] *Vollständiges Gesang Büchlein* (Durlach, 1667), p. 44.

O MENSCH, SCHAU JESUM CHRISTUM AN

Hymn, by Daniel Specht, in five 6-line stanzas (1663).   Melody, annoymous (1555) to ' Der Herr Gott sei gepreiset'.

298

i O Mensch, schau Jesum Christum an,
Den wahren Mensch und Gott,
Der für uns hat genug gethan
Durch seinen bittern Tod :
Was vor Marter, Angst und Schmerz
Durchdrang sein treues Herz !

ii Am Kreuze stund er ausgestrackt,
Trug eine Dornenkron,
Hieng wund und blutig, blass und nackt,
Voll Schmerzen, Spott und Hohn :
Aus sein'r offnen Seit' entsprang
Der wahre Seelen-Trank.

iii Er sprach : Es ist vollendet nun,
Was Gott versöhnen kann.
Der Sünder, welche Busse thun,
Nehm ich mich treulich an :
Gieb, Vat'r, deinen Willen drein,
Lass mein Volk Erbe sein.

iv Den Trost kriegt ich aus Jesu Mund
In meines Herzens-Schrein
In seiner letzten Todes-Stund
Und schloss ihn bei mir ein :
Lass geschehn, Herr Jesu Christ,
Der du mein Heiland bist.

i Behold thy Saviour Christ, O man,
True Man and very God,
Who for us crossed death's farthest span
And bore our sins' dark load !
Keen, alas, the aching smart
Distressed His breaking heart !

ii Upon the Cross He hung for us
And wore the crown of thorn,
Was wounded sore and died for us,
His side with spear-thrusts torn.
From His wounds a fountain flowed
That life on us bestowed.

iii He spake : ' O God, 'tis finished all,
The sacrifice is paid :
All sinners unto life I call
Who have repentance made.
Father, grant me lovingly,
That they salvation see ! '

iv To Jesu's words I steadfast hold,
And clasp them to me close,
When death stood ready to enfold
Him there in life's last throes.
Jesu, satisfy my heart
That Thou my Saviour art !

Fischer-Tümpel.[1]

Tr. C. S. T.

[1] Bd. v. No. 473.

O TRAURIGKEIT

Hymn, by Johann Rist, in eight 5-line stanzas (1641)   Melody, anonymous (1628).

299

i O Traurigkeit !
   O Herzeleid !
   Ist das nicht zu beklagen ?
   Gott des Vaters einig Kind
   Wird ins Grab getragen.

ii O grosse Noth !
    Gott selbst liegt todt,
    Am Kreuz ist er gestorben,
    Hat dadurch das Himmelreich
    Uns aus Lieb erworben.

iv Dein Bräutigam,
    Das Gotteslamm,
    Liegt hier mit Blut beflossen,
    Welches er ganz mildiglich
    Hat für dich vergossen.

viii O Jesu du,
      Mein Hilf und Ruh !
      Ich bitte dich mit Thränen :
      Hilf, dass ich mich bis ins Grab
      Nach dir möge sehnen.

U.L.S. 112.

i O grief of heart !
   O bitter smart !
   How can my tongue declare it ?
   God's own Son, our Saviour dear,
   In the tomb lies buried.

ii O dreadful need !
    Our Lord lies dead !
    The Cross accursèd bears Him,
    That from hell He might us win,
    Heavenward with Him soaring.

iv O God's dear Lamb,
    Who bore our blame,
    Thou liest wounded sorely.
    See the precious blood that flowed
    That we might redeemed be !

viii O Jesu blest,
      My Help, my Rest !
      With tears do I entreat Thee,
      That when from the tomb I rise
      These eyes may behold Thee.

Tr. C. S. T.

O WELT, ICH MUSS DICH LASSEN

Hymn, by Paul Gerhardt, in sixteen 6-line stanzas (1647).   Melody (1539), to ' O Welt, ich muss dich lassen', of secular origin.

300

i O Welt, sieh hier dein Leben
  Am Stamm des Kreuzes schweben,
  Dein Heil sinkt in den Tod !
  Der grosse Fürst der Ehren
  Lässt willig sich beschweren
  Mit Schlägen, Hohn und grossem Spott.

* iii Wer hat dich so geschlagen,
  Mein Heil ! und dich mit Plagen
  So übel zugericht ?
  Du bist ja nicht ein Sünder,
  Wie wir und unsre Kinder,
  Von Uebelthaten weisst du nicht.

iv Ich, ich und meine Sünden,
  Die sich wie Körnlein finden
  Des Sandes an dem Meer,
  Die haben dir erreget
  Das Elend, das dich schläget,
  Und das betrübte Marterheer.

i O man, list to His sighing
  Who for thy sake hangs dying,
  Thy Saviour on the Tree :
  The Lord of earth and heavèn,
  His soul with anguish riven,
  A sacrificial Lamb for thee.

iii Who hath, Lord, dared to smite Thee,
  Who falsely doth indict Thee,
  Misjudge and wound Thee so ?
  Of sin Thy soul is guiltless,
  As we and ours are witness
  To sin's long roll of ill and woe.

iv 'Tis I and my misdoing,
  As ocean's billows flowing,
  Unnumbered as the sand,
  'Tis I that have Thee wounded,
  To judgement, death, have hounded,
  And 'gainst Thee guiltless raised my hand.

U.L.S. 113.

Tr. C. S. T.

O WELT, ICH MUSS DICH LASSEN

Hymn, by Paul Gerhardt, in sixteen 6-line stanzas (1647).   Melody (1539), to ' O Welt, ich muss dich lassen ', of secular origin.

301

i O Welt, sieh hier dein Leben
   Am Stamm des Kreuzes schweben,
   Dein Heil sinkt in den Tod !
   Der grosse Fürst der Ehren
   Lässt willig sich beschweren
   Mit Schlägen, Hohn und grossem Spott.

ii Tritt her, und schau mit Fleisse,
   Sein Leib ist ganz mit Schweisse
   Des Blutes überfüllt.
   Aus seinem edlen Herzen,
   Vor unerschöpften Schmerzen,
   Ein Seufzer nach dem andern quillt.

* v Ich bin's, ich sollte büssen
   An Händen und an Füssen
   Gebunden in der Höll.
   Die Geisseln und die Banden,
   Und was du ausgestanden,
   Das hat verdienet meine Seel.

i O man, list to His sighing
   Who for thy sake hangs dying,
   Thy Saviour on the Tree :
   The Lord of earth and heavèn,
   His soul with anguish riven,
   A sacrificial Lamb for thee.

ii Draw near and mark with pity
   His scarred and bleeding body,
   The pallid hues of death !
   And hear how sore He sigheth,
   How painfully expireth
   His feeble, halting, anguished breath !

v 'Tis I should show contrition,
   Deserving of perdition,
   Condemned to deepest hell !
   The tortures that await Thee,
   The thongs that tear and bind Thee,
   Myself should scar, I know right well !

U.L.S. 113.

Tr. C. S. T.

O WELT, ICH MUSS DICH LASSEN

Hymn, by Paul Gerhardt, in sixteen 6-line stanzas (1647). Melody (1539), to 'O Welt, ich muss dich lassen', of secular origin.

302

i O Welt, sieh hier dein Leben
   Am Stamm des Kreuzes schweben,
   Dein Heil sinkt in den Tod !
   Der grosse Fürst der Ehren
   Lässt willig sich beschweren
   Mit Schlägen, Hohn und grossem Spott.

*iii Wer hat dich so geschlagen,
   Mein Heil ! und dich mit Plagen
   So übel zugericht ?
   Du bist ja nicht ein Sünder,
   Wie wir und unsre Kinder,
   Von Uebelthaten weisst du nicht.

*iv Ich, ich und meine Sünden,
   Die sich wie Körnlein finden
   Des Sandes an dem Meer,
   Die haben dir erreget
   Das Elend, das dich schläget,
   Und das betrübte Marterheer.

U.L.S. 113.

i O man, list to His sighing
   Who for thy sake hangs dying,
   Thy Saviour on the Tree :
   The Lord of earth and heavèn,
   His soul with anguish riven,
   A sacrificial Lamb for thee.

iii Who hath, Lord, dared to smite Thee,
   Who falsely doth indict Thee,
   Misjudge and wound Thee so ?
   Of sin Thy soul is guiltless,
   As we and ours are witness
   To sin's long roll of ill and woe.

iv 'Tis I and my misdoing,
   As ocean's billows flowing,
   Unnumbered as the sand,
   'Tis I that have Thee wounded,
   To judgement, death, have hounded,
   And 'gainst Thee guiltless raised my hand.

Tr. C. S. T.

O WELT, ICH MUSS DICH LASSEN

Hymn, by Paul Gerhardt, in sixteen 6-line stanzas (1647). Melody (1539), to 'O Welt, ich muss dich lassen', of secular origin.

303

i O Welt, sieh hier dein Leben
  Am Stamm des Kreuzes schweben,
  Dein Heil sinkt in den Tod !
  Der grosse Fürst der Ehren
  Lässt willig sich beschweren
  Mit Schlägen, Hohn und grossem Spott

vi Du nimmst auf deinen Rücken
   Die Lasten, die mich drücken
   Viel sehrer als ein Stein.
   Du wirst ein Fluch, dagegen
   Verehrst du mir den Segen,
   Dein Schmerzen muss mein Labsal sein.

viii Du springst ins Todes Rachen,
    Mich frei und los zu machen
    Von solchem Ungeheur.
    Mein Sterben nimmst du abe,
    Vergräbst es in dem Grabe:
    O unerhörtes Liebesfeur !

i O man, list to His sighing
  Who for thy sake hangs dying,
  Thy Saviour on the Tree :
  The Lord of earth and heavèn,
  His soul with anguish riven,
  A sacrificial Lamb for thee.

vi For me the weight Thou bearest,
   With love the best and rarest,
   Of my so sore misdeed.
   The curse that I've deservèd
   Upon Thee, Lord, is turnèd :
   My blessing is Thy grievous need !

viii To death art Thou deliverèd
    That we may all be severed
    From death and misery.
    No more hath hell power o'er me,
    For death has bowed before Thee,
    Who lovest me so wondrously.

U.L.S. 113.   *Tr. C. S. T.*

O WELT, ICH MUSS DICH LASSEN

Hymn, by Paul Gerhardt, in sixteen 6-line stanzas (1647). Melody (1539), to ' O Welt, ich muss dich lassen', of secular origin.

304

i O Welt, sieh hier dein Leben
  Am Stamm des Kreuzes schweben,
  Dein Heil sinkt in den Tod !
  Der grosse Fürst der Ehren
  Lässt willig sich beschweren
  Mit Schlägen, Hohn und grossem Spott.

ii Tritt her, und schau mit Fleisse,
  Sein Leib ist ganz mit Schweisse
  Des Blutes überfüllt.
  Aus seinem edlen Herzen,
  Vor unerschöpften Schmerzen,
  Ein Seufzer nach dem andern quillt.

v Ich bin's, ich sollte büssen
  An Händen und an Füssen
  Gebunden in der Höll.
  Die Geisseln und die Banden,
  Und was du ausgestanden,
  Das hat verdienet meine Seel.

i O man, list to His sighing
  Who for thy sake hangs dying,
  Thy Saviour on the Tree :
  The Lord of earth and heavèn,
  His soul with anguish riven,
  A sacrificial Lamb for thee.

ii Draw near and mark with pity
  His scarred and bleeding body,
  The pallid hues of death !
  And hear how sore He sigheth,
  How painfully expireth
  His feeble, halting, anguished breath.

v 'Tis I should show contrition,
  Deserving of perdition,
  Condemned to deepest hell !
  The tortures that await Thee,
  The thongs that tear and bind Thee,
  Myself should scar, I know right well !

U.L.S. 113.

Tr. C. S. T.

O WELT, ICH MUSS DICH LASSEN

Hymn, by Paul Gerhardt, in sixteen 6-line stanzas (1647).   Melody (1539), to ' O Welt, ich muss dich lassen', of secular origin.

305

i O Welt, sieh hier dein Leben
  Am Stamm des Kreuzes schweben,
  Dein Heil sinkt in den Tod !
  Der grosse Fürst der Ehren
  Lässt willig sich beschweren
  Mit Schlägen, Hohn und grossem Spott.

ix Ich bin, mein Heil, verbunden
  All Augenblick und Stunden
  Dir überhoch und sehr.
  Was Leib und Seel vermögen,
  Das soll ich billig legen
  Allzeit an deinen Dienst und Ehr

x Nun, ich kann nicht viel geben
  In diesem armen Leben,
  Eins aber will ich thun :
  Es soll dein Tod und Leiden,
  Bis Leib und Seele scheiden,
  Mir stets in meinem Herzen ruhn.

               U.L.S. 113.

i O man, list to His sighing
  Who for thy sake hangs dying,
  Thy Saviour on the Tree :
  The Lord of earth and heavèn,
  His soul with anguish riven,
  A sacrificial Lamb for Thee.

ix From henceforth and for ever
  I'm bound to Thee, my Saviour,
  In thought, and deed, and word !
  The soul within me liveth
  My Saviour ever singeth,
  To sound His praise and glory stirred.

x Lord, 'tis a feeble offer
  To Thee my soul doth proffer,
  So little has't to give.
  Yet will I e'er remember
  The love of my Redeemer,
  Nor falter ever while I live.

               Tr. C. S. T.

O WELT, ICH MUSS DICH LASSEN

*Hymn, by Paul **Flemming**, in fifteen 6-line stanzas (1642).   Melody (1539), to ' O Welt, ich muss dich lassen', of secular origin.*

306

i In allen meinen Thaten
   Lass ich den Höchsten rathen,
   Der alles kann und hat :
   Er muss zu allen Dingen,
   Solls anders wohl gelingen,
   Selbst geben Segen, Rath und That.

iv Ich traue seiner Gnaden,
   Die mich für allem Schaden,
   Für allem Uebel schützt.
   Leb ich nach seinen Sätzen :
   So wird mich nichts verletzen,
   Und nichts mir fehlen, was mir nützt.

* xv So sei nun, Seele, deine,
   Und traue dem alleine,
   Der dich geschaffen hat.
   Es gehe, wie es gehe :
   Dein Vater aus der Höhe
   Der weiss zu allen Sachen Rath.

U.L.S. 646.

i Whate'er the task He sendeth,
   To God my soul submitteth,
   Who all things well did plan.
   His love all mortals guideth,
   Success 'tis He provideth,
   And blessing showers on every man.

iv Upon His grace relying,
   The powers of hell defying,
   I vanquish every foe.
   If God's Word e'er I follow,
   Come weal, or care, or sorrow,
   Then all's for best, right well I know.

xv Let nought, my soul, affright thee,
   Thy trust in God still plight thee,
   Who hath thy being given !
   Whatever ills dismay thee,
   Thy Father's love will stay thee,
   His counsel guide to highest heaven.

Tr. C. S. T.

O WELT, ICH MUSS DICH LASSEN

Hymn, by Paul Flemming, in fifteen 6-line stanzas (1642).   Melody (1539), to 'O Welt, ich muss dich lassen', of secular origin.

307

i In allen meinen Thaten
   Lass ich den Höchsten rathen,
   Der alles kann und hat :
   Er muss zu allen Dingen,
   Solls anders wohl gelingen,
   Selbst geben Segen, Rath und That.

x Leg ich mich späte nieder,
   Erwach ich frühe wieder,
   Lieg oder zieh ich fort :
   In Schwachheit und in Banden,
   Und was mir stösst zu Handen,
   So tröstet mich sein kräftig Wort.

* xv So sei nun, Seele, deine,
   Und traue dem alleine,
   Der dich geschaffen hat.
   Es gehe, wie es gehe :
   Dein Vater aus der Höhe
   Der weiss zu allen Sachen Rath.

U.L.S 646.

i Whate'er the task He sendeth,
   To God my soul submitteth,
   Who all things well did plan.
   His love all mortals guideth,
   Success 'tis He provideth,
   And blessing showers on every man.

x Whene'er to rest I take me,
   When morning's sun awakes me,
   Where'er I muse or go,
   In trouble or elation,
   Desponding or vexation,
   God's Word gives comfort, well I know.

xv Let nought, my soul, affright thee,
   Thy trust in God still plight thee,
   Who hath thy being given !
   Whatever ills dismay thee,
   Thy Father's love will stay thee,
   His counsel guide to highest heaven.

Tr. C. S. T.

O WELT, ICH MUSS DICH LASSEN

Hymn, by Paul Flemming, in fifteen 6-line stanzas (1642).   Melody (1539), to ' O Welt, ich muss dich lassen', of secular origin.

308

[Strings obbligati]

i In allen meinen Thaten
  Lass ich den Höchsten rathen,
  Der alles kann und hat :
  Er muss zu allen Dingen,
  Solls anders wohl gelingen,
  Selbst geben Rath und That.

xii Ihm hab ich mich ergeben,
  Zu sterben und zu leben,
  Sobald er mir gebeut.
  Es sei heut oder morgen :
  Dafür lass ich ihn sorgen ;
  Er weiss die rechte Zeit.

* xv So sei nun, Seele, deine,
  Und traue dem alleine,
  Der dich geschaffen hat.
  Es gehe, wie es gehe :
  Dein Vater aus der Höhe
  Weiss allen Sachen Rath.

i Whate'er the task He sendeth,
  To God my soul submitteth,
  Who all things well did plan.
  His love all mortals guideth,
  Success 'tis He provideth,
  When faileth wit of man.

xii I give myself unto Him,
  In dying and in living,
  I know Him and I trust.
  So if to-day death cometh
  And loud a summons soundeth,
  God wills and knoweth best.

xv Let nought, my soul affright thee,
  Thy trust in God still plight thee,
  Who hath thy being given !
  Whatever ills dismay thee,
  Thy Father's love will stay thee,
  His counsel guide to heaven.

U.L.S. 646.

Tr. C. S. T.

O WELT, ICH MUSS DICH LASSEN

Hymn, by Paul Gerhardt, in nine 6-line stanzas (1647).   Melody (1539), to ' O Welt, ich muss dich lassen', of secular origin.

309

i Nun ruhen alle Wälder,
  Vieh, Menschen, Städt und Felder,
  Es schläft die ganze Welt :
  Ihr aber, meine Sinnen,
  Auf, auf ! ihr sollt beginnen,
  Was eurem Schöpfer wohlgefällt.

vii Mein Augen stehn verdrossen,
    Im Hui sind sie geschlossen :
    Wo bleibt dann Leib und Seel ?
    Nimm sie zu deinen Gnaden,
    Sei gut für allen Schaden,
    Du Aug und Wächter Israel !

viii Breit aus die Flügel beide,
     O Jesu, meine Freude,
     Und nimm dein Küchlein ein :
     Will Satan mich verschlingen,
     So lass die Englein singen :
     Dies Kind soll unverletzet sein !

ix Auch euch, ihr meine Lieben,
   Soll heute nicht betrüben
   Kein Unfall noch Gefahr.
   Gott lass euch ruhig schlafen,
   Stell euch die güldnen Waffen
   Ums Bett und seiner Engel Schaar !

i Now all the woods are sleeping,
  And night and stillness creeping
  O'er city, man, and beast ;
  But thou, my heart, awake thee,
  To prayer awhile betake thee,
  And praise Thy Maker e'er thou rest.

vii My heavy eyes are closing ;
    When I lie deep reposing,
    Soul, body, where are ye ?
    To helpless sleep I yield them,
    O let Thy mercy shield them ;
    Thou sleepless Eye, their guardian be !

viii My Jesus, stay Thou by me,
     And let no foe come nigh me,
     Safe sheltered by Thy wing ;
     But would the foe alarm me,
     O let him never harm me,
     But still Thine angels round me sing !

ix My loved ones, rest securely,
   From every peril surely
   Our God will guard your heads ;
   And happy slumbers send you,
   And bid His hosts attend you,
   And golden-armed watch o'er your beds.

U.L.S. 529.

Tr. Catherine Winkworth.[1]

[1] *Chorale Book for England* (Lond. 1865), No. 169.

329

O WIE SELIG SEID IHR DOCH, IHR FROMMEN

Hymn, by Simon Dach, in six 4-line stanzas (1635). Melody, by Johann Crüger (1649).

310

i O wie selig seid ihr doch, ihr Frommen,
  Die ihr durch den Tod zu Gott gekommen :
  Ihr seid entgangen
  Aller Noth, die uns noch hält gefangen.

ii Muss man hier doch wie im Kerker leben,
   Da nur Sorge, Furcht und Schrecken schweben :
   Was wir hie kennen,
   Ist nur Müh und Herzeleid zu nennen.

iv Christus wischet ab euch alle Thränen ;
   Habt das schon, wonach wir uns erst sehnen ;
   Euch wird gesungen,
   Was durch keines Ohr allhie gedrungen.

U.L.S. 840.

i Blest of men are they beyond all telling
  Whom the Lord hath called to share His dwelling,
  Through death arisen
  From earth's noisome, dark, corrupting prison.

ii Here below, as in a dungeon bounded,
   We by sin and darkness are surrounded ;
   Our sight sees dimly,
   Fear upon our anxious souls sits grimly.

iv Christ will wipe away all tears and sorrow ;
   Pain is ours to-day, but joy to-morrow
   Where, lo! entrancing,
   Songs of praise th' elect are ever chanting.

Tr. C. S. T.

O WIE SELIG SEID IHR DOCH , IHR FROMMEN

Hymn, by Simon Dach, in six 4-line stanzas (1635). Melody, anonymous (1566), to ' Ach, wie gross ist Gottes Güt und Wohlthat'

311

i O wie selig seid ihr doch, ihr Frommen,
  Die ihr durch den Tod zu Gott gekommen :
  Ihr seid entgangen
  Aller Noth, die uns noch hält gefangen.

v Ach, wer wollte denn nicht gerne sterben
  Und den Himmel für die Welt ererben ?
  Wer wollt hie bleiben,
  Sich den Jammer länger lassen treiben ?

vi Komm, o Christe, komm, uns auszuspannen ;
   Lös uns auf und führ uns bald von dannen !
   Bei dir, o Sonne,
   Ist der frommen Seelen Freud und Wonne.

                    U.L.S. 840.

i Blest of men are they beyond all telling
  Whom the Lord hath called to share His dwelling,
  Through death arisen
  From earth's noisome, dark, corrupting prison.

v Let us then to heaven our thoughts be raising,
  Little worth our earthly lot appraising.
  Here's vain abiding ;
  Heaven we seek, all other things deriding

vi Come, Lord Christ, and from earth's snares release us ;
   Quickly haste to succour us, Lord Jesus,
   And Thou, O Spirit,
   Through Whose grace alone can we find merit !

                    Tr. C. S. T.

O WIR ARMEN SÜNDER

Hymn, by Hermann Bonn, in six irregular stanzas (1542).   Melody, anonymous (1527), to 'Ach wir armen Menschen'.

i O wir ar - men Sün - der!   uns - re Mis - se - that
iii So nicht wä - re kom - men   Chris - tus in die Welt,
vi Da - rum wolln wir lo - ben,   dan - ken al - le - zeit

i Hap - less sin - ners are we !   our of - fence is great !
iii Had not Christ come to us,   born in - to this world,
vi Where - for let us praise Him   with th'e - ter - nal host,

Da - rin wir em - pfan - gen   und ge - bo - ren sind,
Und an sich ge - nom - men   un - ser arm Ge - stalt,
Dem Va - ter und Soh - ne   und dem Heil - gen Geist !

Born in sin we all   were and in e - vil state.
Sure - ly had we one day   in - to hell been hurled !
Bless - ed Son and Fa - ther   and the Ho - ly Ghost !

Hat ge - bracht uns al - le   in sol - che gro - sse Noth.
Und für un - ser Sün - de   ge - stor - ben wil - lig - lich :
Bit - ten, dass sie wol - len   be - hü - ten uns vor Arg,

Sore have we in - vi - ted   our God's a - ven - ging ire,
But He came to save us,   and coun - ted not the loss,
Pray - ing our pe - ti - tion may   at Their throne be heard,

*Bach has a 𝄐 here.

312

O WIR ARMEN SÜNDER

Dass wir un-ter-wor - - fen sind dem ew-gen Tod.
Hät - ten wir musst wer - - den ver-dammt e - wig-lich,
Und dass wir stets blei - - ben bei seim heil-gen Wort.

And His con-dem-na - - tion, e - ver-last-ing fire.
Shame and death en-dur - - èd, yea, the ve - ry Cross.
To keep us from e - - vil 'neath God's ho - ly Word.

Ky - rie e - - - lei - - son! Chri - - - ste

O Lord, hear us now! O Christ

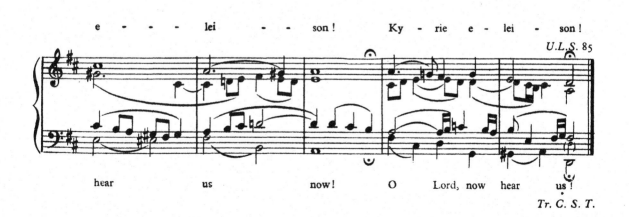

e - - - lei - - son! Ky - rie e - lei - son!

U.L.S. 85

hear us now! O Lord, now hear us!

Tr. C. S. T.

333

PUER NATUS IN BETHLEHEM

Hymn (Latin), 14th cent.; (German) in ten 3-line stanzas (1543). Melody (1553).

313

i Puer natus in Bethlehem,
  Alleluja!
Unde gaudet Jerusalem.
  Alleluja! Alleluja!

iii Cognovit bos et asinus,
  Alleluja!
Quod puer erat dominus.
  Alleluja! Alleluja!

iv Reges de Saba veniunt,
  Alleluja!
Aurum, thus, myrrham offerunt.
  Alleluja! Alleluja!

v De matre natus virgine,
  Alleluja!
Sine virili semine.
  Alleluja! Alleluja!

vii In carne nobis similis,
  Alleluja!
Peccato sed dissimilis.
  Alleluja! Alleluja!

viii Ut redderet nos homines,
  Alleluja!
Deo et sibi similes.
  Alleluja! Alleluja!

ix In hoc natali gaudio,
  Alleluja!
Benedicamus Domino.
  Alleluja! Alleluja!

x Laudetur sancta trinitas,
  Alleluja!
Deo dicamus gratias.
  Alleluja! Alleluja!

Tucher.[1]

i A Child is born in Bethlehem,
  Alleluja!
Exult for joy, Jerusalem!
  Alleluja! Alleluja!

iii The ox and ass in neighb'ring
    stall,
  Alleluja!
See in that Child the Lord of all.
  Alleluja! Alleluja!

iv And kingly pilgrims, long fore-
    told,
  Alleluja!
From east bring incense, myrrh
    and gold.
  Alleluja! Alleluja!

v He comes, a mortal maiden's son,
  Alleluja!
Yet earthly father hath He none.
  Alleluja! Alleluja!

vii Our feeble flesh and His the same,
  Alleluja!
Our sinless kinsman He became,
  Alleluja! Alleluja!

viii That we, from deadly thrall set free,
  Alleluja!
Like Him, and so like God, should
    be.
  Alleluja! Alleluja!

ix Come then, and on this natal day,
  Alleluja!
Rejoice before the Lord and pray.
  Alleluja! Alleluja!

x And to the Holy One in Three,
  Alleluja!
Give thanks and praise eternally.
  Alleluja! Alleluja!

Tr. H. M. MacGill.[2]

i Ein Kind geborn zu Bethlehem,
  Alleluja!
Des freuet sich Jerusalem.
  Alleluja! Alleluja!

iii Das Öchslein und das Eselein
  Alleluja!
Erkannten Gott den Herren fein.
  Alleluja! Alleluja!

*iv Die Kön'g aus Saba kamen dar,
  Alleluja!
Gold, Weihrauch, Myrrhen
    brachtn sie dar.
  Alleluja! Alleluja!

v Sein Mutter ist die reine Magd,
  Alleluja!
Die ohn ein Mann geboren hat.
  Alleluja! Alleluja!

* vii Es ist gar uns gleich nach dem
    Fleisch,
  Alleluja!
Der Sünden nach ist's uns nicht
    gleich.
  Alleluja! Alleluja!

viii Damit er ihm uns machet gleich,
  Alleluja!
Und wieder brächt zu Gottes
    Reich.
  Alleluja! Alleluja!

ix Für solche gnadenreiche Zeit,
  Alleluja!
Sei Gott gelobt in Ewigkeit.
  Alleluja! Alleluja!

x Gelobt sei die Dreieinigkeit
  Alleluja!
Und Gott der Herr in Ewigkeit.
  Alleluja! Alleluja!

Tucher.[3]

[1] Bd. i. No. 22.   [2] *Songs of the Christian Creed* (Lond. 1876), No. 35.   [3] Bd. i. No. 23.

SCHMÜCKE DICH, O LIEBE SEELE

Hymn, by Johann Franck, in nine 8-line stanzas (1649 & 1653).   Melody, by Johann Crüger (1649).

314

i Schmücke dich, o liebe Seele,
 Lass die dunkle Sündenhöhle ;
 Komm ans helle Licht gegangen,
 Fange herrlich an zu prangen.
 Denn der Herr voll Heil und Gnaden
 Will dich jetzt zu Gaste laden ;
 Der den Himmel kann verwalten,
 Will jetzt Herberg in dir halten.

ii Eile, wie Verlobte pflegen,
 Deinem Bräutigam entgegen,
 Der da mit dem Gnadenhammer
 Klopft an deine Herzenskammer.
 Oeffn ihm bald die Geistespforten ;
 Red ihn an mit schönen Worten :
 Komm, mein Liebster, lass dich küssen ;
 Lass mich deiner nicht mehr missen.

iv Ach wie hungert mein Gemüthe,
 Meschenfreund, nach deiner Güte ;
 Ach wie pfleg ich oft mit Thränen
 Mich nach dieser Kost zu sehnen ;
 Ach wie pfleget mich zu dürsten
 Nach dem Trank des Lebensfürsten ;
 Wünsche stets dass mein Gebeine
 Sich durch Gott mit Gott vereine.

* ix Jesu, wahres Brod des Lebens,
 Hilf, dass ich doch nicht vergebens
 Oder mir vielleicht zum Schaden
 Sei zu deinem Tisch geladen.
 Lass mich durch dies Seelenessen
 Deine Liebe recht ermessen,
 Dass ich auch, wie jetzt auf Erden,
 Mög dein Gast im Himmel werden.

i O, my soul, prepare to meet Him,
 Purified, transformed, receive Him !
 See, His presence shines upon Thee !
 Lift Thy heart ! in praise essay thee !
 For the Lord, with love unbounded,
 Bids thee share the feast He founded ;
 He in highest heaven Who reigneth
 Thee to taste His banquet deigneth.

ii Lo ! He knocketh at thy portal.
 See, He offers life immortal !
 Comely as Thy Bridegroom greet Him,
 Lowly hear His voice and meet Him.
 Open wide the hind'ring gateway,
 Reverent murmur to Him straightway
 ' I am Thine, dear Lord ; receive me,
 Take my heart, nor ever leave me !'

iv Lord, I hunger for Thy spirit,
 Thou Who died'st for man's demerit.
 Ah, how oft with eager yearning
 Have I to Thy feast been turning,
 Sorely striving, spent and worsted,
 For the Cup of Life have thirsted !
 Grant me now the precious favour,
 To be one with God my Saviour !

ix Bread of Life, all grace conveying,
 See me now Thy will obeying ;
 Of Thy Table, here before me,
 May I not be deemed unworthy.
 Let me in Thy banquet measure
 All the greatness of my treasure.
 As on earth Thy guest Thou mak'st me,
 So in heaven one day instate me !

U.L.S. 287.   *Tr. C. S. T.*

SCHWING DICH AUF ZU DEINEM GOTT

Hymn, by Paul Gerhardt, in eleven 8-line stanzas (1653).   Melody, a reconstruction (? by Bach) of 'Meine Hoffnung stehet feste' (1680).

315

i Schwing dich auf zu deinem Gott,
 Du betrübte Seele !
Warum liegst du Gott zum Spott
 In der Schwermuthshöhle ?
Merkst du nicht des Satans List ?
 Er will durch sein Kämpfen
Deinen Trost, den Jesus Christ
 Dir erworben, dämpfen.

* ii Schüttle deinen Kopf und sprich :
 Fleuch, du alte Schlange ;
Was erneurst du deinen Stich,
 Machst mir angst und bange ?
Ist dir doch der Kopf zerknickt,
 Und ich bin durchs Leiden
Meines Heilands dir entrückt
 In den Saal der Freuden.

vi Stürme, Teufel, und du Tod !
 Was könnt ihr mir schaden ?
Deckt mich doch in meiner Noth
 Gott mit seiner Gnaden :
Der Gott, der mir seinen Sohn
 Selbst verehrt aus Liebe,
Dass der ewge Spott und Hohn
 Mich dort nicht betrübe.

i In the Lord put thou thy trust
 When care on thee presseth.
E'en when helpless in the dust,
 'Tis not God distresseth.
Doubting Him thou'rt Satan's prey,
 Whose fell plots would snare thee,
Toiling ever, night and day,
 For his own to share thee.

ii Christian, courage take and say,
 ' Satan, hence ! avaunt ye !
Put thy feeble darts away,
 Cease to vex and taunt me !
Crushed is now thy horrid head
 By my Saviour's anguish.
Through His Cross to joy I'm led,
 Nevermore to languish '

vi So then, Satan, Death, and Hell
 No more can distress me !
God is near, I know full well,
 And His love will bless me.
God Who gave me His dear Son
 Out of hell to draw me,
Who salvation for me won,
 Will to grace restore me.

SEELENBRÄUTIGAM

Hymn, by Adam Drese, in fifteen 6-line stanzas (1697).   Melody, by (?) Drese (1698).

316

i Seelenbräutigam,
  Jesu, Gottes Lamm,
  Habe dank für deine Liebe,
  Die mich zieht aus reinem Triebe
  Von der Sünden Schlamm,
  Jesu, Gottes Lamm !

ii Deiner Liebe Glut
  Stärket Muth und Blut.
  Wenn du freundlich mich anblickest
  Und an deine Brust mich drückest :
  Macht mich wohlgemuth
  Deiner Liebe Glut.

iii Wahrer Mensch und Gott,
  Trost in Noth und Tod,
  Du bist darum Mensch geboren,
  Zu ersetzen, was verloren,
  Durch dein Blut so roth,
  Wahrer Mensch und Gott !

iv Meines Glaubens Licht
  Lass verlöschen nicht :
  Salbe mich mit Freudenöle,
  Dass hinfort in meiner Seele
  Ja verlösche nicht
  Meines Glaubens Licht.

i Bridegroom, all mine own,
  Jesu, God's dear Son,
  Take my heart for all Thy loving,
  All Thy care and wise protecting
  From sin's scars and shame,
  Jesu, God's dear Son !

ii Thy love all divine
  Doth enkindle mine.
  When Thy friendly glance is on me,
  And upon Thy breast Thou fold'st me,
  All my heart's aflame
  With Thy love divine.

iii Jesu, God and Man,
  Lived on earth a span,
  Came from heaven to dwell among us,
  And salvation sure has won us.
  Red Thy life-blood ran,
  Jesu, God and Man !

iv Clear and holy Light,
  Ever shine Thou bright !
  With the oil of faith anoint me
  That I ne'er may disappoint Thee,
  Shining clear and bright,
  Clear and Holy Light !

U.L.S. 779.

Tr. C. S. T.

SEELENBRÄUTIGAM

Hymn, by Adam Drese, in fifteen 6-line stanzas (1697). *Melody, by* (?) *Drese* (1698).

317

i Seelenbräutigam,
  Jesu, Gottes Lamm,
  Habe dank für deine Liebe,
  Die mich zieht aus reinem Triebe
  Von der Sünden Schlamm,
  Jesu, Gottes Lamm !

ii Deiner Liebe Glut
  Stärket Muth und Blut.
  Wenn du freundlich mich anblickest
  Und an deine Brust mich drückest :
  Macht mich wohlgemuth
  Deiner Liebe Glut.

v So werd ich in dir
  Bleiben für und für ;
  Deine Liebe will ich ehren
  Und in dir dein Lob vermehren,
  Weil ich für und für
  Bleiben werd in dir.

vi Held aus Davids Stamm :
  Deine Liebesflamm
  Mich ernähre, und verwehre,
  Dass die Welt mich nicht versehre,
  Ob sie mir gleich gram :
  Held aus Davids Stamm.

i Bridegroom all mine own,
  Jesu, God's dear Son,
  Take my heart for all Thy loving,
  All Thy care and wise protecting
  From sin's scars and shame,
  Jesu, God's dear Son !

ii Thy love all divine
  Doth enkindle mine.
  When Thy friendly glance is on me,
  And upon Thy breast Thou fold'st me,
  All my heart's aflame
  With Thy love divine.

v In Thee, Lord, I'd bide,
  Ever in Thee hide,
  Thy dear love for ever telling,
  Sing Thy praise and might excelling,
  While in Thee I hide,
  Ever in Thee bide.

vi Lion of David's stem,
  Send Thy Spirit's flame.
  Never let my soul be wounded,
  Be in earth's fell snares confounded,
  Nor be put to shame,
  Lion of David's stem !

U.L.S. 779.

Tr. C. S. T.

SEI GEGRÜSSET, JESU GÜTIG

Hymn, by Christian Keimann, in five 6-line stanzas (1663).   *Melody by* (?) *Gottfried Vopelius* (1682).

318

i Sei grüsset, Jesu gütig,
   Über alle Mass sanftmüthig !
   Ach wie bist du doch zerrissen,
   Und dein ganzer Leib zerschmissen,
   Lass mich deine Lieb ererben
   Und darinnen selig sterben.

i Jesu, Saviour, heed my greeting !
   Kind and gentle is Thy being.
   Long the torture Thou hast suffered,
   Deep the insults to Thee offered.
   Let me all Thy love inherit,
   And meet death in Thy sure merit !

ii O mein Jesu, Gott und mein Heil,
   Meines Herzens Trost und mein Theil,
   Beut mir deine Hand und Seiten,
   Wenn ich werde sollen streiten.
   Lass mich deine Lieb ererben
   Und darinnen selig sterben.

ii Jesu, Master, dearest treasure,
   Christ, my Saviour, my heart's pleasure,
   Hands and piercèd side, O show me,
   Should I tempted be to doubt Thee !
   Let me all Thy love inherit,
   And meet death in Thy sure merit !

iv O ! du weiss und rothe Quelle,
   Kühle meine matte Seele :
   Wenn ich werd im Tode liegen,
   Hilf mir ritterlich obsiegen.
   Lass mich deine Lieb ererben
   Und darinnen selig sterben.

iv O Thou fountain ever flowing,
   Gracious comfort e'er bestowing,
   When Death lays his hand upon me
   Help me then to meet him boldly !
   Let me all Thy love inherit,
   And meet death in Thy sure merit !

v O ! wie freundlich kannst du laben,
   Jesu, alle, die dich haben ;
   Die sich halten an dein Leiden,
   Können seliglich abscheiden.
   Lass mich deine Lieb ererben
   Und darinnen selig sterben.

v Sweet refreshment floweth freely
   To Thy children stayed upon Thee.
   On Thy Passion, Lord, relying,
   Nought I fear the hour of dying.
   Let me all Thy love inherit,
   And meet death in Thy sure merit !

Fischer-Tümpel.[1]

Tr. C. S. T.

[1] Bd. iv. No. 16.

SINGEN WIR AUS HERZENSGRUND

Hymn, anonymous, in six 7-line stanzas (c. 1560). Melody, anonymous (1544), to ' Da Christus geboren war'

319

i Singen wir [all] aus Herzensgrund,
Loben Gott mit unserm Mund !
Wie er Güt an uns beweist,
So hat er uns auch gespeist :
Wie er Thier und Vogl ernährt
Also hat er uns bescheet,
Welchs wir jetzt haben verzehrt.

* iv Gott der die Erde hat zug'richt,
Lässts an Nahrung mangeln nicht ;
Berg und Thal, die macht er nass,
Dass dem Vieh auch wächst sein Gras ;
Aus der Erden Wein und Brod
Schaffet Gott und giebt uns satt,
Davon Mensch sein Leben hat.

* vi Wir danken sehr und bitten ihn,
Dass er geb des Geistes Sinn,
Dass wir solches recht verstehn,
Stets nach sein Geboten thun,
Seinen Namen machen gross,
In Christo ohn Unterlass ;
So singn wir das Gratias.

i Sing ye to God with heart and voice,
Praise Him all and loud rejoice !
On us goodness He hath poured,
For us harvest's plenty stored.
He Who everything that lives
Keepeth, man his being gives
And his every need perceives.

iv Well hath our God the world ordained !
Good things on us He hath rained ;
His the valleys and the hills,
Herbs and pasture-feeding rills,
His the autumn's harvest sheaves.
Earth with plenty fair He wreathes,
Life into our being breathes.

vi Now thank we Him and praise Him too
Who doth our dull sense renew,
Maketh us to grow in grace
And t'ward His law set our face.
His name come now, glorify,
Sing with joy and melody,
' Gratias ' to God on high !

Tucher.[1]

Tr. C. S. T.

[1] Bd. i. No. 600.

SINGT DEM HERRN EIN NEUES LIED

Hymn, by Matthäus Apelles von Löwenstern, a translation of Psalm cxlix, in four 8-line stanzas (1644). Melody, by von Löwenstern (1644).

320

Psalm cxlix.

i Singt dem Herrn ein neues Lied,
  Die Gemeine soll ihn loben,
  Weil er ihren Grenzen Fried
  Hat versprochen hoch von oben.
  Israel sich freue dessen,
  Welcher ihn gemachet hat,
  Und in Aengsten schaffet Rath :
  Seiner soll er nicht vergessen.

ii Zion über deinen Gott
   Freue dich sammt deinem Saamen,
   Halt in Ehren sein Gebot,
   Lobe seinen werthen Namen :
   Nimm die Pauken, nimm die Saiten,
   Such herfür das Harfen-Spiel,
   Weil er's selbst so haben will,
   Seine Wunder auszubreiten.

iii Denn der Herr hat Lust an dir,
    Als an seinem eignen Volke
    Er lässt schweben für und für,
    Über dir die Gnaden-Wolke.
    Herrlich hilft er auch dem Armen ;
    Wenn er ihm zu Fusse fällt,
    Sein Vertrauen auf ihn stellt,
    Will er seiner sich erbarmen.

i Sing a new song to the Lord,
  Let the congregation praise Him,
  Who to us doth peace afford,
  Looking down on earth so loving.
  Israel therefore rejoice ye
  For the good things He hath done !
  Help when tribulations come,
  Be assured, He'll ne'er deny ye.

ii Praise, O Zion, praise thy God,
   Let thy children loudly praise Him,
   In high honour Him adore,
   To His name fine anthems raising !
   Sound the strings in jubilation,
   With the harp make merry sound,
   Lauding Him, as are ye bound,
   Tell His deeds to every nation.

iii For in us He pleasure takes,
    We on earth His people chosen ;
    Ever brings He for our sakes
    Over us His clouds of blessing.
    To the poor He gives salvation :
    Should our foot in danger slide,
    From above our need is spied,
    Help He sends with expedition.

M. A. v. Löwenstern.[1]

Tr. C. S. T.

[1] *Fruelings-Mayen* (Breslau, 1644), No. 10.

SO GIEBST DU NUN, MEIN JESU, GUTE NACHT

Hymn, by August Pfeiffer, in twenty-four 4-line stanzas (1688).   Melody, anonymous (1694).

321

* Bach has a 𝄐 here.

i So giebst du nun, mein Jesu, gute Nacht ?
  So stirbst du denn, mein allerliebstes Leben ?
  Ja, du bist hin, dein Leiden ist vollbracht :
  Mein Gott ist todt, sein Geist ist aufgegeben. *(bis)*

ii Mein Schatz ist hin, den meine Seele liebt ;
  Der neigt sein Haupt, dem sich der Himmel bücket !
  Der mir und aller Welt das Leben giebt,
  Wird von dem Tod ins finstre Grab gezücket. *(bis)*

iii Kommt, ihr Geschöpfe, kommet doch herbei !
  Klagt euren Herrn ! ihr Erden-Klüfte, zittert !
  Du Abgrund, brich und gieb dein Angst-Geschrei !
  Ihr Gräber, reisst ! ihr harten Felsen, splittert ! *(bis)*

iv Ach traur't mit mir ! Ich seh, der Held im Streit,
  Des Vaters Wort, die Zuflucht aller Frommen,
  Der Menschen Heil, der Herr der Herrlichkeit,
  Der Lebensfürst ist schmählich umgekommen. *(bis)*

Fischer-Tümpel.[1]

i Now must Thou then, my Saviour, say farewell ?
  And is it death that lays cold hands upon Thee ?
  'Tis so ! My Lord now ends His mortal spell :
  Alas ! He's dead, His soul of life is weary. *(bis)*

ii He was my All I loved with all my heart.
  Now sinks His head, before which heaven fell prostrate
  He Who to all the world did life impart
  Is now of death's dark cav'rnous grave the inmate. *(bis)*

iii O come, ye faithful souls, and with me sigh !
  Come, mourn your Lord ! O earth, with terror tremble
  And hell below, send up a piteous cry !
  Ye dead, arise ! Ye rocks, to pieces crumble! *(bis)*

iv Come, mourn with me the Hero of our race,
  The Father's Word, the Hope of all that's mortal,
  Salvation's Lord, the King of heaven's high place !
  The Prince of Life hath entered death's dark portal.

Tr. C. S. T.

[1] Bd. iv.   No. 589.

SOLLT ICH MEINEM GOTT NICHT SINGEN

Hymn, by Paul Gerhardt, in twelve 10-line stanzas (1653). Melody, by Johann Schop (1641), to 'Lasset uns den Herren preisen'.

SOLLT ICH MEINEM GOTT NICHT SINGEN

i Sollt ich meinem Gott nicht singen ?
  Sollt ich ihm nicht fröhlich sein ?
  Denn ich seh in allen Dingen,
  Wie so gut ers mit mir mein.
  Ist doch nichts als lauter Lieben,
  Das sein treues Herze regt,
  Das ohn Ende hebt und trägt
  Die in seinem Dienst sich üben.
  Alles Ding währt seine Zeit,
  Gottes Lieb in Ewigkeit.

ii Wie ein Adler sein Gefieder
  Über seine Jungen streckt,
  Also hat auch hin und wieder
  Mich des Höchsten Arm gedeckt,
  Alsobald im Mutterleibe,
  Da er mir mein Wesen gab
  Und das Leben, das ich hab
  Und noch diese Stunde treibe.
  Alles Ding währt seine Zeit,
  Gottes Lieb in Ewigkeit.

xii Weil denn weder Ziel noch Ende
  Sich in Gottes Liebe findt,
  Ei ! so heb ich meine Hände
  Zu dir, Vater, als dein Kind ;
  Bitte, wollst mir Gnade geben,
  Dich aus aller meiner Macht
  Zu umfangen Tag und Nacht,
  Hier in meinem ganzen Leben,
  Bis ich dich nach dieser Zeit
  Lob und lieb in Ewigkeit.

U.L.S. 722.

i Shall I not loud praises sing Thee ?
  Shall I not give thanks, O Lord ?
  When I see how well and truly
  Dost to me Thy gifts afford ?
  Deep Thy love, so true and tender,
  Is upon my head outpoured,
  Endlessly on all is showered
  Who their duty to Thee render.
  All things mortal have their day ;
  God's love stands eternally !

ii As an eagle o'er her nestling
  Spreads her shelt'ring wings above,
  So am I from all molesting
  Warded by my Saviour's love.
  Since of old my mother bore me,
  And God callèd me to life,
  Guarded have I been from strife,
  Till this hour by His sure mercy.
  All things mortal have their day ;
  God's love stands eternally !

xii So then, since Thy love's unceasing,
  Nor my need can ever fail,
  Hear me, Lord, Thy grace beseeching,
  Let it e'er for me avail !
  May it keep me strong and steady,
  Serving Thee with all my might,
  Never halting day or night,
  Be my days or few or many,
  Till I meet beyond the skies
  Thou Thyself in Paradise.

Tr. C. S. T.

STRAF MICH NICHT IN DEINEM ZORN

Hymn, by Johann Burchard Freystein, in ten 8-line stanzas (1697). Melody, anonymous (1694), to ' Straf mich nicht in deinem Zorn'.

323

i Mache dich, mein Geisti, bereit,
Wache, fleh und bete,
Dass dich nicht die böse Zeit
Unverhofft betrete ;
Denn es ist
Satans List
Über viele Frommen
Zur Versuchung kommen.

vii Bete aber auch dabei
Mitten in dem Wachen ;
Denn der Herre muss dich frei
Von dem allen machen,
Was dich drückt
Und bestrickt,
Dass du schläfrig bleibest
Und sein Werk nicht treibest.

* x Drum so lasst uns immerdar
Wachen, flehen, beten,
Weil die Angst, Noth und Gefahr
Immer näher treten ;
Denn die Zeit
Ist nicht weit,
Da uns Gott wird richten
Und die Welt vernichten.

i Ready be, my soul, alway,
Watch ye, pray unceasing !
Else shall come the Judgement day
On thee all unheeding.
O beware !
Satan's lure
Offereth temptation
For thy soul's damnation.

vii And when night around thee falls,
Ever pray unceasing !
Pray to God no ill appals,
Hostile round thee creeping,
Do thee harm
Or alarm.
Pray He watchful make thee,
Fulfil His work in thee.

x Therefore let us all be found
Watchful, prayerful ever !
Peril sore and griefs abound,
To us drawing nearer.
Comes the day
God will pay
Judgement on our scorning ;
Day of wrath and mourning !

U.L.S. 564.

Tr. C. S. T.

STRAF MICH NICHT IN DEINEM ZORN

C. P. E. Bach (1765 and 1784) associates the melody with its proper hymn, by Johann G. Albinus, in seven 8-line stanzas (1692, 1697).

Psalm vi.

i Straf mich nicht in deinem Zorn,
  Grosser Gott, verschone !
Ach, lass mich nicht sein verlorn,
  Nach Verdienst nicht lohne.
    Hat die Sünd
    Dich entzündt :
  Lösch ab in dem Lamme
  Deines Grimmes Flamme.

ii Zeig mir deine Vaterhuld,
  Stärk mit Trost mich Schwachen !
Ach, Herr, hab mit mir Geduld,
  Mein Gebeine krachen :
    Heil die Seel
    Mit dem Oel
  Deiner grossen Gnaden,
  Wend ab allen Schaden.

vii Vater, dir sei ewig Preis
  Hier und auch dort oben ;
Wie auch Christo gleicherweis,
  Der allzeit zu loben :
    Heilger Geist,
    Sei gepreist,
  Hoch gerühmt, geehret,
  Dass du mich erhöret.

i Not in wrath, O mighty God,
  Not in anger smite us !
We must perish if Thy rod
  Justly should requite us.
    We are nought ;
    Sin hath brought,
  Lord, Thy wrath upon us ;
  Yet have mercy on us !

ii Show me now a Father's love,
  And His tender patience,
Heal my wounded soul, remove
  These too sore temptations !
    I am weak,
    Father, speak
  Now of peace and gladness,
  Comfort Thou my sadness !

vii Father, hymns to Thee we raise,
  Here and soon in heavèn ;
And the Son and Spirit praise,
  Who our bonds have riven ;
    Evermore
    We adore
  Thee Whose grace hath stirred us,
  And Whose pity heard us.

U.L.S. 349.

Tr. Catherine Winkworth [1]

[1] *Chorale Book for England* (Lond. 1865), No. 41.

VALET WILL ICH DIR GEBEN

Hymn, by Valerius Herberger, in five 8-line stanzas (1613).   Melody, by Melchior Teschner (1613).

324

i Valet will ich dir geben,
   Du arge, falsche Welt ;
   Dein sündlich böses Leben
   Durchaus mir nicht gefällt.
   Im Himmel ist gut wohnen ;
   Hinauf steht mein Begier.
   Da wird Gott ehrlich lohnen
   Dem, der ihm dient allhier.

ii Rath mir nach deinem Herzen,
   O Jesu Gottes Sohn :
   Soll ich ja dulden Schmerzen,
   Hilf mir, Herr Christ, davon ;
   Verkürz mir alles Leiden,
   Stärk meinen blöden Muth :
   Lass mich selig abscheiden,
   Setz mich in dein Erbgut.

iv Verbirg mein Seel aus Gnaden
   In deiner offen Seit ;
   Rück sie aus allem Schaden
   Zu deiner Herrlichkeit.
   Der ist wohl hie gewesen,
   Wer kommt ins himmlisch Schloss ;
   Der ist ewig genesen,
   Wer bleibt in deinem Schooss.

i Farewell, farewell for ever,
   Thou false and evil world !
   Thy ways are ill, and never
   On them my eyes are turned.
   In heaven's my habitation,
   With God is my desire ;
   For out of every nation
   He calls who served Him here.

ii Thy counsel ever give me,
   Lord Jesu, God's dear Son !
   When trouble comes upon me,
   Deliver me therefrom !
   In sorrow stand beside me,
   Confirm my halting will,
   Through death's dark gateway guide me,
   With joy in heavèn fill !

iv In grace from Thy side flowing
   O wash my spirit white !
   From earth's vain things withdrawing,
   Soon bring her to Thy sight !
   O well is he and happy
   O'er whom Thou throw'st Thy wing !
   He'll reign with Thee in glory
   Who close to Thee doth cling.

U.L.S. 580.

Tr. C. S. T.

VALET WILL ICH DIR GEBEN

Hymn, by Valerius Herberger, in five 8-line stanzas (1613).   Melody, by Melchior Teschner (1613).

325

i Valet will ich dir geben,
  Du arge, falsche Welt ;
  Dein sündlich böses Leben
  Durchaus mir nicht gefällt.
  Im Himmel ist gut wohnen ,
  Hinauf steht mein Begier.
  Da wird Gott ehrlich lohnen
  Dem, der ihm dient allhier.

* iii In meiner Herzens Grunde
  Dein Nam und Kreuz allein
  Funkelt all Zeit und Stunde :
  Drauf kann ich fröhlich sein.
  Erschein mir in dem Bilde
  Zu Trost in meiner Noth,
  Wie du, Herr Christ, so milde
  Dich hast geblut zu Tod.

v Schreib meinen Nam aufs beste
  Ins Buch des Lebens ein,
  Und bind mein Seel gar feste
  Ins Lebensbündelein
  Der, die im Himmel grünen
  Und vor dir leben frei :
  So will ich ewig rühmen,
  Dass dein Herz treue sei.

i Farewell, farewell for ever,
  Thou false and evil world !
  Thy ways are ill, and never
  On them my eyes are turned.
  In heaven's my habitation,
  With God is my desire ;
  For out of every nation
  He calls who served Him here.

iii Within my deepest being
  Thy Name and Cross always
  Shine bright and glow unceasing
  To yield me joy and praise.
  O ever let me see Thee,
  To comfort my last breath,
  As on the Cross of glory
  Thou once did'st hang in death.

v O may my name be written
  Within Thy Book of Doom !
  May I to Thee be knitten
  And to Thy Kingdom come !
  There shall I ever living
  Be happy, saved, and free,
  Thy praise for ever singing,
  And own Thy clemency.

U.L.S. 580.

Tr. C. S. T.

VATER UNSER IM HIMMELREICH

Hymn, by Johann Heermann, in seven 6-line stanzas (1630).   Melody, anonymous (1539).

326

i So wahr ich lebe, spricht dein Gott,
  Mir ist nicht lieb des Sünders Tod ;
  Vielmehr ist dies mein Wunsch und Will,
  Dass er von Sünden halte still,
  Von seiner Bosheit kehre sich
  Und lebe mit mir ewiglich.

* vi Heut lebst du : heut bekehre dich !
  Eh morgen kommt, kanns ändern sich :
  Wer heut ist frisch, gesund und roth,
  Ist morgen krank, ja wohl gar todt.
  So du nun stirbest ohne Buss,
  Dein Leib und Seel dort brennen muss.

* vii Hilf, o Herr Jesu, hilf du mir,
  Dass ich noch heute komm zu dir
  Und Busse thu den Augenblick,
  Eh mich der schnelle Tod hinrück ;
  Auf dass ich heut und jederzeit
  Zu meiner Heimfahrt sei bereit.

                    U.L.S. 395.

i 'Now as I live,' of old God spake,
  'The sinner from his doom I'll take !
  For rather pleasing 'tis to Me
  That he from sin's embrace should flee,
  Cast off the chain of evil ways,
  And live with Me above always.'

vi Amend your ways while yet you may !
   To-morrow comes, too late to pray.
   To-day is with us ; use it well,
   Lest morning find your soul in hell.
   Repentant, then, approach your end ;
   So shall your soul to God ascend.

vii O Christ, Lord Jesu, help Thou me
    My footsteps to direct to Thee,
    And bring me contrite to Thy throne !
    And if Thou summonest me soon,
    To-day, to-morrow, home on high,
    Lord, may I ready be to die !

                    Tr. C. S. T.

VATER UNSER IM HIMMELREICH

Hymn, by Martin Luther, a version of The Lord's Prayer in nine 6-line stanzas (1539). Melody, anonymous (1539).

327

i Vater unser im Himmelreich,
  Der du uns alle heissest gleich
  Brüder sein und dich rufen an
  Und willt das Beten von uns han :
  Gieb, dass nicht bet allein der Mund ;
  Hilf, dass es geh aus Herzens Grund.

* iv Dein Will gescheh, Herr Gott, zugleich
  Auf Erden, wie im Himmelreich:
  Gieb uns Geduld in Leidenszeit,
  Gehorsam sein in Lieb und Leid:
  Wehr und steur allem Fleisch und Blut,
  Das wider deinen Willen thut.

vi All unser Schuld vergieb uns, Herr,
  Dass sie uns nicht betrübe mehr,
  Wie wir auch unsern Schuldigern
  Ihr Schuld und Fehl vergeben gern.
  Zu dienen mach uns all bereit
  In rechter Lieb und Einigkeit.

i Our Father in the heaven Who art,
  Who tellest all of us, in heart
  Brothers to be, and on Thee call,
  And wilt have prayer from one and all,
  Grant that the mouth not only pray,
  From deepest heart O help its way.

iv Thy will be done, the same, Lord God,
  On earth as in Thy high abode;
  In pain give patience for relief,
  Obedience too in love and grief;
  All flesh and blood keep off and check
  That 'gainst Thy will makes a stiff neck.

vi Forgive, Lord, all our trespasses,
  That they no more may us distress,
  As we our debtors gladly let
  Pass all their trespasses and debt.
  To serve make us all ready be
  In honest love and unity.

U.L.S. 572.

Tr. George Macdonald.[1]

[1] *Exotics* (Lond. 1876), p. 91.

VATER UNSER IM HIMMELREICH

Hymn, by Martin Luther, a version of The Lord's Prayer, in nine 6-line stanzas (1539). Melody, anonymous (1539).

328

i Vater unser im Himmelreich,
　Der du uns alle heissest gleich
　Brüder sein und dich rufen an
　Und willt das Beten von uns han :
　Gieb, dass nicht bet allein der Mund ;
　Hilf, dass es geh aus Herzens Grund.

* iv Dein Will gescheh, Herr Gott, zugleich
　Auf Erden, wie im Himmelreich :
　Gieb uns Geduld in Leidenszeit,
　Gehorsam sein in Lieb und Leid :
　Wehr und steur allem Fleisch und Blut,
　Das wider deinen Willen thut.

vii Führ uns, Herr, in Versuchung nicht,
　Wenn uns der böse Geist anficht.
　Zur linken und zur rechten Hand
　Hilf uns thun starken Widerstand,
　Im Glauben fest und wohl gerüst
　Und durch des Heilgen Geistes Trost.

U.L.S. 572.

i Our Father in the heaven Who art,
　Who tellest all of us, in heart
　Brothers to be, and on Thee call,
　And wilt have prayer from one and all,
　Grant that the mouth not only pray,
　From deepest heart O help its way.

iv Thy will be done, the same, Lord God,
　On earth as in Thy high abode ;
　In pain give patience for relief,
　Obedience too in love and grief ;
　All flesh and blood keep off and check
　That 'gainst Thy will makes a stiff neck.

vii Into temptation lead us not,
　When th' evil spirit battles hot
　Upon the right and the left hand,
　Help us with vigour to withstand,
　Firm in the faith, armed 'gainst a host,
　Through comfort of the Holy Ghost.

Tr. George Macdonald.[1]

[1] *Exotics* (Lond. 1876), p. 91.

VATER UNSER IM HIMMELREICH

Hymn, by Martin Moller, a free translation of 'Aufer immensam, Deus, aufer iram', in seven 6-line stanzas (1584). Melody, anonymous (1539).

329

Aufer immensam, Deus.

i Nimm von uns, Herr, du treuer Gott,
  Die schwere Straf und grosse Ruth,
  Die wir mit Sünden ohne Zahl
  Verdienet haben allzumal.
  Behüt vor Krieg und theurer Zeit,
  Vor Seuchen, Feur und grossem Leid !

iii Ach, Herr Gott, durch die Treue dein
   Mit Trost und Rettung uns erschein !
   Beweis an uns dein grosse Gnad
   Und straf uns nicht auf frischer That :
   Wohn uns mit deiner Güte bei ;
   Dein Zorn und Grimm fern von uns sei.

* vii Leit uns mit deiner rechten Hand
    Und segne unsre Stadt und Land :
    Gieb uns allzeit dein heiligs Wort,
    Behüt vors Teufels List und Mord :
    Verleih ein seligs Stündelein,
    Auf dass wir ewig bei dir sein.

U.L.S. 579.

i Put far from us, O faithful God,
  Thine anger sore and vengeful rod !
  Our sins are great and numberless,
  Deserving judgement, we confess.
  Keep from us war and pestilence
  And hold us in Thy providence !

iii O Lord God, through Thy mercy's grace,
   Reveal the glory of Thy face ;
   Bestow on us Thy gracious care,
   Nor angry drive us to despair,
   But ever keep us one with Thee,
   Repentant and from judgement free !

vii O Lord, stretch forth Thy mighty hand
    To guard and bless our fatherland !
    Preserve Thy Word among us pure,
    Protect us from sin's crafty lure,
    Grant one day that we die in Thee,
    And live with Thee eternally !

Tr. C. S. T.

VATER UNSER IM HIMMELREICH

Hymn, by Martin Moller, a free translation of 'Aufer immensam, Deus, aufer iram', in seven 6-line stanzas (1584). **Melody**, *anonymous (1539).*

Aufer immensam Deus.

i Nimm von uns, Herr, du treuer Gott,
  Die schwere Straf und grosse Ruth,
  Die wir mit Sünden ohne Zahl
  Verdienet haben allzumal.
  Behüt vor Krieg und theurer Zeit,
  Vor Seuchen, Feur und grossem Leid !

iii Ach, Herr Gott, durch die Treue dein
  Mit Trost und Rettung uns erschein !
  Beweis an uns dein grosse Gnad
  Und straf uns nicht auf frischer That :
  Wohn uns mit deiner Güte bei ;
  Dein Zorn und Grimm fern von uns sei.

vii Leit uns mit deiner rechten Hand
  Und segne unsre Stadt und Land :
  Gieb uns allzeit dein heiligs Wort,
  Behüt vors Teufels List und Mord :
  Verleih ein seligs Stündelein,
  Auf dass wir ewig bei dir sein.

U.L.S. **579.**

i Put far from us, O faithful God,
  Thine anger sore and vengeful rod !
  Our sins are great and numberless,
  Deserving judgement, we confess.
  Keep from us war and pestilence
  And hold us in Thy providence !

iii O Lord God, through Thy mercy's grace,
  Reveal the glory of Thy face ;
  Bestow on us Thy gracious care,
  Nor angry drive us to despair,
  But ever keep us one with Thee,
  Repentant and from judgement free !

vii O Lord, stretch forth Thy mighty hand
  To guard and bless our fatherland !
  Preserve Thy Word among us pure,
  Protect us from sin's crafty lure,
  Grant one day that we die in Thee,
  And live with Thee eternally !

Tr. C. S. T.

VATER UNSER IM HIMMELREICH

Hymn, by Martin Moller, a free translation of 'Aufer immensam, Deus, aufer iram', in seven 6-line stanzas (1584).   Melody, anonymous (1539).

331

Aufer immensam, Deus.

i Nimm von uns, Herr, du treuer Gott,
  Die schwere Straf und grosse Ruth,
  Die wir mit Sünden ohne Zahl
  Verdienet haben allzumal.
  Behüt vor Krieg und theurer Zeit,
  Vor Seuchen, Feur und grossem Leid !

v Die Sünd hat uns verderbet sehr ;
  Der Teufel plagt uns noch viel mehr ;
  Die Welt und unser Fleisch und Blut
  Uns allezeit verführen thut.
  Solch Elend kennst du, Herr, allein :
  Ach lass es dir befohlen sein !

* vii Leit uns mit deiner rechten Hand
  Und segne unsre Stadt und Land :
  Gieb uns allzeit dein heiligs Wort,
  Behüt vors Teufels List und Mord :
  Verleih ein seligs Stündelein,
  Auf dass wir ewig bei dir sein.

U.L.S. 579.

i Put far from us, O faithful God,
  Thine anger sore and vengeful rod !
  Our sins are great and numberless,
  Deserving judgement, we confess.
  Keep from us war and pestilence
  And hold us in Thy providence !

v Sin sore besets us everywhere,
  And for us Satan lays his snare.
  The world, and e'en our flesh and blood,
  Do all conspire against our good.
  Our trouble is not hid from Thee ;
  Have mercy, Lord, and set us free !

vii O Lord, stretch forth Thy mighty hand
  To guard and bless our fatherland !
  Preserve Thy Word among us pure,
  Protect us from sin's crafty lure,
  Grant one day that we die in Thee,
  And live with Thee eternally !

Tr. C. S. T.

VERLEIH UNS FRIEDEN GNÄDIGLICH

Hymn, by Martin Luther, a translation of 'Da pacem, Domine' (1529), with an additional unmetrical stanza (1566). Melody, an adaptation (1531) of 'Veni Redemptor gentium', with unmetrical addendum (1566).

*Ver-leih uns Frie-den gnä-dig-lich, Herr Gott, zu unsern Zei - ten; Es,

Lord, in Thy mer-cy grant us peace In all our time and na - tion. 'Tis

ist ja doch kein an-drer nicht, Der für uns könn-te strei - ten, Denn

none but Thou canst give re-lease; Thou art our great Sal - va - tion, And

du, un-ser Gott al-lei-ne. Gieb un-sern Für-sten und der Ob-rig-keit Fried

our a-vail-ing Cham-pi-on. Grant to our prince and to all ma-gis-trates peace

und gut Re-gi-ment, dass wir un-ter ih-nen ein ge-ruh-ig und stil-les

and good re-gi-ment; that un-der them al-way we be qui-et-ly gov-erned,

¹ *U.L.S.* 220. *Tr. C. S. T.*

Da pacem, Domine.

Da pacem, Domine, in diebus nostris, quia non est alius qui pugnet pro nobis, nisi tu Deus noster.

V. Fiat pax in virtute tua

R. Et abundantia in turribus tuis.

Oratio. Deus, a quo sancta desideria, recta consilia, et justa sunt opera: da servis tuis illam, quam mundus dare non potest, pacem: ut et corda nostra mandatis tuis dedita, et hostium sublata formidine, tempora sint tua protectione tranquilla. Per Dominum Jesum Christum nostrum. Amen.

VERLEIH UNS FRIEDEN GNÄDIGLICH

Hymn, by Martin Luther, a translation of " Da pacem, Domine ' (1529), with an additional unmetrical stanza (1566). Melody, an adaptation (1531) of 'Veni Redemptor gentium', with unmetrical addendum (1566).

VERLEIH UNS FRIEDEN GNÄDIGLICH

[1] U.L.S. 220. Tr. C. S. T.

The Collect for Peace.

O God, who art the author of peace and lover of concord, in knowledge of whom standeth our eternal life, whose service is perfect freedom; Defend us Thy humble servants in all assaults of our enemies; that we, surely trusting in Thy defence, may not fear the power of any adversaries; through the might of Jesus Christ our Lord. *Amen.*

VOM HIMMEL HOCH DA KOMM ICH HER

Hymn, by Paul Gerhardt, in eighteen 4-line stanzas (1667). Melody, by (?) M. Luther (1539), to ' Vom Himmel hoch'.

334

i Schaut, schaut, was ist für Wunder dar ?
Die schwarze Nacht wird hell und klar,
Ein grosses Licht bricht dort herein,
Ihm weichet aller Sternen-Schein.

* viii Schaut hin ! dort liegt im finstern Stall,
Des Herrschaft gehet über all :
Da Speise vormals sucht ein Rind,
Da ruht jetzt der Jungfrauen Kind.

xvii Es danke Gott, wer danken kann,
Der unser sich so hoch nimmt an
Und sendet aus des Himmels-Thron
Uns, seinen Feinden, seinen Sohn.

xviii Drum stimmt an mit der Engel Heer :
Gott in der Höhe sei nun Ehr,
Auf Erden Friede jeder Zeit,
Den Menschen Wonn und Fröhlichkeit.

Fischer-Tümpel.[1]

i Behold ! what wondrous thing is this
That lights with brilliance all the skies ?
Lo ! shines a star so glorious bright
That into day is turned the night !

viii For see, here in a manger lies
The Lord of earth, of sea, of skies !
Where oxen in the stall are fed
The Son of Mary makes His bed.

xvii So, thank we God with heart and voice !
Yea, every living thing rejoice !
For God sends to us from His throne
His dearly loved and only Son.

xviii Now, glory be to God on high,
So sing the angels in the sky ;
On earth be peace to one and all
Who one t'ward other show good will !

Tr. C. S. T.

[1] Bd. iii. No. 485.

VOM HIMMEL HOCH DA KOMM ICH HER

Hymn, by Martin Luther, in fifteen 4-line stanzas (1535).   Melody, by (?) M. Luther (1539).

335

i Vom Himmel hoch da komm ich her,
  Ich bring euch gute neue Mähr.
  Der guten Mähr bring ich so viel,
  Davon ich singn und sagen will.

ii Euch ist ein Kindlein heut geborn
   Von einer Jungfrau auserkorn,
   Ein Kindelein so zart und fein,
   Das soll eur Freud und Wonne sein.

* xiii Ach, mein herzliebes Jesulein,
       Mach dir ein rein sanft Bettelein,
       Zu ruhen in meins Herzens Schrein,
       Dass ich nimmer vergesse dein.

xv Lob, Ehr sei Gott im höchsten Thron,
   Der uns schenkt seinen eingen Sohn !
   Dess freuet sich der Engel Schaar
   Und singet uns solch's neues Jahr.

U.L.S. 55.

i From heaven above to earth I come
  To bear good news to every home ;
  Glad tidings of great joy I bring,
  Whereof I now will say and sing.

ii To you this night is born a Child
   Of Mary, chosen mother mild ;
   This little Child, of lowly birth,
   Shall be the joy of all your earth.

xiii Ah, dearest Jesus, Holy Child,
     Make Thee a bed, soft, undefiled,
     Within my heart, that it may be
     A quiet chamber kept for Thee.

xv Glory to God in highest heaven,
   Who unto man His Son hath given !
   While angels sing with pious mirth
   A glad New Year to all the earth.

Tr. Catherine Winkworth.[1]

[1] *Chorale Book for England* (Lond. 1865), No. 30.

VOM HIMMEL HOCH DA KOMM ICH HER

Hymn, by Paul Gerhardt, in sixteen 4-line stanzas (1653).   Melody, by (?) M. Luther (1539), to ' Vom Himmel hoch'.

336

i Wir singen dir, Immanuel,
  Du Lebensfürst und Gnadenquell,
  Du Himmelsblum und Morgenstern,
  Du Jungfrau'n Sohn, Herr aller Herrn.

* ii Wir singen dir mit deinem Heer
  Aus aller Kraft Lob, Preis und Ehr,
  Dass du, o längst gewünschter Gast,
  Dich nunmehr eingestellet hast.

v Nun du bist hier, da liegest du,
  Hältst in dem Kripplein deine Ruh ;
  Bist klein, und machst doch alles gross,
  Bekleidst die Welt, und kommst doch bloss.

xvi Ich will dein Hallelujah hier
  Mit Freuden singen für und für,
  Und dort in deinem Ehrensaal
  Solls schallen ohne Zeit und Zahl.

U.L.S. 58.

i We sing Thy praise, Immanuel,
  Thou Fount of grace, thou Foe of hell,
  Thou Flower of heaven, thou Morning Star,
  Maid Mary's Son, yet greater far !

ii We laud Thee with the hosts of heaven.
  Praise, honour, might, and power be given
  To Thee, O long-expected Guest,
  Who with Thy sight this earth hath blessed !

v Now here Thou liest, welcome Guest,
  And in a manger tak'st Thy rest,
  So frail, yet makest all things great,
  Naked, yet bring'st us great estate.

xvi And so, we Alleluja raise
  And forth to all men tell Thy praise,
  Till one day in Thy halls above
  ·Thy love for ever shall we prove.

Tr. C. S. T.

VON GOTT WILL ICH NICHT LASSEN

Hymn, by Ludwig Helmbold, in nine 8-line stanzas (1563-4). Melody (1571), of secular origin ('Ich ging einmal spazieren').

337

i Von Gott will ich nicht lassen,
  Denn er lässt nicht von mir :
  Führt mich auf rechter Strassen
  Da ich sonst irret sehr.
  Er reicht mir seine Hand ;
  Den Abend wie den Morgen
  Thut er mich wohl versorgen,
  Sei, wo ich woll im Land.

iii Auf ihn will ich vertrauen
  In meiner schweren Zeit :
  Es kann mich nicht gereuen ;
  Er wendet alles Leid.
  Ihm sei es heimgestellt ;
  Mein Leib, mein Seel, mein Leben
  Sei Gott dem Herrn ergeben :
  Er schaffs, wies ihm gefällt.

iv Es thut ihm nichts gefallen,
  Denn was mir nützlich ist.
  Er meints gut mit uns allen,
  Schenkt uns den Herren Christ,
  Ja seinen lieben Sohn :
  Durch ihn er uns bescheret,
  Was Leib und Seel ernähret :
  Lobt ihn ins Himmels Thron.

i From God shall nought divide me,
  For He is true for aye,
  And on my path will guide me,
  Who else should often stray ;
  His ever bounteous hand
  By night and day is heedful,
  And gives me what is needful,
  Where'er I go or stand.

iii If sorrow comes, He sent it,
  In Him I put my trust ;
  I never shall repent it,
  For He is true and just,
  And loves to bless us still ;
  My life and soul, I owe them
  To Him Who did bestow them :
  Let Him do as He will.

iv Whate'er shall be His pleasure
  Is surely best for me ;
  He gave His dearest treasure
  That our weak hearts might see
  How good His will t'ward us ;
  And in His Son He gave us
  Whate'er could bless and save us—
  Praise Him Who loveth thus !

U.L.S. 640.

Tr. Catherine Winkworth.[1]

[1] *Chorale Book for England* (Lond. 1865), No. 140.

VON GOTT WILL ICH NICHT LASSEN

Hymn, by Ludwig Helmbold, in nine 8-line stanzas (1563-4).   Melody (1571), of secular origin ('Ich ging einmal spazieren').

338

i Von Gott will ich nicht lassen,
Denn er lässt nicht von mir :
Führt mich auf rechter Strassen
Da ich sonst irret sehr.
Er reicht mir seine Hand ;
Den Abend wie den Morgen
Thut er mich wohl versorgen,
Sei, wo ich woll im Land.

v Lobt ihn mit Herz und Munde,
Dass er uns beides schenkt.
Das ist ein sel'ge Stunde,
Darin man sein gedenkt ;
Sonst verdirbt alle Zeit,
Die wir zubringn auf Erden :
Wir sollen selig werden
Und bleibn in Ewigkeit.

vi Auch wenn die Welt vergehet
Mit ihrem Stolz und Pracht,
Kein Ehr noch Gut bestehet,
Welchs vor war gross geacht :
Wir werden nach dem Tod
Tief in die Erd begraben :
Wenn wir geschlafen haben,
Will uns erwecken Gott.

i From God shall nought divide me,
For He is true for aye,
And on my path will guide me,
Who else should often stray ;
His ever bounteous hand
By night and day is heedful,
And gives me what is needful,
Where'er I go or stand.

v O praise Him, for He never
Forgets our daily need ;
O blest the hour whenever
To Him our thoughts can speed ;
Yea, all the time we spend
Without Him is but wasted
Till we His joy have tasted,
The joy that hath no end.

vi For when the world is passing
With all its pomp and pride,
All we have been amassing
No longer may abide ;
But in our earthly bed,
Where softly we are sleeping,
God hath us in His keeping,
To wake us from the dead.

U.L.S. 640.

Tr. Catherine Winkworth.[1]

[1] *Chorale Book for England* (Lond. 1865), No. 140.

VON GOTT WILL ICH NICHT LASSEN

Hymn, by Ludwig Helmbold, in nine 8-line stanzas (1563-4).   Melody (1571), of secular origin (' Ich ging einmal spazieren ').

339

i Von Gott will ich nicht lassen,
 Denn er lässt nicht von mir :
 Führt mich auf rechter Strassen,
 Da ich sonst irret sehr.
 Er reicht mir seine Hand ;
 Den Abend wie den Morgen
 Thut er mich wohl versorgen,
 Sei, wo ich woll im Land.

viii Darum ob ich schon dulde
 Die Widerwärtigkeit,
 Wie ich auch wohl verschulde
 Kommt doch die Ewigkeit,
 Ist aller Freuden voll ;
 Dieselb ohn einigs Ende,
 Dieweil ich Christum kenne,
 Mir widerfahren soll.

ix Das ist des Vaters Wille,
 Der uns geschaffen hat ;
 Sein Sohn hat Guts die Fülle
 Erworben und Genad ;
 Auch Gott der Heilig Geist
 Im Glauben uns regieret,
 Zum Reich der Himmel führet :
 Ihm sei Lob, Ehr und Preis !

i From God shall nought divide me,
 For He is true for aye,
 And on my path will guide me,
 Who else should often stray ;
 His ever bounteous hand
 By night and day is heedful,
 And gives me what is needful,
 Where'er I go or stand.

viii Then, though on earth I suffer
 Much trial, well I know
 I merit ills still rougher,
 And 'tis to heaven I go ;
 For Christ I know and love,
 To Him I now am hasting,
 And gladness everlasting
 With Him this heart shall prove.

ix For such His will Who made us ;
 The Father seeks our good ;
 The Son brought grace to aid us,
 And saved us by His blood ;
 His Spirit rules our ways,
 By faith in us abiding,
 To heaven our footsteps guiding ;
 To Him be thanks and praise !

U.L.S. 640.   Tr. Catherine Winkworth.[1]

[1] *Chorale Book for England* (Lond. 1865), No. 140.

VON GOTT WILL ICH NICHT LASSEN

Hymn, by Ludwig Helmbold, in nine 8-line stanzas (1563-4).   Melody (1571), of secular origin ('Ich ging einmal spazieren').

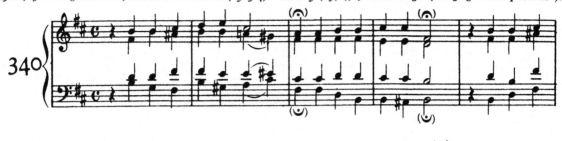

i Von Gott will ich nicht lassen,
   Denn er lässt nicht von mir :
   Führt mich auf rechter Strassen,
   Da ich sonst irret sehr.
   Er reicht mir seine Hand ;
   Den Abend wie den Morgen
   Thut er mich wohl versorgen,
   Sei, wo ich woll im Land.

* v Lobt ihn mit Herz und Munde,
   Dass er uns beides schenkt.
   Das ist ein sel'ge Stunde,
   Darin man sein gedenkt ;
   Sonst verdirbt alle Zeit,
   Die wir zubringn auf Erden :
   Wir sollen selig werden
   Und bleibn in Ewigkeit.

vi Auch wenn die Welt vergehet
   Mit ihrem Stolz und Pracht,
   Kein Ehr noch Gut bestehet,
   Welchs vor war gross geacht :
   Wir werden nach dem Tod
   Tief in die Erd begraben :
   Wenn wir geschlafen haben,
   Will uns erwecken Gott.

i From God shall nought divide me,
   For He is true for aye,
   And on my path will guide me,
   Who else should often stray ;
   His ever bounteous hand
   By night and day is heedful,
   And gives me what is needful,
   Where'er I go or stand.

v O praise Him, for He never
   Forgets our daily need ;
   O blest the hour whenever
   To Him our thoughts can speed ;
   Yea, all the time we spend
   Without Him is but wasted
   Till we His joy have tasted,
   The joy that hath no end.

vi For when the world is passing
   With all its pomp and pride,
   All we have been amassing
   No longer may abide ;
   But in our earthly bed,
   Where softly we are sleeping,
   God hath us in His keeping,
   To wake us from the dead.

U.L.S. 640.   *Tr. Catherine Winkworth.*[1]

[1] *Chorale Book for England* (Lond. 1865), No. 140.

VON GOTT WILL ICH NICHT LASSEN

Hymn, by Ludwig Helmbold, in nine 8-line stanzas (1563-4).   Melody (1571), of secular origin ('Ich ging einmal spazieren ').

341

i Von Gott will ich nicht lassen,
  Denn er lässt nicht von mir :
  Führt mich auf rechter Strassen,
  Da ich sonst irret sehr.
  Er reicht mir seine Hand ;
  Den Abend wie den Morgen
  Thut er mich wohl versorgen,
  Sei, wo ich woll im Land.

viii Darum ob ich schon dulde
  Die Widerwärtigkeit,
  Wie ich auch wohl verschulde :
  Kommt doch die Ewigkeit,
  Ist aller Freuden voll ;
  Dieselb ohn einigs Ende,
  Dieweil ich Christum kenne,
  Mir widerfahren soll.

* ix Das ist des Vaters Wille,
  Der uns geschaffen hat ;
  Sein Sohn hat Guts die Fülle
  Erworben und Genad ;
  Auch Gott der Heilig Geist
  Im Glauben uns regieret,
  Zum Reich der Himmel führet :
  Ihm sei Lob, Ehr und Preis !

i From God shall nought divide me,
  For He is true for aye,
  And on my path will guide me,
  Who else should often stray ;
  His ever bounteous hand
  By night and day is heedful,
  And gives me what is needful,
  Where'er I go or stand.

viii Then, though on earth I suffer
  Much trial, well I know
  I merit ills still rougher,
  And 'tis to heaven I go ;
  For Christ I know and love,
  To Him I now am hasting,
  And gladness everlasting
  With Him this heart shall prove.

ix For such His will Who made us ;
  The Father seeks our good ;
  The Son brought grace to aid us,
  And saved us by His blood ;
  His Spirit rules our ways,
  By faith in us abiding,
  To heaven our footsteps guiding ;
  To Him be thanks and praise !

U.L.S. 640.

Tr. Catherine Winkworth.[1]

[1] *Chorale Book for England* (Lond. 1865), No. 140.

WACHET AUF, RUFT UNS DIE STIMME

Hymn, by Philipp Nicolai, in three 12-line stanzas (1599).   Melody, by Nicolai (1599).

342

WACHET AUF, RUFT UNS DIE STIMME

i Wachet auf ! ruft uns die Stimme
Der Wächter sehr hoch auf der Zinnen :
Wach auf, du Stadt Jerusalem !
Mitternacht heisst diese Stunde !
Sie rufen uns mit hellem Munde :
Wo seid ihr klugen Jungfrauen ?
Wohlauf, der Bräutgam kömmt !
Steht auf, die Lampen nehmt !
Hallelujah !
Macht euch bereit
Zu der Hochzeit :
Ihr müsset ihm entgegen gehn.

ii Zion hört die Wächter singen ;
Das Herz thut ihr vor Freuden springen :
Sie wachet und steht eilend auf.
Ihr Freund kommt vom Himmel prächtig,
Von Gnaden stark, von Wahrheit mächtig :
Ihr Licht wird hell, ihr Stern geht auf.
Nun komm, du werthe Kron,
Herr Jesu, Gottes Sohn !
Hosianna !
Wir folgen all
Zum Freudensaal,
Und halten mit das Abendmahl.

* iii Gloria sei dir gesungen
Mit Menschen und englischen Zungen,
Mit Harfen und mit Cymbeln schön.
Von zwölf Perlen sind die Pforten
An deiner Stadt ; wir sind Consorten
Der Engel hoch vor deinem Thron.
Kein Aug hat je gespürt,
Kein Ohr hat mehr gehört
Solche Freude.
Dess sind wir froh :
Io, io !
Ewig *in dulci jubilo.*

U.L.S. 690.

i Wake from sleep ! hark, sounds are falling !
The watchman from the height is calling—
Awake, awake, Jerusalem !
Hours of night are quickly flying ;
O hear the voice of warning crying !
Where be ye, virgins heedless all ?
Awake ! the Bridegroom comes !
Awake ! and trim your lamps !
Alleluja !
For Him prepare
A feast most rare,
To greet Him eager forward go !

ii Zion hears the watchman calling
And on her heart deep joy is falling.
She waits and watches, limbs alert.
Down from heaven her Lord comes glorious,
So full of grace, in truth victorious,
Her Star, her Light, illumes the earth.
Thou'rt come who wear'st the crown,
Lord Jesus, God's dear Son !
Alleluja !
We follow all
Within Thy hall
To sup with Thee and heed Thy call.

iii Let all creatures now adore Thee,
All men and angels bow before Thee,
With harps and cymbals well attuned !
Enter we Thy pearl-built portals
To swell the throng of Thine immortals,
Where angels circle round Thy throne.
No eye hath seen, nor ear
Was ever blest to hear
Such rejoicing.
Wherefore, sing out
And joyous shout
Io ! in dulci jubilo !

Tr. C. S. T.

WÄR GOTT NICHT MIT UNS DIESE ZEIT

Hymn, by Martin Luther, a translation of Psalm cxxiv, in three 7-line stanzas (1524).   Melody, by (?) Johann Walther (1524).

343

Psalm cxxiv.

i Wär Gott nicht mit uns diese Zeit,
  So soll Israel sagen,
  Wär Gott nicht mit uns diese Zeit :
  Wir hätten musst verzagen,
  Die so ein armes Häuflein sind,
  Veracht von so viel Menschenkind,
  Die an uns setzen alle.

ii Auf uns so zornig ist ihr Sinn :
  Wo Gott hätt das zugeben,
  Verschlungen hätten sie uns hin
  Mit ganzem Leib und Leben ;
  Wir wärn, als die ein Fluth ersäuft
  Und über die gross Wasser läuft
  Und mit Gewalt verschwemmet.

* iii Gott Lob und Dank, der nicht zugab,
  Dass ihr Schlund uns möcht fangen.
  Wie ein Vogel des Stricks kommt ab,
  Ist unser Seel entgangen.
  Strick ist entzwei und wir sind frei :
  Des Herren Name steht uns bei,
  Des Gottes Himm'ls und Erden.

i If God were not upon our side,
  Then let Israel say it ;
  If God were not upon our side,
  We had been quite dismayèd.
  A poor, a lowly flock are we,
  'Gainst whom the world rails mightily
  And sets on us in anger.

ii So wrathful truly was their mien,
  In fury 'gainst us blowing,
  Quick swallowed up we all had been
  From mortal ken and knowing.
  As by the waters of a flood
  We had been drownèd where we stood
  And utterly destroyèd.

iii But, praise to God ! -His might hath closed
  The lion's mouth that gapèd !
  As from a snare the bird uprose,
  So is our soul escapèd !
  The snare's in twain, we're free again.
  Stands fast and true the Lord's great name ;
  O'er heaven and earth He reigneth.

U.L.S. 250.

Tr. C. S. T.

WARUM BETRÜBST DU DICH, MEIN HERZ

Hymn, by (?) Hans Sachs, in twelve (fourteen : 1565) 5-line stanzas (1560). Melody, anonymous (1565).

344

i Warum betrübst du dich, mein Herz ?
  Bekümmerst dich und trägest Schmerz
  Nur um das zeitlich Gut ?
  Vertrau du deinem Herrn und Gott,
  Der alle Ding erschaffen hat.

ii Er kann und will dich lassen nicht ;
  Er weiss gar wohl, was dir gebricht :
  Himmel und Erd ist sein.
  Mein Vater und mein Herre Gott,
  Der mir beisteht in aller Noth !

iii Weil du mein Gott und Vater bist,
  Dein Kind wirst du verlassen nicht,
  Du väterliches Herz.
  Ich bin ein armer Erdenkloss,
  Auf Erden weiss ich keinen Trost.

* xi Der zeitlich Ehr will gern entbehrn :
  Wollst mich des Ewigen gewährn,
  Das du erworben hast
  Durch deinen herben bittern Tod :
  Dess bitt ich dich, mein Herr und Gott !

U.L.S. 701.

i Why art thou so cast down, my heart ?
  Why anxious and in trouble art
  O'er earth's poor fleeting joys ?
  Have trust in God, be not dismayed !
  Thee and all things else He hath made.

ii He will not leave Thee in thy need,
  He knoweth well what thou dost plead,
  Who heaven and earth doth own.
  The Lord, thy God and Father, will
  Stand at thy side in every ill.

iii Lord, Thou my God and Father art !
  I know Thou'st given to me Thy heart
  Nor wilt forget Thy child.
  I am but dust, a thing of clay,
  Yet have I Thee my course to lay.

xi Earth's dazzling lure I'd all resign
  If heavèn's glories were but mine,
  Which Christ for me has won
  On Calvary's accursèd tree.
  O Lord my God, give ear to me !

Tr. C. S. T.

WARUM BETRÜBST DU DICH, MEIN HERZ

Hymn, by (?) Hans Sachs, in twelve (fourteen : 1565) 5-line stanzas (1560).   Melody, anonymous (1565).

345

i Warum betrübst du dich, mein Herz ?
　Bekümmerst dich und trägest Schmerz
　Nur um das zeitlich Gut ?
　Vertrau du deinem Herrn und Gott,
　Der alle Ding erschaffen hat.

iii Weil du mein Gott und Vater bist,
　Dein Kind wirst du verlassen nicht,
　Du väterliches Herz.
　Ich bin ein armer Erdenkloss,
　Auf Erden weiss ich keinen Trost.

xii Alles, was ist auf dieser Welt,
　Es sei Silber, Gold oder Geld,
　Reichthum und zeitlich Gut :
　Das währt nur eine kleine Zeit
　Und hilft doch nicht zur Seligkeit!

xiii Ich dank dir, Christ, o Gottes Sohn,
　Dass du mich solchs erkennen lan
　Durch dein göttliches Wort.
　Verleih mir auch Beständigkeit
　Zu meiner Seelen Seligkeit !

　　　　　　U.L.S. 701.

i Why art thou so cast down, my heart ?
　Why anxious and in trouble art
　O'er earth's poor fleeting joys ?
　Have trust in God, be not dismayed !
　Thee and all things else He hath made.

iii Lord, Thou my God and Father art!
　I know Thou'st given to me Thy heart
　Nor wilt forget Thy child.
　I am but dust, a thing of clay,
　Yet have I Thee my course to lay.

xii The world around may boast its wealth,
　Its silver, gold, and precious pelf,
　Its pomp and passing lure.
　It lasteth but a little time,
　And helps no whit to heavèn's shine.

xiii I thank Thee, Lord God, evermo,
　For all Thou deignest me to know
　Within Thy Holy Word.
　Now grant me constant readiness
　To meet my end in happiness !

　　　　　　Tr. C. S. T.

WARUM BETRÜBST DU DICH, MEIN HERZ

Hymn, by (?) Hans Sachs, in twelve (fourteen : 1565) 5-line stanzas (1560).   Melody, anonymous (1565).

346

i Warum betrübst du dich, mein Herz ?
  Bekümmerst dich und trägest Schmerz
  Nur um das zeitlich Gut ?
  Vertrau du deinem Herrn und Gott,
  Der alle Ding erschaffen hat.

xii Alles, was ist auf dieser Welt,
   Es sei Silber, Gold oder Geld,
   Reichthum und zeitlich Gut :
   Das währt nur eine kleine Zeit
   Und hilft doch nicht zur Seligkeit !

xiii Ich dank dir, Christ, o Gottes Sohn,
    Dass du mich solchs erkennen lan
    Durch dein göttliches Wort.
    Verleih mir auch Beständigkeit
    Zu meiner Seelen Seligkeit!

xiv Lob, Ehr und Preis sei dir gesagt
    Für alle dein erzeigt Wohlthat ;
    Und bitt ich demüthig :
    Lass mich nicht von deim Angesicht
    Verstossen werden ewiglich.

U.L.S. 701.

i Why art thou so cast down, my heart ?
  Why anxious and in trouble art
  O'er earth's poor fleeting joys ?
  Have trust in God, be not dismayed !
  Thee and all things else He hath made.

xii The world around may boast its wealth,
   Its silver, gold, and precious pelf,
   Its pomp and passing lure.
   It lasteth but a little time,
   And helps no whit to heavèn's shine.

xiii I thank Thee, Lord God, evermo,
    For all Thou deignest me to know
    Within Thy Holy Word.
    Now grant me constant readiness
    To meet my end in happiness !

xiv Praise, honour, power to Thee be done
    For all that Thou for man hast won !
    And but one thing I ask :
    Ne'er put me distant from Thy sight
    Nor let my sin condemn me quite !

Tr. C. S. T.

WARUM SOLLT ICH MICH DENN GRÄMEN

Hymn, by Paul Gerhardt, in twelve 8-line stanzas (1653).   Melody, by Johann G. Ebeling (1666).

347

i Warum sollt ich mich denn grämen?
  Hab ich doch
  Christum noch :
  Wer will mir den nehmen?
  Wer will mir den Himmel rauben,
  Den mir schon
  Gottes Sohn
  Beigelegt im Glauben?

xi Herr, mein Hirt, Brunn aller Freuden!
  Du bist mein,
  Ich bin dein ;
  Niemand kann uns scheiden.
  Ich bin dein ; weil du dein Leben
  Und dein Blut
  Mir so gut
  In den Tod gegeben.

xii Du bist mein, weil ich dich fasse,
  Und dich nicht,
  O mein Licht,
  Aus dem Herzen lasse.
  Lass mich, lass mich hingelangen,
  Da du mich
  Und ich dich
  Leiblich werd umfangen!

i Wherefore, soul of mine, art grieving?
  Christ thy Lord
  Will afford
  All that thou art needing.
  Nothing heaven can e'er take from me;
  Faith knows well
  All is well,
  Christ doth there await me.

xi Fount of grace, all joy excelling!
  Thou art mine,
  I am Thine,
  Ne'er from Thee departing.
  Thine I am ; for Thou hast givèn
  Thine own life
  That from strife
  I may pass to heavèn.

xii Thou art mine ! let me embrace Thee !
  From my sight,
  My soul's Light,
  Never I'll displace Thee.
  Bring me soon to Thee in glory,
  Where I'll see
  Rapturously
  Thee and love Thee alway !

U.L.S. 784.

Tr. C. S. T.

WARUM SOLLT ICH MICH DENN GRÄMEN

Hymn, by Paul Gerhardt, in fifteen 8-line stanzas (1653).   Melody, by Johann G. Ebeling (1666).

348

i Fröhlich soll mein Herze springen
  Dieser Zeit,
  Da vor Freud
  Alle Engel singen.
  Hört, hört, wie mit vollen Chören
  Alle Luft
  Laute ruft :
  Christus ist geboren !

viii Ei, so kommt und lasst uns laufen,
  Stellt euch ein
  Gross und klein,
  Kommt mit grossen Haufen.
  Liebt den, der vor Liebe brennet,
  Schaut den Stern,
  Der uns gern
  Licht und Labsal gönnet.

* xv Ich will dich mit Fleiss bewahren,
  Ich will dir
  Leben hier,
  Dir will ich abfahren.
  Mit dir will ich endlich schweben
  Voller Freud
  Ohne Zeit
  Dort im andern Leben.

i All my heart to-day rejoices,
  As I hear,
  Far and near,
  Sweetest angel voices ;
  ' Christ is born ! ' their choirs are singing,
  Till the air
  Everywhere
  With their joy is ringing.

viii Come then, let us hasten yonder !
  Here let all,
  Great and small,
  Kneel in awe and wonder.
  Love Him Who with love is yearning ;
  Hail the Star
  That from far
  Bright with hope is burning !

xv Thee, dear Lord, I'll ever cherish,
  Live to Thee,
  And with Thee
  Dying, shall not perish ;
  But shall dwell with Thee for ever,
  Far on high
  In the joy
  That can alter never.

U.L.S. 35.

Tr. Catherine Winkworth.[1]

[1] *Chorale Book for England* (Lond. 1865), No. 31.

WAS BETRÜBST DU DICH, MEIN HERZE

Hymn, by Zacharias Hermann, in twelve 8-line stanzas (1690). Melody, by Bach.

349

i Was betrübst du dich, mein Herze ?
Warum grämst du dich in mir ?
Sage, was für Noth dich schmerze ?
Warum ist kein Muth bei dir ?
Was für Unglück hat dich troffen,
Und wo bleibt dein freudig Hoffen ?
Wo ist deine Zuversicht,
Die zu Gott sonst war gericht ?

ii Denke nicht, du seist verlassen
Und Gott achte deiner nicht :
Seine Hände, die dich fassen,
Und sein gnädig Angesicht
Haben Acht auf deine Tritte,
Deine Thränen, deine Schritte ;
Alle Trübsal, die dich quält,
Wird genau von Gott gezählt.

iii Geht dirs nicht nach deinem Willen ;
Ei so gehts nach Gottes Rath ;
Der wird doch sein Wort erfüllen,
Das er zugesaget hat :
Das er die, so ihm vertrauen
Und auf seine Güte schauen,
Die auf seinen Wegen gehn,
Nicht will lassen hülflos stehn.

i Why cast down, my heart within me ?
Wherefore art disquieted ?
Say then, what doth wound and press thee ?
Why's thy wonted courage fled ?
Wherefore comes thy loud complaining ?
God's in heaven, o'er earth is reigning.
Courage take, O anxious heart !
God from thee can nothing part.

ii Do not think thou art forsaken,
Or that God ne'er giveth heed.
Into His thy hands He's taken
And thy welfare hath decreed.
Well He knoweth what doth vex thee
And thy tears call down His pity.
Whatsoe'er may be the ill,
Ointment on it God will spill.

iii Let your will to God be yielded :
Be assured He knoweth best.
Everything shall be fulfillèd
As His Word makes manifest :
That all they who trust Him wholly,
And His counsels follow solely,
Never shall be put to shame,
But their dearest hopes obtain.

WAS BIST DU DOCH, O SEELE, SO BETRÜBET

Hymn, by Rudolf Friedrich von Schultt, in eight 5-line stanzas (1704).   Melody, anonymous (1704).

350

Bach has a ⌢ here.

i Was bist du doch, o Seele so betrübet
   Dass dir der Herr ein Kreuz zu tragen giebet ?
   Was grämst du dich
   So ängstiglich,
   Als würdest du drum nicht von Gott geliebet ?

ii Wie bist du so unruhig und bekümmert,
   Weil dich die Freudensonne nicht aufschimmert ?
   Was sorgest du,
   Bist voll Unruh ?
   Dadurch wird ja dein Zustand nur verschlimmert.

vii Harr' nur und trau auf Gott in allem Leiden,
   Und lass dich keine Noth von ihm abscheiden,
   Hör, was er sagt,
   Sei unverzagt,
   Mein Kind, ich will dich mir zum Preis bereiten.

viii Drum, Seele, sei getrost zu Gott erhoben,
   Sein hülfreich Antlitz zeigt sich dir von oben,
   Er ist dein Gott,
   Hilft dir aus Noth,
   Du sollt ihn hier und dort mit Freuden loben.

Schemelli.[1]

i Why, O my soul, art thou cast down within thee ?
   Because thy Lord a Cross to bear has given thee ?
   Why dost thou sigh
   So bitterly,
   Forgetting God with love doth e'er regard thee ?

ii Why restless art, by grief and care oppressèd ?
   Dost think ne'er shines on thee God's sunlight blessèd ?
   Why moans thy heart
   So sore a smart,
   With grief and heavy weight of woe distressèd ?

vii Have faith in God, whate'er thy future may be ;
   No matter what He sends, let nought dismay thee !
   To Him give heed
   Who hath decreed
   And in His praise to sound thy voice hath willed thee.

viii And so, my soul, look up to God above thee !
   His countenance doth beam with love upon thee.
   He is thy Lord ;
   Then be assured,
   Lift up thy voice and sing His praises alway !

Tr. C. S. T.

[1] *Musicalisches Gesangbuch* (Leipzig, 1736), p. 533.

WAS GOTT THUT, DAS IST WOHLGETHAN

Hymn, by Samuel Rodigast, in six 8-line stanzas (1676). Melody, by (?) Johann Pachelbel (1690).

351

i Was Gott thut, das ist wohlgethan :
　 Es bleibt gerecht sein Wilie.
　 Wie er fängt meine Sachen an,
　 Will ich ihm halten stille.
　 Er ist mein Gott,
　 Der in der Noth
　 Mich wohl weiss zu erhalten;
　 Drum lass ich ihn nur walten.

ii Was Gott thut, das ist wohlgethan :
　 Er wird mich nicht betrügen.
　 Er führet mich auf rechter Bahn :
　 So lass ich mich begnügen
　 An seiner Huld
　 Und hab Geduld ;
　 Er wird mein Unglück wenden :
　 Es steht in seinen Händen.

* vi Was Gott thut, das ist wohlgethan :
　 Dabei will ich verbleiben.
　 Es mag mich auf die rauhe Bahn
　 Noth, Tod und Elend treiben.
　 So wird Gott mich
　 Ganz väterlich
　 In seinen Armen halten ;
　 Drum lass ich ihn nur walten.

i What God ordains aione is right,
　 His Word's a rock and bideth.
　 Where'er He guides me, day and night,
　 In Him my heart confideth.
　 He is my God
　 Who hath withstood
　 Fierce foes upon me pressing.
　 For ever will I trust Him.

ii What God ordains alone is right,
　 He never will deceive me.
　 Upon my path He giveth light,
　 And loving doth relieve me.
　 In His sure grace
　 My trust I place
　 Wherever He may lead me,
　 Well knowing He will speed me.

vi What God ordains alone is right,
　 Therewith will I content me,
　 Though trouble's ever in my sight
　 And pain and death are sent me.
　 My Father's care
　 Is ever near,
　 His strong right hand doth shield me.
　 To Him I trusting yield me.

U.L.S. 607.

Tr. C. S. T.

WAS GOTT THUT, DAS IST WOHLGETHAN

Hymn, by Samuel Rodigast, in six 8-line stanzas (1676). Melody, by (?) Johann Pachelbel (1690).

352

*i Was Gott thut, das ist wohlgethan :
Es bleibt gerecht sein Wille.
Wie er fängt meine Sachen an,
Will ich ihm halten stille.
Er ist mein Gott,
Der in der Noth
Mich wohl weiss zu erhalten ;
Drum lass ich ihn nur walten.

iii Was Gott thut, das ist wohlgethan :
Er wird mich wohl bedenken.
Er, als mein Arzt und Wundermann,
Wird mir nicht Gift einschenken
Für Arzenei.
Gott ist getreu ;
Drum will ich auf ihn bauen
Und seiner Gnade trauen.

v Was Gott thut, das ist wohlgethan :
Muss ich den Kelch gleich schmecken,
Der bitter ist, nach meinem Wahn :
Lass ich mich doch nicht schrecken,
Weil doch zuletzt
Ich werd ergötzt
Mit süssem Trost im Herzen,
Da weichen alle Schmerzen.

i What God ordains alone is right,
His Word's a rock and bideth.
Where'er He guides me, day and night,
In Him my heart confideth.
He is my God
Who hath withstood
My foes upon me pressing.
For ever will I trust Him.

iii What God ordains alone is right,
He holds me in His keeping.
Physician wise, He knows my plight,
And for my good is seeking.
His love can heal.
His word is leal ;
So therefore will I trust Him,
Nor from my heart e'er thrust Him.

v What God ordains alone is right ;
My cup of woe I drain it.
It shall not e'er pass from my sight,
Resignèd here I drink it,
Assured at last
I'll hold Him fast
In trusting love unfeignèd,
Who hath my soul maintainèd.

U.L.S. 607.

Tr. C. S. T.

378

WAS GOTT THUT, DAS IST WOHLGETHAN

Hymn, by Samuel Rodigast, in six 8-line stanzas (1676).   Melody, by (?) Johann Pachelbel (1690).

353

i Was Gott thut, das ist wohlgethan :
　Es bleibt gerecht sein Wille.
　Wie er fängt meine Sachen an,
　Will ich ihm halten stille.
　Er ist mein Gott,
　Der in der Noth
　Mich wohl weiss zu erhalten;
　Drum lass ich ihn nur walten.

iv Was Gott thut, das ist wohlgethan :
　Er ist mein Licht und Leben,
　Der mir nichts Böses gönnen kann ;
　Ich will mich ihm ergeben
　In Freud und Leid.
　Es kommt die Zeit,
　Da öffentlich erscheinet,
　Wie treulich er es meinet.

* vi Was Gott thut, das ist wohlgethan :
　Dabei will ich verbleiben.
　Es mag mich auf die rauhe Bahn
　Noth, Tod und Elend treiben :
　So wird Gott mich
　Ganz väterlich
　In seinen Armen halten ;
　Drum lass ich ihn nur walten.

i What God ordains alone is right;
　His word's a rock and bideth.
　Where'er He guides me, day and night,
　In Him my heart confideth.
　He is my God
　Who hath withstood
　My foes upon me pressing.
　For ever will I trust Him.

iv What God ordains alone is right,
　He is my Light, my Beacon.
　Against my foemen doth He fight ;
　I ne'er shall be forsaken.
　Come joy or woe,
　Where'er I go,
　He on my path is shining,
　My welfare true designing.

vi What God ordains alone is right,
　Therewith will I content me,
　Though trouble's ever in my sight
　And pain and death are sent me.
　My Father's care
　Is ever near,
　His strong right hand doth shield me.
　To Him I trusting yield me.

U.L.S. 607.

Tr. C. S. T.

WAS GOTT THUT, DAS IST WOHLGETHAN

Hymn, by Samuel Rodigast, in six 8-line stanzas (1676).   Melody, by (?) Johann Pachelbel (1690).

354

i Was Gott thut, das ist wolgethan :
  Es bleibt gerecht sein Wille.
  Wie er fängt meine Sachen an,
  Will ich ihm halten stille.
  Er ist mein Gott,
  Der in der Noth
  Mich wohl weiss zu erhalten ;
  Drum lass ich ihn nur walten.

i What God ordains alone is right,
  His Word's a rock and bideth.
  Where'er He guides me, day and night,
  In Him my heart confideth.
  He is my God
  Who hath withstood
  My foes upon me pressing.
  For ever will I trust Him.

ii Was Gott thut, das ist wolgethan :
  Er wird mich nicht betrügen.
  Er führet mich auf rechter Bahn :
  So lass ich mich begnügen
  An seiner Huld
  Und hab Geduld ;
  Er wird mein Unglück wenden :
  Es steht in seinen Händen.

ii What God ordains alone is right,
  He never will deceive me.
  Upon my path He giveth light,
  And loving doth relieve me.
  In His sure grace
  My trust I place
  Wherever He may lead me,
  Well knowing He will speed me.

iii Was Gott thut, das ist wolgethan :
  Er wird mich wohl bedenken.
  Er, als mein Arzt und Wundermann,
  Wird mir nicht Gift einschenken
  Für Arzenei.
  Gott ist getreu ;
  Drum will ich auf ihn bauen
  Und seiner Gnade trauen.

iii What God ordains alone is right,
  He holds me in His keeping.
  Physician wise, He knows my plight,
  And for my good He's seeking.
  His love can heal.
  His word is leal ;
  So therefore will I trust Him,
  Nor from my head e'er thrust Him.

U.L.S. 607.

Tr. C. S. T.

WAS GOTT THUT, DAS IST WOHLGETHAN

Hymn, by Samuel Rodigast, in six 8-line stanzas (1676).   Melody, by (?) Johann Pachelbel (1690).

355

[Horns I. II. obbligati]

* i Was Gott thut, das ist wohlgethan :
    Es bleibt gerecht sein Wille.
    Wie er fängt meine Sachen an,
    Will ich ihm halten stille.
    Er ist mein Gott,
    Der in der Noth
    Mich wohl weiss zu erhalten;
    Drum lass ich ihn nur walten.

i What God ordains alone is right,
    His Word's a rock and bideth.
    Where'er He guides me, day and night,
    In Him my heart confideth.
    He is my God
    Who hath withstood
    My foes upon me pressing.
    For ever will I trust Him.

v Was Gott thut, das ist wohlgethan :
    Muss ich den Kelch gleich schmecken,
    Der bitter ist, nach meinem Wahn :
    Lass ich mich doch nicht schrecken,
    Weil doch zuletzt
    Ich werd ergötzt
    Mit süssem Trost im Herzen,
    Da weichen alle Schmerzen.

v What God ordains alone is right ;
    My cup of woe I drain it.
    It shall not e'er pass from my sight,
    Resignèd here I drink it,
    Assured at last
    I'll hold Him fast,
    In trusting love unfeignèd,
    Who hath my soul maintainèd.

vi Was Gott thut, das ist wohlgethan :
    Dabei will ich verbleiben.
    Es mag mich auf die rauhe Bahn
    Noth, Tod und Elend treiben.
    So wird Gott mich
    Ganz väterlich
    In seinen Armen halten ;
    Drum lass ich ihn nur walten.

vi What God ordains alone is right,
    Therewith will I content me,
    Though trouble's ever in my sight
    And pain and death are sent me.
    My Father's care
    Is ever near,
    His strong right hand doth shield me.
    To Him I trusting yield me.

U.L.S. 607.

Tr. C. S. T.

WAS GOTT THUT, DAS IST WOHLGETHAN

Hymn, by Samuel Rodigast, in six 8-line stanzas (1676).   Melody, by (?) Johann Pachebel (1690).

356

[Trumpet obbligato]

i Was Gott thut, das ist wohlgethan :
   Es bleibt gerecht sein Wille.
   Wie er fängt meine Sachen an,
   Will ich ihm halten stille.
   Er ist mein Gott,
   Der in der Noth
   Mich wohl weiss zu erhalten;
   Drum lass ich ihn nur walten.

v Was Gott thut, das ist wohlgethan :
   Muss ich den Kelch gleich schmecken,
   Der bitter ist, nach meinem Wahn :
   Lass ich mich doch nicht schrecken,
   Weil doch zuletzt
   Ich werd ergötzt
   Mit süssem Trost im Herzen,
   Da weichen alle Schmerzen.

* vi Was Gott thut, das ist wohlgethan :
   Dabei will ich verbleiben.
   Es mag mich auf die rauhe Bahn
   Noth, Tod und Elend treiben.
   So wird Gott mich
   Ganz väterlich
   In seinen Armen halten ;
   Drum lass ich ihn nur walten.

i What God ordains alone is right,
   His Word's a rock and bideth.
   Where'er He guides me, day and night,
   In Him my heart confideth.
   He is my God
   Who hath withstood
   My foes upon me pressing.
   For ever will I trust Him.

v What God ordains alone is right ;
   My cup of woe I drain it.
   It shall not e'er pass from my sight,
   Resignèd here I drink it,
   Assured at last
   I'll hold Him fast,
   In trusting love unfeignèd,
   Who hath my soul maintainèd.

vi What God ordains alone is right,
   Therewith will I content me,
   Though trouble's ever in my sight
   And pain and death are sent me.
   My Father's care
   Is ever near,
   His strong right hand doth shield me.
   To Him I trusting yield me.

U.L.S. 607.

Tr. C. S. T.

WAS MEIN GOTT WILL, DAS G'SCHEH ALLZEIT

Hymn, by Albrecht, Markgraf of Brandenburg-Culmbach, in four 10-line stanzas (c. 1554). Melody, anonymous (c. 1529), to the secular ' Il me souffit de tous mes maulx '.

357

* i Was mein Gott will, das g'scheh allzeit,
   Sein Will der ist der beste.
   Zu helfen den er ist bereit,
   Die an ihn glauben feste.
   Er hilft aus Noth,
   Der fromme Gott,
   Und tröst die Welt mit Maszen :
   Wer Gott vertraut,
   Fest auf ihn baut,
   Den will er nicht verlassen.

ii Gott ist mein Trost, mein Zuversicht,
   Mein Hoffnung und mein Leben :
   Was mein Gott will, dass mir geschicht,
   Will ich nicht widerstreben.
   Sein Wort ist wahr :
   Denn all mein Haar
   Er selber hat gezählet.
   Er hüt und wacht,
   Stets für uns tracht,
   Auf dass uns gar nichts fehlet.

iii Nun muss ich Sünder von der Welt
   Hinfahrn in Gottes Willen
   Zu meinem Gott : wanns ihm gefällt,
   Will ich ihm halten stille.
   Mein arme Seel
   Ich Gott befehl
   In meiner letzten Stunden :
   Du frommer Gott,
   Sünd, Höll und Tod
   Hast du mir überwunden.

i Whate'er God wills is best alway
   And ever justly grounded.
   E'er ready He to guide our way
   If faith on Him's sure founded.
   Our God in need
   Doth help indeed,
   He chastens but in measure.
   Who trusts in God
   Stands like a rod,
   Forsaken shall be never.

ii God's comforts all my life sustain,
   In Him's my hope and being.
   Whate'er He wills will I maintain,
   Without resistance yielding.
   His Word is clear—
   That every hair
   Upon my head is numbered.
   He ever wakes,
   Close guard He takes ;
   Our every need's remembered.

iii Now must I, laden deep with sin,
   Forth from this earth betake me,
   To meet my God, His grace to win ;
   Resigned I hear Him call me.
   In my last hour
   Upon His power
   My hope and faith are planted.
   For at His breath
   Hell, Sin, and Death
   Lie low, by Jesus conquered !

U.L.S. 641.

Tr. C. S. T.

WAS MEIN GOTT WILL, DAS G'SCHEH ALLZEIT

Hymn, by Albrecht, Markgraf of Brandenburg-Culmbach, in four 10-line stanzas (c. 1554). Melody, anonymous (c. 1529), to the secular ' Il me souffit de tous mes maulx '.

358

i Was mein Gott will, das g'scheh allzeit,
Sein Will der ist der beste.
Zu helfen den er ist bereit,
Die an ihn glauben feste.
Er hilft aus Noth,
Der fromme Gott,
Und tröst die Welt mit Maszen :
Wer Gott vertraut
Fest auf ihn baut,
Den will er nicht verlassen.

ii Gott ist mein Trost, mein Zuversicht,
Mein Hoffnung und mein Leben :
Was mein Gott will, dass mir geschicht,
Will ich nicht widerstreben.
Sein Wort ist wahr ;
Denn all mein Haar
Er selber hat gezählet.
Er hüt und wacht,
Stets für uns tracht,
Auf dass uns gar nichts fehlet.

* iv Noch eins, Herr, will ich bitten dich,
Du wirst mirs nicht versagen :
Wenn mich der böse Feind anficht,
Lass mich, Herr, nicht verzagen.
Hilf und auch wehr,
Ach Gott, mein Herr,
Zu Ehren deinem Namen.
Wer das begehrt,
Der wird gewährt ;
Drauf sprech ich fröhlich : Amen !

i Whate'er God wills is best alway
And ever justly grounded.
E'er ready He to guide our way
If faith on Him's sure founded.
Our God in need
Doth help indeed,
He chastens but in measure.
Who trusts in God
Stands like a rod,
Forsaken shall be never.

ii God's comforts all my life sustain,
In Him's my hope and being.
Whate'er He wills will I maintain,
Without resistance yielding.
His word is clear—
That every hair
Upon my head is numbered.
He ever wakes,
Close guard He takes ;
Our every need's remembered.

iv And so, dear Lord, I Thee entreat,
Thine ear incline unto me,
And when Death's solemn call I meet
Thy gracious mercy show me !
O Lord, then raise
My soul to praise
Thy name in highest heaven !
Thy creatures frail
Thou wilt not fail ;
Wherefore, Lord, sing we ' Amen ' !

U.L.S. 641.

Tr. C. S. T.

WAS MEIN GOTT WILL, DAS GSCHEH ALLZEIT

Hymn, by Paul Gerhardt, in twelve 10-line stanzas (1647). Melody, anonymous (c. 1529), to the secular ' Il me souffit de tous mes maulx'.

359

i Ich hab in Gottes Herz und Sinn
Mein Herz und Sinn ergeben.
Was böse scheint, ist mir Gewinn ;
Der Tod selbst ist mein Leben.
Ich bin ein Sohn
Dess, der den Thron
Des Himmels aufgezogen ;
Ob er gleich schlägt
Und Kreuz auflegt,
Bleibt doch sein Herz gewogen.

ii Das kann mir fehlen nimmermehr ;
Mein Vater muss mich lieben.
Wenn er mich auch gleich wirft ins Meer,
So will er mich nur üben
Und mein Gemüth
In seiner Güt
Gewöhnen fest zu stehen ;
Halt ich dann Stand,
Weiss seine Hand
Mich wieder zu erhöhen.

* x Ei nun, mein Gott, so fall ich dir
Getröst in deine Hände.
Nimm mich, und mach du es mit mir
Bis an mein letztes Ende,
Wie du wohl weisst,
Dass meinem Geist
Dadurch sein Nutz entstehe,
Und deine Ehr
Je mehr und mehr
Sich in ihr selbst erhöhe.

i To God's all gracious providence
My heart and soul are yielded.
Through death to life He calls me hence ;
In loss my gain's revealèd.
He is my own
And on His throne
In heavèn now is reigning.
Whate'er befall
Or fears appal,
His love can know no waning.

ii My Father's love mine truly is,
Not ever will it fail me.
My soul may toss on stormy seas ;
'Tis but to test and prove me.
He guides my will,
With grace doth fill,
E'er helpful by me standing.
So, by His grace,
I run my race
And fulfil His commanding.

x And so, my God, I come to Thee,
On Thy great love relying.
Take me, and my sure Helper be
Till life's last breath is flying !
O let Thy will
Incline me still
And prosper my endeavour !
To Thy great praise
My voice I raise,
Extolling Thee for ever.

U.L.S. 708.   Tr. C. S. T.

WAS MEIN GOTT WILL, DAS G'SCHEH ALLZEIT

Hymn, by Paul Gerhardt, in twelve 10-line stanzas (1647). Melody, anonymous (c. 1529), to the secular 'Il me souffit des tous mes maulx'.

360

i Ich hab in Gottes Herz und Sinn
Mein Herz und Sinn ergeben.
Was böse scheint, ist mir Gewinn ;
Der Tod selbst ist mein Leben.
Ich bin ein Sohn
Dess, der den Thron
Des Himmels aufgezogen ;
Ob er gleich schlägt
Und Kreuz auflegt,
Bleibt doch sein Herz gewogen.

v Zudem ist Weisheit und Verstand
Bei ihm ohn alle Massen ;
Zeit, Ort und Stund ist ihm bekannt
Zu Thun und auch zu Lassen.
Er weiss, wann Freud,
Er weiss, wann Leid,
Uns, seinen Kindern, diene ;
Und was er thut,
Ist alles gut,
Obs noch so traurig schiene.

*xii Soll ich denn auch des Todes Weg
Und finstre Strasse reisen :
Wohlan ! so tret ich Bahn und Steg,
Den mir dein Augen weisen.
Du bist mein Hirt,
Der alles wird
Zu solchem Ende kehren,
Dass ich einmal
In deinem Saal
Dich ewig möge ehren.

i To God's all gracious providence
My heart and soul are yielded.
Through death to life He calls me hence ;
In loss my gain's revealèd.
He is my own
And on His throne
In heavèn now is reigning.
Whate'er befall
Or fears appal,
His love can know no waning.

v How great the wisdom of our God !
How wise His understanding !
Both time and space obey His nod
And fulfil His commanding.
He sorrow sends
Or gladness lends,
As best it seemeth to Him.
His every deed
Supplies our need,
However dark their planning.

xii So, though I tread death's cheerless ways,
Its sunless pathways tracing,
Thy loving hand all fear allays,
My feeble courage bracing.
Thou art my Guide,
And by my side
To mansions fair wilt call me,
To where on high
Eternally
Thy praises echo loudly.

U.L.S. 708.

Tr. C. S. T.

WAS MEIN GOTT WILL, DAS GSCHEH ALLZEIT

Hymn, by Paul Gerhardt, in eighteen 10-line stanzas (c. 1653) Melody, anonymous (c. 1529), to the secular 'Il me souffit de tous mes maulx.

361

i Barmherzger Vater, höchster Gott,
Gedenk an deine Worte :
Du sprichst : Ruf mich an in der Noth,
Und klopf an meine Pforte.
So will ich dir
Errettung hier,
Nach deinem Wunsch erweisen,
Dass du mit Mund
Und Herzengrund
In Freuden mich sollst preisen.

viii Wenn der Gerecht in Nöthen weint,
Will Gott ihn fröhlich machen,
Und die zerbrochnes Herzens Feind,
Die sollen wieder lachen.
Wer Fromm will sein,
Muss in der Pein
Und Jammerstrasse wallen ;
Doch steht ihm bei
Des Höchsten Treu
Und hilft ihn aus dem allen.

* ix Ich habe dich ein Augenblick,
O liebes Kind, verlassen ;
Sieh, aber, sieh, mit grossem Glück
Und Trost ohn alle Massen
Will ich dir schon
Die Freudenkron
Aufsetzen und verehren.
Dein kurzes Leid
Soll sich in Freud
Und ewig Heil verkehren.

i Father, O gracious, heavenly Lord,
Thy Holy Word has taught me,
That whosoever's on Thee called
Shall swift receive Thy mercy ;
My plaint Thou'lt hear,
Or far or near,
And hearken to my crying.
So shall my heart
Thy praise impart
Who turn'st to joy my sighing.

viii The righteous soul that cries in need
Shall know and feel God near him.
From heavèn comfort comes with speed
And joy to such as fear Him.
And though he go
In paths of woe
And mid distresses languish,
God's help is nigh
And from on high
Descends to still his anguish.

ix ' I had, perchance, forgotten thee,
O child of man, a moment ;
But soon thou shalt in heavèn see
And taste love's full enjoyment.
A crown of joy
Without alloy
Shalt thou be ever wearing,
Thy span of bliss
Be measureless,
Eternal glory sharing.'

Fischer-Tümpel.[1]

Tr. C. S. T.

[1] Bd. iii. No. 449.

WAS MEIN GOTT WILL, DAS G'SCHEH ALLZEIT

Hymn, by Albrecht, Markgraf of Brandenburg-Culmbach, in four 10-line stanzas (c. 1554). Melody, anonymous (c. 1529), to the secular 'Il me souffit de tous mes maulx'.

362

* i Was mein Gott will, das g'scheh allzeit,
   Sein Will der ist der beste.
   Zu helfen den er ist bereit,
   Die an ihn glauben feste.
   Er hilft aus Noth,
   Der fromme Gott,
   Und tröst die Welt mit Maszen :
   Wer Gott vertraut,
   Fest auf ihn baut,
   Den will er nicht verlassen.

ii Gott ist mein Trost, mein Zuversicht,
   Mein Hoffnung und mein Leben :
   Was mein Gott will, dass mir geschicht,
   Will ich nicht widerstreben.
   Sein Wort ist wahr :
   Denn all mein Haar
   Er selber hat gezählet.
   Er hüt und wacht,
   Stets für uns tracht,
   Auf dass uns gar nichts fehlet.

iii Nun muss ich Sünder von der Welt
   Hinfahrn in Gottes Willen
   Zu meinem Gott : wanns ihm gefällt,
   Will ich ihm halten stille.
   Mein arme Seel
   Ich Gott befehl
   In meiner letzten Stunden :
   Du frommer Gott,
   Sünd, Höll und Tod
   Hast du mir überwunden.

i Whate'er God wills is best alway
   And ever justly grounded.
   E'er ready He to guide our way
   If faith on Him's sure founded.
   Our God in need
   Doth help indeed,
   He chastens but in measure.
   Who trusts in God
   Stands like a rod,
   Forsaken shall be never.

ii God's comforts all my life sustain,
   In Him's my hope and being.
   Whate'er He wills will I maintain,
   Without resistance yielding.
   His Word is clear—
   That every hair
   Upon my head is numbered.
   He ever wakes,
   Close guard He takes ;
   Our every need's remembered.

iii Now must I, laden deep with sin,
   Forth from this earth betake me,
   To meet my God, His grace to win ;
   Resigned I hear Him call me.
   In my last hour
   Upon His power
   My hope and faith are planted.
   For at His breath
   Hell, Sin, and Death
   Lie low, by Jesus conquered !

U.L.S. 641.

Tr. C. S. T.

WAS MEIN GOTT WILL, DAS G'SCHEH ALLZEIT

Hymn, by Albrecht, Markgraf of Brandenburg-Culmbach, in four 10-line stanzas (c. 1554). Melody, anonymous (c. 1529), to the secular 'Il me souffit de tous mes maulx'.

363

*i Was mein Gott will, das g'scheh allzeit, Sein Will der ist der beste Zu helfen den er ist bereit, Die an ihn glauben feste ! Er hilft aus Noth, Der fromme Gott, Und tröst die Welt mit Maszen : Wer Gott vertraut, Fest auf ihn baut, Den will er nicht verlassen.	i Whate'er God wills is best alway And ever justly grounded. E'er ready He to guide our way If faith on Him's sure founded Our God in need Doth help indeed, He chastens but in measure. Who trusts in God Stands like a rod, Forsaken shall be never
ii Gott ist mein Trost, mein Zuversicht, Mein Hoffnung und mein Leben : Was mein Gott will, dass mir geschicht, Will ich nicht widerstreben. Sein Wort ist wahr, Denn all mein Haar Er selber hat gezählet. Er hüt und wacht, Stets für uns tracht, Auf dass uns gar nichts fehlet.	ii God's comforts daily me sustain, In Him's my hope and being. Whate'er He wills will I maintain, Without resistance yielding. His Word is clear— That every hair Upon my head is numbered. He ever wakes, Close guard He takes ; Our every need's remembered.
iv Noch eins, Herr, will ich bitten dich, Du wirst mirs nicht versagen : Wann mich der böse Feind anficht, Lass mich, Herr, nicht verzagen. Hilf und auch wehr, Ach Gott, mein Herr, Zu Ehren deinem Namen. Wer das begehrt Der wird gewährt ; Drauf sprech ich fröhlich : Amen !	iv And so, dear Lord, I Thee entreat, Thine ear incline unto me, And when Death's solemn call I meet Thy gracious mercy show me ! O Lord, then raise My soul to praise Thy name in highest heavèn ! Thy creatures frail Thou wilt not fail ; Wherefore, Lord, sing we ' Amen ' !

U.L.S. 641.   Tr. C. S. T.

WAS WILLST DU DICH, O MEINE SEELE, KRÄNKEN

Hymn, by Dietrich von dem Werder, in nine 10-line stanzas (1653). *Melody, anonymous (1682).*

364

WAS WILLST DU DICH, O MEINE SEELE, KRÄNKEN

i Was willst du dich, o meine Seele, kränken !
  Meinst du, dass Gott nicht kann an dich gedenken ?
  Er weiss gar wohl, wann er dir helfen soll ;
  Denn er ist selbst der Gnad und Güte voll.
  Halt ihm nur stille ;
  Es gehet so sein Wille.
  Wie kann er dich denn lassen in den Banden.
  Du bist ja seine Braut.
  Wer hofft in Gott, und dem vertraut,
  Wird nimmermehr zu Schanden.

ix Trotz Teufel, Welt, Tod, und der Höllen Rachen,
   Gott ist mein Gott, dem alle meine Sachen,
   Mein Kreuz, Leib, Seel und Leben heimgestellt,
   Dabei lass ichs, er machs, wies ihm gefällt.
   Ich halt ihm stille,
   Was Gott will ist mein Wille,
   Sein Trost befreit mich aller Sünden-Banden,
   Drauf bleib ich fest gebaut.
   Wer hofft in Gott und dem vertraut,
   Wird nimmermehr zu Schanden.

Wagner.[1]

i How now, my soul, why makest sore complaining ?
  Dost e'er suppose that God thy prayer's disdaining ?
  Right well He knows whenever thou'rt in need.
  E'er pitiful is He and helps with speed.
  To Him hold closely :
  He willeth, so it shall be.
  How can'st suppose He'll leave thee here to languish ?
  He loves thee as His bride.
  Whoe'er trusts God, puts else beside,
  Shall never know shame's anguish.

ix So, Death and Satan both I do contemn them.
   God is my God and I His own possession.
   And if a Cross I bear, I know 'tis best,
   I leave it all to Him and am at rest.
   I hold Him closely :
   He willeth, so it shall be.
   He'll loose the bonds of sin wherein I languish,
   And so I calm abide ;
   For who trusts God, puts else beside,
   Shall never know shame's anguish.

Tr. C. S. T.

[1] *Vollstandiges Gesangbuch,* vi. 188.

WELT, ADE! ICH BIN DEIN MÜDE

Hymn, by Johann Georg Albinus, in nine 8-line stanzas (1649). Melody and harmonization by Johann Rosenmüller (1649), as used by Bach.

WELT, ADE! ICH BIN DEIN MÜDE

*i Welt, ade! ich bin dein müde,
  Ich will nach dem Himmel zu:
  Da wird sein der rechte Friede
  Und die stolze Seelenruh.
  Welt, bei dir ist Krieg und Streit,
  Nichts denn lauter Eitelkeit:
  In dem Himmel allezeit
  Friede, Ruh und Seligkeit.

ii Wenn ich werde dahin kommen,
  Bin ich aller Krankheit los
  Und der Traurigkeit entnommen,
  Ruhe sanft in Gottes Schooss.
  Welt, bei dir u.s.w.

iv Unaussprechlich schöne singet
  Gottes auserwählte Schaar:
  Heilig, heilig, heilig! klinget
  In dem Himmel immerdar.
  Welt, bei dir u.s.w.

v Nichts ist hier, als stetes Weinen,
  Keine Freude bleibet nicht:
  Will uns gleich die Sonne scheinen,
  So verhemmt die Nacht das Licht.
  Welt, bei dir u.s.w.

U.L.S. 842.

i World, farewell! of thee I'm weary,
  'Tis toward heaven my way I'd take.
  There await me, no more dreary,
  Peace and rest that nought can break.
  In the world are war and strife,
  Unrest and deceit are rife.
  But in heaven is holy joy,
  Peace and love without alloy.

ii When to heavèn God shall call me,
  All life's troubles pass away,
  Perfect peace shall e'er befall me
  In His blessèd arms alway.
  In the world, *etc., etc.*

iv Hark how gloriously singing
  Sounds the far angelic band,
  Holy, holy, holy! ringing
  Clear throughout the heavenly strand!
  In the world, *etc., etc.*

v Here on earth are tears and sorrow;
  Joy and gladness ne'er abide.
  Though the sun shines, each to-morrow
  Through the shades of night is spied.
  In the world, *etc., etc.*

Tr. C. S. T.

WELTLICH EHR UND ZEITLICH GUT

Hymn, by Michael Weisse, in ten 7-line stanzas (1531). Melody (1555), the descant of Weisse's original (1531) tune.

366

i Weltlich Ehr und zeitlich Gut,
  Wollust und aller Übermuth
  Ist eben wie ein Gras,
  Alle Pracht und stolzer Ruhm
  Verfällt als ein Wiesenblum :
  O Mensch, bedenk eben das
  Und versorge dich noch bass !

ii Dein End bild dir täglich für,
  Gedenk der Tod ist für der Thür
  Und will mit dir davon,
  Er klopft an und du musst h'raus,
  Und da wird nichts anders aus :
  Hättest du nun recht gethan,
  So fündest du guten Lohn.

vii Christus redet offenbar
  Und spricht zu aller Menschen Schaar :
  Wer mit mir herrschen will,
  Der nehm auch sein Kreuz auf sich,
  Unterwerf sich williglich
  Und halt sich nach mein'm Beispiel,
  Thu nicht, wie sein Adam will.

viii O Mensch, sie an Jesum Christ,
  Sofern er dir zum Fürbild ist,
  Und untergib dich gar :
  Nimm auf dich sein süsses Joch
  Und folg ihm doch treulich nach,
  So kommst du zur Engelschaar,
  Die des wartet immerdar.

i Earth's frail pomp and vanities,
  Delights and vain frivolities,
  Shall wither as the grass.
  All its might and boasted power
  Falleth as a faded flower.
  This is truth ! it close embrace,
  And with care pursue thy course !

ii Live as though the day were near
  When thou before God must appear.
  When death knocks at the door,
  His dread summons must obey,
  When he calls thou must not stay.
  If thou hast fulfilled God's law
  He will welcome thee, be sure.

vii Christ, when here on earth He lived,
  Spake oftentimes to those He loved ·
  ' He who would call him Mine
  Must here bear his Cross, as I,
  Take its burden willingly,
  To My will his own resign,
  And for Mammon never pine '.

viii Do as Jesus bids thee do,
  Him only as thy Pattern know
  And strive to learn His will !
  His yoke cheerful on you take,
  All you do, do for His sake !
  Journey ever on until
  Angels' songs your senses fill.

Tucher.[1]

Tr. C. S. T.

[1] Bd. i. No. 515.

WENN ICH IN ANGST UND NOTH

Hymn, by Matthäus Apelles von Löwenstern, a version of Psalm cxxi in seven 4-line stanzas (1644). Melody, by M. A. von Löwenstern (1644).

367

* Bach has a 𝄐 here.

Psalm cxxi.

i Wenn ich in Angst und Noth mein Augen heb empor
  Zu deinen Bergen, Herr, mit Seufzen und mit Flehen,
  So reichst du mir dein Ohr,
  Dass ich nicht darf betrübt von deinem Antlitz gehen.

ii Mein Schutz und Hülfe kömmt, o treuer Gott, von dir,
  Der du das Firmament und Erdreich hast gegründet;
  Kein Mensch kann helfen mir
  Vor deinem Gnaden-Thron allein man Rettung findet.

iii Du schaffest, dass mein Fuss mir nicht entgleiten kann;
  Du leitest selber mich auf allen meinen Wegen
  Und zeigest mir die Bahn,
  Wenn mir die Welt, der Tod und Teufel Stricke legen.

iv Du Hüter Israel, du schläfst noch schlummerst nicht;
  Dein Augen Tag und Nacht ob denen offen bleiben,
  Die sich in deine Pflicht
  Zur Kreuz-Fahn durch dein Blut, o Jesu, lassen
    schreiben.

Fischer-Tümpel.[1]

i When in my deepest woe my gaze I lift on high
  To heaven's far distant height, where Thou, O Lord, art
    reigning,
  Thou answerest my cry.
  I hear and am content, my will to Thine resigning.

ii My Shield and Helper true, O mighty Lord, Thou art,
  Who hath the firmament and earth's great frame created;
  No man can cure my smart,
  'Tis by Thy grace alone my woes can be abated.

iii My footsteps dost Thou lead and guidest them aright;
  My pathways dost direct, nor lett'st me from them
    wander.
  Thou'rt with me in the fight
  When Sin and Satan's wiles my soul from Thee would
    sunder.

iv Shepherd of Israel that slumbers not nor sleeps,
  Thy people day and night Thine eye with love beholdeth,
  Each one who fealty keeps,
  Who neath Thy blood-stained flag in service loyal
    enrolleth.

Tr. C. S. T.

[1] Bd. i. No. 385.

WENN MEIN STÜNDLEIN VORHANDEN IST

Hymn, by Nikolaus Herman, in four (five : 1574) 7-line stanzas (1562).   Melody, by Herman (1569).

368

i Wenn mein Stündlein vorhanden ist
　Und soll hinfahrn mein Strasse :
　So g'leit du mich, Herr Jesu Christ,
　Mit Hilf mich nicht verlasse !
　Mein Seel an meinem letzten End
　Befehl ich, Herr, in deine Händ :
　Du wollst sie mir bewahren !

ii Mein Sünd mich werden kränken sehr,
　Mein G'wissen wird mich nagen ;
　Denn ihr sind viel, wie Sand am Meer :
　Doch will ich nicht verzagen ;
　Gedenken will ich an dein Tod,
　Herr Jesu, und dein Wunden roth :
　Die werden mich erhalten.

iii Ich bin ein Glied an deinem Leib,
　Dess tröst ich mich von Herzen !
　Von dir ich ungeschieden bleib
　In Todesnoth und Schmerzen :
　Wenn ich gleich sterb, so sterb ich dir ;
　Ein ewigs Leben hast du mir
　Durch deinen Tod erworben.

i When my last hour is close at hand,
　And I must hence betake me,
　Do Thou, Lord Jesus, by me stand,
　Nor let Thine aid forsake me ;
　To Thy blest hands I now commend
　My soul, at this my earthly end,
　And Thou wilt safely keep it.

ii My sins, dear Lord, disturb me sore,
　My conscience cannot slumber,
　But I will cleave to Thee the more,
　Though they the sands outnumber ;
　I will remember Thou didst die,
　Will think on Thy most bitter cry,
　Thy sufferings shall uphold me.

iii Since I was graft into the Vine,
　So will I comfort borrow ;
　For Thou wilt surely keep me Thine
　Through fear, and pain, and sorrow ;
　Yea, though I die, I die to Thee,
　And Thou through death didst win for me
　The right to life eternal.

U.L.S. 843.

Tr. Catherine Winkworth.[1]

[1] *Chorale Book for England* (Lond. 1865), No. 193.

WENN MEIN STÜNDLEIN VORHANDEN IST

Hymn, by Nikolaus Herman, in four (five : 1574) 7-line stanzas (1562).   Melody, by Herman (1569).

369

[Violin obbligato]

i Wenn mein Stündlein vorhanden ist
Und soll hinfahrn mein Strasse :
So g'leit du mich, Herr Jesu Christ,
Mit Hilf mich nicht verlasse !
Mein Seel an meinem letzten End
Befehl ich, Herr, in deine Händ :
Du wollst sie mir bewahren !

* iv Weil du vom Tod erstanden bist,
Werd ich im Grab nicht bleiben ;
Mein höchster Trost dein Auffahrt ist :
Tods Furcht kann sie vertreiben ;
Denn wo du bist, da komm ich hin,
Dass ich stets bei dir leb und bin :
Drum fahr ich hin mit Freuden !

v So fahr ich hin zu Jesu Christ,
Mein Arm thu ich ausstrecken ;
So schlaf ich ein und ruhe fein,
Kein Mensch kann mich aufwecken,
Denn Jesus Christus, Gottes Sohn,
Der wird die Himmelsthür aufthun,
Mich führn zum ewgen Leben.

U.L.S. 843.

i When death at last my spirit calls
And to my doom shall take me,
O guide me, that no ill befalls,
And never, Lord, forsake me !
My soul I place within Thy hand
To comfort her at my last end.
I know well Thou'lt preserve me.

iv Since thou from death hast risen again,
The grave's not my last dwelling.
Thou art in heaven, hast conquered pain,
The powers of hell dispelling.
To where Thou art Thou bidd'st me come,
In heaven with Thee to make my home.
I go my way rejoicing.

v My course is set to heaven above ;
To Christ I hence betake me.
Asleep in Him and in His love
No mortal hand can wake me.
Lord Christ, fair victor in the strife,
From heaven shall call my soul to life,
And bliss eternal grant me !

Tr. C. S. T.

WENN MEIN STÜNDLEIN VORHANDEN IST

Hymn, by Nikolaus Herman, in four (five : 1574) 7-line stanzas (1562). Melody, by Herman (1569).

370

i Wenn mein Stündlein vorhanden ist
  Und soll hinfahrn mein Strasse :
  So g'leit du mich, Herr Jesu Christ,
  Mit Hilf mich nicht verlasse !
  Mein Seel an meinem letzten End
  Befehl ich, Herr, in deine Händ :
  Du wollst sie mir bewahren !

ii Mein Sünd mich werden kränken sehr,
  Mein Gwissen wird mich nagen ;
  Denn ihr sind viel, wie Sand am Meer :
  Doch will ich nicht verzagen ;
  Gedenken will ich an dein Tod,
  Herr Jesu, und dein Wunden roth :
  Die werden mich erhalten.

iii Ich bin ein Glied an deinem Leib,
  Dess tröst ich mich von Herzen !
  Von dir ich ungeschieden bleib
  In Todesnoth und Schmerzen :
  Wenn ich gleich sterb, so sterb ich dir ;
  Ein ewigs Leben hast du mir
  Durch deinen Tod erworben.

U.L.S. 843.

i When my last hour is close at hand,
  And I must hence betake me,
  Do Thou, Lord Jesus, by me stand,
  Nor let Thine aid forsake me ;
  To Thy blest hands I now commend
  My soul, at this my earthly end,
  And Thou wilt safely keep it.

ii My sins dear Lord, disturb me sore,
  My conscience cannot slumber,
  But I will cleave to Thee the more,
  Though they the sands outnumber ;
  I will remember Thou didst die,
  Will think on Thy most bitter cry,
  Thy sufferings shall uphold me.

iii Since I was graft into the Vine,
  So will I comfort borrow ;
  For Thou wilt surely keep me Thine
  Through fear, and pain, and sorrow ;
  Yea, though I die, I die to Thee,
  And Thou through death didst win for me
  The right to life eternal.

Tr. Catherine Winkworth.[1]

[1] *Chorale Book for England* (Lond. 1865), No. 193.

WENN MEIN STÜNDLEIN VORHANDEN IST

Hymn, by Nikolaus Herman, in four (five : 1574) 7-line stanzas (1562). Melody, by Herman (1569).

371

i Wenn mein Stündlein vorhanden ist
Und soll hinfahrn mein Strasse :
So g'leit du mich, Herr Jesu Christ,
Mit Hilf mich nicht verlasse !
Mein Seel an meinem letzten End
Befehl ich, Herr, in deine Händ :
Du wollst sie mir bewahren !

iv Weil du vom Tod erstanden bist,
Werd ich im Grab nicht bleiben ;
Mein höchster Trost dein Auffahrt ist :
Tods Furcht kann sie vertreiben ;
Denn wo du bist, da komm ich hin,
Dass ich stets bei dir leb und bin :
Drum fahr ich hin mit Freuden !

v So fahr' ich hin zu Jesu Christ,
Mein Arm thu ich ausstrecken ;
So schlaf ich ein und ruhe fein,
Kein Mensch kann mich aufwecken,
Denn Jesus Christus, Gottes Sohn,
Der wird die Himmelsthür aufthun,
Mich führn zum ewgen Leben.

i When Death at last my spirit calls
And to my doom shall take me,
O guide me, that no ill befalls,
And never, Lord, forsake me !
My soul I place within Thy hand
To comfort her at my last end.
I know well Thou'lt preserve me.

iv Since Thou from death hast risen again,
The grave's not my last dwelling.
Thou art in heaven, hast conquered pain,
The powers of hell dispelling.
To where Thou art Thou bidd'st me come,
In heaven with Thee to make my home.
I go my way rejoicing.

v My course is set to heaven above ;
To Christ I hence betake me.
Asleep in Him and in His love
No mortal hand can wake me.
Lord Christ, fair victor in the strife,
From heaven shall call my soul to life,
And bliss eternal grant me !

U.L.S. 843.

Tr. C. S. T.

WENN MEIN STÜNDLEIN VORHANDEN IST

Hymn, by Nikolaus Herman, in four (five : 1574) 7-line stanzas (1562). Melody, by Herman (1569).

372

[Trumpet obbligato]

i Wenn mein Stündlein vorhanden ist
Und soll hinfahrn mein Strasse :
So g'leit du mich, Herr Jesu Christ,
Mit Hilf mich nicht verlasse !
Mein Seel an meinem letzten End
Befehl ich, Herr, in deine Händ :
Du wollst sie mir bewahren !

iv Weil du vom Tod erstanden bist,
Werd ich im Grab nicht bleiben ;
Mein höchster Trost dein Auffahrt ist :
Tods Furcht kann sie vertreiben ;
Denn wo du bist, da komm ich hin,
Dass ich stets bei dir leb und bin :
Drum fahr ich hin mit Freuden !

* v So fahr ich hin zu Jesu Christ,
Mein Arm thu ich ausstrecken ;
So schlaf ich ein und ruhe fein,
Kein Mensch kann mich aufwecken,
Denn Jesus Christus, Gottes Sohn,
Der wird die Himmelsthür aufthun,
Mich führn zum ewgen Leben.

i When death at last my spirit calls
And to my doom shall take me,
O guide me, that no ill befalls,
And never, Lord, forsake me !
My soul I place within Thy hand
To comfort her at my last end.
I know well Thou'lt preserve me.

iv Since Thou from death hast risen again,
The grave's not my last dwelling.
Thou art in heaven, hast conquered pain,
The powers of hell dispelling.
To where Thou art Thou bidd'st me come,
In heaven with Thee to make my home.
I go my way rejoicing.

v My course is set to heaven above ;
To Christ I hence betake me.
Asleep in Him and in His love
No mortal hand can wake me.
Lord Christ, fair victor in the strife,
From heaven shall call my soul to life,
And bliss eternal grant me !

U.L.S. 843.

Tr. C. S. T.

WENN WIR IN HÖCHSTEN NOTHEN SEIN

Hymn, by Paul Eber, in seven 4-line stanzas (c. 1560). Melody, by Louis Bourgeois (1547), to 'Leve le cœur, ouvre l'oreille'.

373

i Wenn wir in höchsten Nothen sein
Und wissen nicht, wo aus noch ein,
Und finden weder Hilf noch Rath,
Ob wir gleich sorgen früh und spat :

ii So ist dies unser Trost allein,
Dass wir zusammen insgemein
Dich anrufen, o treuer Gott,
Um Rettung aus der Angst und Noth ;

iii Und heben unser Aug und Herz
Zu dir in wahrer Reu und Schmerz,
Und suchen der Sünd Vergebung
Und aller Strafen Linderung,

iv Die du verheissest gnädiglich
Allen, die darum bitten dich
Im Namen deins Sohns Jesu Christ,
Der unser Heil und Fürsprech ist.

U.L.S. 583.

i When in the hour of utmost need
We know not where to look for aid,
When days and nights of anxious thought
Nor help nor counsel yet have brought,

ii Then this our comfort is alone :
That we may meet before Thy throne,
And cry, O faithful God, to Thee,
For rescue from our misery ;

iii To Thee may raise our hearts and eyes,
Repenting sore with bitter sighs,
And seek Thy pardon for our sin,
And respite for our griefs within :

iv For Thou hast promised graciously
To hear all those who cry to Thee,
Through Him Whose name alone is great,
Our Saviour and our Advocate.

Tr. Catherine Winkworth.[1]

[1] *Chorale Book for England* (Lond. 1865), No. 141.

WENN WIR IN HÖCHSTEN NÖTHEN SEIN

Hymn, by (?) Bodo von Hodenberg, in fifteen 4-line stanzas (1646).   Melody, by Louis Bourgeois (1547), to 'Leve le cœur, ouvre l'oreille'.

374

i Vor deinen Thron tret ich hiemit,
  O Gott, und dich demüthig bitt .
  Wend dein genädig Angesicht
  Von mir blutarmen Sünder nicht.

ii Du hast mich, o Gott Vater mild,
  Gemacht nach deinem Ebenbild ;
  In dir web, schweb und lebe ich,
  Vergehen müsst ich ohne dich.

vi Wenn Sünd und Sathan mich anklagt
  Und mir das Herz im Leib verzagt,
  Alsdann brauchst du dein Mittler Amt,
  Dass mich der Vater nicht verdammt.

viii Gott Heilger Geist, du höchste Kraft,
  Dess Gnade in mir alles schafft :
  Ist etwas gut am Leben mein,
  So ist es wahrlich lauter dein.

Fischer-Tümpel.[1]

i Before Thy throne, my God, I stand,
  Myself, my all, are in Thy hand ;
  O show me Thine approving face,
  Nor from Thy son withhold Thy grace.

ii O God, my Father, Thou hast laid
  Thy likeness on me, whom Thou'st made ;
  In Thee is all my being here,
  With Thee beside me nought I fear.

vi Should Sin and Satan hold me thrall,
  Should heart grow faint and fears appal,
  Sure still Thou dost behind me stand
  And stay Thy just, avenging hand.

viii O Holy Spirit, power divine,
  Fill full this erring heart of mine.
  Of good repute whate'er there be
  In me is found, it comes from Thee.

Tr. C. S. T.

[1] Bd ii. No. 396.

WER GOTT VERTRAUT

Hymn, by Joachim Magdeburg, in three 12-line stanzas (1597 : st. i 1571). Melody, by Magdeburg (1571).

375

i Wer Gott vertraut,
   Hat wohl gebaut
*Im Himmel und auf Erden :
   Wer sich verlässt
   Auf Jeşum Christ,
*Dem muss der Himmel werden.
   Darum auf dich
   All Hoffnung ich
   Ganz fest und steif thu setzen :
   Herr Jesu Christ,
   Mein Trost du bist
*In Todes Noth und Schmerzen.

ii Und wenns gleich wär
   Dem Teufel sehr
*Und aller Welt zuwider :
   Dennoch so bist
   Du, Jesu Christ,
*Der sie all schlägt darnieder.
   Und wenn ich dich
   Nur hab um mich
   Mit deinem Geist und Gnaden :
   So kann fürwahr
   Mir ganz und gar
*Wed'r Tod noch Teufel schaden.

i Who puts his trust
   In God most just
*Hath built his house securely ;
   He who relies
   On Jesu Christ
*Shall reach his heaven most surely.
   Then fixed on Thee
   My trust shall be,
   For Thy truth cannot alter ;
   While mine Thou art,
   Not death's worst smart
*Shall make my courage falter.

ii Though fiercest foes
   My course oppose,
*A dauntless front I'll show them.
   My champion Thou,
   Lord Christ, art now,
*Who soon shalt overthrow them !
   And if but Thee
   I have in me
   With Thy good gifts and Spirit,
   Nor death nor hell,
   I know full well,
*Shall hurt me, through Thy merit.
                    Tr. Catherine Winkworth.[1]

U.L.S. 642.

[1] *Chorale Book for England* (Lond. 1865), No. 145.   * The 3rd, 6th and last lines of each stanza are repeated.

WER NUR DEN LIEBEN GOTT LÄSST WALTEN

Hymn, by Emilie Juliane, Countess of Schwarzburg-Rudolstadt, in twelve 6-line stanzas (1695).   Melody, by Georg Neumark (1657), to 'Wer nur den lieben Gott'.

376

*i Wer weiss, wie nahe mir mein Ende !
Hin geht die Zeit, her kommt der Tod :
Ach, wie geschwinde und behende
Kann kommen meine Todesnoth !
Mein Gott, ich bitt durch Christi.Blut :
Machs nur mit meinem Ende gut !

iii Herr, lehr mich stets mein End bedenken
Und, wenn ich einstens sterben muss,
Die Seel in Jesu Wunden senken,
Und ja nicht sparen meine Buss.
Mein Gott, u.s.w.

iv Lass mich bei Zeit mein Haus bestellen,
Dass ich bereit sei für und für
Und sage stets in allen Fällen :
Herr, wie du willt, so schicks mit mir !
Mein Gott, u.s.w.

xii Ich leb indess in Gott vergnüget
Und sterb ohn alle Kümmerniss.
Mir gnüget, wie mein Gott es füget ;
Ich glaub und bin es ganz gewiss : ·
Durch deine Gnad und Christi Blut
Machst du's mit meinem Ende gut.

U.L.S. 609

i Who knows when life's last hour approacheth?
Time fast doth fly and death draws near :
How swift on life death's call encroacheth,
And sounds his summons stern and drear !
Lord God, in Christ's dear name I pray,
In that last hour my spirit stay !

iii Lord, let me e'er for death be ready,
And, when his hand's upon me laid,
In Jesu's loving bosom rest me,
Repentant, pardoned, unafraid.
Lord God, etc.

iv While yet there's time let me prepare me
To meet the summons when it falls,
To say with honest heart and steady :
'Lord, I am Thine, whate'er befalls'.
Lord God, etc.

xii My life at peace with God proceedeth,
Nor death can rouse a thought of fear.
Content I take what He decree-eth,
For faith is strong, my course is clear.
Lord, through Thy blood once shed for me,
O bid me hence to rest with Thee !

Tr. C. S. T.

WER NUR DEN LIEBEN GOTT LÄSST WALTEN

Hymn, by Georg Neumark, in seven 6-line stanzas (1657). Melody, by Neumark (1657).

377

i Wer nur den lieben Gott lässt walten
  Und hoffet auf ihn allezeit :
  Den wird er wunderlich erhalten
  In aller Noth und Traurigkeit.
  Wer Gott, dem Allerhöchsten, traut,
  Der hat auf keinen Sand gebaut.

ii Was helfen uns die schweren Sorgen ?
  Was hilft uns unser Weh und Ach ?
  Was hilft es, dass wir alle Morgen
  Beseufzen unser Ungemach ?
  Wir machen unser Kreuz und Leid
  Nur grösser durch die Traurigkeit.

iii Man halte nur ein wenig stille
   Und sei doch in sich selbst vergnügt,
   Wie unsers Gottes Gnadenwille,
   Wie sein Allwissenheit es fügt.
   Gott, der uns ihm hat auserwählt,
   Der weiss auch sehr wohl, was uns fehlt.

U.L.S. 675.

i He who will suffer God to guide him,
  And trusteth Him in all his ways,
  Shall ever know that God's beside him
  In hours of trial and evil days.
  He whom God's mighty love hath filled
  Upon a rock his castle's built.

ii Of what avail our bitter sorrow ?
  'Tis not despair that brings relief.
  What profit if each new to-morrow
  Still finds us languishing in grief ?
  We but increase our load of care
  By tame surrender to despair.

iii Be still and wait on God's good pleasure,
   And be content with what He sends.
   E'er find in His good will thy treasure,
   And know His wisdom rules thine ends.
   God as His children us doth own
   And all our needs to Him are known.

Tr. C. S. T.

WER NUR DEN LIEBEN GOTT LÄSST WALTEN

Hymn, by Christoph Tietze, in eight 6-line stanzas (1663). Melody, by Georg Neumark (1657), to ' Wer nur den lieben Gott lässt walten'.

378

*i Ich armer Mensch, ich armer Sünder
   Steh hier vor Gottes Angesicht :
   Ach Gott, ach Gott, verfahr gelinder
   Und geh nicht mit mir ins Gericht.
   Erbarme dich, erbarme dich,
   Gott, mein Erbarmer, über mich !

ii Wie ist mir doch so angst und bange
   Von wegen meiner grossen Sünd :
   Hilf, dass ich wieder Gnad erlange,
   Ich armes und verlornes Kind.
   Erbarme dich, erbarme dich,
   Gott, mein Erbarmer, über mich !

iii Mein kläglich und beweglich Klagen,
   Ach Herr, wie lang erhörst du nicht ?
   Wie kannst du das Geschrei vertragen ?
   Hör, was der arme Sünder spricht :
   Erbarme dich, erbarme dich ;
   Erhöre mich, erhöre mich !

vi Sprich nur Ein Wort, so werd ich leben ;
   Sprich, dass der arme Sünden hör :
   Ich habe dir die Sünd vergeben ;
   Hinfürder sündige nicht mehr !
   Erbarme dich, erbarme dich,
   O mein Erbarmer, über mich !

i Before God's awful throne I place me,
   A sinner frail and mortal wight.
   Deal with me, Lord, in love, I pray Thee,
   Nor drive me broken from Thy sight !
   Have mercy on me, Saviour mine,
   Absolve me, make me wholly Thine !

ii So sorely does my sin distress me,
   And weigh me down with guilty mien.
   O grant me, Lord, to feel Thy mercy,
   Thy child forlorn on Thee doth lean !
   Have mercy on me, Saviour mine,
   Absolve me, make me wholly Thine !

iii O wilt Thou never heed my crying ?
   Thy countenance why hast Thou turned ?
   Why art Thou comfort still denying ?
   O hear the heart that's for Thee burned !
   Have mercy on me, Saviour mine,
   And to my plaint Thine ear incline !

vi Speak but one word, and I am happy,
   Speak to my soul that she may hear :
   ' Thy sin have I forgiven wholly,
   Thou art made whole, now sin no more '
   Have mercy on me, Saviour mine,
   Absolve me, make me wholly Thine !

U.L.S. 376.

Tr. C. S. T.

WER NUR DEN LIEBEN GOTT LÄSST WALTEN

Hymn, by Georg Neumark, in seven 6-line stanzas (1657). Melody, by Neumark (1657).

379

i Wer nur den lieben Gott lässt walten
  Und hoffet auf ihn aliezeit,
  Den wird er wunderlich erhalten
  In aller Noth und Traurigkeit.
  Wer Gott, dem Allerhöchsten, traut,
  Der hat auf keinen Sand gebaut.

iv Er kennt die rechten Freudenstunden ;
   Er weiss wohl, wenn es nützlich sei.
   Wenn er uns nur hat treu erfunden,
   Und merket keine Heuchelei :
   So kommt Gott, eh wirs uns versehn,
   Und lässet uns viel Guts geschehn.

* vii Sing, bet und geh auf Gottes Wegen,
    Verricht das Deine nur getreu
    Und trau des Himmels reichem Segen :
    So wird er bei dir werden neu.
    Denn welcher seine Zuversicht
    Auf Gott setzt, den verlässt er nicht.

U.L.S. 675.

i He who will suffer God to guide him,
  And trusteth Him in all his ways,
  Shall ever know that God's beside him
  In hours of trial and evil days.
  He whom God's mighty love hath filled
  Upon a rock his castle's built.

iv He knows the hour when joy is seemly,
   And giveth it with lavish hand :
   He will reward our faith supremely
   If we are loyal servants found.
   He answ'reth, though our deeds are ill,
   And with good things our heart doth fill.

vii Sing, pray, and follow God unceasing,
    And to His will be steadfast, true !
    So shalt thou win from heaven a blessing,
    Thy covenant with God renew.
    Whoso on Him with faith is set
    Shall ne'er forgotten be nor let !

Tr. C. S. T.

WER NUR DEN LIEBEN GOTT LÄSST WALTEN

Hymn, by Georg Neumark, in seven 6-line stanzas (1657). Melody, by Neumark (1657).

380

i Wer nur den lieben Gott lässt walten
　Und hoffet auf ihn allezeit :
　Den wird er wunderlich erhalten
　In aller Noth und Traurigkeit.
　Wer Gott, dem Allerhöchsten, traut,
　Der hat auf keinen Sand gebaut.

v Denk nicht in deiner Drangsalshitze,
　Dass du von Gott verlassen seist,
　Und dass Gott der im Schoosse sitze,
　Der sich mit stetem Glücke speist :
　Die Folgezeit verändert viel,
　Und setzet jeglichem sein Ziel.

* vii Sing, bet und geh auf Gottes Wegen,
　Verricht das Deine nur getreu
　Und trau des Himmels reichem Segen :
　So wird er bei dir werden neu.
　Denn welcher seine Zuversicht
　Auf Gott setzt, den verlässt er nicht.[1]

U.L.S. 675.

i He who will suffer God to guide him,
　And trusteth Him in all his ways,
　Shall ever know that God's beside him
　In hours of trial and evil days.
　He whom God's mighty love hath filled
　Upon a rock his castle's built.

v Think not when trial thee defieth,
　That God His face from thee hath turned.
　'Tis not the man He ne'er denieth
　Who only His regard hath earned.
　God works in a mysterious way,
　And every man receives his pay.

vii Sing, pray, and follow God unceasing,
　And to His will be steadfast, true !
　So shalt thou win from heaven a blessing,
　Thy covenant with God renew.
　Whoso on Him with faith is set
　Shall ne'er forgotten be nor let !

Tr. C. S. T.

[1] Bach's text of st. vii differs from the original.

WER NUR DEN LIEBEN GOTT LÄSST WALTEN

Hymn, by Emilie Juliane, Countess of Schwarzburg-Rudolstadt, in twelve 6-line stanzas (1695). Melody, by Georg Neumark (1657), to 'Wer nur den lieben Gott lässt walten'.

i Wer weiss, wie nahe mir mein Ende !
  Hin geht die Zeit, her kommt der Tod :
  Ach, wie geschwinde und behende
  Kann kommen meine Todesnoth !
  Mein Gott, ich bitt durch Christi Blut :
  Machs nur mit meinem Ende gut !

iii Herr, lehr mich stets mein End bedenken
   Und, wenn ich einstens sterben muss,
   Die Seel in Jesu Wunden senken
   Und ja nicht sparen meine Buss.
   Mein Gott, *u.s.w.*

iv Lass mich bei Zeit mein Haus bestellen,
   Dass ich bereit sei für und für
   Und sage stets in allen Fällen :
   Herr, wie du willt, so schicks mit mir !
   Mein Gott, *u.s.w.*

*xii Ich leb indess in Gott vergnüget
   Und sterb ohn alle Kümmerniss.
   Mir gnüget, wie mein Gott es füget ;
   Ich glaub und bin es ganz gewiss :
   Durch deine Gnad und Christi Blut
   Machst dus mit meinem Ende gut.

U.L.S. 609.

i Who knows when life's last hour approacheth ?
  Time fast doth fly and death draws near :
  How swift on life death's call encroacheth,
  And sounds his summons stern and drear !
  Lord God, in Christ's dear name I pray,
  In that last hour my spirit stay !

iii Lord, let me e'er for death be ready,
   And, when his hand's upon me laid,
   In Jesu's loving bosom rest me,
   Repentant, pardoned, unafraid.
   Lord God, *etc.*

iv While yet there's time let me prepare me
   To meet the summons when it falls,
   To say with honest heart and steady :
   ' Lord, I am Thine, whate'er befalls'.
   Lord God, *etc.*

xii My life at peace with God proceedeth,
   Nor death can rouse a thought of fear.
   Content I take what He decrec-eth,
   For faith is strong, my course is clear.
   Lord, through Thy blood once shed for me,
   O bid me hence to rest with Thee !

Tr. C. S. T.

WER NUR DEN LIEBEN GOTT LÄSST WALTEN

Hymn, by Georg Neumark, in seven 6-line stanzas (1657). Melody, by Neumark (1657).

382

i Wer nur den lieben Gott lässt walten
  Und hoffet auf ihn allezeit,
  Den wird er wunderlich erhalten
  In aller Noth und Traurigkeit.
  Wer Gott, dem Allerhöchsten, traut,
  Der hat auf keinen Sand gebaut.

vi Es sind ja Gott sehr schlechte Sachen,
  Und ist dem Höchsten alles gleich,
  Den Reichen klein und arm zu machen,
  Den Armen aber gross und reich :
  Gott ist der rechte Wundermann,
  Der bald erhöhn, bald stürzen kann.

* vii Sing, bet und geh auf Gottes Wegen,
  Verricht das Deine nur getreu
  Und trau des Himmels reichem Segen :
  So wird er bei dir werden neu.
  Denn welcher seine Zuversicht
  Auf Gott setzt, den verlässt er nicht.

U.L.S. 675.

i He who will suffer God to guide him,
  And trusteth Him in all his ways,
  Shall ever know that God's beside him
  In hours of trial and evil days.
  He whom God's mighty love hath filled
  Upon a rock his castle's built.

vi God's purposes are well contrivèd,
  And to His hands it comes with ease
  The rich of wealth are swift deprivèd,
  The poor are raisèd from their knees.
  Yea, God alone can marvels do,
  Lift up and doom to ruin too.

vii Sing, pray, and follow God unceasing,
  And to His will be steadfast, true !
  So shalt thou win from heaven a blessing,
  Thy covenant with God renew.
  Whoso on Him with faith is set
  Shall ne'er forgotten be nor let !

Tr. C. S. T.

WERDE MUNTER, MEIN GEMÜTHE

Hymn, by Johann Rist, in twelve 8-line stanzas (1642).   Melody, by Johann Schop (1642).

383

i Werde munter, mein Gemüthe,
  Und ihr Sinnen, geht herfür,
  Dass ihr preiset Gottes Güte,
  Die er hat gethan an mir :
  Da er mich den ganzen Tag
  Vor so mancher schweren Plag
  Hat erhalten und ergötzet,
  Dass mich Satan nicht verletzet.

ii Lob und Dank sei dir gesungen,
   Vater der Barmherzigkeit,
   Dass mir ist mein Werk gelungen,
   Dass du mich vor allem Leid
   Und vor Sünden mancher Art
   So getreulich hast bewahrt,
   Auch den Feind hinweg getrieben,
   Dass ich unbeschädigt blieben.

iii Keine Klugheit kann ausrechen
    Deine Güt und Wunderthat ;
    Ja kein Redner kann aussprechen,
    Was dein Huld erwiesen hat.
    Deiner Wohlthat ist zu viel ;
    Sie hat weder Mass noch Ziel.
    Herr, du hast mich so geführet,
    Dass kein Unfall mich berühret.

i Sink not yet, my soul, to slumber,
  Wake, my heart, go forth and tell
  All the mercies without number
  That this bygone day befell ;
  Tell how God hath kept afar
  All things that against me war,
  Hath upheld me and defended,
  And His grace my soul befriended.

ii Father, merciful and holy,
   Thee to-night I praise and bless,
   Who to labour true and lowly
   Grantest ever meet success ;
   Many a sin and many a woe,
   Many a fierce and subtle foe
   Hast Thou checked that once alarmed me,
   So that nought to-day has harmed me.

iii Yes, our wisdom vainly ponders,
    Fathoms not Thy loving thought ;
    Never tongue can tell the wonders
    That each day for us are wrought ;
    Thou hast guided me to-day
    That no ill hath crossed my way,
    There is neither bound nor measure
    In Thy love's o'erflowing treasure.

U.L.S. 537.

Tr. Catherine Winkworth.[1]

[1] *Lyra Germanica* (2nd Series), p. 78.

The Score of Cantata No. 146 does not indicate the words selected by Bach.

WERDE MUNTER, MEIN GEMÜTHE

Hymn, by Johann Rist, in twelve 8-line stanzas (1642). Melody, by Johann Schop (1642).

384

i Werde munter, mein Gemüthe,
Und ihr Sinnen, geht herfür,
Dass ihr preiset Gottes Güte,
Die er hat gethan an mir :
Da er mich den ganzen Tag
Vor so mancher schweren Plag
Hat erhalten und ergötzet,
Dass mich Satan nicht verletzet.

v Herr, verzeihe mir aus Gnaden
Alle Sünd und Missethat,
Die mein armes Herz beladen
Und so gar vergiftet hat,
Dass auch Satan durch sein Spiel
Mich zur Hölle stürzen will.
Da kannst du alleine retten ;
Strafe nicht mein Uebertreten !

* vi Bin ich gleich von dir gewichen,
Stell ich mich doch wieder ein ;
Hat uns doch dein Sohn verglichen
Durch sein Angst und Todespein.
Ich verleugne nicht die Schuld ;
Aber deine Gnad und Huld
Ist viel grösser als die Sünde,
Die ich stets in mir befinde.

i Sink not yet, my soul, to slumber,
Wake, my heart, go forth and tell
All the mercies without number
That this bygone day befell ;
Tell how God hath kept afar
All things that against me war,
Hath upheld me and defended,
And His grace my soul befriended.

v Of Thy grace I pray Thee pardon
All my sins, and heal their smart ;
Sore and heavy is their burden,
Sharp their sting within my heart ;
And my foe lays many a snare
But to tempt me to despair,
Only Thou, dear Lord, canst save me,
Let him not prevail against me.

vi Have I e'er from Thee departed,
Now I seek Thy face again,
And Thy Son, the loving-hearted,
Made our peace through bitter pain.
Yes, far greater than our sin,
Though it still be strong within,
Is the love that fails us never,
Mercy that endures for ever.

Tr. Catherine Winkworth.[1]

U.L.S. 537.

[1] *Lyra Germanica* (2nd Series), p. 78.

WERDE MUNTER, MEIN GEMÜTHE

Hymn, by Martin Jahn, in nineteen 8-line stanzas (1661).   Melody, by Johann Schop (1642), to ' Werde munter, mein Gemüthe'.

385

i Jesu, meiner Seelen Wonne,
Jesu, meine beste Lust,
Jesu, meine Freuden-Sonne,
Jesu, dir ist ja bewusst,
Wie ich dich so herzlich liebe
Und mich ohne dich betrübe.
Drum, o Jesu, komm zu mir,
Und bleib bei mir für und für.

* ii Jesu, mein Hort und Erretter,
Jesu, meine Zuversicht,
Jesu, starker Schlangentreter,
Jesu, meines Lebens-Licht !
Wie verlanget meinem Herzen,
Jesulein, nach dir mit Schmerzen !
Komm, ach komm ! ich warte dein,
Komm, o liebstes Jesulein !

vi Wohl mir, dass ich Jesum habe !
O wie feste halt ich ihn,
Dass er mir mein Herze labe,
Wenn ich krank und traurig bin.
Jesum hab ich, der mich liebet
Und sein Leben für mich giebet.
Ach ! drum lass ich Jesum nicht,
Wenn mir gleich das Herze bricht.

Fischer-Tümpel.[1]

i Jesu, fondest, dearest treasure,
Jesu, source of joy and Sun,
Jesu, best and purest pleasure,
Jesu, well to Thee is known
That indeed I truly love Thee,
That without Thee life is lonely !
Come, O Jesu, come to me,
Bide with me eternally !

ii Jesu, Refuge, dearest Saviour,
Jesu, hold me in Thy sight,
Jesu, Death's all-conquering Slayer,
Jesu, brightest guiding Light !
How for Thee my lone heart sigheth !
With what love to Thee it crieth !
Come, O come ! for Thee I pine ;
Dearest Jesu, make me Thine !

vi O how dear is Jesu's loving !
Firmly to Him will I cling.
His dear love is e'er removing
Life's dark shadows, smart, and sting.
He is mine and me He loveth,
Him my lonely soul receiveth,
From Him never will I part,
For 'twould break my loving heart.

Tr. C. S. T.

[1] Bd. v. No. 497.

WERDE MUNTER, MEIN GEMÜTHE

Hymn, by Martin Jahn, in nineteen 8-line stanzas (1661).   Melody, by Johann Schop (1642), to ' Werde munter, mein Gemüthe'.

386

i Jesu, meiner Seelen Wonne,
Jesu, meine beste Lust,
Jesu, meine Freuden-Sonne,
Jesu, dir ist ja bewusst,
Wie ich dich so herzlich liebe
Und mich ohne dich betrübe.
Drum, o Jesu, komm zu mir,
Und bleib bei mir für und für.

ii Jesu, mein Hort und Erretter,
Jesu, meine Zuversicht,
Jesu, starker Schlangentreter,
Jesu, meines Lebens-Licht !
Wie verlanget meinem Herzen,
Jesulein, nach dir mit Schmerzen !
Komm, ach komm! ich warte dein,
Komm, o liebstes Jesulein !

xvii Jesus bleibet meine Freude,
Meines Herzens Trost und Saft,
Jesus steuret allem Leide,
Er ist meine Lebens Kraft,
Meiner Augen Lust und Sonne,
Meiner Seelen Schatz und Wonne.
O ! drum lass ich Jesum nicht
Aus dem Herzen und Gesicht.

Fischer-Tümpel.[1]

i Jesu, fondest, dearest treasure,
Jesu, source of joy and Sun,
Jesu, best and purest pleasure,
Jesu, well to Thee is known
That indeed I truly love Thee,
That without Thee life is lonely !
Come, O Jesu, come to me,
Bide with me eternally !

ii Jesu, Refuge, dearest Saviour,
Jesu, hold me in Thy sight,
Jesu, Death's all-conquering Slayer,
Jesu, brightest guiding Light !
How for Thee my lone heart sigheth !
With what love to Thee it crieth !
Come, O come ! for Thee I pine ;
Dearest Jesu, make me Thine !

xvii Jesus all my joy remaineth,
My heart's solace and my Stay,
All my wounds to heal He deigneth,
On Him all my need I lay.
He's my heart's fond hope and treasure,
My soul's rapture, dearest pleasure,
He is with me day and night,
Ever in my heart and sight.

Tr. C. S. T.

[1] Bd. v. No. 497.

WERDE MUNTER, MEIN GEMÜTHE

Hymn, by Johann Rist, in twelve 8-line stanzas (1642).   Melody, by Johann Schop (1642).

387

i Werde munter, mein Gemüthe,
   Und ihr Sinnen, geht herfür,
   Dass ihr preiset Gottes Güte,
   Die er hat gethan an mir :
   Da er mich der ganzen Tag
   Vor so mancher schweren Plag
   Hat erhalten und ergötzet,
   Dass mich Satan nicht verletzet.

iv Dieser Tag ist nun vergangen,
   Die betrübte Nacht bricht an ;
   Es ist hin der Sonne Prangen,
   So uns all erfreuen kann.
   Stehe mir, o Vater bei,
   Dass dein Glanz stets vor mir sei
   Und mein kaltes Herz erhitze,
   Ob ich gleich im Finstern sitze.

* vi Bin ich gleich von dir gewichen,
   Stell ich mich doch wieder ein ;
   Hat uns doch dein Sohn verglichen
   Durch sein Angst und Todespein.
   Ich verleugne nicht die Schuld ;
   Aber deine Gnad und Huld
   Ist viel grösser als die Sünde,
   Die ich stets in mir befinde.

i Sink not yet, my soul, to slumber,
   Wake, my heart, go forth and tell
   All the mercies without number
   That this bygone day befell ;
   Tell how God hath kept afar
   All things that against me war,
   Hath·upheld me and defended,
   And His grace my soul befriended.

iv Now the Light, that nature gladdens,
   And the pomp of day is gone,
   And my heart is tired and saddens
   As the gloomy night comes on.
   Ah then, with Thy changeless light
   Warm and cheer my heart to-night,
   As the shadows round me gather
   Keep me close to Thee, my Father.

vi Have I e'er from Thee departed,
   Now I seek Thy face again,
   And Thy Son, the loving-hearted,
   Made our peace through bitter pain.
   Yes, far greater than our sin,
   Though it still be strong within,
   Is the love that fails us never,
   Mercy that endures for ever.

U.L.S. 537.

Tr. Catherine Winkworth.[1]

[1] *Lyra Germanica* (2nd Series), p. 78.

WERDE MUNTER, MEIN GEMÜTHE

Hymn, by Martin Jahn, in nineteen 8-line stanzas (1661).   Melody, by Johann Schop (1642), to 'Werde munter, mein Gemüthe'.

388

i Jesu, meiner Seelen Wonne,
   Jesu, meine beste Lust,
   Jesu, meine Freuden-Sonne,
   Jesu, dir ist ja bewusst,
   Wie ich dich so herzlich liebe
   Und mich ohne dich betrübe.
   Drum, o Jesu, komm zu mir.
   Und bleib bei mir für und für.

ii Jesu, mein Hort und Erretter,
   Jesu, meine Zuversicht,
   Jesu, starker Schlangentreter,
   Jesu, meines Lebens-Licht!
   Wie verlanget meinem Herzen,
   Jesulein, nach dir mit Schmerzen!
   Komm, ach komm! ich warte dein,
   Komm, o liebstes Jesulein!

vi Wohl mir, dass ich Jesum habe!
   O wie feste halt ich ihn,
   Dass er mir mein Herze labe,
   Wenn ich krank und traurig bin.
   Jesum hab ich, der mich liebet
   Und sein Leben für mich giebet.
   Ach! drum lass ich Jesum nicht,
   Wenn mir gleich das Herze bricht.

Fischer-Tümpel.[1]

i Jesu, fondest, dearest treasure,
   Jesu, source of joy and Sun,
   Jesu, best and purest pleasure,
   Jesu, well to Thee is known
   That indeed I truly love Thee,
   That without Thee life is lonely!
   Come, O Jesu, come to me,
   Bide with me eternally!

ii Jesu, Refuge, dearest Saviour,
   Jesu, hold me in Thy sight,
   Jesu, Death's all-conquering Slayer,
   Jesu, brightest guiding Light!
   How for Thee my lone heart sigheth!
   With what love to Thee it crieth!
   Come, O come! for Thee I pine;
   Dearest Jesu, make me Thine!

vi O how dear is Jesu's loving!
   Firmly to Him will I cling.
   His dear love is e'er removing
   Life's dark shadows, smart, and sting.
   He is mine and me He loveth,
   Him my lowly soul receiveth,
   From Him never will I part,
   For 'twould break my loving heart.

Tr. C. S. T.

[1] Bd. v. No. 497.

416

WIE BIST DU, SEELE, IN MIR SO GAR BETRÜBT

Hymn, by Tobias Zeutschner, in six 4-line stanzas (c. 1699). Melody, anonymous (1675), to 'O Weltregierer der von dem Himmel schaut'.

389

* **Bach has a** 𝆏 **here.**

i Wie bist du, Seele, in mir so gar betrübt?
  Dein Heiland lebet, der dich ja treulich liebt.
  Ergieb dich gänzlich seinem Willen,
  Er kann allein dein Trauern stillen.

ii Bist du in Nöthen, ach harre nur auf Gott,
  Ihm dich vertraue in Seel und Leibes Noth.
  Der vormals Herzens-Angst gewendet,
  Der ists, der noch dir Hülfe sendet.

iv Bist du in Jesu, in deinem Heiland, reich,
  Kein Kaiser, König ist diesem Reichthum gleich.
  Hast du nicht, was dich hier ergötzet,
  G'nug! wenn der Himmel dies ersetzet.

vi Drum, liebe Seele, wirf alles Trauern hin,
  Geduldig leide, nicht kränke deinen Sinn.
  Ergiebst du dich hier Gottes Willen,
  Dort wird er dich mit Freud erfüllen.

Fischer-Tümpel.[1]

i Why art, within me, my spirit, so downcast?
  Thy Saviour liveth, Whose love doth hold thee fast.
  To Him give ear, thy will resigning,
  Be sure He'll answer thy repining.

ii Art thou in trouble, then take thy plaint to God,
  Both soul and body, for well He knows their need.
  He Who of old felt pain and anguish
  Will never suffer thee to languish.

iv Art not in Jesus, thy blessèd Saviour, rich?
  Has earth a sovereign who wieldeth power such?
  Hast not here what flesh satisfieth?
  Take heart! thee heaven one day receiveth.

vi Then, O my spirit, put all thy cares aside!
  Patient in suffering, content and cheerful bide!
  If here God's word Thou loyal fulfillest,
  Then Heaven will give thee joy the richest.

Tr. C. S. T.

[1] Bd. v. No. 486.

WIE SCHÖN LEUCHTET DER MORGENSTERN

Hymn, by Philipp Nicolai, in seven 12-line stanzas (1599).   Melody, by (?) Nicolai (1599).

390

i Wie schön leuchtet der Morgenstern
Voll Gnad und Wahrheit von dem Herrn,
Die süsse Wurzel Jesse !
Du Sohn Davids aus Jakobs Stamm,
Mein König und mein Bräutigam,
Hast mir mein Herz besessen :
Lieblich,
Freundlich,
Schön und herrlich,
Gross und ehrlich,
Reich von Gaben,
Hoch und sehr prächtig erhaben.

v Herr Gott Vater, mein starker Held,
Du hast mich ewig vor der Welt
In deinem Sohn geliebet ;
Dein Sohn hat mich ihm selbst vertraut :
Er ist mein Schatz, ich bin sein Braut,
Sehr hoch in ihm erfreuet.
Eia,
Eia.
Himmlisch Leben
Wird er geben
Mir dort oben :
Ewig soll mein Herz ihn loben.

* vi Zwingt die Saiten in Cithara
Und lasst die süsse Musica
Ganz freudenreich erschallen,
Dass ich möge mit Jesulein,
Dem wunderschönen Bräutgam mein,
In steter Liebe wallen.
Singet,
Springet ;
Jubilieret,
Triumphieret ;
Dankt dem Herren :
Gross ist der König der Ehren.

i How brightly shines yon Morning Star
Whose beams shed blessing near and far,
The Stem whence Jesse sprang forth !
Great David's Son of Jacob's line,
My King and Bridegroom, He is mine,
My love on Him is poured forth.
Glorious !
Gracious !
Fair ! Victorious !
Great honorious !
Rich in blessing,
Power supreme and might possessing !

v O God, Thou Champion of our race,
Who e'er from time's remotest space
Through Thy dear Son hast loved me,
Jesus hath given me His dear heart,
I am of Him so close a part,
My soul in Him is happy.
Glory !
Glory !
O the wonder !
Jesus yonder
Calls me to Him
Evermore to love and praise Him !

vi The strings attune, the organs sound,
Be all our joy with music crowned,
In gladness voices blending !
Lord Jesus deigns with us to mate,
A heavenly Bridegroom passing sweet,
In union never ending !
Sing ye,
Speed ye !
Joyful be ye !
Triumph sound ye !
Tell the story :
Great is He, the King of Glory !

WIE SCHÖN LEUCHTET DER MORGENSTERN

Hymn, by Philipp Nicolai, in seven 12-line stanzas (1599).   Melody, by (?) Nicolai (1599).

391

i Wie schön leuchtet der Morgenstern
  Voll Gnad und Wahrheit von dem Herrn,
  Die süsse Wurzel Jesse !
  Du Sohn Davids aus Jakobs Stamm,
  Mein König und mein Bräutigam,
  Hast mir mein Herz besessen :
  Lieblich,
  Freundlich,
  Schön und herrlich,
  Gross und ehrlich,
  Reich von Gaben,
  Hoch und sehr prächtig erhaben.

iii Geuss sehr tief in mein Herz hinein,
  Du heller Jaspis und Rubin,
  Die Flamme deiner Liebe :
  Und erfreu mich, dass ich doch bleib
  An deinem auserwählten Leib
  Ein lebendige Rippe.
  Nach dir
  Ist mir,
  Süss und holde
  Himmelsrose !
  Krank und glimmet
  Mein Herz, durch Liebe verwundet.

iv Von Gott kommt mir ein Freudenschein,
  Wenn du mit deinen Aeugelein
  Mich freundlich thust anblicken.
  O Herr Jesu, mein trautes Gut !
  Dein Wort, dein Geist, dein Leib und Blut
  Mich innerlich erquicken.
  Nimm mich
  Freundlich
  In dein Arme,
  Dass ich warme
  Werd von Gnaden :
  Auf dein Wort komm ich geladen.

i O Morning Star, how fair and bright
  Thou beamest forth in truth and light !
  O Sovereign meek and lowly,
  Thou Root of Jesse, David's Son,
  My Lord and Bridegroom, Thou hast won
  My heart to serve Thee solely !
  Holy !
  Holy !
  Thou art glorious,
  All victorious,
  Rich in blessing,
  Rule and might o'er all possessing.

iii Thou Heavenly Brightness ! Light Divine !
  O deep within my heart now shine,
  And make Thee there an altar !
  Fill me with joy and strength to be
  Thy member, ever joined to Thee
  In love that cannot falter ;
  Loving
  Longing
  Doth possess me,
  Turn and bless me,
  For Thy gladness
  Eye and heart here pine in sadness.

iv But if Thou look on me in love,
  There straightway falls from God above
  A ray of purest pleasure ;
  Thy Word and Spirit, Flesh and Blood,
  Refresh my soul with heavenly food,
  Thou art my hidden treasure ;
  Let Thy
  Mercy
  Warm and cheer me !
  O draw near me.
  Thou hast taught us
  Thee to seek since Thou hast sought us.

U.L.S. 437.

Tr. Catherine Winkworth.[1]

[1] *Chorale Book for England* (Lond. 1865), No. 149.

419

WIE SCHÖN LEUCHTET DER MORGENSTERN

Hymn, by Philipp Nicolai, in seven 12-line stanzas (1599).   Melody, by (?) Nicolai (1599).

392

i Wie schön leuchtet der Morgenstern
Voll Gnad und Wahrheit von dem Herrn,
Die süsse Wurzel Jesse !
Du Sohn Davids aus Jakobs Stamm,
Mein König und mein Bräutigam,
Hast mir mein Herz besessen :
Lieblich,
Freundlich,
Schön und herrlich,
Gross und ehrlich,
Reich von Gaben,
Hoch und sehr prächtig erhaben.

iv Von Gott kommt mir ein Freudenschein,
Wenn du mit deinen Aeugelein
Mich freundlich thust anblicken.
O Herr Jesu, mein trautes Gut !
Dein Wort, dein Geist, dein Leib und Blut
Mich innerlich erquicken.
Nimm mich
Freundlich
In dein Arme,
Dass ich warme
Werd von Gnaden :
Auf dein Wort komm ich geladen.

vii Wie bin ich doch so herzlich froh,
Dass mein Schatz ist das A und O,
Der Anfang und das Ende :
Er wird mich doch zu seinem Preis
Aufnehmen in das Paradeis ;
Dess klopf ich in die Hände.
Amen !
Amen !
Komm du schöne
Freudenkrone,
Bleib nicht lange :
Deiner wart ich mit Verlangen.

i How brightly shines yon Morning Star
Whose beams shed blessing near and far,
The Stem whence Jesse sprang forth !
Great David's Son of Jacob's line,
My King and Bridegroom, He is mine,
My love on Him is poured forth.
Glorious !
Gracious !
Fair ! Victorious !
Great, honorious !
Rich in blessing,
Power supreme and might possessing !

iv Upon me God hath deigned to shine
In favour and with love divine,
My soul with rapture filling.
Thy Word and Spirit, Flesh and Blood,
Are now, O Lord, my heavenly food,
Strength in my soul instilling.
Friendly
Treat me,
Warm and cheer me,
Ever hold me
In Thy fealty,
Constant to Thy Word e'er keep me !

vii On Jesus all my love is cast,
With joy I hail Him, First and Last,
Beginning and the Ending.
He calls on me to sing His praise
And live with Him in Paradise,
My life to Him commending.
Amen !
Amen !
O come quickly,
Thou'rt my Glory !
Let me meet Thee !
All my soul goes forth to greet Thee.

Tr. C. S. T.

WIE SCHÖN LEUCHTET DER MORGENSTERN

Hymn, by Philipp Nicolai, in seven 12-line stanzas (1599).   Me'ody, by (?) Nicolai (1599).

393

[Horn I.II. obbligati]

i Wie schön leuchtet der Morgenstern
Voll Gnad und Wahrheit von dem Herrn,
Die süsse Wurzel Jesse !
Du Sohn Davids aus Jakobs Stamm,
Mein König und mein Bräutigam,
Hast mir mein Herz besessen :
Lieblich,
Freundlich,
Schön und herrlich,
Gross und ehrlich,
Reich von Gaben,
Hoch und sehr prächtig erhaben.

vi Zwingt die Saiten in Cithara
Und lasst die süsse Musica
Ganz freudenreich erschallen,
Dass ich möge mit Jesulein,
Dem wunderschönen Bräutgam mein,
In steter Liebe wallen.
Singet,
Springet ;
Jubilieret,
Triumphieret ;
Dankt dem Herren :
Gross ist der König der Ehren.

* vii Wie bin ich doch so herzlich froh,
Dass mein Schatz ist das A und O,
Der Anfang und das Ende :
Er wird mich doch zu seinem Preis
Aufnehmen in das Paradeis ;
Dess klopf ich in die Hände.
Amen !
Amen !
Komm du schöne
Freudenkrone,
Bleib nicht lange :
Deiner wart ich mit Verlangen.

i How brightly shines yon Morning Star
Whose beams shed blessing near and far,
The Stem whence Jesse sprang forth !
Great David's Son of Jacob's line,
My King and Bridegroom, He is mine,
My love on Him is poured forth.
Glorious !
Gracious !
Fair ! Victorious !
Great, honorious !
Rich in blessing,
Power supreme and might possessing !

vi The strings attune, the organs sound,
Be all our joy with music crowned,
With gladness voices blending !
Lord Jesus deigns with us to mate,
A heavenly Bridegroom passing sweet,
In union never ending !
Sing ye,
Speed ye !
Joyful be ye !
Triumph sound ye !
Tell the story :
Great is He, the King of Glory !

vii On Jesus all my love is cast,
With joy I hail Him, First and Last,
Beginning and the Ending.
He calls on me to sing His praise
And live with Him in Paradise,
My life to Him commending.
Amen !
Amen !
O come quickly,
Thou'rt my Glory !
Let me meet Thee !
All my soul goes forth to greet Thee.

U.L.S. 437.

Tr. C. S. T.

WIE SCHÖN LEUCHTET DER MORGENSTERN

Hymn, by Philipp Nicolai, in seven 12-line stanzas (1599). Melody, by (?) Nicolai (1599).

394

[Violin Obbligato]

i Wie schön leuchtet der Morgenstern
Voll Gnad und Wahrheit von dem Herrn,
Die süsse Wurzel Jesse !
Du Sohn Davids aus Jakobs Stamm,
Mein König und mein Bräutigam,
Hast mir mein Herz besessen :
Lieblich,
Freundlich,
Schön und herrlich,
Gross und ehrlich,
Reich von Gaben,
Hoch und sehr prächtig erhaben.

* iv Von Gott kommt mir ein Freudenschein,
Wenn du mit deinen Aeugelein
Mich freundlich thust anblicken.
O Herr Jesu, mein trautes Gut !
Dein Wort, dein Geist, dein Leib und Blut
Mich innerlich erquicken.
Nimm mich
Freundlich
In dein Arme,
Dass ich warme
Werd von Gnaden :
Auf dein Wort komm ich geladen.

vii Wie bin ich doch so herzlich froh,
Dass mein Schatz ist das A und O,
Der Anfang und das Ende.
Er wird mich doch zu seinem Preis
Aufnehmen in das Paradeis ;
Dess klopf ich in die Hände.
Amen !
Amen !
Komm du schöne
Freudenkrone,
Bleib nicht lange :
Deiner wart ich mit Verlangen.

i How brightly shines yon Morning Star
Whose beams shed blessing near and far,
The Stem whence Jesse sprang forth !
Great David's Son of Jacob's line,
My King and Bridegroom, He is mine,
My love on Him is poured forth.
Glorious !
Gracious !
Fair ! Victorious
Great, honorious !
Rich in blessing,
Power supreme and might possessing !

iv Upon me God hath deigned to shine
In favour and with love divine,
My soul with rapture filling.
Thy Word and Spirit, Flesh and Blood,
Are now, O Lord, my heavenly food,
Strength in my soul instilling.
Friendly
Treat me.
Warm and cheer me,
Ever hold me
In Thy fealty,
Constant to Thy Word e'er keep me !

vii On Jesus all my love is cast,
With joy I hail Him, First and Last,
Beginning and the Ending.
He calls on me to sing His praise
And live with Him in Paradise,
My life to Him commending.
Amen !
Amen !
O come quickly !
Thou'rt my Glory !
Let me meet Thee !
All my soul goes forth to greet Thee.

Tr. C. S. T.

U.L.S. 437.

WIR CHRISTENLEUT

Hymn, by Christoph Runge, in eight 6-line stanzas (1653). Melody, by (?) Caspar Fuger, the younger (1593), to 'Wir Christenleut'.

395

i Lasst Furcht und Pein (*bis*)
  Weit von euch sein,
  Denn ich will euch jetzt grosse Freud anzeigen,
  Und mein Bericht
  Will diese Pflicht,
  Dass ihr zu dem sollt Herz und Ohren neigen.

* iv Seid froh, dieweil (*bis*)
  Jetzt euer Heil
  Ist heut ein Gott und auch ein Mensch geboren :
  Der, welcher ist
  Der Herr und Christ,
  In Davids Stadt von vielen auserkoren.

vii Dank sag ich dir (*bis*),
  O meine Zier,
  Dass du ein Mensch, als ich war ganz verloren,
  Ach mir zu gut,
  In Fleisch und Blut
  Gekommen, bist also ein Mensch geboren.

Fischer-Tümpel.[1]

i Let fear and pain, (*bis*)
  No more remain !
  Good tidings of great joy I bring to all men.
  Now what I tell
  Consider well :
  Incline your ears and let your hearts sing ' Amen '.

iv Give praise and sing ! (*bis*)
  Salvation's King
  From heaven to earth as mortal man's descended.
  He lies, ye wist,
  Both Man and Christ,
  In David's city fair mid oxen tended.

vii Now, thanks and praise (*bis*)
  To Thee we raise,
  Who as a Man art born to come among us.
  How wondrous good !
  Our flesh and blood
  Thou bear'st, salvation evermore to win us.

Tr. C. S. T.

[1]Bd. iii. No. 514.

WIR CHRISTENLEUT

Hymn, by Caspar Fuger, in five 6-line stanzas (1592).   Melody, by (?) Caspar Fuger, the younger (1593).

396

i Wir Christenleut (*bis*)
  Habn jetzund Freud,
  Weil uns zu Trost ist Christus Mensch geboren,
  Hat uns erlöst.
  Wer sich dess tröst
  Und glaubet fest, soll nicht werden verloren.

ii Ein Wunderfreud ! (*bis*)
  Gott selbst wird heut
  Von Maria ein wahrer Mensch geboren.
  Ein Jungfrau zart
  Sein Mutter ward,
  Von Gott dem Herren selbst dazu erkoren.

* iii Die Sünd macht Leid ; (*bis*)
  Christus bringt Freud,
  Weil er zu uns in diese Welt ist kommen.
  Mit uns ist Gott
  Nun in der Noth :
  Wer ist, der uns als Christen kann verdammen ?

U.L.S. 57.

i Come, Christian folk, (*bis*)
  Your joy be spoke,
  For Christ is born and man salvation bringeth.
  Who to Him cleaves,
  In faith believes,
  Shall never die, but life in heaven receiveth.

ii How wonderful ! (*bis*)
  To do His will
  God's Son as Man is come from heaven among us.
  He's born the Child
  Of maiden mild,
  Whom God of old did choose, His mother glorious.

iii Sin's wage is death ! (*bis*)
  But Christ brings life ;
  To us God from His throne hath sent salvation.
  He's on our side
  When ills betide.
  The Christian none shall bring to condemnation.

Tr. C. S. T.

WIR CHRISTENLEUT

Hymn, by Caspar Fuger, in five 6-line stanzas (1592).   Melody, by (?) Caspar Fuger, the younger (1593).

397

i Wir Christenleut (*bis*)
 Habn jetzund Freud,
 Weil uns zu Trost ist Christus Mensch geboren,
 Hat uns erlöst.
 Wer sich dess tröst
 Und glaubet fest, soll nicht werden verloren.

iv Drum sag ich Dank (*bis*)
 Mit dem Gesang
 Christo dem Herrn, der uns zu gut Mensch
  worden,
 Dass wir durch ihn
 Nun all los sein
 Der Sünden Last und unträglichen Bürden.

* v Hallelujah ! (*bis*)
 Gelobt sei Gott !
 Singen wir all aus unsers Herzens Grunde :
 Denn Gott hat heut
 Gemacht solch Freud,
 Der wir vergessen solln zu keiner Stunde.

                    U.L.S. 57.

i Come, Christian folk, (*bis*)
 Your joy be spoke
 For Christ is born and man salvation bringeth.
 Who to Him cleaves,
 In faith believes,
 Shall never die, but life in heaven receiveth.

iv Wherefore give praise ! (*bis*)
 Your voices raise
 To God as Child of man on earth conceivèd !
 For we from sin
 Release shall win,
 And from its burden ever be relievèd.

v Alleluja ! (*bis*)
 Give thanks to God !
 Sing out with heart and voice, all people living !
 For God's dear Son
 Salvation's won :
 So evermore to Him be praise unceasing !

                    Tr. C. S. T.

WIR GLAUBEN ALL AN EINEN GOTT, SCHÖPFER

Hymn, by Martin Luther, a free version of the Nicene Creed, in three 10-line stanzas (1524). Melody, from the plainsong of the 'Credo' (1524).

WIR GLAUBEN ALL AN EINEN GOTT, SCHÖPFER

i wah - - ren, Al - lem Un - fall will er weh - ren, Kein
ii bo - - ren Durch den Heil - gen Geist im Glau - ben; Für
iii e - - ben; Hie all Sünd ver - ge - ben wer - den. Das

i vides us, Thro' all snares and per - ils leads us, Wat - -
ii mo - - ther, That lost man might life in - her - - it; Made
iii mun - - ion. We be - lieve our sins for - giv - - en, And

i Leid soll uns wi - der - fah - - ren. Er sor -
ii uns, die wir warn ver - lo - - ren, Am Kreuz
iii Fleisch soll auch wie - der le - - ben: Nach die.

i -ches that no harm be - tides - - us; He car - - - - -
ii true Man, our Eld - er Bro - - ther, Was cru - - - - -
iii that life with God in heav - - en, When we

i - - get für uns, hüt und -
ii - - ge - stor - ben, und vom
iii - - sem E - lend ist be -

i - - eth for - us, day and
ii - - ci - fi - èd for man's
iii - - are raised up, shall be

i wacht; Es steht al - - les in sei - ner Macht.
ii Tod Wie - der auf - er - stand - en durch Gott.
iii reit Uns ein Le - ben in E - wig - keit.[1]

i night, All things are gov - ern'd by His might.
ii sin, And rais'd by God to life a - gain.
iii ours, Our por - tion in e - ter - ni - ty.[2]

[1] *U.L.S.* 253.   [2] *Chorale Book for England* (Lond. 1865).   App. vi.

WO GOTT DER HERR NICHT BEI UNS HÄLT

Hymn, by Johann Gigas (Heune), in six 7-line stanzas (1561).   Melody, anonymous (1535), to ' Wo Gott der Herr '.

399

i Ach, lieben Christen, seid getrost :
  Wie thut ihr so verzagen,
  Weil uns der Herr heimsuchen thut ?
  Lasst uns von Herzen sagen :
  Die Straf wir wohl verdienet han !
  Solches bekenn ein jedermann ;
  Niemand darf sich ausschliessen.

iii Kein Frucht das Waizenkörnlein bringt,
  Es fall denn in die Erden :
  So muss auch unser irdisch Leib
  Zu Staub und Aschen werden,
  Eh er kommt zu der Herrlichkeit,
  Die du uns, Herr Christ, hast bereit
  Durch deinen Gang zum Vater.

* vi Wir wachen oder schlafen ein ;
  So sind wir ja des Herren !
  Auf Christum wir getaufet sein ;
  Der kann dem Satan wehren.
  Durch Adam auf uns kommt der Tod :
  Christus hilft uns aus aller Noth ;
  Drum loben wir den Herren.

U.L.S. 577.

i Now comfort take, good Christians all !
  Why stand ye so dejected ?
  What though our God now chasteneth us
  Who have His counsels flouted ?
  How justly falls His chastening hand
  Our hearts, now contrite, understand
  And bow to His correcting.

iii E'en as to earth the grain doth fall
  That soon to harvest riseth,
  So must our body vile decay
  As in earth's care it lieth ;
  Thence glorified it soon shall fly
  To those far mansions in the sky
  Where Christ hath gone before us.

vi For, though we wake and though we sleep,
  The Lord will ever shield us ;
  Who hath baptized us faith will keep,
  To Satan will not yield us.
  Through Adam's sin death on us came ;
  But Christ the Victim's borne the blame.
  Praise God, then, for His goodness !

Tr. C. S. T.

WO GOTT DER HERR NICHT BEI UNS HÄLT

Hymn, by Johann Gigas (Heune), in six 7-line stanzas (1561). Melody, anonymous (1535), to 'Wo Gott der Herr'.

i Ach, lieben Christen, seid getrost :
  Wie thut ihr so verzagen,
  Weil uns der Herr heimsuchen thut ?
  Lasst uns von Herzen sagen :
  Die Straf wir wohl verdienet han !
  Solches bekenn ein jedermann ;
  Niemand darf sich ausschliessen.

vi Wir wachen oder schlafen ein,
  So sind wir ja des Herren !
  Auf Christum wir getaufet sein ;
  Der kann dem Satan wehren.
  Durch Adam auf uns kommt der Tod ;
  Christus hilft uns aus aller Noth ;
  Drum loben wir den Herren.

vii Gelobt sei Gott im höchsten Thron,
  Der Vater aller Gnaden,
  Der uns aus Lieb gegeben hat
  Sein Sohn für unsern Schaden ;
  Gelobt der Tröster Heilig Geist :
  Wollt uns am letzten End beistehn,
  Und helf uns selig sterben.

U.L.S. 577.

i Now comfort take, good Christians all !
  Why stand ye so dejected ?
  What though our God now chasteneth us
  Who have His counsels flouted ?
  How justly falls His chastening hand
  Our hearts, now contrite, understand
  And bow to His correcting.

vi For, though we wake and though we sleep,
  The Lord will ever shield us ;
  Who hath baptized us faith will keep,
  To Satan will not yield us.
  Through Adam's sin death on us came ;
  But Christ the Victim's borne the blame.
  Praise God, then, for His goodness !

vii So, praise our God on heaven's far throne,
  The Father of all blessing,
  Whose love hath given us His dear Son
  To bear our sin and suffering !
  And praisèd be the Holy Ghost
  Who guideth when we need it most !
  May we in death confess Him !

Tr. C. S. T.

WO GOTT DER HERR NICHT BEI UNS HÄLT

Hymn, by Martin Luther, a version of Psalm cxxiv in three 7-line stanzas (1524).   Melody, anonymous (1535).

401

Psalm cxxiv.

i Wär Gott nicht mit uns diese Zeit,
  So soll Israel sagen,
  Wär Gott nicht mit uns diese Zeit :
  Wir hätten musst verzagen,
  Die so ein armes Häuflein sind,
  Veracht von so viel Menschenkind,
  Die an uns setzen alle.

ii Auf uns so zornig ist ihr Sinn :
   Wo Gott hätt das zugeben,
   Verschlungen hälten sie uns hin
   Mit ganzem Leib und Leben ;
   Wir wärn, als die ein Fluth ersäuft
   Und über die gross Wasser läuft
   Und mit Gewalt verschwemmet.

iii Gott Lob und Dank, der nicht zugab,
    Dass ihr Schlund uns möcht fangen.
    Wie ein Vogel des Stricks kommt ab,
    Ist unser Seel entgangen.
    Strick ist entzwei und wir sind frei :
    Des Herren Name steht uns bei,
    Des Gottes Himm'ls und Erden.

i If God were not upon our side,
  Let Israel declare it ;
  If God were not upon our side
  We had been all dismayèd.
  A poor, a lowly flock are we,
  'Gainst whom the world rails mightily
  And sets in anger on us.

ii Their wrath so mighty 'gainst us rose,
   We quickly had been swallowed,
   Both life and limb had ta'en our foes
   Who madly on us followed.
   We were as men by waters drowned,
   Or they in ships no line may sound,
   By angry storm-seas tumbled !

iii But thanks to God Whose might doth close
    The lion's mouth that gapèd !
    As from a snare the bird uprose,
    So is our soul escapèd.
    The snare's in twain, we're free again !
    Stands fast and true the Lord's great name :
    O'er earth and heaven He reigneth !

U.L.S. 250.

Tr. C. S. T.

WO GOTT DER HERR NICHT BEI UNS HÄLT

Hymn, by Justus Jonas, a version of Psalm cxxiv, in eight 7-line stanzas (1524).   Melody, anonymous (1535).

402

Psalm cxxiv.

i Wo Gott der Herr nicht bei uns hält,
  Wenn unsre Feinde toben,
  Und er unser Sach nicht zufällt
  Im Himmel hoch dort oben ;
  Wo er Israels Schutz nicht ist
  Und selber bricht der Feinde List :
  So ists mit uns verloren.

* vii Die Feind sind all in deiner Hand,
  Dazu all ihr Gedanken ;
  Ihr Anschlag ist dir wohl bekannt :
  Hilf nur, dass wir nicht wanken.
  Vernunft wider den Glauben siecht,
  Aufs künftig will sie trauen nicht,
  Da du wirst selber trösten.

* viii Den Himmel und auch die Erden
  Hast du, Herr Gott, gegründet :
  Dein Licht lass uns helle werden,
  Das Herz uns werd entzündet,
  In rechter Lieb des Glaubens dein
  Bis an das End beständig sein ;
  Die Welt lass immer murren.

U.L.S. 254.

i Had not the Lord been on our side
  When foemen rudely mocked us,
  And had He not their plots defied
  As from on high He watched us,
  Had He Israel's shield not been
  And made our cause to victory lean,
  We had been all destroyèd.

vii Our foes, great God, are in Thy hand,
  Wherefore our praise we give Thee.
  Their evil arts dost Thou withstand,
  Help Thou our need we pray Thee !
  'Tis Faith 'gainst Reason war doth wage :
  No weapon is her heritage
  But trust in Thy great mercy.

viii The heaven above, the earth below,
  Hast Thou, O Lord, both founded.
  A kindly light upon us show,
  Nor let us be confounded.
  Inflame our hearts with love to Thee
  Until life's end, eternally ;
  So, let the world deride us !

Tr. C. S. T.

WO GOTT DER HERR NICHT BEI UNS HÄLT

Hymn, by Justus Jonas, a version of Psalm cxxiv, in eight 7-line stanzas (1524)   Melody, anonymous (1535).

403

Psalm cxxiv.

i Wo Gott der Herr nicht bei uns hält,
  Wenn unsre Feinde toben,
  Und er unser Sach nicht zufällt
  Im Himmel hoch dort oben ;
  Wo er Israels Schutz nicht ist
  Und selber bricht der Feinde List :
  So ists mit uns verloren.

ii Was Menschenkraft und Witz anfäht,
  Soll uns billig nicht schrecken :
  Er sitzet an der höchsten Stätt ;
  Der wird ihrn Rath aufdecken,
  Wenn sie's aufs klügste greifen an,
  So geht doch Gott ein ander Bahn ;
  Es steht in seinen Händen.

iv Sie stellen uns wie Ketzern nach,
  Zu unserm Blut sie trachten ;
  Noch rühmen sie sich Christen hoch,
  Die Gott allein gross achten :
  Ach Gott, der theure Name dein
  Muss ihrer Schalkheit Deckel sein !
  Du wirst einmal aufwachen.

v Aufsperren sie den Rachen weit
  Und wollen uns verschlingen ;
  Lob und Dank sei Gott allezeit :
  Es wird ihn nicht gelingen.
  Er wird ihr Strick zerreissen gar
  Und stürzen ihre falsche Lahr :
  Sie werden Gott nicht wehren.

U.L.S. 254.

i Had not the Lord been on our side
  When foemen rudely mocked us,
  And had He not their plots defied
  As from on high He watched us,
  Had he Israel's shield not been
  And made our cause to victory lean,
  We had been all destroyèd.

ii No wit of man or mortal might
  To dread or fear can move us.
  God sitteth crowned upon the height
  And giveth comfort to us.
  When crafty plots the foemen lay,
  Their schemings God will swift dismay,
  And to His keeping take us.

iv They name us heretics in scorn
  And for our life they clamour.
  Yet Christians all of them were born
  And call our God their Saviour.
  O God, that sacred name of Thine
  Doth cover their unjust design ;
  Thou wilt not let it prosper !

v Their grinning jaws are open wide,
  Their timid prey to swallow.
  But thanks to God, in Whom we bide,
  Their arts are known and shallow.
  He will their planning overthrow
  Nor let their plots to harvest grow ;
  They never shall maintain them.

Tr. C. S. T.

WO GOTT DER HERR NICHT BEI UNS HÄLT

Hymn, by (?) David Denicke, in ten 7-line stanzas (1646).   Melody, anonymous (1535), to ' Wo Gott der Herr'.

404

[Trumpets I.II. Obbligati.]

i O Gott, der du aus Herzengrund
Die Menschen Kinder liebest,
Und uns zu aller Zeit und Stund
Viel Gutes reichlich giebest :
Wir danken dir, dass deine Treu
Bei uns ist alle Morgen neu
In unserm ganzen Leben.

* ix Lass deine Kirch und unser Land
Der Engel Schutz empfinden,
Dass Fried und Heil in allem Stand
Sich bei uns möge finden ;
Lass sie des Teufels Mord und List,
Und was sein Reich und Anhang ist,
Durch deine Kraft zerstören.

* x Zuletzt lass sie an unserm End
Den Satan von uns jagen,
Und unsre Seel in deine Hand
Und Abrahams Schoos tragen,
Da alles Heer dein Lob erklingt
Und Heilig ! Heilig ! Heilig ! singt
Ohn einiges aufhören.

Fischer-Tümpel.[1]

i O God, Who plenteous founts of love
Upon Thy children pourest,
And in Thy mansions fair above
Rich treasure for them storest,
We thank Thee, Who art good and true,
Whose mercies every morning flow,
And fall in showers upon us !

ix Grant us, O Lord, Thine angel band
May have us in their keeping,
Bring joy and peace on every hand,
Nor e'er be far or sleeping :
O let them curb the devil's might
And drive him powerless from sight,
E'er in Thy strength prevailing.

x And when at last Death sounds his call,
From Satan bid them tear us,
And to Thy presence, one and all,
In heaven above to bear us,
Where every soul Thy praises sings,
Where Holy ! Holy ! Holy ! rings
With ceaseless Allelujas.

Tr. C. S. T.

[1]Bd. ii. No. 370.

WO GOTT ZUM HAUS NICHT GIEBT SEIN GUNST

Hymn, by (?) Johann Kolross, a version of Psalm cxxvii, in five 4-line stanzas (1525). Melody, anonymous (1535)

405

Psalm cxxvii.

i Wo Gott zum Haus nicht giebt sein Gunst,
  So arbeit jedermann umsonst.
  Wo Gott die Stadt nicht selbst bewacht,
  So ist umsonst der Wächter Macht.

iii Nun sind sein Erben unsre Kind,
    Die uns von ihm gegeben sind :
    Gleich wie die Pfeil ins Starken Hand,
    So ist die Jugend Gott bekannt.

iv Es soll und muss dem g'schehen wohl,
   Der dieser hat sein Köcher voll ;
   Sie werden nicht zu Schand noch Spott,
   Vor ihrem Feind bewahrt sie Gott.

v Ehr sei dem Vater und dem Sohn,
  Sammt Heilgem Geist in Einem Thron :
  Welch's ihm auch also sei bereit
  Von nun an bis in Ewigkeit.

i If God withdraweth, all the cost
  And pains that build the house are lost ;
  If God the city doth not keep,
  The watchful guards as well may sleep.

iii 'Tis all in vain till God has blest ;
    He can make rich, yet give us rest.
    Children and friends are blessings too,
    If God our Sovereign make them so.

iv Happy the man to whom He sends
   Obedient children, faithful friends !
   How sweet our daily comforts prove
   When they are seasoned with His love.

v To Father, Son, and Holy Ghost,
  The God Whom heaven's triumphant host
  And suffering saints on earth adore,
  Be glory now and evermore !

U.L.S. 688.

Isaac Watts.[1]

[1] *Psalmodia Germanica* (Lond. 1722), p. 35.

MELODIES WITH CONTINUO
(Figured and Unfigured)

ACH, DASS ICH DIE LETZTE STUNDE

406

Hymn, by Erdmann Neumeister, in six 8-line stanzas (1717). Melody, by Bach (1736).

AUF, AUF, DIE RECHTE ZEIT IST HIER

407

Hymn, by Martin Opitz, in seven 4-line stanzas (1628). (Fischer-Tümpel, i, 293.) Melody, anonymous (1736).

AUF, AUF, MEIN HERZ, MIT FREUDEN

408

Hymn, by Paul Gerhardt, in nine 8-line stanzas (1647). (Fischer-Tümpel, iii, 388.) Melody, by Johann Crüger (1648).

BEGLÜCKTER STAND GETREUER SEELEN

409

Hymn, by Ulrich Bogislaus von Bonin, in eight 8-line stanzas (1727).   Melody, anonymous (1698), to ' Entfernet euch, ihr matten Kräfte'.

BESCHRÄNKT, IHR WEISEN DIESER WELT

410

Hymn, by Christoph Wegleiter, in twelve 10-line stanzas (1703).   (U.L.S. 298).   Melody, by Bach (1736).

BRICH ENTZWEI, MEIN ARMES HERZE

Hymn, by David Trommer, in eight 8-line stanzas (1670). (Fischer-Tümpel, iv, 227.) Melody, anonymous (1715).
The penultimate line is sung thrice and part of the last line is repeated.

BRUNNQUELL ALLER GÜTER

Hymn, by Johann Franck, in eight 8-line stanzas (1653). (U.L.S. 163) Melody, anonymous (1653).

CHRIST LAG IN TODESBANDEN

[See No. 37 supra.]

DAS WALT MEIN GOTT

Hymn, by David von Schweinitz, in twelve 7-line stanzas (1650).   (F.T. iv. 430.)   Melody, found only in Krebs' MS.

DER LIEBEN SONNEN LICHT UND PRACHT

Hymn, by Christian Scriver, in nine 8-line stanzas (1684).   (U.L.S. 508.)   Melody, anonymous (1708).

DER TAG IST HIN, DIE SONNE GEHET NIEDER

Hymn, by Johann Christoph Rube, in nine 4-line stanzas (1714).   Melody (French), 1542

DER TAG MIT SEINEM LICHTE

Hymn, by Paul Gerhardt, in seven 10-line stanzas (1666). (U.L.S. 514.) *Melody, by Jakob Hintze (1670).*

DICH BET ICH AN, MEIN HÖCHSTER GOTT

Hymn, by Johann Gottfried Olearius, in seven 6-line stanzas (1686). Melody, by Bach (1736).

DIE BITTRE LEIDENSZEIT BEGINNET ABERMAL

Hymn, by (?) Heinrich Elmenhorst, in four 9-line stanzas (1681).   Melody, by Joh. Wolfgang Franck (1681).
Part of the last line must be repeated to fit the melody.

DIE GÜLDNE SONNE

Hymn, by Paul Gerhardt, in twelve 10-line stanzas (1666). (U.L.S. 449.) Melody, anonymous (1708).

DIR, DIR, JEHOVAH, WILL ICH SINGEN

Hymn, by Bartholomäus Crasselius, in eight 6-line stanzas (1697). (U.L.S. 556.) Melody, by Bach (1725).

EINS IST NOTH, ACH HERR, DIES EINE

Hymn, by Johann Heinrich Schröder, in ten 8-line stanzas (1697).   *(U.L.S. 302.)*   *Melody, by Bach (1736).*

ERMUNTRE DICH, MEIN SCHWACHER GEIST

[See No. 83 supra.]

ERWÜRGTES LAMM, DAS DIE VERWAHRTEN SIEGEL

424

Hymn, by Ulrich Bogislaus von Bonin, in eight 6-line stanzas (1735).   Melody, anonymous (1704), to 'Mein Freund zerschmelzt'

ES GLÄNZET DER CHRISTEN INWENDIGES LEBEN

425

Hymn, by Christian Fr. Richter, in eight 8-line stanzas (1704).   Melody, anonymous (1704).

ES IST NUN AUS MIT MEINEM LEBEN

Hymn, by Magnus Daniel Omeis, in seven 8-line stanzas (1673). (Fischer-Tümpel, v. 169.) Melody, anonymous (1715).
The last line must be repeated to fit the melody.

ES IST VOLLBRACHT! VERGISS JA NICHT

Hymn, by Joh. Eusebius Schmidt, in six 6-line stanzas (1714). (U.L.S. 96.) Melody, anonymous (1714.

ES KOSTET VIEL, EIN CHRIST ZU SEIN

428

Hymn, by Christian Friedrich Richter, in seven 6-line stanzas (1704). Melody, anonymous (1704).

The last line must be repeated to fit the melody.

GIEB DICH ZUFRIEDEN UND SEI STILLE

429

[See No. 116 *supra*.]

GIEB DICH ZUFRIEDEN UND SEI STILLE

430

[See No. 116 supra.]

GIEB DICH ZUFRIEDEN UND SEI STILLE

431

Hymn, by Paul Gerhardt, in fifteen 7-line stanzas (1666). (U.L.S. 622.) Melody, anonymous (1725).

GIEB DICH ZUFRIEDEN UND SEI STILLE

Hymn, by Paul Gerhardt, in fifteen 7-line stanzas (1666). (U.L.S. 622.) Melody, by Jakob Hintze (1670).

GOTT LEBET NOCH

Hymn, by Joh. Friedrich Zihn, in seven 10-line stanzas (1688). Melody, anonymous (1714)

GOTT, WIE GROSS IST DEINE GÜTE

Hymn, by Georg Christian Schemelli, in four 10-line stanzas (1736).   Melody, by Bach (1736).

HERR CHRIST, DER EINIG GOTTS SOHN

[*See No. 131 supra.*]

HERR, NICHT SCHICKE DEINE RACHE

Hymn, by Martin Opitz, in ten 8-line stanzas (1634). (Fischer-Tümpel, i 297.) Melody, by Louis Bourgeois (1547), to 'Mon Dieu, preste moy l'aureille'.

HIER LIEG ICH NUN, O VATER ALLER GNADEN

Hymn, by Johann Arndt, in six 4-line stanzas (1612). Melody, by Bach (post 1736).

ICH BIN JA, HERR, IN DEINER MACHT

438

Hymn, by Simon Dach, in eight 8-line stanzas (1648). (U.L.S. 825.) Melody, by Heinrich Albert (1648).

ICH FREUE MICH IN DIR

439

Hymn, by Caspar Ziegler, in four 8-line stanzas (1697). (U.L.S. 38.) Melody, anonymous (1646), to ' Gross ist, o grosser Gott'.

ICH HALTE TREULICH STILL

Hymn, by J. H. Till, in twelve 8-line stanzas (1736). Melody, by Bach (1736).

ICH LASS DICH NICHT

Hymn, by Wolfgang Christoph Dessler, in nine 10-line stanzas (1692). (Fischer-Tümpel, v 397.) Melody, anonymous (1727).
The last line of each stanza must be repeated to fit the melody.

ICH LIEBE JESUM ALLE STUND

Hymn, by (?) Georg Christian Schemelli, in six 6-line stanzas (1736).   Melody, anonymous (1736).

The first three syllables of the last line of each stanza must be repeated to fit the melody.

ICH STEH AN DEINER KRIPPEN HIER

Hymn, by Paul Gerhardt, in fifteen 7-line stanzas (1653).   (U.L.S. 39.)   Melody, by Bach (1736).

IHR GESTIRN, IHR HOHEN LÜFTE

444

[See No. 191 supra.]

JESU, DEINE LIEBESWUNDEN

445

Hymn, by 'C. W.', in eight 4-line stanzas (1736). Melody, anonymous (1736).

JESU, JESU, DU BIST MEIN

Hymn, anonymous, in eight 8-line stanzas (1687).   Melody, by Bach (1736)

JESU, MEINES GLAUBENS ZIER

Hymn, by Gottfried Wilhelm Sacer, in five 8-line stanzas (1714)   (Fischer-Tümpel, iv, 620.)   Melody, anonymous (1714).

JESU, MEINES HERZENS FREUD

[*See No. 215 supra.*]

JESUS IST DAS SCHÖNSTE LICHT

Hymn, by Christian Fr. Richter, in nine 8-line stanzas (1704). Melody, anonymous (1704).

JESUS, UNSER TROST UND LEBEN

450

Hymn, by Ernst Christoph Homburg, in eight 7-line stanzas (1659). (Fischer-Tümpel, iv 351.) Melody, anonymous (1714).

KEIN STUNDLEIN GEHT DAHIN

451

Hymn, by Michael Franck, in ten 7-line stanzas (1688). (Fischer-Tümpel, iv 273.) Melody, anonymous (1698).

KOMM, SÜSSER TOD

452

Hymn, anonymous, in ten 7-line stanzas (1725). Melody, by Bach (1736).

KOMMT, SEELEN, DIESER TAG

453

Hymn, by Valentin Ernst Löscher, in seven 8-line stanzas (1713). Melody, by Bach (1736).

KOMMT WIEDER AUS DER FINSTERN GRUFT

Hymn, by Valentin Ernst Löscher, in seven 7-line stanzas (1713). Melody, by Bach (1736).

LASSET UNS MIT JESU ZIEHEN

LASSET UNS MIT JESU ZIEHEN

Hymn, by Siegmund von Birken (Betulius), in four 10-line stanzas (1652). (U.L.S. 767.) Melody, by Johann Schop (1641),
to ' Lasset uns den Herren preisen '.

LIEBES HERZ, BEDENKE DOCH

456

Hymn, by Christian Jakob Koitsch, in nine 8-line stanzas (1714). Melody, anonymous (1714).

LIEBSTER GOTT, WANN WERD ICH STERBEN

457

[See No. 233 supra.]

LIEBSTER HERR JESU, WO BLEIBST DU SO LANGE

458

Hymn, by Christoph Werner, or Christoph Weselovius, in seven 6-line stanzas (1676). *Melody, by Bach* (1736).
The last five syllables of the fifth, and the last three syllables of the last, line of each stanza must be repeated to fit the melody.

LIEBSTER IMMANUEL, HERZOG DER FROMMEN

[*See No. 234 supra.*]

MEIN JESU, DEM DIE SERAPHINEN

Hymn, by Wolfgang Christoph Dessler, in eight 8-line stanzas (1692). (U.L.S. 422.) Melody, anonymous (1704).

MEIN JESU, WAS FÜR SEELENWEH

461

Hymn, by Georg Christian Schemelli, in six 12-line stanzas (1736).   *Melody, by Bach* (1736).

MEINES LEBENS LETZTE ZEIT

462

[See No. 256 supra.]

NICHT SO TRAURIG, NICHT SO SEHR

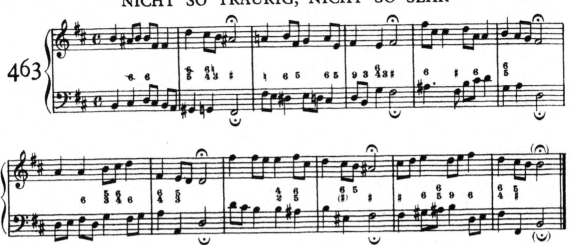

Hymn, by Paul Gerhardt, in fifteen 6-line stanzas (1647). (U.L.S. No. 698.) Melody, anonymous (1714).

NUR MEIN JESUS IST MEIN LEBEN

Hymn, anonymous, in six 12-line stanzas (1698). Melody, anonymous (1698).

O DU LIEBE MEINER LIEBE

Hymn, by Elisabeth von Senitz, in seven 8-line stanzas (1697). (U.L.S. 107, wrongly attributed to Joh. Angelus.) Melody, by (?) Christian Knorr von Rosenroth (1684), to 'Hat der Himmel gleich viel Wege'.

O EWIGKEIT, DU DONNERWORT

[See No. 282 supra.]

O FINSTRE NACHT, WANN WIRST DU DOCH VERGEHEN

Hymn, by Georg Friedrich Breithaupt, in ten 8-line stanzas (1704). Melody, by Bach (1736).

O JESULEIN SÜSS, O JESULEIN MILD

Hymn, by (?) Valentin Thilo, in six 5-line stanzas (1650). Melody, anonymous (1650), to ' Komm, heiliger Geist, mit deiner Genad '.

O LIEBE SEELE, ZIEH DIE SINNEN

Hymn, by (?) Georg Christian Schemelli, in twelve 10-line stanzas (1736). Melody, by Bach (1736).

O WIE SELIG SEID IHR DOCH, IHR FROMMEN

[See No. 310 supra.]

SCHAFFS MIT MIR, GOTT, NACH DEINEM WILLEN

471

Hymn, by Benjamin Schmolck, in eleven 6-line stanzas (1725).   Melody, by Bach (1725).

SEELEN-BRÄUTIGAM

472

[See No. 317 supra.]

SEELENWEIDE

473

Hymn, by Adam Drese, in twelve 6-line stanzas (1695).   Melody, anonymous (1708).

SEI GEGRÜSSET, JESU GÜTIG

[See No. 318 supra.]

SELIG, WER AN JESUM DENKT

Hymn, by 'A. G. B.', in three 7-line stanzas (1736).   Melody, anonymous (1736).

SO GEHST DU NUN, MEIN JESU, HIN

476

Hymn, by Caspar Fr. Nachtenhöfer, in four 10-line stanzas (1667). (U.L.S. 781, with a fifth stanza.) Melody, by (?) Christoph Wagner (1699).

SO GIEBST DU NUN, MEIN JESU, GUTE NACHT

477

[*See No. 321 supra.*]
The last line of each stanza must be repeated to fit the melody.

SO WUNSCH ICH MIR ZU GUTER LETZT

Hymn, by Johann Rist, in fourteen 8-line stanzas (1641).   (Fischer-Tümpel ii. 210.)   Melody, anonymous (1736).

STEH ICH BEI MEINEM GOTT

Hymn, by Johann Daniel Herrnschmidt, in fourteen 8-line stanzas (1714).   Melody, anonymous (1714).

VERGISS MEIN NICHT, DASS ICH DEIN NICHT VERGESSE

480

Hymn, by Gottfried Arnold, in six 7-line stanzas (1697). Melody, anonymous (1698), to 'Wie wohl ist mir, dass ich nunmehr entbunden'.

VERGISS MEIN NICHT

481

Hymn, by (?) Georg Christian Schemelli, in five 7-line stanzas (1736). Melody, by Bach (1736).

The first four syllables of the first line and the whole of the last line in each stanza must be repeated to fit the melody.

WARUM BETRÜBST DU DICH

Stanza, by (?) Bach (1725).   Melody, by Bach (1725).

WAS BIST DU DOCH, O SEELE, SO BETRÜBET

[See No. 350 supra.]

WER NUR DEN LIEBEN GOTT LÄSST WÄLTEN

484

[See No. 378 supra.]

WIE WOHL IST MIR, O FREUND DER SEELEN

485

Hymn, by Wolfgang Christoph Dessler, in six 10-line stanzas (1692). (U.L.S. 438.) Melody, by Bach (1725).

WO IST MEIN SCHÄFLEIN, DAS ICH LIEBE

486

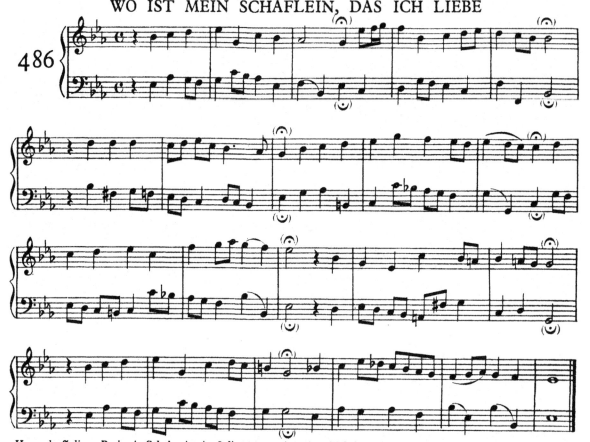

Hymn, by Juliana Patientia Schultt, in nine 8-line stanzas (1701). Melody, anonymous (1698), to ‘ Wo ist der Schönste, den ich liebe ? ’.

WO SOLL ICH FLIEHEN HIN

487

[*See No. 27 supra.*]

MELODIES WITHOUT CONTINUO

GOTT, MEIN HERZ DIR DANK ZUSENDET

488

Hymn, by Emilie Juliane, Countess of Schwarzburg-Rudolstadt, in six 8-line stanzas (1682). (F.T. v. 609.) Melody, by Bach.

ICH G'NÜGE MICH AN MEINEM STANDE

489

Hymn, by Caspar Neumann, in eleven 6-line stanzas. Melody, by Bach.

MEINE SEELE, LASS ES GEHEN

490

Hymn, by Joh. Christoph Rube, in six 6-line stanzas (1712). Melody, by Bach.

APPENDICES

APPENDIX I

CRITICAL NOTES ON THE TEXTS

The following abbreviations are used:

1765 = ' Johann Sebastian Bachs vierstimmige Choralgesänge gesammlet von Carl Philipp Emanuel Bach. Erster Theil. Berlin und Leipzig, gedruckt und zu finden bey Friedrich Wilhelm Birnstiel, Königl. privil. Bucbdrucker, 1765.'

1769 = ' Johann Sebastian Bachs vierstimmige Choralgesänge. Zweyter Theil. Berlin und Leipzig. Gedruckt und zu finden bey Friderich Wilhelm Birnstiel, Königl. privil. Buchdrucker, 1769.'

1784 = ' Johann Sebastian Bachs vierstimmige Choralgesänge. Erster Theil. Leipzig, bey Johann Gottlob Immanuel Breitkopf, 1784.'

1785 = ' Johann Sebastian Bachs vierstimmige Choralgesänge. Zweyter Theil. Leipzig, bey Johann Gottlob Immanuel Breitkopf, 1785.'

1786 = ' Johann Sebastian Bachs vierstimmige Choralgesänge. Dritter Theil. Leipzig, bey Johann Gottlob Immanuel Breitkopf, 1786.'

1787 = ' Johann Sebastian Bachs vierstimmige Choralgesänge. Vierter Theil. Leipzig, bey Johann Gottlob Immanuel Breitkopf, 1787.'

1832 = ' 371 vierstimmige Choralgesänge von Johann Sebastian Bach. Dritte Auflage. Eigenthum der Verleger. Leipzig, bey Breitkopf & Härtel. Pr. 3 Thlr' [n.d., but Vorwort signed by ' C. F. Becker, Organist an der Petrikirche, Leipzig, den 9 December 1831.'

1843 = ' Joh. Seb. Bachs vierstimmige Kirchengesänge. Geordnet und mit einem Vorwort begleitet von C. F. Becker, Organisten an der Nicolaikirche und Lehrer an der Musikschule zu Leipzig. Eingetragen in das Archiv des Vereins. Mit Johann Sebastian Bach's Portrait. Leipzig, 1843. Verlag von Robert Friese.' [The collection was issued in six Parts, 1842–43, and with the general title page quoted here.]

1885 = ' 371 vierstimmige Choralgesänge von Johann Sebastian Bach. Vierte Auflage. Leipzig, Breitkopf & Härtel.' [n.d. The Edition, while it follows 1832, represents a new type-setting. C. F. Becker and A. Dörffel were the editors. The current imprint of this edition was revised by E. Naumann in 1897.]

1892 = Jahrgang XXXIX of ' Johann Sebastian Bach's Werke. Herausgegeben von der Bach-Gesellschaft zu Leipzig.' [The volume, edited by F. Wüllner, contains Bach's ' Choräle, Lieder und Arien.' The Vorwort is dated ' Köln, im December 1892.'

BG. = The volumes published by the Bachgesellschaft 1850–1900.

' Bach's Cantata Texts ' = ' Joh. Seb. Bach. Cantata Texts sacred and secular. With a reconstruction of the Leipzig Liturgy of his period. By Charles Sanford Terry. London. 1926.'

' Bach's Chorals ' = ' Bach's Chorals. By Charles Sanford Terry.' 3 vols. Cambridge. 1915–1921.

BOHT = ' Bach's Original Hymn-Tunes for congregational use. Edited, with Notes, by Charles Sanford Terry. Oxford. 1922.'

Dretzel 1731 = 'Das Evangelischen Zions Musicalische Harmonie, Oder: Evangelisches Choral-Buch, Worinnen Die wahre Melodien, derer so wohl in denen beeden Marggrafthümern Bayreuth und Onoltzbach, als auch in der Stadt Nürnberg, deren Gebiete und andern Evangelischen Gemeinen üblichen Kirchen-Lieder . . . herausgegeben von Cornelio Heinrich Dretzeln, Organ. zu St Aeg. Nürnberg, zufinden bey Wolfgang Moritz Endters seel. Tochter, Mayrin und Sohn. Gedruckt bey Lorenz Bieling, 1731.'

Erk = Johann Sebastian Bach's mehrstimmige Choralgesänge und geistliche Arien. Zum ersten Mal unverändert nach authentischen Quellen mit ihren ursprünglichen Texten und mit den nöthigen kunsthistorischen Nachweisungen herausgegeben von Ludwig Erk. 1 Theil. Leipzig, C. F. Peters.' [n.d., but die Vorrede is dated ' Berlin, den 8 December 1850 '.]

= Ditto ' 2 Theil ' [n.d., but das Vorwort is dated ' Berlin, den 8 October 1865 '].

Freylinghausen 1704 = ' Geistreiches Gesang-Buch, Den Kern Alter und Neuer Lieder, Wie auch die Noten der unbekannten Melodeyen . . . von Johann Anastasio Freylinghausen, Past. Adj. Halle. Gedruckt und verlegt im Wäysen-Hause, 1704 '. [The Vorrede is dated September 22, 1703.]

Freylinghausen 1714 = ' Neues Geist-reiches Gesang-Buch, auserlesene, so Alte als Neue, geistliche und liebliche Lieder, Nebst den Noten der unbekanten Melodeyen . . . von Johann Anastasio Freylinghausen, Past. Adj. Halle. Gedruckt und verlegt im Waysenhause MDCCXIV. Mit Königl. Preussisch Privilegio.' [The Vorrede is dated September 28, 1713.]

H = Handschrift P. 831 in the Musik Abteilung of the Preuss. Staatsbibliothek. Its outer leaf bears the inscription: ' Johann Sebastian Bachs vierstimmige Choralgesaenge. Gesamlet von Carl Philipp Emanuel Bach. Erster und zweyter Theil.' [See Introduction.]

König 1738 = ' Harmonischer Lieder-Schatz, oder Allgemeines Evangelisches Choral-Buch, Welches die Melodien derer so wohl alten als neuen biss hieher eingeführten Gesänge unsers Teutschlandes in sich hält . . . von Johann Balthasar König, Directore Chori Musices in Franckfurt am Mayn. Auf Kosten des Autoris. Anno 1738.' [The Vorbericht is dated September 8, 1738.]

Krebs MS = Six hymn tunes preserved by Joh. Ludwig Krebs, printed in Spitta, iii, 401.

Leipzig 1729 = ' Das vollstandige und vermehrte Leipziger Gesang-Buch . . . Vormahls von Vopelio, jetzo aber aufs neue verbessert und vermehrt herausgegeben . . . Sebastian Heinrich Barnbeck, Leipzig, 1729.' [Later editions were edited by Carl Gottlob Hofmann and published by Barnbeck in 1740 and 1744.]

Naumann = ' Joh. Seb. Bach. Geistliche Lieder und Arien aus Schemelli's Gesangbuch und dem Notenbuch der Anna Magdalena Bach. Für eine Singstimme mit Pianoforte (Orgel oder Harmonium).' [Ed. Breitkopf, No. 4738, 1901.] [An edition, arranged for a lower voice, by Friedrich Martin, was published in 1923. Ed. Breitkopf, No. 4738.]

Reimann 1747 = ' Singende und musicirende Engel im Innern einer Kirche darstellend. J. B. Reimans, Org. v. Hirschb[erg], Samlung alter und neuer Melodien Evangel. Lieder, gestochen und verlegt von C[hristoph] H[einrich] Lau, Org.' [n.d., but dedication, by Lau, dated March 1747.]

Richter = Johann Sebastian Bachs Werke. Für Gesang. Gesammtausgabe für den praktischen Gebrauch. VII. Choralgesänge. Verlag von Breitkopf & Härtel in Leipzig.' [n.d., but Vorwort, signed by Bernh. Friedr. Richter, dated ' Leipzig, am Johannistage 1898.']

Schein 1627 = Cantional, Oder Gesangbuch Augspurgischer Confession . . . so in Chur- und Fürstenthümen Sachsen, insonderheit aber in beyden Kirchen und Gemeinen allhier zu Leipzig gebräuchlich. Verfertiget, und mit 4, 5 und 6 Stimmen Componiret von Johan-Hermano Schein, Grünhain, Directore der Music daselbsten. Cum Priv. Elect. Sax. 1627. In verlegung des Autoris und bey demselben auff der Schulen zu S. Thomas daselbst zu finden.'

APPENDIX I

Schemelli 1736 = ' Musicalisches Gesang-Buch, Darinnen 954 geistreiche, sowohl alte als neue Lieder und Arien, mit wohlgesetzten Melodien, in Discant und Bass, befindlich sind ; Vornemlich denen Evangelischen Gemeinen im Stifte Naumburg-Zeitz gewidmet . . . herausgegeben von George Christian Schemelli, Schloss-Cantore daselbs . . . Leipzig 1736. Verlegts Bernhard Christoph Breitkopf, Buchdr.' [The Vorrede, dated April 24, 1736, acknowledges Bach's contribution of new melodies and reharmonization of old ones.]
Seiffert = ' Seb. Bach's Gesänge zu G. Chr. Schemellis " Musicalischem Gesangbuch ". Leipzig 1736. Mit ausgearbeitetem generalbass herausgegeben von Max Seiffert. Berlin, 1925.'
Telemann 1730 = ' Fast allgemeines Evangelisch-Musicalisches Lieder-Buch . . . in dieser bequemen Forme herausgegeben von Georg Philip Telemann . . . Hamburg, gedruckt bei Philip Ludwig Stromer 1730.'
Vetter 1709 = ' Musicalische Kirch- und Hauss-Ergötzlichkeit, bestehend in denen gewöhnlichen geistlichen Liedern so durchs gantze Jahr bey öffentlichem Gottesdienste gesungen werden . . . mit sonderbahren Fleiss aufgesetzet von Daniel Vettern, Organisten zu St Nicolai in Leipzig. Zu finden bei dem Autore. Druckts Christoph Friedrich Rumpff.' [n.d., but the Dedication is dated August 26, 1709. Part II, containing 48 more melodies, appeared in 1713.]
Vopelius 1682 = ' Neu Leipziger Gesangbuch, Von den schönsten und besten Liedern verfasset . . . Mit Fleiss verfertiget und herausgegeben von Gottfried Vopelio, von Zittau, itziger Zeit bey der Schulen zu S. Nicol. Cantore . . . Leipzig, In Verlegung Christoph Klingers, Buchh. Druckts Gallus Niemann, 1682.' [The Vorrede is dated September 24, 1681.]
Winterfeld = ' Der evangelische Kirchengesang und sein Verhältniss zur Kunst des Tonsatzes, dargestellt von Carl von Winterfeld. Leipzig 1843.' [Vols. 2 and 3 in 1845, 1847.]
Witt 1715 = ' Psalmodia sacra, Oder: Andächtige und schöne Gesänge . . . In dem Fürstenthum Gotha und Altenburg, auf nachfolgende Art zu singen und zu spielen . . . Gotha, Verlegts Christoph Reyher, 1715.' [An edition of the work, entitled ' Neues Cantional, mit dem General-Bass,' is in the British Museum (C.7.).]
Wüllner = ' Joh. Seb. Bachs Werke. Nach der Ausgabe der Bachgesellschaft. Lieder und Arien. Für vierstimmigen gemischten Chor. Veröffenlichungen Neuen Bachgesellschaft. Jahrgang 1, Heft 2 [1901].'
Zahn = ' Die Melodien der deutschen evangelischen Kirchenlieder, aus den Quellen geschöpft und mitgeteilt von Johannes Zahn. Gütersloh, 1889.' [Vols. 2-6 appeared in 1890-1893.]

1—**H.** No. 152; **1769**, No. 152; **1785**, No. 148.

H., entitled ' Uns ist ein Kind geborhen '; **1769** and **1785**, ' Uns ist ein Kindlein heut gebohrn.' There are two hymns bearing the latter title: **1892**, No. 161, prints the first stanza of the 1560 text, a hymn for whose association with the melody there is no authority (*cf.* Zahn, Nos. 2574–79).

H. and **1769**, first chord   bar 4 Bass

2—**H.** No. 182; **1769**, No. 182; **1785**, No. 177.

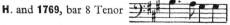

H. and **1769**, bar 8 Tenor

3—**H.** No. 192; **1769**, No. 192; **1785**, No. 186.

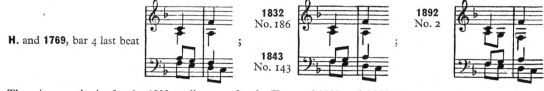

H. and **1769**, bar 4 last beat

There is no authority for the **1892** reading, nor for the Tenor of **1832** and **1843**. Erk, No. 152 (in E mi.)
Telemann 1730, Dretzel 1731, König 1738, Reimann 1747, all include the hymn and melody (Zahn, No. 1831). The hymn was in Leipzig use (Leipzig 1729, 1740, 1744) and is without a melody in Schemelli 1736 (No. 584).

4—**1786**, No. 279; **BG.** x, 288 (Cantata 48) (*c.* 1740).

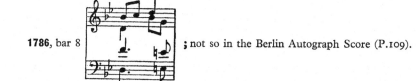

1786, bar 8   ; not so in the Berlin Autograph Score (P.109).

Bach's two versions of the melody (*cf.* No. 5) differ in details but derive from Vopelius (1682).

5—**H.** No. 44; **1765**, No. 44; **1784**, No. 40.
6—**1786**, No. 262; **BG.** 1, 72 (Cantata 2) (*c.* 1740).

1786, bar 5 Tenor   is not found in the original Parts in the Thomasschule.

Bach's text of the melody (*cf.* Nos. 7 and 8) is generally constant and conventional.

7—**1786**, No. 253; **BG**. xviii, 254 (Cantata 77) (*c.* 1725).

BG. xviii, bars 4 and 9 Tenor ; so in Berlin Autograph Score (P.68) and modern vocal

scores.   Since the original Score bears signs of haste, the preferable **1786** text is adopted. **1832**, No. 253, and **1843**, No. 3B. follow **1786**.

1786, bars 5 and 10 Alto ;not in P.68.

„ , bar 14 Bass ; not in P.68.

8—**H**. No. 3; **1765**, No. 3; **1784**, No. 3; **BG**. xxxii, 43 (Cantata 153) (1727).

1765 and **1784**, bars 7–9 ; also **1832**, No. 3, and **1843**, No. 3 C.

It is noteworthy that the editor corrected **H**'s version of these bars in **1765**, and that **1784** confirmed his preference.   On the other hand, **H**. is supported by the Berlin Original Parts (St. 79), which, however, are not positively autograph. That **H**'s reading is authoritative may be accepted.

9—**H**. No. 160 ; **1769**, No. 160; **1785**, No. 156; **1787**, No. 307; **BG**. I, 94 (Cantata 3) (*c.* 1740).

H. and **1769**, bar 6, first beat   . **1787**, bar 7, second beat

Bach's melodic line (*cf.* No. 10) is consistent and conventional (Zahn, No. 533).

10—**1786**, No. 217; **BG**. xxxii, 58 (Cantata 153) (1727ʼ.

11—**H**. No. 43; **1765**, No. 43; **1784**, No. 39.

H. and **1765**, bar 4 Bass ; a misprint.

The melody was current in Leipzig from 1709 as a hymn tune (Zahn, No. 3573). The hymn was in Leipzig use (Leipzig 1729, 1740, 1744) and is tuneless in Schemelli 1736 (No. 66).

12—**H**. No. 52; **1765**, No. 52; **1784**, No. 48; **BG**. v (I) 216 (Cantata 26) (*c.* 1740).

In **H**., **1765**, and **1784**, the small notes are the vocal Bass.

The   Berlin   Autograph   Score   (P.47),   bar   4   Tenor,   has . The variation

 is found in all the other three texts, and, being preferable, is adopted.

It is observable that, though the melody was current in various forms, Bach's text here and in the earlier ' Orgelbüchlein ' is uniform. It is based on a reconstruction of the original tune, probably by Joh. Crüger (Zahn No. 1887).

13—**H**. No. 157; **1769**, No. 157; **1785**, No. 153.

H. and **1769**, bar 1 Bass ; an error.

Erk (No. 158)
Richter (No. 17)   } bar 4 Soprano ; all three 18th cent. texts;
1892, No. 10   **1832**, No. 153; **1843**, No. 114.

1785 and **1832** (but not **1843**), bar 7 Soprano

14—**BG**. xxxiii, 46 (Cantata 162) (1715).

The melody appears for the first time in this Cantata and has been, probably inaccurately, attributed to Bach. The problem is discussed in *Bach's Chorals*, ii, 435. Since it was not Bach's habit to associate unfamiliar melodies with familiar hymns, it may be supposed that the melody had a Weimar vogue. It occurs nowhere else in Bach's music.

15—**1786**, No. 249.

Bach's melody is generally uniform in Nos. 15, 16, 17, excepting the final line. In No. 16 he uses a form which differs from the other two.

16—**1787**, Nos. 312, 352; **BG.** xxiv, 48 (Cantata 112) (1731).

The two settings in **1787** differ in details and also from the Thomasschule Original Parts. The inclusion of the two settings in 1787 was probably due to an oversight, the first being entitled ' Allein Gott in der Höh' sei Ehr' ', and the second ' Der Herr ist mein getreuer Hirt '. The text of No. 16 follows the Original Parts, from which **1787** shows the following variations:

No. 312, bar 10 Tenor

„   last bar Soprano

No. 352, bar 3 Alto

„   bar 7 Tenor

„   bar 8 Alto

„   bar 10 Tenor

17—**H.** No. 129; **1769**, No. 129; **1785**, No. 125; **1787**, No. 325; **BG.** xxiii, 116 (Cantata 104) (c. 1725).

It is clear that this harmonization survived in two, and probably three versions. The Cantata Choral is reproduced in **1787**, No. 325, which, however, shows the following variations:

1787, No. 325, bars 4 and 5

„   bar 5 last note Bass

„   bar 9   ; also 1785, No. 125.

H., **1769**, and **1785** are all in G ma., and preserve another form of the Cantata Choral, from which they differ as follows:

H., **1769**, **1785**, bar 5 Alto

H., **1769**, bar 9 Alto

„   „   last line

„   „   show the same error in the last Bass bar   . **1785** adopts the same

harmonization for this closing line, excepting the Tenor, which reads:

18—**H.**, No. 13; **1765**, No. 13; **1784**, No. 13; **BG.** vii, 114 (Cantata 33) (*c.* 1740).

H., 1765, 1784, bar 7 Soprano  ; this conforms with Bach's otherwise uniform statement of the closing cadence, but is not supported by Prof. Schubring's Autograph Score.

H., 1765, bar 9 Tenor ; an error.

1765, bar 12 Bass ; a sharp is added in the Druckfehler before the 3rd note.

H., 1765, 1784, the small notes are the vocal Bass.

19—**1787**, No. 358.
1892, No. 9, bar 14 Bass ; so also **1843**, No. 13B, and Richter (No. 15).

20—**H.**, No. 132; **1769**, No. 132; **1785**, No. 128.

H. and **1769**, bars 6 and 7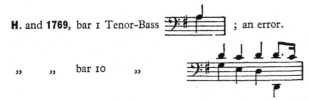

1785, bar 1 Bass, first note

Zahn (Nos. 3837–42) records no version of the 1691 melody similar to and earlier than Bach's. It may be attributed to him. Dretzel 1731, König 1738, and Reimann 1747, use a number of variants (Zahn, Nos. 3839–3842.) The hymn was in Leipzig use (Leipzig, 1729, 1740, 1744) and is tuneless in Schemelli 1736 (No. 535). Erk omits the Choral.

21—**H.**, No. 163; **1769**, No. 163; **1785**, No. 159.

H. and **1769**, bar 1 Tenor-Bass ; an error.

„ „ bar 10 „

The form of the melody adopted by Bach appears to be his own, a variation of the 1531 *cantus* published by Johann Crüger in 1640 (Zahn, No. 1646), repeated by Witt (1715), and therefore familiar to Bach from his Weimar years. Telemann 1730 and König 1738 use Crüger's text. The hymn was in Leipzig use (Leipzig 1729, 1740, 1744). Erk (No. 160), in A.

22—**H.**, No. 186; **1769**, No. 186; **1785**, No. 180.
It may be noted that bars 4 and 8 of Crüger's original melody (Zahn, No. 258) are as follows:

Telemann 1730, Dretzel 1731, König 1738, include the hymn and melody. Reimann 1747 uses an original tune (Zahn, Nos. 258, 259). The hymn was not in Leipzig use, but is included, tuneless, in Schemelli 1736 (No. 127). Erk omits the Choral.

23—**1786**, No. 208.
The melody is that of 'Erschienen ist der herrlich Tag' (No. 86 *infra*) much altered.

24—**H.**, No. 5; **1765**, No. 5; **1784**, No. 5; **1787**, No. 308.

H. and **1765**, bars 9–10 Tenor-Bass

H., bar 14 Tenor

1765, bar 11 Tenor

1787 (in A flat to 'Ein Lämmlein geht '), bar 16

Erk (No. 161), in A flat (1785 text).

25—**H.**, No. 128; **1769**, No. 128; **1785**, No. 124.

1892, No. 16, bar 3 Bass  ; Richter (No. 24) also adopts the unwarrantable G sharp.

This form of Staden's melody is not found in print earlier than 1769 and may be attributed to Bach. König 1738 and Reimann 1747 both use a reconstruction printed in Dretzel 1731 (Zahn, 824). The hymn was in Leipzig use (Leipzig 1729, 1740, 1744).

26—**H.**, No. 28; **1765**, No. 28; **1784**, No. 25; **BG.** xxx, 260 (Cantata 148) (c. 1725).

H., **1765**, **1784**, bar 4 Bass ⟨music⟩ ; so **1832**, No. 25.

„ „ „ bar 10 Bass ⟨music⟩ ; so **1832**, No. 25.

„ „ „ in A mi. (to ' Wo soll ich fliehen hin '); so **1832**.
The Cantata text rests upon a copy of the original Score by Gottlob Harrer, Bach's successor at St Thomas's. The other texts merit equal consideration.
Excepting line 4, Bach's treatment of the melody in his five Leipzig Cantatas (cf. Nos. 27–30) is uniform. In the Organ Preludes he follows another text of the *cantus* (cf. ' Bach's Chorals ', iii, 345).

27—**1786**, No. 281; **BG.** xx (i), 194 (Cantata 89) (c. 1730).
The small notes in bars 7 and 8 are the vocal Bass of **1785**.
1786, entitled ' Wo soll ich fliehen hin '.

28—**1787**, No. 303; **BG.** I, 150 (Cantata 5) (1735).

29—**BG.** xxxvii, 212 (Cantata 188) (1731).
W. Friedemann Bach's hand is suspected in this Cantata.

30—**1787**, No. 330; **BG.** xxviii, 164 (Cantata 136) (c. 1725 or later).

BG., bar 4 Tenor ⟨music⟩

„ „ 9 „ ⟨music⟩

In each of the three chords distinguished by an asterisk an essential note is supplied by the Violin *obbligato*. In the text of No. 30 they are substituted in the Tenor part, as in **1787**.

„ „ 12 „ ⟨music⟩

1787 „ 12 Bass ⟨music⟩ ; so **1832**, No. 331; **1843**, No. 25 D.

„ „ 13 Tenor ⟨music⟩ ; „ „ (with minor close)

1787, entitled ' Wo soll ich fliehen hin '.

31—**H.**, No. I; **1765**, No. I; **1784**, No. 1.
Many variants of the melody are found. Bach's approximates to the Leipzig tradition (Schein 1627) (Zahn, No. 5269f).

32—**H.**, No. 14; **1765**, No. 14; **1784**, No. 10; **BG.** vii, 300 (Cantata 38) (c. 1740).
H., **1765**, **1784**, and **BG.**, both F's in bar 2 Alto are sharpened. Erk (No. 166), following the Viola part.

has ⟨music⟩ , which is preferable. **BG.** Score is not autograph.

BG., bar 3 Alto ⟨music⟩ ; all other texts (also **1832**, No. 10; **1843**, No. 10)

The Thomasschule Original Parts show no accidental before the second note. The Berlin Score is not autograph.
The small notes are the vocal Bass of **H.**, **1765**, and **1784**. The Cantata Continuo only includes the small notes in bars 10 and 13.

33—**1787**, No. 339.

      Telemann 1730 and Reimann 1747 include the hymn and melody (Zahn, No. 5393). The hymn was in Leipzig use (Leipzig 1729, 1740, 1744) and is included, tuneless, in Schemelli 1736 (No. 484). Erk omits the Choral.

34—**1786**, No. 230.

35—**1786**, No. 197.

      Erk (No. 171), in E mi.

36—**BG.** xvi, 214 (Cantata 66) (1731).

37—**H.**, No. 19; **1765**, No. 19; **1784**, No. 15.

      H., bar 3 Tenor, lacks accidental before 5th note (C).

      With minor variations, Bach's *cantus* is uniform and conventional (*cf.* Nos. 38–41). Erk omits the Choral.

38—**1787**, No. 370.

      Erk omits the Choral.

39—**H.**, No. 189; **1769**, No. 189; **1785**, No. 184; **BG.** I, 124 (Cantata 4) (*c.* 1740).

      H., **1769**, **1785**, in D mi.

H., **1785**, bar 10 Soprano   ; so **1832**, No. 184; **1843**, No. 15B; Erk (No. 172).

1769, **BG.**, bar 10 Soprano   ; so Thomasschule Original Parts.

      The C natural is preferable, and, since the Original Parts are not entirely autograph, is adopted.

H., bar 11 Bass   ; corrected in **1769**.

40—**BG.** xxxii, 154 (Cantata 158) (? Weimar).

      The Choral is not in Erk in this form (see No. 41).

41—**1786**, No. 261.

      A variation of No. 40 (*supra*), from which it differs chiefly in the Alto of the second part. Erk (No. 173) prints this version.

42—**H.**, No. 67; **1765**, No. 67; **1784**, No. 65.

      Erk omits the Choral.

43—**BG.** I, 210 (Cantata 7) (*c.* 1740).

44—**H.**, No. 123; **1769**, No. 124; **1785**, No. 119; **BG.** xxxv, 198 (Cantata 176) (1735).

BG., bar 14, first beat Tenor-Bass

BG. and **1785**, bar 17 Tenor   ; **H.** and **1769** have D natural.

H., bar 18 Soprano   , an error.

      H., **1769**, **1785**, the small notes are the vocal Bass.

45—**1786**, No. 245.

      Erk (No. 169), in A mi.

46—**1786**, No. 210.

1892, No. 23; Erk, No. 170; **1843**, No. 163, bar 7 Tenor   ; **1832**, No. 210, as **1786**.

      Reimann 1747 includes the hymn and melody (Zahn, No. 993). The hymn was in Leipzig use (Leipzig 1729, 1740, 1744).

47—**H.**, No. 58; **1765**, No. 58; **1784**, No. 55; **BG.** xxvi, 20 (Cantata 121) (*c.* 1740).

H., bar 4 Soprano   ; an error corrected in **1765**.

      Erk (No. 175), following the Berlin original Parts, bar 14 Bass.   The C sharp is found in all 18th century texts; so also **1832**, No. 56 and **1843**, No. 55.

H., **1765**, **1784**, bar 15 Tenor 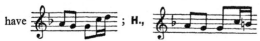 ; not in Berlin Autograph Score (P. 867).

„   „   „, small notes are the vocal Bass. In the Cantata the Tenor phrase at bar 13-end is broken by a repetition of ' in Ewigkeit.'

48—**H.**, No. 8; **1765**, No. 8; **1784**, No. 7.

1892, No. 28, bar 6 Alto

Since the Editor of **1892** was ignorant of the existence of **H.**, his text here must be attributed to a desire to remove the high D from the Alto part. Both 18th century prints, as also **1832**, **1843**, and Erk (No. 176)

have   ; **H.**,

Bach here uses a version of the last line of the melody that dates from 1662. In No. 49 he prefers the composer's original (1607) text (Zahn, No. 132).

49—**1787**, No. 315.

With minor differences, the setting is the opening chorus of Cantata 95 (**BG.** xxii, 131), without the instrumental interludes.

50—**1786**, No. 198; **1787**, No. 306.

The two settings are identical. They may be attributed to the pre-Leipzig period; for Bach employs the same version of the *cantus* as he used in the ' Orgelbüchlein '. That form, significantly, is found in Witt, No. 95 (1715). In the St John Passion (Nos. 51, 52 *infra*) Bach uses another version of the melody, in Leipzig use and dating from 1598. (See ' Bach's Chorals ', ii, 491; iii, 132.)

Erk omits the Choral.

51—**H.**, No. 77; **1765**, No. 77; **1784**, No. 80; **BG.** xii (1), 43 (St John Passion) (1723).

52—**H.**, No. 117; **1769**, No. 117; **1785**, No. 113; **BG.** xii (1), 121 (St John Passion) (1723).

53—**1786**, No. 200.

Bach's melodic line approximates closely to Reimann 1747 (Zahn, No. 6240B). Both vary the original by substituting B natural for B flat in bars 1 and 7.

54—**1786**, No. 196.

Reimann 1747 includes the hymn and melody (Zahn 2503). The hymn was not in Leipzig use after 1740; it is found only in Leipzig 1729.

Erk (No. 178), in D mi.

55—**H.**, No. 168; **1769**, No. 168.

This is one of the five Chorals in **H.** and **1765–69** omitted from **1784–87**. Four of them are expressly repudiated by C. P. E. Bach (Preface **1765**) as spurious. The present Choral is not named, and by implication therefore may be deemed authentic. See Introduction, *supra* p. iv.

56—**1787**, No. 310.

König 1738 sets the melody to another hymn (Zahn, No. 5391). The hymn was in Leipzig use (Leipzig 1729, 1740, 1744) and is included, tuneless, in Schemelli 1736 (No. 5).

Erk omits the Choral.

57—**1786**, No. 228.

1786, last bar Alto

58—**H.**, No. 166; **1769**, No. 166; **1785**, No. 162.

H. and **1769**, bar 12 Tenor

As in the ' Orgelbüchlein ', Bach uses a six-lined version of the melody which appeared first in Witt (1715). Telemann 1730 and König 1738 also use it (Zahn, No. 381c). On Bach's relations with Witt's Hymn-book, see ' Bach's Chorals ', iii, 29.

59—**1787**, No. 313.

Erk omits the Choral: Apparently it belongs to Bach's early period.

1787, last bar Tenor

60—**H.**, Nos. 56, 183; **1765**, No. 56; **1769**, No. 183; **1784**, No. 52; **1785**, No. 178; **BG.**, xxvi, 40 (Cantata 122) (*c.* 1742)

H., No. 183, **1769**, No. 183, bar 2 Tenor   otherwise the texts are identical. The small

notes are the vocal Bass elsewhere than in the Cantata.

61—**1786**, No. 224.

Other than the original, to which Bach's version is superior, Zahn (No. 673) does not find the tune in any 18th century text. The hymn was in Leipzig use (Leipzig 1729, 1740, 1744) and is in Schemelli 1736 (No. 7).

62—**H.**, No. 80; **1765**, No. 80; **1784**, No. 75.

Bach proposed to include the melody in the ' Orgelbüchlein '. The similarity of his and Witt's (No. 415) version of it is therefore worthy of remark. Telemann 1730, Dretzel 1731, König 1738, and Reimann 1747, all include it (Zahn, No. 4217). The hymn was not in Leipzig use after 1744 (Leipzig 1729, 1740); Schemelli 1736 (No. 8).

63—**1786**, No. 239.

König 1738 and Reimann 1747 include the hymn, the former to a melody found in Freylinghausen 1714 (Zahn, No. 4796). The hymn was not in Leipzig use and is not in Schemelli 1736.

Erk omits the Choral.

64—**H.**, No. 158; **1769**, No. 158; **1785**, No. 154.

H. and **1769**, bar 5

„   „   bars 6–7 Bass

Bach uses the Leipzig (Schein 1627) version of the ancient melody (Zahn, No. 335e).
Erk omits the Choral.

65.—**H.**, No. 162; **1769**, No. 162; **1785**, No. 158.

H. and **1769**, bar 4

„   „   bar 11

„   „   bar 12 Alto

Erk omits the Choral.

66—**1786**, No. 207.
Bach adopts the Leipzig (Schein 1627) form of the melody in preference to the more popular version by Joh. Crüger (Zahn, No. 370c), which Reimann 1747 uses.
Erk (No. 184), in E mi.

67—**1786**, No. 231.
Bach adopts the Leipzig (Schein 1627; Vopelius 1682) form of the melody (Zahn, No. 5001), as also do König 1738 and Reimann 1747.

68—**1786**, No. 232.
The hymn and its melody are in Freylinghausen 1704; the hymn was in Leipzig use (1729, 1740, 1744), but is not in Schemelli 1736.
Erk omits the Choral.

69—**H.**, No. 131; **1769**, No. 131; **1785**, No. 127.
Here and in the Organ Preludes Bach's text of the melody is invariable.
Erk omits the Choral.

70—A. M. Bach's ' Notenbuch ' (1725); **1786**, No. 209.

1786, bar 3 Soprano

„   bar 6   „

„   bar 8   „

„   bar 11 Tenor

„   bar 14 Soprano

Dretzel 1731, König 1738, and Reimann 1747 use the Freylinghausen 1704 melody (Zahn, No. 3067). Bach's not only is set to the hymn in Schemelli 1736 (No. 421 infra), but was probably in Leipzig use, since the hymn is found in Leipzig 1729, 1740, 1744.

71—**H.**, No. 46; **1765**, No. 46; **1784**, No. 42; **BG**. xvi, 246 (Cantata 67) (*c.* 1725).
The small notes are the vocal Bass of **H.**, **1765**, and **1784**.

72—**BG**. xxiv, 158 (Cantata 116) (1744).
Erk prints the Choral twice (Nos. 22, 186). They only differ from each other and from **BG** in the Alto part

of bar 7, whose last note in No. 186 is  . Erk gives 'a lost MS' as his authority, and the

emendation as 'conjectural'.

The Autograph Score differs from the Thomasschule Original Part in bar 9 Soprano:

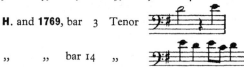

73—**H.**, No. 169; **1769**, No. 169; **1785**, No. 164.

H. and **1769**, bar 3 Tenor

,, ,, bar 14 ,,

The hymn is in Vopelius (1682) and was later in Leipzig use (Leipzig 1729, 1740, 1744).

74—**H.**, No. 92; **1765**, No. 92; **1784**, No. 86; **BG**. xii (2), 104 (Cantata 56) (1731 or 1732).
The small notes are the vocal Bass of **H.**, **1765**, and **1784**. The Cantata Continuo is with the vocal Bass in bars 7–8.
In No. 75 (*infra*) Bach treats the opening line of Crüger's melody more freely. Here (No. 74) he keeps to the Leipzig (1649) text.

75—**H.**, No. 141; **1769**, No. 141; **1785**, No. 137.

76—**H.**, Nos. 104, 130; **1769**, Nos. 104, 130; **1785**, Nos. 100, 126; **BG**. ii, 252 (Cantata 18) (1714).
The texts are identical except in key. **H.** No. 104, **1769**, No. 104, and **1785**, No. 100 are uniform with **BG.**, but are set to Johannes Agricola's (?) 'Ich ruf zu dir, Herr Jesu Christ' (See No. 190 *infra*). The other settings are in A. mi., to Spengler's hymn.
Erk (No. 189) prints the G mi. setting.

77—**H.**, No. 23; **1765**, No. 23; **1784**, No. 20.

H., bar 9 Alto

1765, bars 8, 11, text defective, corrected in Druckfehler.
All three (*cf.* Nos. 78 and 79) vocal settings of Luther's tune are uniform in its text and differ from that employed in the 'Orgelbüchlein'. The latter's melody is uniform with Witt (No. 482). The three vocal settings follow the Leipzig use (Zahn, No. 7377*a*). See 'Bach's Chorals', iii, 155.

78—**1786**, No. 250.

Erk (No. 190), bar 6 Alto . His variation is not sanctioned.

79—**1786**, No. 273; **BG**, xviii, 378 (Cantata 80) (1730).
The small notes in bars 5 and 13 are the vocal Bass of **1786**.

80—**1786**, No. 280.
The hymn and melody are in Freylinghausen (1704), Dretzel 1731, and König 1738. Bach's version is greatly superior (Zahn, No. 7127) and certainly reveals his revision. Reimann 1747 uses another derivative (Zahn, No. 7131). The hymn was in Leipzig use (Leipzig 1729, 1740, 1744) and is in Schemelli 1736 (No. 112).

81—**H.**, No. 37; **1765**, No. 37; **1784**, No. 33.

H. and **1765**, bar 1 Soprano

H., bar 3 Soprano

H. and **1765**, bar 4 Tenor, last beat

,, ,, ,, ,, 5 Bass, last beat

,, ,, ,, ,, 13 Alto

Erk omits the Choral.

82—**H.**, No. 100; **1765**, No. 100; **1784**, No. 72; **BG**. i, 176 (Cantata 6) (1736).

1765 and **1784**, last bar Tenor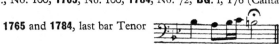

APPENDIX I

83—**1787**, No. 342; **BG.** ii, 32 (Cantata 11) (*c.* 1735).

1787, penult. bar Alto

The small notes are the vocal Bass of **1787**.
Bach, here and in Nos. 84 and 85, adopts Joh. Crüger's (1648) widely used reconstruction of Schop's melody. (Zahn, No. 5741*b*).

84—**H.**, No. 10; **1765**, No. 10; **1784**, No. 9; **1787**, No. 360; **BG.** v (2), 59 (Christmas Oratorio) (1734).

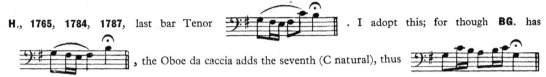

H., **1765**, **1784**, **1787**, last bar Tenor . I adopt this; for though **BG.** has , the Oboe da caccia adds the seventh (C natural), thus

The small notes are the vocal Bass of **H.**, **1765**, **1784**, but not **1787**. **1787** is set to Joh. Rist's 'Du Lebensfürst Herr Jesu Christ'.

85—**H.**, No. 106; **1769**, No. 106; **1785**, No. 102; **BG.** x, 126 (Cantata 43) (*c.* 1735).

BG. (Autograph Berlin Score [P. 44, adn. 6]) bar 11–12 Alto  ; the reading of all the

other texts is preferable and is adopted.

BG. last bar Tenor ; the other texts have ;

86—**BG.** xvi, 233 (Cantata 67) (*c.* 1725).
Here and in No. 87 Bach follows the Leipzig (Schein 1627) form of the melody (Zahn, No. 1743).

87—**H.**, No. 20; **1765**, No. 20; **1784**, No. 17; **BG.** xxx, 122 (Cantata 145) (1729 or 1730).

H., penultimate bar Bass ; an error, repeated, but corrected, in **1765**.

H., **1765**, and **1784**, in E mi.

88—**H.**, No. 181; **1769**, No. 181; **1785**, No. 176.

H., **1769**, and **1785**, bar 14 Tenor  this produces consecutive octaves between the Soprano

and Tenor in the last chord of bar 14 and the first of bar 15.

H. and **1769**, bar 14 Alto .

Erk omits the Choral.

89—**H.**, No. 4; **1765**, No. 4; **1784**, No. 4; **BG.** xx (i), 134 (Cantata 86) (*c.* 1725).
Bach's melodic text in Nos. 89–93 is uniform and conventional.

90—**1787**, No. 289; **BG.** I, 274 (Cantata 9) (1731 or later).

1787, bar 9 Alto 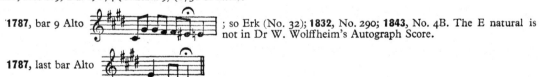 ; so Erk (No. 32); **1832**, No. 290; **1843**, No. 4B. The E natural is not in Dr W. Wolffheim's Autograph Score.

1787, last bar Alto

The small notes in **BG.** only.

91—**1787**, No. 334; **BG.** xxxii, 96 (Cantata 155) (1716).

1787, bar 6 Tenor-Bass  ; so **1832**, No. 335; **1843**, No. 4C.

Erk (No. 33)   „   „

92—**1787**, No. 328; **BG**. xiii (1), 148 (Three Wedding Chorals).

1787, bar 2 Bass  ; so **1832**, No. 329

„ „ 3 „ ; so „

„ „ 6 Alto ; so „

„ „ 7, 2nd beat ; so „

„ „ 10, last beat Tenor ; so „

„ „ 11 Bass ; so „

1787 and **BG**. are set to ' Sei Lob und Ehr dem höchsten Gut '.

93—**1786**, No. 248; **1787**, No. 353; **BG**, xxiv, 172 (Cantata 117) (*c.* 1733).
      The duplication of the Choral in **1786** and **1787** was clearly due to the former's defective text. **1787** differs from **BG**. slightly.

1787, bars 1–2  ; bar 3 Alto

The vocal Bass of **1787** is uniform with the Continuo of **BG**.

1786, bars 1–2 ; bar 5 Alto

; bar 5 Bass

„ bar 6 Alto ; bar 7 Tenor

„ bar 9 Alto ; bar 10 Tenor

1786, 1787, and **BG**. are set to ' Sei Lob und Ehr dem höchsten Gut '.

94—**1786**, No. 216; **BG**. xii (2), 190 (Cantata 60) (1732).

1786, bar 15 Alto

The vocal Bass of **1786** is uniform with the Continuo of **BG**.

Erk (No. 195), bar 3 Tenor ; the D sharp is not in the Berlin Score (P. 461 adn. 1), nor in the original Parts.

95—**H**., No. 30; **1765**, No. 30; **1784**, No. 27.
      Bach proposed to introduce the melody into the " Orgelbüchlein " (*cf.* " Bach's Chorals," iii, 53); it had little vogue in his period.

96—**H.**, No. 171; **1769**, No. 171; **1785**, No. 166.
For the Tenor of bar 10 I follow **H. 1769** has
The Editor of **1769** misread **H.**'s 3rd and 4th notes,
and the Editor of **1785** changed the 5th to avoid consecutive fifths with the Soprano.

Bach proposed to introduce the melody into the 'Orgelbüchlein' (*cf.* 'Bach's Chorals', ii, 41). It is associated
with the hymn in Telemann 1730, König 1738, Freylinghausen 1741, and Reimann 1747 (Zahn, No. 4298).
The hymn was in Leipzig use (Leipzig 1729, 1740, 1744) and is tuneless, in Schemelli 1736 (No. 390).

97—**1786**, No. 238.
The hymn is in Freylinghausen (1714), but did not pass into Leipzig use until 1740 (Leipzig 1740, 1744).
König 1738 and Reimann 1747 include it (Zahn, No. 1423), but it is not in Schemelli 1736.

98—**1787**, No. 351.
Bach's statement of the melody (*cf.* Nos. 99-101) is uniform and conventional.
Erk omits the Choral.

99—**H.**, No. 17; **1765**, No. 17; **1784**, No. 16.

1765, bar 12 Soprano   ; corrected in the Druckfehler.

100—**BG.** xvi, 325 (Cantata 69) (*c.* 1730).
This Choral and No. 101 differ only in a few bars. Their separate existence is probably due to the fact that this
Cantata did double duty, for the Twelfth Sunday after Trinity and also for the Council Election service, when,
in No. 100, drums and trumpets were added to the orchestra.

101—**1787**, No. 332.
Erk (No. 199) includes the Choral as in No. 100 *supra*.

102—**BG.** xvi, 354 (Cantata 70) (1716).
Bach's melodic line (*cf.* Nos. 103-109) is practically uniform, and conventional.

103—**H.**, No. 33; **1765**, No. 33; **1784**, No. 29; **BG.**, vii, 80 (Cantata 32) (*c.* 1740).
The vocal Bass of **H.**, **1765**, **1784** is uniform with the Continuo of **BG.**, excepting the 3rd beat of bar 3 and
the last bar.

104—**H.**, No. 84; **1765**, No. 84; **1784**, No. 76; **BG.** v (1), 360 (Cantata 30) (1738).
H., **1765**, **1784**, in G ma. Their vocal Basses are uniform with the Continuo of **BG.**

105—**H.**, No. 71; **1765**, No. 71; **1784**, No. 67; **BG.** vii, 348 (Cantata 39) (1732).
H., **1765**, **1784**, in G ma.

   „   „   „   bar 7 Bass

106—**H.**, No. 66; **1765**, No. 66; **1784**, No. 63; **1786**, No. 256; **BG.**, xxix, 124 (Cantata 194) 1723).

H., **1765**, **1784**, in G ma.
   „   „   „   bar 7 Tenor   ; 1786

   „   „   „   vocal Bass uniform with Continuo of **BG.**
1786 (set to 'Jesu, deine tiefe Wunden'; see No. 108), uniform with **BG.** vocal parts (except bar 7 Tenor).
Erk (Nos. 35, 202) gives both texts in B flat.

107—**BG.** ii, 288 (Cantata 19) (1726).
Two texts of this Choral exist: one in No. 107, the other in No. 108. Erk (No. 38) prints the former. No. 107
is scored for trumpets and drums (the festival orchestra on St Michael's Day). No. 108 perhaps was designed
for ferial use, when the normal orchestra merely duplicated the vocal parts.

108—**1787**, No. 297.
1787, set to Gerhardt's 'Weg, mein Herz, mit dem Gedanken'. See No. 103.

109—**1786**, Nos. 254, 282; **BG.** v (i), 188 (Cantata 25) (*c.* 1731).
1786, No. 254, entitled 'Weg, mein Herz': No. 282, 'Freu dich sehr'.

   „   No. 254, bar 2 Alto   ; bar 2 Tenor

   „   „   bar 7 Soprano   ; last bar Tenor

   „   No. 282 bar 11 Bass   ; last bar Tenor

110—**H.**, No. 9; **1765**, No. 9; **1784**, No. 8; **BG.** vii, 394 (Cantata 40) (1723).

H., 1765, 1784 bar 2 Soprano

„ „ „ bars 4 and 16 Soprano

„ „ „ bar 6 Soprano

„ „ „ bar 7 Bass, small notes.

Telemann 1730, Dretzel 1731, König 1738, Freylinghausen 1741, include the hymn and melody (Zahn, No. 7880). The hymn was in Leipzig use (Leipzig 1729, 1740, 1744) and is also in Schemelli 1736 (No. 189).

111—**H.**, No. 167; **1769**, No. 167; **1785**, No. 163.
The hymn was not in Leipzig use and is not in Schemelli 1736. Zahn (No. 2339) finds the melody in only one 18th century Hymn-book.
Erk omits the Choral.

112—**H.**, No. 164; **1769**, No. 164; **1785**, No. 160; **BG.** xvi, 118 (Cantata 64) (1723).

H and **1769** bar 8 Alto

A variant text in **BG.** xvi, p. xv has the following:

Bar 6 Alto

Bar 3

Bar 7 Tenor

Bach's statement of the melody is uniform and conventional (*cf.* Nos. 113–15).
The Continuo of **BG.** is uniform with the vocal Bass of **H., 1769, 1785.**

113—**H.**, No. 57; **1765**, No. 57; **1784**, No. 53; **BG.** xxii, 32 (Cantata 91) (*c.* 1740).

H., 1765, 1784, bar 2 Bass ; bar 7 Bass

H., bar 8, 2nd beat ; 1765 ; 1784 (sic)

BG. bar 9, last beat ; the Alto and Bass notes differ from the Berlin Autograph Score (P. 869), whose text, as in No. 113, corresponds with **H., 1765.** In **1784** the Tenor C is sharpened.

Omitting the Horns and Timpani, the Cantata setting is also in **BG.** xvi, 371, with minor differences, as a variant to No. 112 *supra.*

114—**1787**, No. 287.
Erk omits the Choral.

115—**BG.** v (2), 110 (Christmas Oratorio) (1734).

Erk (No. 207), first Soprano note

116—**1786**, No. 271
Gerhardt's hymn is included in Freylinghausen 1704 and 1741, Telemann 1730, Schemelli 1736, König 1738 (Zahn, Nos. 7414, 7415) and Leipzig 1740, 1744. König employs a melody with which Bach also was familiar (see No. 431 *infra*).

117—**1786**, No. 225.

    The hymn was not in Leipzig use before 1740 (Leipzig 1740, 1744).

    Erk omits the Choral.

118—**H.**, No. 138; **1769**, No. 137; **1785**, No. 134.

    Bach proposed to insert a Prelude on the melody in the 'Orgelbüchlein' ('Bach's Chorals', iii, 38).

Erk (No. 209) prints the first chord of bar 13

119—**H.**, No. 39; **1765**, No. 39; **1784**, No. 34; **BG.** v (2), 208 (Christmas Oratorio, 1734).

H., **1765**, **1784**, bar 4 last chord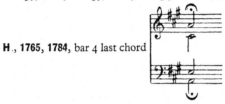

    „   „   „ vocal Bass uniform with Continuo of **BG.** (except bar 6).

    „   „   „ set to the melody's original words, a hymn not used by Bach elsewhere.

120—**H.**, No. 184; **1769**, No. 184; **1785**, No. 181.

H., and **1769**, bar 8 Tenor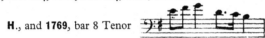

    Bach proposed to include a Prelude on this little-used melody in the 'Orgelbüchlein' ('Bach's Chorals', iii, 58).

    Erk omits the Choral.

121—**1786**, No. 234.

    A harmonization of the figured Choral in Schemelli 1736 (see No. 433 *infra*). Freylinghausen 1714 uses the same melody. Dretzel 1731, König 1738, and Reimann 1747 prefer other tunes (Zahn, Nos. 7953, 7954, 7957). The hymn was in Leipzig use (Leipzig 1729, 1740, 1744).

1786, bar 30 Bass 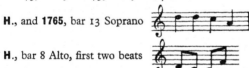 , an error.

122—**H.**, No. 75; **1765**, No. 75; **1784**, No. 70.

H., and **1765**, bar 13 Soprano

H., bar 8 Alto, first two beats

    Bach proposed to introduce a Prelude on the melody in the 'Orgelbüchlein' (Bach's Chorals', iii, 46).

    Erk (No. 213), one tone higher.

123—**H.**, No. 21; **1765**, No. 21; **1784**, No. 18.

    1765, errors in bars 2, 4, 7, 12, corrected in the Druckfehler. It is observable that in the 'Orgelbüchlein'

Bach writes the first line of the melody  , following Witt 1715 (No. 5). *Cf.*

    'Bach's Chorals', iii, 176.

124—**H.**, No. 198; **1769**, No. 198; **1785**, No. 192.

H. and **1769**, bar 13

    Dretzel 1731, König 1738 and Reimann 1747 include the hymn, but to other melodies (Zahn, No. 2851, 2853). It was in Leipzig use (Leipzig 1729, 1740, 1744).

125—**H.**, No. 93; **1765**, No. 93; **1784**, No. 90; **BG.** xii (2), 132 (Cantata 57) (*c.* 1740).

H., **1765**, **1784**, bar 10 Tenor

    Bach's melodic text is much freer than in No. 126 *infra*. Zahn (No. 1912) does not indicate any 18th century text uniform with Bach's, to whom this variation of the melody may be attributed.

126—**BG**. xxviii, 196 (Cantata 137) (1732); **BG**. xli, 174 ('Herr Gott Beherrscher') (*post* 1734).
BG., xli, Choral in D.

127—**1786**, No. 235; **1787**, No. 318.
1787, set to the Latin 'Sanctus'.

1786, bar 4 Alto

   ,,   bar 8 Tenor

   ,,   bar 16 Soprano

   ,,   bar 17 Tenor

128—**H**., Nos. 26, 87; **1765**, Nos. 26, 87; **1784**, Nos. 23, 88; **BG**. v (1), 272 (Cantata 28) (c. 1736).

H., **1765**, **1784**, bar 9 Soprano   ; bar 11 Soprano

  ,, ,, ,, bar 12 ,,

1765, No. 87 bar 12 Bass

All the texts, except **BG**., have the lower A in bar 5 Bass.
H., No. 26, **1765**, No. 26, **1784**, No. 23, set to Gerhardt's 'Zeuch ein zu deinen Thoren'.

The conventional form of the first phrase of the melody was   (Zahn, No. 5267).

Bach followed Witt (No. 56) in his variation of it.

129—**H**., No. 103; **1769**, No. 103; **1785**, No. 99; **BG**. ii, 198 (Cantata 16) (1724).

H., **1769**, **1785**, bar 2 Soprano   ; **H**., bar 3 Tenor

H., **1769**, **1785**, **BG**., bar 4, all have G sharp as the last Alto note. The Berlin Autograph Score (P. 45, adn. 5)

has G natural. **1785** prints the bar

The small notes are the vocal Bass in **H**., **1769**, **1785**.

130—**H**., No. 127; **1769**, No. 127; **1785**, No. 123; **BG**. xxxvii, 74 (Cantata 183) (1735).
H., **1769**, **1785**, bar 3 Soprano, *tr*. omitted.

  ,, ,, ,, bar 4 Soprano

  ,, ,, ,, bar 10 Tenor

  ,, ,, ,, last phrase ; **1832**, No. 123, and **1843**, No. 23 C. follow **H**., **1769**, **1785**: but the Berlin Score is autograph (P. 149).

131—**1787**, No. 302; **BG**. xxii, 184 (Cantata 96) (c. 1740).
The small notes are the vocal Bass of **1787**.
Transposed into A, the Choral ends Cantata 132 in the vocal scores.
Erk (No. 217) misprints the Bass in bar 9.

132—**H.**, No. 105; **1769**, No. 105; **1785**, No. 101; **BG**. xxxiii, 88 (Cantata 164) (1715).
133—**H.**, No. 172; **1769**, No. 172; **1785**, No. 167.

H., and **1769**, bars 8 and 9

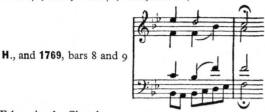

Erk omits the Choral.

134—**BG**. xxvi, 268 (Cantata 130) (*c*. 1740).

Erk (No. 218), first note Tenor  ; Richter (No. 131)

135—Erk (No. 220) prints the setting from an old MS ('von Emanuel Bach?'), as an alternative to No. 134 *supra* in Cantata 130.
136—**1787**, No. 333.
   1787, entitled 'Für deinen Thron tret ich hiemit'.
137—**1786**, No. 205.

   1786, bar 5 from end Soprano   ; so **1832**, No. 205; not in **1843**, No. 158.

   „   last two bars Bass   ;   **1832** } **1892**

1843   „   „   „

See another setting of the Plainsong in Bach's Organ Works (Augener ix, 1154; Novello xviii, 44).
   Erk omits the movement.
138—**BG.**, xxiv, 246 (Cantata 119) (1723).
138A—**BG.**, xxiv, 284 (Cantata 120) (1730).
   In Erk (No. 274) as 'Nun hilf, Herr Christ'.
139—**1786**, No. 212.
   The hymn was not in Leipzig use in Bach's period. Witt (No. 677) has another, but obviously derived, **tune** (Zahn, No. 4842). Telemann 1730, König 1738, and Reimann 1747, all use the 1556 melody (Zahn, No. 4840).
   Erk omits the Choral.
140—**H.**, No. 38; **1765**, No. 38; **1784**, No. 35.

   1784, bar 5 Tenor, last note   ; an error.

Here and in No. 141 Bach clearly takes the tune from two Hymn-books. In No. 140 his first line follows Crüger's text. In No. 141 he adopts a variation of that line which Zahn (No. 3695) notes in König 1738.
   Erk omits the choral.
141—**1787**, No. 286.   Erk omits the Choral.
142—**H.**, No. 140; **1769**, No. 140; **1785**, No. 136.
   Erk omits the Choral.
143—**1786**, No. 226.
   Reimann 1747 is the only 18th century Hymn-book containing the melody. Its text there (Zahn, No. 4711) is **not** uniform with Bach's, whose variation of the sixth line of the stanza is probably his own. The hymn was in Leipzig use (Leipzig 1729, 1740, 1744).
   1892 is disposed, but without good reason, to attribute the melody to Bach.
144—**H.**, No. 78; **1765**, No. 78; **1784**, No. 73.

   1765, bar 4 Bass, last note   ; corrected in the Druckfehler. Bach's statement of the melody

(*cf*. Nos. 145–147) is uniform and conventional.
145—**1786**, No. 266; **BG**. x, 298 (Cantata 48) (*c*. 1740).

   1786, bar 5 Alto, last beat   The Berlin Autograph Score (P. 109) has   ; but the

natural is preferable.

   1786, bar 9 Alto, first note   ; an error.

   „   penult. bar Alto   ; not so in P. 109.

146—**1787**, No. 293; **BG.** xxiv, 80 (Cantata 113) (*c.* 1740).

1787, bar 4 Bass

„   8 bar Alto

„   bar 9 Soprano, *tr* omitted.
„   last bar Tenor; no accidental.

„   bar 10 Alto 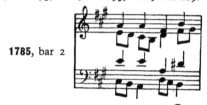 . The Autograph Score in the Musikbiblioltek Peters (MSa R.

No. 3) has A natural.

147—**H.,** No. 98; **1765**, No. 98; **1784**, No. 92; **BG.** xxxiii, 166 (Cantata 168) (*c.* 1725).

H., 1765, 1784, bar 5 Bass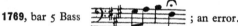

148—**H.,** No. 195; **1769**, No. 195; **1785**, No. 189.

1785, bar 2 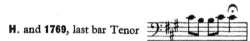 ; **H.** and **1769** can also be read so. But it is probable that the sign indicating a crossing of parts between the Alto and Tenor has been omitted in all.

1769, bar 5 Bass  ; an error.

H. and **1769,** last bar Tenor

Bach proposed to include a Prelude on the melody 'Herr Jesu Christ, wahr Mensch und Gott' in the 'Orgelbüchlein' ('Bach's Chorals', iii, 56). It is impossible to state the actual melody Bach had in mind; probably the tune to which the hymn is set in Witt 1715 (No. 697), a melody Bach has not used elsewhere.

149—**1787**, No. 283; **BG.** xxvi, 160 (Cantata 127) (*c.* 1740).

1787, bar 1

„   bar 11 Bass

150—**H.,** No. 196; **1769**, No. 196; **1785**, No. 190.
    Bach evidently follows Vetter 1713 (*cf.* Zahn, 3302).
    Erk (No. 227) quotes the melody from Reimann 1747, where it appears in a major form. The hymn was not in Leipzig use before 1740 (Leipzig 1740, 1744) and is not in Schemelli.

151—**1786**, No. 221.

1892, No. 85 bar 8 Alto, incorrectly transcribes ; so Richter, No. 149.

1843, No. 172, emends

Erk omits the Choral.

152—**H.,** No. 147; **1769**, No. 147; **1785**, No. 144; **1787**, No. 317.
    The four texts are uniform; but **H.**, **1769**, and **1785** are entitled 'Wer in dem Schutz des Höchsten ist'. Bach's melodic text (*cf.* No. 153) is uniform, excepting the second line.
    Erk omits the Choral.

153—**1787**, No. 316; **BG**. xxxii, 114 (Cantata 156) (1730 or 1729).

Bar 3 Tenor, the original Parts (Thomasschule) have

1787, bar 4 Tenor

Erk (No. 167), prints the Choral under the title 'Aus tiefer Noth schrei ich zu dir'.

154—**1786**, No. 277.
Bach proposed to include a Prelude on the tune in the 'Orgelbüchlein' ('Bach's Chorals', iii, 57). Of his four texts of the melody, the most considerable variation is in the third line of No. 157 *infra*. As this Choral was written before Bach came to Leipzig in 1723 the form he adopts there may have been a Weimar use. It is observable that a similar treatment of that line appears in Witt 1715 (No. 698).
Erk omits the Choral.

155—**BG**. xxx, 299 (Cantata 149) (1731).

156—**H**., No. 60; **1765**, No. 60; **1784**, No. 56; **BG**. xxxv, 157 (Cantata 174) (1729).

H., **1765**, **1784**, bar 8 Alto

„ „ „ bar 10 Tenor, last note G sharp.

„ „ „ bar 18 Tenor, last beat

H., bar 13 Bass ; an error.

Erk (No. 228), bar 13 Alto

157—**H**., No. 111; **1769**, No. 111; **1785**, No. 107; **BG**. xii (1), 131 (St John Passion) (1723).

H., **1769**, **1785**, bar 13 Alto

„ „ „ bar 17 Bass

„ „ „ bar 20 Tenor

158—**BG**. xxxiii, 27 (Cantata 161) (1715).
No. 159 *infra* has the same Bass.
Erk (No. 232), bar 11 Tenor, 4th note G sharp; so Richter (No. 161). Bach's melodic text (*cf.* Nos. 159–168) is conventional and nearly uniform. Probably his treatment of the melody's second line in Nos. 160 and 162 is his own.

159—**1786**, No. 270.
1786, entitled 'Befiehl du deine Wege'.

160—**H**., No. 88; **1765**, No. 88; **1784**, No. 89: **BG**. iv, 248 (St Matthew Passion) (1729).
H., **1765**, **1784**, in B mi., to 'O Haupt voll Blut'.

„ „ „ bar 4 Soprano

1765, bar 9 Bass ; an error.

„ bar 11 Tenor ; an error corrected in the Druckfehler.

The small notes are the vocal Bass of **H**., **1765**, **1784**.

161—**BG**. xxviii, 136 (Cantata 135) (*c*. 1740).
162—**1787**, No. 344; **BG**. v (2), 36 (Christmas Oratorio) (1734).
Excepting the small note in bar 8 the vocal Bass of **1787** is uniform with the Continuo of **BG**.
1787, to 'O Haupt voll Blut'.

163—**H**., No. 24; **1765**, No. 24; **1784**, No. 21; **BG**. xxxii, 46 (Cantata 153) (1727).
164—**1787**, No. 285.
1787, to 'Befiehl du deine Wege'.
Erk omits the Choral.

165—H., No. 86; **1765**, No. 86; **1784**, No. 87; **BG**. iv, 186 (St Matthew Passion) (1729).
    H., 1765, 1784, to ' O Haupt voll Blut '.

166—**1787**, No. 366.
    1787, to ' Befiehl du deine Wege '.

167—H., No. 102; **1769**, No. 102; **1785**, No. 98; **BG**. iv, 51, 53 (St Matthew Passion) (1729).
    H., 1769, 1785, in D, to ' O Haupt voll Blut '.
    BG. iv, 51, in E; **BG**. iv, 53, in E flat.
    Erk (No. 57), in E.

168—H., No. 79; **1765**, No. 79; **1784**, No. 74; **BG**. iv, 214 (St Matthew Passion) (1729).
    H., 1765, 1784, to ' O Haupt voll Blut '.

H., bar 2  ; **1765,** bar 2

169—H., No. 62; **1765**, No. 62; **1784**, No. 58; **BG**. xii (1), 17 (St John Passion) (1723).
    H., 1765, 1784, show the following variations for the vocal Bass of **BG**.

bar 9  ; bar 11

Bach's treatment of the second line of the melody invariably (*cf.* Nos. 170–172) has an individual note. Crüger

wrote  (Zahn, No. 983).

170—H., No. 115; **1769**, No. 115; **1785**, No. 111; **BG**. xii (1), 52 (St John Passion) (1723).

    H., 1769, 1785, bar 8 Tenor last note [♪] .

171—H., No. 85; **1765**, No. 85; **1784**, No. 78; **BG**. iv, 23 (St Matthew Passion) (1729).

    H., 1765, 1784, penult. bar Bass.

172—H., No. 109; **1769**, No. 109; **1785**, No. 105; **BG**. iv, 192 (St Matthew Passion) (1729).

Erk (No. 60), bar 7 Tenor 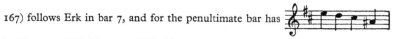 ; penult. bar Soprano

Neither reading is authorized by the Berlin Autograph Score (P. 25) nor any 18th century text. Richter (No.

167) follows Erk in bar 7, and for the penultimate bar has

173—H., No. 173; **1769**, No. 173; **1785**, No. 168.
    After 1644 the melody is found in no 18th century Hymn-book except Reimann 1747 (Zahn, No. 8569).
The hymn was not in Leipzig use, nor is in Schemelli 1736.
    Erk omits the Choral.

174—H., No. 174; **1769**, No. 174; **1785**, No. 171.

    1892, No. 155, bar 6 Bass incorrectly has 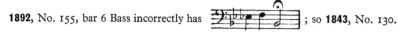 ; so **1843**, No. 130.

Excepting 1644, the melody appears only in König 1738 and Reimann 1747 among 18th century Hymn-books.
The hymn was not in Leipzig use, nor is in Schemelli 1736.
    Erk omits the Choral.

175—H., No. 70; **1765**, No. 70; **1784**, No. 79.

    H., 1765, 1784, penult. bar Alto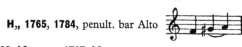

176—**1786**, No. 199; **1787**, No. 301.

The two texts differ only in the Tenor of bar 6. **1786** has [bass clef notation] . The melody was current in

various forms. Bach's is close to Crüger's (1653) (Zahn, No. 4329f).
    Erk omits the Choral.

APPENDIX I

177—**H.**, No. 159; **1769**, No. 159; **1785**, No. 155.

H. and **1769**, bar 11, Alto

A Leipzig use of the melody is betokened by the fact that it is in Vopelius 1682 (Zahn, No. 3687a).
Erk omits the Choral.

178—**1787**, No. 367; **BG.** v (2), 166 (Christmas Oratorio) (1734).
1787 is identical with **BG.** minus the orchestral symphonies; so also **1843**, No. 209.
Erk (No. 235) prints the Choral in its Oratorio form.

179—**1786**, No. 251.
The hymn is included in Dretzel 1731, Schemelli 1736, König 1738, Freylinghausen 1741, and Reimann 1747. It was also in Leipzig use (Leipzig 1729, 1740, 1744. Freylinghausen associates it with Albert's melody, used by Bach in Schemelli 1736 (*infra* No. 439).

180—**1786**, No. 223.
The melody is also in Reimann 1747.
Erk (No. 237), a minor third higher (three flats). He omits the accidental before the last Bass note of bar 2.

181—**H.**, No. 2; **1765**, No. 2; **1784**, No. 2.
Bach proposed to include a Prelude on the melody in the 'Orgelbüchlein' ('Bach's Chorals', iii, 58). His form of the melody, here and in Nos. 182–3 *infra*, does not follow Witt 1715 (No. 411).
Erk omits the Choral.

182—**1787**, No. 340; **BG.** vii, 282 (Cantata 37) (1727).

BG., bar 3 Tenor  ; **1787**, **1832**, and **1843**, all have G natural.

Vocal Score, bar 7, has G sharp as first Soprano and Tenor notes. The Original Score is not autograph, but the figuring forbids the sharp and it is altogether improbable that Bach should have altered the melody on its repetition (*cf.* bar 3). **1787** is supported by **1832**, No. 341, and **1843**, No. 1b.
Erk (No. 63) adopts both the above readings.

1787, bar 8 Tenor

183—**1786**, No. 272.

1786, bar 7 Alto ; an error.

Erk omits the Choral.

184—**H.**, No. 194; **1769**, No. 194; **1785**, No. 188.

H., and **1769**, bar 6, last beat ; so **1892**, No. 96.

Bach proposed to include a Prelude on the melody in the 'Orgelbüchlein' ('Bach's Chorals', iii, 59). It is therefore significant that his melodic line adopts the Witt 1715 (No. 414) form of a tune which exists in many variants.

185—**1786**, No. 229.
Crüger's Gesangbuch (1640) altered 'Herr' to 'O' in the first line of the hymn, a text which was thereafter general.

186—**H.**, No. 64; **1765**, No. 64; **1784**, No. 61; **BG.** xxviii, 80 (Cantata 133) (1735 or 1737).

H., **1765**, **1784**, bar 11

The melody appeared in print first in 1754, in Johann Daniel Müller's 'Vollständiges Hessen-Hanauisches Choral-Buch'. It is found in Bach's autograph twenty years earlier (*cf.* 'Bach's Chorals', ii, 393). That it is his composition is improbable; for in 1738 König used it and also printed a tune obviously related (Zahn, No. 5157):

Both Bach's and König's melodies are reminiscent of 'O Gott, du frommer Gott' (No. 289 *infra*). The hymn was in Leipzig use (Leipzig 1729, 1740, 1744) and is in Schemelli 1736 (No. 194).

187—**H.**, No. 22; **1765**, No. 22; **1784**, No. 19.

1892, No. 98, bar 8, 3rd beat 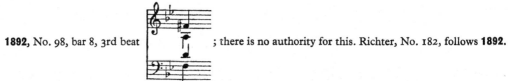 ; there is no authority for this. Richter, No. 182, follows **1892**.

Erk omits the Choral.

188—**1843**, No. 19 B, C, D.
The three settings (transposed by **1843** into G minor, with minor alterations in the text) are from the Organ Chorals (**BG**. xl.). Peters vi, 77 prints A; Novello xviii, 58, B and C; Augener iv, 1101 and v, 1115, A and B.

A, bar 1 Tenor-Bass, Augener has

„ bar 5, one MS (**BG**. xl) has

B, bar 9 Bass, Augener has

„ bars 1–3 Bass, **1843**, has

„ bar 9 Tenor, **1843**, has

C, last chord, **1843**, has

Erk omits the Chorals.
Bach proposed to include a Prelude on the melody in the ' Orgelbüchlein ' (' Bach's Chorals ', iii, 46).

189—**BG**. xxxvii, 118 (Cantata 185) (1715).

Erk (No. 240), bar 7 Soprano

190—**H.**, No. 69; **1765**, No. 69; **1784**, No. 71; **BG**. xxxv, 234 (Cantata 177) (1732).
Excepting **BG**., all the texts are in E minor, the grace notes in bars 2 and 3 are lacking, and the vocal Bass is uniform with the Cantata Continuo (except bars 12, 13, and the first two beats of 14).

191—**H.**, No. 165; **1769**, No. 165; **1785**, No. 161.

H., and **1769**, bar 1 Bass

1785, bar 1 Soprano

Bach's free treatment of the melody for Schemelli 1736 may be studied in No. 444 *infra*. Zahn (No. 3703) does not reveal its occurrence in any other Hymn-book between 1712 and 1830. The hymn was not in Leipzig use in Bach's period.
Erk omits the Choral.

192—**H.**, No. 145; **1769**, No. 145; **1785**, No. 140.

H. and **1769**, bar 3 Alto

The melody had very little vogue. Vopelius 1682 includes it and indicates a Leipzig use.

193—**BG**. xii (2), 50 (Cantata 52) (c. 1730).
Bach's treatment of the melody is generally uniform (*cf.* Nos. 194, 195) and differs markedly from the original 1581 text. The variations, however, are not all his own. Cf. ' Bach's Chorals ', iii, 214.

194—**H.**, No. 81; **1765**, No. 81; **1784**, No. 77; **BG**. v (2), 190 (Christmas Oratorio) (1734).

        H., **1765**, **1784**, bar 4, last note Bass

         ,,   ,,   ,,   bar 8, last note Bass

         ,,   ,,   ,,   bar 6, Alto   ; so in the Berlin Original Score (P. 32) Alto part, but not in Vn. ii.

         ,,   ,,   ,,   bar 6, Bass part uniform with **BG**. Continuo.

         ,,   ,,   ,,   bar 10 Alto   ; so **1832**, No. 77; **1843**, No. 72 A,

195—**H.**, No. 122; **1769**, No. 123 (122); **1785**, No. 118; **BG**. iv, 151 (St Matthew Passion) (1729).
196—**H.**, No. 150; **1769**, No. 150; **1785**, No. 143.

        H. and **1769**, bar 10 Tenor

Erk omits the Choral.

197—**H.**, No. 126; **1769**, No. 126; **1785**, No. 122; **BG**. xx (1), 118 (Cantata 85) (1735).

        H., **1769**, **1785**, bar 4 Bass   ; so **1832**, No. 122.

1843, No. 89 rewrites the bar

Apart from the collection in which it appeared, the melody is not found again in print earlier than **1769**. Its present form, greatly superior to the original, must be attributed to Bach. The hymn was in Leipzig use (Leipzig 1729, 1740, 1744) and is in Schemelli 1736 (No. 613).

198—**1786**, No. 269.
    Bach's four texts of the melody evidently follow two different versions. The last four bars of Nos. 198, 200, 201 indicate a common original. None of them appears in a Cantata and all may date from the pre-Leipzig period. Bach proposed to include a Prelude on the melody in the ' Orgelbüchlein ' (' Bach's Chorals ', iii, 43), and the tune is in Witt 1715 (No. 286), whose last line and Bach's show a close relation. No. 199, on the other hand, clearly follows a Leipzig use (Vetter 1713). *Cf.* Zahn, No. 6804.

199—**1787**, No. 296; **BG**. xviii, 286 (Cantata 78) (*c*. 1740).

        1787, bar 9, Soprano

         ,,   ,,   Bass

200—**H.**, No. 41; **1765**, No. 41; **1784**, No. 37.

        H. and **1765**, bar 11 Bass

201—**1787**, No. 368.
    Erk omits the Choral.
202—**H.**, No. 175; **1769**, No. 175; **1785**, No. 169.
    H. and **1769**, bar 7 Tenor first note D natural.

        1785 penult. bar Soprano   . The original (? 1668) text, which Bach follows closely, has A as the first note, as in **H.**, and **1769**.

    Excepting its original source, the melody is found in no Hymn-book earlier than (Zahn, No. 6335) Reimann 1747. The hymn was not in Leipzig use until 1740 (Leipzig 1740, 1744) and is not in Schemelli 1736.
203—**1786**, No. 243.
    The inclusion of this melody in Vopelius 1682 indicates a Leipzig use.
    Erk omits the Choral.
204—**1786**, No. 244.
    A harmonization of the figured Choral in Schemelli (*infra* No. 446). König 1738 includes the hymn, but to another melody (Zahn, No. 6447).
    Excepting Schemelli (*infra* No. 447), the melody is found in no Hymn-book earlier than 1815.
    Erk omits the Choral.

205—**H.**, No. 63; **1765**, No. 63; **1784**, No. 59; **BG.** xxxii, 168 (Cantata 159) (1729).

    H., **1765**, and **1784**, bar 2 Tenor, a flat is lacking before the last note.

    „   „   „   Bass uniform with the **BG.** Continuo in bars 15–16.

    Bach's melodic line (*cf.* Nos. 206, 207) is uniform. It is noticeable that he does not follow the Leipzig tradition, as in Vopelius 1682 (p. 165), but prefers a version published at Weissenfels 1714 (Zahn, No. 6288).

    Becker (**1843**, No. 59 D.) prints the following setting of the melody ('transposed from D into A'), but does not reveal its source. It occurs nowhere else:

206—**H.**, No. 83; **1765**, No. 83; **1784**, No. 82; **BG.** xii (1), 39 (St John Passion) (1723).

    H., **1765**, **1784**, bar 12 Bass, small notes.

207—**H.**, No. 110; **1769**, No. 110; **1785**, No. 106; **BG.** xii (1), 103 (St John Passion) (1723).

    BG. bar 7 Tenor-Bass, last chord, ♫ The Tenor B accords with the figuring. On the other hand, Bach's Score here is not autograph and is corrected by all the 18th century texts, as well as **1832**, No. 106.

    1843, No. 59 B follows **BG.**, as also do Erk (No. 67) and Richter (No. 193).

208—**1787**, No. 355.

    Of Bach's seven settings of this melody, two (Nos. 209 and 214) are distinguished from the others by the form of the second line ♫ This accords with Crüger's original text, excepting the sharpened fourth note, which being found in Vopelius 1682 and Vetter 1709, indicates Leipzig use. For the second part of the tune Bach follows a variation of Crüger's melody which Zahn (No. 8032) finds first in Georg Philipp Telemann's "Evangelisch-Musicalisches Lieder-buch," published at Hamburg in 1730. In fact, the form is found in two Cantatas (Nos. 64 and 81) which date from the early Leipzig years. It is therefore possible that Telemann

borrowed his distinctive treatment of the penultimate line: ♫ from Bach's use.

    Erk omits the Choral.

209—**H.**, No. 94; **1765**, No. 94; **1784**, No. 96; **BG.** xx (1), 152 (Cantata 87) (1735).

    H., **1765**, **1784**, bar 9 Tenor ♫ ; all to 'Jesu, meine Freude'.

    H., penult. bar Soprano ♫

    H., last bar Bass ♫ ; **1765** ♫ ; corrected in the Druckfehler.

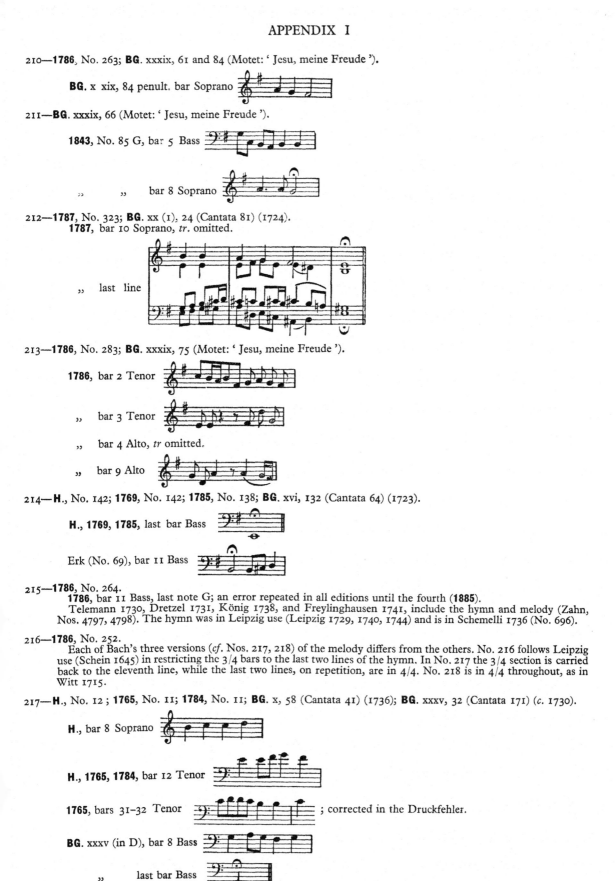

210—**1786**, No. 263; **BG**. xxxix, 61 and 84 (Motet: 'Jesu, meine Freude').

BG. x xix, 84 penult. bar Soprano

211—**BG**. xxxix, 66 (Motet: 'Jesu, meine Freude').

1843, No. 85 G, bar 5 Bass

,,   ,,   bar 8 Soprano

212—**1787**, No. 323; **BG**. xx (1), 24 (Cantata 81) (1724).
1787, bar 10 Soprano, *tr.* omitted.

,,   last line

213—**1786**, No. 283; **BG**. xxxix, 75 (Motet: 'Jesu, meine Freude').

1786, bar 2 Tenor

,,   bar 3 Tenor

,,   bar 4 Alto, *tr* omitted.

,,   bar 9 Alto

214—**H.**, No. 142; **1769**, No. 142; **1785**, No. 138; **BG**. xvi, 132 (Cantata 64) (1723).

H., **1769**, **1785**, last bar Bass

Erk (No. 69), bar 11 Bass

215—**1786**, No. 264.
1786, bar 11 Bass, last note G; an error repeated in all editions until the fourth (**1885**).
Telemann 1730, Dretzel 1731, König 1738, and Freylinghausen 1741, include the hymn and melody (Zahn, Nos. 4797, 4798). The hymn was in Leipzig use (Leipzig 1729, 1740, 1744) and is in Schemelli 1736 (No. 696).

216—**1786**, No. 252.
Each of Bach's three versions (*cf.* Nos. 217, 218) of the melody differs from the others. No. 216 follows Leipzig use (Schein 1645) in restricting the 3/4 bars to the last two lines of the hymn. In No. 217 the 3/4 section is carried back to the eleventh line, while the last two lines, on repetition, are in 4/4. No. 218 is in 4/4 throughout, as in Witt 1715.

217—**H.**, No. 12 ; **1765**, No. 11; **1784**, No. 11; **BG**. x, 58 (Cantata 41) (1736); **BG**. xxxv, 32 (Cantata 171) (*c.* 1730).

H., bar 8 Soprano

H., **1765**, **1784**, bar 12 Tenor

1765, bars 31–32 Tenor   ; corrected in the Druckfehler.

BG. xxxv (in D), bar 8 Bass

,,   last bar Bass

218—**1787**, No. 326; **BG**. xxxvii, 257 (Cantata 190) (1725).

1787, bar 13 Tenor

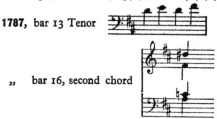

„ bar 16, second chord

„ Bass uniform with **BG**. Continuo.

219—**H.**, No. 179; **1769**, No. 179; **1785**, No. 174.

H. and **1769**, bar 1 Soprano

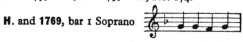

1785, penult. bar Alto ; so **1832**, No. 174; but not **1843**, No. 133.

Erk (No. 249), one tone higher.

220—**H.**, No. 34; **1765**, No. 34; **1784**, No. 30.

H., and **1765**, bar 4 Tenor

1892, No. 110, bar 2 Tenor queries the D sharp. It is unmistakeable in **H.**, 1765, 1784.

221—**H.**, No. 180; **1769**, No. 180; **1785**, No. 175.
    Erk (No. 251), in D.

222—**1787**, No. 337; **BG**, xxx, 95 (Cantata 145) (1729 or 1730).

223—**H.**, No. 133; **1769**, No. 133; **1785**, No. 129.

H. and **1769**, bar 9 Tenor, last note

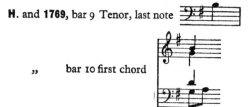

„ bar 10 first chord

Telemann 1730, Dretzel 1731, König 1738, Freylinghausen 1741, and Reimann 1747, include the hymn and melody (Zahn, No. 5395). The hymn was in Leipzig use (Leipzig 1729, 1740, 1744) and is in Schemelli 1736 (No. 615.)

224—**H.**, No. 193; **1769**, No. 193; **1785**, No. 187.

H. and **1769**, bar 3 Tenor

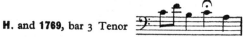

225—**BG**. xli, 238 (' Gott der Hoffnung ').
    The authenticity of this Cantata is very questionable.

226—**BG**. xii (2), 164 (Cantata 59) (1735); **BG**. xxxv, 177 (Cantata 175) (1735).

BG. xii (2), bars 10 and 21 Alto(10)  ; (21)

227—**H.**, No. 73; **1765**, No. 73; **1784**, No. 69; **BG**. xxxix, 57 (Motet: ' Der Geist hilft '). (1729.)

H., bar 4 last beat Tenor-Bass  ; **1765** and **1784**

1784, bar 8 Alto

H., **1765**, **1784**, bar 8 Bass

BG. (autograph), bar 13 last note Tenor, lacks an accidental to supersede the signature. All three 18th century texts have E flat.

    H., **1765**, **1784**, last bar Tenor: *tr.* omitted. All three texts are in G.

228—BG. xxxix, 125 (Motet: ' Komm, Jesu, komm ').
Erk omits the Choral.

229—1787, No. 369; **BG.** xviii, 146 (Cantata 74) (1735).

1787, bar 2 Bass

„ bar 3 Soprano

„ bar 12, second half

„ last bar Tenor

Vocal Score, bar 8 Alto, third beat 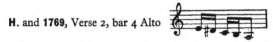 ; the F sharp is neither in **1787** nor in the Berlin Original Parts (St. 103).

230—H., No. 51; **1765,** No. 51; **1784,** No. 46; **BG.** xxiii, 230 (Cantata 108) (1735).
Excepting bar 3 from the end, the Bass of **H., 1765, 1784** is uniform with the Cantata Continuo.

231—H., No. 134; **1769,** No. 134; **1785,** No. 132.

H. and **1769,** Verse 2, bar 4 Alto

„ „ bar 5 Bass, fourth note, sharp lacking.

„ „ bar 10 Alto, first beat

H. Verse 2, bar 10 Bass, last beat 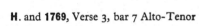 ; **1769** omits 7th quaver

H. and **1769,** Verse 3, bar 7 Alto-Tenor

„ „ bar 9 Bass, first beat

None of the texts is phrased for vocal use.
Erk omits the Choral.

232—1786, No. 218.
It would appear (Zahn, No. 6863) that Bach was original in his association of the melody with Opitz's hymn. Telemann 1730, König 1738, and Reimann 1747 set the tune to another text. The hymn was not in Leipzig use in Bach's period, nor is it in Schemelli 1736.
Erk omits the Choral.

233—H., No. 47; **1765,** No. 47; **1784,** No. 43; **BG.** i, 241 (Cantata 8) (c. 1725).

H. 1765, 1784, bar 5 Bass

„ „ „ bar 12 Soprano-Tenor, the grace note is lacking.
„ bar 12 Bass, first half of bar is omitted.

1765, penult. bar Tenor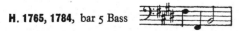

234—**H.**, No. 200; **1769**, No. 200; **1785**, No. 194; **BG.** xxvi, 60 (Cantata 123) (*c.* 1740).
    H. and **1769**, bar 1 Alto, third note lacks sharp.

1785, bar 7 Soprano ; a typographical error.

H., **1769**, **1785**, bar 7 Tenor ; not so in Berlin Autograph Score (P. 875).

BG. and vocal Score, bar 7 Bass ; repeated by Richter (No. 229). Not in P. 875

1785, bar 9 Alto ; not so in Berlin Autograph.

H. and **1769**, bar 11 Bass ; not so in Berlin Autograph.

Erk (No. 258), bar 13 Bass ; an error.

1785, bar 14 Alto ; not so in Berlin Autograph.

235 A—**H.**, No. 137; **1769**, No. 138; **1785**, No. 131; **1787**, No. 327.

    H., **1769**, **1785**, bar 2 Alto

    ,, ,, ,, bar 7 Soprano

    ,, ,, ,, bar 9 Alto

    ,, ,, ,, bar 9 Bass

    1769 and **1785**, bar 7 Tenor : **H.**, bar 7, lost chord

    H., bar 8 Alto

Erk omits the Choral.

    B—**BG.** xl, 25; **1843**, No. 96 A.
    The setting is among Kirnberger's collection of Bach's Organ Choralvorspiele.
    1843, No. 96B, also prints the Organ Choral included in Augener's (viii, 1101) and Novello's (xviii, 72) editions.

236—**1786**, No. 227.
    1786, bar 9 Bass, fourth note lacks sharp.

    ,, bar 17 Soprano ; an error.

    1892, No. 121, bar 19 Soprano  ; the emendation is unwarranted. Bach's text is true to the original (Zahn, No. 975).
    Erk omits the Choral.

237—**1786**, No. 276.
    Erk omits the Choral.

238—**H.**, No. 59; **1765**, No. 59; **1784**, No. 54; **BG**. xxxii, 16 (Cantata 151) (*c.* 1735-40).

H., 1765, 1784, bar 5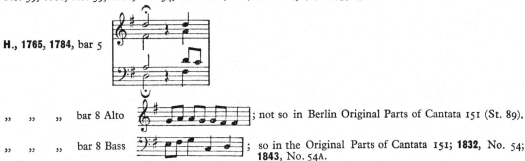

„ „ „ bar 8 Alto 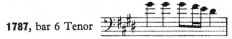 ; not so in Berlin Original Parts of Cantata 151 (St. 89).

„ „ „ bar 8 Bass ; so in the Original Parts of Cantata 151; **1832**, No. 54; **1843**, No. 54A.

239—**BG.** xiii (1), 70 (Cantata 195) (*c.* 1726).

240—**1787**, No. 341.
Erk omits the Choral.

241—**H.**, No. 48; **1765**, No. 48; **1784**, No. 44.
Erk omits the Choral.

242—**1787**, No. 309; **BG.** xii (1), 74 (St John Passion) (1723).
BG set to Postel's stanza.

1787, bar 6 Tenor

The Bass of **1787** is uniform with the Continuo of **BG.**, except bar 5.

243—**BG.** xxviii, 248 (Cantata 139) (*c.* 1740).

244—**1786**, No. 258.
Zahn (No. 1067) does not show Bach's version of the first line of the melody occurring elsewhere. Telemann 1730, Dretzel 1731, König 1738, and Reimann 1747, introduce the hymn and melody. The hymn was in Leipzig use (Leipzig, 1729, 1740, 1744) and is in Schemelli 1736 (No. 49).

245—**H.**, No. 135; **1769**, No. 135; **1785**, No. 130.

246—**1787**, No. 319.
1787, entitled ' Gott sei uns gnädig und barmherzig '.
Erk omits the Choral.

247—**1787**, No. 357; **BG.** i, 303 (Cantata 10) (*c.* 1740).

1787, bar 12 Bass ; so **1832**, No. 358; **1843**, No. 95.

248—**H.**, No. 155; **1769**, No. 155; **1785**, No. 151.

H., bar 6, Soprano

„ and **1769**, bar 7 Alto

Erk omits the Choral.

249—**BG.** xvi, 368 (Cantata 70) (1716).
The setting differs in details from No. 250.
Of Bach's seven settings of the melody, Nos. 253-4-5 differ from the others in the fifth and sixth lines. These, with emendations which appear to be Bach's, are taken from Hammerschmidt's *second* verse, whose melody differs from that of the first, which Bach uses in the other four settings.

Erk (No. 263), bar 1 Bass ; the B natural is unauthoritative.

250—**1787**, No. 347.
The settings differ in details from No. 249.

251—**H.**, No. 156; **1769**, No. 156; **1785**, No. 152; **BG.** xxxii, 82 (Cantata 154) (1724) .

BG., bar 1 Bass ; not so in the Berlin Original Score (P. 130).

H. and **1769**, last bar, Alto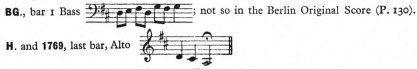

„ „ bars 4 and last, Bass, small notes.

252—**BG.**, xxxii, 140 (Cantata 157) (1727).

253—**1787**, No. 298.
  Erk omits the Choral.

254—**BG.** xxvi, 82 (Cantata 124) (*c.* 1740).

  The original Thomasschule Bass part, bar 4

255—**BG.** xli, 201.
  The concluding Choral of the St Matthew Passion in its original (1729) form.
  Erk does not include the Choral.

256—**1787**, No. 345.

   1787, bar 7 Tenor, first note   ; an error; so **1832**, No. 346

   1843, No. 208 substitutes   ; so **1892**, No. 128.

  A harmonization of the figured Choral in Schemelli 1736 (No. 462 *infra*). König 1738 also includes the hymn and melody. The hymn was not in Leipzig use in Bach's period. **1892**, on no solid ground, is disposed to attribute the melody to Bach.
  Erk omits the Choral.

257—**H.**, No. 53; **1765**, No. 53; **1784**, No. 49.

   H., bar 11 Alto   ; so **1832**, No. 49; but not **1843**, No. 49B.

   „ bar 12 Soprano

258—**1787**, No. 324; **BG.** xx (1), 76 (Cantata 83) (1724).

   1787, bar 8

   „ bar 9 Tenor, last note

   „ bar 13 Soprano-Alto

259—**BG.** xxvi, 110 (Cantata 125) *c* . 1740).

   BG., bar 5, last note Alto 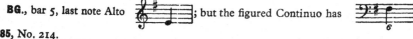 ; but the figured Continuo has

260—**1785**, No. 214.
  Erk omits the Choral.

261—**H.**, No. 153; **1769**, No. 153; **1785**, No. 149.

   H. and **1769**, penult. bar Soprano-Alto

  Gerhardt's popular hymn was included in Schemelli 1736 (No. 574), where it is set to the following melody, originally in Freylinghausen 1714:

                           (Zahn, No. 3342).

  Its relation to Bach's melody is evident. Telemann 1730 (Zahn, No. 3346), Dretzel 1731 (Zahn, Nos. 3347-3350), König 1738 (Zahn, No. 3353), and Reimann 1747 (Zahn, No. 3354) set the hymn to other and original melodies. Bach was at one with his contemporaries in providing a tune for Gerhardt's popular hymn, which was in Leipzig use (Leipzig 1729, 1740, 1744).

262—**H.**, No 101; **1769**, No. 101; **1785**, No. 97; **BG.** xxxiii, 192 (Cantata 169) (1731).

1785, bar 5 Bass

„ bar 8, last note Alto lacks the sharp.

„ bar 13, first half

H., 1769, 1785, bars 14, 15 Bass uniform with Continuo of **BG.**

263—**1784,** No. 36.

264—**H.**, No. 89; **1765**, No. 89; **1784**, No. 83; **BG.** xiii (1), 128 (Cantata 197) (1737).

265—**1787,** No. 329; **BG.** xiii (1), 149 (Three Wedding Chorals).

1787, bar 5 Tenor

„ „ Bass, small notes.

„ bar 8 Bass

„ bar 10

„ bar 12 Soprano-Alto

266—**H.**, No. 36; **1765**, No. 36; **1784**, No. 32.

267—**H.**, No. 191; **1769**, No. 191; **1785**, No. 185.

H. and **1769,** last bar Soprano

Erk omits the Choral.

268—**H.**, No. 188; **1769**, No. 188; **1785**, No. 183.

H. and **1769,** bar 9 Soprano

Erk (No. 272), in A.

269—**1787,** No. 361; **BG.** v (2), 245 (Christmas Oratorio) (1734).
1787, entitled ' Es ist gewisslich an der Zeit '.

270—**1786,** No. 260.

1786, first note Soprano

„ entitled ' Es ist gewisslich an der Zeit '.

271—**H.**, No. 32; **1765**, No. 32; **1784**, No. 28; **BG.** vii, 258 (Cantata 36) (c. 1730).

1765, bar 2 Bass, last note :uncorrected in the Druckfehler.

272—**H.**, No. 176; **1769**, No. 176; **1785**, No. 170; **BG.** xvi, 50 (Cantata 62) (c. 1740).
H., 1769, 1785, in A minor; Bass as Continuo of **BG.**

H., 1769, bar 3 Tenor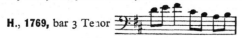

273—**BG.** xxxiii, 104 (Cantata 165) (1724).

274—**BG.** xviii, 316 (Cantata 79) (1735).

275—**H.,** No. 99; **1765**, No. 99; **1784**, No. 93; **1786**, No. 257; **BG.** xxix, 138 (Cantata 194) (1723).
 H., **1765**, **1784**, entitled ' Wach auf, mein Herz, und singe '.
 „ „ „ bar 4 Soprano, no *tr*.

 „ „ „ bar 5 Bass

 1786, penult. bar, Soprano

276—**H.,** No. 7; **1765**, No. 7; **1784**, No. 6; **BG.** ii, 225 (Cantata 17) (1737 or 1727).

 H., **1765**, **1784**, bar 15 Soprano

 BG., bar 18 Soprano ; not so in the Berlin Autograph Score (P. 45, adn. 4).

 H., **1765**, **1784**, bar 22 Alto ; the Berlin Autograph has A sharp.

 1765 and **1784**, first chord bar 34

 1843, No. 6 E prints as a simple Choral the extended setting of the melody in the middle movement of the Motet ' Singet dem Herrn '.

277—**1786**, No. 268.

 1786, bar 7 Alto ; corrected in **1843**, No. 6 A.

 „ bar 14, first note Alto, no flat; corrected in **1843**, No. 6A.

 „ bar 18 Alto ; corrected in **1843**, No. 6A.

 Erk omits the Choral.

278—**1787**, No. 295.
 Erk omits the Choral.

279—**H.,** No. 121; **1769**, No. 121; **1785**, No. 116; **BG.** v (1), 316 (Cantata 29) (1731.

 H. and **1769**, bar 28 Bass ; the last note is G natural in **1785** and the Berlin Autograph Score (P. 166.

 H., **1769**, **1785**, penult. bar Tenor

 „ „ „ Bass uniform with Continuo of **BG.**, excepting bar 26

280—**1786**, No. 222.
 Zahn (No. 4089) notices the repetition of the last line as peculiar to Reimann 1747 in the Hymn-books of Bach's period. Neither Telemann, Dretzel, nor König includes the melody. The hymn was not in Leipzig use in Bach's period, but is in Schemelli 1736 (No. 821).
 Erk omits the Choral.

281—**1786**, No. 240.
 The second line of the melody, as written by Bach, does not appear in a Hymn-book until Telemann's (1730). Witt 1715 differs materially. Hence Bach's setting may be attributed to the middle Leipzig period. The hymn was in Leipzig use (Leipzig 1729, 1740, 1744) and is in Schemelli 1736 (No. 53). *Cf.* Zahn, No. 212B. Dretzel 1731, uses the same, and König 1738 another melody (Zahn, No. 214).
 Erk omits the Choral.

282—**1786**, No. 274.
 The Bass is the same as in No. 467 *infra*.

283—**H.**, No. 29; **1765**, No. 29; **1784**, No. 26; **BG**. ii, 317 and 327 (Cantata 20) (*c.* 1725).

1765, bar 7 Bass [musical notation] ; an error, corrected in the Druckfehler.

284—**1787**, No. 311; **BG**. xli, 114 (' Ehre sei Gott ') (1728).

1787, bar 9 Bass [musical notation]

„ bar 13 Alto [musical notation]

„ bar 13 Bass, the whole of the seventh line an octave lower.

„ penult. bar Soprano-Tenor [musical notation]

285—**1786**, No. 255; **BG**. xvi, 120 (Cantata 64) (1723).

1786 (' Was frag ich nach der Welt '), bar 9 Bass [musical notation]

286—**1786**. No. 290; **BG**. xxii, 127 (Cantata 94) (1735); **BG**. xvi, 372 (Cantata 64) (1723).

1786 (' Was frag ich nach der Welt '), bar 11, last chord Soprano-Alto [musical notation] ; an error.

„ bar 12 Alto, third note (G) lacks a sharp.

„ bar 13 Alto, last note [musical notation]

„ bar 15 Tenor, „ „ [musical notation]

BG. xvi, last line Soprano-Alto [musical notation]

This setting was used in Cantata 64 as a variant of No. *285 supra*.

287—**H.**, No. 90; **1765**, No. 90; **1784**, No. 84; **BG**. x, 186 (Cantata 45) (*c.* 1740).
H., **1765**, **1784**, Bass uniform with Continuo of **BG**.

288—**BG**. xxvi, 184 (Cantata 128) (*c.* 1735).

Erk (No. 279), following a copy of the Original Score, bar 4 Alto [musical notation]

„ bar 6 Tenor [musical notation]

Neither of these readings is found in the Autograph Score owned by Frau Radecke, Winterthur.

289—**1787**, No. 336; **1843**, No. 205B; **BG**. v (1), 150 (Cantata 24) (1723).
The Choral lacks the orchestral interludes which accompany it in the Cantata.

BG., bar 2 Tenor, last note, [musical notation]

„ bar 3 Alto [musical notation] ; Bass [musical notation]

„ bar 5 Bass, last beat [musical notation]

„ bar 6 Tenor, last beat [musical notation]

„ bar 7 Soprano [musical notation]

„ bar 8 Bass [musical notation]

BG., bar 11 Alto, fifth note (E) lacks flat.

„ bars 13–14

Erk omits the Choral, which, in the Cantata, is extended by orchestral interludes.

290—**1787,** No. 314.
Erk omits the Choral.

291—**H.,** No. 82; **1765,** No 82; **1784,** No. 81.; **BG.** x, 236 (Cantata 46) (*c.* 1725).

1765, bar 5 Tenor, last note

BG., bar 8 Bass

„ bar 11 Bass

H., bar 15 Bass

BG., bar 16 Tenor

„ bar 18 Alto F natural.
Erk (No. 280) includes the orchestral interludes, as in **BG.**

292—**H.,** No. 16; **1765,** No. 16; **1784,** No. 14.
Differing in key, the Choral is closely similar to No. 293 (Erk, No. 106).

293—**BG.,** xxxvii, 95 (Cantata 184) (1731).

294—**H.,** No. 178; **1769,** No. 178; **1785,** No. 173.

H., bar 2, last note Soprano-Alto

The Choral is found in no Hymn-book prior to 1851. The hymn was not in Leipzig use in Bach's period, nor is it in Schemelli 1736.
Erk omits it.

295—**1786,** No. 236; **1787,** No. 294.

1787 (' Herr Jesu Christ, meins Lebens Licht '), bar 1 Bass

1786 (' O Jesu, du mein Bräutigam '), bar 3 Bass

„ bar 5 Alto, D sharp.
1787, bar 8 Alto, first note G sharp; an error.

„ bar 9 Alto

Erk omits the Choral.

296—**H.,** No. 170; **1769,** No. 170; **1785,** No. 165.

H. and **1769,** bar 4, third and fourth beats Tenor-Bass

„ „ bar 8, Soprano

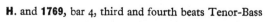

297—**1786**, No. 201; **1787**, No. 305.

1786, bar 5 Alto

Erk omits the Choral.

298—**1786**, No. 203.
   1786, bar 12 Alto. F natural.
   „ penult. bar Alto, first note (E) lacks flat.
   Winterfeld (iii, 285) wrongly attributes the melody to Bach. The hymn was not in Leipzig use in Bach's period, nor is it in Schemelli 1736.
   Erk (No. 282), in A mi.

299—**H.**, No. 74; **1765**, No. 74; **1784**, No. 60.
   Erk omits the Choral.

300—**H.**, No. 54; **1765**, No. 54; **1784**, No. 50; **BG.**, iv, 164 (St Matthew Passion) (1729).
   H., **1765**, **1784**, entitled ' In allen meinen Thaten '.

301—**H.**, No. 120; **1769**, No. 120; **1785**, No. 117; **BG.** iv, 42 (St Matthew Passion) (1729).
   H., **1769**, **1785**, entitled ' Nun ruhen alle Wälder '.
   „   „   „   bar 10 Bass, the final note (E) lacks natural. In the Berlin Autograph Score (P. 25) the natural is distinct.

302—**H.**, No. 65; **1765**, No. 65; **1784**, No. 62; **BG.** xii (1), 31 (St John Passion) (1723).
   H., **1765**, **1784**, entitled ' Nun ruhen alle Wälder '.
   H., bar 9 Alto, last note (F sharp) lacking.

   BG., bar 10 Alto, last beat ; the suggested D sharp is authorized neither by the Berlin Original Score (P. 28) nor any text until **1843**, No. 50A. See No. 304 *infra*.

303—**1786**, No. 275.
   1786, entitled ' O Welt, sieh hier dein Leben '.

   1892, No. 143, bar 5, third beat, Soprano-Tenor  ; the alteration is unwarranted. *Cf.* No. 307 *infra*.

Erk omits the Choral.

304—**1787**, No. 362.
   1787, entitled ' O Welt, sieh hier dein Leben '. The Choral is a variation of No. 302 *supra*.

305—**1787**, No. 365.
   1787, entitled ' O Welt, sieh hier dein Leben '.
   Erk omits the Choral.

306—**1787**, No. 354; **BG.** x, 150 (Cantata 44) (*c.* 1725).

   1787 (' Nun ruhen alle Wälder '), last bar Tenor

307—**H.**, No. 107; **1765**, No. 107; **1785**, No. 103; **BG.** ii, 98 (Cantata 13) (*c.* 1740).
   H., **1765**, **1785**, entitled ' Nun ruhen alle Wälder '.
   „   „   „   bars 1–3, Bass uniform with **BG.** Continuo.

308—**BG.** xxii, 230 (Cantata 97) (1734).
   Erk does not include the Choral.

309—**1787**, No. 288.
   1787, entitled ' Nun ruhen alle Wälder '.

   1787, bar 6 Alto, last beat

Erk omits the Choral.

310—**1786**, No. 213.
   This popular hymn was in Leipzig use (Leipzig 1729, 1740, 1744) and is in Schemelli 1736 (No. 894).

311—**1786**, No. 219.
   The melody is in Vopelius 1682 and therefore was in Leipzig use. It will be observed that Bach introduces the opening of the other melody (No. 310) into the first Tenor bar.

312—1786, No. 202.

1786, bar 5 Soprano　[music notation]　; an error.

　„　bar 14 Alto, last note (D) lacks accidental.

　„　bar 18 Soprano　[music notation]　; corrected in **1843**, No. 156.

Erk omits the Choral.

313—H., No. 11; **1765**, No. 12; **1784**, No. 12; **BG.** xvi, 152 (Cantata 65) (1724).

H., 1765, 1784, bar 14

　　In the original, the second line of the melody was sung to the repeated last three syllables of the first line of each stanza.　The substitution of 'Alleluja!' has involved a slight alteration of Bach's phrasing.

314—H., No. 25; **1765**, No. 25; **1784**, No. 22;　**BG.** xxxv, 322 (Cantata 180) (c. 1740).
H., 1765, 1784, in E flat.

H., and 1765, bar 5 Tenor　[music notation]

315—H., No. 144; **1769**, No. 144; **1785**, No. 142; **BG.** vii, 387 (Cantata 40) (1723).

H. and 1769, bar 8 Bass　[music notation]

1785, bar 9 Bass　[music notation]　; the second B is flattened in the Berlin Autograph (P. 63).

　„　bar 11 Alto　[music notation]

H. and 1769, bar 11 Soprano　[music notation]

　„　　„　bar 14, Bass　[music notation]

　　The melody in Vetter 1713 (No. 87), represents the Leipzig use. Bach's is a great improvement upon it and probably his own. Zahn (No. 6295B) notes a MS of it in 1750.

316—1785, No. 141.

1785 bar 4 Tenor, last beat　[music notation]

　　The Choral, excepting bars 6 and 7, is generally identical with No. 317 *infra* (Erk, No. 287). Hymn and melody are in Freylinghausen 1704, Dretzel 1731, König 1738, Reimann 1747, and Schemelli 1736 (see No. 472 *infra*). The hymn was not in Leipzig use before 1740 (Leipzig 1740, 1744).
　　1843, No. 104A shows minor modifications.

317—H., No. 146; **1769**, No. 146.

H., bar 3 Soprano　[music notation]　.　See No. 472 *infra*.

318—H. No. 177; **1769**, No. 177; **1785**, No. 172.

H., and 1769, bar 2 Bass　[music notation]

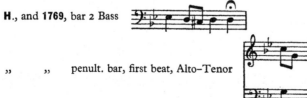

　„　　„　penult. bar, first beat, Alto-Tenor

　　It is noteworthy that here, as in the Organ Prelude on the melody, Bach follows Witt 1715, and not Vopelius's original Leipzig text. *Cf.* ' Bach's Chorals ', iii, 292. Bach's Bass is uniform with No. 474 *infra*.

319—**H.**, No. 113; **1769**, No. 113; **1785**, No. 109; **BG.** xxxvii, 191 (Cantata 187) (1732).

    H., **1769**, **1785**, bar 6 Tenor   ; not so in the Berlin Autograph Score (P. 84).

    H., penult. bar Alto   ; an error.

    Erk (No. 289) inserts a *tr.* in bars 3, 5, 7, which is not in the voice parts of the Cantata nor the 18th century texts.

320—**1786**, No. 246.
    The hymn was not in Leipzig use in Bach's period and is not in Schemelli 1736.
    Reimann 1747 uses another melody (Zahn, No. 6425).
    Erk omits the Choral.

321—**1786**, No. 206.

    1786, bar 3 Soprano

      „   bar 5 Tenor

    1786, bar 9 is omitted; it is supplied from the figuring of No. 477 *infra*.
    The hymn and melody are in Schemelli (No. 315). König 1738 uses another melody (Zahn, No. 850). The hymn was in Leipzig use (Leipzig 1729, 1740, 1744).
    Erk omits the Choral.

322—**1786**, No. 220.
    Cf. ' Lasset uns ' (No. 455 *infra*).
    The association of the melody with Gerhardt's hymn appears first in Witt 1715 (No. 387). While Bach's version of the melody seems to be in a large measure original, its familiarity with Witt's text is evident.
    Erk omits the Choral.

323—**H.**, No. 42; **1765**, No. 42; **1784**, No. 38; **BG.** xxiv, 132 (Cantata 115) (c. 1740).

    H., **1765**, **1784**, last bar Tenor

     „   „   „   in E flat.
    Telemann 1730, Dretzel 1731, König 1738, Freylinghausen 1741, Reimann 1747, include the melody (Zahn, No. 6274). The hymn was in Leipzig use (Leipzig 1729, 1740, 1744) and is in Schemelli 1736 (No. 945).

324—**H.**, No. 27; **1765**, No. 27; **1784**, No. 24.

    1885, No. 24; bar 9 Bass   ; probably the correct reading.

    Erk omits the Choral.

325—**H.**, No. 112; **1769**, No. 112; **1785**, No. 108; **BG.** xii (1), 95 (St John Passion) (1723).

    H., **1769**, **1785**, bar 3 Soprano   ; in the Berlin Original Score the last note is G.

326—**H.**, No. 114; **1769**, No. 114; **1785**, No. 110; **BG.** xxiii, 66 (Cantata 102) (1731).

    1785, bar 8 Soprano

      „   penult. bar Alto

327—**H.**, No. 50; **1765**, No. 50; **1784**, No. 47; **BG.** xii (1), p. xvi.
    The Choral is No. 9 of the St John Passion as it appeared in the first and second version of that work. It is curious that the Choral found its way into **H.**, **1765**, and **1784** in this form rather than as in No. 328 *infra*.

    BG., bar 6 Alto

      „   „   Tenor

      „   bar 11 Bass

328—**BG.** xii (1), 18 (St John Passion).

329—**BG**. xxiii, 32 (Cantata 101) (*c.* 1740).
 The setting is closely similar to No. 330. Erk prints it in the Cantata form.

330—**1787**, No. 291 ('Nimm von uns, Herr').
 Cf. No. 329 *supra.*

331—**1786**, No. 267; **BG**. xx (1), 214 (Cantata 90) (*c.* 1740).

 1786, bar 8 Alto  ; in the Autograph Berlin Score (P. 83) the last note is G natural.

332—**H**. No. 97; **1765**, No. 97; **1784**, No. 91; **1786**, No. 259 ; **BG**. x, 91 (Cantata 42) (1731).

 1786, bar 10 Tenor

 ,,   ,,   Alto

 ,,   bar 11, Tenor-Bass, fourth beat

 ,,   bar 15 Alto

 H., **1765**, **1784**, Bass uniform with Continuo of **BG**. except in bars 13 ( ), 19–21, 23.

333—**1786**, No. 215; **BG**. xxvi, 131 (Cantata 126) (*c.* 1740).
 1786, bar 9 Tenor, fifth note C natural.
 ,,   bar 12 ,, first note C.
 ,,   bar 15 Bass, second note F sharp.
 ,,   in G mi.

334—**BG**. v (2), 66 (Christmas Oratorio) (1734).

335—**H**., No. 49; **1765**, No. 49; **1784**, No. 45; **BG**. v (2), 47 (Christmas Oratorio) (1734).
 In the Oratorio the lines of the hymn are separated by orchestral interludes and the following variations of the Bass are found:

 Bar 4

 ,, 5

 ,, 6–8

 Erk (No. 295) prints the Choral in its Oratorio form.

336—**1787**, No. 343; **BG**. v (2), 90 (Christmas Oratorio) (1734).

 In the Oratorio the lines of the hymn are separated by orchestral interludes. Bar 7 there appears thus:

 Erk (No. 296) prints the Choral in its Oratorio form.   The Oratorio movement is in 12/8. **1843**, No. 45 B, in D.

337—**1787**, No. 331.
 Zahn (No. 5264) does not reveal an earlier example of Bach's distinctive variation of the opening line. It is found neither in Vopelius, Schein, Vetter, nor Witt.
 Erk omits the Choral.

338—**H**., No. 118; **1769**, No. 118; **1785**, No. 114.
 H. and **1769**, entitled ' Helft mir Gott's Güte preisen '.
 Erk omits the Choral.

339—**1787**, No. 363.
 Erk omits the Choral.

340—**BG**. xli, 259 (Cantata: ' Lobt ihn mit Herz un Munde ').
 Bach's authorship of the Cantata is very questionable.
 Erk does not include the Choral.

341—**H.**, No. 197; **1769**, No. 197; **1785**, No. 191; **BG.** xviii, 104 (Cantata 73) (*c.* 1725).

1786, bar 5 Bass, last note

H., 1769, 1785, bar 8 Tenor ; Erk (No. 46)

I have adopted the text of the Tenor in the Berlin Original Parts (St. 566).

H. and **1769**, bar 8 Bas

1769, penult. bar Bass ; an error.

1785,   ,,   Tenor

H., 1769, 1785, in A mi.

342—**H.**, No. 185; **1769**, No. 185; **1785**, No. 179; **BG.** xxviii, 284 (Cantata 140) (1731 or 1742).

Bar 10. The Thomasschule Original Tenor Part has

H. and **1769**, bar 29 Alto

  ,,   ,,   **1785**, small Bass notes throughout.

343—**H.**, No. 187; **1769**, No. 187; **1785**, No. 182; **BG.** ii, 132 (Cantata 14) (1735).

H. 1769, 1785, bar 5, last beat and following chord

H. and **1769**, bar 12 Alto, second note (A) lacks flat.

1785, last bar Alto

H., 1769, 1785, Bass uniform with the Cantata Continuo, excepting the last three bars.

344—**H.**, No. 96; **1769**, No. 96; **1784**, No. 94; **BG.** x, 274 (Cantata 47) (1720).

345—**H.**, No. 148; **1769**, No. 148; **1785**, No. 145.
    H. has for signature three sharps, a slip corrected in **1769**.
    Erk omits the Choral.

346—**1787**, No. 299.
    Erk (No. 121), in F mi.

347—**1787**, No. 356.
    1843, No. 102 B, bar 7 Alto, has F sharp, an unnecessary emendation adopted by **1892**, No. 169.
    ,,   ,,   bar 12   ,,   F sharp throughout   ,,   ,,   ,,   ,,
    Erk omits the Choral.

348—**H.**, No. 143; **1769**, No. 143; **1785**, No. 139; **BG.** v (2), 124 (Christmas Oratorio) (1734).

H., bar 2 Alto ; the F sharp is preferable to the F natural, and mitigates the consecutive

fifths between Soprano and Alto. But F natural is found in all the other texts. **1785** has

1785, bar 10 Tenor-Bass

H. and **1769**, bar 12, Alto-Tenor, third beat

„   „   **1785**, last bar Bass

„   „   „   Bass uniform with the Oratorio Continuo

349—**1786**, No. 237.

1885, No. 237, bar 12 Alto 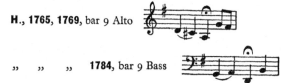 ; **1892**, No. 170 repeats the unnecessary emendation.
The melody is found in no Hymn-book earlier than 1855 (Zahn, No. 6830). But the hymn was in Leipzig use (Leipzig 1729, 1740, 1744) and is in Schemelli 1736 (No. 632).

Erk omits the Choral.

350—**H.**, No. 199; **1769**, No. 199; **1785**, No. 193.

A harmonization of the figured Choral in Schemelli (No. 483 *infra*). The hymn was not in Leipzig use in Bach's period. The hymn and melody are included in Freylinghausen 1704 and 1741, Dretzel 1731, and König 1738 (Zahn, No. 1837).

351—**BG.** xxii, 276 (Cantata 99) (*c.* 1733).

352—**H.**, No. 68, 190; **1765**, No. 68; **1769**, No. 190; **1784**, No. 64; **BG.** xxx, 87 (Cantata 144) (*c.* 1725).

H., **1765**, **1769**, bar 9 Alto

„   „   „   **1784**, bar 9 Bass

The authenticity of the Cantata is challenged.

353—**BG.** xvi, 379 (Cantata 69) (1724).

Cantata 69 (' Lobe den Herrn, meine Seele ') did double duty in 1724. This Choral was probably used on one of the occasions, but does not appear in the Score of the Cantata (see ' Bach's Cantata Texts ', p. 405). Set a minor third lower, it differs only in a few details from No. 356 *infra*; and is as closely related to No. 354 *infra*.

354—**1787**, No. 292.
Cf. Nos. 353 *supra* and 356 *infra*.

355—**1787**, No. 346; **BG.** xiii (1), 147 (Three Wedding Chorals) (? 1749).

1787, first line

„   Bass uniform with **BG.** Continuo, excepting bars 3, 11.

356—**BG.** ii, 78 (Cantata 12) (1724 or 1725).
Cf. Nos. 353 and 354 *supra*.

357—**BG.** xviii, 84 (Cantata 72) (*c.* 1726).

358—**BG.** xxiv, 28 (Cantata 111) (*c.* 1740).

359—**H.**, No. 45; **1765**, No. 45; **1784**, No. 41; **BG.** xvi, 166 (Cantata 65) (1724).

1784, bar 12 Alto ; the first note (F sharp) is F natural in **H.** and **1765**.

360—**BG.** xxii, 68 (Cantata 92) (*c.* 1740).

Erk (No. 130), first bar Soprano The Vn. i and Ob. i, ii, have G sharp in the Thomasschule

Original Parts. The Soprano part has G natural. That G natural is correct is proved by the Berlin Original Score (P. 873), whose existence was unknown to Erk and to the Editor of **BG.** xxii.

361—**H.**, No. 124; **1769**, No. 124B; **1785**, No. 120; **1787**, No. 348; **BG.** xxiii, 94 (Cantata 103) (1735).

1787, entitled 'Ich hab in Gottes Herz und Sinn'

H., **1769**, **1785**, bar 5 Alto

   ,,   ,,   ,,   ,, Tenor

   ,,   ,,   ,,   ,, 11–12 Bass

1787, bar 11 Alto

362—**H.**, No. 119; **1769**, No. 119; **1785**, No. 115; **BG.** iv, 83 (St Matthew Passion) (1729).

      H. 1769, **1785**, bar 8, last note Tenor, G sharp. In the Berlin Autograph Score (P. 25) the note lacks an accidental.

363—**1786**, No. 265; **BG.** xxx, 92 (Cantata 144) (*c.* 1725).

      BG. and **1786**, bar 4 Alto ; the Berlin Autograph Score (P. 134) has A as the second note.

364—**1786**, No. 241.

      The melody is found in no 18th century Hymn-book, but the hymn was in Leipzig use in Bach's period (Leipzig 1729, 1740, 1744). It is not in Schemelli 1736. König 1738 includes the hymn, but to another melody (Zahn, No. 7845).

      Erk omits the Choral.

365—**H.**, No. 154; **1769**, No. 154; **1785**, No. 150; **BG.** v (1), 244 (Cantata 27) (1731).

H., **1769**, **1785**, bar 6 Soprano II

   ,,   ,,   ,,   ,, 8 Alto

   ,,   ,,   ,,   ,, 8 Tenor-Bass

   ,,   ,,   ,,   ,, 11 Alto

   ,,   ,,   ,,   ,, 14 Alto

   ,,   ,,   ,,   ,, 15 Alto

   ,,   ,,   ,,   ,, 17 Alto

   ,,   ,,   ,,   ,, 21 Bass

      Bach's Cantata setting exactly follows the text of Rosenmüller as in Vopelius 1682, p. 947. Winterfeld (ii, No. 110) prints Rosemüller's original text. It differs materially from the Bach-Vopelius version only

in bar 7 Bass :   and bar 13 Bass

366—**1785**, No. 211.

      Freylinghausen 1741 and Reimann 1747 include the hymn and melody (Zahn, No. 4975). The hymn was not in Leipzig use in Bach's period, nor does Schemelli 1736 include it.

      Erk omits the Choral.

367—**H.**, No. 151; **1769**, No. 151; **1785**, No. 174.

      Zahn (No. 4233) does not note the melody in any 18th century Hymn-book earlier than Gotha 1726. It is not in Schein, Vopelius, or Vetter. It appears in Dretzel 1731, König 1738, and Reimann 1747. Zahn does not observe Bach's variation of Löwenstern's third line. The hymn was not in Leipzig use in Bach's period, nor does Schemelli 1736 include it.

      Erk omits the Choral.

368—**1787**, No. 321.
  Erk omits the Choral.

369—**BG.** xxii, 153 (Cantata 95) (1732).

370—**H.**, No. 55; **1765**, No. 55; **1784**, No. 51.

  H., bar 14, Tenor-Bass, first note

371—**1787**, No. 350.
  Erk omits the Choral.

372—**BG.** vii, 50 (Cantata 31) (1715).

373—**H.**, No. 72; **1765**, No. 72; **1784**, No. 68.
  Erk (No. 306), in G.

374—**1786**, No. 247.
  Erk omits the Choral.

375—**H.**, No. 139; **1769**, No. 139; **1785**, No. 135.

  H., and **1769**, bar 6 Tenor

  „ „ „ „ 10 Bass

Bach proposed to include a Prelude on the melody in the ' Orgelbüchlein ' (Bach's Chorals ', iii, 49).
Erk omits the Choral.

376—**1786**, No. 204; **BG.** xxxiii, 122 (Cantata 166) (c. 1725).
  1786, Bass uniform with Cantata Continuo.

377—**H.**, No. 149; **1769**, No. 149; **1785**, No. 146.

  H. and **1769**, bar 4 Bass, first note

  „ „ „ „ 9 Tenor

Erk omits the Choral.

378—**1787**, No. 338; **BG.** xxxv, 292 (Cantata 179) (1724).

  1787, bar 3 Soprano

  „ bar 5 Alto, third beat F natural; the Berlin Autograph Score (P. 146) has F sharp.

  1787, bar 5 Tenor

  BG., bar 6 Tenor, C sharp. The Editor's emendation is not authorized; the Autograph Score, like **1787**, has C natural.

  1787, bar 8 Tenor

  „ „ 10 Soprano

379—**H.**, No. 108; **1769**, No. 108; **1785**, No. 104; **BG.** xx (1), 178 (Cantata 88) (1732).
  H., **1769**, **1784**, bars 8–9 Bass, small notes.

380—**H.**, No. 76; **1765**, No. 76; **1784**, No. 66; **BG.** xiii (1), 144 (Cantata 197) (1737).

  H., **1765**, **1784**, penult. bar Tenor

381—**H.**, No. 116; **1769**, No. 116; **1785**, No. 112; **BG.** xx (1), 98 (Cantata 84) (1731 or 1732).

382—**BG.** xxii, 94 (Cantata 93) (1728).

383—**BG.** xxx, 190 (Cantata 146) (c. 1740).

  BG., bar 1 Alto   ; so in one copy of the Score; another has G for the third crotchet (as in Erk, No. 308).

384—**H.**, No. 125; **1769**, No. 125; **1785**, No. 121; **BG.** iv, 173 (St Matthew Passion) (1729).

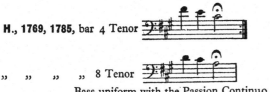

H., 1769, 1785, bar 4 Tenor

„ „ „ „ 8 Tenor

„ „ „ Bass uniform with the Passion Continuo.

385—**1786**, No. 233; **BG.** xxxii, 65 (Cantata 154) (1724).
    BG., bar 6 Tenor, third and fourth crotchets D natural. Both **1786** and the Berlin Original Score (P. 130) have D sharp.

1786, bar 9 Soprano

The setting closely resembles No. 386 *infra*.

386—**1787**, No. 364.
    1787, entitled ' Jesu meiner Seelen Wonne '.
    The setting closely resembles No. 385 *supra*. Erk (No. 138) prints them as a single text without any indication of their differences.

387—**H.**, No. 95; **1765**, No. 95; **1784**, No. 95; **BG.** xii (2), 86 (Cantata 55) (1731 or 1732).

388—**1787**, No. 349.
    1787, entitled ' Jesu, meiner Seelen Wonne '.
    Erk omits the Choral.

389—**1786**, No. 242.
    Reimann 1747 uses the melody. König 1738 prefers an original tune (Zahn, No. 4094). The hymn was not in Leipzig use in Bach's period, nor is it in Schemelli.

390—**BG.** vii, 243 (Cantata 36) (c. 1730).
    It is evident (*cf.* No. 391 *infra*) that this Choral survived in more than one text. The present setting differs from No. 391 in the second part, but not materially. Erk (No. 144) prints this setting as based upon the three non-Cantata texts (*infra* No. 391), but does not expose their differences. It is observable (*cf.* Nos. 391–394 *infra*), in bars 3–6 of the second part of the hymn, that Bach's text is not constant. In Nos. 390, 393, he follows Crüger's version (1640). In Nos. 391, 392 he adopts the form in Vopelius 1682. In No. 394 he prefers an older version. The No. 394 version is found also in Witt 1715 and Bach uses it in his Organ Prelude.

391—**H.**, No. 91; **1765**, No. 91; **1784**, No. 85; **1786**, No. 195; **1787**, No. 304.
    H., 1765, 1784, 1786, bar 3 Soprano, the appogiatura before the second crotchet is omitted.

„ „ „ „ Bass

1786, bar 9   **1786,** bar 10 Soprano

H., 1765, 1784, bars 10–11

H., 1765, 1784, 1786, bar 12 Bass

Erk (No. 145) prints the Choral as from **1784, 1786, 1787** without exposing their differences.

392—**1785**, No. 278.

1785, bar 3 Alto  ; corrected in **1832**, No. 278.

1843, No. 77B alters bar 6 Bass to

Erk omits the Choral.

393—**BG.** i, 51 (Cantata 1) (*c.* 1740).

394—**1787**, No. 322; **BG.** xxxv, 69 (Cantata 172) (1724 or 1725).
1787, bars 1–7 Tenor—

1787, bar 6 Alto   **1787**, last bar Alto

1787, last bar Tenor

„ bar 7   **1787**, bar 8 Bass

395—**1787**, No. 359; **BG.** v (2), 126 (Christmas Oratorio) (1734).

1787, bar 2 Bass

„ last bar Bass

396—**1787**, No. 320; **BG.** vii, 377 (Cantata 40) (1723).

1787, bar 3 Alto   ; the last note is E flat in the Berlin Autograph Score (P. 63).

BG., last bar Tenor   ; the last note lacks an accidental in the Autograph Score and **1787**.

397—**H.**, No. 61; **1765**, No. 61; **1784**, No. 57; **BG.** xxiii, 324 (Cantata 110) (*post* 1734).

398—**H.**, No. 136; **1769**, No. 136; **1785**, No. 133.

H., and **1769**, bar 4 Bass

„ „ „ bar 24, Alto-Tenor-Bass

H. has minor errors in bars 10, 11, 24, corrected in **1769**.
Erk omits the setting.

399—**1787**, No. 300; **BG.** xxiv, 108 (Cantata 114) (*c.* 1740).
1787, entitled ' Ach, lieben Christen, seid getrost '.
BG., bar 8, has E flat in Alto and Bass; first and second beats. The Peters Autograph Score lacks accidentals.

400—**H.**, No. 35; **1765**, No. 35; **1784**, No. 31.

H. and **1765**, bar 9 Bass, last beat

„ „ „ , **1784**, entitled ' Ach, lieben Christen, seid getrost '.

401—**1787**, No. 284.
1787, entitled ' Wär Gott nicht mit uns diese Zeit '.

402—**BG.** xxxv, 272 (Cantata 178) (*c.* 1740).

Erk (No. 148), following J. N. Forkel's MS., last bar Tenor

Erk (No. 315) reprints the Choral ' from the Original Parts ' in the Thomasschule. It differs from his No. 148

only in the last bar of the Tenor, which reads

403—**1787**, No. 335.
404—**BG**. xli, 258 (Cantata, ' Siehe, es hat überwunden').
The authenticity of the Cantata is exceedingly questionable.
405—**H.**, No. 161; **1769**, No. 161; **1785**, No. 157.
406—Schemelli, No. 831. Harmonized in Naumann, No. 1; Seiffert, No. 56; four-part, **BOHT.**, No. 1; Wüllner, **No. 1.**
Not in Erk.
407—Schemelli, No. 171. Harmonized in Naumann, No. 2; Seiffert, No. 11; four-part, Wüllner, No. 2. Zahn, Naumann, and Seiffert are disposed to attribute the melody to Bach. But *cf.* ' Bach's Chorals ', ii, 75.
Not in Erk.
408—Schemelli, No. 320. Harmonized in Naumann, No. 3; Seiffert, No. 27; four-part, Wüllner, No. 3.
409—Schemelli, No. 570. Harmonized in Naumann, No. 4; Seiffert, No. 39; four-part, Wüllner, No. 4.
Not in Erk.
410—Schemelli, No. 689. Harmonized in Naumann, No. 5; Seiffert, No. 47; four-part, BOHT., No. 2; Wüllner, No. 5.
Not in Erk.
411—Schemelli, No. 303. Harmonized in Naumann, No. 6; Seiffert, No. 24; four-part, Wüllner, No. 6.
412—Schemelli, No. 355. Harmonized in Naumann, No. 7; Seiffert, No. 29; four-part, Wüllner, No. 7.
Not in Erk.
413—**BG**. xl, 12. The Choral is appended to three MSS of the Organ Prelude. See ' Bach's Chorals ', iii, 118; and No. 37–41 *supra.*
Not in **1892** or Erk.
414—Krebs MS. Harmonized in Naumann, App. No. 5. See ' Bach's Chorals ', ii, 73, 78.
Not in **1892** or Erk.
415—Schemelli, No. 39. Harmonized in Naumann, No. 8; Seiffert, No. 2; four-part, Wüllner, No. 8.
Erk (No. 18) supplies a conjectural figuring.
416—Schemelli, No. 40. Harmonized in Naumann, No. 9; Seiffert, No. 3; four-part, Wüllner, No. 9; **1843**, No. 183.
Not in Erk.
417—Schemelli, No. 43. Harmonized in Naumann, No. 10; Seiffert, No. 4; four-part, Wüllner, No. 10.
Not in Erk.
418—Schemelli, No. 396. Harmonized in Naumann, No. 11; Seiffert, No. 31; four-part, BOHT., No. 3; Wüllner, No. 11.
Not in Erk.
419—Schemelli, No. 258. Harmonized in Naumann, No. 12; Seiffert, No. 17; four-part, Wüllner, No. 12.
Schemelli, bar 6 from end, figures the second crotchet $\frac{6}{4\sharp}$
Not in Erk.
420—Schemelli, No. 13. Harmonized in Naumann, No. 13; Seiffert, No. 1; four-part, Wüllner, No. 13.
Not in Erk.
421—Schemelli, No. 397. Harmonized in Naumann, No. 14; Seiffert, No. 32. Four-part, BOHT., No. 4; Wüllner, No. 14; No. 70 *supra*; Erk, No. 19.
422—Schemelli, No. 112. Harmonized in Naumann, No. 15; Seiffert, No. 7. Four-part, BOHT., No. 5; Wüllner, No. 15; **1843**, No. 202.
Not in Erk.
423—Schemelli, No. 187. Harmonized in Naumann, No. 16; Seiffert, No. 12. Four-part, Wüllner, No. 16; Nos. 83–85 *supra.*
Not in Erk.
424—Schemelli, No. 580. Harmonized in Naumann, No. 17; Seiffert, No. 43. Four-part, Wüllner, No. 17.
Not in Erk.
425—Schemelli, No. 572. Harmonized in Naumann, No. 18; Seiffert, No. 40. Four-part, Wüllner, No. 18.
Not in Erk.
426—Schemelli, No. 847. Harmonized in Naumann, No. 19; Seiffert, No. 57. Four-part, Wüllner, No. 19.
Not in Erk.
427—Schemelli, No. 306. Harmonized in Naumann, No. 20; Seiffert, No. 25. Four-part, Wüllner, No. 20.
Not in Erk.
428—Schemelli, No. 522. Harmonized in Naumann, No. 21; Seiffert, No. 38. Four-part, Wüllner, No. 21.
429 ⎱ A. M. Bach's ' Notenbuch ' (1725). Harmonized in Naumann, Nos. 22, 23. Four-part, BOHT., No. 6; Wüllner,
430 ⎰ Nos. 22, 23; No. 116 *supra.*
Erk (Nos. 43, 44) figures the Continuo.
431—A. M. Bach's ' Notenbuch ' (1725).
The melody is found only in König 1738 and is conjecturally attributed to him by Zahn, No. 7419. Probably Zahn is correct; for the melody closely resembles another in the same collection (Zahn, No. 1815) which appears there in print for the first time.
Not in Erk.
432—Schemelli, No. 647. Harmonized in Naumann, No. 24; Seiffert, No. 45. Four-part, Wüllner, No. 24.

1892, No. 24, bar 9, figures the first crotchet $\flat \atop (?\natural)$

433—Schemelli, No. 488. Harmonized in Naumann, No. 25; Seiffert, No. 37. Four-part, Wüllner, No. 25; No. 121 *supra.*
434—Schemelli, No. 360. Harmonized in Naumann, No. 26; Seiffert, No. 30. Four-part, BOHT., No. 7; Wüllner, No. 26.
Not in Erk.
435—Peters, Orgelwerke, v. 107.
The Choral concludes an Organ Prelude on the melody ' Vom Himmel hoch da komm ich her ' and survives in the MSS of Bach's pupil J. L. Krebs.
Not in **1892**, or Erk.
436—Schemelli, No. 78. Harmonized in Naumann, No. 27; Seiffert, No. 5. Four-part, Wüllner, No. 27.
Not in Erk.
437—Krebs MS. Harmonized in Naumann, App. No. 4. Four-part, BOHT., No. 8.
Not in **1892** or Erk.

438—Schemelli, No. 861. Harmonized in Naumann, No. 28; Seiffert, No. 58. Four-part, BOHT., No. 9; Wüllner, No. 28; **1843**, No. 197B.
    See No. 179 *supra* for Bach's own melody.
    Not in Erk.

439—Schemelli, No. 194. Harmonized in Naumann, No. 29; Seiffert, No. 13. Four-part, Wüllner, No. 29.
    Not in Erk. See No. 186 *supra* for another melody.

440—Schemelli, No. 657. Harmonized in Naumann, No. 30; Seiffert, No. 46. Four-part, BOHT., No. 10; Wüllner, No. 30.
    Not in Erk.

441—Schemelli, No. 734. Harmonized in Naumann, No. 31; Seiffert, No. 51. Four-part Wüllner, No. 31.
    Not in Erk.

442—Schemelli, No. 737. Harmonized in Naumann, No. 32; Seiffert, No. 52. Four-part, Wüllner, No. 32.
    Naumann and Seiffert are disposed to attribute the melody to Bach. Arnold Schering (*Bach-Jahrbuch* **1924**, p. 122) finds it commonplace.
    Not in Erk.

443—Schemelli, No. 195. Harmonized in Naumann, No. 33; Seiffert, No. 14. Four-part, BOHT., No. 11; Wüllner, No. **33**.
    Arnold Schering (*Bach-Jahrbuch* 1924, p. 120) does not regard the melody as bearing the stamp of Bach's individuality. Neither Naumann nor Seiffert supports his opinion.
    Not in Erk.

444—Schemelli, No. 197. Harmonized in Naumann, No. 40; Seiffert, No. 15. Four-part, Wüllner, No. 40; **1843**, No. 121A.
    Not in Erk.

445—Schemelli, No. 139. Harmonized in Naumann, No. 35; Seiffert, No. 10. Four-part, Wüllner, No. 35.
    Both Naumann and Seiffert attribute the melody to Bach. But see ' Bach's Chorals ', ii, 100, and *Bach-Jahrbuch* 1924, p. 120.
    Not in Erk.

446—Schemelli, No. 741. Harmonized in Naumann, No. 34; Seiffert, No. 53. Four-part, BOHT., No. 12; Wüllner, No. 34; No. 204 *supra*.
    Not in Erk.
    1892, No. 34, figuring defective in bars 7 and 13; Seiffert, in bars 13, 15.

447—Schemelli, No. 119. Harmonized in Naumann, No. 36; Seiffert, No. 8. Four-part, Wüllner, No. 36.
    Not in Erk.

448—Schemelli, No. 696. Harmonized in Naumann, No. 37; Seiffert, No. 48. Four-part, Wüllner, No. 37.
    For another melody, see No. 215 *supra*.
    Not in Erk.

449—Schemelli, No. 463. Harmonized in Naumann, No. 38; Seiffert, No. 33. Four-part, Wüllner, No. 38.
    Not in Erk.

450—Schemelli, No. 333. Harmonized in Naumann, No. 39; Seiffert, No. 28. Four-part, Wüllner, No. 39.
    1892, No. 39, incorrectly figures bar 19, second crotchet 6–4–3.
    Not in Erk.

451—Schemelli, No. 869. Harmonized in Naumann, No. 41; Seiffert, No. 60. Four-part, Wüllner, No. 41.

452—Schemelli, No. 868. Harmonized in Naumann, No. 42; Seiffert, No. 59. Four-part, BOHT., No. 13; Wüllner, No. **42**.

453—Schemelli, No. 936. Harmonized in Naumann, No. 43; Seiffert, No. 67. Four-part, BOHT., No. 14; Wüllner, No. **43**.

454—Schemelli, No. 938. Harmonized in Naumann, No. 44; Seiffert, No. 68. Four-part, BOHT., No. 15; Wüllner, No. 44.
    Not in Erk.
    1892, No. 44, bar 5, incorrectly figures fourth quaver sharp third.

455—Schemelli, No. 281. Harmonized in Naumann, No. 45; Seiffert, No. 18. Four-part, Wüllner, No. 45.
    Not in Erk.

456—Schemelli, No. 467. Harmonized in Naumann, No. 46; Seiffert, No. 34. Four-part, Wüllner, No. 46.

457—Schemelli, No. 873. Harmonized in Naumann, No. 47; Seiffert, No. 61. Four-part, Wüllner, No. 47; No. 233 *supra*.

458—Schemelli, No. 874. Harmonized in Naumann, No. 48; Seiffert, No. 62. Four-part, BOHT., No. 16; Wüllner, No. 48.
    Not in Erk.

459—Schemelli, No. 761. Harmonized in Naumann, No. 49; Seiffert, No. 54. Four-part, Wüllner, No. 49; No. 234 *supra*
    1843, No. 150.

460—Schemelli, No. 121. Harmonized in Naumann, No. 50; Seiffert, No. 9. Four-part Wüllner, No. 50.
    Not in Erk.

461—Schemelli, No. 283. Harmonized in Naumann, No. 51; Seiffert, No. 19. Four-part, BOHT., No. 17; Wüllner, No. **51**.
    Not in Erk.

462—Schemelli, No. 881. Harmonized in Naumann, No. 52; Seiffert, No. 63. Four-part, Wüllner, No. 52; No. 256 *supra*.
    Not in Erk.

463—Schemelli, No. 574. Harmonized in Naumann, No. 53; Seiffert, No. 41. Four-part, Wüllner, No. 53.
    For Bach's own melody see No. 261 *supra*.
    Not in Erk.

464—Schemelli, No. 700. Harmonized in Naumann, No. 54; Seiffert, No. 49. Four-part, Wüllner, No. 54.
    Not in Erk.

465—Schemelli, No. 284. Harmonized in Naumann, No. 55; Seiffert, No. 20. Four-part, Wüllner, No. 55.
    Not in Erk.

466—A. M. Bach's ' Notenbuch ' (1725). Harmonized in Naumann, No. 56. Four-part Wüllner, No. 56; No. 282 *supra*.

467—Schemelli, No. 891. Harmonized in Naumann, No. 57; Seiffert, No. 64. Four-part, BOHT., No. 19; Wüllner, No. 57.
    Not in Erk.

468—Schemelli, No. 203. Harmonized in Naumann, No. 58; Seiffert, No. 16. Four-part, Wüllner, No. 58.
    Not in Erk.

469—Schemelli, No. 575. Harmonized in Naumann, No. 59; Seiffert, No. 42. Four-part, BOHT., No. 21; Wüllner, No. 59.

470—Schemelli, No. 894. Harmonized in Naumann, No. 60; Seiffert, No. 65. Four-part, Wüllner, No. 60; No. 310 *supra*.

471—A. M. Bach's ' Notenbuch ' (1725). Harmonized in Naumann, No. 61. Four-part, BOHT., No. 22; Wüllner, No. 61.

472—Schemelli, No. 472. Harmonized in Naumann, No. 62; Seiffert, No. 35. Four-part, Wüllner, No. 62; No. 317 *supra*.
473—Schemelli, No. 710. Harmonized in Naumann, No. 63; Seiffert, No. 50. Four-part, Wüllner, No. 63.
    Not in Erk.
474—Schemelli, No. 293. Harmonized in Naumann, No. 65; Seiffert, No. 22. Four-part, Wüllner, No. 65; No. 318 *supra*.
475—Schemelli, No. 292. Harmonized in Naumann, No. 64; Seiffert, No. 21. Four-part, Wüllner, No. 64.
    Zahn, Seiffert, and Naumann attribute the melody to Bach. But see ' Bach's Chorals ', ii, 118, and *Bach-Jahrbuch* 1924, p. 121.
    Not in Erk.
476—Schemelli, No. 296. Harmonized in Naumann, No. 66; Seiffert, No. 23. Four-part, Wüllner, No. 66.
    Not in Erk.
477—Schemelli, No. 315. Harmonized in Naumann, No. 67; Seiffert, No. 26. Four-part, Wüllner, No. 67; No. 321 *supra*.
    Not in Erk.
478—Schemelli, No. 901. Harmonized in Naumann, No. 68; Seiffert, No. 66. Four-part, Wüllner, No. 68.
    Zahn, Seiffert, and Naumann attribute the melody to Bach. But see ' Bach's Chorals ', ii, 119, and *Bach-Jahrbuch*, 1924, p. 121.
    Not in Erk.
479—Schemelli, No. 945. Harmonized in Naumann, No. 69; Seiffert, No. 69. Four-part, Wüllner, No. 69.
480—Schemelli, No. 475. Harmonized in Naumann, No. 70; Seiffert, No. 36. Four-part, Wüllner, No. 70.
    Not in Erk.
481—Schemelli, No. 627. Harmonized in Naumann, No. 71; Seiffert, No. 44. Four-part, BOHT., No. 23; Wüllner, No. 71.
    Not in Erk.
482—A. M. Bach's ' Notenbuch ' (1725); Krebs MS. Harmonized in Naumann, No. 72. Four-part, BOHT., No. 24; Wüllner, No. 72.
    Not in Erk.
483—Schemelli, No. 779. Harmonized in Naumann, No. 73; Seiffert, No. 55. Four-part Wüllner, No. 73; No. 350 *supra*.
484—**BG**. xl, 3; Peters, v. 57.
    Not in **1892** or Erk.
485—A. M. Bach's ' Notenbuch ' (1725). Harmonized in Naumann, No. 74. Four-part, BOHT., No. 26; Wüllner, No. 74.
    Not in Erk.
486—Schemelli, No. 108. Harmonized in Naumann, No. 75; Seiffert, No. 6. Four-part, Wüllner, No. 75.
    Not in Erk.
487—**BG**. xxxiii, 64 (Cantata 163) (1715).
    Not in Erk.
488—Krebs MS. Harmonized in Naumann, App. No. 6.
    Other than this one, the hymn lacks a melody (see ' Bach's Chorals ', ii, 87). It was in Leipzig use (Leipzig 1729, 1740, 1744), but is not in Schemelli 1736.
489—Krebs MS. Harmonized in Naumann, App. No. 8. Zahn (No. 2960) records no printed tune to this hymn earlier than 1785. It is noteworthy, therefore, that Kittel, another pupil of Bach's, is presumed to have preserved a second melody for it (Zahn, No. 2959). The hymn is in Schemelli (No. 449), but without a melody of its own. Krebs' tune, therefore, may have been sketched for the projected enlarged edition of Schemelli's Hymn-book. The hymn, however, was in Leipzig use (Leipzig 1729, 1740, 1744).
490—Krebs MS. Harmonized in Naumann, No. 7.
    Bach was familiar with the hymn in Witt 1715. König 1738 set it to another melody (Zahn, No. 3764). Schemelli 1736 included the hymn (No. 667), but without a melody. Bach's, probably, was prepared for the projected enlarged edition. (See ' Bach's Chorals ', ii, 109.) But the hymn was in Leipzig use (Leipzig 1729, 1740, 1744).
    Bar 6 Soprano, Spitta has E natural as the second note.

APPENDIX II

METRICAL INDEX OF THE MELODIES

Metre		Number

TWO LINES

11.12 (*Iambic*)	57

THREE LINES

8.8.8	313
10.10.10 (*Iambic*)	173

FOUR LINES

Alcaic

11.11.9.9	389

Iambic

7.6.7.6	48, 49
7.7.7.7	273–275
8.6.8.6	237–240, 281
8.7.8.7	22, 184
8.8.8.8 ...	2, 9, 10, 34, 45, 47, 58–61, 64, 66, 82, 88,
	133–136, 142, 148, 224, 225, 267, 295,
	334–336, 373, 374, 405
8.8.9.9	407
10.10.11.11	25
10.11.10.11	321, 477
11.11.9.9	389
11.11.10.10	68, 416, 434
11.11.11.5	46, 169–172, 236, 297
12.12.13.13	244
12.13.6.13 (or 6.6 6.7 6.7)	367

Trochaic

7.7.7.7	271, 272
8.7.8.7	445
10.10.7.5	97

Trochaic-Iambic

8.8.7.8	220
10.10.5.10	310, 311, 470

FIVE LINES

Amphibrachic-Iambic

10.9. 8.8. 10	468

Dactylic

14.14. 4.7 8	125, 126

Iambic

6.6 6.6. 6	21
8.8. 6. 8.8	344–346
8.8.7. 8.7	55
8.8. 8.4. 8	187, 188
8.8. 8.8. 4	23, 86, 87
8.8. 8.8. 10	120
11.11. 4.4. 11	3, 350, 483

Iambic-Trochaic

4.4 7.7. 6	299
8.7. 8.7. 8	332, 333
8.7. 8.8. 5 (4) (3)	112–115
8.8. 8.7. 4	69

Mixed

9.9. 11.10. 5	262–264

Trochaic

8.6. 8.8.8	12

Trochaic-Iambic

8. 6.5. 7.6	219

SIX LINES

Alcaic

5.6. 5.6. 9.10	280

Dactylic

11.11. 10.10. 11.11	458

Metre		Number

Iambic

4.4.7. 4.4.7	4, 5
4.4.11. 4.4.11	395–397
4. 7.6. 7.7.6	62
6.6. 7.7. 7.7	26–30, 487
7.7.6. 7.7.6	192, 308
7.7.6. 7.7.8	300–307, 309
7.7. 7.7. 8. 11	111
8.7. 8.7. 8.7	442
8.7. 8.7. 8.8	241–243
8. 7.11. 8. 11.11	418
8.8.7. 4.4.7	193–195
8.8.7. 8.8.7	54, 197, 229, 230
8.8. 8.8.8. 8.8 ...	1, 149, 175, 326–331
8.8. 9.9. 10.8	427
8.11. 10.11. 10.4	428
9.8. 9.8. 8.8	124, 376–382, 471, 484
9.8. 9.8. 9.9	489
9.10. 9.10. 10.10	70, 421
11.10. 11.10. 8.12	424
11.11. 11.11. 11.11	185

Iambic-Trochaic

8.5. 8.4. 7.7	257–259
8.6. 8.6. 7.6	298

Trochaic

4.4.7. 4.4.7	473
5.5. 8.8. 5.5	316, 317, 472
6.6. 6.6. 6.6	123, 150
7.7. 7.7. 7.7	261, 463
7.8. 7.8. 7.7	221, 222, 248–255
7.8. 7.8. 8.8	235
8.7.7. 8.7.7	11
8.7. 8.7. 8(7). 8(7)	119, 140, 141, 177, 178, 191, 444, 490
8.8.7. 8.8.7	20
8.8. 8.8. 8.8	318, 474

SEVEN LINES

Dactylic

11.10. 11.10. 5.5.10	234, 456

Iambic

4. 4.4. 6. 7.7. 6	414
4.6. 7.7. 6.6. 4	481
6.6.8. 4.8. 8.8	451
7.6. 7.6. 7.7.6	96, 131, 132, 435
7.6. 7.6. 8.7.6	176
7.7. 7.7. 7.7. 8	296
8.6. 8.6. 4.4.7	71, 72
8. 7.7. 6.6. 6.4	452
8.7. 8.7. 8.8.7	6–8, 15–17, 32, 89–93, 95, 143–147,
	151–153, 268–270, 343, 368–372,
	399–404, 443, 454
9.8. 9.8. 9.6.7	228
11.11.10. 11.13. 8.4	480

Iambic-Trochaic

6.6. 6.6. 7.6.5	196
9.8. 9.8. 9.9.8	116, 429–432

Sapphic

5.6. 5.6. 5.6.5	67

Trochaic

6.6. 7.7. 6.7.6	63
7.4. 7.4. 7.4. 6	215, 448
7(8).7. 7.7. 7.7.7	319
7.8. 7.6. 7.3.6	139
7.8. 7.8. 7.4.7	475
8.8. 7.7. 8.8.8	450

Metre					Number
Trochaic-Iambic					
7.8.6. 7.7. 7.7 ...	...	...	...	...	366

EIGHT LINES
Amphibrachic

Metre					Number
12.11. 12.11. 6.6. 12.12	...	...	...		425

Iambic

Metre					Number
6.6. 6.6. 6.6. 6.6	...	...	...	...	440
6.6. 6.6. 8.8. 7.7	...	...	...	...	291
6.7. 6.7. 6.6. 6.6		73, 186, 265, 266, 284–290, 439, 453			
6.7. 6.7. 6.7. 6.7	...	...	...	...	479
7.6. 7.6. 6.6. 6.6	...	...	...	...	408
7.6. 7.6. 6. 7.7.6		...	31, 128–130, 337–341		
7.6. 7.6. 7.6. 7.6		...33, 56, 158–168, 181–183, 223, 324, 325			
8.7. 8.7. 4.4. 7.7	...	...	...	...	351–356
8.7. 8.7. 6.6. 8.8	...	...	...	...	415
8.7. 8.7. 8.7. 8.7	...	...	...	...	292, 293
8.7. 8.7. 8.8. 7.7	...	...	...	...83–85, 423	
8.8.7. 8.8.7. 8.8		117, 282, 283, 466			
8.8. 8.8. 8.8. 8.8	...	...	...	...	81
8.8.9. 8.8.9. 8.8	...	...	...	...	179, 438
8.9. 8.9. 8.9. 8.9	...	...	...	...	478
9. 8.8. 9. 9.8. 9.8	...	...	...	...	486
9.8. 9.8. 4.4. 8.8	...	...	...	...	409
9.8. 9.8. 9. 8.8. 9	...	...	...	...	460
9.9.8. 9.9.8. 8.4	...	...	...	...	426
11.8 11.8. 8.8. 9.9	...	...	...	...	467

Iambic-Trochaic

7.7. 7.7. 7.8(7). 8.4	...	...	...	37–41, 413	

Trochaic

6.5. 6.5. 6.4. 6.8	...	...	...	...	53
6.6.5. 6.6.5. 8.8	...	...	...	...	412
7.6. 7.6. 3.3. 6.6	...	...	...	...	323
7.6. 7.6. 7.6. 7.6	...	50–52, 202, 205–207, 315			
7.8. 7.8. 6. 8.8. 4	...	...	...	...	256, 462
7.8. 7.8. 7. 8.8. 7	...	...	...	...	449
7.8. 7.8. 7. 8. 7.7. 8	...	...	...	...	320
7.8. 7.8. 8.7. 8.7	...	...	...	...	456
7.8. 7.8. 8.7. 7.7	...	...	...	...	204, 446
7. 8.8. 7. 8.7. 8.7	...	...	...	...	447
8. 3.3. 6. 8. 3.3. 6	...	...	...	...	347, 348
8.7. 8.7. 7.7. 7.7	...	...	...	...	365
8.7. 8.7. 7.7. 8.8		102–109, 233, 383, 384, 387, 457, 488			
8.7. 8.7. 8.7. 8.7	...	...	...	...	406, 465
8.7. 8.7. 8.8. 7.7		13, 14, 74, 75, 198–201, 349, 385, 386, 388			
8.8. 7.7. 8.8. 7.7	...	...	...	...	232, 436
8.8. 8.8. 8.8. 8.8	...	...	...	...	314

Trochaic-Amphibrachic

8.7. 8.7. 12.12. 11.11	...	...	...	...	80, 422

Trochaic-Iambic

4.6. 4.6. 4.6. 4.6	...	...	...	...	174
8.8. 8.8. 5.5. 2.7	...	...	...	...	411

NINE LINES
Iambic

4.6.6. 4.6.6. 9.9.4	...	...	...	...	94
8.7. 8.7. 8.7. 8.7.7	...	...	...	42–44, 98–101	
8.7. 8.7. 8.8.8. 5.8	...	...	...	...	18, 19

Iambic-Dactylic

12.12.13. 12.12.13. 10.10.13	...	...	...	...	419

Metre					Number
Iambic-Trochaic					
8.7. 8.7. 5(6).5.5. 6.7	...	...	...	...	77–79
8.7. 8.7. 8.7. 4.6.7	...	...	...	...	189, 190
9.8. 9.8. 4.5. 4.5.5	...	...	...	...	429–432

Irregular

8.8. 9.8. 8.8. 8.9. 8	...	...	...	...	226, 227

TEN LINES
Iambic

4.4. 8.4. 4.4. 4.4. 4.4. 8	...	...	...	180	
4.7. 4.4. 11. 6.6.6. 7.4	...	...	...	441	
7.7. 7.7.6. 7.7. 7.7.6	...	...	...	417	
8.6. 8.6. 8.8.6. 7.7.7.(6)	...	...	...	65	
8.7. 8.7. 4.4.7. 4.4.7	...	76, 357–363, 476			
8.7. 8.7. 8.8.7. 8.8.7	...	...	...	24	
8.9. 8.9. 8.8. 9.9. 8.8	...	...	...	410	
9.8. 9.8. 5.5.4. 5.5.10	...	...	...	469	
9.8. 9.8. 9.9.8. 9.9.8	...	...	...	485	
11.11. 10.10. 5.7.11. 6.8.7	...	...	...	364	

Iambic-Amphibrachic

5.5. 5.5. 10. 5.6. 5.6. 10	...	...	...	420	

Iambic-Trochaic

4.7. 8.7. 8.7. 8.8. 7.7	...	...	...	121, 433	
8.8. 8.8. 8.8. 8.8. 8.8	...	...	...	398	

Mixed

11.8. 11.8. 5. 9.9. 6.7.5	...	...	...	122	

Trochaic

8.7.7. 8.7.7. 8.8. 8.8	...	...	...	110	
8.7. 8.7. 8.7.7. 8.7.7	...	203, 322, 455			
8.7. 8.7. 8.7. 8.7. 8.8	...	...	...	434	

Trochaic-Iambic

6.6.5. 6.6.5. 3.4. 8.6	...	...	...	208–214	

TWELVE LINES
Iambic

4.4.7. 4.4.7. 4.4.7. 4.4.7	...	...	...	375	
6.7.6.6. 6.7.6.6. 6.7.6.7	...	...	...	482	
7.8. 7.8. 7.6. 7.6. 7.6. 7(8).6	...	...	...	276–279	
8.8.7. 8.8.7. 8.8.7. 8.8.7	...	...	...	297	
8.8.7. 8.8.7. 8.8. 8.8. 8.8	...	...	...	154–157	

Iambic-Trochaic

8.8.7. 8.8.7. 2.2. 4.4. 4.8	...	...	390–394, 461		

Trochaic-Iambic

8.7. 8.7. 8.8. 8.8. 5.5. 3.7	...	...	...	464	
8.9.8. 8.9.8. 6.6. 4.4. 4.8	...	...	...	342	

FOURTEEN LINES
Iambic

7.6. 7.6. 7.6. 7.6. 7.7. 7.6. 7.6	...	...	216–218		

Trochaic-Iambic

7.6. 7.6. 7.8.7. 6.6 9. 5.6. 7.5	...	...	260		
7.7. 7.7. 7.7.7. 7.7.7.7. 7.8	...	...	...	118	

IRREGULAR
Nos. 35, 36, 127, 137, 138, 231, 245–247, 312

APPENDIX III

CHRONOLOGICAL TABLE OF THE MELODIES

Date	Number
Pre-Reformation	15–17, 21, 35–36, 45, 47, 50–53, 64, 66, 88–93, 112–115, 118, 122, 137, 138, 224, 225, 245–247, 260, 262–264, 271, 272, 332, 333, 398
1524	6–8, 32, 37–44, 69, 81, 95, 131, 132, 220, 226, 227, 257–259, 268, 343, 413, 435
1525	24, 98–101, 152, 153, 231, 297
1527	292, 293, 312
1529	77–79, 189, 190, 357–363
1530	229, 230
1531	63, 65, 97, 123
1534	57
1535	76, 196, 219, 269, 270, 399–405
1539	300–309, 326–331, 334–336
1540	276–279
1541	18, 19
1542	68, 296, 416
1543	82
1544	181–183, 319
1545	55, 176
1546	267
1547	185, 232, 373, 374, 436
1548	120
1551	102–109, 133–136, 149
1553	313
1554	237–240
1555	298, 366
1560	23, 86, 87
1565	344–346
1566	67, 139, 311
1568	34, 180, 236
1569	128–130, 368–372
1571	337–341, 375
1577	154–157
1581	193–195
1587	273–275
1588	58, 59
1589	1, 2, 187, 188
1591	216–218
1593	144–147, 395–397
1594	96, 295
1595	184
1597	148
1598	31
1599	342, 390–394
1601	71, 72, 158–168, 175
1603	33
1605	56
1609	26–30, 48, 49, 60, 205–207, 223, 487
1611	54
1613	324, 325
1625	4, 5, 9, 10, 25 (circa)
1628	241–243, 299
1632	291
1640	151, 169–172

Date	Number
1641	83–85, 322, 423, 455
1642	119, 177, 198–201, 203, 282, 283, 383–388, 466
1644	46, 173, 174, 244, 280, 320, 367
1646	110, 439
1648	62, 111, 117, 142, 265, 266, 408, 438
1649	22, 74, 75, 140, 141, 310, 314, 365, 470
1650	468
1652	12
1653	208–214, 221, 222, 412
1655	191, 444
1657	376–382, 484
1658	249–255
1660	215, 448
1661	11
1662	3, 94
1663	73
1664	235
1665	125, 126
1666	347, 348
1667	281
1668	202
1670	417, 432
1675	389
1678	13
1679	192, 234, 284–288, 459
1680	80, 315
1681	419
1682	318, 364, 474
1684	465
1686	248
1690	351–366
1691	20
1693	289, 290
1694	150, 197, 321, 323, 477
1698	316, 317, 409, 451, 464, 472, 480, 486
1699	476
1704	80, 350, 424, 425, 428, 449, 460, 483
1708	415, 420, 473
1712	490
1713	61, 233, 457
1714	121, 427, 433, 447, 450, 456, 463, 479
1715	14, 411, 426
1725	431
1726	127, 256, 462
1727	441
1733	414 (circa)
1736	407, 442, 445, 475, 478
1738	186
1742	143
J. S. Bach	70, 116, 178, 179, 204, 228, 261, 294, 349, 406, 410, 418, 421, 422, 429, 430, 434, 437, 440, 443, 446, 452–454, 458, 461, 467, 469, 471, 481, 482, 485, 488, 489, 490
1769	124

APPENDIX IV

INDEX OF THE COMPOSERS

[NOTE.—Unlike the hymn texts, few of the melodies can be associated with an ascertained author. Such as can be, positively or conjecturally, are indexed in the Table below. Melodies not included are by anonymous composers.]

INDEX OF THE AUTHORS

APPENDIX VI

INDEX OF THE HYMNS

Hymn					Set to	Number
Dir, dir, Jehovah, will ich singen	...	...	...	...	Own Melody	70, 421
Du Friedefürst, Herr Jesu Christ					,,	71, 72
Du grosser Schmerzensmann	...				,,	73
Du Lebensfürst, Herr Jesu Christ				...	Ermuntre dich, mein schwacher Geist	83, 85
Du, o schönes Weltegebäude	...	...	...	...	Own melody	74, 75
Durch Adams Fall ist ganz verderbt					,,	76
Ein feste Burg ist unser Gott	...	...	...	...	,,	77–79
Ein Kind geborn zu Bethlehem						313
Ein Lämmlein geht und trägt die Schuld	...				Au Wasserflüssen Babylon	24
Eins ist noth, ach Herr, dies Eine	...	...	...		Own melody	80, 422
Erbarm dich mein, o Herre Gott					,,	81
Erhalt uns, Herr, bei denem Wort					,,	82
Ermuntre dich, mein schwacher Geist	...	...	...		,,	84, 423
Erschienen ist der herrlich Tag	...				,,	86, 87
Erstanden ist der heilig Christ	...				,,	88
Erwürgtes Lamm, das die verwahrten Siegel					,,	424
Es glänzet der Christen inwendiges Leben	...				,,	425
Es ist das Heil uns kommen her	...	...	...		,,	89–91
Es ist genug	...	...	...	...	,,	94
Es ist gewisslich an der Zeit	...	...	...	...	Nun freut euch, lieben Christen gmein	270
Es ist nun aus mit meinem Leben					Own melody	426
Es ist vollbracht! vergiss ja nicht					,,	427
Es kostet viel, ein Christ zu sein					,,	428
Es spricht der Unweisen Mund wohl					,,	95
Es stehn vor Gottes Throne					·,,	96
Es wird schier der letzte Tag herkommen					,,	97
Es wollt uns Gott genädig sein					,,	98–101
Freu dich sehr, o meine Seele	...	...	...	...	,,	102, 107
Freuet euch, ihr Christen alle	...	...	...	...	,,	110
Fröhlich soll mein Herze springen	...	...	...		Warum sollt ich mich denn grämen	348
Für Freuden lasst uns springen	...	...	...		Own melody	111
Gelobet seist du, Jesu Christ	...				,,	112–115
Gieb dich zufrieden und sei stille	...	...	...		,,	116, 429–432
Gott, der du selber bist das Licht	...	...	...		,,	117
Gott der Vater, wohn uns bei	...	...	...		,,	118
Gott des Himmels und der Erden					·,,	119
Gott hat das Evangelium	...				,,	120
Gott lebet noch	...	...			·,,	121, 433
Gott, mein Herz dir Dank zusendet	...				,,	488
Gott sei gelobet und gebenedeiet	...				,,	122
Gott Vater, sende deinen Geist	...				Kommt her zu mir, spricht Gottes Sohn	229
Gott, wie gross ist deine Güte	...	...	...	...	Own melody	434
Gottes Sohn ist kommen	...	...	...		,,	123
Gottlob, es geht nunmehr zum Ende	...	...	...		··	124
Hast du denn, Jesu, dein Angesicht gänzlich verborgen				...	·,,	125
Heilig, heilig, heilig	...	...	...	...	,,	127
Helft mir Gotts Güte preisen	...	...	...		,,	128, 129
Herr Christ, der einig Gotts Sohn					,,	131, 132, 435
Herr Gott, dich loben alle wir	...				,,	133, 135
Herr Gott, dich loben wir	...	...	...		,,	137, 138
Herr, ich denk an jene Zeit	...	...	...		,,	139
Herr, ich habe missgehandelt	...	...	...		,,	140, 141
Herr Jesu Christ, dich zu uns wend	...	...	...		,,	142
Herr Jesu Christ, du hast bereit	...	...	...		,,	143
Herr Jesu Christ, du höchstes Gut	...	...	...		,,	144, 146, 147
Herr Jesu Christ, ich schrei zu dir	...	...	...		Herr Jesu Christ, du höchstes Gut	145
Herr Jesu Christ, wahr Mensch und Gott	...	...			Own melody	148, 149
Herr, nicht schicke deine Rache	...	...	...		,,	436
Herr, nun lass in Friede	...	...	...	...	,,	150
Herr, straf mich nicht in deinem Zorn	...	...			,,	151
Herr, wie du willt, so schicks mit mir	...	...			,,	153
Herzlich lieb hab ich dich, o Herr	...	...			,,	154–157
Herzlich thut mich verlangen	...	...	...		,,	158
Herzliebster Jesu, was hast du verbrochen	...	...			,,	169–172
Heut ist, o Mensch, ein grosser Trauertag	...	...			,,	173
Heut triumphiret Gottes Sohn					,,	175
Hier lieg ich nun, o Vater aller Gnaden	...	...			,,	437
Hilf, Gott, dass mirs gelinge	...	...	...	...	,,	176
Hilf, Herr Jesu, lass gelingen	...	...	...	...	,,	177, 178

Hymn	Set to	Number
Ich armer Mensch, ich armer Sünder	Wer nur den lieben Gott lässt walten	378
Ich bin ja, Herr, in deiner Macht	Own melody	179, 438
Ich dank dir, Gott	„	180
Ich dank dir, lieber Herre	„	181–183
Ich dank dir schon durch deinen Sohn	„	184
Ich danke dir, Herr Gott, in deinem Throne	„	185
Ich freue mich in dir	„	186, 439
Ich freue mich in dir	O Gott, du frommer Gott	284
Ich gnüge mich an meinem Stande	Own melody	489
Ich hab in Gottes Herz und Sinn	Was mein Gott will, das g'scheh allzeit	359, 360
Ich hab mein Sach Gott heimgestellt	Own melody	187, 188
Ich halte treulich still	„	440
Ich ruf zu dir, Herr Jesu Christ	„	189, 190
Ich lass dich nicht	„	441
Ich liebe Jesum alle Stund	„	442
Ich steh an deiner Krippen hier	„	443
Ich steh an deiner Krippen hier	Nun freut euch, lieben Christen gmein	269
Ihr Gestirn, ihr hohlen Lüfte	Own melody	191, 444
Ihr Gestirn, ihr hohlen Lüfte	Gott des Himmels und der Erden	119
In allen meinen Thaten	Own melody	192
In allen meinen Thaten	O Welt, ich muss dich lassen	306–308
In dich hab ich gehoffet, Herr	Own melody	193, 195
In dulci jubilo	„	196
Ist Gott mein Schild und Helfersmann	„	197
Jesu, deine Liebeswunden	„	445
Jesu, deine tiefe Wunden	Freu dich sehr, o meine Seele	108
Jesu, der du meine Seele	Own melody	198–201
Jesu, der du selbsten wohl	„	202
Jesu, du mein liebstes Leben	„	203
Jesu, Jesu, du bist mein	„	204, 446
Jesu Leiden, Pein und Tod	„	205–207
Jesu, meine Freude	„	208, 210–214
Jesu, meiner Seelen Wonne	Werde munter, mein Gemüthe	385, 386, 388
Jesu, meines Glaubens Zier	Own melody	447
Jesu, meines Herzens Freud	„	215, 448
Jesu, nun sei gepreiset	„	216–218
Jesus Christus, unser Heiland, Der den	„	219
Jesus Christus, unser Heiland, Der von	„	220
Jesus ist das schönste Licht	„	449
Jesus, meine Zuversicht	„	221
Jesus, unser Trost und Leben	„	450
Kein Stündlein geht dahin	„	451
Keinen hat Gott verlassen	„	223
Komm, Gott Schöpfer, Heiliger Geist	„	224, 225
Komm, Heiliger Geist, Herre Gott	„	226, 227
Komm, Jesu, komm	„	228
Komm, süsser Tod, komm, selge Ruh	„	452
Kommt her zu mir, spricht Gottes Sohn	„	229, 230
Kommt, lasst euch den Herren lehren	Freu dich sehr, o meine Seele	105
Kommt, Seelen dieser Tag	Own melody	453
Kommt wieder aus der finstern Gruft	„	454
Kyrie, Gott Vater in Ewigkeit	„	231
Lass, o Herr, dein Ohr sich neigen	„	232
Lasset uns mit Jesu ziehen	„	455
Lasst Furcht und Pein	Wir Christenleut	395
Liebes Herz, bedenke doch	Own melody	456
Liebster Gott, wann werd ich sterben	„	233, 457
Liebster Herr Jesu, wo bleibst du so lange	„	458
Liebster Immanuel, Herzog der Frommen	„	234, 459
Liebster Jesu, wir sind hier	„	235
Lobe den Herren, den mächtigen König der Ehren ...	Hast du denn, Jesu, dein Angesicht gänzlich verborgen	126
Lobet den Herren, denn er ist sehr freundlich	Own melody	236
Lobt Gott, ihr Christen alle gleich	„	237, 238, 240
Mache dich, mein Geist, bereit	Straf mich nicht	323
Machs mit mir, Gott, nach deiner Güt	Own melody	241, 242
Mein Augen schliess ich jetzt in Gottes Namen zu ...	„	244
Mein Jesu, dem die Seraphinen	„	460
Mein Jesu, was für Seelenweh	„	461
Meine Seele erhebt den Herren	„	245–247
Meine Seele, lass es gehen	„	490
Meinen Jesum lass ich nicht, Jesus	„	248

APPENDIX VI

Hymn	*Set to*	*Number*
Valet will ich dir geben...	Own melody	324, 325
Vater unser im Himmelreich	,,	327, 328
Vergiss mein nicht, dass ich dein nicht vergesse	,,	480
Vergiss mein nicht, Mein	,,	481
Verleih uns Frieden gnädiglich	,,	332, 333
Vom Himmel hoch da komm ich her	,,	335
Von Gott will ich nicht lassen	,,	337–341
Vor deinen Thron tret ich hiemit	Herr Gott, dich loben alle wir	136
Vor deinen Thron tret ich hiemit	Wenn wir in höchsten Nöthen sein	374
Wach auf, mein Herz, und singe	Nun lasst uns Gott dem Herren	275
Wachet auf, ruft uns die Stimme	Own melody	342
Wär Gott nicht mit uns diese Zeit	,,	343
Wär Gott nicht mit uns diese Zeit	Wo Gott der Herr nicht bei uns hält	401
Warum betrübst du dich	Own melody	482
Warum betrübst du dich, mein Herz	,,	344–346
Warum sollt ich mich denn grämen	,,	347
Was alle Weisheit in der Welt	Christ unser Herr zum Jordan kam	44
Was betrübst du dich, mein Herz	Own melody	349
Was bist du, o Seele, so betrübet	,,	350, 483
Was frag ich nach der Welt	O Gott, du frommer Gott	285, 286
Was Gott thut, das ist wohlgethan	Own melody	351–356
Was mein Gott will, das g'scheh allzeit	,,	357, 358, 362–363
Was willst du dich, o meine Seele, kränken	,,	364
Weg, mein Herz, mit dem Gedanken	Freu dich sehr, o meine Seele	103
Welt, ade! ich bin dein müde	Own melody	365
Weltlich Ehr und zeitlich Gut	,,	366
Wenn ich in Angst und Noth	,,	367
Wenn mein Stündlein vorhanden ist	,,	368–372
Wenn wir in höchsten Nöthen sein	,,	373
Wer Gott vertraut	,,	375
Wer in dem Schutz des Hochsten ist	Herr, wie du willt, so schicks mit mir	152
Wer nur den lieben Gott lässt walten	Own melody 377, 379, 380, 382, 484	
Wer weiss wie nahe mir mein Ende	Wer nur den lieben Gott lässt walten	376, 381
Werde munter, mein Gemüthe	Own melody	383, 384, 387
Wie bist du, Seele, in mir so gar betrübt	,,	389
Wie schön leuchtet der Morgenstern	,,	390–394
Wie soll ich dich empfangen	Herzlich thut mich verlangen	162
Wie wohl ist mir, o Freund der Seelen	Own melody	485
Wir Christenleut	,,	396, 397
Wir glauben all an einen Gott	,,	398
Wir singen dir, Immanuel	Vom Himmel hoch da komm ich her	336
Wo Gott der Herr nicht bei uns hält	Own melody	402, 405
Wo Gott zum Haus nicht giebt sein Gunst	,,	403
Wo ist mein Schäflein das ich liebe	,,	486
Wo soll ich fliehen hin	,,	487
Wo soll ich fliehen hin	Auf meinen lieben Gott	26, 27, 28, 30
Wohl dem, der sich auf seinen Gott	Machs mit mir, Gott, nach deiner Güt	243
Zeuch ein zu deinen Thoren	Helft mir Gotts Güte preisen	130

APPENDIX VII

CHRONOLOGICAL TABLE OF THE HYMNS

Date	Number
Pre-Reformation	35, 36, 196, 313
1515	55
1524	6, 7, 32, 37–41, 47, 69, 76, 81, 89–91, 95, 98–101, 112–115, 118, 122, 131, 132, 219, 220, 224–227, 257–260, 262–264, 268, 271, 272, 343, 398, 401–403, 413, 435
1525	15, 24, 297, 405
1526	45
1527	292, 293
1529	65, 77–79, 137, 138, 189, 190, 332, 333
1530	230
1531	16, 21, 50–53, 63, 97, 176, 296, 366
1533	193, 195
1535	181–183, 335
1539	327, 328
1540	18, 19, 276–279
1541	42, 43, 231
1542	82, 312
1543	313
1544	57, 64, 88, 123
1548	120
1549	267
1554	133, 135, 152, 357, 358, 362, 363
1556	34, 270
1559	180
1560	23, 54, 86, 87, 236–238, 240, 319, 344–346, 373
1561	399, 400
1562	368–372
1563	148, 149, 337–341, 347
1566	67
1570	66
1571	154–157, 375
1575	273, 274
1580	128, 129
1582	153
1584	329–331
1585	96
1586	184
1587	9
1588	58, 59, 144, 146, 147
1589	187, 188
1591	216–218
1592	31, 396, 397
1595	60
1597	161, 375
1598	17
1599	342, 390–394
1601	1, 71, 72, 175
1605	158
1607	29
1608	61, 420
1609	48, 49, 223
1610	151, 295
1611	2, 10, 223
1612	185, 437
1613	4, 5, 62, 324, 325
1618	56
1620	102, 107, 145
1625	25
1628	407
1629	241, 242
1630	26–28, 30, 106, 109, 169–172, 287, 289, 290, 295, 326, 487
1632	291
1633	205–207
1634	436
1635	310, 311, 470
1636	22, 265, 266
1637	232
1638	143
1640	139
1641	83–85, 117, 198–201, 203, 299, 423, 478
1642	119, 177, 178, 192, 194, 282, 283, 306–308, 383, 384, 387, 466
1644	46, 108, 173, 174, 244, 280, 320, 367
1646	8, 110, 136, 374, 404
1647	24, 103, 239, 261, 275, 300–305, 309, 359, 360, 408, 463
1648	3, 68, 105, 111, 179, 438
1649	140, 141, 314, 365
1650	414, 468
1651	142, 226
1652	12–14, 455
1653	33, 44, 74, 75, 130, 159, 162–166, 208, 210–214, 221, 229, 269, 315, 322, 336, 347, 348, 361, 364, 395, 412, 443
1655	119, 191, 444
1656	160, 167, 168
1657	197, 377, 379, 380, 382
1658	249–255
1659	209, 450
1660	215, 448
1661	11, 385, 386, 388
1662	94
1663	73, 150, 202, 235, 298, 318, 378, 474, 484
1666	116, 417, 429–432
1667	334, 476
1668	125
1670	411
1671	104, 285, 286
1673	288, 426
1675	92, 93
1676	20, 351–356, 458
1679	234, 459
1680	126
1681	419
1682	124, 488
1684	415
1686	418
1687	204, 446
1688	321, 433, 451, 477
1690	349
1692	121, 243, 281, 323, 441, 460, 485
1695	376, 381, 473
1697	70, 80, 186, 228, 284, 316, 317, 323, 421, 422, 439, 465, 472, 480
1698	464
1699	389
1700	222, 233, 294, 457
1701	486
1703	410
1704	350, 425, 428, 449, 467, 483
1712	490
1713	453, 454
1714	416, 427, 447, 456, 479
1717	406
1725	452, 471, 482
1726	256, 462
1727	409
1735	424
1736	248, 434, 440, 442, 445, 461, 469, 475, 481
Undated	489

APPENDIX VIII

THE HYMNS DISTINGUISHED BY THEIR SEASONS

(a) THE CHRISTIAN YEAR

Advent	Nos. 97, 120, 123, 162, 268, 270, 271, 272, 282, 283, 342
Christmas	Nos. 1, 21, 47, 60, 65, 84, 110, 111, 112, 113, 114, 115, 119, 131, 132, 186, 191, 194, 196, 237, 238, 239, 240, 269, 284, 313, 334, 335, 336, 348, 395, 396, 397
New Year	Nos. 58, 59, 60, 128, 129, 177, 178, 216, 217, 218
Epiphany	No. 194
Passiontide	Nos. 24, 50, 51, 52, 54, 55, 73, 108, 160, 167, 168, 169, 170, 171, 172, 173, 174, 176, 202, 205, 206, 207, 296, 297, 298, 299, 300, 301, 302, 303, 304, 305, 312, 318, 321
Easter	Nos. 35, 36, 37, 38, 39, 40, 41, 53, 86, 87, 88, 175, 219, 221, 222
Ascensiontide ...	Nos. 23, 83, 85, 267
Whitsuntide ...	Nos. 66, 130, 176, 224, 225, 226, 227, 229, 262, 263, 264
Trinity	Nos. 15, 44, 118, 127, 137, 138, 231

(b) SAINTS' AND OTHER HOLY DAYS

St John Baptist ...	Nos. 42, 43, 104
Feasts of the B.V.M.	Nos. 245, 246, 247, 257, 258, 259
St Michael	Nos. 96, 133, 134, 135, 404

(c) TIMES AND SACRAMENTS

Morning	Nos. 25, 31, 56, 61, 62, 117, 119, 136, 180, 181, 182, 183, 184, 185, 275, 327, 328, 390, 391, 392, 393, 394
Evening	Nos. 34, 45, 64, 67, 68, 124, 136, 244, 281, 309, 323, 383, 384, 387
Baptism	Nos. 42, 43
Confirmation ...	Nos. 25, 80, 248, 249, 250, 251, 252, 253, 254, 255
Holy Communion ...	Nos. 16, 17, 22, 122, 127, 143, 220, 295, 314
Thanksgiving ...	Nos. 57, 92, 93, 126, 134, 137, 138, 236, 265, 266, 273, 274, 276, 277, 278, 279, 280, 319, 320, 322
Penitential ...	Nos. 4, 5, 11, 18, 19, 26, 27, 28, 30, 32, 81, 140, 141, 144, 146, 147, 151, 152, 161, 189, 190, 198, 199, 200, 201, 291, 312, 323, 326, 329, 330, 331, 374
Tribulation ...	Nos. 3, 8, 9, 24, 29, 33, 76, 103, 106, 109, 116, 121, 125, 145, 153, 159, 163, 164, 165, 166, 192, 193, 195, 197, 223, 230, 232, 234, 243, 261, 306, 307, 308, 315, 337, 338, 339, 340, 341, 344, 345, 346, 347, 349, 350, 351, 352, 353, 354, 355, 356, 357, 358, 359, 360, 361, 362, 363, 364, 367, 373, 375, 377, 378, 379, 380, 381, 382, 389, 399, 400, 401-403
Sickness and Death ...	Nos. 10, 12, 13, 14, 48, 49, 74, 75, 94, 102, 107, 124, 139, 148, 149, 150, 158, 179, 187, 188, 228, 233, 241, 242, 256, 257, 258, 259, 260, 294, 295, 310, 311, 318, 323, 324, 325, 365, 366, 368, 369, 370, 371, 372, 376, 381

(d) GENERAL

Nos. 2, 6, 7, 20, 46, 63, 69, 70, 71, 72, 77, 78, 79, 80, 82, 89, 90, 91, 95, 98, 99, 100, 101, 105, 142, 154, 155, 156, 157, 203, 204, 208, 209, 210, 211, 212, 213, 214, 215, 235, 248, 249, 250, 251, 252, 253, 254, 255, 285, 286, 287, 288, 289, 290, 292, 293, 306-308, 316, 317, 332, 333, 343, 385, 386, 388, 390, 391, 392, 393, 394, 398, 405

Discographies by Travis & Emery:

Discographies by John Hunt.

1987: From Adam to Webern: the Recordings of von Karajan.

1991: 3 Italian Conductors and 7 Viennese Sopranos: 10 Discographies: Arturo Toscanini, Guido Cantelli, Carlo Maria Giulini, Elisabeth Schwarzkopf, Irmgard Seefried, Elisabeth Gruemmer, Sena Jurinac, Hilde Gueden, Lisa Della Casa, Rita Streich.

1992: Mid-Century Conductors and More Viennese Singers: 10 Discographies: Karl Boehm, Victor De Sabata, Hans Knappertsbusch, Tullio Serafin, Clemens Krauss, Anton Dermota, Leonie Rysanek, Eberhard Waechter, Maria Reining, Erich Kunz.

1993: More 20th Century Conductors: 7 Discographies: Eugen Jochum, Ferenc Fricsay, Carl Schuricht, Felix Weingartner, Josef Krips, Otto Klemperer, Erich Kleiber.

1994: Giants of the Keyboard: 6 Discographies: Wilhelm Kempff, Walter Gieseking, Edwin Fischer, Clara Haskil, Wilhelm Backhaus, Artur Schnabel.

1994: Six Wagnerian Sopranos: 6 Discographies: Frieda Leider, Kirsten Flagstad, Astrid Varnay, Martha Moedl, Birgit Nilsson, Gwyneth Jones.

1995: Musical Knights: 6 Discographies: Henry Wood, Thomas Beecham, Adrian Boult, John Barbirolli, Reginald Goodall, Malcolm Sargent.

1995: A Notable Quartet: 4 Discographies: Gundula Janowitz, Christa Ludwig, Nicolai Gedda, Dietrich Fischer-Dieskau.

1996: The Post-War German Tradition: 5 Discographies: Rudolf Kempe, Joseph Keilberth, Wolfgang Sawallisch, Rafael Kubelik, Andre Cluytens.

1996: Teachers and Pupils: 7 Discographies: Elisabeth Schwarzkopf, Maria Ivoguen, Maria Cebotari, Meta Seinemeyer, Ljuba Welitsch, Rita Streich, Erna Berger.

1996: Tenors in a Lyric Tradition: 3 Discographies: Peter Anders, Walther Ludwig, Fritz Wunderlich.

1997: The Lyric Baritone: 5 Discographies: Hans Reinmar, Gerhard Hüsch, Josef Metternich, Hermann Uhde, Eberhard Wächter.

1997: Hungarians in Exile: 3 Discographies: Fritz Reiner, Antal Dorati, George Szell.

1997: The Art of the Diva: 3 Discographies: Claudia Muzio, Maria Callas, Magda Olivero.

1997: Metropolitan Sopranos: 4 Discographies: Rosa Ponselle, Eleanor Steber, Zinka Milanov, Leontyne Price.

1997: Back From The Shadows: 4 Discographies: Willem Mengelberg, Dimitri Mitropoulos, Hermann Abendroth, Eduard Van Beinum.

1997: More Musical Knights: 4 Discographies: Hamilton Harty, Charles Mackerras, Simon Rattle, John Pritchard.

1998: Conductors On The Yellow Label: 8 Discographies: Fritz Lehmann, Ferdinand Leitner, Ferenc Fricsay, Eugen Jochum, Leopold Ludwig, Artur Rother, Franz Konwitschny, Igor Markevitch.

1998: More Giants of the Keyboard: 5 Discographies: Claudio Arrau, Gyorgy Cziffra, Vladimir Horowitz, Dinu Lipatti, Artur Rubinstein.

1998: Mezzos and Contraltos: 5 Discographies: Janet Baker, Margarete Klose, Kathleen Ferrier, Giulietta Simionato, Elisabeth Höngen.

1999: The Furtwängler Sound Sixth Edition: Discography and Concert Listing.

1999: The Great Dictators: 3 Discographies: Evgeny Mravinsky, Artur Rodzinski, Sergiu Celibidache.

1999: Sviatoslav Richter: Pianist of the Century: Discography.

2000: Philharmonic Autocrat 1: Discography of: Herbert Von Karajan [Third Edition].

2000: Wiener Philharmoniker 1 - Vienna Philharmonic & Vienna State Opera Orchestras: Disc. Part 1 1905-1954.

2000: Wiener Philharmoniker 2 - Vienna Philharmonic & Vienna State Opera Orchestras: Disc. Part 2 1954-1989.

2001: Gramophone Stalwarts: 3 Separate Discographies: Bruno Walter, Erich Leinsdorf, Georg Solti.

2001: Singers of the Third Reich: 5 Discographies: Helge Roswaenge, Tiana Lemnitz, Franz Völker, Maria Müller, Max Lorenz.

2001: Philharmonic Autocrat 2: Concert Register of Herbert Von Karajan Second Edition.

2002: Sächsische Staatskapelle Dresden: Complete Discography.

2002: Carlo Maria Giulini: Discography and Concert Register.

2002: Pianists For The Connoisseur: 6 Discographies: Arturo Benedetti Michelangeli, Alfred Cortot, Alexis Weissenberg, Clifford Curzon, Solomon, Elly Ney.

2003: Singers on the Yellow Label: 7 Discographies: Maria Stader, Elfriede Trötschel, Annelies Kupper, Wolfgang Windgassen, Ernst Häfliger, Josef Greindl, Kim Borg.

2003: A Gallic Trio: 3 Discographies: Charles Münch, Paul Paray, Pierre Monteux.

2004: Antal Dorati 1906-1988: Discography and Concert Register.

2004: Columbia 33CX Label Discography.

2004: Great Violinists: 3 Discographies: David Oistrakh, Wolfgang Schneiderhan, Arthur Grumiaux.

2006: Leopold Stokowski: Second Edition of the Discography.

2006: Wagner Im Festspielhaus: Discography of the Bayreuth Festival.

2006: Her Master's Voice: Concert Register and Discography of Dame Elisabeth Schwarzkopf [Third Edition].

2007: Hans Knappertsbusch: Kna: Concert Register and Discography of Hans Knappertsbusch, 1888-1965. Second Edition.

2008: Philips Minigroove: Second Extended Version of the European Discography.

2009: American Classics: The Discographies of Leonard Bernstein and Eugene Ormandy.

Discography by Stephen J. Pettitt, edited by John Hunt:
1987: Philharmonia Orchestra: Complete Discography 1945-1987

Available from: Travis & Emery at 17 Cecil Court, London, UK.
(+44) 20 7 240 2129. email on sales@travis-and-emery.com .

Music and Books published by Travis & Emery Music Bookshop:

Mellers, Wilfrid: Beethoven and the Voice of God

Mellers, Wilfrid: Caliban Reborn - Renewal in Twentieth Century Music

Mellers, Wilfrid: François Couperin and the French Classical Tradition

Mellers, Wilfrid: Harmonious Meeting

Mellers, Wilfrid: Le Jardin Retrouvé, The Music of Frederic Mompou

Mellers, Wilfrid: Music and Society, England and the European Tradition

Mellers, Wilfrid: Music in a New Found Land: ... ... American Music

Mellers, Wilfrid: Romanticism and the Twentieth Century (from 1800)

Mellers, Wilfrid: The Masks of Orpheus: ...... the Story of European Music.

Mellers, Wilfrid: The Sonata Principle (from c. 1750)

Mellers, Wilfrid: Vaughan Williams and the Vision of Albion

Panchianio, Cattuffio: Rutzvanscad Il Giovine.

Pearce, Charles: Sims Reeves, Fifty Years of Music in England.

Pettitt, Stephen: Philharmonia Orchestra: Complete Discography 1945-1987

Playford, John: An Introduction to the Skill of Musick.

Purcell, Henry et al: Harmonia Sacra ... The First Book, (1726)

Purcell, Henry et al: Harmonia Sacra ... Book II (1726)

Quantz, Johann: Versuch einer Anweisung die Flöte traversiere zu spielen.

Rameau, Jean-Philippe: Code de Musique Pratique, ou Methodes.

Rastall, Richard: The Notation of Western Music.

Rimbault, Edward: The Pianoforte, Its Origins, Progress, and Construction.

Rousseau, Jean Jacques: Dictionnaire de Musique

Rubinstein, Anton : Guide to the proper use of the Pianoforte Pedals.

Sainsbury, John S.: Dictionary of Musicians. Vol. 1. (1825). 2 vols.

Simpson, Christopher: A Compendium of Practical Musick in Five Parts

Spohr, Louis: Autobiography

Spohr, Louis: Grand Violin School

Tans'ur, William: A New Musical Grammar; or The Harmonical Spectator

Terry, Charles Sanford: Four-Part Chorals of J.S. Bach. (German & English)

Terry, Charles Sanford: Joh. Seb. Bach, Cantata Texts, Sacred and Secular.

Terry, Charles Sanford: The Origins of the Family of Bach Musicians.

Tosi, Pierfrancesco: Opinioni de' Cantori Antichi, e Moderni

Van der Straeten, Edmund: History of the Violoncello, The Viol da Gamba ...

Van der Straeten, Edmund: History of the Violin, Its Ancestors... (2 vols.)

Walther, J. G.: Musicalisches Lexikon ober Musicalische Bibliothec (1732)

Travis & Emery Music Bookshop
17 Cecil Court, London, WC2N 4EZ, United Kingdom.
Tel. (+44) 20 7240 2129

Music and Books published by Travis & Emery Music Bookshop:

Anon.: Hymnarium Sarisburense, cum Rubris et Notis Musicus

Agricola, Johann Friedrich from Tosi: Anleitung zur Singkunst. (Faksimile 1757)

Bach, C.P.E.: edited W. Emery: Nekrolog or Obituary Notice of J.S. Bach.

Bateson, Naomi Judith: Alcock of Salisbury

Bathe, William: A Briefe Introduction to the Skill of Song

Bax, Arnold: Symphony #5, Arranged for Piano Four Hands by Walter Emery

Burney, Charles: The Present State of Music in France and Italy

Burney, Charles: The Present State of Music in Germany, The Netherlands …

Burney, Charles: An Account of the Musical Performances ... Handel

Burney, Karl: Nachricht von Georg Friedrich Handel's Lebensumstanden.

Burns, Robert (jnr): The Caledonian Musical Museum (1810 volume)

Cobbett, W.W.: Cobbett's Cyclopedic Survey of Chamber Music. (2 vols.)

Corrette, Michel: Le Maitre de Clavecin

Crimp, Bryan: Dear Mr. Rosenthal … Dear Mr. Gaisberg …

Crimp, Bryan: Solo: The Biography of Solomon

d'Indy, Vincent: Beethoven: Biographie Critique

d'Indy, Vincent: Beethoven: A Critical Biography

d'Indy, Vincent: César Franck (in French)

Fischhof, Joseph: Versuch einer Geschichte des Clavierbaues

Frescobaldi, Girolamo: D'Arie Musicali per Cantarsi. Primo Libro & Secondo Libro.

Geminiani, Francesco: The Art of Playing the Violin.

Handel; Purcell; Boyce; Green et al: Calliope or English Harmony: Volume First.

Hawkins, John: A General History of the Science and Practice of Music (5 vols.)

Herbert-Caesari, Edgar: The Science and Sensations of Vocal Tone

Herbert-Caesari, Edgar: Vocal Truth

Hopkins and Rimboult: The Organ. Its History and Construction.

Hunt, John: some 40 discographies – see list of discographies

Isaacs, Lewis: Hänsel and Gretel. A Guide to Humperdinck's Opera.

Isaacs, Lewis: Königskinder (Royal Children) A Guide to Humperdinck's Opera.

Lacassagne, M. l'Abbé Joseph : Traité Général des élémens du Chant.

Lascelles (née Catley), Anne: The Life of Miss Anne Catley.

Mainwaring, John: Memoirs of the Life of the Late George Frederic Handel

Malcolm, Alexander: A Treaty of Music: Speculative, Practical and Historical

Marx, Adolph Bernhard: Die Kunst des Gesanges, Theoretisch-Practisch

May, Florence: The Life of Brahms

Mellers, Wilfrid: Angels of the Night: Popular Female Singers of Our Time

Mellers, Wilfrid: Bach and the Dance of God

Travis & Emery Music Bookshop
17 Cecil Court, London, WC2N 4EZ, United Kingdom.
Tel. (+44) 20 7240 2129

CPSIA information can be obtained at www.ICGtesting.com
Printed in the USA
BVOW09s0723260116

433326BV00011B/27/P